AF273085

From Ritual to Refuse

Faunal exploitation by the elite of Chinikihá, Chiapas, during the Late Classic period

Coral Montero López

Archaeopress Pre-Columbian Archaeology 14

Archaeopress Publishing Ltd
Summertown Pavilion
18-24 Middle Way
Summertown
Oxford OX2 7LG

www.archaeopress.com

ISBN 978-1-80327-024-1
ISBN 978-1-80327-025-8 (ePdf)

© Archaeopress and and Coral Montero López 2022

All rights reserved. No part of this book may be reproduced, or transmitted, in any form or by any means, electronic, mechanical, photocopying or otherwise, without the prior written permission of the copyright owners. This book is available direct from Archaeopress or from our website www.archaeopress.com

Contents

List of Figures

Chapter seven

Chapter eight

Chapter nine

Chapter ten

'Emissaries had been sent to the fringes of the kingdom, two or three days walk away, to obtain deer, which were increasingly scarce, for the great feasts'

David Webster (2002:14), describing the great lengths hunters needed to go in order to bring back deer for ceremonies at Copán during the Late Classic period.

In loving memory of Maestro Oscar Polaco,

the teacher, the friend

Preface

This zooarchaeological analysis investigates the faunal exploitation patterns of the Maya inhabitants from Chinikihá, a Late Classic period (AD 700-850) site in the periphery of Palenque, in Chiapas Mexico. The research presented here was originally conducted as part of my PhD dissertation, which in turn was derived from my Master of Archaeology studies. My fascination with bones and taphonomical processes began even earlier, in my days as a young university student at Universidad de las Américas Puebla, in México. From the first osteology class, I was hooked. Just as many of my fellow students chose to specialise in ceramics or obsidian, I knew that my archaeological material of preference would be human and animal bones.

My PhD studies were conducted during 2008 and 2010, with the final version of my Doctoral dissertation completed in 2013. The final edits for publication were done over subsequent years while working full-time, moving interstate several times in Australia, and enduring the hard COVID lockdowns in Victoria.

The Late/Terminal Classic period was a time characterised by an increasing political competitiveness amongst larger sites, concluding in environmental and dietary changes that are well documented (see Emery 2010 for a summary). However, little is known of how smaller or secondary sites responded to increased environmental and dietary pressures. Therefore, I centred on the study of a large faunal assemblage located behind a palatial structure, which was analysed through the application of standard zooarchaeological and isotope analyses.

The assemblage of Chinikihá probably represents the discarded remains of several feasting events in a one single deposit, *Operación* 114. While most of the anthropological and archaeological feast markers are present, there are specific zooarchaeological markers which had ambiguous results. As such, the identification of feasting based exclusively on zooarchaeological markers is not possible. In the absence of complimentary data, such as ceramics or macrobotanical remains, and without a thorough analysis of the taphonomic history of the context, there are very few animal-based markers that could be used to define the deposit. Nevertheless, the contextual data reveals a structured behaviour that departs from the processing and consuming of the common everyday meal and provides new information on faunal exploitation patterns by elite groups in a smaller polity in the Maya Lowlands.

The results of this analysis suggest that there was little change in the way faunal resources were exploited during the Late Classic period, indicating continuity in the way the elite at Chinikihá managed the faunal resources that were available to them. The minor changes which could be observed in the deposit were more suggestive of changes in the depositional history and the integration of the materials into the archaeological record than of changes in faunal resource exploitation.

The results from Chinikihá provide new evidence for faunal exploitation in the Maya Lowlands, and coincide with published data from other sites, confirming that there was no noticeable change in the consumption patterns of fauna in ritual activities through the Late/Terminal Classic period, and therefore, there is no evidence of the so-called 'environmental collapse'. Furthermore, there is some continuity in the exploitation pattern from elite contexts through that period, maintaining the emphasis on a few species of high utility, such as the white-tailed deer and the dog. A pattern of consumption based on prime-aged animals, and more specifically, the use of meaty portions such as the haunch was observed at Chinikihá. Finally, this study suggests that there was intensification in feasting activities by the elite of Chinikihá, as a means to display their power to other rival polities, especially during the Late Classic period, a period of increased political interactions.

I could not have completed this research without my strong support group. First of all, I am forever in debt to Dr Rodrigo Liendo Stuardo from Instituto de Investigaciones Antropológicas (IIA-UNAM) for allowing me to continue with the analysis of Chinikihá's material during my PhD studies. I also acknowledge the collaborative and friendly team of students who along with me, embarked in studying the complex deposit that is *Operación* 114: Atasta Flores, Keiko Teranishi, Flavio Silva, Esteban Mirón, and Felipe Trabanino. I want to thank Rodrigo Liendo, Esteban Mirón, and Felipe Trabanino for allowing me to use and reproduce some of their dissertation images in this publication. I am also indebted to my dissertation co-directors, Professors Richard Cosgrove and Peter Mathews from La Trobe University in Bundoora, Australia, who always had kind words of encouragement, and made enormous contributions to the final document.

A special thank-you goes to the committee of three external examiners, Prof Joaquín Arroyo Cabrales

(Laboratorio de Arqueozoología 'M. en C. Ticúl Álvarez' at the Sub-Dirección de Laboratorios, Instituto Nacional de Antropología e Historia at Mexico City), Dr Kitty Emery (Environmental Archaeology, Florida Museum of National History at the University of Florida at Gainesville), and Dr Sean Ulm (Department of Anthropology, Archaeology, and Sociology, James Cook University at Cairns) for reading the dissertation and making thoughtful contributions that enriched the final version. Consequently, this publication is slightly different from the dissertation I submitted for graduation.

I would also like to express my thanks to Pedro Morales, Edith Cienfuegos, Francisco Oterc, and Rafael Puente Martínez from Laboratorio de Isotópos Estables, from Instituto de Geología (IG-UNAM), for processing and conducting the isotope analyses, and their friendship that has resulted in several collaborative papers and possibly many more to come. Dr José Reyes Gasca from Instituto de Física (IF-UNAM) kindly ran the *Crystallinity Index* (CI) analysis on three samples.

At Instituto Nacional de Antropología e Historia (INAH), I would like to thank Maestro Oscar Polaco, a great friend and mentor who pointed me in the right direction when I got interested in analysing faunal material in 2005. He took the time to teach and train me, and for that, I will be always in his debt. Thank you to all the personnel at Laboratorio de Zooarqueología (INAH), especially Dr Joaquín Arroyo Cabrales, Dra Fabiola Guzmán, Maestra María Teresa Olivera, and Aurelio Ocaña for all their support at the laboratory, and for granting access to the reference material. Biologist Belén Chávez helped me during the washing and sorting processes while I was in Mexico City.

Last but not least, I want to thank my family and friends in Mexico and Australia; without their support I would have not been able to complete my studies in record time. To my parents, Salvador and María del Carmen, a big thank-you for always believing in my crazy dreams and never cutting my wings short. To my partner James Robertson, I want to thank the patience, love, and support during the editing process in the crazy year of 2020. Without your support, lockdown in Melbourne would have been ten times worse.

My trip to Mexico in 2009 to conduct fieldwork and laboratory analysis was covered by a Faculty of Humanities and Social Sciences Grant, and two separate School of Historical Research Grants, both from La Trobe University. During my stay at the PhD program at La Trobe University in Melbourne, financial support was provided by La Trobe University Postgraduate Research Scholarship (LTUPRS) and EIPRS (Endeavour International Postgraduate Research Scholarship). I also received financial support from Beca Complemento from Secretaría de Educación Pública (SEP), granted to Mexican students conducting Postgraduate studies overseas.

The original text from the dissertation was edited and proofread by Alexandra Byrne, and the images for this publication were digitalised by Dr Emiliano Gallaga Murrieta and Aliruth Rivera. I also would like to thank Dr Simon Martin and Prof. Peter Mathews for providing me with original drawings that significantly enriched this text.

Introduction

Problem statement

The celebration of feasts among the Maya has been recognized as an important ritual activity in which commoners and the elite engaged diachronically and for myriad sociopolitical purposes. At the domestic level, feasts were celebrated to venerate ancestors and to celebrate other life cycle landmarks, such as births, weddings, deaths. Feasts among the elite have received particular attention, as the royal classes used them as a means of controlling and displaying their power (Clark and Blake 1994; Dietler 2001; Dietler and Hayden 2001).

Feasts in the Maya area have been extensively studied using varying approaches largely centering on the analysis of ceramics to identify feasting behaviour. The remains of feasts are usually identified by a higher proportion of serving wares, and the presence of decorated vessels (LeCount 2001; Reents-Budet 2000). The identification of possible feasting deposits has also been achieved by their association with specific architectural features (Eppich 2009; Hendon 2003; Joyce and Henderson 2007; LeCount 2001).

Nonetheless, the study of the faunal remains associated with those contexts has often been interpreted in different ways, from secondary domestic refuse, to the remnants of feasts at different scales. When numerous faunal remains often accompany large quantities of ceramic fragments and other ritual paraphernalia, many researchers tend to categorize such evidence as the remains of feasts sponsored by the elite. Zooarchaeologically, feasts have been defined by high frequencies of favoured food species and their body portions, high proportions of whole animals, and the presence of exotic species (Dabney *et al.* 2004; Emery *et al.* 2009; Twiss 2008). The presence of these characteristics is not exclusive to feasting deposits, especially in societies where some animals were used for both domestic and ritual activities. In the Maya area for example, similar set of characteristics has been used to define other type of contexts, such as hunting shrines (Emery *et al.* 2009), and other activities associated with the elite, further confusing the subject. Although we now know more about the patterns of exploitation of fauna resources and their accessibility to different social groups, specific studies to test if these are the result of feasting hav been scarce (Pohl 1994; Shaw 1991; Yaeger 2000). This dissertation contributes to the study and identification of feasting from a zooarchaeological perspective through the analysis of faunal remains, and to the understanding of ritual consumption of fauna and its association with social inequality, through the complementary analysis of faunal remains and a collection of human remains, both from the archaeological site of Chinikihá.

This research is partly derived from a previous study, in which it has been impossible to answer the questions (Montero 2008), and the necessity of embracing the complexity of the context in such a way that would allow meaningful results to be obtained. In the past it was considered that there was too little information available for conducting regional comparisons in Maya zooarchaeology; however, this is no longer the case (Emery 2004a). Presently, there are a number of zooarchaeological studies that have been undertaken in the Maya area, though only a limited number are similar to the context located behind the Palace at Chinikihá— the subject of this analysis—and therefore comparable. I believe that it is through comparing and contrasting similar contexts that the patterns of feasting behaviour involving the use of faunal resources will emerge.

Research problem

Animal and human bones are probably one of the most common materials encountered in any archaeological project around the world. Both have the potential to provide information such as the health and diet of individuals as well as activities conducted in past societies and the relationship between humans and their environment. Furthermore, the combination of faunal remains, large quantities of ceramics, and other ceremonial materials often exclusive to the elite, allows us to explore the concepts of differential access and consumption patterns by different tiers of the Late Classic period society, especially in ritual activities, such as feasting events. Unlike other ritual activities, feasting does not have a unique material signature that can be used for its identification in the archaeological record in an exclusive way. However, feasting deposits, as the accumulated outcome of a repeated event, may result in a highly structured context that can be analysed by dissecting particular aspects, such as differential access to meat resources and butchering practices.

For Chinikihá, new data from new excavations, and a multi-disciplinary analysis involving isotope analysis and more thorough zooarchaeological analysis are used here to study the exploitation of animals in the context in which they appear. A holistic approach, and an emphasis on the taphonomic history and context formation is chosen now to explore the symbolism of faunal resources and their use by the higher classes, in order to address questions about feasting in the Maya Lowlands promoted by the elite. Elites engaged in the consumption of unusually large quantities of meat in celebratory feasts, not only to establish and maintain power in their own communities, but also to help them reinforce the status of their own cities in view of the complex political situation that dominated the Late Classic period.

Some of the questions that need to be answered in this dissertation include: Can we identify feast through the analysis of faunal remains? What are the zooarchaeological markers of feasts, if any? Ultimately, is it possible to identify different patterns of consumption and processing of animals for feasting events that could be helpful when identifying differences in a long-term deposit?

Aims

The aim of this study is to explore the faunal exploitation and patterns of utilisation at Chinikihá by the elite during the Late Classic period. More specifically, the use of zooarchaeological and isotope analysis is tested in order to identify feasting activities. More particular objectives include:

- To test if feasting can be identified in the archaeological record using a set of defined anthropological and zooarchaeological markers, especially in a deposit associated with the elite in Chinikihá.
- To use isotope analysis first to provide a baseline of plants and animals values expected for δ^{13}C and δ^{15}N to measure corn and consumption from a set of animal and human archaeological samples. This data will then be used to check if there was a differential access pattern among the members of the elite.
- To compare the different *Operaciones* while establishing if there were spatial differences in the distribution of faunal remains. Comparisons will also be carried at the inter-site level in order to see how Chinikihá's results are integrated in a regional exploitation pattern.
- Using the distribution of the materials inside a context that possibly reflects feasting, the objective would be to see how many consumption episodes can be identified, through the taphonomic analysis.
- The information generated from the analysis of Chinikihá also lends itself to the exploration of predictions regarding dietary failure during the Late/Terminal Classic period and how did

it affect the exploitation patterns of the elite (see Emery 2010). Finally, all the information generated is then inserted in the debate about what the role of the feasts sponsored by the ruling elites during the Late/Terminal period would have been.

Research design

To pursue this understanding, I will start by introducing the concept of feasting and the archaeological markers that have been proposed in literature to define it. More specifically, in recent years, there have been new studies conducted on feasting throughout the world, including the Maya area, resulting in a set of zooarchaeological markers that can be used to identify feasting through the analysis of bones. The main objective of this study is then to analyse Chinikihá's assemblage to identify whether a set of zooarchaeological markers can be used to establish a positive identification of feast remains. Feasting in the Mayan area during the Late/Terminal Classic period was particularly important, as local elite groups used it for many purposes, including to differentiate themselves from the rest of the population, and as a means to display their power to other elites.

Archaeological deposits with hundreds of faunal bones, mixed with ceramic fragments, exotic goods, and other ritual artefacts have been identified in many instances as feasting remains. However, these practices are not exclusive to the upper classes, and there is enough data to confirm that there is enough data to confirm that the rituals of the Maya elite derive from domestic rituals and that this was a long-standing tradition in all of Mesoamerica. The distribution of exotic or restricted goods, including meat, is not homogeneous even among members of the elite, possibly indicating a diffuse range of social status. These deposits can also be the result of other activities, thereby creating further difficulties in the assessment of such sites. Therefore, Chapter two aims to describe all the other types of contexts that may resemble a feasting deposit.

Chapter three is focused on the socio-political environment that existed during the Classic period. The complexity of this period resulted in an increase of construction activities and a growth of social networks, leading to the presence of numerous archaeological contexts that included faunal remains, such as caches, burials, and offerings. Such sites share many common traits with feasting sites, further complicating the problem of identifying a context as a feasting deposit. A description of these terms is presented in order to allow a comparison between the archaeological markers for each. This is to demonstrate that assigning a specific behaviour as the single activity involved in the creation of a context containing faunal remains can be problematic. Chapter four offers a brief description of Chinikihá and each of the *Operaciones* where the faunal bones were found.

Chapter five lays out the zooarchaeological methodology used in this research, while the methodology and background information for the isotope analysis in the Maya area is presented in Chapter six. The results of the zooarchaeological analysis are presented in Chapter seven, with the detailed analysis of *Operación* 114, a context behind the Palace at Chinikihá, presented in Chapter eight, as this context may have been the final deposit of a series of feasting events. In Chapter nine, the results from the isotopic analysis are presented. The combined use of the data obtained from the zooarchaeological and the isotopic analysis is discussed and integrated in Chapter ten, with the conclusions presented at the end.

Chapter one

Theoretical background to feasting: activities in archaeology

The analysis of animal remains as evidence of ritual activities in archaeology has been discussed in detail by several authors (for extensive reviews, see Fogelin 2007; Miracle and Milner 2002; O'Day *et al.* 2004). In addition to the study of animal bones for the purpose of understanding changes in subsistence patterns, many studies have focused on variations in access to food stuffs based on status and food preference, two concepts that are usually associated with the emergence of a powerful ruling class or elite and the mechanisms applied to create and maintain their power and identity (see Gumerman 1997 and Smith 2006 for extensive reviews). One of those mechanisms is feasting, identified as 'any sharing of special food (in quality, preparation, or quantity) by two or more people for a special (not everyday) event' (Hayden 2001; Hayden and Villeneuve 2011:434). As such, feasting has been intimately related to the emergence of inequality and social complexity. While for some authors feasting has been considered a continuation or extension of the domestic and private sphere (Potter and Ortman 2004:175), this study will focus on the public aspects of ritual feasting, including the manipulation by the elite of access to foods considered of 'high status' (Curet and Pestle 2010).

The concept of feasting has been treated extensively in both the anthropological and archaeological literature (for a review of the past 100 years, see Hayden and Villeneuve 2011) with an emphasis on the ethnographic evidence of feasting and its markers (Dietler 2001; Dietler and Hayden 2001; Hayden 2001; Jackson and Scott 2003; Pauketat *et al.* 2002). Ethnographic analogues have then been applied with some success to the study of archaeofaunal remains, but such applications have not been without complication. One obvious issue is the questions of whether anthropological criteria for identifying feasts are applicable to the archaeological record and to what extent. Although some archaeologists have engaged in establishing criteria for the identification of feasting more suited to archaeological research (Hayden 2001; Rosenswig 2007), the general application of the anthropological markers to the study of feasting in archaeology has failed to recognise the numerous dimensions of certain socially significant foods (Curet and Pestle 2010:416), and furthermore the different behaviours that may be associated with such foods. It is therefore necessary to identify specific behavioural markers associated with a feast in order to understand feasting properly (Hayden and Villeneuve 2011:441). In

the present study, the Chinikihá assemblage is compared with the more traditional anthropological markers of feasting in order to examine whether the archaeological deposits are a result of feasting.

As a social practice, consumption of food is a ritual activity that can be seen as a series of events that are usually patterned (Sullivan 1989; Vogt 1993). Therefore, animal use in relation to food consumption can be highly ritualised and feasts may be considered ritual activities which serve both symbolic and political agendas (deFrance 2009:106). In this sense, it is important to identify the role of a particular feast and what the motivation was for the feasting event.

Furthermore, identifying the function associated with a context containing faunal remains is in itself a complex process. Faunal remains in archaeology have been identified in a wide variety of contexts, including burials, trash middens, and 'special contexts', where their presence has created interpretative challenges for scholars, particularly in identifying the nature of the context in which they appear, and ultimately, the identification of the associated behaviour. In many instances, the presence of a large number of faunal remains mixed with a large number of ceramic fragments in a given context has been determined to be the result of feasting behaviour. Therefore, determining which animal bones are present in the archaeological record, and understanding how they came to be present (the taphonomic history), is important and is addressed in Chapter two.

In this chapter, defining what constitutes a feast and how feasting activities have been identified in the archaeological record is the main objective, using ethnographic data as well as zooarchaeological markers for feasting. The discussion is then centred more specifically on the faunal remains and other artefacts associated with the celebration of feasts. This is followed by a description of feasting in Mesoamerica, drawing in examples from the Maya area, in order to create a *corpus* of archaeological examples of possible feasting deposits that will serve as a background to the study of the assemblage from Chinikihá.

Defining a feast

Feasts at their basic level, are defined as a communal consumption of food and/or drink that is generally different from an everyday meal (Dietler and Hayden 2001:3; Hayden 2001:28; Brown 2001:370). Feasting as a activity is an almost universal practice and is imbued with various meanings on economic, social and symbolic levels, dependent upon the scenario. As an economic factor, it is intimately related to surplus production and the use, control and distribution of products (Hayden 2001:25-27). Socially, feasts are important because they facilitate the creation and maintenance of extended social networks (Brown 2001:386; Kan 1989). Finally, the symbolic aspect of a feast is related to ritual behaviour and the celebration of socially important events (Hayden 1996). Most importantly, feasts usually have highly ritualised components that possess material correlates (Dietler 1996:89; Hayden 2001:28), making feasts the perfect focus when analysing ritual activities. These material correlates or markers are discussed towards the end of this chapter.

Feasts are therefore multifaceted, and because of this, the present study will focus on the role of feasts in the socio-political arena, although the economic and symbolic aspects of feasting are also considered and integrated in the discussion. Firstly, the nature of a feast as an activity that is recurrent, organised and patterned is presented, followed by a discussion of how it may be identifiable in the archaeological record.

Feasting as a repetitive behaviour

Individual feasting events are intangible acts that cannot be observed directly (Dietler and Hayden 2001:7); however, it is through the patterning of such a repetitive behaviour that it can be inferred. Moreover, feasts do not necessarily happen as a single event, but can be composed of separate episodes, days, months, or even years apart (Wiessner 2001:125). Therefore, some patterning should be expected. It is necessary then, if social interaction is studied, to understand the role that feasts have, as well as the different consumption patterns and how these have changed through time (Dietler and Hayden 2001). The study of feasting is therefore a powerful tool in establishing an understanding of a whole range of cultural processes, especially in complex societies (Hayden 2001:24).

It has been observed then, in general, that feasts have material correlates in the frequencies of artefacts, the locations in which they occur, and their spatial association to specific structures. In this sense, different aspects of a feast can be examined, such as the spatial component, and the artefactual data, that may include ceramics, and faunal materials (Dietler and Hayden 2001:9). Thus, feasts do have a series of material correlates that are present and identifiable in the archaeological record (Brown 2001; Hayden 2001). To identify feasting as a ritual activity, it is necessary to

understand that feasting occurs with other ritual acts (Brown 2001:370) that distinguish it. The feasting place must be considered an articulator of social relations (Dietler 2001). In this chapter, complex societies and the use of feasts as a means to achieve social change or maintain continuity is examined.

Feasting and social change

One of the main reasons for an anthropological study of feasts is to identify the social component that is inherent in this activity. As feasts have been defined as the consumption of food by more than one individual (Dietler and Hayden 2001), feasting involves food sharing and food distribution, where sharing serves to bond larger groups together and distribution creates a temporary imbalance, and often requires a later return. Distribution also facilitates the construction of social inequality (Wiessner 2001:116). In short, feasts involve social change (Dietler and Hayden 2001:16).

Regardless of their purposes, feasts and 'particularly competitive feastings may have played a pivotal role in cultural evolution' (Hayden 1996:127), especially in societies where there was food production and surplus. Some of the earliest examples of feasting have been recovered in the Levante, dating to the Natufian period (Munro and Grosman 2010), and such events become more important during the period of agricultural transition that propelled the development of food production (Twiss 2008). Feasting is widely recognized in other parts of the world, including among the Inca in South America and throughout the American chiefdoms (Jackson and Scott 2003; Lau 2002; Pauketat *et al.* 2002; Sandefour 1988; Stocker and Davis 2004). In more complex societies, feasts are an integral part of the social component and as such, the activity that can be manipulated by groups or individuals (Clarke 2001:148). Hence, if the aim is to understand the celebration of feasts and accompanying display of resources, it is imperative to understand the emergence of factionalism and how feast markers are intertwined with the rest of the markers of complex societies, such as in the case of the Andean region or the Maya area, two areas where feasting and social inequality have been extensively studied (Brown 2007; Costin and Earle1989; D´Altroy 1994; Sandefur 1988).

For example, in Perú, during the Late Intermediate period and in areas outside Cuzco, imitating old rituals to display ancestral ties to the Wari would provide political legitimacy to local lords. This was achieved by copying the burial system, and imitating the ceramics used in offerings and feasts (McEwan 2006:94-95). Feasting and drinking with the ancestors was a highly ritualised behaviour and served as a way of controlling the populatous by the elite (McEwan 2006:96). In this type of feast, large amounts of food and other goods are displayed to the public, and as such, can be considered under the 'costly signalling theory', where what seems to be unconditional generosity and wasteful behaviour on behalf of the sponsor actually serves to strengthen them and at the same time promote promote collective cooperation among the attendants (Bliege Bird and Smith 2005).

Feasts were also common among less complex societies, and studies regarding their occurrence in hunter/gatherer societies and early chiefdoms have been conducted (Hayden 2001). What all feasts have in common is that they require the consumption of communal food in public spaces by a gathering of people and the creation of status related goods (D'Altroy 1994:175-176). Feasts must then have a material signature that reflects patterns of a social structure which can be identifiable in the material record (Hayden 2001; Wiessner 2001:116).

Feasting involves also some sort of display, whether it is display of food, objects, individuals, or groups. Most of the evidence for a feast among these societies relies on the vast quantities of large ceramic vessels and the significant proportions of animal remains which appear in the archaeological record. Complex societies have a series of specific archaeological markers, such as the presence of multiple socio-political entities, an increase in the population mobility and the existence of ceremonial and symbolic representations of new social classes (D'Altroy 1994; Rosenswig 2007). Artefacts or structures built for display include special vessels, platforms, graves or houses (Wiessner 2001:116). In summary, the analysis of feasting remains has been key in identifying a relationship between feasts and political acts celebrating alliances between governing elites, as suggested by Brumfiel (1987) and Pohl (1994).

The role of feasts

Feasts are defined as the sharing of food by two or more people and there are therefore numerous types of feasts with differing purposes and roles (Hayden 2001). Feasts are rituals that adopt different forms, depending on their goal; they may be linked to an exclusive sphere, such as the religious, social or political sectors. Just like ritual may cross over multiple spheres of actions (Grant 1991), so too can feasting, further complicating the process of identifying the function of a specific feast context (deFrance 2009:147; Wiessner 2001:116). In the next section, I discuss the role of feasts in the religious, social, and political spheres.

Feasts and the religious sphere

Feasts are commonly divided into two types, secular and sacred, however despite this distinct separation, the two types are complementary (Wiessner 2001:125). Secular and sacred feasts can usually be distinguished from one another by the differences in the size of the feast in question. Large secular feasts usually involved a display in a competitive context, making them more distinctly identifiable (Wiessner 2001:125-126). According to some authors, feasts can also be classified according to their spatial organisation, and the availability of access to the required spaces. They can be open or private, depending on the inclusion or exclusion of certain segments of the society. Communal feasts involve all the inhabitants of a site, and promote solidarity, while private or closed feasts are exclusive to a group of people, and are usually identified in direct association to a specific structure, especially inside inner patios of residential complexes belonging to the elite (D'Altroy 1994:175-176). Dietler (1996) nominates this last type as 'diacritical', where feasts are hosted by the ruling class and are exclusive to their kind.

Feasts and the social sphere

Feasts can have different purposes, including the veneration of ancestors (Kansa and Campbell 2004; Lau 2002), the mobilisation of labour and social resources (Gero 1990; Hastorf 1993; Wells 2007), and the promotion of alliances with or incorporation of other polities. Other feasts that may have a social role include those that are seen at the household level and include ceremonies of initiation, marriage, or death, as well as to provide compensation owed or assemble a labour force. If any inferences are to be drawn from the material culture, there is an underlying assumption when assessing such a site that the social role of feasting is understood. The assessment must involve analysis based on specific contexts and the resultant patterning (Dietler and Hayden 2001:7-8).

Feasts and the political sphere

Political feasts are a key component in the emergence of centralised societies and their expansion to include other polities (Morris 1982). Feasts in the political sphere tend to be sponsored by individuals seeking self-promotion or increased prestige (Clark and Blake 1994:17). Such individuals or 'aggrandisers' control the resources and obtain power during periods of political turmoil and regeneration (Conlee 2006). Aggrandisers may use feasting in a competitive way to establish and maintain influence within their social group, internally or externally. In this sense, the importance of feasts relies on the creation and maintenance of social relations between different groups of people that are inserted into a regional political community (Dietler 2001:68-69). Internally, feasts create social debt and the corresponding reciprocation (Clark and Blake 1994; Wells 2007) and create a state of imbalance between those giving and those receiving, with feasts playing an important role in the emergence of social inequality (Clarke 2001; Dietler 2001). These actions, therefore, generate compromises through the act of giving presents and reciprocation (McAnany 1995:31-32), which in turn can be seen as a mechanism of cohesion. Externally, aggrandisers may use feasts for auto-promotion and warfare (Pohl and Pohl 1994:141). Together, the sponsorship of local feasts not only increases the collective power and status of the domestic lineage, but it also serves to display their power to other polities (McAnany 1995:118).

Feast and social inequality

The study of feasting allows exploration of inequality between, and within social strata. At the smallest unit of organisation, the household, gender differences are seen through the production of goods related to the subsistence economy (Cohodas 2002; Hendon 2002; McKillop 2004:122; Robin 2006). It has been observed gender differences may be reproduced or alternatively transformed during a feasting event; division of labour and the benefits obtained by each gender can also be identified (Dietler and Hayden 2001:11). In this sense, feasts are not only a mechanism for differentiating between individuals, but also to establish positions of dominance and subordination (Hendon 2003:207). For instance, at the household level, ethnographic data have shown that it is the women who transform food into feasts, in which the men are the main beneficiaries (Dietler and Hayden 2001:11, although see McKillop 2004:122).

When studying inequality between social strata, it is expected that elites had greater access to resources than the rest of the society (Fried 1967:186), probably resulting in a better diet and therefore better health. Nevertheless, this inequality is not always clear and as such, distinguishing between contexts associated with the elite and contexts associated with commoners can be difficult. The archaeofaunal assemblage from a ceremonial context associated with the elite class appears similar to ceremonial contexts associated with other social strata. This is probably because both result from the refuse patterns of a single group, and in many instances, everyday artefacts are used during feasts (Bíró and Montero 2008; Hamblin 1984:10). There are numerous examples of the use of ordinary artefacts as part of ritual feasts; extensive studies of such use have been conducted in the American Southwest and at some sites in the Maya region (Masson 1999; Pohl 1983; Potter and Ortman 2004:174).

This study explores the material correlates of communal feasts sponsored by the elite class to generate inequality and maintain their status, and the role of feasts in the socio-political arenas.

Anthropological markers of feasting

Michael Dietler and Brian Hayden's (2001) work on feasting has been fundamental in understanding the application of anthropological feast markers to archaeological study. In short, the difference between daily meals and feasts are marked by the quantity of food, and the quality, including delicacies or ritually marked foods (Dietler 1996; Hayden 2001; Kirch 2001:169). In some cases, further differentiation includes the ways and places in which feast foods were consumed (Kirch 2001:169). As a repetitive ritual act that is reflected in patterning of material culture, feasts are expected to be archaeologically recognizable (LeCount 2001:935). For example, the display of wealth by the ruling class in feasting events can be observed in archaeology by the presence of high concentrations of ceramics, the presence of large quantities of animal bones and valuable goods, as seen in the Andean area and in some sites in the Maya area (D'Altroy 1994:176).

Feasts are expected to have material correlates that can be identified in the archaeological record. These have been called 'signatures' or markers (Hayden 2001:40-41), and include various types of indicators that share some common traits. In this dissertation, they are grouped into six main categories: specific faunal and botanical products, food preparation and presentation, location of preparation and feasting areas, location of disposal features, associated prestige items and display, and other items (Table 1). These criteria can then be used to analyse the archaeological record.

While the first four categories do have a material correlate that can be recognized in the archaeological record, some of the associated prestige items and display that accompany a ritual in many instances do not leave a trace in feasting deposits but can be inferred from iconography and ethnographic accounts. In a similar way, those traits identified as 'other' are not usually present in the archaeological record, or where they are present, are not necessarily associated with other feasting markers but instead can provide indirect information about feasting activities. In this case, therefore, the focus will be on the four main categories, through which feasting may be further explored in the archaeological record.

Specific fauna and botanical products

The identification of a feast context has been based largely on the presence of food items that are exotic or have been prepared differently from those consumed in everyday meals (Hayden (2001:40). This is particularly evident in societies where meat or alcoholic beverages are not part of everyday meals (Clarke 2001:149); the presence of exotic fauna and evidence of alcoholic

SPECIFIC FAUNA AND BOTANICAL PRODUCTS	Food	Rare or labour-intensive plant or animal species (especially condiments, spices, and domestic animals)
		Special 'recreational' foods (e.g. tobacco, opium, cannabis, and alcohol)
		Quantity of food items
		Evidence of waste of food items (e.g. deposition of articulated joints, unprocessed bone)
	Resource characteristics	Abundance, intensified exploitation, invulnerability to overexploitation
	Food-storage facilities	Stables, storage pits, granaries
FOOD PREPARATION AND PRESENTATION	Preparation vessels	Unusual types (e.g. for beer-making, chilli-grinding, perhaps initial appearance of cooking pots)
		Unusually large sizes of vessels
		Unusual quantities of preparation vessels
	Food-preparation facilities	Unusual size of facilities (e.g. several hearths in a row)
		Unusual location or construction of facilities
	Serving vessels	Unusual material quality or type (e.g. first occurrence of pottery or highly decorated or specially finished pottery, large gourds, stone bowls)
		Unusual size of serving vessels
		Unusual quantities of serving vessels
LOCATION OF PREPARATION AND FEASTING AREAS	Feasting facilities	Special structures (temporary vs. permanent) for highest-ranking guests and hosts, or for large number of people
		Special display facilities, scaffolds, poles, or other features
	Special locations	Mortuary or remote locations that are clearly not habitation sites (e.g. in front of Megalithic tombs, at henge monuments, inside caves)
		Loci associated with nuclear households, residential corporate households, large feasting middens or central community spaces
LOCATION OF DISPOSAL FEATURES	Special food-disposal features	Bone dumps
		Special refuse fires containing feasting items
		Feasting middens
ASSOCIATED PRESTIGE ITEMS AND DISPLAY	Associated prestige items	Presence or absence, and relative abundance of prestige items typically used in different types of feasts (e.g. ritual display items, feathers, shell jewellery)
		The destruction of wealth or prestige items (via intentional breakage or burial)
	Ritualised items of etiquette	Smoking or other narcotic paraphernalia
		Ritualised vessels for consumption of alcohol, chocolate, kava, or other prestige drinks
	Paraphernalia for public rituals	Dance masks or costume elements
OTHER ITEMS	Record-keeping devices	The presence or absence and frequency of tally sticks or counting tokens
	Existence of aggrandisers	Wealthy burials; social or site hierarchies; large residences with high storage per capita
	Pictorial and written records of feasts	Symbolic pictograms

Table 1. Archaeological signatures of feasts (Modified from Hayden 2001:40).

drinks in a specific context can be identified as evidence of feasting (Hayden 2001). In particular, such evidence in abundance is a strong indicator of a feast event (Wiessner 2001:117).

Foods consumed at feasts are called festive or high cuisine (Dietler 1996:98). During feasts, food is shared or redistributed among a large group of people, thus leaving remains at the site where the feast occurred (Wiessner 2001:116). This sharing or redistribution can be seen in the archaeological record by the presence of the animals or artefacts that were featured during the event, and the large concentrations in which they appear (Wiessner 2001).

In societies that use domestic animals for feasting, the frequencies in which animals of different age and size are present, as well as the distribution of body portions by their utility index, can also be used in order to identify the type of feasts in which they were consumed (Hayden 2001:49). According to Hayden (2001:49), in domestic feasts, the presence of low utility body portions such as the skull is expected, while in larger feasts, high utility cuts will predominate. This is particularly helpful when studying societies that use the same animals for ritual and non-ritual activities (Crabtree 2002). Finally, the bone remains which result from feasting may display evidence of special or different treatment in comparison with bones recovered from refuse contexts associated with domestic consumption, such as differential burning or breakage patterns (Brown 2002).

In the Maya feasts, common food stuffs such as corn, beans, and squash may be present in addition to the exotic items such as meat (Brown 2001:380). Meat was probably consumed in smaller proportions at the household or domestic level, but in public or elite-sponsored feasts, evidence of the consumption of meat from large mammals, such as dog and deer, is present in larger proportions (Brown 2001). In comparison, in the Mantaro region of Perú, access to the meat of large mammals, in the form of camelids, was restricted exclusively to the royal class as a consequence of the expansion of the Inca (D'Altroy 1994). However, guinea pigs (*Cavia porcellus*) were preferred for feasts, due to their symbolism (Sandefur 1988).

Nonetheless, this distinction may be more difficult to identify in the Maya area, due to the utilisation of the same animals for the higher and lower classes and due to the refuse practices of this group (secondary discard, cleaning, reuse, and so on). In the Maya area, during the Postclassic and Colonial periods, meat was probably exclusive to the higher classes (Masson 1999); however, during the Classic period, access to meat was less limited, though the best cuts were restricted

to the elite. There is an extensive body of references for the consumption of deer, especially the haunch, among the Maya (Emery 1997:400; Pendergast 1992; see Montero 2008 for discussion). It seems that the key to the identification of a feasting event is the presence of numerous faunal remains, especially those favoured by the elite, such as the deer (Navarro 2009:108).

Zooarchaeologically, feasting deposits have been identified 'in high frequencies in which preferred species appear as food, especially with a high representation of the entire body or in the large proportions in which the meatiest sections appear' (Emery *et al.* 2009:787). Other authors add that deposits from feasting should be characterised by a low diversity of species represented (Kelly 2001:351), and a high amount of waste, as represented by the presence of articulated remains (Jackson and Scott 2003:555).

One example of particular interest, due to its similarity to *Operación* 114 from Chinikihá as discussed below, was found at Group B of Xunantunich, Belize, located 100m away from the palace. This deposit has been identified as a midden or special-use deposit that contained more than 800 deer bones representing at least nine individual animals, as well as other fauna, such as peccary, dog, puma, and rabbit (Freiwald 2010:412). From the deer, limb bones are more common than axial parts; however, other feasting contexts found throughout the site (such as deposits associated with Structures 23 and 25) presented both limb and axial elements. In Group B, another feasting deposit was identified based on the ceramics rather than faunal remains, primarily service wares including open bowls and plates (LeCount 1999). Other examples will be touched upon when discussing *Operación* 114 in Chapter ten.

Food preparation and presentation

Feasts are usually documented in archaeology because of their unusually large scale (Hayden 2001:47), with uncommonly large quantities of artefacts or diverse artefact styles (Wiessner 2001:116). This is especially true in the case of the ceramics used to hold sacred foods and drinks. Such ceramic containers may become sanctified and have a symbolic role (Brown 2007:3). According to Hayden (2001:47), the size of ceramic vessels for preparation and consumption is usually a good indicator of the size of feasts (Conlee 2006:111). On the other hand, a feast may not necessarily result in the presence of large quantities of vessels in an archaeological context, for example, in societies like the Enga, serve food in banana and breadfruit leaves (Wiessner 2001:140, endnote 6). However, in societies where ceramics were routinely used for the preparation, consumption, and storage of food, the relative presence of the ceramics related to each activity can provide some guidance in the identification of a feasting context (see LeCount 2001).

In the Maya area, information about the types of ceramics that were used in feasts can be found in the iconography. The typical forms used during rituals and public feasts include highly-decorated vessels sometimes accompanied by a short description of the ritual for which they were used (Reents-Budet 1994, 2000, 2001), or indicating their contents (McKillop 2004:244). Sumptuous polychrome ceramics are also a clear indicative of a ritual activity (LeCount 2001). Common vessels represented in feasting scenes include a combination of plates, usually with *tamales*, cylinder vases, with or without a lid, a bowl, and a jar (Reents-Budet 2000:1026). Archaeologically, the type and quantity in which certain ceramics appear, may indicate their use in feasts (LeCount 2001). LeCount (2001:944-945) suggests that serving wares are a better indicator for feasting than cooking and preparation ceramics, as serving items display wealth and status. Herein, it is suggested that, as cooking techniques do not differ between private and public consumption, cooking ware is not an ideal marker to indicate feasting. The differentiation must then be established based on the proportion in which serving wares are present, including large bowls and plates, and polychrome vases (Hendon 2003:218; LeCount 2001:945), where a ratio of 2:1 would be expected, regardless of the nature of the feast, including feasts for ancestor veneration (Hageman 2004), or competitive feasts celebrated by the elite (Clark and Blake 1994; Hayden 1996).

LeCount (2001:946) also stresses that the context of consumption is as important as the ceramics when distinguishing feast patterns. Perhaps the only example where the location in which the preparation and consumption of feasts occurred has been identified at the site of Cerén, which is uncharacteristically well preserved. At this site, one specific structure, Structure 10, was identified as a primarily a non-domestic facility used for the storage of ritual paraphernalia, and the preparation of food, based on the presence of extremely large ceramic pieces and a very low proportion of serving wares (Brown and Gerstle 2002:100). Evidence of food included butchered animals and plant remains. The ceramics present include utilitarian vessels, mainly jars, large storage vessels with no handles, indicating little or no mobility, very few painted serving vessels, and no censer, or miniatures (Beaudry-Corbett *et al.* 2002:125, table 13.7). This has been interpreted as the location where feasts would have been prepared (Brown 2001).

Combinations of specific forms may also suggest feasting as, in many Maya sites, polychrome plates, bowls, jars, and cylindrical vases with a lid are routinely found (Reents-Budet 2000). Plates and dishes for serving *tamales* and vases for drinking chocolate are usually related to diachronical feasting sponsored by lineage-based households (LeCount 2001). Furthermore, information on what the plates might have contained is sometimes texts, with some displaying a specific glyph for plates used for *tamales*, a cooked, vegetal-wrapped mass of maize dough usually stuffed with meat (Taube 1989:31), in particular those made with venison, a type of food often related to feasts among the elite (Zender 2000:1044). The consumption of deer meat in feasting events has been studied and will be discussed below. What becomes apparent here is that the importance of vessels as containers of ritual foods, and their transformation from a common receptacle to being themselves sacred by holding the ritual foods, or by displaying motifs that make them symbolic (Brown 2007:9).

From this discussion, it is possible to see the great importance of polychrome vessels, and their relation to feasts and other communal rituals promoted by the elite. During the Formative period, the establishment of a communal identity was created through the display of incised motifs on serving wares that were probably contributed by different households. With the emergence of elite class and the consolidation of their power, the use of these motifs was abandoned, and the inclusion of decorative polychrome ceramics was adopted, their use becoming common throughout the whole Maya area for the Classic period (McKillop 2004:246). The production of these vessels was controlled by the elite class and distribution occurred primarily in the palaces (Ball 1993), with the elites also maintaining control of other crafts, such as textile, shell, and ornament manufacture (Emery and Aoyama 2007; Halperin and Foias 2010; McKillop 2004), and in some cases producing these goods themselves (Emery 2010). Therefore, the use of polychrome ceramics would stress the acquisitive power of the high class and their use in public feasts would serve as a vehicle to convey their power, through the gifting and exchange of polychrome vessels during public events. Such events would have helped to support the social networks establishing alliances and enmities between elites who attended the celebrations (Halperin and Foias 2010).

Location of preparation and feasting areas

Feasting facilities range from temporary structures to more permanent ones and be located in remote areas or nearby ceremonial or domestic structures. Institutionalised competition or promotional activities undertaken by the elites are more often related to a permanent structure (Hayden 2001:40). The physical location of possible feasting context is probably one of the best indicators for a positive or negative identification, as there is an intrinsic relationship between the architectural structures where food was prepared and eaten which has been observed in the Maya region (Brown 2001:378).

In the Maya area, feasts are not limited to a specific setting, as it is well known that feasts occurred from the household unit to the public arena. However, ritual and other communal feasts may have occurred more frequently in open and public spaces, and at specific times. This manipulation of the built space is an attempt by the governing class to assert their power (Ashmore 1989). The emergence of state ritual is often bound to specific types of architecture (Marcus 1999), whether it is open ceremonial plazas (Clark 2004; Inomata 2006:810), palaces (Webster 2001:130) or ballcourts (Scarborough 1991:130). The development of any centralised polity relies on the execution of public events within a built environment, or 'theatrical performances', where displayers and observers meet (Inomata 2006:805).

Demarest (2004:96) mentions that feasts were held in patios situated near temples and shrines, where other ritual activities were carried out, including animal sacrifice. There is no doubt that ritual activities were performed in plazas, as confirmed by the carving and placing of stelae in plazas directly associated with these celebrations (Grube 1992). It is assumed that a large number of spectators would have observed the ritual activities being carried out at the plazas, emphasising the public character of rituals. One example is the relation between feasting events and ballcourts (Bíró and Montero 2008; Brown 2001; Conlee 2006:111; Fox 1996; Masson and Peraza Lope 2004). Fox (1996:494) studied the relationship between feasting events and ballcourts and concluded '[...] the coordination and sequencing of ballgames and feasts was not coincidental, therefore, but rather a deliberate strategy of ruling and emerging elites to produce public dramas through the manipulation of ritual.'

Pictorial information of feasts is also found depicted on the ceramics themselves during the Classic period, suggesting that feasting would also have taken place inside some structures (Reents-Budet 2000). A more private form of feast would have occurred inside royal palaces when visitors from other regions, local leaders with petitions, and leaders of subordinate polities bearing tribute would be received in formal audiences (Demarest 2004:95-96).

It is also important to stress that feasting deposits have been identified in domestic deposits associated with elite families, such as N14-2 deposit in El Perú-Waka' (Eppich 2009), or Group B deposit at Xunantunich (Freiwald 2010), but mostly, these contexts tend to

appear associated with a main ceremonial structure at the centre of sites (Montero 2008; Reents-Budet 2000).

The location and conduct of feasts may also shed light on who was in charge of preparing ritual foods. Among contemporary Yucatec Maya, it is the men who prepare foods for ritual consumption, occupying different activity areas and methods of preparation. While women at the household level prepare food by cooking stews on the hearth, men prepare roasts and *tamales* that are cooked in an underground pit (O'Connor 2000).

Location of disposal features

Feasting generates a huge number of discarded materials and these materials are usually found near the places where they were consumed (Dietler and Hayden 2001:9; Murray 1980). In the sense that feasting is a ritual action, it can be classified as 'ceremonial trash', a term designated for ritual artefacts that are discarded after their use-life has come to an end, or they have become obsolete. These items may or may not be damaged at the time of their disposal and are usually associated with sacred spaces (Walker 1995). Such ceremonial trash can be differentiated from other refuse containing bones, as debris from ritual activities is not treated in the same way as ordinary trash.

More recently, archaeomelogists placing emphasis on the study of discard and abandonment behaviours have become more and more common, as a means to explain social organisation and ritual (LaMotta and Schiffer 2005:122). In the 'behavioural archaeology' framework, the accumulation of traces of events and processes through time are studied, aided by the use of ethnological observations (LaMotta and Schiffer 2005:123). According to LaMotta and Schiffer (2005:123), ritual discard is discernible, and can be positively identified among other archaeological materials. However, because in many instances ritual artefacts are utilitarian, some people fail to identify the ritual component of these discard deposits (Walker 1995:79). Furthermore, it is because archaeologists have had difficulty in identifying the ritual correlates, they tend to merge them into the same behavioural disposal practice (Walker 1995:76).

Ritual feasting middens have a tendency to contain higher concentrations of serving vessels compared with storage vessels (Clayton *et al.* 2005:126). In this sense, since storage vessels, are related to preparation areas, their presence in a specific context would not necessarily indicate the consumption of a feast, but rather food preparation. When studying refuse disposal, it is important to consider '[...] the categorization of objects as garbage, the distinction between clean and dirty, the nature of food preparation, diet and consumption, reuse and recycling, population size, animal roles, and the abandonment and post-abandonment activities' (Marciniak 1999:301). This information, along with the study of the taphonomic histories of the deposit (Lyman 1994), will help us to identify the role of animals and ultimately, of feasts in the archaeological record.

The identification of disposal areas associated with feasting among the Maya is a complex topic. The Maya did not deposit trash within living spaces (Guderjan *et al.* 2003:32), but removed it and re-deposited it in other areas, sometimes forming short-time middens (Sharer and Sedat 1987:261). Therefore, the discarding of food associated with a structure does not necessarily represent a direct consumption or the use of those spaces, exclusively by the elite (Emery 2007a; Montero 2008; Pendergast 2004; Sharer and Sedat 1987:261). Until recently, it was thought that the absence of food remains associated with elite structures was a consequence of the Maya cleaning practices, as they would have kept the spaces free of trash (Adams 1977:146; Marken and González Cruz 2007:150). Nevertheless, a few contexts found at the core of the sites suggest that at least some of these remains were being disposed of near the structures where the consumption may have happened. Therefore, these remains might represent the diet of the occupants of such structures. There are now a few examples of ritual use of animals and ceramics that can be identified as feasting material. It has been suggested that in order to distinguish between ritual and domestic use, the proportion of serving wares compared to ritual ceramic items is a useful indicator (Clayton *et al.* 2005:126), and the predominance of faunal remains that represent the meatier or the best cuts from large game in comparison to other less desirable parts (see Emery 2010).

The Maya of the Classic period, especially in densely occupied settlements, are well known for their management of garbage. Recent studies have found that not all the trash was discarded in the same pattern or in the same place (Hutson and Stanton 2007). The Maya would gather and remove it from the liveable areas in buildings, or incorporate it as a construction fill (Chase and Chase 1998a). Some authors suggest that, in the rare event that garbage is found in its primary deposit—called *de facto* trash—it should be fully studied (Chase *et al.* 2004:15), as it allows us to understand the formation process that was involved in its creation.

In many instances, the interpretation of refuse discard among the Maya was based heavily on an economic framework (Emery 2004b), especially if it was the result of an industry, such as tool production. Therefore, a full understanding of the discard pattern requires recognition of other aspects, such as the symbolic and ritual spheres (Emery and Aoyama 2007).

Correlating the anthropological markers with the archaeological record

The study of feasting and its appearance in the archaeological record has recently increased, resulting in a theoretical framework that can be then used to identify elites and analyse social change and interrelationships (Gumerman 1997; Pauketat *et al.* 2002; Rosenwig 2007; Twiss 2008). Feast deposits in these cases have been identified by the presence of specific characteristics that set these contexts apart from others of a more mundane nature. These include but are not limited to large quantities of ceramics, food remains, and exotic prestige goods that suggest their association to the elite classes (Lau 2002).

Nevertheless, feasts are tremendously variable and their role or the motivation behind them can be transformed very quickly in a short period of time, complicating their individual identification in the archaeological record (Rosenwig 2007:3; Twiss 2008:419). What most archaeologists discover are deposits reflecting many individual feasting episodes, or 'a palimpsest of many different feasts' (Rosenwig 2007:6), which form what is sometimes known as the 'festive landscape' (Dietler 2001:93; Rosenwig 2007:6). Because of these limitations, it is suggested that the study of feasting activities focus not on a single feasting episode, but the average outcome of various feasts (Rosenwig 2007).

Ritual processing and consumption of animals as food as part of such feast activities has been identified around the world, although these cases are isolated, and evidence sometimes appears to be very scarce. In the Old World, it has been proposed that feasting goes back to the Upper Palaeolithic period (50,000-10,000BP) with the emergence of modern human behaviour (Hayden 2009). More reliable evidence for feasting appears during the Pre-Pottery Neolithic (*c.* 10,200-7500 BP/9700-6250 BC) when feasting activity increases with the intensification of agriculture (Twiss 2008). As social complexity emerges, feasts become more and more common. Ultimately, the identification of a feast in the archaeological record is generally based on the concept that they represent a different pattern from that produced by everyday meals. It mainly involves food consumption in a shared way by different persons. Regardless of the type (secular or ritual, public or private), all feasts are similar in some ways. Several authors have identified a series of feasting markers that are commonly derived from ethnographic studies and archaeological contexts (Munro and Grosman 2010:15365; Twiss 2008) and are presented in Table 2.

Zooarchaeological markers for feasting

From Table 2, it is possible to observe that some of the markers directly refer to faunal remains, a characteristic

Common aspect of feasting	Material correlates
Consumption of large quantities of food and drink	Unusually large and dense concentrations of food remains
	Facilities for storage of foods (vessels, pens)
	Large amounts of food preparation/serving vessels
	Large cooking facilities (hearths)
	Special disposal practices
High frequency of processing carcasses	High frequency of cut marks
High frequency of young animals	Large proportion of unfused bones
Consumption of rare or costly to obtain foods	Presence of rare or labour-intensive species or preparations
Emphasis on large animals	Remains of large species, wild or domestic
Low frequency of post-depositional modifications	Low proportions of carnivore and rodent gnawing
Consumption of alcohol and other drug substances	Remains of drinking paraphernalia
	Macrobotanical remains (hallucinogens)
Use of special locations	Non-habitational sites
	Unusually large or elaborate facilities
Public rituals	Food remains associated with human remains/graves
Performances (singing, dancing, music)	Costume, musical instruments
Display of wealth and/or status	Presence of prestige items (destroyed)
Food wastage	Discard of edible material (joints, minimally processed bones)
Use of special serving paraphernalia	Unusual quality, decoration of serving equipment

Table 2. Feasting markers and their material correlates in archaeology (Modified from Twiss 2008:420, Table 1).

consistently identified in several zooarchaeological studies around the world (see Twiss 2008). Therefore, based on these exclusive zooarchaeological markers, this study has gathered an extended list of characteristics that can be used as markers to identify feasting through the analysis of faunal remains. These include, but are not limited to:

- High density of faunal and ceramic remains
- Special location or in a setting in association with ritual activities
- Associated cooking and preparation areas
- Special foods, rarely eaten or costly to obtain
- High proportions of butchered and processed remains
- Special contexts that may be discrete deposits
- High proportions of symbolically important species
- Focus on one species and low species diversity
- High frequency of young or immature animals
- Presence of articulated remains
- Less taphonomic modifications of bones in feasting contexts

A brief description of each is presented here as the basis of each marker, but these descriptions are considered and put to test in the analysis of the materials presented the next chapters.

High density of faunal and ceramic remains

Feasting deposits are usually very compact deposits, with little or no soil between refuse materials and containing very high numbers of bones and ceramics in comparison to other deposits of domestic or other nature. In Perú, a midden associated with ancestor veneration, produced more than 100kg of faunal bones, and a large number of ceramic fragments, with notable quantities of decorated fragments characterising the assemblage (Lau 2002). The amount of materials from this context contrasted sharply with other middens within the same settlement, as the second largest deposit contained only 3kg of bones. In the Maya region, a high density of faunal remains seems to be one of the characteristics used in the initial identification of feasts, with several examples in the literature. While a large number of examples of such contexts dating to the Classic period have been identified, relatively few have been observed outside this period, some examples being Blackman Eddy for the Preclassic (Brown 2007), and Laguna de On (Masson 1999) for the Postclassic period. High density deposits are especially common during the Late Classic period, and have been identified in sites of different ecological settings, such as Altun Ha (Pendergast 1992), Chichen Itzá (Götz 2008, 2005), Dzibilchaltún (Götz 2004), Xunantunich (Freiwald 2010), Lagartero (Koželsky 2005), Copán (Hendon 2003), Trinidad de Nosotros (Moriarty and Foias 2006), and El-Perú Waka (Eppich 2009).

Special location or in a setting in association with ritual activities

Although feasts can occur within a domestic household, larger and more public feasting events tend to occur in association with special structures, or in special settings. Structures can be purpose-built for the occasion, or existing ritual structures may be used to host a feast (Twiss 2008:424). In other instances, feasting participants will congregate in special settings, such as caves (Munro and Grosman 2010). Large quantities of ritual or symbolic paraphernalia found in these settings are usually considered a good archaeological marker for a feast or feasts (Twiss 2008:424).

Feasts can be associated with residential areas (for family and ancestor veneration), or with larger structures, where feasting remains are used as fill. The feasts associated with a large structure may represent the gathering of people for temple construction (LeCount 1996), where food would be provided by the elites who sponsored the construction. The relationship between feasting and labour recruitment for the construction of public structures has been documented for other areas including Cerro Lampay, Perú (Vega-Centeno and Lafosse 2007) and Xunantunich, Belize (LeCount 1996).

Associated cooking and preparation areas

Feasts are large-scale meals that would require large amounts of labour for the preparation of foodstuffs. Some authors suggest that a cooking area should be in the vicinity of a feast deposit, as foods would be processed and prepared and served near the location where people gathered to consume the communal meal. Evidence of cooking activities as inferred by the presence of one or several hearths, charcoal, and ash deposits have been found in association with feast deposits in Perú (Lau 2002:287), and several sites in the Maya region, a good example of which is found at the site of Blackman Eddy, Belize (Brown 2007). Linda Brown (2002:138) also mentions that one feature associated with feasting events among contemporary Maya groups in Guatemala is the cooking hearth. Calcined bone and broken ceramic pots (*ollas*) exhibiting evidence of fire exposure may also be present.

Special foods, rarely eaten or costly to obtain

Several authors have suggested that meat is a vital component of feasts, especially large animals that will supply copious amounts of meat, but also, are prestige conveyors, as they are owned or access-restricted to some segments of society (Clarke 2001; Kelly 2001; Twiss 2008). Meat in some societies may be considered itself as special food, not consumed as part of the daily meal, where diets are predominantly based on plants (Clarke 2001; Twiss 2008:422). In other societies, some animals might be seen as costly because they are not usually eaten, or they are difficult to obtain or process. This includes animals that are imported from other ecological areas, or those that require a major labour investment to process. The presence of non-local animals is therefore a good marker. In some coastal sites in the Maya area, the presence of deer portions from inland areas indicates their importance in the performance of ritual activities (Pohl 1990:168). Carnivores in general, but more specifically the jaguar and gray fox, are included in feasting deposits, and were considered to be difficult to obtain. Although there are references to the consumption of gray fox in the Maya area (Hamblin 1984:145; Wing and Steadman 1980:326), they are rarely found in domestic middens.

Storage facilities for food, and storing vessels

Storage facilities include portable or non-portable ceramic vessels and baskets, but also structures or enclosed areas where animals would be 'stored' for future use. In this sense, large containers were used for grains, and wild and domestic fauna were kept in pens. Pens have been identified in different regions, including China (Jing and Flad 2005:253), and among contemporary Tangan people from Papua New Guinea, who keep pigs in pens, raising them in advance for future feasts (Twiss 2008:419). In the Maya area, it has been suggested that wild animals may have been kept in captivity (Pohl 1976), but evidence is very scarce.

Special contexts that may be discrete deposits

Not all feasts will produce middens, although large collections of food remains are likely to be the remnants of feasting (Twiss 2008:419). Indeed, once feasting behaviour becomes more and more common, accumulations of feasting debris become larger and more public. These in turn become more worthy of special disposal, along with other 'ceremonial trash' (Walker 1995). Therefore, it is expected that these remains are deposited or disposed of in special locations. The intentional placement of feasting remains may be marked by the deposit of an offering or other marker at the bottom of the deposit. LeCount (1996) describes the inaugural deposit of a cache of two complete vessels at the bottom of a deposit and four broken vessels over the plastered floor that capped it.

High proportions of symbolically important species

This includes wild and domesticated animals that hold an important symbolic role. In early societies, large domesticates were the norm in feasting deposits, as they were considered to enhance prestige (Twiss 2008:423). In the Early Neolithic period, the auroch, while also regarded as symbolically important, was well suited to feeding large numbers of people due to its size, making it a preferable option for a feast (Munro and Grosman 2010). In the Maya region, where few domesticated animals existed, the domestic dog was not an everyday meal item, but was the preferred food choice during feasts in the Preclassic and Classic period (Clutton-Brock and Hammond 1994; deFrance 2009:142). Large animals such as deer and peccary were also chosen, especially during the Classic period (Emery 2007a). Remains of these two species are some of the most commonly recorded, as both held very important symbolic roles in ceremonies and were associated with fertility rituals (Pohl and Feldman 1982). Deer and dogs are also very symbolically important because they may have been used as a substitute for human sacrifice (Pohl 1994).

Another example of the symbolic use of animals is the clear selection of animals of a specific sex—each sex possessed its own symbolism. At Domuztepe, in Turkey, female animals were chosen as special value was placed on their milking and breeding properties (Kansa and Campbell 2004). Obviously, the importance of the species present in feasting deposits is related to the type of society with which they are associated; therefore, the important species within each society should be identified and considered as part of the zooarchaeological analysis.

Focus on one species and low species diversity

In feasting ceremonies, the focus on special or symbolic species is indicated by the presence of a significantly high proportion of these species, and a relatively low diversity in the faunal assemblage. In Perú, the *Chinchawas* midden contained mainly camelids that produced a large amount of meat, with a low representation of small animals, including guinea pigs (*Cavia* sp.) (Lau 2002:289). This is interesting as guinea pigs are symbolically significant, but do not necessarily produce large amounts of meat. In the Maya region, Mary Pohl (1994:135) examined the traditions documented during the Early Historical period and concluded that it is possible that the control that the elites maintained over access to important animals may have resulted in a preponderance of such species in ritual feasts sponsored by the elites. As mentioned

above, deer were of great importance because they provided a considerable amount of meat consumed in a short period of time (Pohl 1994:138). The choice of certain taxa for feasts may or may not be constrained by their availability, since in many cases, the animals most commonly available were not the focus of a feasting event. This stresses the fact that it is a culturally defined behaviour. For example, in contexts associated to the elite of Colhá, deer and dog meat were mostly consumed rather than fish, despite the common availability of fish in the swampy surroundings of the site (Pohl 1994).

Nevertheless, low diversity is not necessarily a prerequisite of feasting, and it usually depends on the nature of the feast. Some feasts are defined by a variety of food stuffs which would be absent from daily meals (Twiss 2008:422). Greater diversity however, may also be reflected in the ways food is prepared, resulting in a larger variety of cooking vessels than those expected in a normal meal and therefore reflected in the ceramic remains of an archaeological context (Twiss 2008:422).

High frequency of young or immature animals

Selection of young animals, identified mostly by the presence of immature teeth and unfused long bones, is seen as a result of feasting. These physical characteristics are indicative of prime age individuals (Stiner 1990). In many deposits around the world there is a marked preference for prime-aged animals as they ensure a large meat return (Kansa and Campbell 2004), especially for medium and large mammals. Younger animals also have more palatable meat, therefore, the targeting of a specific age group may be culturally prescribed. A clear selection of young camelids has been observed in a feasting deposit in *Chinchawas*, Perú (Lau 2002:289). In a feasting event at the site of Blackman Eddy, white-tailed and brocket deer were yearlings or younger animals (Brown 2007).

High proportions of butchered and processed remains

The presence of butchering, filleting and dismembering cut marks signal that animals were being processed for food, rather than deposited complete as an offering. Feasting contexts with a high proportion of butchered animals are common in different periods and areas around the world (Munro and Grosman 2010; Stocker and Davis 2004). Although most researchers agree that a high proportion of butchered remains are a distinctive marker of feasting, it is not always the case. At the site of Domuztepe (5550 BC), located in southern Turkey, domestic animals were the norm, with concentrated quantities of cattle, sheep/goat and dog remains being found in a ritual context known as the Death Pit (Kansa and Campbell 2004). While cattle and large animals presented cut marks, several dog bones were found complete with no butchering marks present, but according to the authors (Kansa and Campbell 2004:9) the absence of cut marks may represent a different cooking and/or consumption pattern for the special event. However, when processing marks are present, they are not expected to indicate a departure from the usual methods of food preparation.

On a related point, the presence of particular body portions may suggest specific targeting of certain segments. Some researchers have noted that specific body portions dominate feasting contexts, for example, at the Palace of Nestor site, long bones and mandibles dominated the assemblage (Stocker and Davis 2004:183) in contrast with other deposits, where all body parts are present (Kansa and Campbell 2004:181).

Presence of articulated remains

The presence of articulated joints of an animal carcass, or the presence of significant number of complete or unprocessed bones, is also commonly cited in examples of feasting (Hayden 2001:49; Kelly 2001:347). However, it is necessary to emphasise two important points. The amount of waste is directly related to the size of the animals, the larger the animal, the larger the amount of waste. Secondly, the larger the feast, the greater the amount of waste that can be expected (as seen through the presence of bone reduction) (Hayden 2001:49). Also, the presence of the articulated segments of a carcass may provide information on the process by which a feasting context was formed, as they suggest that the feasting remains were deposited when fresh and covered rapidly (Munro and Grosman 2010). Complete, articulated remains may also indicate that animals were not processed as thoroughly as in daily life (Kansa and Campbell 2004). The presence of articulated joints also indicates that there is some food wastage, as joints are minimally processed, and discarded with edible meat still attached to them (Twiss 2008:422). Evidence of food waste as a means to identify feasts is more relevant when there are historical data available on the consumption patterns practised in a society, although it is possible to apply the same logic to prehistoric sites (Milner and Miracle 2002a:3).

Taphonomic modifications of bones in feasting contexts

It would be assumed expected that the remains of a feast would be deposited in one single event, and subsequently covered with relative speed. Therefore, it would be expected that few post-depositional modifications would affect the assemblage. As a guide, it is considered that feasting deposits would depart from everyday consumption and disposal patterns and display less burning, carnivore gnawing and fracturing.

Another expected feature of feasting deposits would be that they are usually well-preserved as a combined result of their sometimes-privileged location in association with buildings that help to preserve them, and the fact that they are subjected to minimal exposure as a consequence of their rapid deposit following the conclusion of the feasting ceremony. In a feasting midden located in Late Classic Group B at Xunantunich, animal bones display little damage and only 0.9% of the bones display exposure to carnivore gnawing (Freiwald 2010:411). This deposit is similar to the figures from Postclassic Cozumel, with 1.96% of the materials presenting gnawing (Hamblin 1980:327). The low presence of post-depositional modifications suggests that both deposits were covered up soon after they were deposited. In the case of Xunantunich, a plaster floor sealed the context (Freiwald 2010:411).

Feasting in Mesoamerica and the Maya area

Feasts have been widely studied in Mesoamerica (Fox 1996; LeCount 2001; Pohl 1994; Rosenswig 2007), and it is considered that the intensification of feasting events seems to be related to periods of political and social tension. During the Formative period (1450-1250 BC) at the site of Cuauhtémoc in the southern Soconusco region of México, Rosenwig (2007:2) has identified a correlation between the presence of sponsored feasting and the emergence of a newly stratified society. Feasts were promoted by the elite groups in order to promote social cohesion, but also as a medium for the display of their elevated status. In the Maya region, one period of extensive political complexity is the Late/Terminal Classic period, and feasting events during this time have been studied as a proxy for the study of social inequality (Hendon 2003).

Feasting was not necessarily restricted to the higher classes, but instead seems to have been very prevalent among the rest of the population (McAnany 1995:31-32). Nonetheless, the interest in this dissertation is related to the emergence of inequality in Mesoamerica, which is accompanied by the reproduction and display of power by the high classes, specifically through competitive feasting (see Dietler and Hayden 2001; Hayden and Villeneuve 2011). Types of feasts have has been widely studied through the production and use of ceramics (LeCount 2001; Navarro 2009; Reents-Budet 2000), their relationship to specific architectural structures, such as ballcourts (Fox 1996), other ceremonial buildings (Eppich 2009), and palaces (Pohl 1994).

Feasts and social inequality

For the Maya region, the study of feasts has received significant attention, as a number of important papers have appeared recently in the archaeological and ethnographical literature (Anderson 2010; Christenson 2010; Dahlin *et al.* 2010; Eppich 2009; Goldstein and Hageman 2010; LeCount 2001). The interpretation of feasting events in this area has been conducted through the analysis of a different materials, including palaeobotanical remains (Christenson 2010; Goldstein and Hageman 2010), and the consumption of ritual beverages made of cacao (Joyce and Henderson 2007), but few have used the analysis of animal bones (Brown 2007; Montero 2008). A number of limitations inhibit the identification of Mayan feasts, including the generally poor preservation of bones and ceramics and the intrinsic path by which ritual artefacts enter the archaeological record. This situation created an interpretative challenge because the iconography mentions frequent feasting events and it is clear that feasts as a ritual activity would have occurred regularly. Archaeological identification of clear feasting episodes is few because in many instances, similar contexts display the same artefacts, and yet they are the result of different activities, as discussed in the earlier part of this chapter.

In the Maya area, evidence of feasting among the elite has been discussed for several sites, including Lagartero (White *et al.* 2004), Xunantunich (Freiwald 2010), Blue Creek (Clayton *et al.* 2005), and Copán (Hendon 2002), among others. In Copán there is enough evidence to consider that preparation of food for feasts was not state controlled. Ceramics used for feast-food preparation have been found in non-dominant houses (Hendon 2003). This stands in clear contrast to craft production, which was controlled by the elite, as seen in different sites in the Maya area (Emery 2007a, 2010; Hendon 2003:222). It is therefore expected that these domestic groups in charge of food production would have to contribute with some food for the elite-sponsored feasts. An example of this comes from a small-scale feast at the Preclassic site of Blackman Eddy in Belize, where the presence of large quantities of ceramics and diverse fauna were interpreted as the result of a communal gathering where participants were obliged to contribute with something, in a 'pot luck' style (Brown 2007:16); this would generate a high diversity in the archaeofaunal assemblage (Jackson and Scott 2003:555).

Another example where feasting remains were the result of the cooperation among different segments of the society all contributing to a communal feast, also comes from Copán (Hendon 2003). While Masson (2004a:101) suggests that the acquisition of fauna at the domestic level may reflect the local hunting and fishing practices, the presence of specific game animals indicates management of these resources by the elite. One such controlled resource was dog meat, and there is evidence of feasts during the Preclassic

period at the site of Colhá, Belize, where dogs seem to have been a significant dietary item (Shaw 1991). Therefore, the proportion of resources that may have been contributed by the general population and those controlled and utilised by the elite should be considered when studying feasts in this area (*sensus* Rice 1981).

Feasting also seems to be a long-term activity that continued into the Classic, Postclassic and Colonial periods (deFrance and Hanson 2008). It served different purposes, such as ancestor veneration, and delimiting land ownership (McAnany 1995:100-101). Ultimately, feasts have been studied in order to explore the socio-political changes that were promoted by the ruling class. During the Classic period, a major increase in population and associated ceremonial sites may also have put stress on the demand for resources, and the necessity for the centralised management of these goods and their distribution (Teeter 2001). Elites would most likely have required payment for their services from the population, including their intercession to the gods for a good harvest (Pohl 1983:100). Long-term dynasties would have controlled the acquisition and re-distribution of goods to the population, but also would have consumed large amounts of resources themselves in the form of competitive feasts and other rituals involving the conspicuous consumption of goods (Emery 2004c). According to Pohl (1983:100), some redistribution of goods would have been expected, especially during feasting events during the Classic period, such as the *Cuch* ceremony.

Rulers used feasts to establish economic and political relationships with other polities (LeCount 1999; McKillop 2004:122, 140), and through diplomatic acts that included royal visits, marriages, and military alliances (Martin and Grube 2000; McKillop 2004:122). In many instances, it is possible that the elite accomplished several of these goals during a single feast event. New powerful lineages would also have used feasts to display their authority (Rosenwig 2007). During the Classic period, a major growth in the construction of structures in the ceremonial centres would have led to celebratory feasts related to the dedication of the buildings, and termination rituals for structures being built or abandoned. Festivals associated with calendar dates were also recurrent during this time, possibly resulting in the celebration of cyclical feasts (Hendon 2003), although this practice might have started in the Late Preclassic (Rice and Rice 2004:88). The celebration of K'atun-endings is best known from the Late Classic, reflected in a series of architectural complexes with a stelae-altar depicting the ruler commemorating the end of the K'atun, such as those related to *Yax Pasaj Chan Yoaat*, a Copán ruler, and the magnificent carved stelae from Quiriguá (see Martin and Grube 2000). In the Long Count of the Maya calendric system, a K'atun represents a period of 20 years (7200 days), or 20 Tun (a year, or stone).

The remains of all such events from the Classic period would have resulted in the presence of numerous rich deposits that would have included a wide range of artefacts, including numerous ceramic fragments, lithic tools, bones and shell, and even scattered and isolated human remains. Examples of termination or dedication feasts and sacrificial deposits were associated with diverse structures, such as the N14-2 dedication deposit in El Perú-Waka', with the staircase of a central structure (Eppich 2009), and the middens around the ballcourt at Trinidad de Nosotros (Moriarty and Foias 2006). These contexts have been interpreted as the result of open, public feasting and other ritual ceremonies involving food (Dahlin *et al.* 2010:215), that not only served to establish the hierarchy of the ruling elite within the community, but also displayed power and mitigated conflict with neighbouring settlements (Moriarty and Foias 2006:1135). The site of Lagartero, Chiapas, has been identified as a location in which a feast may have been held on one or several occasions (Koželsky 2005). There are abundant remains of service wares, particularly clay figurines and vases for drinking cacao which suggests that this feasting was conducted by the elite (Koželsky 2005:31-32; LeCount 2001). Koželsky (2005:32) concluded that due to the large size of this context, it is possible that it may have been an open or public feast.

During the Late phase of the Classic period, an emphasis was placed on royal lineages and the acknowledgment of these lineages as the ruling classes. This may have been a consequence of the association between rulers and the supernatural, where rulers were seen as divine, such as in the case of Palenque. It is possible then that the focus on the royal families would have derived partially from the concentrated construction efforts and remodelling of elite residences, consequently increasing the appearance of ritual contexts associated with palaces and other such structures. There also is evidence to suggest that feasting was occurring at a more private level, and that these events were exclusionary. In these cases, it is considered that there would be a distinct difference between the feast items associated with this class and those of the general population (White 2005:358). For the Postclassic, it is possible to observe continuity in the celebration of ritual activities by the elite, including the sites of Laguna de On, Santa Rita Corozal and Mayapan, especially those festivities that involved calendric celebrations, and the display and affirmation of power by the rulers (see Masson 1999 for discussion).

Domestic, state-controlled feasting, and gender relations

The study of feasts in Mesoamerica not only allows us to explore gender relations in the production and consumption of feasts, but also the production of ritual goods found in ritual contexts in general, from household to elite contexts. There is a clear difference in the activities performed by females and males in elite residential areas, thus the objects associated with each gender have an accordingly specific spatial distribution, for example in the distribution of bone needles and spindle whorls (female sphere), and scribe tools (male sphere) (Aoyama 2009; Inomata *et al.* 2002). These male/female behavioural spheres have been identified in Formative Oaxaca (Flannery and Winter 1976) and modern Zinacantán (Vogt 1969:83-84). Nonetheless, in her study of Copán, Hendon (1997) has argued that there were no divisions of male and female spaces in domestic compounds. Inomata and colleagues (2002:326) argue that this difference is due to the fact that the objects in Aguateca and Oaxaca represent the areas where they were actually used, and not discarded.

Tools and other implements used by women and men during the preparation of feasts, and other objects that circulated during feasts commonly appear in feasting deposits. For example, woven mantas, presumably made by women, were presented as gifts to feast attendants (Pohl and Feldman 1982), stressing the importance of female labour in the gift-giving and goods circulation which occurred during feasts (McAnany 1995:32). Bone needles and perforators often appear in feasting deposits. Lithic implements, primarily obsidian blades also appear regularly in feasting deposits. These would have been used by the hunters or specialists preparing animal carcasses for the feast and are usually referred to as male tools (Montero 2008). Other artefacts that were circulated include high-quality polychrome vessels, objects that appear in both elite and non-elite burials, confirming the participation of the whole population in such events (McAnany 1995:33). Therefore, it would be expected that tools used in the production of textiles, such as needles and spindle whorls, would be present in feasting contexts.

Limitations in identifying feasting in the archaeological record

One should always keep in mind that identifying the behaviour behind an archaeological deposit may be problematic. It is understood that there are at least three limitations in the identification of feasting. First, the problem of using the concepts and markers defined in the anthropological literature. Archaeologists all around the world have borrowed the concepts and feasting markers developed by Dietler and Hayden (2001), and applied them to the study of different archaeological deposits, including different time intervals, and different social organisation. In some cases, this is a valid exercise, especially in socially stratified or complex societies, however it is not necessarily applicable to other types of societies, particularly when studying the competitive feast where the available resources are limited for any reason, and when a sharing egalitarian ethic dominates the social relationships as in hunter/gatherer societies (Hayden 1996).

The second limitation is that of time, since in many instances it is not possible to identify if a feasting context is the result of a single or multiple episodes. This problem is not specific to feasting deposits, but most animal bone deposits result from a combination of actions, so that their precise duration simply cannot be identified (Marciniak 1999). Identifying individual episodes may be as difficult as pinpointing individual households when the deposit is the result of sharing a refuse context (Pendergast 2004). Sometimes even when paying close attention to the formation process of the contexts themselves, and their taphonomic histories, it is markedly difficult to separate the different components (social, ritual, and political) that may be intermixed (Wiessner 2001), resulting in a 'cumulative palimpsest', where archaeological deposits are a result of the superimposition of successive activities (Bailey 2007:204). More specifically in zooarchaeology (Marciniak 1999:301), it is rare that a bone assemblage will be the result of a single event, but rather, such deposits form through long-term processes, where

individual and collective actions collide, resulting in palimpsests, 'formed as a result of overlapping, multiple events in the exploitation of different animal species and subsequent transformation of remaining bones.' Because of their nature, palimpsests are largely seen as problematic in archaeology, usually referring to a material record that is incomplete (Bailey 2007:203). However, if we are to deal with this specific type of context, we must develop specific tools to dissect contexts that may reflect the true nature of a palimpsest (Bailey 2007:219).

Third, identifying the purpose of the feast may not be as easy in the archaeological record, as it is in ethnographic studies. Identifying what the reason was behind the act of feasting may explain why the remains appear where they are, why they were deposited in a particular manner and other contextual data that could be used to understand the presence of the deposit. Is the feast inclusionary or exclusive to the elites? Was it to celebrate an alliance or to accompany the desecration of a building? Access to oral and written information about the reasons for celebrating a feast is a privilege that many archaeologists do not enjoy, and they are therefore left with the task of assigning possible causes based only on what the results of their data look like.

Chapter two

The presence of faunal remains in different contexts: the Maya case

In this chapter, the discussion will focus on the nature of the ritual deposit, considering the presence of faunal remains in a myriad of contexts that share common characteristics, but are the result of different behaviours. Then, I will discuss the nature of feasting deposits, and the parameters of what can be considered good indicators of feasting activities, providing some examples of feasting in the archaeological record, especially for Mesoamerica. In the second section I will discuss the use of two of the most commonly encountered objects in ritual contexts, animal bones and plant remains, followed by a discussion of their use and symbolism among the Maya.

Identifying the nature of the deposit

Ritual contexts among the ancient Maya have been widely analysed through the study of such elements as votive offerings and burials (see Kunen *et al.* 2002 for discussion). These deposits are considered the material residue of ritual actions, and as such, are understood to be embued with meaning (Joyce 2001). In this sense, it is the archaeologist's task to identify the behaviour that resulted in the deposit of these materials. Nevertheless, identifying ritual behaviour is one of the most difficult tasks (Kunen *et al.* 2002), and archaeologists will often refer to the presence of a specific element in the archaeological record in order to define the context as ritual. For example, the inclusion of disarticulated human remains in a cache dominated by faunal remains or lithics may suggest that the whole context is of a ritual nature (Becker 1992; Kunen *et al.* 2002:197; Tiesler 2007). In many instances, the materials present in a ritual context are the same or similar and include exotic goods, bones, and smashed or broken ceramic fragments. This has resulted in a seemingly endless typology of contexts where all of these materials are included. Therefore, it is a polythetic set of attributes that, when combined in different ways, leads to slight differences in context typology.

In an attempt to avoid confusion, Kunen and colleagues have proposed a method of identifying ritual events based on the relationship between artefacts and context in which they appear (Kunen *et al.* 2002:197). There is a wide range of contexts defined as 'ritual' including offerings, termination rituals, middens, and even burials. In the literature, a ritual context may not always be identified as the same type by different researchers.

The identification will depend on the specific material analysed and the approach taken by the archaeologist conducting the study. Below I will briefly discuss the role of faunal remains within ritual contexts and the applications of zooarchaeology to this study.

The study of materials which result from a ritual process can be approached by analysing the way they are buried or disposed, that is, in what manner they enter the archaeological record. Objects present in a ritual deposit following the conclusion of ritual behaviour are classified as 'ceremonial trash' (Walker 1995).

Presence of faunal remains in different contexts

In early research, the overall characteristics of the faunal remains recovered from a site were presented without reference to a specific context and without a direct association with structures. The aim was to produce a taxonomic list, usually prepared by zoologists, of the species that were present. However, in the 1950s, an effort was made by archaeologists to integrate faunal analyses as part of larger archaeological projects. These studies focused on contexts that were distinct—'special deposits' such as caches and burials or culturally modified bones and bone artefacts (Emery 2004c:196). The analysis of subsistence patterns since the 1970s has been summarised by Emery (2004c). In more recent times, and with the application of new methods and techniques, zooarchaeologists in the Maya area started to pursue regional comparisons in the use of faunal remains (Wing 1981; Emery 2004d). In México, zooarchaeological studies include not only the taxonomical identification, but also, a growing interest in the 'incorporation in ideological explanations, assigning religious or ritual values to the fauna' (Corona-M. 2008:75). According to Emery (2004c), a growing interest in explaining the social behaviour behind faunal assemblages has opened the door to the study of ritual activities. This includes the study of feasting and other ceremonies involving repetitive use of animals; therefore, it is crucial that the function of the contexts in which faunal remains appear be correctly described and identified.

In many instances, one or more elements (bones, broken ceramics, etc.) are not present, and the definition or function of a context as a ritual deposit has been assigned depending on their spatial relationship to an architectural structure (Chase and Chase 1998a:300). Artefacts are then seen as part of a system, reflecting the activities that were conducted by the inhabitants of such a building (Chase *et al.* 2004:15). However, when all the elements are present, the type of context may be differentiated by the proportion and condition in which each artefact occur. The complexity in defining these contexts is best exemplified by the site of Seibal. Pohl (1985a:133) identified some late Classic deposits as *in situ* middens around structures. In a later paper, this author refers to the same deposit as construction fill (Pohl 1990:162). Clearly, defining the nature of the archaeofaunal sample is a difficult enterprise when the taphonomic history is not considered.

Another example that illustrates the problematic task of defining these contexts is the archaeofaunal assemblage recovered from the archaeological site of Lagartero, Chiapas dating to the Late Classic period. First, it was defined as a termination ritual midden related to an end-of-cycle ceremony (Ekholm 1990:455), mainly because of the presence of plain and polychrome ceramics, figurines, pendants, shell ornaments, musical instruments, weaving tools, and stone tools, but also because of its relationship with a permanent structure. However, more recently Koželsky (2005:1-2) has noted that the midden at Lagartero does not resemble other known termination deposits, and argues that this context, with its high proportion of consumable animals with symbolic importance, is best characterised as the result of a feasting event. White-tailed deer dominates this deposit, along with dog and rabbit remains, differentiating it from other similar contexts (Koželsky 2005). Furthermore, White and colleagues (2004:144) conducted an isotopic analysis of deer and dog remains recovered from the context and concluded that some of them were deliberately fed maize in preparation for ritual use. While the ceremonial nature of this context is clearly identifiable, the interpretation of the assemblage depends on the angle from which it is approached.

This dilemma illustrates how crucial it is to fully understand the context in which faunal remains appear, determining first if there is a direct association between garbage and the original occupants of the building (Chase *et al.* 2004:14). Additionally, other sources of bias must be considered, including the extent of preservation (Moholy-Nagy 2003:58), the various ways employed by the Maya for handling and disposing of garbage and furthermore, the recovery techniques utilised and experience in the excavation of such deposits by archaeologists (Chase *et al.* 2004:15). With these examples in mind, it is considered necessary to explore the diversity of contexts in which the same artefacts appear.

Not all fauna is present in the same contexts, as not all contexts are equal. It has been suggested that caches, burials, caves, and *cenotes* (sink holes) are conceptually linked to rulership and lineage worship (Moholy-Nagy 1978 in Pohl 1983:56). Additionally, the *Cuch* ceremony, usually performed with the accession of a new ruler, would be associated to ancestor veneration (Pohl 1981).

The Maya considered burials, caves, and *cenotes* as places charged with symbolism, and this would certainly extend to the objects that were deposited in them. Thus, it is plausible that the fauna found in these contexts may also be analysed as a unit (Pohl 1983:102). During the Classic period, reptiles, birds, and particularly marine fish, were commonly dedicated in ceremonial offerings, and according to Pohl (1983:76-77, table 3.2) this fauna contrasts with that found in domestic deposits. In a comparison between fauna found in ritual and refuse deposits, Pohl (1983) found that ritual fauna is rare in midden deposits, whereas in refuse deposits deer was found more often and in close association with the elite. Other animals that appear in association with deer include peccary, turkey, turtles, and dogs (Foreman 2004; Pohl 1983).

From the distribution of faunal species by site, it is possible to observe that not all species were used in the same manner; furthermore, not all body parts are represented equally, suggesting there was a symbolic value placed on different body parts that lead to their presence in some contexts and not in others. For example, although the deer is more common in deposits located in the ceremonial centre, usually associated with the elite (Pohl 1976), it is also possible to find deer in ritual deposits in *cenotes* and caves, and in the latter, skull elements, possibly from *Mazama* sp. are predominant (Hopkins 1992; Pohl 1983:89).

In cenotes, Pohl (1983:91) mentions that tarsal bones (astragali and calcanea) may have been deposited as tokens of the sacrificial haunch, as the 'meatier parts of the deer may have been removed for ritual consumption', or 'were sometimes saved, perhaps for ceremonial feasting or as raw material for tools'. The difference seems to be in the type of body parts present by context. On the other hand, dogs are disproportionately represented by skulls and teeth, and their distribution is not restricted to a specific context, with the same segments appearing in similar proportions in ritual and domestic deposits (Pohl 1983:93).

Deer is not only associated with fertility ceremonies, but also with ancestor veneration, and political inauguration (Pohl 1981, 1983, 1985b, 1990; Pohl and Feldman 1982). In this sense, deer was consumed in a communal way, during public feasts (Brown 2002:158). In regards to ancestor veneration, we can see that the earliest ceremonial offerings begin to appear parallel to the emergence of elite lineages during the Late Preclassic, and continuing well into the Classic period (Pohl 1983:98). But probably the most significant association is that of feasting events organised to commemorate ancestors (McAnany 1995). These events, although most probably sponsored by the elite (Fox 1996; Masson and Peraza Lope 2008) were also a convergence point for other sections of the society, including minor elites and non-elite individuals (McAnany 1995:33).

The taphonomic history of the deposit: different types of context, same materials?

To discuss ritual and feasting among the Maya, it is necessary to understand the processes by which ritual is contextualised within the built environment (Fox 1996:483). In the Maya literature, there are numerous descriptions of large concentrations of objects that were deposited around buildings. Among the most common objects are large quantities of ceramics, lithic tools, shell, and bone. However, it is important to differentiate those contexts that reflect truly intentional and finite deposits, from those that are formed by a diversity of artefacts that may be the result of a mix of behaviours, such as construction fills and sheet middens. The former type includes those deposits that are ritual or symbolically charged, while construction fills and middens are mixed deposits, where materials resulting from a myriad of activities may end up together. As the rest of this section will centre on the discussion of the ritual deposits, here I will only mention that mixed deposits are found near or around structures, but they do not reflect necessarily the status of the people who inhabited the buildings or the activities that were carried out inside. An example is construction fills for building palaces, where mixed refuse from different social classes ends up in the same context.

Contexts where faunal materials have been found have been interpreted in different ways, sometimes as special deposits, termination/dedication deposits, caches and votive offerings, ritual middens, and even burials. There seems to be a constellation of categories used to describe these items, creating confusion in their interpretation. Ultimately, the aim of the archaeologist should be to identify the behaviour that produced the context, in order to gain a better understanding of the formation processes that produce these confusing deposits (Kunen *et al.* 2002:200, Walker 1995). It is only then that we will be able to create equitable comparisons between deposits and, as result, be able to explain any behavioural variation. Also, in focusing on the behaviour, we can avoid the trap of introducing false variability due to the bias of the excavator and their differing definitions of context.

To understand such deposits, it is necessary to consider the relationship that exists between these contexts and the structures within which they appear (Kunen *et al.* 2002:197). In the next section, I offer a brief discussion of ritual contexts and their association with the built space. This is by no means exhaustive, but I consider that it illustrates the difficulty of identifying the behaviour behind the creation of a context. It is also important to stress that all of the deposits detailed here may be part of a large continuum of ritual activities, making it impossible to define the boundaries between one type and another.

Special deposits

Unusual deposits containing human and/or animal bones placed as a result of activities other than those related to subsistence are commonly found in the archaeological record around the world, and usually categorised as 'special deposits' (Grant 1991:109; Hamerow 2006). These deposits are thought to be the result of a single event or sequential events (Moholy-Nagy and Coe 2008:3), and may or may not be in direct association with a building, appearing in a wide array of deposits, such as pits, ditches and graves (Hamerow 2006:2). Special contexts are usually differentiated by their nature or their association with other archaeological remains (Grant 1991:109). In special deposits, it is clear that there is a deliberate and careful placement of the objects, and they are generally thought to be ritual in nature (Grant 1991; Hamerow 2006:2). However, in some cases, a failure to distinguish between economic and ritual activities (Grant 1991:109), has resulted in special deposits being mistaken for domestic rubbish, or waste deposits being interpreted as ritual or symbolic deposits (Hamerow 2006:2). It is therefore important to stress that the domestic/ritual dichotomy usually does not consider the possibility that there might be waste deposited in ritual or symbolic ways, a phenomenon studied in its own terms and grouped as 'ceremonial trash', as discussed below (Hill 1995; Walker 1995).

However, before moving on to other types of deposits, it is important to stress that the formation processes and time intervals represented by these special deposits has been a constant concern for the researchers. In the Late Anglo-Saxon site of Eynsham Abbey, a large deposit was found, containing significant quantities of animal bones, including some that indicate primary butchery, but more importantly, some more unusual species were found, suggesting that the deposit was a result of a high-status event (Hamerow 2006:16). According to Hamerow (2006:16) this context represents a large number of individual animals, the remains of which may have been deposited over a long period of time, or may instead have been intensively deposited as the result of the gathering of a large group of people.

In the Maya area, special deposits have been described as 'associated features and materials that are thought to be the result of a single event or of closely-spaced *sequential* events' (Moholy-Nagy and Coe 2008:2, italics mine). Special deposits may include burials, caches and 'problematical deposits'. However, Moholy-Nagy and Coe (2008:2) stress that this last term should be used exclusively for contexts that 'might be the result of a single event or a sequence of events *widely spaced in time*' (Moholy-Nagy and Coe 2008:2, italics mine). Here the author is stressing the uniqueness of these events, in the sense that they may not only happen once; they are unique events that do not happen on a regular basis, as opposed to those that would be repetitive, which leave a distinguishable pattern in the archaeological record. Examples of sites where such contexts appear include Blue Creek (Guderjan *et al.* 2003), Yaxuná (Suhler 1996), Blackman Eddy (Garber *et al.* 1998), and Flora Creek (Glassman *et al.* 1995). Because of their nature and location, these contexts have been referred to as 'special deposits' in many instances (Guderjan *et al.* 2003:32), but probably represent a residential termination ritual (Guderjan *et al.* 2003:32).

Dedicatory and termination deposits

The practice of laying special deposits of high-valued objects in direct association with architectural structures or dwellings is a common feature around the world and can be referred to as 'foundation deposits' (Hamerow 2006). There are examples of this type of deposits, including Middle to Late Anglo-Saxon sites (Hamerow 2006). Perhaps the most important feature of foundation deposits is that they can be directly associated with the initial construction sequence of buildings (Coe 1959; Hamerow 2006:1; Kunen *et al.* 2002), or associated with the abandonment of a structure (Hamerow 2006:8).

'Dedicatory or commemorative rituals' and subsequent deposits are usually associated with new construction (Freidel and Schele 1989), and are placed before the completion of a structure or when a building is enlarged (Coe 1959:77; Kunen *et al.* 2002; Mock 1998). It seems that it is their physical location in relationship with a structure that defines them. However, other authors (Garber 1983) who focus mainly on the nature of the artefacts deposited argue that if they are complete, they can be considered dedicatory, whereas if they were broken, they should be identified as termination offerings.

It is well known that among the Maya, the practice of remodelling structures was common during the Classic, and this practice may have extended to domestic

households (Coe 1956; Haviland 1981). This may possibly account for the profusion of termination deposits reported in the Maya area, contrasting dramatically with the relative few identified outside this cultural area (Plunket 2002:7).

The practice of placing dedicatory offerings in the Maya area seems to have its roots during the Late Formative, as attested in the site of K'axob (McAnany 2004). At this site, an offering formed by vessels with plant and faunal remains was placed immediately prior to the construction of an ancestor shrine (Masson 2004b:391). The animal remains deposited in the vessels included rows of newborn deer teeth and frog bones (Masson 2004b:391), and both animals were related to fertility rituals during the Protohistoric times (Pohl 1981, 1983). According to Mock (1998:6), dedication offerings may include sacrificial victims including humans and animals, as the presence of these sacrifices was believed to ensure that the building was brought to life. Therefore, dedicatory deposits were placed before the completion of a structure (Coe 1959), and termination offerings were placed on the floor, representing the last use of a building at the time of its abandonment (Chase and Chase 1998a:301).

'Termination offerings' are usually seen as a scatter of purposely smashed objects around structures (Coe 1959), or on occupational surfaces that may be associated with a building defacement (Chase and Chase 1998a; Garber 1983). Garber (1983:802) defined a termination ritual as 'the intentional destruction of jade artefacts in association with the abandonment of architectural structure'. Furthermore, this definition can be extended to other categories of broken artefacts, including ceramics, stelae, and bones, accompanied by an intentional deposit of white marl (Garber 1983, 1989:9). It is this intensive burning and destruction (Pagliaro *et al.* 2003:77), along with the presence of large quantities of elite artefacts, that distinguish termination ritual deposits from domestic middens. Pagliaro and colleagues (2003) also stress that ceramic sherds often appear with sharp edges, suggesting that the materials in these contexts are deposited rapidly and expediently for this ritual. However, this is not necessarily a characteristic of termination deposits, as termination ritual deposits in Aguateca include broken ceramic fragments and lithics that could have been brought in already broken from nearby structures (Aoyama 2009:58-59).

A great diversity of artefacts has been recovered from termination deposits, including grinding stones, as well as chipped stone, and an abundance of valuable goods, such as jade, carved shell, carved bones, musical instruments, and polychrome ceramics, all being objects related to the elite (Aoyama 2009:8). In

Aguateca, many of these artefacts were deposited on the living floors when the residences were abruptly abandoned (Aoyama 2009:8). According to Aoyama, the destruction of buildings was conducted by foreigners (Aoyama 2009:8-9) in order to terminate the city as a political and economic power (Inomata 2003:60). Thus, termination rituals may be performed by locas as an offering to the structure, or by their enemies as part of a larger desecrating ritual. Desecration rituals which included the creation of termination deposits were common practice during the Classic period, and may have been in use since the Preclassic. An example of the execution of such a ritual during the Early Classic period has been identified at Yaxuná (Freidel *et al.* 2010). A possible example of a termination ritual conducted by the elite for the abandonment of a structure has been identified at Structure 11B at Preclassic Cerros, a site identified as a place where male activities were conducted (Scarborough and Freidel 1991:58); however, other authors consider that this termination ritual was conducted by foreigners (Freidel 1992).

Previous excavations have failed to identify similar contexts as the result of ritual activity, therefore forcing a review of their function. However, it should be kept in mind that ritual activities are dynamic and change through time, and so, they may convey multiple purposes (Coe 1990: 930).

Caches and votive offerings

Caches and votive deposits are defined as 'offerings'. Offerings are generally regarded as the tangible residue of ritual behaviour (Moholy-Nagy 1997:298), and are commonly included in burials or votive caches. The objects included in offerings are usually broken and as a result they are also referered to as 'killed deposits, votive offerings, and ritual caches' (Walker 1995:75).

Caches are defined as a type of offering that includes one or more objects placed together, that may or may not be concealed (Becker 1992:191; Coe 1959:77), and that denotes intentionality (Coe 1959). Caches can be distinguished from foundation deposits—including dedication and termination deposits—because they are usually buried in such a way that intrudes into earlier structures or within the construction fills (Coe 1959; Chase and Chase 1998a:300). Caches are often recognisable by the fact that they appear in the form of artefacts placed inisde a pottery vessel, however, a ceramic container is not essential element of a cache (Chase and Chase 1998a:300).

In the Maya area, there are two types of caches, those that define a sacred domain for a broader community, and those that include a diverse set of activities, such as ancestor veneration or the commemoration of historical and calendaric events (Chase and Chase 1998a:314). Items in caches are generally complete and unburnt, with the artefacts intentionally arranged in layers or in specific numbers (Chase and Chase 1998a:314). Also, caches have a consecratory function, and are usually offerings associated with the elite Moholy-Nagy and Coe (2008:2). However, when a cache is in non-elite contexts, it has been defined as a problematic deposit, because of their uncertain function (Moholy-Nagy and Coe 2008:2-3). There is evidence from the Postclassic period indicating that there was continuity between the non-elite and elite practices of making offerings to the ancestors and it is considered likely that this continuity probably also occurred prior to this period (McAnany 1995). All members of society would have been involved, and according to McAnany (1995:33), there was more differentiation based on gender than on social class.

Faunal remains identified from caches usually include complete or semi-complete animals, and although exotic animals often appear to be the preference, this is not always the case. In the Late-Classic site of Xunantunich, a cache associated with a juvenile human burial was found in the centre of a ballcourt, and another cache was identified in association with a platform (Freiwald 2010). The latter consisted of four complete birds, including turkeys (Freiwald 2010:410), a domesticated animal commonly used often in ritual ceremonies during the Postclassic (Thornton *et al.* 2012; Pohl and Feldman 1982). In caches associated with hunting shrines, there seemed to be a preference for medium or large-sized mammals, usually wild species (Brown 2005:137). Caches are offerings associated with the elite, as they controlled ritual through the manipulation of ritual objects (Chase 1985). Thus, caches are a good indicator of social status, and as such, are often found in contexts which differ from more domestic household refuse (Moholy-Nagy 1997:298). Caution must be employed when defining such deposits, as the possibility that evidence of ritual and domestic activities may occur together in the same context does exist (Moholy-Nagy 1997:299).

Disposal and feasting

Upon review of the numerous terminologies and definitions applied to various deposits, it is unsurprising that what may clearly be a ritual deposit could be referred as refuse, with no further interpretation undertaken regarding the associated behaviours by which it was formed. The definition of 'refuse' is itself confusing, as previously discussed in Chapter one. Moholy-Nagy (1997:297) defines 'refuse' as discarded material distinct from biodegradable waste or garbage; it is the result of household activities carried out by elite as well as non-elite groups. When listing the types of materials, Moholy-Nagy stresses that refuse is formed by 'potsherds, with smaller amounts of broken or worn-out artefacts of stone, shell, bone, pottery, and plaster, fragmentary architectural elements, and *bones and shells of animals that were usually eaten*' (Moholy-Nagy 1997:297, italics mine). Middens in Late/Terminal Classic Copán were identified by the absence of collapsing walls, and because they proved to be rich in bones, with the presence of ash, carbon, and some refitted artefacts (Hendon 2003:213). Middens can then be used as proxy to produce very valuable artefactual chronological data and allow us to compare assemblages at a regional level (Guderjan *et al.* 2003:32).

But is it possible to identify the behaviour or the activities that leave these materials behind? And if so, what do they represent? Are they the 'active' elements that were in use during a ritual or are they the discarded materials or garbage from ceremonial activities? In recent times, it has been stressed that ceremonial discard is in itself a specific type of context, not to be confused with other types, such as offerings (Walker 1995). 'Ceremonial trash' has been defined as the repository of artefacts that have finished their use-lives or become obsolete, and they may or may not be intentionally broken at the time of disposal (Walker 1995:75). Walker (1995) mentions that sometimes ceremonial trash occurs within locations that are identified as ceremonial themselves—such as temples, cemeteries, and so on—or in special natural settings, such as a cave or other sites with a remarkable ceremonial connotation.

In the worst case, items that are not well understood, either due to the context in which they appear or as a result of their nature, have been classified under 'ritual/unidentified' (Moholy-Nagy and Coe 2008). That is, ritual is used as a general classification for non-identified materials, assigning them a function *a priori*, that is, as ritual (Walker 1995:79).

At the Preclassic site of Nakbé there have been several rich primary refuse middens found around structures, and these have been interpreted as the result of domestic activities, although in many cases the same materials can also be 'ritual refuse' (Hansen 1998:58). That is, the refuse deposits are a mix of both domestic and ritual objects in the same context. Hansen (1998:58-59) mentions that middens surrounding Preclassic platforms are usually domestic in nature, presenting domestic materials such as broken ceramics, ash, bones, shell, and the remains from lithic production/rejuvenation. On the other hand, evidence of the elites' activities has also been identified by the presence of figurines, polychrome stuccoed and fine ceramics. However, items suggestive of ritual activity such as

incensarios, so common in other ritual settings (Kunen *et al.* 2002:208; McAnany 1995; Rands *et al.* 2002), are missing from this context. In the Long Count of the Maya calendric system, a K'atun represents a period of 20 years (7200 days), or 20 Tun (a year, or stone).

Structure B1 at the Preclassic site of Blackman Eddy in Belize presented a context identified as 'feasting debris' (Brown 2007:16). The feasting event may have been intimately related to the construction sequence of Structure B1. Among the materials present, plant and animal remains have been recovered; the faunal analysis resulted in the identification of more than 200 fragments (MNI = 17), including deer, rabbit and other medium and small sized mammals, as well as birds, fish, freshwater molluscs and reptiles. Of these, deer appeared to be the preferred species (Freiwald in Brown 2007). At least some of the bones had been burnt and presented cut marks, suggesting food preparation. Furthermore, a large proportion of the animals had not yet reached maturity, indicating the intentional selection of young animals for feasting events, as suggested previously by some researchers (Pohl 1983:62; Wing 1975).

Some authors have identified cases which appear to be transposed ritual middens. In such cases, remains have been removed from a ritual feasting midden in a location, and incorporated into construction fill as part of the construction sequence or change in function of a building new location (Clayton *et al.* 2005:119). These contexts usually lack domestic refuse and in general, display characteristics from a true feasting context, however, these deposits are secondary by nature, as they have been moved from their original place. An example of this shift is seen at Blue Creek (Guderjan *et al.* 2003), where Special Deposit 1 may reflect a periodic celebration of rituals that involved the consumption of large amounts of food in a feast (Clayton *et al.* 2005). It is interesting to note that these authors propose that this context may reflect a secondary feast context based on the presence of ceramics in contrast to an evident lack of lithics and faunal remains, both items amply associated with feasting middens (Brown 2001; Masson 1997). The authors' identification of the event as a feast is based on the fact that the context is located at the core of the site and thus its nature must be ritual.

The importance of identifying the context

As discussed above, defining the context is vital for the correct identification of the behaviour that produced the assemblage. The importance of studying and describing the context has been stressed by many authors (Clayton *et al.* 2005; deFrance and Hanson 2008:307; Emery 2003, 2004b, 2004c; LeCount 2001). By doing so, it becomes possible to distinguish ritual from non-ritual behaviour in the archaeological record

(Clayton *et al.* 2005). Diane and Arlen Chase (1998a:326) propose that if the aim is to understand these ritual contexts, one must always keep in mind that these deposits are dynamic, and therefore, it is in the study of their variation in distribution, content and treatment that we will be able to interpret their meaning.

More specifically, when studying assemblages that contain faunal bones, it is important to understand the context in which they appear, and the post-depositional modifications that may have affected them, as this may result in even further variability between contexts (Stanchly 2004). It has been suggested that a record of all post-depositional modifications, including faunal modifications and weathering stages, should be recorded as a possible source of bias (Emery 2004c:207; Hamerow 2006:2). Only after these transformations are acknowledged and studied, it is possible to conduct comparisons between different types of contexts (Emery 2004c).

Furthermore, the importance of temporal changes in the function of a context or its location, and ultimately, the changes in the behaviour that produced them, should also be considered. Differences in ritual processes occur through time, possibly as a response to the changes in the socio-political spheres. It is possible to observe that during the Preclassic and Early Classic periods, caches of layered objects were more numerous and such caches are found in the core of a site; with these deposits, a sacred landscape was being established (Chase and Chase 1998a:324). On the contrary, during the Postclassic, the focus shifts from public to a more private setting, and caches are found in non-central residential compounds (Chase and Chase 1998a:324). In the next chapter, a discussion over the political interaction in the Maya Lowlands is presented, as well as the involvement of Chinikihá within the political and social networks that were present during the Late Classic period. More specifically, focus on the elite groups and the differentiated access to faunal resources during the so-called 'Maya collapse' is put on, and the importance of meat consumption as part of the rituals performed by the elite during this period.

Chapter three

Chinikihá and the sociopolitical situation during the Maya Classic period

Political interaction in the Maya Lowlands during the Late Classic period

During the Classic period, the Maya from the Lowlands came in contact with one another for a variety of reasons, and most settlements were arranged in commercial, social and political networks that extended to other sub-regions of the Maya area. In the following chapter, an explanation of the political framework in which Chinikihá was connected, is presented, as well as a discussion of its chronology, and in particular, the role that Chinikihá played during the Late Classic period (AD 600-850).

Until recently, it was believed that while Chinikihá was already occupied during the Formative period, Palenque was not (Liendo 2009a). However, ceramics dating to the Formative period have been recovered from both Chinikihá and Palenque, suggesting that both sites were occupied at this time (Liendo 2009a). According to Rands (1977) the population was concentrated around the Usumacinta River during the Formative period, with less dense occupation occurring at Palenque and its surrounds. The rich alluvial floodplains associated with the Usumacinta River would have been the ideal place for flood farming (Liendo 2003). This low population away from the river and floodplains continued during the Early Classic period, especially during the Picota phase (AD 150-350), however, the presence of local monochrome ceramics, characteristic of this early phase, at Palenque, Chinikihá and other small settlements on the piedmont, suggests an initial population growth in the region in the form of small villages (Liendo 2003:96).

In the second half of the Early Classic period, or Motiepa phase (AD 350-500), ceramics from Petén, including Aguila Anaranjado and Balanza Negro types, as well as polychromes, have been found at several sites, including Chinikihá and Chancalá (Rands 1977). During the Motiepa phase, the influence from the Petén area diminishes (Liendo 2003), and there is a change in the concentration of the population with a movement from the Usumacinta River to the Palenque, Chinikihá, Chancalá and other piedmont sites (Rands 1977:175). It is during this period that Palenque started to have greater influence over its surroundings (Bishop 1994:31; de Montmollin 1988). Nevertheless, this influence was minimal at the household level, as the agricultural production remained in the hands of the local

producers, who would have built their households near the best soils (Liendo 2003:98). This scenario changed towards the end of the Early Classic period, specifically during the Cascada phase (AD 500-600), when the political centralisation seen in Palenque, Chinikihá, and Chancalá would have impacted the household distribution on the landscape (Liendo 2003:100).

During the Late Classic period, including the Otulum (AD 600-685) and Murciélagos (AD 685-750) phases, a major construction effort took place in Palenque, possibly as a consequence of the importance of this site in the region (Liendo 2003:100). The population was highly concentrated along the main settlements, of which Palenque was the most influential. According to Liendo (2003:160) the agricultural production would have been controlled directly by the elite from Palenque. It is possible that some inhabitants from Palenque would have been mobilised to work on elite-owned land that would have yielded a greater production for the support of the elite; these lands have been identified within a radius of 4km from Palenque (Liendo 2003:160).

Finally, the sphere of influence of Palenque over its surrounding sites expanded even further during the Murciélagos to Balunté phase transition (AD 750-850), possibly as a result of the development of a new way of political integration (Liendo 2009a). In this sense, Palenque could have been the centre of a regional political territory demarcated by inscriptions, with Xupá to the south, Tortuguero to the west and Chinikihá to the east (Liendo 2005a:32).

Independent sites and intra-site relationships: the hieroglyphic evidence

Martin and Grube (1995), through the study of the hieroglyphic data, suggest that the political system of the Maya during the Classic period can be identified as a Dynamic Hegemonic Model. For these authors, the hierarchical relationships among settlements changed when some sites would have reached their peak. This is similar to the model proposed by Marcus (1993), based on the political model that existed in the Yucatán Peninsula at the time of the Conquest. It has been suggested that this model can be traced back the Classic, and probably even the Preclassic, period— an era when there were series of emblem glyphs or

Figure 1a. Emblem glyphs for Chinikihá (original drawings courtesy of Simon Martin, reproduced with permission).

toponyms referring to individual sites (Mathews 1991; Marcus 1976; Schele and Mathews 1991:251).

Emblem glyphs occur in conjunction with the name phrases of royal individuals; therefore, they serve as royal title, emphasising the control over a polity by an individual ruler ('the divine lord of') or dynasty (Mathews 1985). Moreover, to some authors, emblem glyphs refer not only to sites but also to the extended territory they controlled (Marcus 1973; Mathews 1991). So far, there are around 40 emblem glyphs that have been identified from sites varying in size (Martin and Grube 2000:19). Examples of emblem glyphs for specific sites include Copán, Tikal, Dos Pilas, Calakmul, Palenque, and Chinikihá, with the last two presented in Figure 1. Based on the distribution and location of these emblem glyphs, Mathews (1991:29) argued that there are at least 40 or more independent polities by the end of the Late Classic period (AD 790). Palenque's

last Long Count date registered is 9.18.0.0.0, which translates to AD 780. Furthermore, during the Cascada phase (AD 500-600), Throne 1 is erected in Chinikihá (AD 573), depicting a *K'atun*-ending date on the left panel, suggesting that Chinikihá was an independent site at the time (Mathews n/d).

The emphasis placed on the individual ruler is what defines the Classic period, and stands in clear contrast to the Preclassic, where an emphasis was placed on a supernatural power (Martin and Grube 2000:17). The Classic polities were in constant contact with their neighbours as references to other polities appear in the hieroglyphic data. Contact was diverse in form, and included warfare, royal marriage and visits, and hierarchical relationships between polities (Schele and Mathews 1991). Evidence of this contact comes primarily from the epigraphic studies, but in some instances, there is also corroborating data in the

Figure 1b. Emblem glyphs for Palenque (original drawings courtesy of Simon Martin, reproduced with permission).

archaeological record, such as in the case of warfare (Chase and Chase 1998b).

There is a general consensus among Maya scholars that sites were somewhat independent during the Classic period; however, some have argued that all sites were equal and at the same political rank (Freidel 1986; Mathews 1991:29; Sabloff 1986), where others suggest that the interactions between sites were conducted under a ranking system (Martin and Grube 2000:18). In this sense, some authors suggest that some sites were regional states, with at least two 'superstates', Tikal and Calakmul, with which the rest of the cities maintained dynamic interactions (Martin and Grube 1995). The hegemonies of Tikal and Calakmul would have started during the Early Classic period (*c.* 150-500), with a strong hieroglyphic record indicating Calakmul as the superpower that controlled most of the transition between Early and Late Classic periods

(Martin and Grube 2000:20). But during the Late Classic period, around AD 700, the power of Tikal and Calakmul appears to diminish, and other entities begin to fight for control, including Palenque, Piedras Negras, Toniná, and Yaxchilán (Webster 2002:281).

In order to understand the political situation of Chinikihá, it is necessary to discuss its geographical location, as it is an important factor that played a major role in the development of relationships between Chinikihá and other surrounding settlements, primarily with Palenque, its closest and most powerful neighbour, but also with other sites such as Pomoná, and Piedras Negras. In the next section, a brief description of Chinikihá including background information is presented, as well as a discussion of the role of Palenque and its relationship with Chinikihá during the Classic period.

Figure 2. Geographical location of Chinikihá (study area) (credit: Coral Montero López).

Site description and previous archaeological works

Chinikihá is situated in the modern state of Chiapas, in the southern portion of México (Figure 2). Its coordinates are 17° 25' 09" N and 91° 39' 07" W (Grave 1996). Geographically, it belongs to the Usumacinta region (Hammond and Ashmore 1981:21, Figure 2.1), and because of its flora and fauna, it has also been classified as part of the Tierras Bajas Noroccidentales (Sharer 1994). Chinikihá is located on a piedmont and possibly held control of two adjacent valleys: La Primavera and Lindavista. Both valleys may have functioned as natural avenues, connecting the lowlands of the Gulf of México and the Usumacinta River (Liendo 2007a).

Once considered to be a peripheral site of Palenque, the archaeological site of Chinikihá was first described at the end of the 1800s (Maler 1901) and integrated into México's *Atlas Arqueológico* in the 1930s (Marquina 1939). Chinikihá is located 40km southeast of the bigger site of Palenque, covering an area of 0.7km² along the highway that connects the towns of Reforma Agraria (Chiapas) and Gregorio Méndez (Tabasco). With several hundred

built structures and platforms, and some hieroglyphic references to the site on carved stelae, Chinikihá is now known not just to have been the capital of an ancient kingdom but is also understood to have had a major role in the political network of the Usumacinta River and other peripheral sites (Figure 3).

More recent work at Chinikihá includes that conducted by Berlin (1955), and Greene and colleagues (Greene *et al.* 1972); nonetheless, these explorers were focused on describing the monumental constructions and stelae. Robert Rands (1967) created a basic ceramic typology, and the first archaeological excavation at Chinikihá to produce a map was conducted by Alfonso Grave (1996), as part of the larger *Proyecto Especial Palenque*. In similar circumstances, Rodrigo Liendo (2003) visited the site as part of the larger *Proyecto Integración Política en el Señorío de Palenque*, and produced a more accurate map of the distribution of buildings forming the site. During this season, more than 120 structures were registered in the core of the site, including a Palace, a ballcourt, and several other structures varying in size and function (Liendo 2007a). As a consequence, the necessity of a more extensive reconnaissance was acknowledged, and

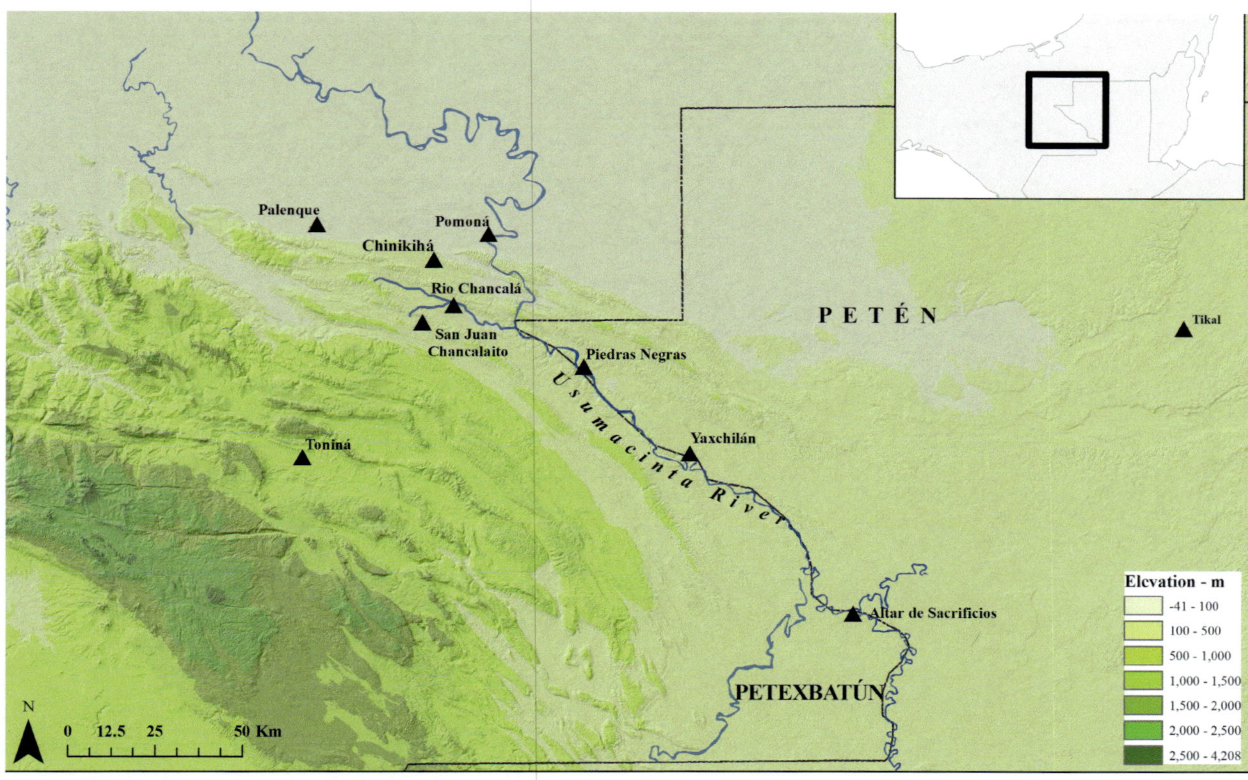

levation obtained from Jarvis A., H.I. Reuter, A. Nelson, E. Guevara, 2008, Hole-filled seamless SRTM data V4, International Centre for Tropical Agriculture (CIAT), ailable from http://srtm.csi.cgiar.org.

Figure 3. Geographical location of the archaeological site of Chinikihá (credit: Coral Montero López).

in 2006 the *Proyecto Arqueológico Chinikihá* (PRACH) was established under the direction of Dr Liendo.

Palenque and Chinikihá: The regional setting

Palenque is an impressive site from the architectural point of view, possessing more than 1600 structures and a population estimated to have been between 6000 and 8000 inhabitants (Liendo 2007b:87), comparable to other important sites, such as Copán. However, there is little information available regarding the dynamic relationships between Palenque and other surrounding sites of minor size (Liendo 2007b). Recent work in the region has increased our knowledge of the settlement patterns in the surrounding area (Liendo 1999, 2003, 2007b). Liendo (1999, 2007b) surveyed the region around Palenque and divided it into five sub-regions:

1. hinterland or central area (Palenque)
2. the area extending between El Lacandón and Nututun
3. the Chancalá River valley
4. the Intermediate Plains near Chacamax River
5. the 'Sierra' area extending from El Lacandón and Chinikihá

According to Liendo (2005b:72), Palenque had control over all these sub-regions with the exception of the 'Sierra' region (Figure 4). Hieroglyphic data suggest that the limits of Palenque were Xupá to the south, Tortuguero to the west and Chinikihá to the east (Liendo 2005a:32; Marcus 1976). Thus, it seems that Chinikihá was outside the sphere of influence of Palenque, at least for some time. With such a big area under its control, it is possible that Palenque controlled the production of goods and extraction of natural resources by smaller polities under its dominance; thus, it may be well possible that Palenque demanded other goods from all the subordinated sites, including agricultural and other resources. Ceramic studies have confirmed that Palenque's role was that of a consumer in the exchange network (Rands and Bishop 1980:42).

Chronologically, it is known that Palenque was occupied during the Preclassic, but little information beyond that is available (Figure 5). In this sense, the earliest ceramic evidence of occupation for Chinikihá dates to the Late Preclassic period (400 BC to AD 100) (Liendo 2007b; Rands 1967, 2007). During the Early Classic period (AD 250-600), which includes the second half of the Picota, and Motiepa and Cascada phases, there is no clear evidence for an early occupation

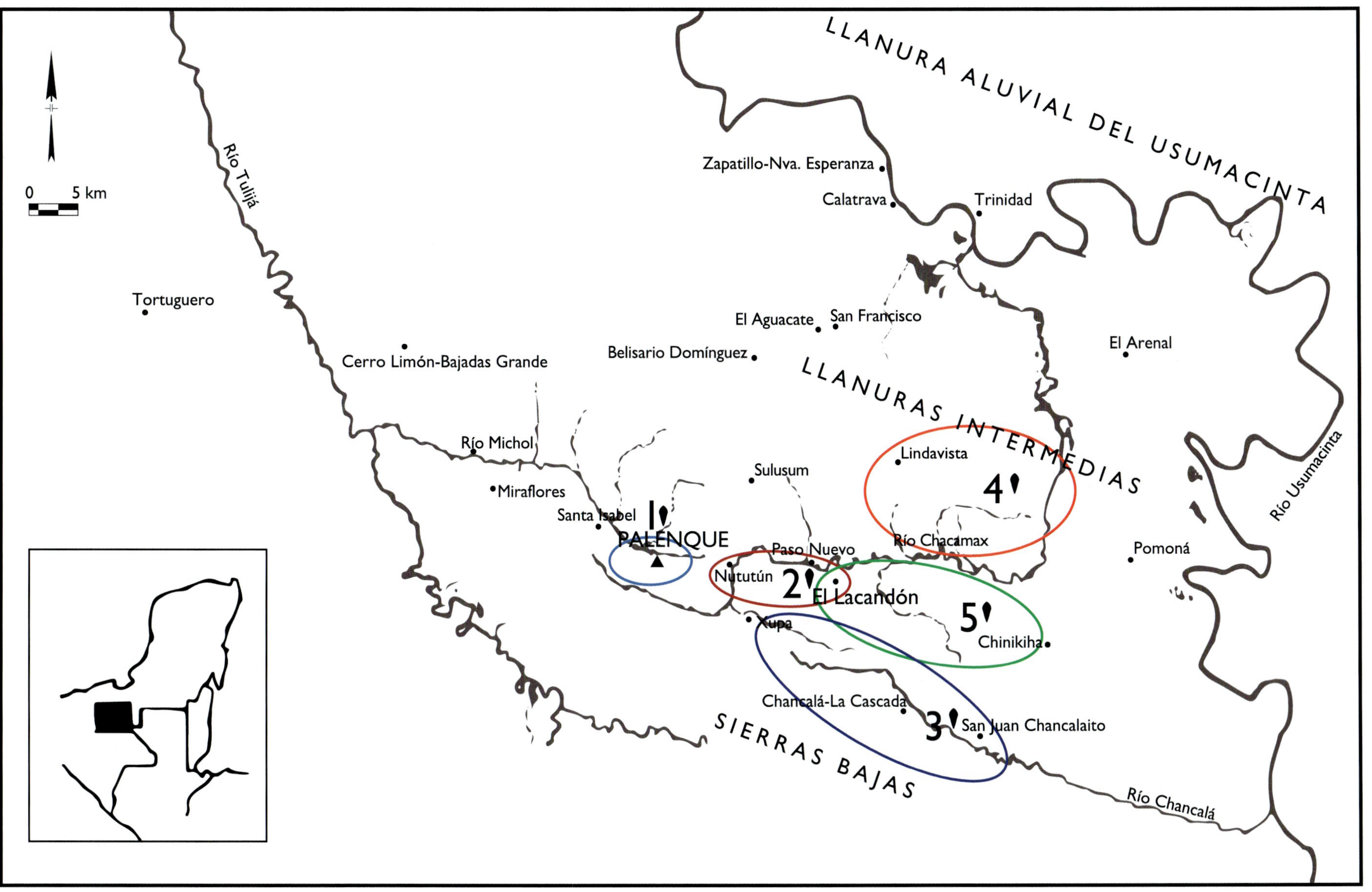

Figure 4. Palenque region and the five sub-regions as defined by Liendo (1996) (modified from López 2005:46).

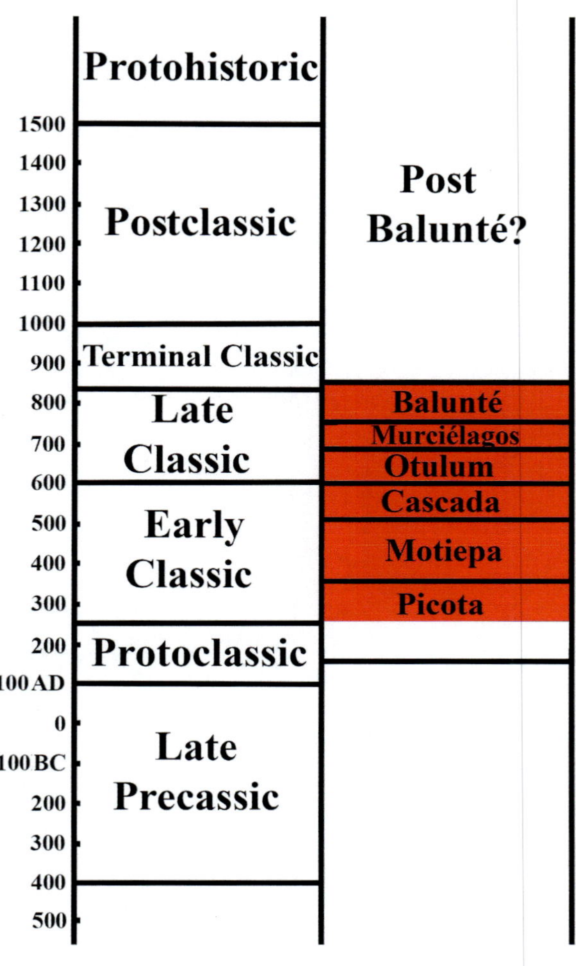

Figure 5. Proposed chronology for Palenque (shaded area represents the main occupation phases at Chinikihá) (modified from Montero 2008:72, Figure 5; Sharer and Traxler 2006:98, Table 2.2).

of the other sites. The emerging of ruling dynasties began in the Early Classic period, resulting in a nucleation phenomenon with new settlements along the Usumacinta River, such as Piedras Negras, Pomoná and Yaxchilán (Golden and Scherer 2006:2). Some authors believe that there is evidence to suggest that these sites were occupied since the Formative period (600-200 BC) (Escobedo and Houston 2004; Garcia Moll 1996, 2003; Rands 1967). Nonetheless, these sites grew to be big settlements, and most probably would have held some influence in their immediate surroundings (Golden and Scherer 2006:2). Chinikihá would have participated in this new regional political system, integrating itself as one of many minor sites in the area (de Montmollin 1988; Liendo 2003).

By the end of the Early Classic period (AD 250-600), Palenque was considered as the capital of this region (Liendo 2005a:31), with the establishment of a dynasty

that started with *K'uk' B'alam* I (Quetzal Jaguar) in AD 431, and continued well into the Late Classic period (AD 600-850), with the last king recorded as *Janaab' Pakal* III (accession date AD 799), a period that stressed the presence of external influences, as it can be seen in the Mexicanised name of *Janaab' Pakal* III as 6 Death (Martin and Grube 2000:175). The Late Classic period encompasses three phases: Otulum (AD 600-685), Murciélagos (AD 685-750), and most of Balunté (AD 750-850). According to Liendo (2003), during the Otulum phase, the first evidence of intensive agriculture appears around Palenque. These lands were possibly controlled and even owned by the elite from Palenque (Liendo 2003). In late Otulum and Murciélagos, Palenque reached its architectural climax, including several monuments, such as the Temple of the Folliated Cross and some buildings of the Palace, stressing Palenque's role as a major Classic Maya centre (Rands 1974).

The transition between the Murciélagos and Balunté phases also saw the appearance of new sites and the growth of others that existed between Palenque and Chinikihá; all these sites were connected by a *sacbé* (road) running east-west (Liendo 2005b:39). This massive change in the surroundings of Palenque may have been implemented with the goal of supporting the increasing core population that inhabited Palenque by this time (Liendo 2005b:40). Nevertheless, during the end of the Balunté phase, most probably around AD 800 or the early Terminal Classic period (AD 830-1000), a marked decline in the production of local polychrome wares is observed, and the appearance of the Fine Orange wares spreading from the north is visible at Palenque around AD 830, a date that some researchers pinpoint as the collapse of this polity (Rands 1974). During the Balunté phase, a shift in populations is also observed with the settling of territory previously vacant in the region (Liendo 2005b:40).

Palenque was most powerful during the Late Classic period under the guidance of *K'inixh Janaab' Pakal* I, also known as 'Pakal', an epoch where the emblem glyph for Palenque is first used (Sharer 1994:291). Pakal's reign was one of the longest (over 60 years), and under his guidance, Palenque was the primary centre ruling over a vast area that included more than 400 settlements of different sizes, and cross-cutting different ecological niches (Liendo 2005a). During Pakal and his sons' reigns, Palenque was subject to a major construction programme, resulting in a great diversity of architectural structures, including a variety of civic-ceremonial structures, such as plazas, a palace and a ballcourt. All of these elements characterise what Liendo (2007b) has defined as Category I sites, definitely including Palenque and probably Chinikihá. Category I sites are known as 'civic-ceremonial', and some other distinctive architectural features are present, including

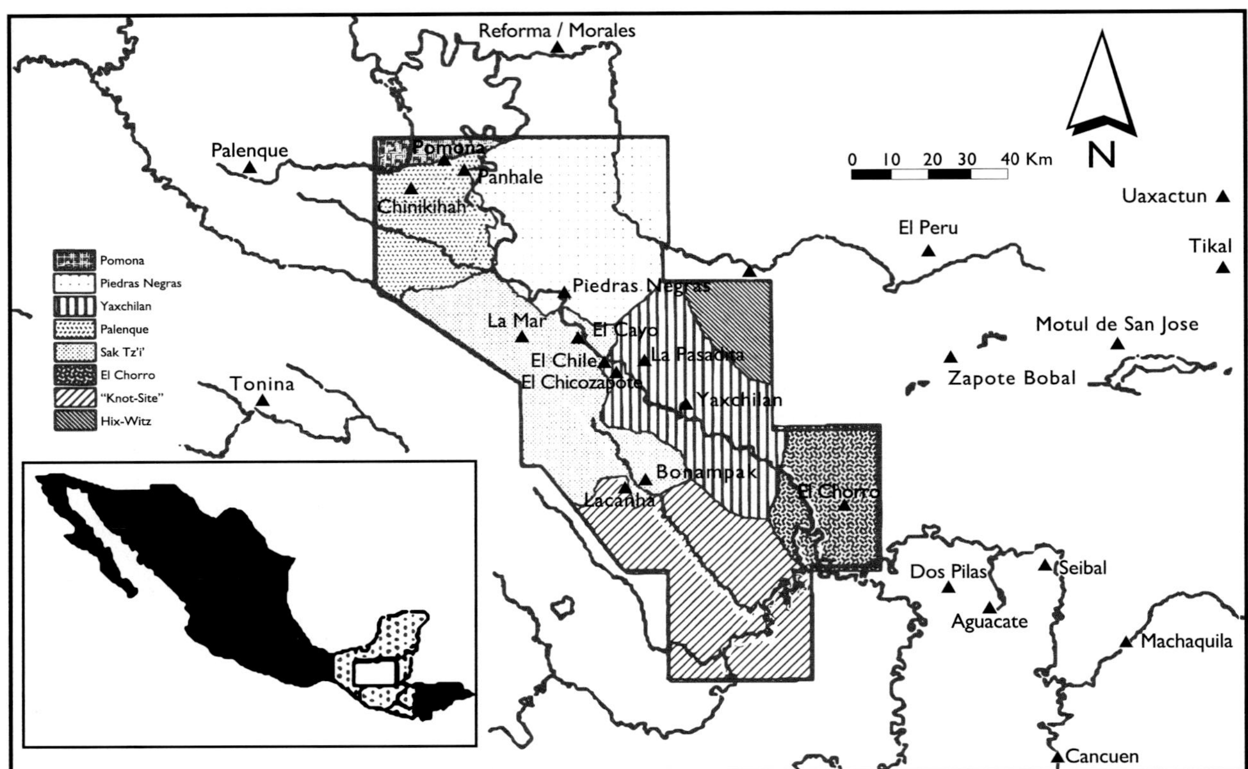

Figure 6. Spheres of influence during the Classic period (modified from Anaya et al. 2003).

a ballcourt, a public plaza, and several platforms and mounds (Flores 2010; Liendo 2009a).

One of the most important features of the Category I sites is the presence of a palatial structure that would indicate several nuclei of political, ideological, and ritual activity within a particular region (Liendo 2007b). The existence of a palace seems to be a direct consequence of the changes that occurred in the political arena, especially during the Classic period. Palaces do not seem to have been present during the Preclassic period, therefore, it is possible that the construction of palaces coincides with the emergence of a few ruling lineages who have managed to centralise the power (McAnany 1995:133). In addition, Rice (2009) proposes a 'palace economy', which is a type of ritual production, where the elites living in palaces held control not only of the production of exotic goods, but also of the surplus of basic foodstuffs.

References to some Category I sites or their rulers exist in the form of emblem glyphs and texts recorded on stelae. Such references also support the idea that these sites were independent entities (Liendo 2005b; Mathews 2001). Certainly, Chinikihá possesses a multi-room palace, a large ballcourt and a plaza surrounded by several platforms and domestic units (Liendo 2005b),

all of which suggest it was an independent polity. Several stelae have been recovered from Chinikihá, and references to local rulers (Maler 1901) and the possible existence of an emblem glyph (Martin and Grube 2000:19) have enabled researchers to classify Chinikihá as a Category I site, in addition to Palenque (Flores 2010; Liendo 2005b). Some evidence also suggest that Chinikihá was not only in contact with Palenque, but also with Pomoná, Toniná, and Piedras Negras. According to Anaya and colleagues (2003), Chinikihá was under Pomoná's sphere of influence during the 7th century AD (Figure 6). However, during the Late Classic, around the 8th century AD, Palenque appears to have emerged as the strongest ruling centre, dominating the whole region, including Chinikihá (Liendo 2005a).

Chinikihá during the Late classic/Terminal period

During the Late Classic, a massive population growth occurred in the larger sites resulting in significant architectural activity, especially during the Otulum-Murciélagos phases (AD 600-750) (Flores 2010; Liendo 2007b:100). This increase in the population would have put different groups in contact; Palenque was well-established as a regional centre, controlling surrounding sites (Liendo 2003). Consequently, inter-site elite interaction also increased (Demarest 2004:113), and rulers came into contact through a diversity of mechanisms that included peaceful relationships established through kinship, alliances, and marriage (Schele and Mathews 1991:228, 245), exchange (Sharer 1994:461-462), the witnessing of throne accessions and royal visits in general (Schele and Mathews 1991:228; Schele and Miller 1986:149). Finally, elites came into contact through warfare (Chase and Chase 1998b). Palenque was not exempt from conflicts and was defeated by Calakmul; other smaller polities also engaged in warfare, one example being the defeat of Lacanhá by Yaxchilán (AD 514), with both sites falling years later to Piedras Negras (AD 573).

Evidence of conflict between Chinikihá and other polities appears on a throne that mentions the capture of a person who may have been a Toniná native in AD 573, a site that is more than 70km away (Martin and Grube 2000:179). The name of the Toniná individual is unknown, but it is possible that it may have been Jaguar Bird Peccary (Martin and Grube 2000:178), a lord that acceded in AD 563. This inscription is important as it suggests a possible local lineage at Chinikihá, involving *K'inich B'ah Tok'* (Stuart and Morales 2003). The fact that this lord used the title *K'inich* (or divine lord), not only testifies to its simulation of Palenque's great lineage, which commenced with *K'uk' Balam* I from Palenque (Grave 1996; Liendo 2005b), but probably his claim to a mystical ancestor. This would have derived in an appropriation of status symbols by the ruling class at Chinikihá. It may also be possible that as a satellite site, Chinikihá's own lineage was substituted by one imposed from Palenque.

Evidence for other types of interaction includes royal visits during calendar-based festivities including a *K'atun* anniversary (Schele and Mathews 1991:228). These occasions would also allow new lineages to display their power and in general, elites became more competitive, and rivalries emerged during these events, not only in this region, but also in the whole of the Maya world (Demarest 2004:110).

All these changes may have converted Chinikihá and other smaller secondary sites into local independent centres (Liendo 2009a), extending to sites along the Usumacinta River. Chinikihá and Chancalá, among other small polities, were negotiating alliances or embarking in warfare with larger polities like Pomoná, Piedras Negras, and Yaxchilán (Anaya 2001, 2005; Golden and Scherer 2006:3). However, the geographical extents of Chinikihá and Chancalá are unknown (Anaya 2001). As an independent polity situated in the political frontier of three larger entities—Palenque, Piedras Negras, and Pomoná—it is expected that Chinikihá would display evidence of a series of fluctuating relationships with these sites, reflected primarily through ceramics

(Liendo 2005a). Furthermore, it would also be expected that Chinikihá would be using similar mechanisms to create a sense of a stable community through 'theatrical' displays of rituals and symbolic objects in events organised by the elite (Inomata 2006). According to Inomata (2006:818), these events or gatherings would have occurred in plazas and on causeways and would have been repeated constantly.

Certainly, all of these interactions are intertwined with economic and political behaviours, in the much broader topic of ritual. It is also possible that the relationships between these sites fluctuated between peace and war. For example, Martin and Grube (2000) note that there are abundant records of large gatherings of people for the celebration of feasts, and for such events, noble visitors from other sites would also have participated.

In this chronological framework, it is possible to hypothesise that during the Late Classic and Terminal periods, the Lowlands region was a very dynamic area with sites interacting in diverse ways. Because of Chinikihá's geographical location, it may have been in a conflict area, and although it may have remained as a relatively independent polity, it was likely to have been engaged in regional warfare, and explicit displays of its power through ceremonies including large feasts, where lords from neighbouring sites would have been invited.

The Maya collapse during the Classic period

Towards the end of the Late Classic/Terminal period, there were a series of abrupt changes and disruptions that are observable in the archaeological record all over the Maya region, in what has been known as 'the Maya collapse'. To account for these changes, two main hypotheses have been proposed, one is based on socio-political changes and the other sees the collapse more as a consequence of environmental factors. Since then, many researchers have embraced either one or the other hypothesis, although presently, most Maya scholars would agree that the collapse can be explained by a combination of these circumstances (Emery 1999:835).

A brief description of the two hypotheses is presented below in order to construct a framework in which to place Chinikihá and the study of the zooarchaeological assemblages that are discussed in this dissertation. Moreover, a description of the dietary failure model during the Late Classic/Terminal periods (Emery 2010) is also presented.

The socio-political hypothesis

During the Late Classic several changes, both ecological and political, occurred in the Maya area that ultimately contributed to the abandonment of many large sites. The Maya collapse has been identified as a period when major sites were abandoned, and this was accompanied by the cessation of the construction of buildings and stelae, and of writing (Culbert 1988). However, recent archaeological works in different regions of the Maya area have found that small populations continued to live in some major sites, leading to the conclusion that the collapse was more of an extensive failure of the elite class, which occurred during the Terminal Classic period (AD 750-1050) (Emery 2010:1).

Status markers seen during the Late Classic period, disappear towards the Terminal period and are definitely rare during the Postclassic, thus it has been proposed that this change was considered 'a cultural adaptation to circumstances that made the costs of maintaining an elite difficult, disadvantageous, or impossible' (Aimers 2007:331), and may be considered as a period of decline or transformation, characterised by the breakdown of divine kingship (Aimers 2007:331). The decline associated with this period was not homogeneous, but rather varied regionally, with a wide array of political and social systems appearing during this period (Demarest *et al.* 2005). In some areas, this transition was more abrupt, with many sites being abandoned, including the Petén region in Guatemala (Aimers 2007:334), and the Usumacinta River, including Piedras Negras, Yaxchilán and Bonampak (Emery 2010:29). Piedras Negras and Yaxchilán may have seen a drastic decline in their populations as a result of disruptions in trading networks following warfare and collapse elsewhere (Aimers 2007: 335). In the Palenque hinterland, the collapse period also impacted the exchange and trade networks in which Palenque (and most probably Chinikihá) participated during earlier periods (Rands 1974).

The environmental hypothesis

As an alternative to the socio-political hypothesis, some authors have proposed a series of ecological factors, such as deforestation, drought, and soil erosion, may have altered the socio-political systems during the Late Classic period, and eventually led to the Maya collapse (Hodell *et al.* 1995; Santley *et al.* 1986). Widespread deforestation seems to have occurred during the Late Classic period as a consequence of agricultural expansion and population growth, which in turn may have affected and limited the dietary choices available during this period (Santley *et al.* 1986; Wright 2006:7). Compounding the problem, it is likely that the Maya elite continued to demand natural resources as tribute, resulting in depletion or over-hunting, particularly of favoured species such as the white-tailed deer (Pohl 1990). It has been proposed that as a result of this exhaustion of natural resources, dependency on corn

increased while access to meat was greatly restricted during this period (Santley *et al.* 1986), as suggested by the presence of markers for nutritional deficiencies and disease on human skeletons (Hooton 1940; Saul 1972; Whittington and Reed 1997).

Nevertheless, new studies in soil erosion and zooarchaeological analyses suggest otherwise. Anselmetti and colleagues (2007:918) conducted a sediment study in Lake Salpeten, northern Guatemala and concluded that intense soil erosion was related to the Preclassic period and decreased towards the Classic, despite human population growth. Soil erosion during the Preclassic may have been related to the introduction of new agricultural techniques, including slash-and-burn practices, which in turn modified the environment, and eventually led to a highly managed landscape that remained stable. This is known as the Maya forest garden (Ford and Nigh 2009).

From a zooarchaeological perspective, Emery (2007a, 2008, 2010), evaluated the hypothesis of over-hunting during the Late and Terminal Classic periods across numerous sites of diverse ecological and temporal settings. She found that despite the Maya hunting practices over more than 4000 years and the environmental changes that occurred during that time, there is no evidence of faunal depletion (Emery 2007a:192). Furthermore, for the Petexbatún area in particular, Emery (2008:631) found that not only faunal species heterogeneity was stable before, during, and after the collapse of the elite, but also that there was an overall hunting efficiency despite drops in the numbers of deer available. Finally, Emery and Thornton (2008a:172) stress that the relationship between the Maya and their environment is complex and that there is no single explanation that is appropriate since the history of each site should be considered.

This suggests that the collapse was discontinuous through time and space, and ranging from a positive impact to no impact at all, depending on the political and environmental setting in which a site was located (Emery 2010:1). Emery (2010:270) concluded that 'neither the ecosystem nor the chemical analysis supports a model of extensive environmental failure, either natural or anthropogenic, as a causal mechanism for the dissolution of Classic Maya society in this region'.

The dietary failure model, diet and differential access to natural resources during the Late Classic/ Terminal period

To test this hypothesis, Emery (2010:121) has proposed several predictions to test the dietary failure model. The author suggests that during this period, those species favoured by the elite class would have been affected by an increased hunting pressure as a consequence of increased competition among the elite members of the society. This would in turn have three consequences: firstly, prior to the collapse, there would have been a rapid increase in the use of those species considered of the greatest value; secondly, there would be an increase in the presence of meatier skeletal portions, especially primary cuts; and thirdly, there would be a generalised inefficiency in the use of carcasses, where only favoured portions were used (Emery 2010:121-122).

Furthermore, Emery (2010:122) suggests that during and immediately after the collapse, famine foods and more efficient use of available resources would be introduced as a reaction to the disappearance of animal populations. This would have resulted not only in the use of a wider range of animals including some not previously considered, but also the use of complete carcasses rather than portions, seen in the archaeological record as changes in the proportion of body parts, changes in species diversity, and finally, changes in the processing of animal resources (Emery 2010:122). Other researchers (Williams *et al.* 2009:40) suggest that after the collapse, elite foods may have become accessible to commoners, as social divisions diminished.

The question of the management of the land by the Maya to increase maize agriculture, and how this affected human and animal populations is relevant to this topic. In particular, understanding the impact of having larger areas for agriculture is then used in order to identify changes in the human diet before, during and after the collapse. Below, it is briefly discussed the temporal differences in the consumption of corn and meat in the Maya region, in order to gain a better picture of the Late Classic/Terminal periods.

A) *Temporal differences in the consumption of corn in the Maya region*

In general, several authors have concluded that there is chronological and spatial variability in corn consumption by humans in the Maya area (Emery and Thornton 2008b; White 1999). It is possible to see that the general trend points towards a temporal variation (White *et al.* 2006a:145), increasing from Late Preclassic to the Classic period (Hammond 1999:94), and probably reaching its highest peak during the Late Classic, as inferred by the ratio of secondary growth forests to agricultural/domestic modified landscapes, when agricultural fields were at their most expansive (Emery and Thornton 2008a:170). From this data, it is possible to assume that there was an increase in corn production that resulted in higher corn consumption by humans and animals during the Late Classic period in

the Maya area. In this sense, much of Emery's work has been focused on studying how maize consumption by humans and animals was affected by ecological factors during the Late Classic period (Emery 1997, 1999, 2010). However, new studies show that maize production was not as affected during this period as previously thought (White *et al.* 2006a:144; Wright 2006:196). In some regions, such as in the Petexbatún, Guatemala, there is enough evidence to suggest that maize production remained stable through time (Emery *et al.* 2000:546).

Regionally, corn consumption was higher in the Lowlands than at coastal sites (Tykot *et al.* 1996; Wright 2006:113), regardless of the chronological period. In general, an increase in corn during the Late Classic period is observable in both human and animal populations (Emery and Thornton 2008b:140), identified through the use of isotope analysis (White *et al.* 2006a). It is interesting, however, that the average corn intake during this period was relatively low for other sites, including large settlements, such as Tikal and Copán (Emery and Thornton 2008a, 2008b) and some coastal sites, including Lamanai (White and Schwarcz 1989). Hence, it has been suggested that there is extreme variability among the ecological settings and time periods within individual sites and this challenges the notion of a single 'Maya menu'. This intra site variability that is observable during the Late Classic period may be due to the individual characteristics of each site. The works of several authors have contested not only the notion of homogeneity, but also stressed the great regional and temporal diversity, according to their geography and ecology, site altitude and land management (Emery *et al.* 2000; Emery and Thornton 2008b; Gerry 1993; Gerry and Krueger 1997; Hammond 1999:95; White 1997; Wright and White 1996).

These different isotope patterns are relevant when studying broader topics, such as socio-political changes, and the so-called collapse during the Late Classic. The traditional argument predicts an increasing reliance on corn when the population increased rapidly during the Classic. As a consequence of the expansion of cornfields, in conjunction with ecological devastation, access to other resources such as wild plants and fauna was minimized (Pohl 1990). However, these models do not take into account the social (war, trade, political activity), or natural (climate, disease) factors and how and what impact they had in each region.

B) *Temporal differences in the consumption of meat in the Maya region*

During the Preclassic period, deer and dog were both consumed; however, the domestic dog (*Canis lupus familiaris*) was the favoured species for rituals. During the Classic, the presence of dog remains in ritual contexts seems to diminish, and the white-tailed deer (*Odocoileus virginianus*) appears to become the most preferred species (Emery 2003, 2007b; White *et al.* 2004). As with corn consumption, it has been argued that the changes observed during this period were possibly a consequence of the unprecedented population growth that occurred particularly during the Late Classic period, which in turn brought changes in the environment by extensive land clearing for agriculture, which would also would have affected access to local species by decreasing the space available for natural resources areas for game hunting (Santley *et al.* 1986:143). Extensive land clearing for agriculture and dense human populations would have resulted in a shortage of meat resources by affecting animal sizes and populations. Santley and colleagues (1986:135) argue that faunal populations, especially white-tailed deer, would have been decimated by 'hunting levels exceeded rates of replacement'. This shortage was not homogeneous among all Maya sites, as some researchers suggest that meat consumption continued to be a significant component in the diet of elite members (Pohl 1994), especially of those species considered as the most valuable. It has been suggested that during the Late Classic period, a more powerful elite emerged which identified itself with the deer, and performed ritual sacrifice and feasting as a means of creating cohesion within a larger population (Bíró and Montero 2008; Masson 1999; Pohl 1994). This in turn would have contributed to the dietary failure that occurred at the end of the Late Classic (Emery 2010; Santley *et al.* 1986). Ethnohistoric accounts mention that meat was consumed in elite-sponsored feasts, and members of the higher classes would have consumed meat more regularly (Tozzer 1941).

Recent zooarchaeological and isotopic analyses suggest that on the contrary, archaeological remains of large mammals, especially white-tailed deer, were particularly abundant during the Late Classic period, although their abundance rapidly decreases by the Terminal Classic period, when greater diversity of species, including exploitation of smaller species, is observed (Emery and Thornton 2008b). Today, researchers agree that meat consumption in the Maya area was variable according to a wide range of factors, much the same as it was with corn consumption. Wright (2006) conducted a recent study testing the ecological model in the Pasión River region by focusing on the biological and social implications of this model. She studied the collapse, evaluating isotopic and palaeopathological evidence, and concluded 'diets were socially and regionally heterogeneous' (Wright 2006:199).

Is there evidence for deer management or semi-domestication?

Since meat was a valuable product that was consumed during feasts, it has been proposed that some faunal domestication may have occurred in order to counteract the apparent scarce faunal resources, and provide access to meat when needed. There is sufficient data to show that the Maya domesticated the dog early on. Most remains of domestic dogs will display isotope values similar to those of humans, thus reflecting the diet of a scavenger (White *et al.* 1993:359, 2001b:91, 2004); nonetheless, evidence that some dogs were purposely fed with corn (and therefore domesticated) is reflected in the isotopic record (Hammond 1999:92; van der Merwe *et al.* 2000; White *et al.* 1993, 2001b, 2004). The isotopic signature of dog remains from votive caches dated to the Preclassic period, confirm that the sacrificed dogs were raised and fed deliberately with corn (White *et al.* 2001b).

Because dogs were domesticated and kept in captivity, some authors have also proposed that similar methods may have been employed for deer, in order to keep up with demands for meat by the ever-growing elite from the Classic period (Masson 1999; Tykot *et al.* 1996). Alternatively, they may have been kept in refuges or parks in forests and savannah regions (Pohl 1985a:138). In earlier works, Pohl (1990, 1995) has suggested that deer were kept in temporary pens, though this may have been only for a short period of time. So far, no pens have been found and, although Pohl (1981) suggests that they existed in Classic Seibal, evidence of an animal being kept in captivity, especially wild large mammals, is not available archaeologically. For the Postclassic period, some researchers suggest that in Mayapan, deer were probably raised and bred in pens or corrals, or that there was a form of forest game management, with the selection of prime-aged animals (Masson and Peraza 2008).

However, the isotopic data suggest that this domestication may have not been straightforward. Isotope analysis of deer from large sites such as Copán, Lagartero, and Tikal (White *et al.* 2004:150) show that most of these animals were hunted in the wild, as their carbon isotope analysis indicate a diet based primarily on wild or C3 plants with the occasional browsing in cornfields (White *et al.* 2001b, 2004). As a result of the deer's opportunistic feeding habits, its diet could potentially serve as a proxy to identify the extent of land modification suffered as a consequence of the agricultural practices. Following this idea, it would be expected that in densely inhabited areas— and including a highly terraced agricultural area— such as Copán and the Petén region, deer isotope values would reflect a high corn intake. However, recent isotope studies (Reed 1994) show that deer were grazing on C3 plants, with a relatively low intake of corn or C4 plants. These results contrast with those from the human burials from those sites, whose values are among the highest for corn intake (Reed 1994). Deer δ^{13}C values for other less populated areas, such as Pasion and Grijalva rivers, show an even a lower intake of corn (Emery and Thornton 2008b; Wright 1993).

According to Emery and Thornton (2008b), the hypothesis of an expansion of corn fields, and reduction of forests during the Classic period, due to a massive increase in human populations (*sensus* Santley *et al.* 1986), would have increased the availability of corn to deer and other herbivores. This would be reflected in higher $\delta^{13}C$ values in their bones (Emery and Thornton 2008b:133). Earlier works (Pohl and Feldman 1982; White *et al.* 2004) stress that deer were common pests that invaded cornfields and/or were raised and fattened with corn for ceremonial purposes.

The only case where there appears to have been a deliberate selection of deer is found in votive caches from Preclassic Cuello (Hammond 1999:92). Nonetheless, some orphaned fawns of deer and peccary appear to have been reared by women and fed corn, in preparation for their sacrifice upon reaching prime age (Pohl 1985a:140). If, however, deer were consuming more corn, not only would it be reflected in the $\delta^{13}C$ values of deer themselves, but in the isotope values of the humans who were consuming the corn-fattened deer.

Summary

Chinikihá is considered a Category I site due its ceremonial architecture, and the existence of a Chinikihá emblem glyph, which indicates that it was an independent polity during some periods of time. Because of its geographical location, it must have participated in the regional political interactions among other larger polities, including Palenque, Pomoná, and Piedras Negras. The presence of early ceramics suggests that Chinikihá was occupied since the Preclassic period, but it was only during the Late Classic period that most civic-ceremonial construction occurred under a new lineage. This increase in population and architectural expansion is seen in the whole region. The traditional model suggests that as populations grew bigger and bigger, there was some pressure on the natural resources that were available. Also, the ruling elites at different sites began to demand more goods for their own ceremonies, including agricultural and faunal resources. In the next chapter, each of the excavation contexts that are examined in the present dissertation are described. Other associated materials, such as ceramics and non-utilitarian artefacts, are also discussed in order to situate the faunal samples within the Late Classic period.

Chapter four

Description of the Chinikihá assemblages

In this chapter, the results of the archaeological excavation and analysis will be presented, describing the collection of materials that resulted from Proyecto Arqueológico Chinikihá (PRACH). This chapter focuses specifically on the collection of faunal remains obtained from *Operación* 114, located behind the Palace at Chinikihá.

The 2006 fieldwork comprised a surface collection and the excavation of several 1x1m tests pits located throughout the site, including *Operaciones* 1, 2 and 3 situated behind the Palace; all material retrieved was analysed by Montero (2008). In 2008, a larger excavation was conducted behind the Palace, in addition to several smaller ones in locations around the site, resulting in several *Operaciones*. Of particular interest to the present study are those *Operaciones* where faunal material was recovered, including *Operaciones* 110 (ceremonial building 'South Acropolis'), *Operaciones* 111, 112, and 115 (North Structure Complex), and *Operación* 114 (behind the Palace) (Figure 7). Outside of Chinikihá, *Operación* 201 (Chancalá) and *Operación* 202 (San Juan Chancalaíto) also produced archaeofaunal material. All of these *Operaciones* will be further detailed in this chapter.

So far, a total of 5575 archaeofaunal remains have been recovered and analysed from Proyecto Arqueológico Chinikihá (Table 3). However, the results from the analysis of the material recovered in 2006 have been presented elsewhere (Montero 2008). The present study addresses the material recovered in 2008, presenting the general results in Chapter six. Particular attention is given to the remains from *Operación* 114, especially regarding the distribution of the favoured species, in order to draw inferences about possible differences or changes throughout the context.

Description of the excavations

I begin by describing the excavations or *Operaciones* from which the faunal remains analysed in this study were recovered. I will commence by describing those *Operaciones* that produced little material, including *Operaciones* 110, 111, 112, 201, and 202. When discussing *Operaciones* 111 and 112, I will also briefly discuss the human burial sample that was used for isotope analysis. Following this, I will provide a more detailed description of *Operación* 114, the focus of my research, taking into consideration the presence of other materials, including ceramics, shell, and macrobotanical remains. This additional information will allow a better understanding of the context, and will place the materials in a chronological framework.

Operación 110

This was a 7 x 3m excavation located in the front part of the staircase that forms the facade of the South Acropolis building (Figure 8). The context has been identified as a series of construction fills, mixed with small discrete refuse deposits, which include fauna and malacological material, ceramic fragments, and large quantities of ash (Liendo 2009b). Two fragments of *manos* or grinding stones were also recovered during the excavation, along with faunal material exhibiting cut marks and other anthropogenic modifications that stress the domestic nature of this deposit.

Location	Season	Total NISP
Operaciones 1, 2, and 3 (1x1 m test pits behind Palace)	2006[a]	375
Operación 114 (grid behind Palace)	2008	3865
Operación 110 (Ceremonial building 'South Acropolis')	2008	129
Operación 201 (Chancalá)	2008	177
Operación 202 (Chancalaíto)	2008	9
Other *Operaciones*	2006[a] and 2008	62
Total		**5575**

[a]data from Montero (2008).

Table 3. Total NISP of faunal material analysed in the present study (this excludes the 2009 fieldwork; note that these numbers do not include shell fragments).

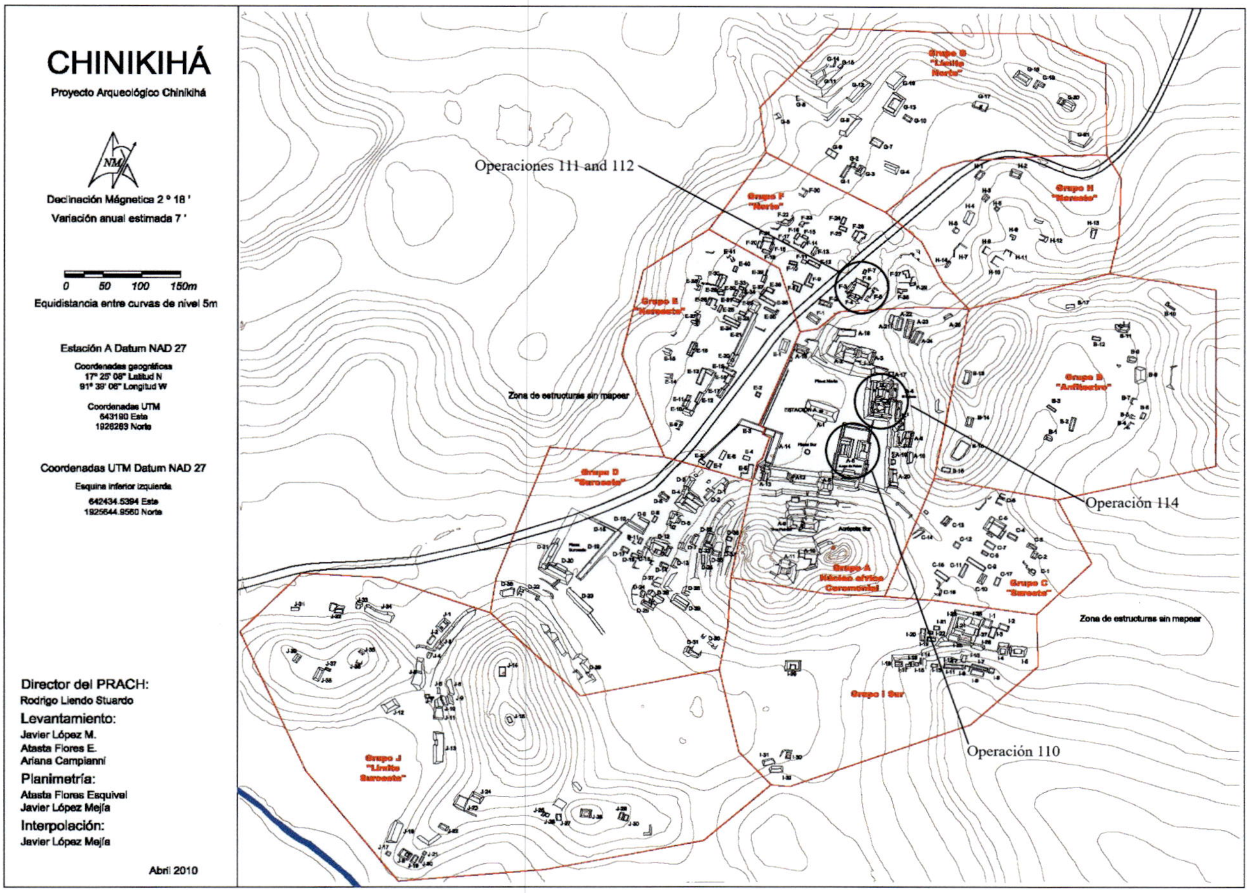

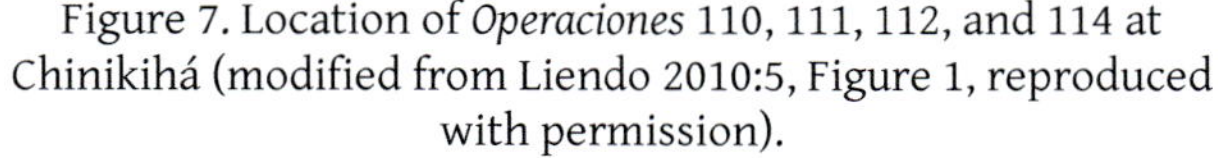

Figure 7. Location of *Operaciones* 110, 111, 112, and 114 at Chinikihá (modified from Liendo 2010:5, Figure 1, reproduced with permission).

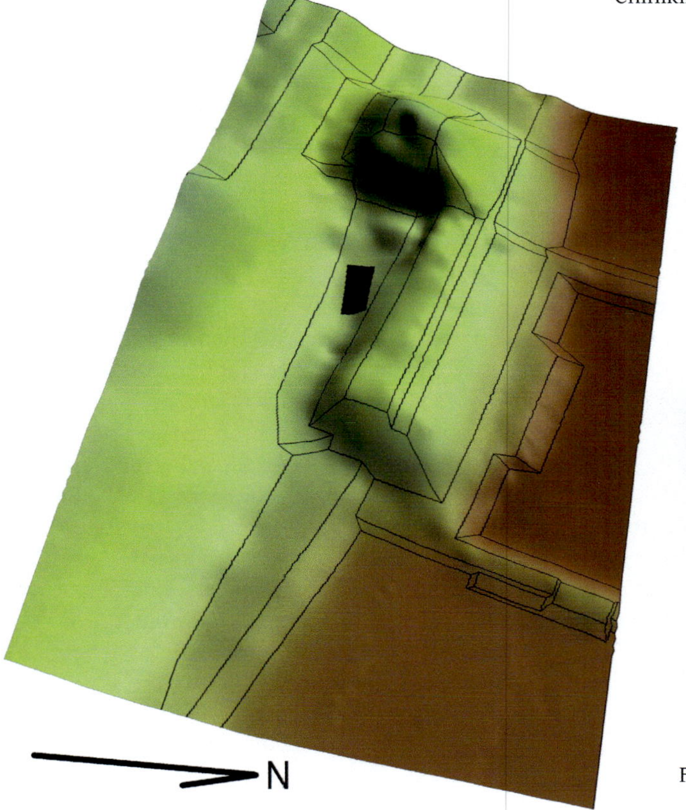

Proyecto Arqueológico Chinikihá

Operación 110

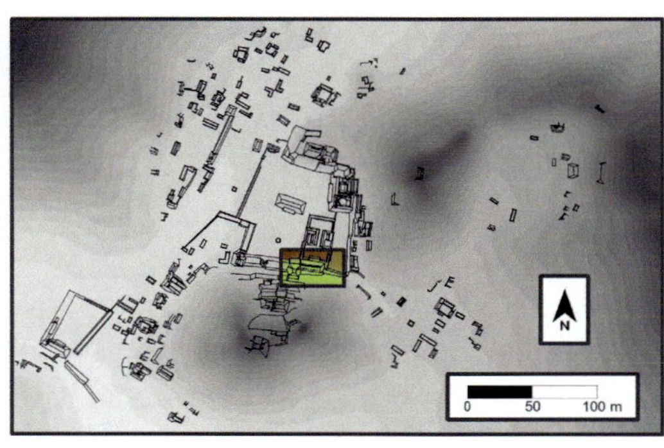

Figure 8. Location of *Operación* 110 (Liendo 2009a:135, reproduced with permission).

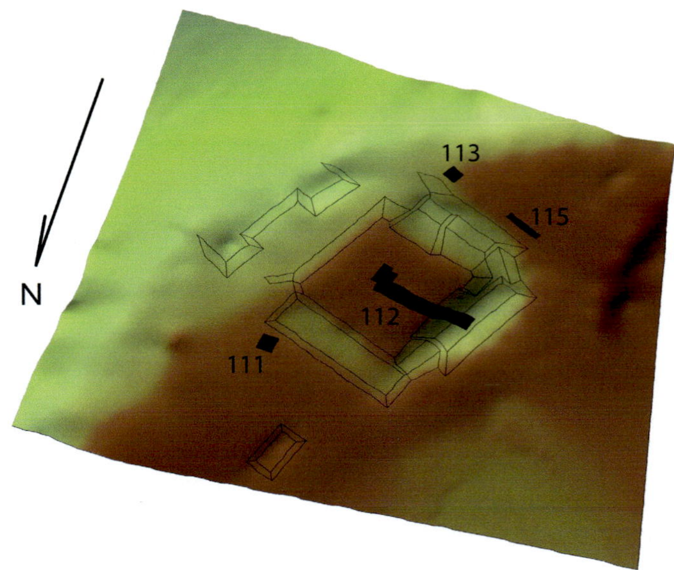

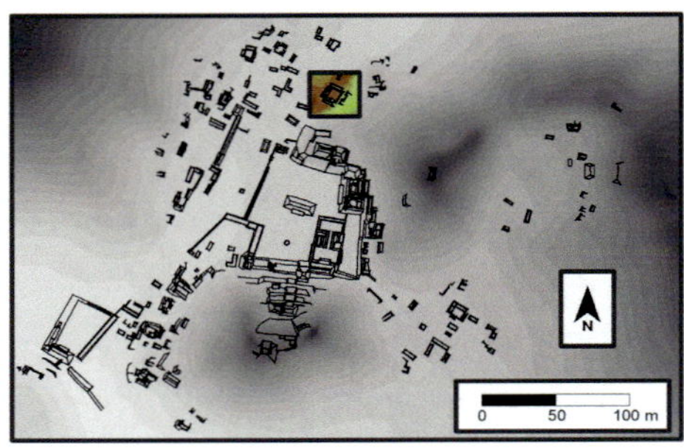

Figure 9. Location of *Operaciones* 111, 112, and 115 (Liendo 2009b:159, reproduced with permission).

Operaciones 111, 112 and 115

These three excavations were conducted in the North Structure complex and resulted in the identification of six formal burials, containing nine individuals, considered to be members of the elite (Montero and Núñez 2011). This domestic complex is located in Sector F, at the north end of Chinikihá, and while *Operación* 111 is an excavation pit outside of a domestic structure, *Operación* 112 is a trench inside the inner patio formed by four surrounding buildings (Liendo 2009b) (Figure 9).

Operación 115 is located on the exterior of the southern structure of the domestic complex. Only two bone fragments were recovered, and no taphonomic modifications were observed. Due to their low frequency and degree of preservation, it is possible that these fragments were redeposited secondarily.

The human burials in Operaciones 111 and 112

An examination of the human burials present in *Operaciones* 111 and 112 will be used to test whether there was a disparity in the accessibility of meat resources between elite individuals and to explore the meat consumption patterns of members of the higher tiers. Formal burials from the Palace would have been more ideal subjects for this study, but no burials have been discovered inside or around it. Although it is well known that during the Classic period there was a major population growth, few human remains have

been identified, and those that have been, were often discovered as a by-product of excavation programmes focused on the architectural areas of sites (Webster 1997) or in unique internments, such as the magnificent tombs of royal personages such as *K'uhul Ajaw* K'inich Janaab' Pakal I in Palenque (e.g. Tiesler and Cucina 2001). A *K'uhul Ajaw* is the highest title given to a ruler during the Classic period, translating to divine or holy lord (Houston and Stuart 2001:59), and this ruler is referenced in texts on stelae and other writings.

In many cases, the location of burials (central or peripheral) within a site has been used to classify them as either elite or non-elite (White *et al.* 2001a; Wright 1994). However, on many occasions, human remains have been located inside the nuclear area which do not necessarily belong to a high status individual. Furthermore, very few excavations in palaces have produced burials, with most of the burial samples coming from domestic residential complexes, for example at Piedras Negras (Scherer *et al.* 2007) and Copán (Reid 1994). Thus, according to Scherer and colleagues (2007:88) status is not necessarily determined by the location of the burials, but by a combination of internment architecture, and associated grave goods where the resulting typology includes commoner, intermediate, elite, and royal classes.

The difference between social classes seems to have become clearer during the Late Classic period, when a shift from acquired to inherited status is evident

Sample	Elem.	Num.	Ind.	Type	Class	Operación	Location	Age	Sex	Dental Modification	Grave Furniture	Dental Pathologies	Anaemia Markers	Periostic Reaction
CM13	40	2	A	Individual	Primary	112	Inner Patio	25-29	F	filing	jade bead	x	x	x
n/a	41	3	A	Individual	Primary	111	Behind North Str.	3-5	n/a	no	n/a	x	no	x
CM14	42	4	A	Collective	Primary	112	Inner Patio	35-39	M	filing	incised vessel	x	x	x
CM15	42	4	B	Collective	Secondary	112	Inner Patio	Middle adult	F	filing/incrust.	no	x	x	x
CM16	42	4	C	Collective	Secondary	112	Inner Patio	40-44	M	no	no	x	x	x
CM17	43	5	A	Individual	Primary	111	Behind North Str.	Middle adult	F	n/a	no	no	x	x
n/a	44	6	A	Collective	Primary	112	Inner Patio	34-39	F	filing	incised vessel	x	x	x
CM18	44	6	B	Collective	Secondary	112	Inner Patio	Mature adult	M	filing/incrust.	no	x	x	x
CM19	45	7	A	Individual	Primary	112	Inner Patio	Adult	M	n/a	plain vessel	no	no	x

n/a: Not present
x: Indicates presence

Table 4. Summary of burial identification at Chinikihá (modified from Liendo 2009b:210-211, Table 1).

(Sharer 1994:490). This change would have been a consequence of the emergence of dynasties during the 5th century AD and the concentration of population in central areas consolidating several sites at a regional scale (Liendo 2009a).

A total of nine human burials were recovered from *Operaciones* 111 and 112, both operations associated with the North Complex, a domestic unit with four structures forming a square, and surrounding a communal inner patio (see Figure 4.3). Some of these inhumations were individual burials, while others were grouped or multiple burials; however, all of the burials are similar in that they were all found in cists built and covered by large river stones and covered with them as well. The presence of complete ceramic vessels associated with some of the individuals as well as the ceramic fragments in the fill of the internments indicates that the entombments occurred during the Balunté phase (AD 750-820) (Luis Núñez, personal communication 2010).

The excavation and complete osteological analysis was conducted by Dr Luis Núñez, from Instituto de Investigaciones Antropológicas at UNAM (IIA-UNAM). A study of the mortuary patterns in Chinikihá as part of a regional system is currently under study by Dr Núñez, and here a brief review of his work is presented (see Table 4). For a complete description of each burial, see Liendo (2009b).

Only two inhumations were found in *Operación* 111, Element 41 and Element 43, and each of them consisted of an individual burial. Neither contained associated objects. *Operación* 112 was originally planned as a 2 x 2m unit in the middle of the inner patio where three burials were discovered, but the discovery of another burial turned this unit into a large trench that extended from the west building to the centre of the patio. Four burials were discovered, including two single ones— Element 40 and Element 45—and two multiple burials, Element 42 (individuals A, B, and C), and Element 44 (individuals A and B).

The associated grave goods, as well as the mortuary patterns seen at Chinikihá, provide a tentative chronological framework for the human burials, confirming them in the Late Classic period (AD 600-850). The mortuary practices at Chinikihá do not differ greatly from other Classic period Maya sites, stressing the existence of a shared belief system (see Chase 1997; Ricketson 1925). Furthermore, the similarity in style found between the vessels used as offerings, and those from other *Operaciones*, attest to the contemporaneity of the burials from the North Complex and *Operación* 114 behind the Palace.

Operación 201 (Chancalá)

Also known as 'La Cascada', the Chancalá site is located in the terrains of Telesecundaria Chancalá, Chiapas in the Chancalá Valley, situated 30km SE of Palenque, and around 15km SW of Tenosique, Tabasco (Flores 2010; Liendo 2009b) (see Figure 3). Although 21 structures were identified at this site, including a ballcourt, palace,

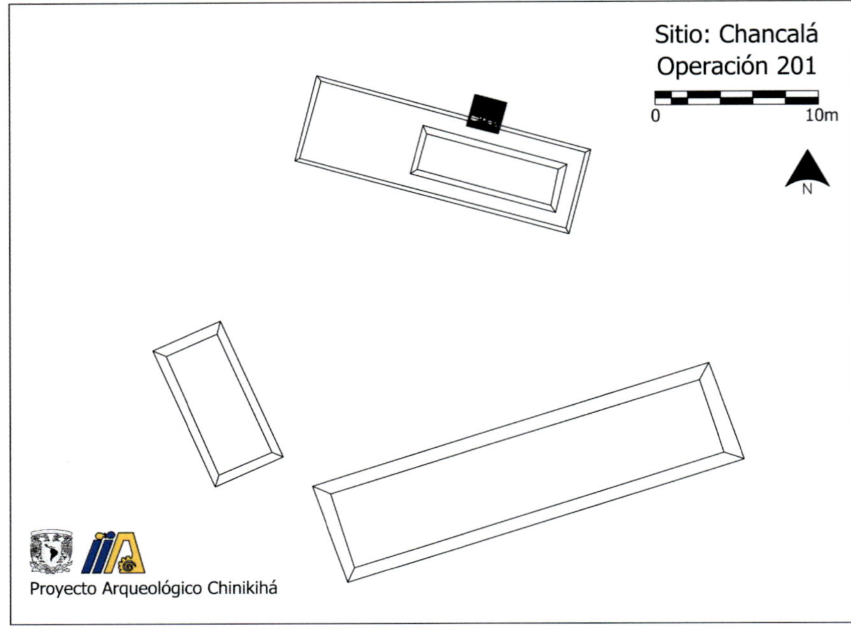

Figure 10. Location of *Operación* 201 in the core of the site of Chancalá (Liendo 2009b:308, reproduced with permission).

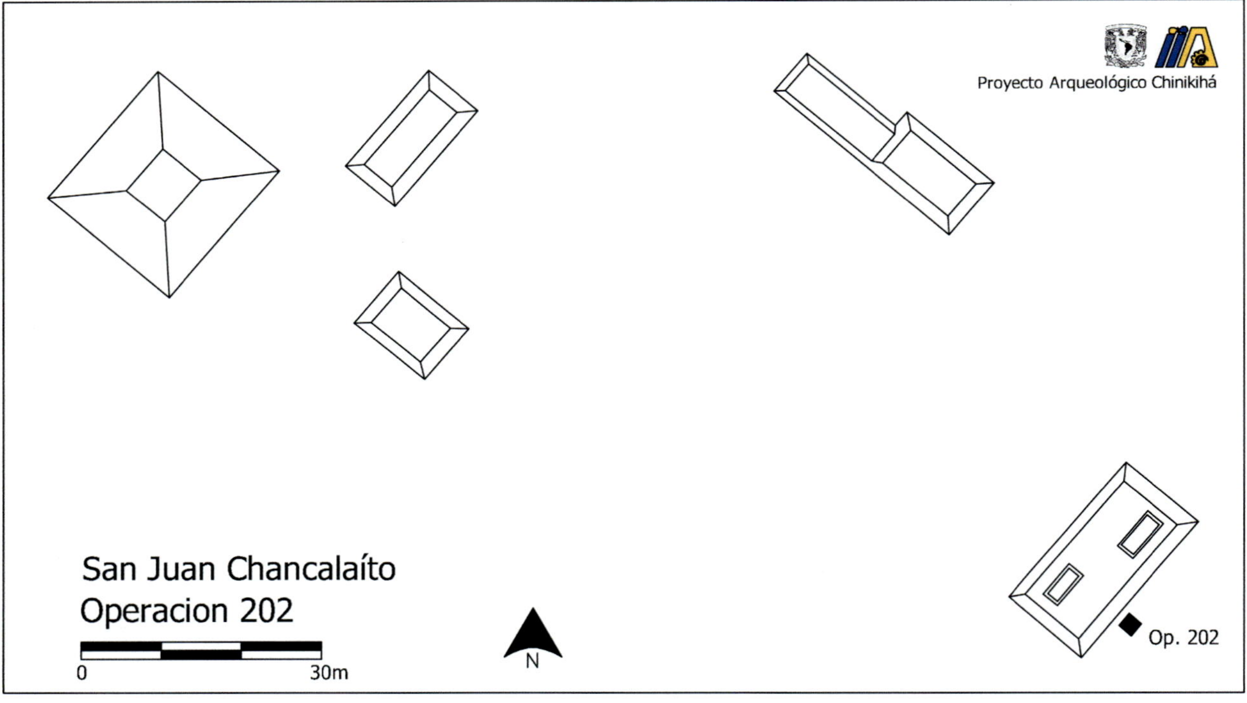

Figure 11. Location of *Operación* 202 in the core of the site of San Juan Chancalaíto (Liendo 2009b:311, reproduced with permission).

a pyramid and a stela (without emblem glyph), it has been classified as a secondary or 'Type I-2' site. The only two sites considered to be 'Type I-1' are Palenque and Chinikihá, due to their grand dimensions (Flores 2010; Liendo 2005b:38).

A 2 x 2m pit was excavated behind a platform which, along with two other structures, forms a central patio (Figure 10). In this test pit, numerous ceramic, lithic, and bone fragments were discovered in what appears to be a midden that served as construction fill for the platform (Liendo 2009b). It is interesting to mention that Liendo (2009b) reports that two semi-complete plates with deer bones were located *in situ*, although the exact location is unknown.

Although no specific dates have been obtained for this context, the ceramics appear to be similar in style to

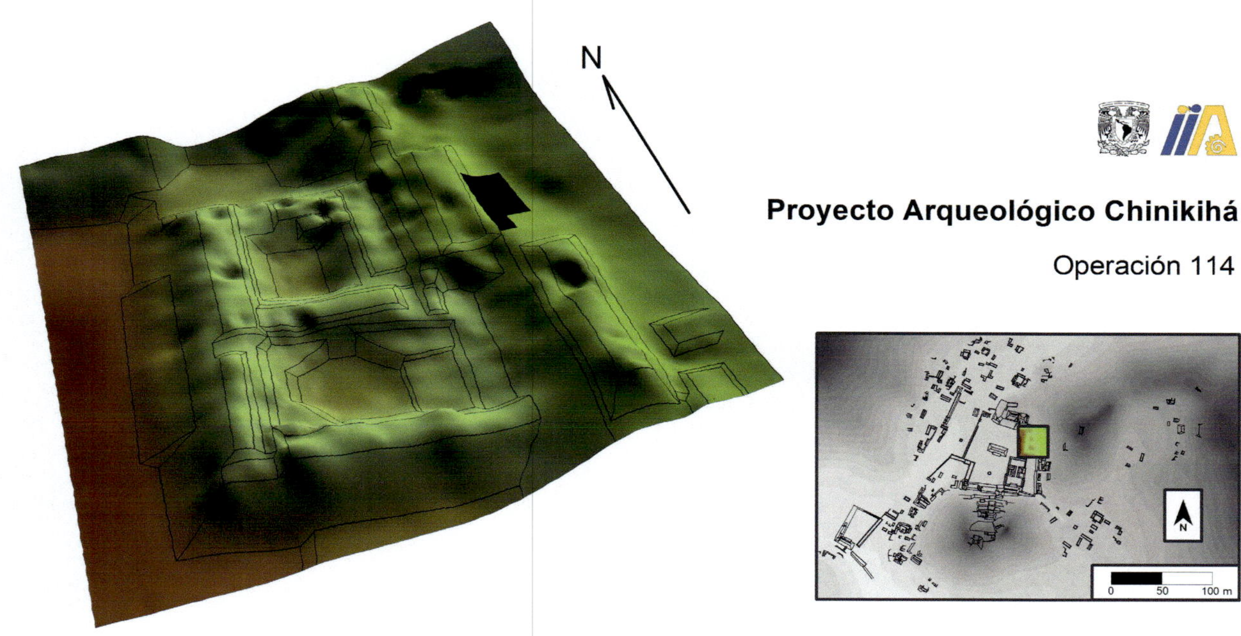

Figure 12. Location of *Operación* 114
(from Liendo 2009b:215, reproduced with permission).

those from the Murciélagos/Balunté phases from Palenque. However, just like Chinikihá, the presence of earlier material, though scarce, suggests an occupation that may have started before the Preclassic period.

Operación 202 (San Juan Chancalaíto)

The valley reconnaissance included San Juan Chancalaíto, also located in the Chancalá valley (Liendo 2009b) (see Figure 3). More than 40 structures were found within 13ha (Liendo 2005a:38). *Operación* 202 is a 2 x 2m pit located at the back of a platform to the east of a plaza formed by three surrounding structures (Figure 11). A large quantity of ceramics was obtained from the surface of an occupation floor, and a preliminary analysis suggests that this site can be dated to the Murciélagos/Balunté phases of the Classic period (Liendo 2009b). Interestingly, almost no animal bones were found in this excavation, in contrast to the excavations at Chinikihá and Chancalá.

Operación 114

This *Operación* was located directly behind the Palace and was laid in a natural corridor formed by the posterior wall of the Palace and a small natural hill, which would have acted as a natural barrier for the eastern side of the site. The northern extremity of this corridor is open, while the southern extension is delimited by the presence of a small platform. The Palace itself is in the

middle section of the archaeological site of Chinikihá and belongs to the architectural group known as 'Group A', or the 'civic-ceremonial centre' (Campiani 2010) (see Figure 7). Within this section of the site, the Palace is situated on a low piedmont on the east side of a large closed plaza, with a ballcourt directly to the south of the Palace and several other large platforms surrounding the plaza, including some ceremonial buildings and domestic units (Figure 12, see inset). Its privileged position within the site stresses the importance of this building and possibly indicates that its inhabitants enjoyed a high status position.

Operación commenced in 2006, during the first season of *Proyecto Arqueológico Chinikihá* (PRACH). During that season, only limited exploratory works were conducted behind the palace, with three 1 x 1m test pits (named *Operaciones* 1, 2 and 3) were excavated. A total of 267 faunal specimens were recovered (Figure 13). It was observed that these deposits were associated with the Palace and as such, it was considered possible that they formed part of an *in situ* deposit.

The zooarchaeological analysis of *Operaciones* 1, 2, and 3 resulted in 65.1% of the faunal remains being identified as white-tailed deer (*Odocoileus virginianus*), with more than half of these identified as juveniles. It is interesting to note that more than half of all the white-tailed deer remains exhibited butchering marks (Montero 2008). It was determined that this context may reflect either

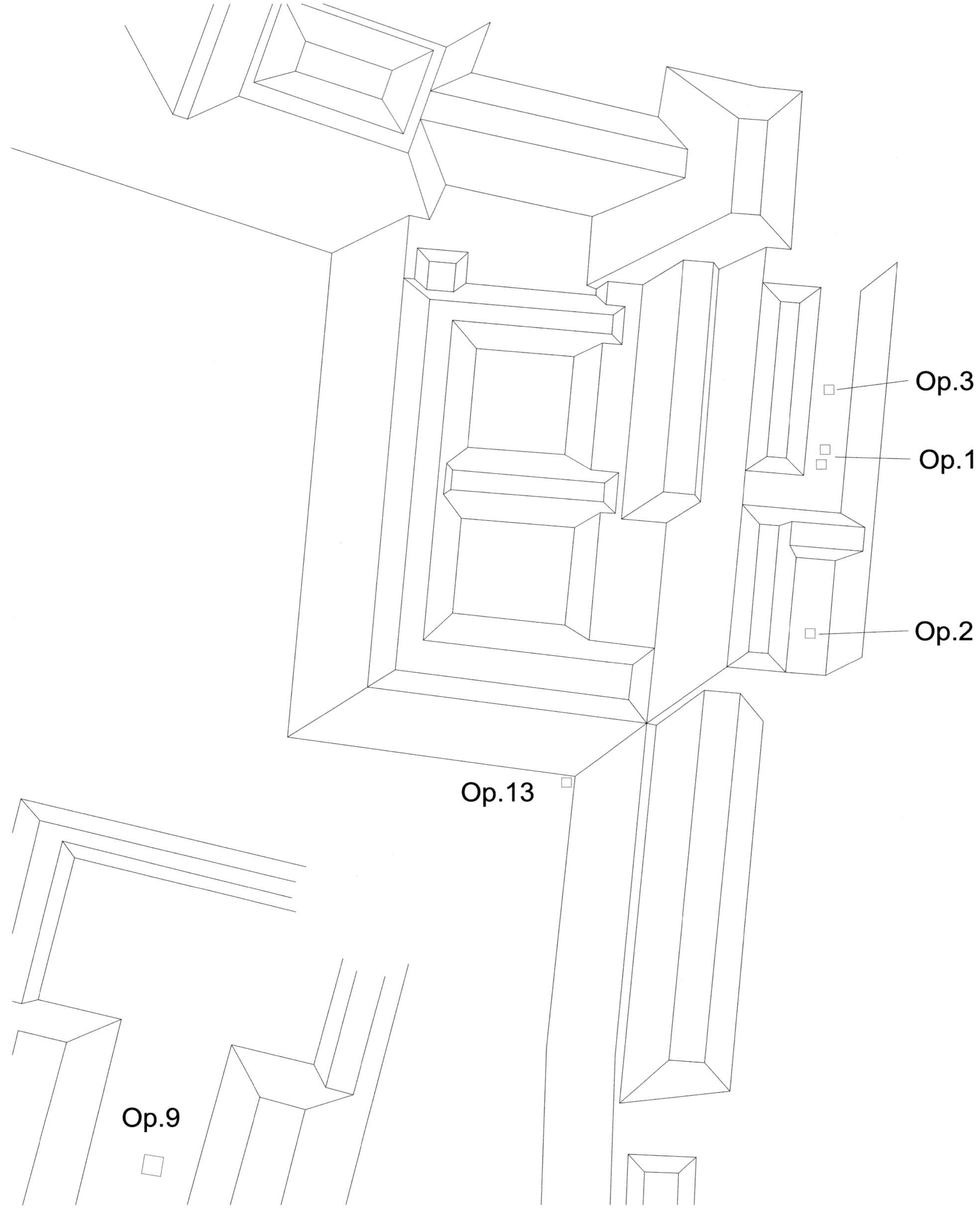

Figure 13. Detail of the location of *Operaciones* 1, 2, and 3 during PRACH 2006 (modified from Liendo 2007a, Figure 5, reproduced with permission).

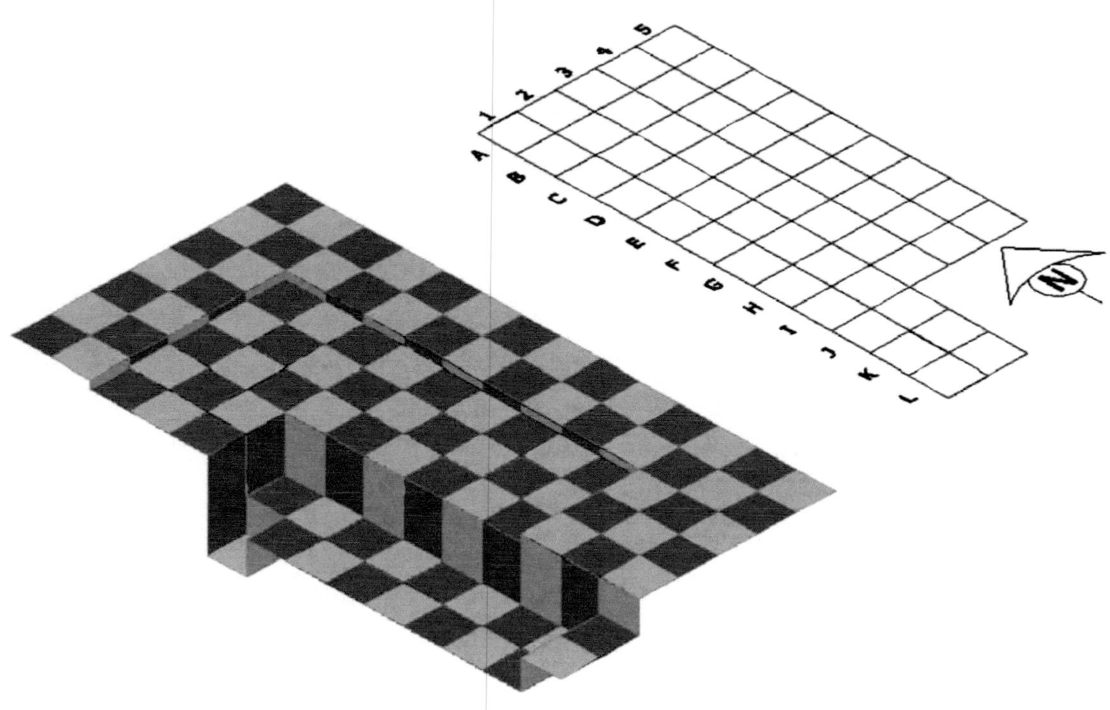

Figure 14. Sketch of the excavation grid of *Operación* 114 (shaded squares were excavated during PRACH 2008) (modified from Trabanino 2008 reproduced with permission).

domestic or ritual activities (Montero 2008:175). Large fragments of ceramic vessels (some of which could be pieced back together), freshwater shell, and lithics, including blades and grinding stones, were also present. These indicated that the deposit could be the result of refuse disposal (Liendo 2009b:216). However, the large quantities of semi-complete and complete bones, as well as individual articulated skeletal elements, and above all, the dominance of a single faunal species, suggested that this deposit could be the result of other processes. It was tentatively identified as a 'problematic deposit' (Montero 2008:175). The presence of human remains, ceramic figurines and whistles, shell ornaments, and carved bones—some of them even with glyphs— contribute to the complexity of this rich deposit.

Another test pit, *Operación* 13, was excavated in the northwest corner of the staircase at the front of the Palace; however, this context only produced 14 faunal specimens. *Operación* 13 may represent the temporary piling of trash near buildings, a common practice by the Maya (Chase and Chase 2000:69). These 'provisional deposits of trash' (Schiffer 1987:65) are a common practice among several past societies who conducted regular clean-ups of the areas they inhabited; trash is piled in areas of low transit, forming secondary and tertiary deposits (Chase and Chase 2000; Hutson *et al.*

2007; Schiffer 1987). This context clearly contrasts to the materials recovered from behind the Palace and suggests differential waste management and disposal practices by the Maya.

In 2008, the second season of PRACH was conducted, with the main objective to complete the excavation of the deposit and identify its physical extent. A 1 x 1m square grid was set up, with a north-south orientation. The grid covered the whole area behind the Palace, from the back wall to the piedmont; however, during this season, only a small section adjacent to the posterior wall of the Palace was excavated. This resulted in a total excavated area of 17m² (Figure 14).

The excavated squares were as follows: E1, E2, F1, F2, G1, G2, G3, H1, H2, I1, I2, J1, J2, K1, K2, L1, and L2. Each of the squares was dug in 10cm artificial spits for control purposes, although natural stratigraphy was also considered. This stratigraphy consisted of five cross-cut natural layers which are described elsewhere (Liendo 2009b:215). The superficial organic layer was removed prior to the excavation of the pits. The first three layers—I, II, and III, from top to bottom—were fully excavated in all the squares with only a few squares reaching Layers IV and V, to a maximum depth of 1.5m. Such depths were reached in the SE corner of

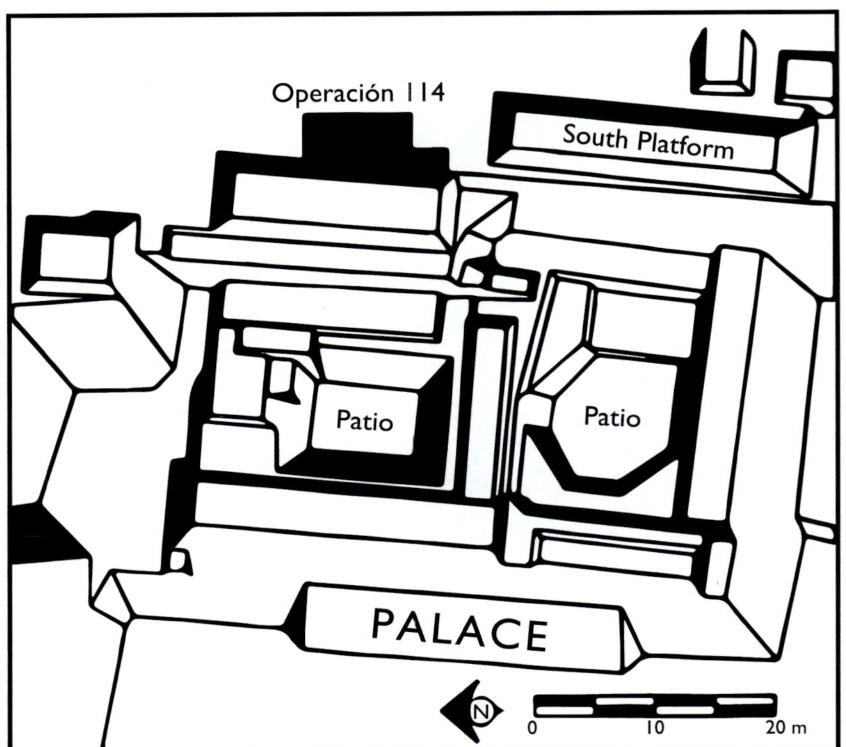

Figure 15. *Operación* 114, located behind the back wall of the Palace and north of the South Platform (modified from Liendo 2009b:216, reproduced with permission).

Figure 16. Profile of excavation showing the stuccoed floor (from Liendo 2009b:217, reproduced with permission).

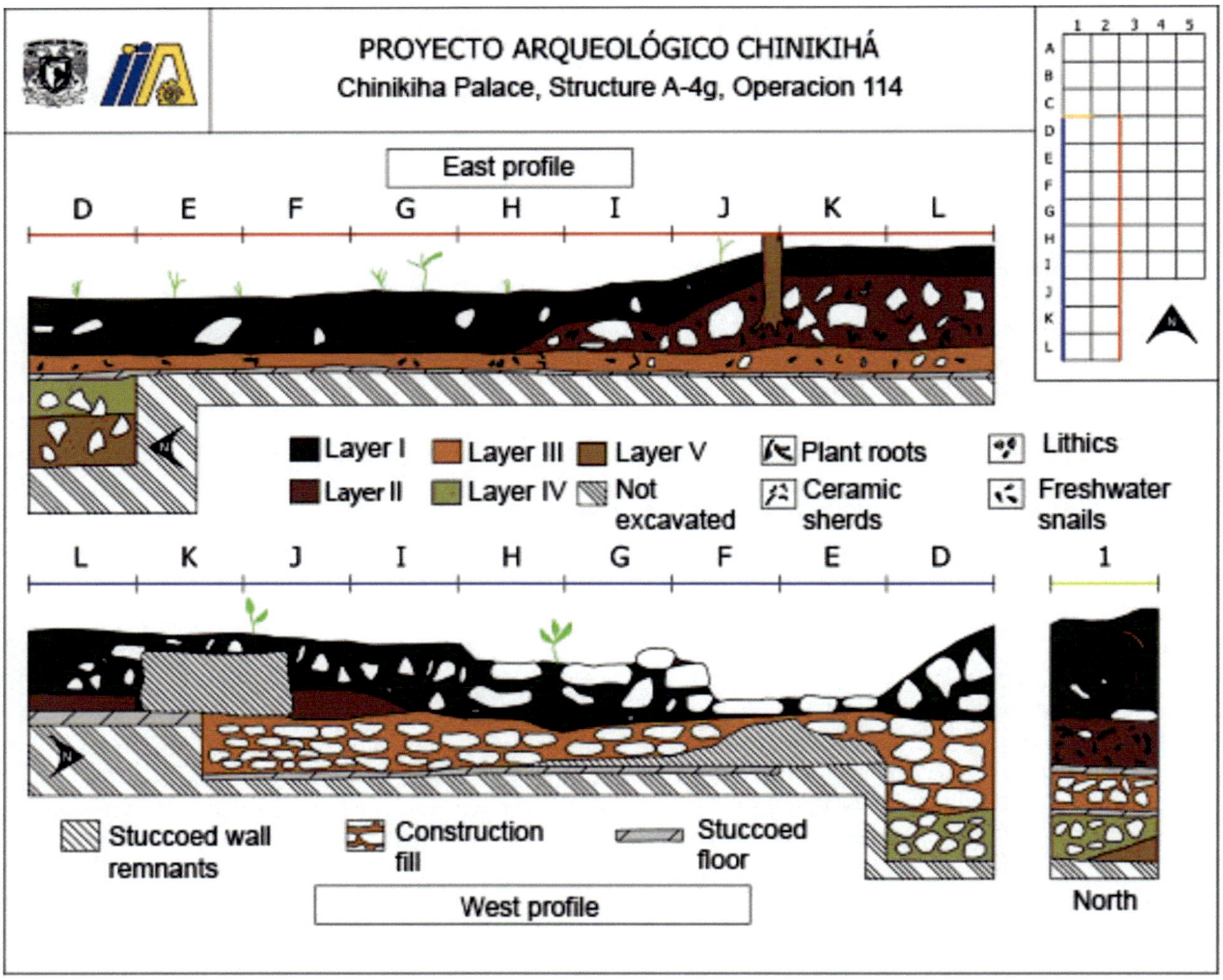

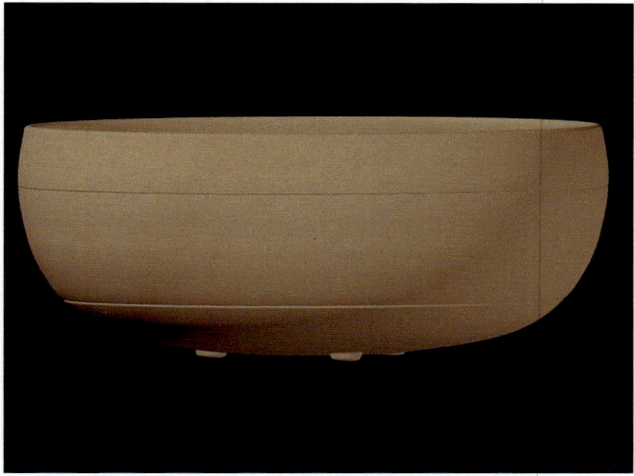 

Figures 17 and 18. Hypothetical reconstruction of an incised tripod vessel (left), and a Murciélagos-Balunté ceramic complex (right) for Chinikihá (courtesy of Esteban Mirón, reproduced with permission).

the grid, formed by squares I, J, K, and L (see Liendo 2009b for a detailed explanation).

During the 2006 season, it was believed that this archaeological deposit has a direct association with the Palace (Liendo 2009b; Montero 2008). However, at the end of the 2008 season, a stuccoed floor was partially uncovered between Layers III and IV, present in all excavated pits and it is probable that this surface was associated with the south platform rather than with the Palace itself (Liendo 2009b:216) (Figure 15). It is believed that this floor represents an occupation surface (Liendo 2009b:216).

The floor was situated consistently between Layers III and IV; however, on top of the floor there was a 10cm sterile layer formed by sand and small pebbles, suggesting that the material above the floor corresponds to a later period in the constructive sequence, where it may have been deposited as part of the construction of the south platform (Liendo 2009b:216). In this sense, the East and West profile drawings show that Layers I, II, and III were above the floor, while Layers IV and V were under it (Figure 16). Furthermore, the incipient presence of a second floor was recorded on the North profile, between Layers II and III, indicating the renovation of the occupational surface, although this floor did not cover the whole area. In terms of the depositional sequence, recent excavations in this area include extensions to the east and south of *Operación* 114, which have revealed that this deposit extends all the way to the south platform (Liendo 2012).

The archaeological materials are not homogeneously distributed within the context, but rather the bulk of the materials were concentrated in squares I, J, K, and L, mixed with large stones covered with mortar

and/or stucco, between Layers I-III. Several discrete concentrations of bones, shell, and fragments of refitted ceramics were discovered among the bulk of the deposit, which help in understanding the formation of the context as well as its depositional history.

Other archaeological materials recovered from Operación 114

Excavations during this season resulted in thousands of faunal bones, freshwater molluscs shells, and ceramic vessel fragments, and lithic tools made of obsidian and flint. There were also a few broken ceramic figurines, representing both humans and animals. Fragments of grinding stones, bone, and shell ornaments, as well as human bones were also recovered in smaller proportions.

More than 17,000 ceramic sherds were recovered from *Operación* 114 during the 2008 season, and these are currently being analysed by Esteban Mirón (UNAM). Most of the ceramics were very well preserved and showed no post-depositional modifications. His preliminary analysis indicates a substantial quantity of ceramics associated with food production, storage, and serving wares, in addition to the presence of ritual vessels. The distribution of ceramics resembles that of the faunal bones, with most of the utilitarian vessels found in squares I, J, K, and L. Food preparation and storage wares include large jars with narrow necks (more than 40cm in diameter), and large unrestricted bowls (more than 40cm in diameter). In terms of the serving wares, these are present in a slightly higher proportion than those used for cooking and storage, and are variable in size, ranging in diameter from small (10cm) to large (40cm). The most common forms include hemispherical bowls, plates, and dishes; many of these forms present globular legs, and are elegantly decorated with iconography inside and out

(Mirón 2012) (Figures 17 and 18). The size, quality, and decoration on many of these ceramics are features found almost exclusively at sites associated with high status groups (Mirón 2012:347). The presence of large serving plates may suggest that they were used to present large amounts of food to a group of people, while the smaller ones suggest personal use of vessels, such as vases for drinking.

Ritual ceramics were also present in small quantities. These include vases (for drinking), musical instruments (whistles, drums), *braseros* (braziers), and *incensarios* (censers), both of which are related to the burning of incense. Based on diagnostic forms, Mirón (2012:347, translation by Montero) also concluded that the ceramic assemblage represents 'the sum of an indeterminate number of activities that were conducted in the immediate vicinity'. These activities may have included domestic and ritual activities conducted by the inhabitants of the Palace.

Felipe Trabanino (UNAM) conducted macrobotanical and phytolith analyses of the organic remains from the midden, using flotation methods. Seeds of *jobo* or hog plum (*Spondias mombin*), *vejuco de uva* or water vine (*Vitis tiliifolia*), and *granadilla* or passionflower (*Passiflora* sp.) were identified, all of which may have been fermented to produce alcoholic or sedative beverages. Such libations were probably used in rituals (Trabanino 2012:234). The use of drugs and fermented beverages is considered to be one of the archaeological markers for feasting events (Hayden 2001:40).

Phytoliths from corn leaves were also found and Trabanino suggests that they may have been used to wrap foodstuffs or placed inside the deposit as an offering. Furthermore, pine needles and palm leaves that may have been used ritually were also identified. Interestingly, a wood charcoal fragment was also analysed and identified as ocote (*Pinus* sp.), a common item in rituals in modern times. Its presence in this context suggests that Chinikihá may have participated in a trade network with the highlands of Chiapas, or the Petén region in Guatemala, via the Usumacinta River (Trabanino 2012:234).

Situating *Operación* 114 in a chronological framework

A temporal range for Chinikihá has been established based on the presence of large numbers of ceramics in deposits from *Operación* 114, as well as vessels accompanying the burials from the North Structure. These can be attributed to a limited number of direct dates, situating them in a chronological framework. Furthermore, the style and pastes displayed also indicate use of the exchange networks that operated across the whole region.

Using the ceramic complex as a temporal proxy

It is important to note that surprisingly, the ceramics from Palenque—and therefore, Chinikihá—have not been studied extensively, except for a few isolated (Jiménez 2009). The fine divisions between phases are tentative, so for the purposes of this study, Palenque's chronological framework has been adopted for Chinikihá. Hence, the ceramic sequence for Chinikihá has been closely paired to Palenque's own analysis, and although a more comprehensive treatment of interaction between Palenque and outlying sites is needed (Rands 2007:25), we can understand the socio-political interactions in which Chinikihá was a part if we compare studies from Palenque. At Palenque, there is a lack of substantial ceramic sequence during the Preclassic when compared to other mayor Maya sites, such as Copán and Tikal (Marken and Straight 2007: 286-287). However, evidence of Preclassic ceramics does exist in nearby sites, including Chinikihá, where early ceramics come mainly from caves and mixed deposits (Rands 2007). Overall, the ceramics in the whole region resemble Olmec wares during the Preclassic period (Marken and Straight 2007: 286-287; Rands 2007:30), stressing the importance of the region in the exchange network between the Olmec region, the Yucatán Peninsula and throughout the Lowlands area (Andrews 1986:41-42). Other connections may have existed between Chinikihá and Piedras Negras in earlier periods (Rands 2007).

During the Early Classic, local wares were produced at Palenque, with a clear influence from the Petén region, located to the southeast of Palenque (Mark and Straight 2007). Nevertheless, once architectural constructions started at Palenque, local wares became more predominant, and the influence from the Petén ceased permanently (Mark and Straight 2007:290). Rands (1967) analysed the ceramics from several sites in the Palenque region, and suggested that the connection between Palenque and Chinikihá was hugely strong during the Classic period.

Recently, a formal attempt to undertake an exclusive study of Chinikihá's ceramics has been made (Jiménez 2009; Mirón 2012). The ceramic pastes are very variable, but locally manufactured. The decoration shows affinities primarily with Palenque, although a small portion of materials resemble those from Piedras Negras, a site situated to the south of Chinikihá, in the Usumacinta River area (Esteban Mirón, personal communication 2010), and the Petén in Guatemala, as well as with Campeche in the Yucatán Peninsula (Jiménez 2009:108).

In terms of the ceramics present in *Operación* 114, a small number dating to the Early Classic period (*c.* 450-600)

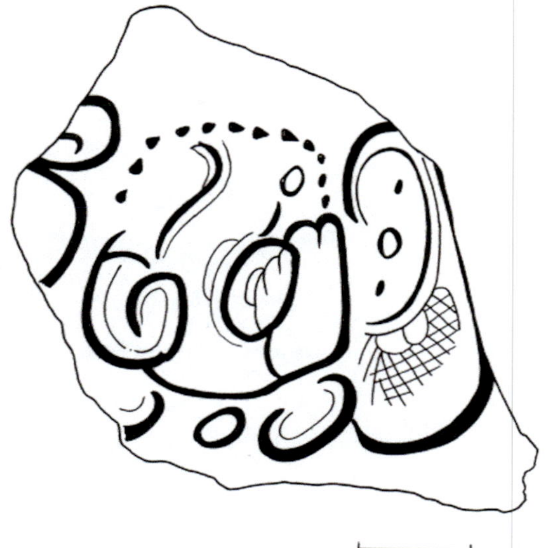

Figure 19. Incised turtle plaque with the glyph 'he/she was born' (original drawing courtesy of Peter Mathews, reproduced with permission).

and Balunté phases (Liendo 2012:175). Stylistically, these materials are similar in form and decoration to the ceramics from Palenque during the same phase (Mirón 2012), placing Layers I, II, and III in the Late Classic period. Furthermore, a fragmented plate with the calendar date of AD 752 was found in this context (Liendo 2012:176), offering solid evidence that this deposit was formed during the Late Classic.

It is interesting to note that other materials with iconography that were found within this location include two turtle plaques with incised glyphs. One of them includes a partial glyph (Figure 19), most possibly a month glyph (left), and the main glyph (right) reads **SIH-ya-ja**, 'he/she was born'; the writing style is consistent with that of the Late Classic period in the Lowlands area (Peter Mathews, personal communication 2011).

Comparing the ceramic assemblage from Operación 114 with other sites

were found underneath the floor, possibly indicating that this floor was an earlier construction phase of the Palace (Liendo 2012:175). Furthermore, some ceramic remains found directly on top of the stuccoed floor were identified as Aguila Naranja (Rodrigo Liendo, personal communication 2011), a type of representative ceramics of the Classic period and related to the Petén area in Guatemala (Liendo 2003:96; Rands 1977). The bulk of the materials in the deposit have been identified as Late Classic period, in particular to the Murciélagos

Tripod and four-legged serving plates are common in other sites, especially in non-domestic contexts (Sheets 2003). The elegance of these plates indicates that their use was reserved for special occasions (Sheets 2003:21). Some of them display glyphs that indicate what they were used for, including *tamales* stuffed with some sort of meat and it is believed that meat was reserved for special occasions (Beaudry-Corbet 2002; Hendon 2003). Two examples found during the Classic period come from Uaxactún, Guatemala (Zender 2000) and Cerén, in El Salvador (Sheets 2003:21). The iconography found on them suggests that at least in some cases, *tamales* were filled with deer meat, as the plates present the *sak chijil/hil waaj* logogram or 'white-venison tamale' (Bíró and Montero 2008; Zender 2000:1044-1050) (Figure 20).

Figure 20. White-venison tamale logogram, or ta SAK-chi-hi-li WAJ (K6080), and ta SAK-ki CHIJ ji-li WAJ on a plate from Uaxactun (circled in red) (modified from Zender 2000:1044, Figure 10).

Figure 21. Examples of ceramic plates possibly for serving tamales: A) three-legged plate with incised decoration from Operación 114; Chinikihá (from Mirón 2012, reproduced with permission); B) plate with waaj glyph from Temple XV, Palenque (modified from López 2006); C) Iconographic representations of plates with tamales (modified from Zender 2000:1046).

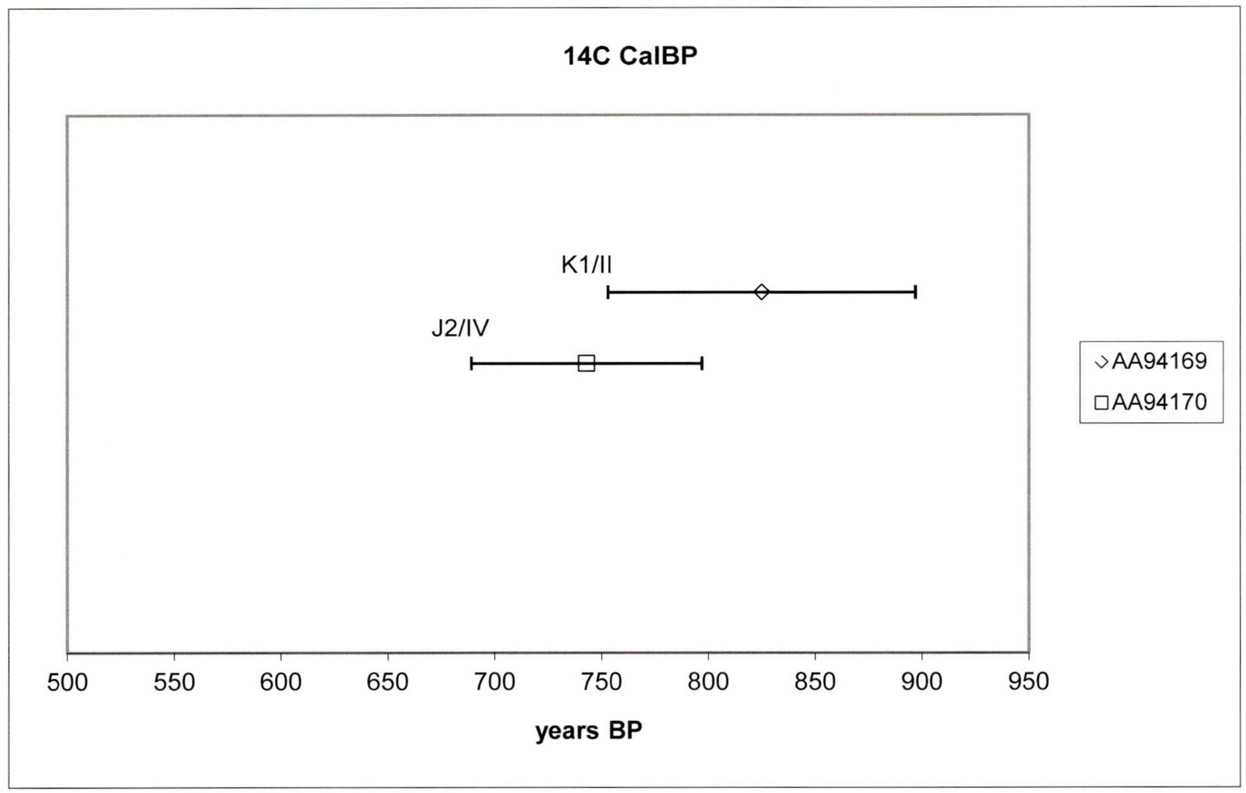

Figure 22. AMS dates from *Operación* 114 showing square/layer.

The large size of some of these plates points to a communal consumption and sharing of special foods during ceremonies, that might have taken place at all levels of the society, from the household level to communal feasts that were probably sponsored by the elite. At the Classic period site of Cerén, an analysis of domestic households showed that decorated four-legged plates were probably used to serve *tamales*, some of which were stuffed with meat including venison, though most were stuffed with maize, amaranth, manioc, and other edible plant foodstuffs (Hendon 2003:208; Sheets 2003). Some of these plates were polychromes and imported from Copán, stressing that domestic ceremonies involving the consumption of meat *tamales* from elegant plates was not overly common (Sheets 2003:21) and probably occurred only on specials occasions.

Closer to Chinikihá, in Late Classic Palenque, a 'plate for eating *tamales*', as suggested by the *waaj* glyph carved on its inner walls, was recovered from a tomb in Temple XV, hinting that it may be possible that similar plates were included in other burials of elite members as offerings of food in the form of meat *tamales* (López 2006:5-6) (Figure 21, letter B). Plates with *tamales* are a common representation in iconography, especially in scenes inside structures where kings and other elite members are being presented with commodities, accompanied by feasting of *tamales* and a fermented drink or a cacao drink (Reents-Budet 2000:1026). The high incidence of these plates in the archaeological record, in association with large quantities of faunal remains, may suggest that feasts were a common activity during the Classic period in the whole Maya area. Examples of feasts in the literature include the archaeological sites of Altun Ha (Reents-Budet 2000) and Lagartero (Koželsky 2005).

Remains of serving wares are usually mixed with other ritual ceramic objects, such as figurines, whistles, and other ritual paraphernalia. For example, in a feasting event at Copán during the Late Classic/Terminal period (*c.* 650-1000), Hendon (2003) identified the presence of food preparation, ritual food serving and eating wares, and long-term storage ceramics. Among the ritual wares, the author identifies fancy bowls and dishes for the consumption of food and drink, as well as other ritual paraphernalia, such as cylinders, figurines, whistles, and *candeleros* (a tubular ceramic container with unknown function), as well as highly decorated vessels used to serve and consume food and drink (including cylindrical vases, plates, bowls, and dishes) (Hendon 2003:218). Vases for drinking fermented drinks, made of cacao or maize, are present in many contexts identified with ritual feasting in the Maya area (Hendon 2003; LeCount 2001; López 2006). The combination of plates for *tamales* and vases for drinking cacao in feasting ceremonies is confirmed by pictorial ceramics containing images of presumed elite members during the Late Classic period

(Reents-Budet 2000:1026). At this point, it is interesting to note that many of these ceramics, including service and ritual vessels, are present in Chinikihá, especially at *Operación* 114.

Direct dating

Only two direct dates from animal bones are available for Chinikihá, both from *Operación* 114; nevertheless, a relative chronology has been established from the ceramic sequence for Chinikihá and the two other sites, Chancalá and San Juan Chancalaíto. The two samples of faunal bone were sent to the University of Arizona AMS Laboratory in Tucson, Arizona for AMS dating (Table 5).

Both samples were fragments of bone from white-tailed deer (*Odocoileus virginianus*). Sample AA94169 (rib) represents Layer II (above the floor), and AA94170 (metacarpus) represents Layer IV (under the floor). Sample AA94169 from Layer II, resulted in a calibrated date of AD 825±72 (Balunté phase), while sample AA94170 from the deeper Layer IV was slightly earlier, with a date of AD 743±54 (Murciélagos phase). The difference between these two dates suggests that the context was formed in a relatively short period of time (less than 100 years) (Figure 22).

A single AMS date was taken by a team of geologists from IIA-UNAM from a soil sample directly under the stuccoed floor, and resulted in an earlier date, which places the deposit under the floor in the Early Classic period (Rodrigo Liendo, personal communication 2011). Interestingly, they conducted some resistance studies over the area, and concluded that the whole deposit was probably laid in a single episode that is related to the construction of new architectural features related to the Palace (Liendo 2012:175). However, concluding that the deposit in *Operación* 114 was the result of a single episode is not straightforward, and part of the analysis presented in Chapter eight is focused on identifying the differences in the distribution of materials within the deposit, in order to infer its function.

In a preliminary analysis of *Operaciones* 1, 2, and 3 from the 2006 season, it was observed that the materials from this context presented different degrees of weathering, as well as a high percentage of bones with faunal modifications, suggesting that it was an open context, at least for some time (Montero 2008). The presence of modified materials was not exclusive to a specific layer, and their presence is mixed with materials that are not modified, indicating differences in the formation process that may have been the result of a series of activities conducted by the inhabitants of Chinikihá. This includes the possibility that materials were placed in this context as part of a general cleaning of occupational surfaces (Montero 2008). This may explain the presence of the materials that were highly eroded

Sample Num.	Lab Num.	Tissue	$d^{13}C$ value	F ($d^{13}C$)	+/- dF ($d^{13}C$)	^{14}C age BP	+/-	Calendric Age cal AD	+/-	Chronological phase
AA94169	X19961A	Rib	-20.6	0.8621	0.0057	1,192	53	825	72	Balunté
AA94170	X19962A	Metacarpus	-20.8	0.8539	0.0047	1,269	44	743	54	Murciélagos

Table 5. AMS dates for Chinikihá (Calibrated with CalPal, http://www.calpal-online.de, accessed on 24 October 2011).

and exhibited extensive modifications resulting from extended exposure, including faunal modifications, such as rodent gnawing.

In contrast, the large deposit of bones that resulted from human consumption, some of which were found still semi-articulated, suggests a rapid deposition (Montero 2008). Hence, one of the objectives of this analysis will be to study all the faunal material from this context in order to make inferences about the formation process and the identification of possible differences in the spatial patterning through time, taking into consideration the presence of the stuccoed floor.

The analysis of the ceramics is as yet incomplete however, Jiménez (2009) conducted a partial analysis of the 2006 ceramics, and Esteban Mirón analysed the cooking vessels from six contexts from Chinikihá, including *Operación* 114 (Mirón 2012, 2014), but were not completed by the time this study was finished. A partial investigation of the macrobotanical remains and charcoal from the 2008 season was conducted by Trabanino (2008, 2012), but is also not yet fully completed. Unfortunately, the analyses of figurines and lithics are in their early stages and no information was available at the time of this writing.

Until the field season of 2008, all faunal remains have been analysed by myself (Montero 2008; Montero and Núñez 2011; Montero *et al.* 2011), and the same methodology is being used to analyse the materials obtained since 2009 by Carlos Varela, from Escuela Nacional de Antropología e Historia (ENAH) from an excavation that extended to the south of *Operación* 114, and other contexts around Chinikihá (Varela 2013). As it can be seen, *Operación* 114 proved to be far more complex than initially thought and a third field season was conducted at the end of 2009. Therefore, the material and information from this last season were not available at the time of writing and are not included in my original dissertation. It is important to stress that once all the archaeological materials have been analysed, they will be integrated in the future, aiming to come up with a heuristic interpretation. However, it is considered likely that the analyses of other archaeological materials will arrive at similar conclusions to those posed here.

Summary

In this chapter, a detailed description of the faunal assemblages found during the 2008 field season of *Proyecto Arqueologico Chinikihá* (PRACH) has been provided. A series of human and faunal remains were recovered from diverse excavations, including *Operaciones* 110, 111, 112, 114, and 115 from Chinikihá, *Operación* 201 from Chancalá, and *Operación* 202 from San Juan Chancalaíto. In *Operación* 112, a set of human burials was identified inside a patio which are also summarised in this chapter.

Of all the *Operaciones* that contained faunal remains, *Operación* 114 is notable as it was the largest deposit (17m²) and presented large quantities of ceramics, lithics, faunal and human bones, as well as numerous malacological remains. Several ceremonial objects were also found within the same context and reflect a possible use by the elite. The context has been situated chronologically within the Late Classic period through the ce ramic analysis, the association to the architectural structures, and two radiocarbon tests from faunal remains. In the next chapter, the zooarchaeological methodology applied to the study of the faunal collection from Chinikihá is presented.

Chapter five

Zooarchaeological methodology

The objective of this chapter is to describe the methodology used to identify and analyse the faunal material recovered by PRACH in 2008. A substantial synthesis of the development of Mayan zooarchaeology has been discussed elsewhere by Emery (2004c). One of the recurrent limitations in Mayan zooarchaeology is that most studies use different methodologies and therefore the results are not comparable, or because data are not yet available to build a robust regional database with which to conduct comparisons (Emery 2004c:198, 2004d, 2010:33).

The present analysis is a continuation of the work carried out previously on archaeofaunal material recovered at Chinikihá from partial excavations and discussed elsewhere (Montero 2008). The results of both analyses are comparable and complementary, since the same methodology was applied to both. This work will subsequently be used as a framework to conduct intra-site comparisons in the Palenque area (Carlos Varela 2013).

The material analysed here represents a diversity of contexts, including domestic and possible ritual discard. However, a greater emphasis has been placed on the analysis of *Operación* 114 because of its importance in understanding the formation processes of a ritual context. The zooarchaeological results for all of the *Operaciones* are presented in Chapter six, but a detailed examination of *Operación* 114 will be discussed in Chapter seven.

Basic quantification (NISP and MNI) of all the material present in the different contexts is presented firstly as an overall analysis, and following this, independently by *Operación*, with special attention to *Operación* 114. A description of all the variables identified is also included, which will then be used to discuss how this methodology can be used in the identification of distinctive consumption patterns, such as repetitive ceremonies or feasting among the Maya elite.

Zooarchaeological analysis

In May and June 2008, excavation works were conducted at Chinikihá. I was able to participate in the excavation of the context behind the Palace, aiming to identify discrete elements among the massive quantity of material. This, however, proved to be a difficult task, since the materials appeared to be distributed homogeneously throughout the deposit. This is probably due to a rather quick sequence of deposition that could have been the result of one or a few events. Although the excavation methodology was planned in order to identify discrete episodes of deposition, this proved an extremely challenging task. Nonetheless, in some cases it was possible to identify a close relationship between certain faunal remains and some ceramic fragments from semi-complete vessels or figurines (Figure 23).

The context was excavated by a large team that followed an agreed methodology described elsewhere (Liendo 2009b). All the recovered archaeological materials were transported to the field laboratory, where local hired staff cleaned parts of the faunal remains. Some soil samples were floated as part of the macrobotanical analysis, and small fragments of animal bone were recovered, and separated. In April 2009, I travelled to Mexico City for five months to conduct the identification and preparation of the isotope analysis. The cleaned material as well as the rest of the unwashed material was then transported to the laboratory at Instituto de Investigaciones Antropológicas at UNAM, where a project member cleaned the remaining bones. All materials were cleaned with running tap water and a soft toothbrush, air-dried, and stored at these facilities. The material was then transported to the Laboratorio de Paleozoología 'Ticúl Álvarez' from Instituto Nacional de Antropología e Historia (INAH) in Mexico City, where conjoining broken fragments were glued back together and taxonomic identification was conducted, with the guidance of Maestro Oscar Polaco.

A database template was created in the computer program *Excel* 2003, and data were recorded for each individual fragment of bone. Basic information included provenance data such as square, stratigraphic layer, species, and element, but also other information was registered, including element, element side, and element portion. This information, plus the age and sex make up the minimal unit of analysis or specimen (as defined by Grayson 1984:16). Other characteristics were also recorded, especially the taphonomic modifications—cultural and non-cultural—such as type of fracture, presence of carnivore and rodent gnawing, weathering stage or erosion, presence of root etching, and insect modifications, location, and type of processing marks—including butchery and other carcass-processing modifications (including cut marks

Figure 23. Remains of a tripod plate, underneath which faunal bones were found, from PRACH 2008 (from Liendo 2010, reproduced with permission).

and burned bone), as well as presence of pathological conditions. Water damage and presence of concretion (calcium carbonate) was also annotated.

Limitations

Although most of the excavation back dirt was collected and bagged, it was not possible to complete the flotation at the time of the 2008 field season, and this work was therefore not conducted until later. However, Trabanino (2008) did carry out some soil flotations, primarily to recover macrobotanical remains, but bone fragments were also retrieved when encountered, and integrated to the main collection by pit and layer. Among the materials recovered by flotation are small fragments of mammal bones and shell fragments; however, it was noted that no small or micro fauna remains were collected, hence the presence of small and/or micro fauna may be limited in this assemblage by a bias towards big mammal fragments. It is well known in zooarchaeology that recovery methods affect sample variability and bias against small animals and elements (James 1997; Quitmyer 2004; Wake 2004).

A few fish bones were recovered from flotation conducted during 2010 but were not integrated in this analysis. Nevertheless, some fish species have relatively large bones and have been recovered by hand in archaeological excavations where there was no flotation or screening (Carr and Fradkin 2008:150). It is possible then that the low frequencies of fish so far obtained at Chinikihá, may indeed be a result of low numbers of fish bones in this assemblage. The absence of fish and other small mammal species may have been a result of cultural preference as, it is understood that in some sites, where sieves were used, no fish remains were recovered (Yaeger 2000). This would also extend to the lack of bird and the few reptile bones (mostly worked turtle bones) that have been recovered, all from *Operación* 114. This absence of riverine and marsh resources in locations where such resources would have been easily accessible to humans has been observed at other sites, including the site of Seibal on the Pasion River (Pohl 1985a), and San Lorenzo, on the Belize River (Yaeger 2000). Thus, the lack of fish in deposits created by the refuse from human consumption may reflect a cultural choice, or differential disposal practices.

Overall, more research needs to be done in order to understand the use of aquatic resources by the Maya (Pohl 1985a:136).

Defining the variables

Different societies use animals in a wide variety of ways. Profane and ritual use may be reflected in the type of animal used, the age, the sex, skeletal completeness, the presence of burned bone, and evidence of butchering patterns (Reitz and Wing 1999:275-276).

Specimen count

The basic counting unit within a given faunal assemblage is the identified *specimen* (Grayson 1984:17) or skeletal part (Lyman 2008:5), and is defined as any individual skeletal remain, whether it is anatomically complete or not. In this analysis, the term *skeletal portion* refers exclusively to a segment of the skeleton, such as hind limb (*sensus* Lyman 2008). Although counting all taxonomic fragments may not be a direct reflection of the life assemblage (Grayson 1978), the results of commensurate quantification of archaeofaunal remains is vital when comparisons between samples are to be carried out (Klein and Cruz-Uribe 1984). In this sense, all quantifications are a measure of abundance of the species present in a specific context. Species frequencies can be calculated in different ways, depending on the objective of the analysis. In this dissertation the Number of Identified Specimens (NISP), and the Minimum Number of Individuals (MNI) are used. All quantified materials are presented as absolute and relative frequencies (NISP) that represent absolute and relative abundances (MNI) (Grayson 1984:17). The objective of this is to counteract the differences in assemblage size when regional comparisons are carried out.

Number of Identified Specimens (NISP)

Also known as the Total Number of Fragments (TNF), this is the simplest measure of frequency of the actual number of identified fragments, being a bone or a tooth, attributed to each taxon, plus those that cannot be attributed to a particular one (Hesse and Wapnish 1985:112; Lyman 2008:27; O'Connor 2000). Many factors affect it, including the transformation from life-to-death-to-deposited assemblage (Klein and Cruz-Uribe 1984), the post-depositional taphonomic history (O'Connor 2000), and the degree of fragmentation (Klein and Cruz-Uribe 1984:25; O'Connor 1985). Perhaps the most important counterpoint is that it assumes that all species are equally affected and therefore, present a similar survival trend (Chaplin 1971:64).

On the other hand, NISP has two obvious advantages, as it is primary data, readily obtainable at the time when bone identifications are done, and these values are cumulative, making them easy to update with subsequent additions of new data (Klein and Cruz-Uribe 1984; Lyman 2008). Rather than a descriptive tool, NISP best reflects a measure for taxonomic abundances (Grayson 1984; Lyman 2008:140), and it is useful for inter-sample statistical comparisons, as it represents the raw data, and is vital for any zooarchaeological analysis. No further calculations of dietary contributions can be derived from NISP figures; thus, I explore this topic and the processing patterns of the species present by comparing the distribution of butchering units, Minimum Number of Elements (MNE), and skeletal completeness (Lyman 1979). Data is presented in tables and basic graphs, and to test for significance of the results, I applied a series of basic univariate statistical tests including analysis of variance (ANOVA), chi-square, Student's t distribution, Kolmogorov-Smirnov D, Kendall's tau, and Spearman's rho, depending on the size of the sub-samples and the assumptions about their distribution. The combination of the data presented in different forms, and the basic statistical analysis of chi-square, can be extremely helpful when analysing the basic components of a deposit (Ringrose 1993).

In the present analysis, refitted specimens were counted as one specimen, as in many cases, these can be the result of breakage during deposition, excavation, or subsequent handling (Reitz and Wing 1999:156). This also includes all epiphyses and diaphyses that are separate—usually unfused due to young age—but belong to the same bone. However, in instances where two or more bones were articulated, they were counted separately, as during the excavation, in most cases, it was not possible to identify if they were laid together, but disarticulated, or existed as an articulated portion. The accuracy of calculating NISP values relies heavily on the specimen identification. Identified specimens are those that could be assigned at least a Family—and where possible a Genus and Species (Lyman 2008). For example, ribs were very fragmented, they were recorded in 'size-related groups', such as small/medium and medium/large mammals (Klein and Cruz-Uribe 1984:19), in line with other works in the Maya area (Emery 2010; Teeter 2001). On the other hand, care was placed to identify vertebrae and ribs, where they were fairly complete, as their presence informs us about carcass processing activities. In some cases, it was possible not only to identify species, but also to record the region on the spine to which the bones belonged.

Minimum Number of Individuals (MNI)

MNI has been extensively used among palaeontologists and was introduced to archaeology by White (1953) as a method to calculate quantity of meat provided by each taxon that was present in the archaeological record. Since then, several authors have used and modified the way MNI is calculated, and an extensive discussion on how MNI has been defined is presented elsewhere (Lyman 2008). It is best defined by Reitz and Wing (1999:194) as 'the smallest number of individuals which is necessary to account for all of the skeletal elements of a particular species found in the site'. Traditionally, MNI considers that for each taxon, the most ubiquitous skeletal element should be identified, with consideration as to whether it is a paired or unpaired bone (O'Connor 2000). However, calculations of MNI can be tedious and are more prone to error than NISP (Klein and Cruz-Uribe 1984), and MNI tends to exaggerate the importance of rare species or other fauna represented by small frequencies (Grayson 1978; Reitz and Wing 1999). In reality it seems very difficult to determine pairs (Lyman 2008:39), therefore MNI is calculated based on the presence of the most commonly occurring sided skeletal element of a taxon in an assemblage. In this sense, vertebrae were not considered for MNI calculations. Despite this, MNI has proved to have an advantage over NISP, because MNI does allow calculation of dietary contribution of a particular species (White 1953).

In this analysis, MNI was calculated using the most common skeletal element, and only for those remains that were identified to the lowest taxonomic level. Complete and fragmentary bones were considered, but no pairing was conducted; where paired elements were identified (left and right), the higher count was included in the calculations (Reitz and Wing 1999:195-198). Skeletal element, age and sex were also considered. MNI was calculated separately for each separate *Operación*, as they represent different cultural units, however, no different MNI was calculated for each stratum, as the remains of a single animal may be scattered vertically, as observed in previous studies (see Montero 2008).

Minimum number of elements (MNE) and skeletal completeness

One of the main questions that any zooarchaeological study should seek to address is the level of bone fragmentation and the origin of this fragmentation. This is not as easy or simple task, but the results of this analysis can provide answers to the following questions: Is the fragmentation the result of human or carnivore activity? Are some body parts more common than others? What parts were targeted, transported, or consumed more often than others?

Although exact details of what was consumed in past societies may never be known, it is possible to identify the most common prey animals, and as a result of this, to understand the dietary preferences within a society (Lyman 1979). The focus can then be shifted from the species consumed to a more specific portions analysis

(Lyman 1979). For this purpose, zooarchaeological concepts such as the Minimum Number of Elements and Skeletal Completeness, have been developed. To gain a better understanding of these concepts, it is necessary to define a skeletal element. A skeletal element refers to a specimen that can be identified as a single specific bone, such as the humerus, while anatomical regions are a group of adjacent skeletal portions, such as a forelimb (Lyman 2008). The analysis by MNE and Skeletal Completeness will be applied only to *Operación* 114, as the rest of the *Operaciones* produced a markedly low number of specimens.

Minimum number of elements (MNE)

MNE is defined simply as 'the minimum number of skeletal elements necessary to account for the specimens under study' (Lyman 2008:218). MNE is derived from the number of elements represented by the fragmentary remains, based on the presence of overlapping landmark features (Reitz and Wing 1999:215). More specifically, MNE considers 'the most common *portion* of each skeletal element and represents the sum of right and left sides for elements that naturally occur in pairs' (Stiner 1994:237, italics mine). In the present study, MNE was calculated following Stiner (1994) and Reitz and Wing (1999), but adapted to fit the data presented here. In calculating MNE, isolated teeth were not considered as their presence tends to over-estimate head counts. Long bone shafts were also not considered, especially when fragmentary or unfused as in many instances they were not identified beyond being assigned to the medium/large mammal category and therefore their presence would be under-estimated.

MNE is subject to the same constraints as MNI, in the sense that MNE is defined by the researcher, and therefore, MNE figures may be not suitable for inter-sample comparisons. Hence, each researcher should state the methodology used to calculate NISP, MNE, and MNI (Lyman 2008:221). Also, as with MNI, MNE results are obtained for each context and should not be summed up in order to obtain a grand total for a whole site. Therefore, one should be aware of its limitations as an analytical tool, and restrict its use to specific contexts. On the other hand, MNE provides different information from that of MNI. NISP and MNI are measures of species abundance, ignoring the specific composition by skeletal parts that form the sample. Two samples with similar NISP and MNI results may show significant disparity in the body parts represented in the sample (Klein and Cruz-Uribe 1984). MNE, as an index to measure skeletal frequency, is useful when aiming to distinguish differences in animal use (Reitz and Wing 1999:202-203). MNE is also helpful when comparing the presence of certain skeletal elements and how they differ when compared to a complete skeleton (Lyman 1994:102). It is because of this quality that MNE will be used in this analysis, as it provides complementary information on dietary input from a particular taxon (Lyman 1979:539).

Skeletal completeness

Measuring skeletal completeness and bone fragmentation can assist in the identification of differences between contexts, for example, whether a deposit is cultural or natural (Lyman 1994). In contexts from around the world which have been defined in definite terms as ritual, such as animal burials, it has been observed that the presence of remains from one or more whole animals can be expected. These include China (Jing and Flad 2005:257) and Mesoamerica; examples being Burial 2 of Teotihuacán, which contained several complete animals, and in the Maya area, a complete but headless deer found at Copán (Williamson 1996:5). This is distinctly incongruent with deposits of domestic refuse, where less complete skeletons are expected (Randolph 1992:371).

In this dissertation skeletal completeness was measured using the formula:

$$d = \log_e X - \log_e Y$$

where d = logged ratio, X is the percentage of each skeletal portion attributed to a particular taxon in the archaeological assemblage, and Y is the percentage of this same portion in a complete skeleton (Reitz and Wing 1999:212).

Another way of analysing skeletal completeness (Stiner 1994:241-242) is the calculation of four indices based on anatomical regions that compare the overall proportion of head elements to a combination of limb parts. Emery (2010:42) combines these indices and proposes the ratio: {limb / (cranial + axial + distal)} to measure the proportion of meat-bearing elements to non-meaty ones. This ratio will be used in this study as it facilitates determining element distribution as a probable result of subsistence patterns.

When processing an animal, the carcass may be divided into anatomical regions, by disarticulation, following the logic of the carcass. Butchering a carcass into smaller portions, then defines a skeletal portion that may include adjacent skeletal elements (e.g. humerus), adjacent anatomical regions (e.g. forelimb), or only parts of these (Reitz and Wing 1999:205); it is comparable to a 'butchering unit', which is culturally defined, and could potentially indicate what was considered consumable (Lyman 1979:539).

However the most important thing to remember is that these concepts are arbitrary and are primarily only used when studying an archaeofaunal collection. As a classification system, different authors have classified the skeletal elements into different anatomical regions, but usually, these categories are skull, vertebrae, upper front and back limbs, lower front and back limbs, and distal elements (Binford 1978; Emery 2010; Reitz and Wing 1999; Stiner 1994). Each of them comprises one or several skeletal elements, according to different criteria depending on the author's own central research question.

Because one of the aims of this study is to explore the processing and consumption patterns of faunal resources, the unit of classification is based on the location of butchering marks, as this will allow the identification of which body parts of the animal were used (Lyman 1976; Perkins and Daly 1968). Butchering marks, mostly resulting from skinning and disarticulation, are located on articulations, and may include several anatomical regions (Reitz and Wing 1999). These are the head (antler, skull, and mandible), neck (atlas, axis, and the rest of the cervical vertebrae), torso (sternum, thoracic and lumbar vertebrae, ribs, and sacrum), upper front limb (scapula and humerus), lower front limb (radio, ulna, carpals, and metacarpals), upper back limb (innominate bones, and femur), lower back limb (patella, tibia, tarsals, and metatarsals), and distal (phalanges). In Table 6, a comparison between different classifications is presented.

As can be seen in Table 6, the way in which the portions have been divided by different authors is notably similar. However, there are some interesting differences, specifically in which category the innominate and the distal elements are considered. The classification of a specific skeletal element in a category can be an arbitrary decision, for example, based on ethnographic observations (Binford 1978; Reitz and Wing 1999:206; Stiner 1994:240). In most cases, these divisions are logical and will follow the animal's own anatomy. In this study, the classifications used by Emery (2010), based on ethnographic descriptions of hunter/butcher choice of meat cuts by the Maya, will be used; however, some minor modifications were made in order to explore more specific distributions of certain elements.

It is important to note that choosing one classification system over the others will ultimately have an impact on the analysis of skeletal elements and their interpretation in terms of the consumption behaviour of a specific group. It will also affect the way the study of skeletal elements contributes to the exploration of other subjects, such as the taphonomic history of a deposit, which body parts are arriving at the site, which ones are considered to be primary discard and

Binford (1978)[a]	Stiner (1994)[a]	Reitz and Wing (1999)[a]	Emery (2010)[b]	Montero (this study)
Antlers, skull, and mandible	Horn/antler	Head (Horn/antler, skull, and mandible)	Cranial (antler, skull)	Head (antler, skull, and mandible)
	Head (Skull and mandible)			
Atlas, axis, and cervical vertebrae	Neck (cervical vertebrae)			Neck (atlas, axis and cervical vertebrae)
Thoracic vertebrae and first two ribs on both sides	Axial column (vertebrae, innominate and sacrum)	Axial (vertebrae, ribs, sternum)	Axial (Neck, spine, and ribs)	Torso (thoracic, lumbar, sternum, ribs, and sacrum)
Lumbar vertebrae, sacrum and pelvis				
Sternum and costal ribs				
Rib slabs				
Front legs (humerus, radio, ulna, carpus, metacarpus, and phalanges)	Upper front limbs (scapula, and humerus)	Forequarter (Scapula, humerus, radius, and ulna)	Upper limb (Scapula and humerus)	Upper front limb (scapula, and humerus)
Rear legs (femur, patella, tibia, tarsus, metatarsus, and phalanges)	Upper hind limb (femur)	Hindquarter (innominate, femur, patella, tibia, and sacrum)	Rear upper limb haunches (innominate, and femur)	Lower front limb (radio, ulna, carpal, and metacarpal)
	Lower front limbs (radio, ulna, carpus, and metacarpus)	Forefoot (carpal, and metacarpus)	Lower limbs (radio/ulna and tibia)	Upper back limb (innominate, femur)
	Lower hind limbs (tibia, tarsus, and metatarsus)	Hind foot (tarsal, and metatarsus)	Distal (carpus/metacarpus, tarsus/metatarsus, and phalanges)	Lower back limb (patella, tibia, tarsal, and metatarsal)
	Feet (phalanges)	Foot (metapodium, phalanges)		Distal (phalanges)

[a] Based on anatomical regions
[b] Based on skeletal regions

Table 6. Comparison between different classifications of skeletal elements.

how the animal carcasses are being butcher or further processed. Therefore, the distribution of specific parts can inform us not only of the activity that was conducted in particular locations, but also which parts a specific group considered more or less valuable. Additionally, preservation of certain elements can be useful when reconstructing the taphonomic history of a deposit.

The method used here will assist in addressing a wide range of issues, including differential survival of skeletal elements with reference to post-depositional taphonomic history and the cultural decisions made by the Maya. It was observed among the modern Maya in Chiapas that these groups place different dietary and utility values on meat portions. At Maya archaeological sites, there is a difference between which skeletal elements are present at sites in different areas, such as inland or coastal regions. Carr (1996:255) suggests that skull fragments are more common in inland processing sites, while on islands, such as Cozumel, there are more antlers and metapodia—bones that are useful as tools.

Similarly, the presence or absence of certain skeletal elements can be evidence for the possibility of a ritual consumption. Previous research suggest that the Maya elite preferred the back limb for ritual consumption (Pohl 1990). Therefore, a large quantity of these bones would be expected in deposits associated with the elite (Montero 2009) and ritual consumption. Images of a lord presented with the haunch of an animal are recurrent in the iconography (Devendhal 2005; Masson 1999), further evidence that the consumption of such portions was practiced during feasts (Bíró and Montero 2008; Emery 2007b). One of the aims of this analysis will be to test if there is a positive correlation between skeletal elements, especially the haunch, and the elite context at Chinikihá.

In testing for MNE and skeletal completeness, isolated teeth were excluded, as it is impossible to determine whether they come from a single cranial element. Hence including them would likely result in a double count of cranial elements. Also, for skeletal completeness, only bones positively identified for sidedness were included. Similarly, those vertebrae not positively identified as cervical, thoracic, or lumbar were also left out. To allow for inter-element comparisons, a standardisation process was conducted, using a modified version of the method proposed by Stiner (1994:240-241). Stiner proposed the use of raw MNE counts, by collapsing them into nine anatomical 'regions', and then standardising them by dividing the raw MNE by the expected number of elements for artiodactyls. The highest ratio may serve as an estimated number of carcasses from which food was obtained (Stiner 1994:241).

Minimum of animal units (MAU) and food utility index (FUI)

Because the presence of skeletal elements closely reflects the methods by which individuals within a single society typically butcher a carcass, a further pair of measures can be derived from MNE. These are Minimum of Animal Units (MAU), and Food Utility Index (FUI). Binford (1984:50) changed MNI to MAU and defined it as 'the minimum number of different specimens referable to a given anatomical part used in classification'. Once MAU values are calculated, the highest value is used as a standard and converted to a normal scale by multiplying it by 100 (%MAU) (Binford 1984:50).

Food Utility Index (FUI) as defined by Metcalfe and Jones (1988) is another index where body parts are ranked according to their utility, which in turn is defined by various factors including decisions based on transportation, and general value of specific sections in an economic framework. The application of FUI is important because it will allow us to see which body portions, especially those of high value or utility, are missing from the context.

Taxonomic identification

Taxa identification was carried out with the aid of Biologist Belem Chávez at the Laboratorio de Paleozoología (INAH). This work was based on comparisons with the reference collection housed there, as well as bibliographical manuals and other references (EA.FLMNH 2003; Olsen 1964, 1982; Schmid 1972). Initially, the remains were sorted by a basic division of identifiable and not identifiable bones, with the latter disregarded hereafter (Klein and Cruz-Uribe 1984:17). This included those fragments that were too small, and/or eroded to be identified at all. However, there were some bones that were identifiable to Class level, and therefore were grouped in a larger more general category, depending on their size. They were grouped in 'small/medium mammal' if they were the size of a domestic dog and smaller and 'medium/large mammal' for animals larger than a dog. The rest of the identifiable material was then further sorted with a greater focus on specific details. All bone fragments that were classified initially as identifiable are included in this analysis.

In order to avoid inter-personal variation, the methodology for the identification of remains was discussed with the laboratory assistant; where there were doubts, identification was resolved following discussion. Finally, the same statistical analysis of the material was conducted in its entirety to maintain comparability with the materials analysed previously (Montero 2008).

Analysis by location

Osteological and malacological material was recovered from different excavation fronts, or *Operaciones* at Chinikihá, following the general excavation plan for PRACH 2008. These include *Operaciones* 110, 111, 112, 114, and 115. Also, two sites located in the valley survey were included. These are San Juan Chancalá (*Operación* 201), and Chancalaíto (*Operación* 202) (see descriptions in Chapter four). These are analysed firstly at site level, as one analytical unit with the objective of observing site patterns. There were then analysed individually, in order to realise intra-site comparisons. Detailed analysis of *Operación* 114 is presented in Chapter eight.

Diversity index

In zooarchaeological analyses, measuring the diversity of a zooarchaeological collection means exploring the composition of an assemblage, where particular taxa are represented (Lyman 2008:173; Reitz and Wing 1999:102). Although they are intrinsically interrelated, their independent calculation permits an exploration of the different properties of a sample (Bobrowsky and Ball 1989:5). Diversity is defined as 'the number of categories represented in a sample or as the way a quantity is distributed among those categories', and intrinsically, this definition refers to two concepts, those of richness (the number of categories) and evenness (the order of abundance) (Jones and Leonard 1989:2). The definition of richness is the number of taxa in a community containing a specified number of individuals (Emery 2010:41; Reitz and Wing 1999:102), and species evenness is calculated as the similarity in abundance of several taxa in a sample (Emery 2010:41).

Diversity, also known as 'heterogeneity', thus assesses the variability in both the number of categories or species and the abundance of individual species with a single value (Bobrowsky and Ball 1989:5). This is to say how many individuals are present in how many species, or as Lyman (2008:174) states '[diversity] signify a family of variables used to describe the structure and composition of faunas and collections of faunal remains'. The analysis of archaeological diversity offers the potential to understand functional and processual relationships (Jones and Leonard 1989:3), represented with one single value.

To calculate diversity, two indices were used: the Simpson's index and the Shannon-Weaver index. To obtain the Simpson's index the following formula was used:

$$D = 1 - \Sigma\{n(n-1)\} / \{N(N-1)\}$$

where: D = heterogeneity, n = specimen count/species, and N = total specimen count (Simpson 1949).

The Shannon-Weaver index—or Shannon-Wiener function—was also obtained because it is crucial to obtain richness and evenness values. It was calculated with the formula:

$$H' = - \Sigma(p_i) (Log_e\ p_i)$$

where: H' = information content in the sample, p_i = the relative abundance of the ith taxon, and Log p_i = the logarithm of p_i (usually the natural logarithm) (Reitz and Wing 1999:105).

As mentioned before, to calculate diversity, richness and evenness have to be computed. Put simply, richness is the variety of species or 'wealth' represented in a sample (Bobrowsky and Ball 1989:5). It is useful when comparing different collections, so sample size also affects its value. Although some researchers just consider the number of taxa present in a sample (Lyman 2008:143), in this study, richness was calculated using an index, namely, Odum's Richness index (Odum 1971), because there is no sample-size dependency with the use of Odum's index (Emery 2010:41). Species richness was calculated using the formula:

$$R = (s - 1 / log\ N)$$

where: s = number of taxa and N = total specimen count.

Species evenness between assemblages was calculated using simple variance based on the proportional abundance of species or frequency (Bobrowsky and Ball 1989:7). Also known as equitability, evenness is calculated here with the following formula:

$$V' = H'/Log\ S$$

where: H' = the Shannon-Weaver function, and S = the number of species in the community (Reitz and Wing 1999:105).

Although NISP can be used when calculating all the indices, MNI counts were preferred here because unlike NISP, MNI are not affected by differential fragmentation among different species, therefore, making it ideal for intra-species comparisons (Cruz-Uribe 1988).

Age, sex, seasonality and mortality profiles

Age

There are two methods of ageing animals, the juvenile-adult distinction—based on epiphyseal fusion and deciduous/permanent teeth distinction—and the continuous distinction, based on dental age classes (Davis 1987:39). As a consequence, different methodologies are applied depending on whether the specimen was a tooth or a bone; age identification is based on dental eruption and/or dental wear, and epiphyseal fusion respectively. For the aging of the white-tailed deer (*Odocoileus virginianus*) remains, Lewall and Cowan (1963), Purdue (1983a), and Severinghaus (1949) were used as a reference. For other large mammals, Reitz and Wing 1999:76) were consulted. For the collared peccari (*Pecari tajacu*), Woodburne (1968) was used to separate juveniles from adult peccaries. For the domestic dog (*Canis lupus familiaris*), the works of Blanco *et al.* (2009) and Crockford (2009) were used. Finally, Hale (1949) and Jones (2006) were useful guides in the estimation of age in rabbits (*Sylvilagus* sp.). When ageing human remains, the works of Bass (1995) and White (1991) were consulted.

For deer teeth, mandibular dental pieces were used (Severinghaus 1949:202), preferably a permanent molar—M1, M2, or M3—complete and still in the alveolus; height, length, and width were measured with an electronic calliper. Molar height was measured according to Klein and Cruz Uribe (1984:46). In order to assign an age for deer teeth, a combination of individual measurements and comparisons with eruption/wear patterns was applied. Age in deer by this method is presented in half yearly increments. When it was possible, a specific age cohort was assigned, but in other instances, it was only possible to classify specimens as juvenile (presence of deciduous teeth), sub-adult (if permanent teeth have erupted but were unworn), and adult (if permanent teeth were worn). Age groups based on dentition eruption/wear include: <12 months (juvenile), 12-24 months (sub-adult), and >24 months (adult).

For the post-cranial specimens, age was based on the timing and order of ossification of epiphyses to diaphyses

(Driesch 1976:4; Edwards *et al.* 1982; Purdue 1983a:1207). It relies on the identification of the fusion stage of the epiphyseal plate, whether the element was initially fused, half-fused or fully fused (Lewall and Cowan 1963:629). The four age classifications used here are: under 12 months, between 12 and 29 months, between 29 and 35 months, and over 35 months of age. These groupings were only used when a specific age cohort can be assigned. These intervals also include the variability in age that a difference in sex might cause, as noted by Purdue (1983a:1212) and Lewall and Cowan (1963).

Other authors do not assign a specific age but base the age groups according to the degree of fusion present between both epiphyses and the diaphysis (Reitz and Wing 1999). According to Reitz and Wing (1999:183) a juvenile has unfused epiphysis in the early fusing category, and presents porous bone whereas a sub-adult specimen is unfused in the middle-late and adults have complete fusion in the late fusing category. When a fragment does not present the late-fusing epiphysis, but presents the early or middle-fusing one, it could be a sub-adult or an adult; therefore, these are considered as indeterminate (Reitz and Wing 1999:183).

However, these terms are comparable to the age intervals proposed previously with a juvenile specimen of 12 months or younger and is characterised by the presence of deciduous teeth, and/or by the presence of totally unfused epiphyses (proximal and distal). Between 12 and 29 months of age, sub-adults present permanent teeth are present (but unworn), and a mix of early, middle and late fusing bones. Between 30-35 months, in the immature individuals, the remaining late epiphyses are fusing. Finally, adults are those who present all of the epiphyses fused, and are over 35 months of age. By 78 months of age, or 6.5 years of age, complete ankylosis of all epiphyses has occurred (Lewall and Cowan 1963:635).

Age identification methods, using teeth eruption/wear and epiphysis fusion, have specific disadvantages, and both suffer from preservation problems. Ageing by teeth seems to offer a narrower age category due to the fact that teeth growth is genetically controlled, as opposed to epiphysis fusion, which is relative to the degree of epiphyseal fusion and is directly related to the differential preservation of some of the skeletal elements, which complicates the task (Davis 1987). Although age seems to be the determinant factor in epiphyseal closure, other factors, such as nutrition and sex, may also affect fusion rates (Purdue 1983a:1212). It can be predicted that the degree of accuracy in identifying a specimen's age will depend greatly on the element itself, whether it is a dental or post-cranial element. Therefore, a comparison between different age profiles that include teeth and epiphyseal fusion

is necessary in order to understand differential age-related survival, and consequently, mortality profiles (Munson and Garniewicz 2003:415; Steele 2003:421). This should allow a better understanding and provide stronger inferences of age profiles.

Sex

Identification of sex in white-tailed deer is not an easy task, and although deer are sexually dimorphic, geographic, and temporal variation can obscure the differences that indicate sex (Purdue 1983b). Perhaps the best way to identify sex is by obtaining several measurements from specific bone elements, for example, the tibia (Purdue 1983b). Sex identification can also be evaluated morphologically by qualitative differences (Purdue 1983b). For white-tailed deer, male animals present pedicels and antlers and females do not, making it easy to identify sex when a complete skull, or at least the frontal bone, is present.

In the post-cranial skeleton, the pelvis is perhaps the best element to look at when sexing deer, specifically by evaluating the frontal pelvic girdle, where determining sex depends on the development and position of the ilio-pectineal eminence (IPE), as stated by Edwards and colleagues (1982). The IPE's position on the edge of the acetabular branch of the pubis exhibits obvious sexual dimorphism and seems consistent after 12 months of age (Edwards *et al.* 1982:545), and among males IPE is a rounded protuberance; in females on the other hand, IPE has a sharp edge, often flattened or shelf-like in appearance (Edwards *et al.* 1982, Table 1).

In conclusion, it can be seen that the deer pelvis presents a clear morphological difference between sexes, a condition that needs to be fulfilled if sexing an animal macroscopically (Chaplin 1971:100). Although it has been observed that the most promising method is measuring when it comes to identifying sex (Klein and Cruz-Uribe 1984:40), in this study, sex was identified morphologically, focusing on the IPE, as time available to conduct the laboratory analysis in Mexico City was limited.

Seasonality and mortality profiles

Seasonality, or the period of the year when an animal is most likely to have been born, is commonly identified by the growth of dentine and cementum that form bands or annuli. These alternating translucent and thick zones can be then counted and compared to individuals of known age (Hillson 2005). For deer, it is commonly done with the incisors (Gilbert 1966) or molars (Kay 1974; Ransom 1966). This method is ideal to age old individuals with more precision, however it is an expensive method if commercially done and it can be time consuming. In a similar fashion, measurements

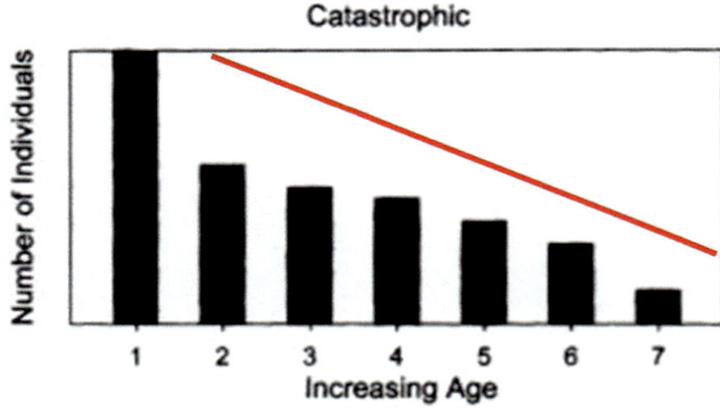

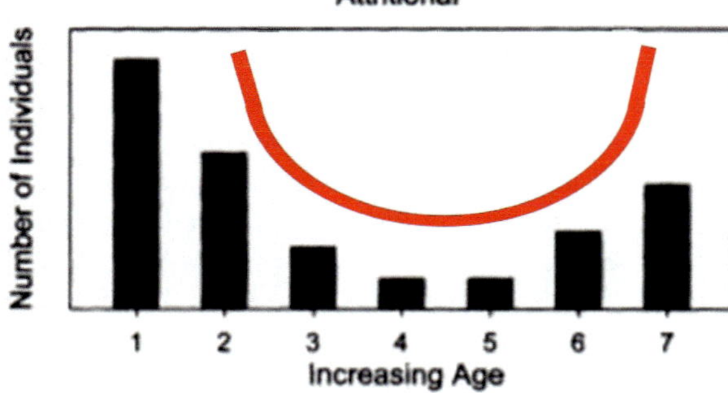

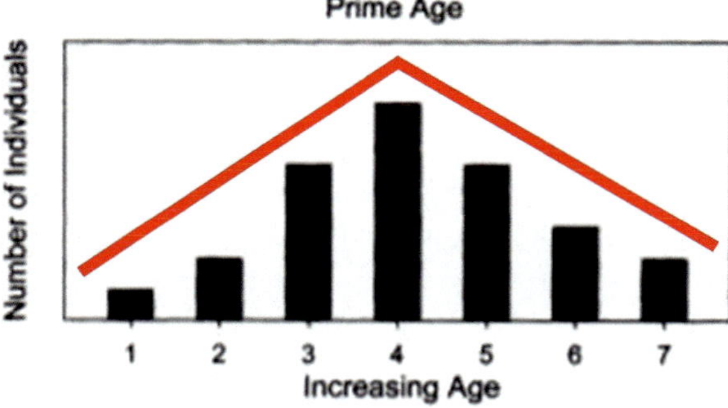

Figure 24. Mortality profiles
(modified from Byers and Hill
2009:303; Figure 3).

of long bone widths can inform us about the size of the animals (Driesch 1976), but again, due to the amount of material and the time constraints, measurements were not taken and instead an alternative, simpler method was used.

Seasonality was identified by a combination of: age intervals based on teeth eruption and epiphyseal fusion in the postcranial skeleton, the presence of antler still attached to male skulls (where possible), and observations of when deer are born in the present day. In North America, deer births occur most commonly between April and September, while in South America, births occur more often during July and November (Álvarez-Romero and Medellín 2005). In the Maya

region, modern figures report that it is common to observe fawns from January to July, with the highest peak between April and June (Jolón 2005:95). It has been observed that white-tailed deer loses the antlers during spring, and sometimes even by February. This period also coincides with the birth of newborns (Álvarez del Toro 1977). In this analysis, June was considered the mid-point for the identification of birth seasonality, which in return, allowed the identification of kill seasonality.

There are three mortality profiles based on the proportions in which each of the age groups appears: catastrophic, attritional and prime-dominated (see Byers and Hill 2009:303). The catastrophic profile results in successively old age classes containing progressively fewer individuals (Klein and Cruz-Uribe 1984:56; Lyman 1994:118). This is also known as a living structure or 'L-shaped', as it reflects a direct proportion of age groups in a living population (Byers and Hill 2009:303). The second, or attritional group, results when individuals in their prime age are underrepresented and extremely young and old animals are overrepresented relative to their abundance in a living population. Attritional profiles generate a 'U-shaped' distribution (Klein and Cruz-Uribe 1984:56; Lyman 1994:118). Disease, malnutrition, and nonhuman predators account for an attritional profile (Steele 2003:420).

Finally, a prime-dominated profile, as its name indicates it, has an elevated proportion of individuals of prime-age while juveniles and old individuals are underrepresented; its presence in an archaeological sample may reflect the targeting of the highest-return individuals in a population (Byers and Hill 2009:301) (Figure 24). Prime-age in ungulates includes those animals with a complete set of permanent teeth, and the entry of animals to their reproductive phase (Stiner 1990:311). The division between prime-age and old adult is based on the degree of teeth occlusal wear, particularly when more than half of the tooth crown is worn away (Stiner 1990:312). Among white-tailed deer, a more uniform wear on all permanent premolars and molars is seen around 6.5 years, with the dentine exposed being more than double the thickness of the enamel (Severinghaus 1949:221). Coincidentally, it is also at 6.5 years that fusion of all postcranial elements is complete (Lewall and Cowan 1963). In this study, prime age is considered to be between 12 months of age to 6.5 years of age, as almost all the epiphyses in the body have completed their fusion by this time, but the animals' weight increase is minimal.

For seasonality and mortality profiles, dental age was used as it is less prone to be affected by diet and environmental factors, as is the case with epiphyseal fusion (Davis 1987). Mortality is calculated as the number of dead individuals per age class (usually in MNI values) (Lyman 1994:118).

The methodology proposed to identify seasonality was taken from Byers and Hill (2009), where each dental piece was assigned an age cohort based on the age groups already defined for white-tailed deer by Severinghaus (1949). Because in most cases, the age identified will cover more than just one cohort, the sum of the probability of an individual falling into any of the groups was identified (Byers and Hill 2009:309). This summed probability was also used to generate mortality profiles.

Combined, the identification of seasonality and mortality profiles can help in discerning if a specific archaeological context was the result of human or nonhuman activities, such as predator behaviour (Steele 2003), and scavenging (Munson and Garniewicz 2003).

Taphonomic modifications

All modifications that were present on the remains in the archaeofaunal collection were recorded, as they provide us with useful information about faunal processing, and the formation process of the archaeological record (Lyman 1994). Because of the natural environmental conditions and the variability of the social practices of the Maya, it is well known that the recovery of faunal remains is skewed by differential preservation, chosen excavation locus, and archaeological recovery techniques (Chase *et al.* 2004:14). It is for this reason, that it is imperative to record carefully the taphonomic modifications that might be present, as well as to identify the taphonomic agent that may have produced them. The modifications that were registered include the type of fracture, faunal modifications, and human modifications.

Degree of fragmentation and type of fracture

A fracture is defined as a localised mechanical failure that results from applying an exterior dynamic force to a bone (Johnson 1985:160). The bone will respond to this force in a predictable way, following its natural anatomy, and the effects will be dependent upon the condition of the bone—whether it was fresh or dry at the time the force was exerted (Hill 1980:135; Lyman 1994:325). This in turn, is based on the microscopic organisation of the collagen fibres specific to each bone fragment (Blasco 1992:136; Johnson 1985:175). Data for the fractures on each specimen were recorded, including presence or absence, agent, condition of the bone when fractured (fresh or dry), type of fracture and location. The type of fracture present on each specimen was recorded, following the typologies by Lyman (1994) and Reitz and Wing (1999:158).

To assess the degree and intensity of fragmentation, several ratios can be calculated including NISP:MNI and NISP:MNE (Lyman 1994:337; Richardson 1980:111). The study of bone fragmentation is important when analysing osteological material possibly derived from human and animal consumption, as it allows an evaluation of the meat and bone marrow processing, tool production, and modes of food preparation employed by past societies (*sensus* Outram 2002) and also allows consideration of the possibility that other taphonomical processes may have contributed to the condition of the bone, such as trampling and secondary deposition by non-human agents.

NISP:MNI informs us only of which species had the highest degree of fragmentation, and how is this reflected on the number of individuals. This method allows for comparisons by location, and species, but does not inform us about which bone or skeletal element is the most fragmented. While the calculation of NISP:MNI is straightforward, NISP:MNE is calculated by using only bone fragments and not complete skeletal elements, as doing so would reduce the proportional difference between the two (Lyman 1994:337). Therefore, I also compared the number of fragmented bones against the presence of complete ones, as these are a common indicator of ritual activity (Twiss 2008). To offset the problem of bone fragmentation and its influence on NISP, bone weights, MNE and MNI were also included. The study of all of these in conjunction with one another, allows us to observe the emergence of patterning in ritual behaviour (Teeter 2001:69).

Faunal modifications

Modifications by animals primarily include carnivore chewing and rodent gnawing, and to a lesser degree, modifications by insects and herbivores (Johnson 1985). Studying such modifications can inform us as to the general condition of the bone, as different animals prefer bones depending on whether they are fresh or dry (Lyman 1994).

The most common agents are carnivores and rodents, the former producing a diversity of marks, such as punctures, scratches, and chewing (Binford 1981; Johnson 1985; Lyman 1994; Montero 2008). It is important to mention that carnivores attack primarily fresh bones, as they are targeting the bone marrow; therefore, carnivore marks are more common on the extremes of long bones or on bone protuberances (White 1992:132-133). On the other hand, rodents target primarily dry bones, as they gnaw bones to prevent the growth of their incisor teeth (Denys 2002:474). Rodent gnawing appears as small, parallel striations that are perpendicular to the long axis of the bone and usually cover large areas of the bone (Binford 1981:49;

Blasco 1992:120-12). Finally, insect modifications were registered when they were present. Insect modifications or 'tunnelling' resemble channelling on cortical bone (Lyman 1994).

Due to the exceptional state of preservation of the collection, it was possible to identify the presence of faunal modifications by simple visual inspection and the use of a magnifying glass. In some cases, the identification of bone modifications was done with the aid of a stereo microscope, aiming to identify the marks and determine the agent of modification.

Human modifications

Although there are many different anthropogenic modifications, two types were considered in this study, those that result from processing a carcass for human consumption and those that result from manufacturing bone and shell tools and ornaments. Modifications resulting from preparing a carcass for its consumption includes cut marks, hack marks and blows, and great attention was paid to registering the presence of cut marks, their frequency, orientation, location on individual bones, and per body segment. Human modification marks are the result of different processes including, but not limited to evisceration, butchering, dismembering, and bone marrow extraction. Different carcass manipulation and processing leads to different cut marks, and it should not be assumed that there will always be marks present, as in many instances, these modifications are not always visible or present on all processed animals (Blasco 1992:112). However, when they are present, they vary greatly according to the type of bone on which they appear, as well as the skill and the tools used by the butcher (Binford 1981:105; Blasco 1992:107). In this study, types of human modification, especially cut marks were classified following the works of Binford (1991), Blasco (1992), and Padró (2000). Special attention was paid to cut marks on articulation ends that may imply butchering and disarticulation processes, as butchering has been defined as the human reduction of a carcass into consumable parts (Lyman 1994:294). Cut marks were registered for all identified fragments, including those in the small/medium mammal and medium/large mammal categories. Interestingly, cut marks were also registered for human remains. In this study, cut marks were counted by presence/absence and location, although the numerous individual marks were not recorded for the analysis.

Technologically, Emery (2010) proposed a generalised model of bone-tool production that accentuates its highly repetitive nature and the standardisation of the process. Emery constructed a sequence of tool production based on a non-elite assemblage (the L4-3 deposit at Dos Pilas from the Terminal Classic period) that was dominated primarily by mammalian long bones. This reflected a stage of the tool reduction hierarchy, which is generally determined by the faunal species and element chosen, including femur, humerus, metacarpal, and tibia. 'Stage 1' is the primary and secondary *debitage* removal, including the removal of epiphyses and other irregularities. 'Stage 2' modifications include the core production and finishing. The resulting diaphysis from the previous stage can now be prepared for the initial cuts, including an 'unsmoothed' horizontal cut to divide the shaft into two segments. Subsequently, one or both segments may be further smoothed.

Modifications which occur during 'Stage 3' include the production of a vertical blank that begins with vertical scoring where the final cuts are going to be located, and a higher percentage of smoothed bones on the exterior and interior. Remains which have been modified to 'Stage 4' exhibit evidence of blank finishing which results in final-sized blanks that are smoothed on both sides; any irregularities that were still present were completely removed at this stage. Finally, 'Stage 5' involves artefact production including various forms such as bone tubes, disks, and ornaments, although the majority can be classified as basic blank forms and/or perforators (Figure 25). Emery (2010:219) also suggests that 'Stage 6' modifications are those from use-wear; however, she found minimal evidence of this at the L4-3 context of Dos Pilas. What Emery found was a dense deposit with almost half of the material representing *debitage* or discards from the manufacture of utilitarian implements, including needles, pins, awls, and other perforators (Emery 2009:459).

Emery (2009) also noticed that this context was different from others, in the taxa and skeletal elements selected for the creation of tools. In the L4-3 assemblage, there seems to be a distinct favouritism exhibited for artiodactyls, especially white-tailed deer, and from this species, metapodials, femurs and tibias are most commonly chosen as raw material, with minimal evidence of crania or axial elements. The abundance of long bones in this tool production context also suggests that the haunches 'were brought in by various hunters and were not the result of a single family's subsistence' (Emery 2009:465).

Typologically, Moholy-Nagy (1994) classified the worked bone and shell from Tikal into three cateogories: technomic, sociotechnic, and idiotechnic, based on their function and the natural environment (habitat) that faunal remains came from. The author identified materials as local and exotic, based on their origin, that is, if they were sourced from the immediate surroundings or were obtained from other ecological niches.

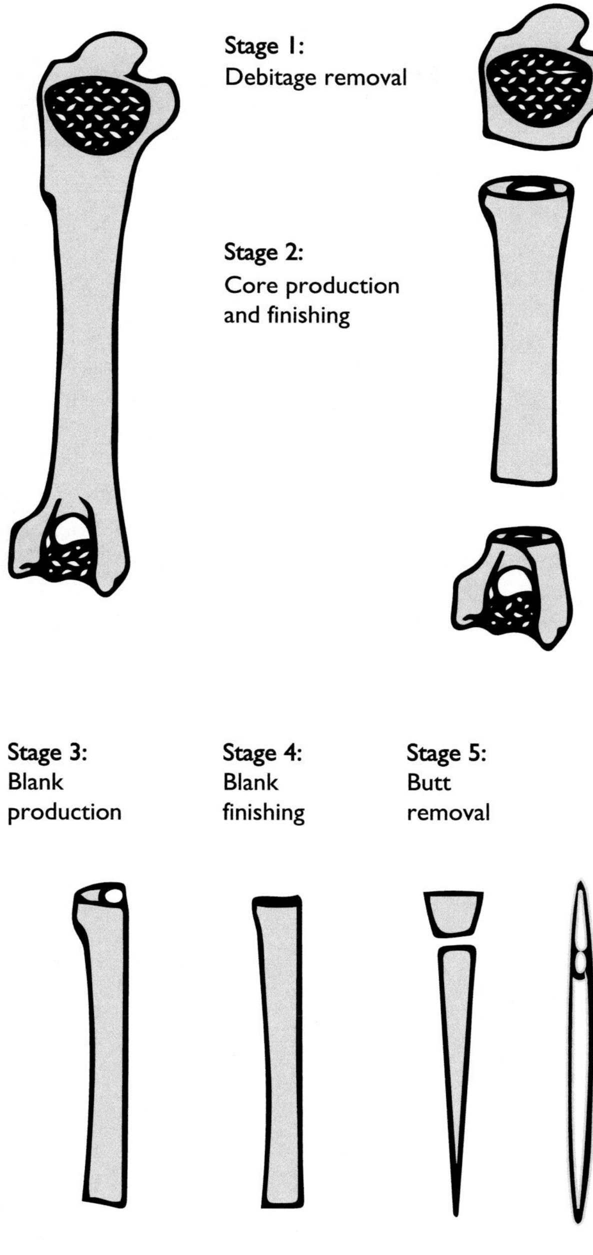

Figure 25. Sequence of bone perforator production (in the form of needle) in the L4-3 assemblage in Dos Pilas (modified from Emery 2009:464, Figure 6a).

According to Moholy-Nagy (1994:110-111), the distribution of specific tools and ornaments varied through time, and the author further classified the worked bone from the Classic period at Tikal into three main groups: domestic tools, higher status and lower status. These three classes have been present since the Preclassic and represent a long tradition; however, it is

the high status objects with an idiotechnic function (a function associated with ritual activities) that appear to have been exclusive to the Classic period, disappearing by the Terminal Classic. Examples of domestic tools include awls, bodkins, pins, needles, perforators, spatulas, *atlatl* (spear thrower), central perforated disks and deer antlers. Higher status objects are stingray spines, clasps for bead bracelets, sets of worked bone with incised hieroglyphs and drawings. Whole amphibians, reptiles, birds, and marine fish can be found in special deposits. Finally, in lower status deposits it is common to find beads, ear spools, dog canines and other kinds of animal teeth perforated for suspension, various types of perforated and unperforated long bone tubes, *pulidores*, glyph-inscribed bones, ladles, pendants, and inlays (Moholy-Nagy 1994). During the Late Classic it is clear that there is specialisation in the manufacture of bone tools and ornaments and that these objects are not associated with the common people (Teeter 2001:342). According to Emery (2003:510), the selection of faunal species by the craft specialists to produce tools or ornaments reflected their social hierarchy. At Petexbatún for example, it is possible to see that the middle/upper classes enjoyed a preferential access to certain species, such as the white-tailed deer, for tool making (Emery 2010). According to Moholy-Nagy (1994:108) it is probable that the elite controlled not only faunal resources, especially those considered exotic, for consumption as foodstuffs, but that they also controlled their use for the production of tools and probably maintained control over even the manufacturing processes by using specialists. Some of the objects are remarkably similar in size, suggesting standardisation.

Weathering stages

Behrensmeyer (1978:161) defines weathering of bone as a process in which inorganic and organic bone components are separated from each other and destroyed by physical and chemical agents. Behrensmeyer proposed six stages (Table 7), numbered zero to five, where five represents the highest degree displayed on the bone surface. This methodology can only be used with mammals over five kilograms (Behrensmeyer 1978:153). Originally, she proposed this classification in order to determine how long a bone was exposed on the surface, and then inferred the amount of time (in years) for that erosion to happen. However, it has been shown that the modifications observable on bones reflect the physical conditions in which the remains were preserved and not the timing (Johnson 1985:184; Lyman and Fox 1989:313).

The terms exfoliation and erosion were also used to define the physical modifications on the bone surface, as these two processes can be informative regarding

Weathering Stage	Description	Range in years since death
0	Greasy, no cracking or flaking, and perhaps with some soft tissue attached	0-1
1	Parallel cracking (longitudinal); articular surfaces perhaps with mosaic cracking	0-3
2	Flaking of outer surface (exfoliation), cracks are present and crack edge is angular	2-6
3	Rough homogeneous compact bone (fibrous texture); weathering penetrates 1-1.5 mm and crack edges are rounded	4-15
4	Coarse fibrous and rough surface; splinters of bone loose on surface; open cracks	6-15
5	Bone falling apart *in situ*; large splinters present; bone material very fragile	6-15

Table 7. Weathering stages according to Behrensmeyer (1978).

context formation. Exfoliation may be the result of the moist/dry cycle to which a bone is subject in a matrix (Polaco *et al.* 1988) and is equivalent to stages 1 and 2 of Behrensmeyer (1978). Furthermore, exfoliation is a process in which the bone is lost in a laminar way, following the longitudinal cracks (Johnson 1985). On the other hand, erosion is produced by trampling and/or wind action over a bone that forces it to be glazed, resulting in bone polish and smooth or rounded edges (Johnson 1985:189; Polaco *et al.* 1988:74).

In this study, an overall weathering stage was scored for each specimen, following Behrensmeyer's (1978:151-152) guidelines; that is, recording the most advanced degree of weathering present on a bone which covers at least one square centimetre of the bone.

Presenting the results and interpretation

The results obtained from the zooarchaeological analysis are presented in Chapters seven and eight. The whole collection of faunal remains from all *Operaciones* is treated as a single assemblage and the results are presented in Chapter seven, following the methodology discussed in this section. Chapter eight will focus on the analysis of *Operación* 114, as this context presented an overwhelming number of specimens used for dietary purposes. Specific analysis based on a series of tests was also conducted in this chapter in order to test regional and intra-site comparisons. The same variables defined in the methodology section were used in Chapter eight, but were combined including:

1. testing for a spatial patterning
2. testing for processing patterns
3. testing for rituality

Finally, the general analysis of the faunal remains and that of *Operación* 114 are integrated and discussed in Chapter ten.

Chapter six

Theoretical background to isotope analysis

There are a wide variety of methods that can be applied to study past diets—including direct analysis of plants, animals, tools, and coprolites. However, these methods do not necessarily reflect the proportions in which food items were consumed (Larsen 1997:270). The reconstruction of palaeodiets has benefited enormously from the development and employment of chemical techniques, which analyses osteological materials directly (White 1999:XII), and allow us to gain direct information from ingestion, rather than collecting evidence of potential consumption (Schoeninger 1989; White 1999:XII). Bone chemistry, especially stable isotopes and trace elemental analysis focusing on alkaline earth elements, such as strontium (Sr), calcium (Ca), and barium (Ba), can characterise past human diet (Larsen 1997:270). Through the analysis of bone chemistry, diet can be directly established, where indirect flora and fauna remains analysis can provide only a framework for potential consumption (White et al. 2006a:144).

While trace element analysis was the first chemical technique to be applied in the study of palaeodiets in Mesoamerica (Wright 1999a:197), recent studies have opted to use stable isotope analysis (mainly $\delta^{13}C$ and $\delta^{15}N$) to investigate ancient subsistence in this vast area (Coyston et al. 1999; Gerry 1997; Gerry and Krueger 1997; Metcalfe et al. 2009; Reed 1994, 1999; Scherer et al. 2007; White 1997; White and Schwarcz 1989; White et al. 2001a, 2001b, 2006a; Whittington and Reed 1997; Williams et al. 2009; Wright 2006; Wright and White 1996).

Use of isotope analysis and its justification

The application of stable isotope analysis has increased considerably in recent times, and in combination with other studies, it can help us gain a better picture of a past society, including the study of human and faunal palaeodiets, animal domestication, reconstruction of palaeoenvironments, migration, and differential access to resources by the members of a group. Of these topics, two are of interest to this analysis: differential access to resources by the inhabitants of a settlement, and animal domestication for ritual purposes.

Because it is difficult to differentiate the status of individual members of Maya society when using more traditional archaeological methods, such as location of the burials, or quantity of grave goods (Chase and Chase 1992), researchers have resorted to isotope analysis as a means of identifying higher quality diets—e.g. consumption of meat—and therefore, possible differences in social status between burials (Coyston et al. 1999; Gerry 1997; Mansell et al. 2006; Powis et al. 1999; Reed 1999; White et al. 1993; Wright 2006).

Also, domestication of wild animals for ritual purposes has been an important topic when discussing the Classic Maya, and the institutionalisation and maintenance of social hierarchies (Bíró and Montero 2008; deFrance 2009), as members of the Maya elite would have differentiated themselves through their patterns of consumption (Pohl 1985a:133). According to some authors, the management of wild animals would have included the raising of deer near the household (Pohl 1995:466), and/or the manipulation of the deer's diet, including feeding them symbolic foodstuffs such as maize (Masson 1999; White and Schwarcz 1989:460-461), which would leave a chemical signature that can be studied through isotope analysis (Emery and Thornton 2008b; Emery et al. 2000; White et al. 2001a, 2001b).

The primary aim of using isotope analysis in this study is to reconstruct the palaeodiet of the faunal remains from the midden with the purpose of exploring the consumption of these resources by the inhabitants of Chinikihá during the Late Classic period. In order to do so, I will examine the food web that was available for human and animal exploitation, through the study of modern and archaeological faunal and floral samples. I will also centre on the faunal archaeological samples to reconstruct the diet and ecology, and discuss the possibility of faunal management or domestication. Finally, because 'we are what we eat' (Tykot 2006:131; Schoeninger 1989:38), the isotope analysis is extended to a human burial sample located in the North Structure, in order to compare and contrast the results from the fauna and human samples from Chinikihá, since 'any valid interpretation based on palaeodiet reconstruction should combine the analysis of human and faunal samples from the same site' (Grupe et al. 2003). Ultimately, the information generated by the human sample will provide evidence regarding the access that members of the elite had to fauna resources, e.g. whether they ate more meat, as is believed to have happened during feasting events.

In this chapter, stable isotopes are explained to provide a background, followed by a brief description of the use of $\delta^{13}C$, and $\delta^{15}N$ isotope analysis in the Maya area. The methodology and sampling techniques used in the present study covered two samples, a human burial sample from the North Structure, identified as members of the elite, and a faunal sample from behind the Palace. The results of these analyses are presented in Chapter eight, where I will discuss the possibility that the high class of Chinikihá enjoyed differential access to faunal and plant resources, drawing also from examples from other sites in the Maya area. Also, the possible inclusion of domesticated fauna will be touched upon. Finally, the isotopic data is be integrated with the results of the zooarchaeological analysis in Chapter ten.

A theoretical background

Isotopes in the environment

An isotope is defined as one of two or more forms that can be present in an element, for example, carbon. These forms have the same number of protons in an atom's nucleus (known as the atomic number), but with different number of neutrons, resulting in different atomic weights (Tykot 2006:131). Radioactive isotopes, such as ^{14}C degrade through time, while stable isotopes (^{13}C and ^{12}C) are not affected. Carbon is omnipresent and forms part of almost all the materials that surround us, including air, oceans, and soil, therefore, living organisms absorb carbon in multiple ways and assimilate it in their own tissues (Katzenberg 2008).

Stable isotopes in bone tissues

Bone is formed primarily by two elements, one organic (collagen), and one mineral (hydroxyapatite or bone apatite), and in both it is possible to find nutritional information (Larsen 1997:290). Collagen contains approximately 35% carbon and 11-16% nitrogen, making it the tissue of choice for carbon and nitrogen isotope analysis (Katzenberg 2008:416). The presence of hydroxyapatite helps the collagen to survive degradation, although it does still degrade over time, depending on post-deposition taphonomic conditions, particularly temperature variations (Roberts *et al.* 2002; Wright and Schwarcz 1996). In contrast to collagen, the carbonate and phosphate fraction, present in the inorganic part of the bone and teeth, have proved to be more resistant to degradation (Wright and Schwarcz 1996). Recent controlled studies have shown that collagen reflects the protein intake, while bone apatite and tooth enamel provide a picture of the total diet (Ambrose and Norr 1993; Krueger and Sullivan 1984; Tieszen and Fagre 1993a, but see Chisholm *et al.* 1982; Schwarcz 2000). Ultimately, the information obtained from both, collagen and apatite, will provide different but complementary dietary information for reconstructing palaeodiet (Tykot *et al.* 2009:168; Wright 2006:80).

Plant ingestion, canopy effect, and tissue fractionation

Wild and domesticated plants photosynthesise atmospheric carbon dioxide (CO_2) that is then metabolised into compounds that we classify as carbohydrates, proteins, and lipids, which are then consumed by an animal, and converted into their body tissues (Tykot 2006:132). Plant consumption provides the pathways for C and N isotopes into the bone (Hedges *et al.* 2006). Therefore, a result from $\delta^{13}C$ isotope analysis will reflect the chosen photosynthesis path. The value of δ shows there are differences on how photosynthesis is carried on among C3 (Calvin-Benson), C4 (Hatch-Slack), and CAM (Crassulacean Acid Metabolism) plants (Larsen 1997:271). C3 plants, usually located in more temperate areas, include a variety of grasses, trees, shrubs, and tubers, with values ranging between -26‰ to -38‰, averaging -22‰ (Tieszen 1991). On the other hand, because C4 plants discriminate less against heavier $\delta^{13}C$ isotope from CO^2, their values are less negative than C3 plants (Larsen 1997:271), ranging from -9‰ to -21‰, with an average of -12.5%. C4 plants are adapted to hot and dry climates and include grasses, such as maize, amaranths, and chenopods (Tieszen 1991). As such, C3 plants are about 14‰ more negative than C4 plants (Larsen 1997). However, in dense forests, the reassimilation of respired CO^2 may have an important effect on plants near the forest floor, that may present values as low as -35‰; this is known as 'canopy effect' (van der Merwe and Medina 1991).

Because of different physiological processes, such as metabolism, what is eaten is not reflected one-to-one in the consumer's remains, but rather, as Henry Schwarcz (2006:316) expresses it, 'you are what you eat, plus an isotopic offset (fractionation)'. Some dietary constituents may be preferentially 'routed' to particular organs or tissues (Schwarcz 1991), resulting in a heterogeneous internal distribution of the stable isotopic signal acquired from the food intake. Thus, the constant relationship between diet and tissue (Δ_{dt}) for every tissue needs to be calculated (DeNiro and Epstein 1978, 1981; Tieszen *et al.* 1983), and failing to acknowledge this fractionation may lead to under- or overestimation of dietary sources (Tieszen *et al.* 1983). However, because in most cases bone is the only organic material to survive in the archaeological record, we need to understand how bone fractionalization works. The 'linear mixing model'—where all carbon atoms from dietary proteins, lipids, and carbohydrates are considered to incorporate into an animal's tissue in the same way—was applied mainly to apatite carbon (Tykot *et al.* 2009:160). More recently, however, it was observed that dietary protein is selectively incorporated and is better reflected in the consumer's collagen, while apatite will reflect the dietary lipids, carbohydrates, and protein (Ambrose and Norr 1993; Tieszen and Fagre

1993). This is known as the 'macronutrient routing model' (Tykot *et al.* 2009). Therefore, apatite values can be taken as the average of carbon content in the diet (the whole diet), while collagen will overemphasise the protein component (Ambrose and Norr 1993).

The values for $^{13}/^{12}C$ of bone collagen ($\delta^{13}C_{col}$) can vary between 1‰ and 6‰, depending on the consumer's size (DeNiro 1987; Krueger and Sullivan 1984; Schwarcz *et al.* 1985); however, it has been accepted that the $\delta^{13}C_{col}$ of a consumer is an average of 5‰ higher than those of the diet (Ambrose 1993; van der Merwe and Vogel 1978). Nonetheless, the 5‰ enrichment works well only with agriculturalist societies or mono-isotopic diets (Gerry and Krueger 1997; Tykot *et al.* 2009), where protein sources are limited. In contrast, wild animals (carnivores and herbivores) and non-agriculturalist societies will obtain protein from different sources, and/or experience secondary fractionation, thus producing a higher variability in $\delta^{13}C_{col}$ (Lee-Thorp *et al.* 1989; White *et al.* 2001a:374-375). This does not seem to affect the diet-apatite relationship; therefore, reconstruction of the whole diet is more robust when done from apatite ($\delta^{13}C_{ap}$) (Ambrose and Norr 1993). Again, there is some fractionation from diet to bone apatite (Tykot *et al.* 2009).

Finally, the ontogeny and turnover rates of collagen and apatite in bone and teeth should be considered, since bone collagen will reflect long-term diet in adults, however a diet high in protein may stimulate a higher rates of bone turnover. Bone apatite is laid down faster than bone collagen, but is still representative of the diet, while tooth enamel apatite is laid down rapidly and not replaced (Tykot *et al.* 1996:356). Therefore, the analysis of dental apatite from tooth enamel will provide information on the diet composition in the early life, because tooth enamel apatite is formed during early development of childhood (Mansell *et al.* 2006). Analysis of tooth enamel apatite from molar 1M will reflect the diet since birth up to 3 years of age (Wright 1999b:437), while that from molar 2M will reflect the diet during childhood (3-7 years), up to 12-16 years of age, when its formation is completed (ElNesr and Avery 1994). Finally, the analysis of tooth enamel apatite from molar 3M will reflect the adult diet (Coyston *et al.* 1999:226).

Isotope measurements

Isotopic indices are measured with a mass spectrometry and are compared against a universal standard that possesses a known value. In the case of carbon, it is relative to the VPDB standard (Vienna PeeDee formation, a marine fossil limestone from South Carolina from a geological formation known as *Belemnitella Americana*), for nitrogen, it is AIR (Ambient Inhalable Reservoir) (Coplen 1994; Craig 1957; Gerry

1997:42, footnote p. 1; Larsen 1997:271). The relative abundance of isotopes is so small that it is expressed in parts per thousand, commonly denominated 'permil' (‰); the index is expressed as $\delta^{13}C$ and $\delta^{15}N$, where the value of δ is calculated with the following formula:

$$\delta\,(‰) = \{[R(sample) - R\,(standard)] / R(standard)\} \times 1000$$

where R = $^{13}C/^{12}C$, or $^{15}N / ^{14}N$ (Craig 1953). VPDB has an established value for δ as 0‰, which works as a reference point for all the samples of unknown value (Gerry 1997). Because the $^{13}C/^{12}C$ ratio is usually lower than that of the reference VPDB standard, the $\delta^{13}C$ values are usually negative (Tykot 2006:132). In general, the average $\delta^{13}C$ for C3 plants is -26‰, while for C4 plants the average $\delta^{13}C$ is -13.0‰ (Deines 1980).

A) *Identifying maize consumption through carbon isotope analysis*

There is not a single isotope index that can isolate any particular diet component, but the values of $\delta^{13}C_{col}$, $\delta^{13}C_{ap}$, and $\delta^{15}N$ are tightly interrelated. For terrestrial herbivores, 'isotopically similar plant proteins and carbohydrates supply carbon to both collagen and apatite respectively, whereas for omnivores and carnivores, lipids from animal foods are also contributors to apatite' (Tykot *et al.* 1996:356). In theory, animals fed on corn, wild or domesticated, when consumed by omnivorous animals—including humans—produce higher isotope values, both in collagen and apatite, though especially in the latter (Tykot 2006: 138).

In terms of identifying corn consumption, it has been proved that $\delta^{13}C_{col}$ reflects this value better (Coyston *et al.* 1999:225). A pure C3 feeder will have a $\delta^{13}C_{col}$ value of -21.5‰, and a strict C4 diet will be $\delta^{13}C_{col}$ ratio of -7.5‰ (Gerry and Krueger 1997:197). Because it is a bimodal distribution, a mix diet of C3 and C4 plants will produce intermediate values between these two extremes (Gerry and Krueger 1997:197).

Although $\delta^{13}C$ values do indicate corn consumption, they do not indicate how much corn was consumed. Several authors have tried to calculate the percentage of corn intake by proposing different formulas (e.g. Gerry and Krueger 1997; Seinfeld *et al.* 2009), both for bone collagen and enamel apatite. For bone collagen, the percentage of C4 plants in a diet has been calculated previously using the following formula:

$$PC4 = (\delta_c - \delta_3 + \Delta_{dc}) / (\delta_4 - \delta_3) \times 100$$

where δ_c = the measured value of the collagen sample, Δ_{dc} = the fractionation factor -5, δ_3 = -26.5‰ (the average value of C3 plants), and δ_4 = -9.5‰ (the average of archaeological maize) (White *et al.* 1993:353; White and Schwarcz 1989:456; Schwarcz *et al.* 1985). Identifying corn consumption levels by this means has a precision of ±8‰ (Schwarcz *et al.* 1985:189).

In order to distinguish if the $\delta^{13}C$ value reflects direct corn consumption or if it is a result of the consumption of herbivore fauna fed with corn, it is necessary to obtain four values: the $\delta^{13}C$ from collagen, the $\delta^{13}C$ from apatite (or structural carbonate), the $\delta^{15}N$ value, and the relationship between the collagen and the apatite, commonly expressed as $\Delta^{13}C_{ap-col}$ or 'spacing' between collagen and apatite in $\delta^{13}C$. The 'spacing' is also a measure used to determine the relative importance of meat in the diet (Krueger and Sullivan 1984; Lee-Thorp *et al.* 1989), and the relationship between carnivore and herbivore diets. The agreed values for this spacing are larger among herbivores than among carnivores, averaging $\Delta^{13}C_{ap-col}$ = 7‰ for herbivores, 5‰ for omnivores, and 3-4‰ for carnivores (Krueger and Sullivan 1984; Lee-Thorp *et al.* 1989). In this analysis, I will combine the results from these four values in order to detect possible differences in the consumption of maize by the animals and humans from the sample from Chinikihá.

B) Identifying animal protein consumption through nitrogen isotope analysis

Traditionally, the spacing between apatite and collagen ($\Delta^{13}C_{ap-col}$) has been calculated using bone collagen and bone apatite to source protein (Krueger and Sullivan 1984; Lee-Thorp *et al.* 1989). The combined used of collagen and apatite data will ensure that protein intake in diet is not over-estimated (Tykot *et al.* 1996:356). The $\delta^{13}C$ values from collagen are determined by the protein from plant resources and reflect the protein component of the diet. On the other hand, $\delta^{13}C$ from the apatite will reflect the total diet (Ambrose and Norr 1993; Tieszen and Fagre 1993a; White *et al.* 2006a:144). However, recent analyses have proved that measurements derived from enamel and dentine, undergo little to no change (Wright and Schwarcz 1999).

Another way of identifying the source of protein is through the analysis of $\delta^{15}N$ and the trophic level of the food source. Nitrogen is fixated in plants when they absorb nitrates and ammonium from the soil, which are then transformed into nitrogen by bacteria. Legumes typically have the lowest value, at 0‰, while plants from hot and arid climates will exhibit higher $\delta^{15}N$ values than plants from forested or temperate areas. Unlike carbon, fractionation of nitrogen isotopes seems to be consistent with increases of 3-4‰, as reflected in the bone collagen (DeNiro and Epstein 1981). Herbivores are in the lowest range (4-8‰), followed by omnivorous animals (9-12‰), with carnivorous animals at the top

(>13‰) (DeNiro and Epstein 1981; Schwarcz 2006:316; Schwarcz and Schoeninger 1991). The analysis of $\delta^{15}N$ isotopes may also assist in differentiating between marine and terrestrial foods, since nitrogen isotopes are usually 4‰ higher in marine plants. In general, the $\delta^{15}N$ values of marine plant consumers are heavier due to a larger fractionation through more trophic levels (Schwarcz and Schoeninger 1991). For most regions, marine vertebrates will exhibit $\delta^{15}N$ values 10‰ higher than those of terrestrial plants and animals (Schoeninger and DeNiro 1984).

Although the remains of fish and molluscs remains are retrieved infrequently from archaeological sites, it must be assumed that the Maya had access to these resources, and it is therefore important to distinguish their consumption where present. However, their values can mimic the results from a high intake of corn, that is, high $\delta^{13}C$ values, making it vital to discern between a high intake of corn or a high intake of seafood through the use of $\delta^{15}N$. Consuming fish would produce a high $\delta^{13}C$ value with a high $\delta^{15}N$ (DeNiro and Walker 1986), because marine creatures follow a different pattern of photosynthesis, with more trophic levels, and therefore marine resources range from 12‰ to 20‰ (Gerry and Krueger 1997:199). In the Maya area, some terrestrial herbivore values have $\delta^{15}N$ that overlap those from reef fish, with values just under 10‰ (White *et al.* 2001a:375). Finally, C3 non-legume plants average 9‰, while legumes are around 1‰ (Whittington and Reed 1997:159).

In general, reef fish will have lower values than those of freshwater fish, which in turn will be slightly higher in $\delta^{15}N$ (Keegan and DeNiro 1988; Katzenberg 2008:426). However, distinguishing between marine and freshwater food sources by $\delta^{15}N$ may be impossible (Schoeninger *et al.* 1983:1382). Furthermore, trophic levels can be affected by many other factors including climate, physiology, and pathological conditions (Heaton *et al.* 1986; Katzenberg and Lovell 1999). Therefore, $\delta^{15}N$ can help us to identify the direct consumption of maize and/or corn-fed animals, as well as of marine/freshwater resources (Chisholm *et al.* 1982; Keegan and DeNiro 1988). As these various results indicate, it is necessary to re-create a realistic food web for each site, which is one of the objectives of this dissertation.

High values of $\delta^{15}N$ can also be helpful when studying childhood diet and infant feeding practices among populations in the archaeological record (Katzenberg *et al.* 1996; White *et al.* 2001a). Because children consuming breast milk possess a $\delta^{15}N$ value enriched up to 2-4‰ relative to their mothers (Fogel *et al.* 1989), it is possible to explore the breastfeeding/weaning process. Therefore, isotope $\delta^{15}N$ analysis can provide a stronger tool to explore both childhood and adulthood diets. This is particularly relevant when studying the possibility of an intra-site differential access to plant and faunal resources. In order to do so, I will combine the information from collagen and apatite, as reflected by on $\delta^{13}C$ and $\delta^{15}N$ isotope ratios.

Brief description of isotope analysis in the Maya area

In the Maya area, the application of isotope analysis to understanding agricultural dispersal began in the 1980s and the beginning of the 1990s, where the most important plant domesticate was maize (*Zea mays*). Not surprisingly, the origin and spread of maize domestication in the Americas has been covered by a large number of studies (see Staller *et al.* 2006 for an extensive study), including some of the earliest works on isotope analysis around the world (DeNiro and Epstein 1981). The earliest $\delta^{13}C$ and $\delta^{15}N$ isotopes were used not only to undertake the study of maize consumption, but also to explore variations in human and animal diets through time, including intra-site analyses (Gerry 1993; Reed 1994; Tykot *et al.* 1996; White and Schwarcz 1989), dietary differences based on differences among social classes, age, and sex (Coyston 1995; Coyston *et al.* 1999; Gerry 1997; Reed 1994), and above all, the exploration of the so-called 'Maya Collapse' during the Late Classic, from an ecological point of view (Emery 1997, 1999; Wright 1994; Wright and White 1996). Landscape modification from the development of cornfields and their impact on human and animal diet was also of central interest during this early period (Emery 1999). In short, $\delta^{13}C$ isotope analysis can be used to document access to maize, resulting in a great variability among different ecological settings and chronological periods (Gerry and Krueger 1997; Tykot 2002; White 1999; Wright 2004).

Because of the relative importance of maize as a staple in diet, and as a symbol in the Maya ideology, some researchers have explored the diet of animals to see if they were purposely fed maize (Emery and Thornton 2008b; Emery *et al.* 2000; White *et al.* 2001a, 2001b). Moreover, isotope analysis of faunal remains, particularly $\delta^{15}N$, can illustrate differences between aquatic and terrestrial protein (Katzenberg 2008; Wright 1993:173). In some instances, isotopic analyses are complemented with trace elements analysis (Reed 1994; Wright 1994), and elaborate zooarchaeological studies (e.g. Emery 2010), allowing a more complete reconstruction of the Maya palaeodiet.

However, two major problems have been identified throughout the history of Maya isotopic analyses. Firstly, these studies rarely considered the diagenetic processes that may have affected the isotopic exchanges. Importantly, however Wright and Schwarcz (1996) demonstrated that these processes must be taken into account when interpreting palaeodiet reconstruction

based on apatite. Secondly, and as a consequence of the general development of isotope methodology (Ambrose and Norr 1993; Tieszen and Fagre 1993a), differences between the values from bone collagen and bone apatite are not well-understood and several authors have pointed out that this also needs to be taken into account when interpreting the results from $\delta^{13}C$ and $\delta^{15}N$ isotope studies (Coyston *et al.* 1999; Tykot *et al.* 1996, 2009).

In the new millennium, new topics and methodologies have been applied to complement isotope analyses, including the reconstruction of past environments, disease and diet, and differences among different social classes, including age and sex-based groups. Among those works with a broader focus on palaeo-environmental reconstruction through the study of faunal diet are those of Kitty Emery, and Christine White (Emery and Thornton 2008b; Emery *et al.* 2000; White *et al.* 2001a). Identifying the relationship between diet and pathology is an effective way of exploring human diet, and differences in gender-based access to ritual goods, including meat, is a topic that is also recurrent in the literature (e.g. White 1997, 2005; Wright and White 1996). The integration of socio-political data with the information obtained from isotope analysis is also incorporated to gain a better understanding of the Classic period and regional comparisons (Scherer *et al.* 2007). More recently, a social dimension has been added to the interpretations from isotope analysis, helping us to understand ideology, gender, economic, and political relationships through the reconstruction of palaeodiets (White *et al.* 2006a:143).

The range of sites studied using isotope analyses in the Maya area is vast and includes archaeological sites from the Preclassic such as Colhá (White *et al.* 2001b), and Kaminaljuyú (Wright and Schwarcz 1999). However, most isotope analysis studies are focused on the Classic period and include numerous Lowland sites such as Piedras Negras (Sherer *et al.* 2007), Xunantunich (Freiwald 2010), Chau Hiix (Metcalfe *et al.* 2009), the Petexbatún region (Emery 1999), and the Pasión River region (Wright 1994, 1997, 1999a, 2006) which together include the sites of Altar de Sacrificios, Seibal, Aguateca, Tamarindito, Itzán, Dos Pilas, Arroyo de Piedra, Punta de Chimino, Quim Chil Hilan, and La Paciencia.

Also, the variability between environmental settings is well represented with sites from riverine zones, such as Lamanai (Coyston *et al.* 1999), and other inland sites, such as Pacbitún (Coyston *et al.* 1999). From the northern Lowlands in the Yucatán Peninsula, only Yaxuná and Chunchucmil have been studied (Mansell *et al.* 2006). For the Postclassic, there is less information available, with inland Mayapán (Wright 2009), and coastal Marco González and San Pedro (Williams *et al.* 2009) being the only sites with recorded isotopic values (Figure 26).

Figure 26. Sites mentioned throughout this work (modified from Emery 2004e: 2).

With reference to this theoretical background, I will interpret the results from the $\delta^{13}C$, and $\delta^{15}N$ isotope analyses from long bone collagen and dental enamel samples obtained from human burials recovered from the North Structure, and several faunal remains from the deposit behind the Palace (*Operación* 114). The methodology for sample preparation is presented below, as well as the sampling methods.

Isotope methodology and techniques

Although there is some variation among researchers in the way bone samples should be prepared to extract the collagen (see Emery *et al.* 2000:541; Emery and Thornton 2008b; Wright 1993:173), the main purpose is to get the sample as free of contaminants as possible. The analytical techniques applied to both human and faunal samples from Chinikihá, are those implemented by Morales (2009) and used routinely at the Laboratorio de Isótopos Estables from Instituto de Geología (IG-UNAM).

Extracting collagen

The techniques for the extraction of collagen from long bones used for $\delta^{13}C$ and $\delta^{15}N$ isotope analysis are explained below. A very similar process was applied to dentine samples, but reagents were usually halved in quantities.

All macro-contaminants (roots, leaves, and debris) are removed, and the samples are then ultrasonically cleaned in distilled water for 15 minutes. Samples are then brushed clean, and rinsed in distilled water, before drying them in a furnace at 60°C for 18 hours. From dry bone, an aliquot between two and four grams is weighed, and ground in an agate mortar and sieved through mesh (150 microns). In the case of teeth, dentine is separated with a dentist's drill from the enamel, leaving the enamel undamaged. The resulting powder is then ground in an agate mortar and sieved through mesh (150 microns).

Then, 20mL of HCl 0.5M (pH<1.0) is added to the aliquot for 30 minutes, agitating the container every five minutes, and decanting the liquid. The process is repeated if required. To remove the humic acids, 10mL of NaOH 0.1M is added for 60 minutes, agitating the container every 15 minutes. At the end of this time, the sample is centrifuged for 10 minutes, and the resulting liquid is then decanted (neutralising the base before discarding). This is then rinsed in approximately 20mL of milli-Q water, repeating three times.

To dissolve the collagen from dentine, 24mL of milli-Q water (adjusting pH to 3 with HCl 0.01M) are added to the solution, which is then put in a closed tube and heated in a furnace to 80°C for 20 hours. The resulting solution is then filtered through a 0.45 microns sieve, and freeze-dried in normal conditions (-52°C, 0.030 mbar) for 12 hours. Finally, 2mg of purified collagen (duplicates) are potted in a 5 x 9mm tin capsule.

The samples were then analysed in a *Thermo Finnigan Delta Plus XL*, with a Dumas elemental analyser attached to the mass spectrometer. This had a precision of 0.2‰ to determine $\delta^{13}C_{VPDB}$ and $\delta^{15}N_{AIR}$ in collagen from dentine and long bone, the techniques from Brock *et al.* (2007) and Hülls *et al.* (2007) were used. $\delta^{13}C_{VPDB}$ and $\delta^{15}N_{AIR}$ values were normalised according to Coplen (1988, Coplen *et al.* 2006), and the $\delta^{13}C_{VPDB}$ analysis for collagen was carried using the reference laboratory materials NBS 22, IAEA CH6, and IAEA CH7, while $\delta^{15}N_{AIR}$ for collagen, results were normalised using IAEAN1, USGS 25, and USGS 26 reference materials.

Extracting apatite

The technique for the extraction of calcium carbonate ($CaCO_3$) from teeth enamel for $\delta^{13}C$ isotope analysis is explained below. The enamel is ground in an agate mortar and then sieved through mesh (150 micron).

To remove all organic material, approximately 5.0mL of H_2O_2 at 30% is added to a minimum of 500mg of enamel for two hours, agitating the receptacle every 15 minutes. Then the sample is centrifuged for 10 minutes, and the resulting liquid is decanted, and rinsed with distilled water. This is repeated three times. To absorb exogenous carbonates, the enamel samples are then treated with a 10mL buffer solution (acetic acid-calcium acetate 1.0M, pH = 4.75), for nine hours. At the end, the solution is centrifuged for 10 minutes, and the resulting liquid is decanted and rinsed with distilled water. This process is again repeated three times.

Finally, enough pure ethanol is added to cover the enamel, this is then heated at 90°C until total evaporation of the solvent has occurred (approximately 12 hours). The result is a final sample of 9.5mg purified enamel. To determine $\delta^{13}C$ from enamel $CaCO_3$, the techniques proposed by McCrea (1950), and Revez *et al.* (2001) were applied. Samples were analysed in a *Gas Bench* attached to a mass spectrometer *Thermo Finnigan MAT 253*. Apatite isotope analyses used LSVEC, NBS-19, and NBS-18 reference materials.

With this methodology, collagen samples from long bone and dentine, and apatite from teeth enamel were obtained and processed. Unfortunately, the extraction of apatite from long bones is achieved by another procedure and as such, apatite from the long bones was not obtained at this stage.

Bone preservation and diagenesis

One fundamental aspect in the application of isotope analysis is the preservation assessment of the samples (collagen and apatite), which will ensure intra-sample comparability. Diagenetic loss of collagen is a common problem and must therefore be discounted as a possible alteration (Ambrose 1990). Various methods exist for assessing the integrity of the collagen recovered from the samples, including the collagen yield per sample, the proportion of carbon and nitrogen (%C and %N), and the atomic ratio of carbon to nitrogen in collagen (C/N), among others. For apatite, the Crystallinity Index (CI) is best suited (Shemesh 1990).

For the $\delta^{13}C$ and $\delta^{15}N$ isotope analyses, either bone collagen or apatite can be used, however due to the incidence of bone diagenesis in the Mayan area, apatite is less likely to produce a consistent result (Wright and Schwarcz 1996). In the present analysis, I will use the isotope values from bone and enamel apatite to address questions about intra-site variation in corn consumption, as suggested by Tykot (2006:138).

Collagen yield

According to Ambrose (1990), percentages are acceptable if they are >3.0% for C, and if N>1.0%. Samples that do not produce enough collagen (less than 1.0%) are also considered unreliable for isotopic analysis (van Klinken 1999). The results for collagen yield of the present analysis were not provided by.

Proportion of carbon and nitrogen (%C and %N)

The proportion of carbon and nitrogen concentrations in bone collagen has also been used to detect diagenesis. According to Ambrose (1990:438), modern bovine tendon values are %C = 47.6, and %N = 16.0, therefore, well-preserved collagen is between 26 and 44 %C, and 11 and 16 %N (van Klinken 1999).

Atomic ratio of carbon to nitrogen in collagen (C/N)

The most common quality markers to identify alterations of the isotopic signal are the collagen yield or concentration and the carbon to nitrogen ratio (C/N), where poor preservation and diagenetic alteration was found to be extremely low concentrations of carbon and nitrogen in collagen (Ambrose 1990:436). DeNiro (1985) suggested that the acceptable range of C/N ratios for archaeological samples is between 2.9 and 3.6. This is because the ratio of collagen in modern bone or intact bone collagen is 3.2 (Katzenberg 2008:418; Wright and White 1996). More recently, in the Maya area, some authors have suggested ranges of 3.0-3.5 (Wright 1993:173), and 2.8-3.8 (Emery *et al.* 2000; Emery and Thornton 2008b). Moreover, Schoeninger and colleagues (1989) indicate that preparation procedures and a low concentration of collagen yield can also produce anomalous C:N ratios, so in order to allow for this, these authors accept values between 2.6-3.4. For the purpose of this analysis, it was considered that values in the 2.8-3.8 range were suitable for isotope analysis.

Crystallinity index (CI)

This value is a measure of post-mortem apatite recrystalinisation (Metcalfe *et al.* 2009:21). According to Shemesh (1990), only those samples with a low crystallinity value of CI<3.8 represent pristine apatite; however, Wright and Schwarcz (1996) suggest that there is diagenesis if bone and enamel apatite CI values fall within the proposed range of 2.8-4.0 and samples that have been affected by mineral diagenesis should not be used for comparisons (Wright and Schwarcz 1996). Before any chemical pre-treatment, three enamel samples (CM04, CM08, and CM09) were submitted to Dr José Reyes Gasca from Instituto de Física (IF-UNAM) for infrared spectrometry.

Sampling

Three groups of samples were obtained for the isotopic analysis. First, modern plants, animals and water sources were collected in order to create a baseline in which to insert the archaeological data. Second, animal teeth and bone were obtained from specimens from *Operación* 114, and third, human teeth and bone were sampled from the burial area situated in the North Complex. The procedure in which each of these three were processed is explained below.

Creating a diet baseline for Chinikihá

Ancient Maya 'menu'

Recent interest in palaeodiet and palaeoenvironmental reconstruction has stressed the necessity of taking into consideration the animals and plants that were available to human groups in a specific geographical region. One method for differentiating resource exploitation and understanding the role of resources in ritual and domestic use, is to chemically analyse bone and plant remains retrieved from the archaeological record. In the Maya area, a focus on palaeodiet reconstruction has been investigated since the 1990s (Coyston 1995; Emery 1997; Gerry 1993; Reed 1994; Wright 1994). Long-distance exchange or trade and local garden hunting are two of the ways the Maya could have obtained valuable resources for common consumption and/or for ritual use.

In order to reconstruct the past diet of the Maya, it is necessary to explore the possible 'menus' that may have been available for consumption. Often the reconstruction of the menu starts by analogy with the modern Maya (Wright 1994:194) who depend mostly on corn and other cultivates. Corn (*Zea mays*) , or maize, is the only C4 plant that the Maya may have consumed routinely. Botanical samples from different contexts in Copán have proved that the most common plant species present was maize (Lentz 1991:272), which was probably the principal staple for all social classes. Other cultivates include beans (*Phaseolus vulgaris*), squash (*Cucurbita moschata*), chayote (*Sechium edule*), and bottle gourd (*Lagenaria sp.*) (Lentz 1991).

In the Maya area, C3 plants include root crops, legumes, vegetables, nuts, and fruits and C4 plants include maize, amaranths, chenopods, and other tropical grasses (Emery *et al.* 2000). Tree fruits were also cultivated and those identified in Copán include ciruela (*Spondias* sp.), avocado (*Persea americana*), nance (*Byrsonima crassifolia*), and possibly zapote (*Pouteria* sp.); wild plants were also consumed and included wild grapes (*Vitis* sp.) (Lentz 1991:277). It is important to note that a number of plants which are commonly available in the present day and are considered likely to have been available in the past, have not been identified in archaeological contexts. This is most probably a consequence of poor preservation, rather than evidence that these species were not exploited by the Maya. These include ramón (*Brosimum alicastrum*), cacao (*Theobroma cacao*), peppers (*Capsicum annuum*), tobacco (*Nicotiana tabacum*), and cotton (*Gossypium* spp.) (Lentz 1991:278-279).

Perhaps the only CAM plants consumed by the Maya were the *nopal* cactus (Opuntia), piñuela (*Bromelia karatas*), and pineapple (*Ananas cosmosus*), but these did not contribute significantly to their diet (White *et al.* 2001a:373, 2004:146), and therefore, no modern samples of these plants were obtained.

Although several isotopic analyses conducted in the Maya area have presented a comparable baseline or a 'model of the food web' formed by modern and archaeological reference collections (Tykot *et al.* 1996; Williams *et al.* 2009; Wright 2006; Wright *et al.* 2010), there has not been one for the Lowlands in Chiapas. The creation of a local baseline is vital to understand the isotopic composition of the available food items that formed a prehistoric menu (Wright 1993:81).

During the summer of 2009, I visited the archaeological sites of Palenque and Chinikihá, and gathered samples of plants that were probably consumed by humans and deer in pre-Hispanic times. Field identification was aided by a local guide at the site of Palenque, and the scientific names were identified in the laboratory posteriorly. It is important to mention that a palaeobotanic study of macrobotanical samples collected at different excavations at Chinikihá is currently being conducted by Felipe Trabanino from IIA-UNAM. Once results become available, samples can be added or deleted from this baseline.

Lab Code	Common name in Spanish (Scientific name)	$\delta^{15}N_{AIR}$	$\delta^{13}C_{VPDB}$
CM 26	Achiote (*Bixa orellana*)	-1.1	-30.24
CM 28F	Cacao (*Theobroma cacao*)	1.07	-30.29
CM 29H	Maiz (*Zea mays*)	3.07	-10.65
CM 30 H	Guaya (*Talisia olivaeformis*)	8.02	-29.50
CM 30 S	Guaya (*Talisia olivaeformis*)	14.09	-26.32
CM 32 H	Ciruela (*Spondias purpurea*)	0.26	-33.52
CM 32 S	Ciruela (*Spondias purpurea*)	4.44	-27.26
CM 33 H	Ejote (*Phaseolus vulgaris*)	1.33	-27.74
CM 33S	Ejote (*Phaseolus vulgaris*)	-0.52	-26.48
CM 34 H	Cabezatábano (*milpa* wild weed)	2.44	-31.06
CM 34 S	Cabezatábano (*milpa* wild weed)	2.31	-29.51
CM 35 S	Pimienta (*Pimienta doica*)	2.13	-25.65
CM 36 H	Palo Mulato (*Bursera simaruba*)	6.71	-26.57
CM 36 S	Palo Mulato (*Bursera simaruba*)	3.16	-25.96
CM 37 H	Guayaba (*Psidium guajava*)	3.17	-30.09
CM 37 S	Guayaba (*Psidium guajava*)	2.1	-25.34
CM 38 S	Calabaza (*Cucurbita sp*)	4.23	-26.85
CM 39H	Ramón (wild) (*Brosimum alicastrum*)	2.43	-27.37
CM 39 S	Ramón (from Palenque)	3.13	-24.69
CM 40	Ramón (wild)	3.44	-24.62
CM 41	Yucca (*Yucca elephantipes*)	3.52	-26.11
CM 42 S	Mango (*Mangifera indica*)	-0.86	-27.67
CM 44	Chive (palm)	3.37	-32.59
CM 45	Shanté (weed)	1.09	-33.37
CM 46	Guácimo (*Guazuma ulmifolia*)	1.62	-30.99
CM 47	Nacta (weed)	2.34	-27.67
CM 48	Chipilín (*Crotalaria langirostra*)	3.3	-28.37
CM 49	Camote (*Ipomoea batatas*)	3.95	-27.50
CM 50	Mostaza (wild) (*Brassica campestris*)	6.31	-28.11
CM 51H	Plátano (*Musa acuminata*)	1.21	-28.57
CM 52	Epazote (*Chenopodium ambrosoides*)	12.39	-27.40
CM 53	Chaya (*Cnidoscolus chayamansa*)	6.12	-29.78
CM 54	Hierbamora (*Solanum americanum*)	7.58	-29.27
CM 55	Chayote (*Sechum edule*)	8.64	-28.22
CM 56	Momo (*Piper auritum*)	9.43	-30.91
CM 57	Papaya (wild) (*Carica papaya*)	0.22	-30.61
CM 58	Higo (*Ficus maxima*)	-0.46	-26.32
CM 59	Holocim (weed)	0.35	-30.53
CM 60	Ñame (*Dioscorea alata*)	1.44	-28.65
CM 61	Jute (*Pachychilus indiorum*)	3.53	-25.25
CM 62	Freshwater fish (*Petenia splendida*)	6.81	-27.93
CM 65	Modern white-tailed deer (*Odocoileus virginiaus*)	6.87	-22.75

*F = fruit
S = seed
H = Leaf

Table 8. Modern reference samples with $\delta^{13}C$ and $\delta^{15}N$ values.

Modern plant and animal samples

A total of 42 plant and animal samples were collected, including 39 plants and three animals. Plant samples were sun-dried, measured and photographed before being packed in resealable bags. Seeds and leaves were separately analysed, according to the plant. Location and altitude were recorded for each sample. These samples were then dried in an oven for three days at 60°C at the Laboratorio de Espectrometría de Masas de Isótopos Estables at Instituto de Geología (IG-UNAM), and processed in a similar fashion as the collagen samples. Furthermore, flesh from a freshwater fish (*Petenia splendida*), and freshwater snails (*Pachychilus* sp.) were also processed. Because white-tailed deer (*Odocoileus virginianus*) is an endangered species and protected under Mexican law, no samples could be obtained on this field trip. However, a modern sample was obtained from the Yucatán region (sample CM62) for comparative purposes. The results are presented in Table 8, with the adjustment of +1.5‰ because of the Industrial Effect or modern anthropogenic decline in $\delta^{13}C$ (Emery *et al.* 2000:540; Tieszen and Fagre 1993b; Stuiver 1978). No other terrestrial mammal samples were collected due to a lack of time; however, published data on modern samples was used to reconstruct the baseline diet at Chinikihá.

Archaeological faunal and human samples

All the archaeological samples were obtained at the archaeological site of Chinikihá, except for one deer from Chancalá. The faunal archaeological samples included nine white-tailed deer, one domestic dog,

Sample ID	Op.	Layer/ Individual	Species
CM02	114	III	white-tailed deer
CM03	114	II	white-tailed deer
CM04	114	III	white-tailed deer
CM05	114	III	white-tailed deer
CM06	114	IV	white-tailed deer
CM07	114	V	white-tailed deer
CM08	114	V	white-tailed deer
CM09	114	IV	white-tailed deer
CM10	114	III	collared peccary
CM11	114	V	human from midden
CM12	201	III	white-tailed deer
CM13	40	2	human burial
CM15	42	4B	human burial
CM16	42	4C	human burial
CM18	44	6B	human burial
CM19	45	7	human burial
CM66	114	III	domestic dog

Table 9. Enamel samples from archaeological teeth.

and one collared peccary, and were obtained from the midden behind the Palace, along with one human mandible that was in the same context. Another five human samples were obtained from the burials excavated in 2008 in the domestic area located in the North Complex. All faunal samples were cleaned at Instituto de Investigaciones Antropológicas at Universidad Nacional Autónoma de México (IIA-UNAM) with tap water and then sun-dried. Human bone samples were selected from the burials that are housed at the Laboratorio de Osteología at IIA-UNAM. Although human bones had been cleaned previously by Dr Luis Núñez from IIA-UNAM, the osteological material was still impregnated with red silt, therefore, they were cleaned once more at IG-UNAM.

All plant, human and faunal bone samples were then pulverised at IIG-UNAM in an agate mortar and screened through 50mm mesh. I conducted the separation into dentine and enamel of the human and faunal teeth with the aid of a portable *Craftman* rotary drill. Both dentine and enamel were then processed in a similar fashion to cortical bone. Edith Cienfuegos and Pedro Morales from IG-UNAM supervised the processing of all samples. Additional help in processing the samples was conducted by personnel at IG-UNAM.

Sampling teeth

Teeth samples for enamel are presented in Table 9. The selection of teeth depended on the preservation state, that is, no teeth with caries or holes were sampled. In the case of the fauna, there were considerably fewer teeth and cranial bones represented in comparison to the rest of the elements, constraining sampling possibilities. Nonetheless, the permanent lower molar 2M was obtained when available. When this molar was missing or was unsuitable, the 3M was sampled instead. Only one premolar was sampled (CM07) however, to provide a broader characterisation of the diet patterns. Teeth from the human samples were selected in a similar fashion. When 2M presented caries or was in poor condition, another molar was selected. When there were jade incrustations or other sort of cultural modifications to the teeth, these were not sampled. In the case of the human sample, the selection of teeth was limited because in two cases (CM14 and CM17) molars were simply not found during excavation.

Ideally, sampling two or three molars from the same individual could help us identify changes in diet later in life. It was not possible to do so in this case, however, the comparison between enamel apatite and long bone collagen provides differences that allow diet and temporal comparisons. Samples representing all three molars were obtained from different individuals, and these will be compared in order to identify variability related to age, as each molar signals a different stage in life. In the near future, sampling two or more teeth for each individual, as well as obtaining different samples from a single tooth in order to explore the possibility of seasonal differences, will be considered.

Sampling bone

Samples for collagen are listed in Table 10. Because faunal remains were mostly disarticulated in the midden, it was impossible to match teeth with long bone from the same individual. Therefore, to be sure that the teeth and the cortical sample would belong to the same individual, a fragment of cortical bone from the mandible. In one case only, it was not possible to sample the mandible and therefore, a fragment of maxillae was then used (CM05), producing good quality collagen for further analysis. In CM08, bone sampling was not possible as the mandible had incised glyphs. For the humans, cortical bone from the femora was preferred, but where such a sample was not possible, the bone collagen sample was obtained from the mandible. This is the case for the human sample obtained from behind the Palace (CM11) since no femur could be matched to the mandible, and in CM18, where the long bones were simply in poor condition. The results of these analyses are presented in Chapter eight.

Sample ID	Operación/ Burial number	Layer/ Individual	Species	Dentine	Long Bone	Notes
CM02	114	III	white-tailed deer	x		
CM03	114	II	white-tailed deer	x	X	
CM04	114	III	white-tailed deer	x	X	
CM05	114	III	white-tailed deer	x	X	
CM06	114	IV	white-tailed deer	x	X	
CM07	114	V	white-tailed deer		X	
CM08	114	V	white-tailed deer	x		No bone sample taken (worked mandible)
CM09	114	IV	white-tailed deer		X	
CM10	114	III	collared peccary	x	x	
CM11	114	V	human from midden	x	x	Bone collagen from mandible
CM12	201	III	white-tailed deer	x		
CM13	40	2	human burial	x	x	
CM14	42	4A	human burial		x	
CM15	42	4B	human burial	x	x	
CM16	42	4C	human burial	x	x	Bone collagen from maxilla;
CM17	43	1	human burial		x	Long bone poor preservation
CM18	44	6B	human burial	x	x	Bone collagen from mandible
CM19	45	7	human burial	x	x	

Table 10. Collagen samples from dentine and long bone for δ13C and δ15N analyses ('x' indicates existence of sample).

Chapter seven

Results of the zooarchaeological analysis

Almost 5000 human and faunal bones, as well as modified bone fragments, and malacological remains were recovered from the PRACH excavations during 2008. This chapter presents the results of the analysis as discussed in the methodology section in Chapter five. I begin by applying a basic zooarchaeological analysis to the whole collection including the identification of the number of identified specimens (NISP), weight, diversity index, and the minimum number of individuals represented (MNI). This information is then used to propose a general model of access to faunal resources by the inhabitants of Chinikihá, while recognising the importance of each species identified, in order to understand the relationship between context and the specific taxa present in each.

Within this assemblage, it was recognised that there were two types of materials, those that resulted from dietary consumption, and modified bone and shell from tool/ornament manufacturing. Thus, the materials were considered together in the overall quantification, but were separated for the analysis by location, identification by age, sex, seasonality, and taphonomic processes, including degree of fragmentation, weathering, and presence of faunal and/or human modifications related to human consumption. These variables are discussed, creating sub-samples by location. In a similar fashion, when dealing with specific analysis, sub-samples were selected from the total count.

The description of materials by *Operación* is then used for comparative purposes to determine the types of contexts where faunal remains were recovered. The main objective of this chapter then is the study of the osteofaunal materials that may have resulted from human consumption, and to explore their distribution throughout the different *Operaciones*; thus, major emphasis is placed on the analysis of the species that may have been exploited for dietary purposes, using sub-samples from the different excavation contexts at Chinikihá. This study provides a series of important insights for the discussion of faunal resource exploitation and the dietary preferences of the elite at Chinikihá during the Late Classic/Terminal period.

Results

Specimens count

All bone and shell fragments recovered from PRACH during 2008 are included in this analysis, resulting in a grand total of 4849 specimens, from which 2522 specimens are bone fragments (52.01%NISP) including fauna and human remains, and 2327 specimens (47.98%NISP), are shell remains. They were recovered from different excavations, including *Operaciones* 110, 111, 112, 114, and 115 from Chinikihá; *Operación* 201 (Chancalá), and *Operación* 202 (San Juan Chancalaíto). One specimen had no information on provenance and was recorded as Not Identified (NI).

Bone fragments recovered by flotation conducted after September 2009 were not considered in this analysis; hence, an underrepresentation of smaller taxa, including small mammals, reptiles, fish, and birds should be expected. Thus, taxonomic diversity and other measurements based on the identified taxa should be considered carefully. Loose unworked teeth and unidentifiable fragments were recorded and are included in Tables 11 and 12, but were not included in further analysis. Loose teeth (NISP = 26) included complete and fragmentary specimens, mostly molars and primarily from three animals, white-tailed deer (N = 20), domestic dog and carnivore (N = 5), and rodent (N = 1), three species that are very common among the Chinikihá assemblage (see Appendix A).

However, such teeth may have become loose as a result of post-depositional factors and could therefore plausibly have come from one of the hemi-mandibles or maxilla which were recovered from the same contexts. Therefore, they were registered but were not considered during further analysis, including MNI and skeletal completeness calculations, as they may have come from an individual already being accounted for by a mandible or maxilla. Isolated teeth were also disregarded when constructing mortality profiles and seasonality calculations. In a similar fashion, a few non-diagnostic bone fragments that were unidentified (N = 25) because of their size and preservation, were noted and recorded, but will be not considered for statistical purposes, as their inclusion does not information about the assemblage (Klein and Cruz-Uribe 1984; Pohl 1976).

In terms of volume, the total faunal assemblage weighed 24,430.1g, and was recovered from 59m². This represents the sum of all the excavated volumes by *Operación*, and includes unmodified material, dietary remains (fauna, humans, and shell), and worked bone and shell (Table 11). *Operación* 114 produced the largest sample by weight (86.55%) and by NISP (79.71%),

Location	Excavated volume (m²)	Weight (g)	%Weight	NISP	%NISP	MNI	%MNI
Operación 110	21	2233.1	9.14	696	14.35	560	23.63
Operación 111	4	66.2	0.27	67	1.38	2	0.08
Operación 112	4	84.9	0.35	20	0.41	17	0.72
Operación 114	17	21144.09	86.55	3865	79.71	1782	75.19
Operación 115	5	22.2	0.09	5	0.10	2	0.08
Operación 201	4	784	3.21	186	3.84	6	0.25
Operación 202	4	61.4	0.25	9	0.19	1	0.04
Not Identified		34.3	0.14	1	0.02		
Total	**59**	**24430.19**	**100.00**	**4849**	**100.00**	**2370**	**100.00**

*MNI calculations do not include modified bone and shell.

Table 11. Summary of NISP, MNI, and weight for all materials by *Operación*.

followed by *Operación* 110 with 9.14% of the total weight and 14.35% of the total NISP. *Operación* 201 was the third largest with 3.21% of the total weight and 3.84% of the total NISP. All other *Operaciones* have significantly less material, representing less than 10% of the total weight and less than 5% of the total NISP calculations.

The obvious difference in sample sizes is due to several factors that need further discussion. The area excavated in each *Operación* is different, with the smaller *Operaciones* being just 4m² (*Operaciones* 111, 112, 115, 201, and 202), while the two largest, *Operaciones* 114 and 110, are 17m² and 21m² respectively. It is interesting to note, however, that the amount of bone remains recovered per *Operación* may not necessarily be related directly to the excavated volume. For example, *Operación* 110 is the largest excavation in terms of its volume (21m²), but it only represents 5.34% of the total NISP, and 1.60% of the total weight. Because all the *Operaciones* are located in the vicinity of a permanent structure, it is possible that all the osteological material has the same survival rates and a similarity in preservation is expected. However, NISP values should be considered carefully, as the fragmentation of the material may be the result of several factors, such as pre and post-depositional fracture patterns and other taphonomical modifications (Klein and Cruz-Uribe 1984; Lyman 2008). Finally, the number of specimens present by *Operación* may be the result of access to faunal resources and reveal the choices and exploitation patterns in each context.

Number of identified specimens (NISP) and taxonomic identification

The number of identified specimens for all the assemblage is presented in Table 12. This includes all bones and shell per *Operación*, including modified and unworked remains. A summary of all taxa can be found in Appendix B. The preservation state of all osteological material allowed an accurate taxonomic identification for the faunal sub-sample, with more than 99% of the sample identified to Class or a more specific level. A combination of factors contributed to the taxonomic level identified for each specimen. The level of identification was largely dependent on the skeletal completeness of the specimens, and the presence of diagnostic elements such as long bone epiphyses and teeth, amongst other factors. The observed spectrum for analysis included a high rate of heavily fragmented specimens, including long bone diaphyses and ribs. The level of taxonomic identification that was obtained for Chinikihá is consistent and comparable with published data for other studies in the Maya area.

The three most numerous species include *jute* shells (*Pachychilus* sp.), a freshwater mollusc, comprising 47.33% of all the assemblage, followed by the remains of large/medium mammals (25.51%), and white-tailed deer (*Odocoileus virginianus*) with 21.24% of the total NISP. All other species are present in low proportions, ranging from 1.38% to almost zero. In regards to the identified species at Chinikihá, some of these were registered for the first time during this analysis, including armadillo (*Dasypus novemcinctus*), gray fox (*Urocyon cinereoargenteus*), and jaguar (*Panthera onca*) while other species have been previously identified at Chinikihá. In the preliminary analysis of three test pits located behind the Palace, it was found that white-tailed deer (*Odocoileus virginianus*) was the predominant species and other species were present in much smaller percentages, including brocket deer (*Mazama* sp.), dog (*Canis lupus familiaris*), agouti (*Dasyprocta punctata*), and collared peccary (*Pecari tajacu*) (Montero 2008).

Following Gautier's (1987) concept of taphonomic groups, it could be assumed that the remains identified as medium/large mammals are probably deer and

Taxon	Op. 110		Op. 111		Op. 112		Op. 114		Op. 115		Op. 201		Op. 202		NI		Total	
	NISP	%NISP	NISP	%NISP	NISP	%NISP	NISP	%NISP	NISP	%NISP	NISP	%NISP	NISP	%NISP	NISP	%NISP	NISP	%NISP
Pachychilus sp.	556	79.89	1	1.49	17	85.00	1719	44.48	2	40.00							2295	47.33
Nephronaias sp.							12	0.31									12	0.25
Pomacea flagellata															1	100.00	1	0.02
Unidentified shell	3	0.43					16	0.41									19	0.39
Testudines							5	0.13									5	0.10
Mammalia	2	0.29	1	1.49			21	0.54			1	0.54					25	0.52
large/medium mammal	121	17.39	55	82.09	2	10.00	954	24.68	3	60.00	98	52.69	4	44.44			1237	25.51
medium/small mammal	4	0.57					53	1.37			10	5.38					67	1.38
Dasypus novemcinctus							1	0.03									1	0.02
Homo sapiens	1	0.14			1	5.00	60	1.55									62	1.28
Carnivora							4	0.10			3	1.61					7	0.14
Canis sp.			1	1.49			4	0.10			2	1.08					7	0.14
Canis lupus familiaris	1	0.14					22	0.57			16	8.60					39	0.80
Urocyon cinereoargenteus							1	0.03									1	0.02
Felidae							1	0.03									1	0.02
Panthera onca							1	0.03									1	0.02
Tapirus bairdii							1	0.03									1	0.02
Artiodactyla							1	0.03									1	0.02
Pecari tajacu							2	0.05									2	0.04
Odocoileus virginianus	4	0.57	1	1.49			964	24.94			56	30.11	5	55.56			1030	21.24
Mazama sp.							1	0.03									1	0.02
Rodentia							1	0.03									1	0.02
Dasyprocta punctata							1	0.03									1	0.02
Sylvilagus sp.	1	0.14					4	0.10									5	0.10
Sylvilagus brasiliensis							1	0.03									1	0.02
Sylvilagus floridanus							1	0.03									1	0.02
Class unknown	3	0.43	8	11.94			14	0.36									25	0.52
Total	696	100.00	67	100.00	20	100.00	3865	100.00	5	100.00	186	100.00	9	100.00	1	100.00	4849	100.00

Table 12. Summary counts for the whole Chinikihá assemblage.

if added to those positively identified as such, the maximum possible percentage of deer increases to 94.56%. In a similar fashion, those remains identified as small/medium mammal can be added to the second most numerous category, the domestic dog, and this would result in a maximum total of 4.46%. These percentages are probably closer to the real faunal frequencies. However, due to the high fragmentation rate of these remains, it was impossible to identify age or sex, and the remains identified only as small/medium or medium/large mammals were kept separate from those of deer and dog, so as not to affect the age/sex analysis of the latter categories. For all other statistical analyses these categories were treated as separate entities. Although it is very probable that the medium/large mammals are in fact deer remains, they were not grouped together as this would have complicated the possibility of creating a comparison with the rest of the taxa. The sum of medium/large mammals and deer NISP would have resulted in an overwhelming presence of deer that would have prevented observations of significant results from any other species. All other variables including presence of faunal and human modifications, and weathering stages, were registered and therefore, small/medium mammal and medium/large mammal categories are included in the statistical analysis, but again maintained as separate categories.

The distribution of species is not homogeneous for all *Operaciones*, and again, this may be related to the sample size, where those *Operaciones* that had the highest NISP values, are also those that had the most species present. *Operación* 114 (3865 NISP) resulted in 26 taxonomic groups, followed by *Operación* 110 (696 NISP) with 10, and *Operación* 201 (186 NISP) with seven taxa respectively. *Operación* 111 (67 NISP) had six taxa, while the rest of the *Operaciones* had three and two taxa present only.

Bone and shell modified in order to produce tools and ornaments include the following species: *jute* (*Pachychilus* sp.), river clam (*Nephronaias* sp.), apple snail (*Pomacea flagellata*), tapir (*Tapirus bairdii*), white-tailed deer (*Odocoileus virginianus*), and human (*Homo sapiens*). Other fragments which displayed modifications from manufacturing processes, and which could only be identified to limited extents due to these modifications, included turtle, mammal, carnivore, and unidentified shell fragments. Worked bone and shell were kept separate and were not included in the MNI calculations and other analyses, but were described and discussed separately.

Minimum number of individuals (MNI)

A minimum number of individuals (MNI) was calculated for the faunal assemblage, disregarding loose teeth and worked bone and shell, as well as fragments identified only to Class level (small/medium and medium/large mammals) because they could potentially be any species. In the same manner, no MNI was calculated for those fragments identified to Order or Family (carnivores, artiodactyls, and *Canis* sp., and *Sylvilagus* sp., and so on). This decision was made due to the fact that each of these fragments could potentially be assigned a MNI of 1, which would likely overemphasise its importance within the assemblage. Hence, MNI values were calculated only for those fragments identified to the level of Species. The minimum number of individuals calculated from the total NISP of 4707 unworked specimens was 2370 (Table 13). By location, *Operación* 114 again produced the highest figure with 1782 MNI, followed by *Operación* 110 with 560 MNI, and *Operación* 112 with 17 MNI. This result is in accordance with the frequencies for NISP; however, due to the presence of more *jute* remains in *Operación* 112, this context produced a higher number of MNI, exceeding that of *Operación* 201, as it was initially anticipated. MNI values however, are approximate and very conservative, so the real number of individuals ranges somewhere between the conservative MNI and the maximum fragments represented by NISP (Grayson 1984).

By species, the most numerous in terms of MNI were *jute* with a count of 2293. The most prominent mammal species is white-tailed deer with 54 MNI, followed by human remains that represent nine individuals, and domestic dog with 7 MNI. Armadillo, gray fox, collared peccary, agouti, forest rabbit and cottontail represent one MNI each. The apparent high number of MNI for *jute* is due to the fact that each shell is considered an individual. However, the amount of meat that each of them produces is small and it would be necessary to eat numerous individuals in order to consume a comparable amount of meat to that produced by the other species that are present in the assemblage. By weight, *jute* represents 31.65%, while white-tailed deer remains comprise 59.06%. All other species represent less than 1% of the total weight, with large/medium mammal fragments weighting 7.45%. Unfortunately, it was not possible to obtain the weight for all the human remains; therefore weight for human remains is marked as not applicable.

If *jute* is removed from the calculations, as well as the material identified to Family level, there is a major presence of white-tailed deer (*Odocoileus virginianus*), with 41.59% of all the specimens (n = 1004). The abundance of deer is enhanced even further when the second most abundant species, human remains (*Homo sapiens*) only comprises 2.49% (n = 60) of the sample, followed by the domestic dog (*Canis lupus familiaris*) with 1.57% (n = 38). All other taxa represent less than 1% each. These include rabbits (*Sylvilagus* sp., *Sylvilagus*

Taxon	Op. 110		Op. 111		Op. 112		Op. 114		Op. 115		Op. 201		Op. 202		Total					
	NISP	MNI	NISP	MNI	NISP	MNI	NISP	MNI	NISP	MNI	NISP	MNI	NISP	MNI	NISP	%NISP	MNI	%MNI	Weight (g)	%
Pachychilus sp.	556	556	1	1	16	16	1718	1718	2	2					2293	48.71	2293	96.75	7616.5	31.65
large/medium mammal	119		55		2		943		2		97		4		1222	25.96	0	0.00	1793.1	7.45
medium/small mammal	4						53				10				67	1.42	0	0.00	41.4	0.17
Dasypus novemcinctus							1	1							1	0.02	1	0.04	8	0.03
Homo sapiens	1	1			1	1	58	7							60	1.27	9	0.38	n/a	n/a
Carnivora							2				2				4	0.08	0	0.00	34.4	0.14
Canis sp.			1				2								3	0.06	0	0.00	18.1	0.08
Canis lupus familiaris	1	1					22	2			15	4			38	0.81	7	0.30	171.89	0.71
Urocyon cinereoargenteus							1	1							1	0.02	1	0.04	4.7	0.02
Felidae							1								1	0.02	0	0.00	6.6	0.03
Panthera onca							1	1							1	0.02	1	0.04	11.4	0.05
Artiodactyla							1								1	0.02	0	0.00	10.4	0.04
Pecari tajacu							2	1							2	0.04	1	0.04	83.4	0.35
Odocoileus virginianus	3	2	1	1			942	48			53	2	5	1	1004	21.33	54	2.28	14213.1	59.06
Mazama sp.							1								1	0.02	0	0.00	12.2	0.05
Dasyprocta punctata							1	1							1	0.02	1	0.04	11.7	0.05
Sylvilagus sp.	1						4								5	0.11	0	0.00	21.5	0.09
Sylvilagus brasiliensis							1	1							1	0.02	1	0.04	5.2	0.02
Sylvilagus floridanus							1	1							1	0.02	1	0.04	2.5	0.01
Total	**685**	**560**	**58**	**2**	**19**	**17**	**3755**	**1782**	**4**	**2**	**177**	**6**	**9**	**1**	**4707**	**100.00**	**2370**	**100.00**	**24066.09**	**100.00**

Table 13. NISP, MNI and weight by Species per *Operación* (worked bone not included).

	Op. 110	Op. 111	Op. 112	Op. 114	Op. 115	Op. 201	Op. 202
NISP total by *Operación*	129	57	3	2037	2	177	9
NISP deer	3	1	0	942	0	53	5
%NISP deer	2.33	1.75	0.00	46.24	0.00	29.94	55.56
NISP dog	1	0	0	22	0	15	0
%NISP dog	0.78	0.00	0.00	1.08	0.00	8.47	0.00
NISP human	1	0	1	58	0	0	0
%NISP human	0.78	0.00	33.33	2.85	0.00	0.00	0.00

Table 14. Percentage of deer, dog, and human remains present by *Operación*.

brasiliensis and *Sylvilagus floridanus*), collared peccary (*Pecari tajacu*), armadillo (*Dasypus novemcinctus*), gray fox (*Urocyon cinereoargenteus*), jaguar (*Panthera onca*), and brocket deer (*Mazama* sp.), each of these species is only represented by a single specimen (n = 1), and all were retrieved from *Operación* 114.

Among the mammals, therefore, the most frequently are white-tailed deer, human and domestic dog. Centering the analysis in those three taxa, and when tallied by *Operación*, deer is the most frequent species where deer has been identified (Table 14). However, the proportions of the three taxa in each *Operación* are slightly different when the total NISP per *Operación* is considered and is dependent on the total number of taxa being identified within each context. The *Operación* with the highest proportion of deer is *Operación* 202 with 55.56%, while in *Operación* 114, deer comprises 46.24% of the assemblage, but only 29.94% in *Operación* 201. In all other *Operaciones*, deer represents a very low proportion or is not present at all. Human remains resulted in a higher percentage in *Operación* 112 (33.33%NISP), while in *Operación* 114 humans comprise only 2.85% of the total.

The other *Operación* in which human remains were present was *Operación* 110, where one specimen represents 0.78% of that *Operación*. Finally, the presence of domestic dog is proportionally higher in *Operación* 201 (8.47%), while in *Operación* 114 domestic dog makes up 1.08% and 0.78% for *Operación* 110. Although %NISP is affected by the total number of specimens and taxa identified for each location, comparisons between the three most frequent mammals and their relative presence within each *Operación*, could potentially reveal tendencies in the preferences for access to certain taxa in each context. Nevertheless, it should be kept in mind that this distribution may also be influenced by the type of context and other factors, such as how each specimen entered the archaeological record and what taphonomic agents have affected them.

Distribution of skeletal elements

The distribution by skeletal elements for all *Operaciones* is presented in Table 15. This includes only those specimens that were identified by skeletal element and taxa, while the categories of small/medium and medium and medium/large mammal fragments were excluded. In regards to the taxa grouped as Artiodactyla, all skeletal elements are present, especially in *Operación* 114, while Carnivora and Lagomorpha are represented mainly by long bones from the upper and lower limbs, with all other skeletal elements occurring less frequently. The pelvic and shoulder girdles occur more frequently among the human remains, while other taxa are represented by long bones, including the agouti (one femur), and the armadillo (one tibia). The distribution of skeletal elements is not homogeneous by *Operación*, and while *Operación* 114 contains all skeletal elements, all the other *Operaciones* have skeletal elements present in smaller frequencies. *Operación* 115 had no skeletal elements identified.

Diversity index

Diversity index was measured by the combination of richness and evenness values, and was calculated by the Simpson's Heterogeneity index and the Shannon-Weaver's Diversity index (Table 16). Due to the low NISP and MNI values of *Operación* 115, it was not possible to obtain any results for its diversity. In a similar fashion, results for richness were not obtained for *Operaciones* 111, 112, and 202 due to their low MNI values. Of all the *Operaciones*, *Operación* 114 yielded the richest assemblage (2.226) with the most taxa identified, followed by *Operaciones* 110 and 201. In terms of evenness, *Operaciones* 110, 111, 114, and 201 have the lower evenness values, while *Operaciones* 112 and 202 are the most evenly distributed. The Shannon-Weaver diversity index results are extremely interesting, with *Operación* 201 having the most diversity (1.1128), while *Operación* 114 had the most taxa identified, but produced a low index (0.75), similar to that from *Operaciones* 112 and 202, meaning that most of

Skeletal element	Op. 110	Op. 111	Op. 112	Op. 114	Op. 115	Op. 201	Op. 202
Antler				2			
Skull		1		74, **8**, _1_, 7h		6, **1**	
Indet. vertebrae				64, **2**, 1h		12	2
Cervical vertebrae				114, 1h		2	
Thoracic vertebrae				126, 3h		3	
Lumbar vertebrae				138, 3h		1	
Sacrum				18			
Sternum				5			
Rib				1, **1**, 4h		1	
Clavicle			1h	10h			
Scapula		1		114, 10h		2	1
Humerus				26, **1**, 1h		3	1
Radius				28, **4**, 1h		3, 7	
Ulna				16, **1**, 1h		1, **1**	
Carpal				6, **1**			
Metacarpus				11, **3**		5, **3**	
Innominate	2, **1**			120, **1**, _2_, 7h		7	
Femur	1			26, **1**, _3_, 1h, 1*		2, **1**	
Patella				3			
Tibia				9, **3**, 1*		3	
Fibula				3h			
Tarsal	1			26		3, 2	1
Metatarsus				10, **1**, 5h		1	
Phalanges	1h			5, **2**			
Metapodium				2			
Long bone				2			

Table 15. Distribution of skeletal elements (NISP) by Operación, grouped by Order: Artiodactyla (regular), Carnivora (Bold), Lagomorpha (underlined), humans (h), and other fauna (*).

Location	Odum's Richness	Simpson's Heterogeneity	Evenness	Shannon-Weaver's Diversity
Op. 110	1.4426	0.8333	0.2135	0.3826
Op. 111	n/a	n/a	0.1605	0.1763
Op. 112	n/a	n/a	0.9183	0.6365
Op. 114	2.226	0.7074	0.2426	0.7500
Op. 115	n/a	n/a	n/a	n/a
Op. 201	0.5581	0.5333	0.6914	1.1128
Op. 202	n/a	n/a	0.9911	0.6870

Table 16. Results for richness, heterogeneity, evenness, and diversity index by *Operación*.

the specimens are identifiable to few taxonomic species. This result is due to the presence of a single dominant species, the white-tailed deer.

As can be seen from these results, diversity, richness, and evenness are very susceptible to sample size (Grayson 1984:159-160; Kintigh 1989, Reitz and Wing 1999:107), making it difficult to compare different samples of diverse size. Nonetheless, it was possible to compare to a general level the values for Chinikihá with published data from different contexts from other Maya sites (Table 17). Koželsky (2005:31) calculated the Shannon Weaver's diversity index for different contexts and different sites, gathering information from published data. In order to be able to compare directly between sites, this author did not include decapods, gastropods or humans in her analysis, focusing exclusively on mammals. The author found that the highest value was that of a midden created by feasting activities in Lagartero (2.98), followed by a context in the centre of Aguateca (2.20), which had the most taxa identified, but with a focus on canid, deer, and rabbits. The context with the lowest diversity index is Actun Polbiche (0.75) and represents ritual activities, with a high selection of one species (dogs).

Site	Shannon-Weaver's Diversity
Lagartero (feasting midden)	2.98
Aguateca (centre)	2.20
Piedras Negras (palace)	1.64
Dos Pilas (periphery)	1.59
Actun Polbiche (ritual)	0.92
Chinikihá (Op. 114)	0.75

Table 17. Comparison of the Shannon-Weaver's Diversity index for other Maya sites.

To conduct comparisons with Koželsky's results, I removed the same taxa as she did from the analysis (decapods, gastropods and human remains), but kept modified bone, producing a Shannon-Weaver's diversity index of 1.10 for *Operación* 114, suggesting again that there is a strong selection for a small number of taxa. This index also shows the impact of a few, highly abundant selected species present in this *Operación*. This is interesting as it confirms that in contexts resulting from specific activities, including ritual feasting (Koželsky 2005).

Importance of taxa represented

The species identified in the Chinikihá assemblage are important in the Maya region as food and for ritual purposes. In this section, I discuss their importance based on their presence in the assemblage. They are grouped by Order and are ordered from most frequent to least frequent.

Artiodactyla

There are two families present in the sample: the Cervidae and the Tayassuidae. Within the Cervidae, there were two species identified, the white-tailed deer (*Odocoileus virginianus*), and the brocket deer (*Mazama* sp.). Within the Tayassuidae, there were also two species, the collared peccary (*Pecari tajacu*), and the white-lipped peccary (*Tayassu pecari*), but in the Chinikihá assemblage only the former was identified. The white-tailed deer is native to the Maya lowlands and is present all over the North American continent (Hall 1981:1092), the smaller brocket deer is found more frequently in the Yucatán Peninsula. In México, and especially in Chiapas, white-tailed deer is highly adaptable and is present in all types of ecosystems, although primarily in open fields surrounded by shrubs (Álvarez del Toro 1977:115), while the brocket deer prefers savannah environments. The collared peccary inhabits grasslands and forests less than 3000m above the sea level (Emmons and Feer 1997). Being herbivorous, the deer browses and grazes on different shrubs, seeds, and fruits (Alcerreca and Robles 2005). It has been mentioned that in the Maya area, the deer browse near cornfields because they like the salty ash of burned fields, as well as the new shoots of corn (Schlesinger 2001). Palo mulato or *chakaj* leaves (*Bursera simaruba*) and ramón fruits (*Brosimum alicastrum*) are also mentioned as favourite plants eaten by deer (Mandujano and Rico-Gray 1991). In the tropical dry forest regions of México, the white-tailed deer eats an average annual diet of 20 plant species, but concentrates more on herbs and grasses during the rainy season. Fruits and deciduous leaves of trees and bushes are important during the dry period (Arceo *et al.* 2005).

The collared peccary (*Pecari tajacu*) occupies a wide range of environments, including forests and grasslands, while the white-lipped peccary is restricted to more dense forests (Reid 1997), and was commonly used as food by the Maya (Emery 2007b:58). The peccary would have been hunted for their high meat yield, yet very few peccary remains are present in the archaeological context; their low frequency is especially obvious in middens and other contexts resulting from human consumption (Fridberg 2005). On the other hand, worked peccary bones are relatively more frequent, although restricted to certain deposits, those either ritual of origin, or associated to the elite (Masson and Peraza Lope 2008; Emery 2007b).

Representations of deer are common in hieroglyphic inscriptions and other pictorial media. There are two broad categories of deer representation, those that present deer as a god in mythical images, and those that represent the deer as food in more mundane images. In contemporary ethnographic studies and iconographic analyses among the Maya, it has been suggested that deer represents the solar god, and thus its sacrifice would assure fertility and result in good harvests (Montoliú 1976; Pohl 1983:98). The important association between deer, fertility, and agricultural prosperity, especially regarding maize, is observed in the images of ritually sacrificed deer. This probably relates to the renewal *cuch* or cargo ceremony (Pohl 1981). In these images, the 'Deer God' or *Huk Sip* is the patron of hunting, and usually represented as a full-sized deer or as an old man, with some physical characteristics of the deer, such as the long ears and antlers (Stone and Zender 2011:78). According to Stone and Zender (2011:78), the 'Deer God' seems 'to take responsibility for the burning of forest to make agricultural land', hence, the importance to appease him with many offerings and sacrifices that often included deer (Stone and Zender 2011; Tozzer 1967). According to Landa, other animals that have been related to fertility include monkey, peccary, dog, jaguar, fish, snake, armadillo, crocodile and turtle, while during Postclassic times, turkey was used as a substitute (Pohl 1983:65).

In the Maya region, white-tailed deer seems to have been preferred over the brocket deer, with numerous deposits containing white-tailed deer remains in higher frequencies than brocket deer (Foreman 2004:34). Deer remains from the Late Classic period abound in the Maya region including sites such as Seibal (Pohl 1985a, 1985b), Altar de Sacrificios (Olsen 1972), Toniná (Soto 1998), Tikal (White *et al.* 2004), Piedras Negras (Emery 2001), Copán (Pohl 1995), and Yaxchilán (Soto and Polaco 1994). Examples of peccary remains have been found sporadically since the Preclassic period, at sites such as Seibal and Cerros (Carr 1985; Pohl 1976). More examples of Tayassuidae remains have been identified from the Classic period, from a variety of sites, including Uxmal, Copán, Luubantun, and the Petexbatún area (Collins 2002; Emery 2010; Kidder 1947; Wing 1975). Since peccaries are species that may have had different uses, including ritual and non-ritual, it is difficult to assess if they were restricted to one segment of society (Fridberg 2005).

Definite evidence about the preference of the higher classes for large mammals including deer and peccary is observable during the Postclassic period (Masson 1999). With bone fragments displaying butchering marks and located in the vicinity of elite dwellings, some authors have proposed that the members of the high class were in charge of meat redistribution (Masson 1999:101). Thus, just like with the deer, access to peccary may have been reserved for the high classes, and furthermore, this practice may be very ancient. The differential procurement and use of artiodactyls other than deer continued during the Postclassic, as seen at Mayapán (Masson and Peraza Lope 2008:178-179).

In Chinikihá, of all the fauna analysed in this study, deer is by far the most frequent species, with all body parts represented in different frequencies. This is the case especially in *Operación* 114, with lower frequencies at other contexts, except *Operaciones* 112 and 115 where no deer remains were retrieved. In contrast, the other two artiodactyls, the brocket deer and the peccary, are present in minimal numbers, probably a reflection of their differing habitat preferences. Only one specimen of brocket deer (hemi-mandible) was identified, and it was found in *Operación* 114. Collared peccary is accounted for only by two specimens, also found in *Operación* 114, and these are two hemi-mandibles, possibly from the same individual. A single possible cut mark was found on one hemi-mandible, suggesting its dietary role.

Carnivora

The carnivores are represented by two families, Canidae and Felidae. Within the former, the domestic dog (*Canis lupus familiaris*) and the gray fox (*Urocyon cinereoargenteus*) were identified, while in the Felidae, there were two specimens, one identified as jaguar (*Panthera onca*) and another specimen identified as Felidae.

The presence of domestic dog in archaeological contexts is very ubiquitous and is often associated with human occupation. This may be a reflection of the significant role it played in Mesoamerica as one of the only two only true domesticated animals, along with the much later domesticated turkey (*Meleagris gallopavo*). Often, the dog was an animal used for many different purposes, including as a pet for companionship and a hunting aide, but also was used ritual and as food. Evidence for the consumption of dogs as food has been observed not only in other parts of Mesoamerica (Wing 1978), but also at several sites in North America (Tito *et al.* 2011) and South America (Schwartz 1997). The exploitation of dogs for food has been documented from the Preclassic period, with dogs being regarded as an alternative but secure source of meat compared to that obtained from the wild (Clutton-Brock and Hammond 1994). Furthermore, changes in dog consumption have been linked directly to changes in the availability of wild animals (Shaw 1999).

Discussions regarding dogs in Mesoamerican archaeology, are often focussed on the famous Mexican hairless dog, also known by its Nahuatl name, *xoloitzcuintle*. This breed originated on the west coast of México and from there spread to the rest of Mesoamerica (Valadéz *et al.* 2009). For a long time it has been believed that the hairless dog was almost exclusively fattened on corn in order to be eaten or sacrificed (Stone and Zender 2011:79); however, the variability of assemblages in which it appears suggests that there were not specific uses for specific breeds of dog (Valadéz *et al.* 2009). In fact, it is common to see two or more breeds mixed in the same deposits (Blanco *et al.* 1999). In the Maya area, at least two examples of *xoloitxcuintle* have been reported, including dog burials at the site of Chac Mool, Quintana Roo and one dentary at the coastal site of Champotón in Campeche (Valadéz *et al.* 2009). In many of the analyses it is not possible to identify what type of dog is present; in Mesoamerica there were at least three or four variants (Olsen 1974).

Dog remains in the archaeological record in the Maya area appear in both, food and ceremonial contexts. It has been documented that dogs were an important resource since the Late Preclassic period (Pohl 1985b: 109; Clutton-Brock and Hammond 1994), with examples at the site of Colhá (Shaw 1991) and Cerros (Carr 1985). During the Preclassic and Classic periods, dog remains have been identified in middens and other deposits with other food remains, strongly indicating their use as food (Clutton-Brock and Hammond 1994). During the

Postclassic, dogs were used for sacrifice and in other rituals, as seen at Cozumel Island (Hamblin 1984). Dog sacrifices have been registered at Chac Mool, Quintana Roo, where more than 35 dogs were sacrificed in association with a New Year ceremony (Valadéz *et al.* 2009).

In Chinikihá, dog is the second most common mammal, excluding humans, and is present in *Operaciones* 110, 201, and 114, being most abundant in the latter. There are a total of 38 dog specimens, from which 57.89% (n = 22) are in *Operación* 114, and 39.47% (n = 15) are in *Operación* 201. Most of the dog remains do not exhibit anthropogenic modifications that would result from processing them as food. Only one fragment of pubic bone and a few other bones have been fractured when fresh, thus the role of dogs as food in these two contexts has been primarily inferred from the Maya literature. It is interesting to mention however, that dog remains in other sites do not present anthropogenic modifications; therefore, the form of preparing dogs for their consumption could be one that does not require deep cuts that would leave marks on the bones.

The gray fox (*Urocyon cinereoargenteus*) inhabits thick forests and brush lands, and is a common species that inhabits all of North America (Hall 1981:943-944). It also adapts well to disturbed areas including agricultural land (Reid 1997:255). Gray fox remains have been identified as food remains in some archaeological deposits, including Cozumel Island and Seibal, and the Petén and Petexbatún areas (Hamblin 1984; Pohl 1990; Emery 2010; Teeter 2001). One skull fragment was recovered from *Operación* 114 at Chinikihá.

The geographical range of the jaguar (*Panthera onca*) includes a variety of habitats, from rain forests to grasslands (Emmons and Feer 1997). In North America, it can be found from Arizona to Panama, along the west and east mountain ranges; in southern México, it can be found in Chiapas and the Yucatán Peninsula, in Central America, it is found everywhere (Hall 1981:1039). Jaguars are opportunistic carnivores and are the only natural predator of deer and peccaries. The aggressive nature of this animal was probably the characteristic that motivated warriors to wear jaguar heads, skins, paws or other parts as a badge of honour (Saunders 1994: 107; Stone and Zender 2011:83). Unfortunately, many of these artefacts do not survive and we therefore do not know how extensive this practice was; however, representations of jaguar skins in pictorial material, suggest that these items were very common. Osteological remains from jaguars, are almost exclusively present in contexts associated with the elite, as it was a conspicuous sign of wealth, probably obtained as tribute (Stone and Zender 2011:83). Furthermore, the elite contexts where jaguar remains have been found are usually ritual contexts and

imply a non-food use (Emery 2007b:59). In Chinikihá, there was only one fragment of an ulna found in *Operación* 114 that was identified as jaguar. No cut marks or other taphonomical modifications were observed, thus it is difficult to make any suggestions about its use, as it could have been included in this deposit by non-human agents. However, it is interesting to note that jaguars' ulnae are used for making *Chak* scepters, or royal standards (Emery 1998, 2007b), both associated with the elite.

Representations of carnivores, especially dogs, are also very common in the Maya iconography and appear in a wide range of examples, including images of dogs on painted vessels, sculptured in stone, and as zoomorphic figurines (Shaw 1991).

Lagomorpha

There are two species of Lagomorpha represented in the Chinikihá assemblage, the forest rabbit (*Sylvilagus brasiliensis*) and the cottontail (*Sylvilagus floridanus*). The forest rabbit is found in the edges of forests, clearings and secondary growth in tropical lowlands, while the cottontail is more common in the arid highlands and savannas (Reid 1997:251). Although rabbits are small, they are heavily targeted for their meat and fur, thus, it would be expected that high percentages of rabbit remains would be found in the archaeological record.

The rabbit is usually associated with the Moon deities, and with the underworld and wet environments (Stone and Zender 2009:85). Iconographic representations of rabbits are less numerous than those of the deer or jaguar, but just like these two animals, rabbits are related to the elite. Archaeologically, the association between rabbits and the elite is reflected in contexts where rabbit remains are recovered from deposits connected to the elite (Emery 2007a:61). Rabbits are present at Seibal, Tikal, Cozumel Island, and in the Petén and Petexbatún regions (Emery 2010; Hamblin 1984; Moholy-Nagy 1997; Pohl 1990). Despite being well represented at some of these sites, quantities of rabbit remains seem to be relatively low during the Late Classic period. This is interesting as rabbits were probably a very numerous resource, and yet, rabbit remains are usually scarce in the archaeological record. Their low frequency may be due to several factors, including the fact that rabbit bones are small and could be more affected by post-depositional influences, such as carnivore gnawing, and/or differential preservation. Rabbits, along with other smaller species such as armadillo and small rodents, are more common in the savannah, and their presence outside this ecological niche, could represent their importation to the lowlands (Emery 2007a:57). In the Chinikihá assemblage, rabbit remains included one femur of *Sylvilagus brasiliensis*, one innominate of

Sylvilagus floridanus; and three femora, one innominate, and one hemi-mandible which were identified only as *Sylvilagus* sp.

Edentata

The only species identified within this Order was the nine-banded long-nosed armadillo (*Dasypus novemcinctus*), an animal that is common in the southern part of México and is present all over Chiapas. Armadillos prefer to live in secondary habitats, including grasslands (Emmons and Feer 1997:39), and the margins of *milpas*. Archaeologically, the bones of this species usually appear in low numbers at different sites, such as in Late Classic Seibal (Pohl 1990:150, Table 1). However, armadillo dermal plaques, or scutes, are more regularly found, especially in ritual assemblages such as burials, as seen in Caracol (Teeter 2001:369). In Chinikihá, only one tibia was recovered from an armadillo from *Operación* 114. No signs of modification were observed, thus, its use as food cannot be confirmed, although it is well known that the Maya nowadays eat armadillo that they capture with the aid of traps in their *milpas*.

Rodentia

In the Chinikihá assemblage, there were two specimens identified within this order, agouti (*Dasyprocta punctata*) and one specimen identified as a rodent. Agoutis are cheek-teeth hypsodont animals that are terrestrial, but enter water readily, generally living in burrows. The geographical distribution of the agouti extends to Central America, until Panamá, and is present in all of the lowlands in Chiapas, where it shares habitats with the other group forming this family, the pacas (*Cuniculus paca*) (Hall 1981:858). The agouti is commonly used as food (Emery 2007b); however, it usually appears in low frequencies in archaeological contexts, with few examples reported from few sites including Piedras Negras (Emery 2007b), Caracol (Teeter 2001), and Lagartero (Koželsky 2005). A single agouti femur was found in *Operación* 114.

Perissodactyla

Baird's tapir (*Tapirus bairdii*) is commonly found from Veracruz to Panamá (Hall 1981:1075). Although tapirs are big animals and yield a lot of meat (more than 150kg), tapir remains are not particularly frequent in the archaeological record, appearing in very low frequencies at Caracol and the Petexbatún region, usually restricted to ritual deposits (Emery 2004c, 2010; Teeter 2001). Specimens recovered from a trash midden at Lagartero (Koželsky 2005), and several fragments recovered from the Postclassic site of Laguna de On (Masson 1999:117) suggest that this species was consumed in ceremonial rites or feasts. In the Chinikihá assemblage, only one modified rib fragment was found at *Operación* 114; it displays use-wear marks from being used as some sort of tool, possibly as an *alisador* or *pulidor*, this is, a polishing tool. With one single specimen, it is impossible to know if tapir was consumed locally or if the rib arrived as raw material or already worked to Chinikihá.

Testudines

Two types of turtle have been previously identified at Chinikihá, the mud turtle (*Kinosternon* sp.) and the river turtle (*Dermatemys mawii*) (Montero 2008). In addition to deer meat, the Maya elite also seem to have favoured turtle for the tenderness and white colour of the meat (Álvarez and Ocaña 1994; Emery 2007b:60). Once the turtle meat was consumed, its carapace was used both for utilitarian purposes, such as the manufacture of ornaments, and for ritual purposes, such as the creation of drums (Emery 2007b:59). Examples of sites where turtle remains are frequent include Piedras Negras (Emery 2001, 2007b), and Palenque (Zúñiga 2000), both sites considered to have had access to riverine resources. At Chinikihá, five turtle plaques were found, mostly from the plastron; these were identified as *Dermatemys mawii* and *Kinosternon* sp. All five fragments were polished and at least four of them contained carved glyphs on their anterior facet. No other skeletal element was found from the turtle skeleton that could suggest that these turtles were first eaten and then the plaques worked. This contrasts drastically with the faunal assemblage from nearby Palenque, where the majority of turtle remains—including five species— are represented by postcranial elements and plaques, suggesting their importance as food and as raw material (Nieto-Calleja 2005; Zúñiga 2000). Therefore, for Chinikihá, the presence of the carved plaques in the assemblage suggests that they arrived as raw material ready to be carved, or that they were worked at Chinikihá, where they may possibly have had a use-life, following which they were discarded, when broken. It is possible though that there is a change through time in the use of turtles as a resource, from their use as a dietary component during the early Classic period, to a more restricted use, in a non-subsistence role, during the Terminal Classic period. This change, however, may alternatively be related to a change in the methods of preparation (Emery 2010:134).

Shell remains

Invertebrates were an important resource among the Maya in the past, used as food, for ritual uses, and for the manufacture of tools; they continue to be utilised by the Maya in the present day. A wide variety of molluscs exist in the region, but the most common in archaeological assemblages are the freshwater

Figures 27 and 28. 'La Cueva del Shote', restaurant in Palenque, Chiapas (left) where a snack made of jute snails (Pachychilus sp.) cooked with momo leaves (Piper spp.) is still served nowadays (right) (Photographs by Coral Montero López).

bivalves and gastropods (Emery 1986). Evidence from such assemblages suggests that the most common invertebrate in the diet was *jute* (*Pachychilus* sp.), including two sub-species (*P. indiorum* and *P. glaphyrus*) (Healy *et al.* 1990). In the present day, *jute* is regarded as a poor man's food (Healy *et al.* 1990) and are considered a non-preferential resource (Nations 1979), eaten primarily in periods of protein scarcity. This gastropod seems to have been important as a supplementary food source when there was not enough animal protein available, especially for children and women (Nations 1979:569). During my short stay in the town of Palenque in 2009 I observed the preparation of a snack made of *jute* snails cooked in water with *momo* (*Piper* spp.) leaves. This 'soup' was served in a small restaurant, as a free snack for people buying a drink (see Figures 27 and 28). The preference of consuming *jute* and other shells in soups was also observed by other researchers in Belize (Healy *et al.* 1990; Powis 2004), suggesting a long Pan-Maya tradition. It is possible that the techniques of preparation may not have changed since pre-Hispanic times.

Remains of *Pachychilus* sp. or *jute*, as they are known in Spanish, have been identified in diverse contexts ranging from domestic to ritual deposits (Halperin *et al.* 2003; Healy *et al.* 1990). Its ubiquity across a diversity of sites suggests that it was highly regarded by the Maya not only for its caloric contribution, but for other functions. Among the modern Lacandón Maya, the shell is ground and turned into powdered lime that is then used to process corn (Nations 1979). *Jute* and other shells are symbolically related to the concepts of fertility and the underworld (Halperin *et al.* 2003), thus, their presence in caves and other ritual deposits is not uncommon.

During the Late Classic period, access to this and other riverine resources such as turtles was probably restricted to the high class, as *jute* shell remains are common in elite contexts, including palaces, and ritual deposits such as votive caches, and burials (Emery 2007b:60; Halperin *et al.* 2003). The most notable characteristic of *jute* shells in ritual contexts is that they are complete, with no apex removal, and they display no evidence of being cooked (Halperin *et al.* 2003). Such remains from ritual contexts are in contrast with contexts where massive amounts of *jute* shells have been identified with other faunal remains, as well as well-made ceramics and lithics, these remains have been identified as the products of human consumption as a result of feasting (Stanchly and Iannone 1997; Halperin *et al.* 2003:214). It is common to find these deposits in construction fill or in middens associated with ceremonial structures (Healy *et al.* 1990).

At Chinikihá, large quantities of *jute* were recovered from several contexts including *Operaciones* 110, 111, 114 and 115 (see Table 12). Shells of different size were retrieved from this assemblage, which, according to some authors, can be useful in differentiating between the two sub-species (Solís 2011). Quantity and weight were noted, but it was not possible to identify every specimen to species due to their fragmentary state or the absence of diagnostic parts; thus, they were grouped under the generic *Pachychilus* sp. classification. Shell remains that were the result of consumption were not identified individually, but were counted by location and grouped by genus level, so limited information is available on the exploitation of freshwater molluscs. Nevertheless, some observations were made. Most of these shells displayed human modification expressed by removal of the apex or spire. This suggests the two species served dietary purposes and supports data previously published for other archaeological sites (Halperin *et al.* 2003; Healy *et al.* 1990; Moholy-Nagy 1978). Once the apex is removed the molluscs need to be cooked or boiled; if boiled for long time, it is also possible to remove the meat without having to cut the apex (Emery 2010:127). It seems that the preferred form of preparing the molluscs for consumption involves both cutting the spire and boiling. These two methods are still observed nowadays, as recorded by this author in the town of Palenque, and in modern Guatemala (Halperin *et al.* 2003:215).

Other molluscs commonly represented in Maya sites include apple snails (*Pomacea flagellata*), a large snail rich in protein (Covich 1983; Moholy-Nagy 1978), and two bivalves (*Nephronaias* sp. and *Psoronaias* sp.) (Powis 2004). Although there are few reports about the dietary consumption of apple snails this species along with the bivalves were most commonly used to manufacture ornaments (Moholy-Nagy 1978). Worked shell in Chinikihá appears generally in the form of pendants and beads and is discussed in the next section.

Origin of fauna by environmental zone

From the previous descriptions, it is possible to observe that some taxa exclusively specific environments, such as the freshwater molluscs which appear only in riverine environments. Other species however, can be found in several environmental zones, but usually have a predilection for one or two environments. Following Emery (2010), microenvironmental zones around Chinikihá were identified, and the different species present in the Chinikihá assemblage were grouped according to the main habitat they inhabit. These are: riverine or lacustrine and their associated shorelines, perennial swamps, canopy forest, *guamil* or high bush, *milpa* or agricultural land, and residential (Table 18). It is possible to observe that faunal resources were obtained from these seven habitats, and were acquired in different proportions. Because *jute* remains are very numerous, riverine/lacustrine resources account for 68.48% of the whole sample.

It was considered that the *milpa* was the primary habitat of the white-tailed deer, and as such this zone contained the second greatest abundance of faunal resources (29.80%), followed by the residential microenvironment (1.13%). The zone with the most diversity is the *guamil* (Emery 2010:81*)*, also known as *acahual* in the Yucatán area. This is a disturbed zone that is the preferred setting for a variety of animals, including the gray fox (*Urocyon cinereoargenteus*), raccoon (*Procyon lotor*), cottontail (*Sylvilagus floridanus*), collared peccary (*Pecari tajacu*), and agouti (*Dasyprocta punctata*), all of which

Habitat	Taxon	NISP	%NISP
Riverine/Lacustrine	*Pachychilus* sp.	2295	68.12
	Nephronaias sp.	12	0.36
Sub-total		2307	68.48
Shorelines		1	
	Pomacea flagellata		0.03
	Kinosternon sp.	1	0.03
	Dermatemys mawii	1	0.03
Sub-total		3	0.09
Perennial swamps	*Mazama* sp.	1	0.03
	Tapirus bairdii	1	0.03
Sub-total		2	0.06
Canopy forest or *majahual*	*Pecari tajacu*	2	0.06
	Dasyprocta punctata	1	0.03
	Felidae	1	0.03
	Sylvilagus floridanus	1	0.03
	Panthera onca	1	0.03
Sub-total		6	0.18
Guamil or *acahual*	*Urocyon cinereoargenteus*	1	0.03
	Dasypus novemcinctus	1	0.03
	Sylvilagus sp.	5	0.15
	Sylvilagus brasiliensis	1	0.03
Sub-total		8	0.24
Milpa	*Odocoileus virginianus*	1004	29.80
	Artiodactyla	1	0.03
Sub-total		1005	29.83
Residential	*Canis lupus familiaris*	38	1.13
Sub-total		38	1.13
Total		**3369**	**100.00**

Table 18. Distribution by habitat of faunal resources present in the Chinikihá assemblage.

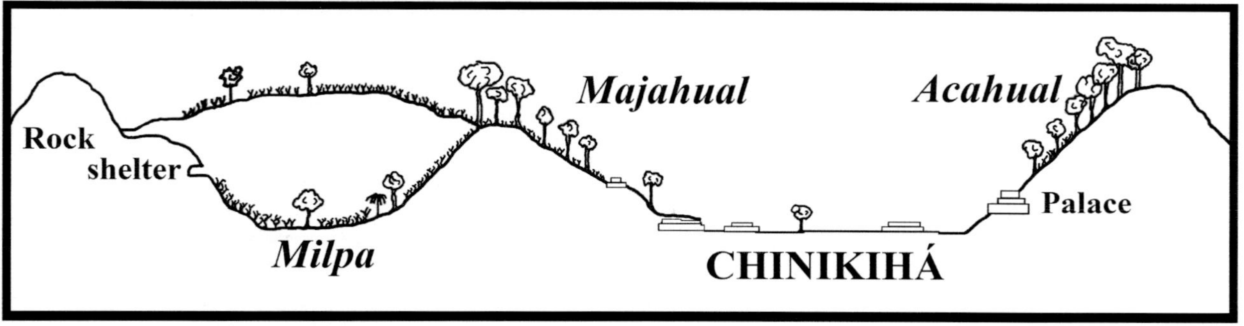

Figure 29. Distribution of environmental zones around Chinikihá (modified from
Trabanino 2012:231, Figure 7.3, reproduced with permission).

are present in this sample, or have been previously identified at Chinikihá (Montero 2008). Although white-tailed deer (*Odocoileus virginianus*) can be found in the *guamil*, its presence in farming lands (*milpa*) is important because it is considered a crop pest (Emery 2010:82).

The presence of the brocket deer (*Mazama* sp.) and forest rabbit (*Sylvilagus brasiliensis*) remains in the assemblage indicate that some animals were acquired from the deeper parts of dense forests; although brocket deer also likes to wander around perennial swamps, and can be attracted to the *milpa*. The representation of deep rain forest animals is supported by the presence of macrobotanical remains identified from the midden, such as *palo mora* (*Machura tinctoria*), a tree valued for its wood (Trabanino 2008). It is interesting to mention that Felipe Trabanino (2012) also identified the presence of exotic plants such as *granadilla* (*Passiflora* sp.) and datura (*Datura stramonium*), species that are commonly used as drugs and are one of the archaeological signatures of a feasting events (Hayden 2001:40).

Other resources that may have been acquired from the immediate vicinity include freshwater snails and reptiles, including apple snail (*Pomeacea flagellata*) and mud turtles (*Kinosternon* sp.), which inhabit ponds and rivers in the wetlands (Carr and Fradkin 2008). Finally, the tapir (*Tapirus bairdii*) is the only animal present in this sample that definitely comes from swampy areas. Nowadays, the tapir is not common in Chiapas, but probably in the past, it was present all over the state (Ceballos and Oliva 2005:61, Figure. 29), making it locally available.

The presence of species from different environmental zones informs us about the exploitation patterns established by the inhabitants of Chinikihá (Figure 29). According to Trabanino (2012), the people from Chinikihá may have exploited the zones surrounding the settlement in order to obtain the plants and animals that they required for food, housing, ceremonies and other uses.

This author also suggests that it is possible that the Maya from Chinikihá, may have managed and transformed the environments, by re-forestation and regeneration (Trabanino 2012:226). A similar management of land has been proposed for other sites during the Late Classic period, including Copán (Fedick 2010).

Temporal and geographic variation in faunal consumption

The faunal composition at Chinikihá points towards a local exploitation, with few animals being brought from more distant areas. This is similar to the exploitation pattern seen in many Maya sites, with differing faunal compositions occurring between sites on the coast and inland. Nevertheless, it is important to note that the distribution of faunal resources is not homogeneous for all sites and several changes through time are also identifiable. During the Preclassic period, a very local pattern of exploitation is seen (Götz 2008; Pohl 1985b:109), especially focusing on those species from the *milpa* and residential zones. This is what some authors have identified as 'garden hunting' (Ford 1991). During the Preclassic period, the presence of dog and deer in inland sites is relatively high (Wing 1981), while in riverine and coastal sites, turtle and fish are more common (Carr and Fradkin 2008; Emery 2010; Masson 2004a; Wing and Scuder 1991). For example, in Preclassic Cerros there was a marked preference for resources from nearby swampy areas (Carr and Fradkin 2008:149), while is the opposite in the Petexbatún area (Emery 2010:83), despite the fact that a swamp environment was as accessible there as in Cerros. What is interesting here is that Carr and Fradkin (2008:149) suggest that the composition of the faunal assemblage observed in Cerros is a reflection of the farming practices that would focus on the high-grounds during the wet season and in the pockets of moisture around the swamps in the dry season. Furthermore, these authors implied that the Maya farmers may have been also in charge of the animal acquisition (Carr and Fradkin 2008).

Towards the end of the Preclassic period, and probably as a consequence of environmental changes that put stress on local resources, several sites started to expand their hunting areas and include larger animals, a tendency that would prevail during the Classic period (Shaw 1991:92). Local exploitation seems to be the norm during the Early phases of the Classic period (McKillop 1984:32). However, faunal exploitation patterns may have begun to transform during this period, changing from the procurement of resources at a primarily domestic level to the development of a regional exchange system, resulting in the presence of remains from larger animals in the Classic period, probably a reflection of the control over faunal resources maintained by the elite (Shaw 1999).

During the Late/Terminal Classic period, favoured species included turtle, deer, peccary, and in lesser proportions, dog, armadillo, agouti, paca, and rabbit; freshwater resources are common in riverine or sites near lakes, such as Trinidad. Emery and Thornton (2008) analysed the materials from Motul de San José, and concluded that large mammals are more often associated with elite contexts during this period. White-tailed deer seems to have been the preferred species during the Late Classic period at various sites, including the Petexbatún region (Emery 2010), the Pasion River region (Pohl 1990), Copán (Collins 2002), and Tikal (Pohl 1990).

Small fauna such as dog, armadillo, rabbit, peccary, and other small/medium sized animals are more common during the Preclassic and Postclassic (Pohl 1976, 1985b:110). Freshwater molluscs are more common in Preclassic sites (Pohl 1985b:109), but are consistently present throughout the Classic period in riverine sites such as in the Petexbatún area (Emery 2010:134). Fish in general does not appear to have been a significant resource until the Postclassic (Emery 1997:46), and the presence of fish during the Classic period seems to be restricted to elite or ritual contexts (McKillop and Winemiller 2004). However, the overall lack of fine screening or wet sieving refuse deposits in most Late Classic sites may have obscured the ubiquity of ichthyic remains (Freiwald 2010). A recent study of the fish remains from a trash midden from Group IV in Palenque (Varela 2019) revealed that fish was indeed one of the most important resources to have been exploited by the Maya, but had not been identified in the past due lack of fine sieving (see Zúñiga 2000).

Around Chinikihá, fauna has been studied at Palenque, Yaxchilán, Piedras Negras and Toniná. In the Palace at Palenque, a series of middens and construction fills with fauna remains have been excavated. Again, a pattern of exploitation of local species has been observed, with a high quantity of turtle, fish and *jute* (Olivera 1997;

Valentín 2007). Interestingly, the zooarchaeological analysis of the materials present in the Palace concluded that the most abundant animals were turtle (*Dermatemys mawii*), a variety of freshwater fish and molluscs (Zúñiga 2000). Mammals including white-tailed deer and domestic dog were in very small proportions, suggesting that in Palenque, the exploitation of fauna was conducted largely at a local level. Nieto-Calleja (2005) identified the presence of turtle as part of a possible feast associated with a termination ritual for one of the structures in the Palace. The preference for freshwater resources seen at Palenque may reflect a local partiality or may alternatively be a consequence of the 'modifications to the immediate environment surrounding Palenque, which may have affected the consumption of mammals' (López 2006:7).

Exploitation of local resources is also seen at Yaxchilán, where the dominant species is white-tailed deer, but freshwater resources are also common, especially turtle plaques used for ritual purposes (Soto 1998, Soto and Polaco 1994). The largest concentration of materials was recovered from construction fills, where most of the bone assemblage showed signs of weathering and exposure to the environment before being finally deposited. In addition to deer and turtle, dog and brocket deer are also present. Deer and dog remains present a high frequency of cut marks and other processing modifications that were the result of human consumption and the manufacturing of tools (Soto 1998:82).

At the site of Toniná, several domestic contexts provide information about faunal exploitation outside the ceremonial centres. Álvarez and colleagues (1990) identified that the dominant species were deer and dog, and in minor proportions rabbit, armadillo and turkey were present. Exotic species were also found, including shark teeth, ray spines and marine shell. These authors concluded that white-tailed deer must have been the preferred animal for all social classes, and the presence of coastal materials suggest that lower classes also had access to exotic goods.

Analysis by location: results

As osteological material was recovered from different contexts, including those associated with a variety of structures, ranging from ceremonial to residential structures, each context is described separately. A summary of NISP and MNI for all *Operaciones* is presented in Table 7.3. In the next paragraphs, I discuss each *Operación* individually, focusing exclusively on the mammal sub-sample.

Operación 110

In this context, a very high proportion of the material was very fragmented and identification to Species level

Taxon	NISP	%NISP	MNI	%MNI
medium/large mammal	119	92.25		
small/med mammal	4	3.10		
Canis lupus familiaris	1	0.78	1	25.00
Odocoileus virginianus	3	2.33	2	50.00
Sylvilagus sp.	1	0.78		
Homo sapiens	1	0.78	1	25.00
Total	**129**	**100.00**	**4**	**100.00**

Table 19. NISP and MNI calculations for *Operación* 110.

Taxon	NISP	%NISP	MNI	%MNI
medium/large mammal	55	96.49		
Odocoileus virginianus	1	1.75	1	100.00
Canis sp.	1	1.75		
Total	**57**	**100.00**	**1**	**100.00**

Table 20. NISP and MNI calculations for *Operación* 111.

Taxon	NISP	%NISP	MNI	%MNI
medium/large mammal	2	66.67		
Homo sapiens	1	33.33	1	100.00
Total	**3**	**100.00**	**1**	**100.00**

Table 21. NISP and MNI calculations for *Operación* 112.

Taxon	NISP	%NISP	MNI	%MNI
medium/large mammal	2	100.00		
Total	**2**	**100.00**		

Table 22. NISP and MNI calculations for *Operación* 115.

was only possible in few instances. More than 95%NISP of the bones were too fragmented to identify the species (Table 19), and were therefore only identified to either medium/large mammal (92.25%NISP; n = 119), or small/medium mammal (3.10%NISP; n = 4). Species identified in *Operación* 110 include deer (2.33%NISP; n = 3), dog (0.78%NISP; n = 1), and rabbit (0.78%NISP; n = 1). One human fragment (phalange) was also recovered (0.78%NISP). White-tailed deer was the most numerous in terms of both NISP and MNI, comprising half the amount of the individuals (50%, n = 2). It is probably though, that the small/medium mammal fragments are from dog or other similar-sized animal, and the medium/large mammal fragments are from deer, thus potentially increasing the percentages for these species.

It can be assumed, based on the location of this context, that it is domestic debris used as construction fill. The material also exhibits different stages of weathering and some bones have carnivore chewing marks that indicate that these materials were exposed for some time, and may have been brought from elsewhere (Pendergast 2004:241) as a result of cleaning activities (Schiffer 1987:59). Therefore, this context may represent a secondary deposit (Pendergast 2004), or even tertiary deposition (Hutson *et al.* 2007:453).

Operaciones 111, 112, and 115

These three *Operaciones* are located in the North Structure Complex, and are therefore presented together. The results from *Operación* 111 identified a large proportion of fragments only as medium/large mammal (96.49%NISP, n = 55), with only two specimens identified to a more narrow classification, including one white-tailed deer, and one identified as a canid (1.75%NISP respectively) (Table 20). The material from *Operación* 111 has no cut marks or other human modifications, and exhibits a range of different weathering stages, making it hard to identify whether it was the result of domestic activities.

However, due to the variability present in the material, it is suggested here that *Operación* 111 may be part of a construction fill.

Very little material was retrieved from *Operación* 112 (NISP = 3), with two fragments identified as medium/large mammal (66.67%NISP) and one human fragment (33.33%NISP) (Table 21). The fragments identified from *Operación* 112 may be part of the construction fill used for the burials, and it is possible that the fragment of human bone may be from a disturbed burial located in the surrounding area.

Lastly, only two fragments were recovered from *Operación* 115, and they were identified as medium/large mammal (Table 22). Neither bone fragment has cut marks, one is very eroded and the other is not. The low frequency of faunal remains recovered from this *Operación* prevents further analysis.

Operación 114

Operación 114 represents the largest assemblage analysed in this study, with 2037 fragments and 64 individuals; however, almost half of the material was only identified as medium/large mammals (46.29%) and small/medium mammals (2.60%). From the identified species, white-tailed deer (*Odocoileus virginianus*) is the most common species (46.24%NISP), and has an MNI of 48. Human remains (*Homo sapiens*) are the second most common taxa representing 2.85% of NISP and resulted in a MNI of seven. Domestic

Taxon	NISP	%NISP	MNI	%MNI
medium/large mammal	943	46.29		0.00
small medium mammal	53	2.60		0.00
Dasypus novemcinctus	1	0.05	1	1.56
Carnivora	2	0.10		0.00
Canis sp.	2	0.10		0.00
Canis lupus familiaris	22	1.08	2	3.13
Urocyon cinereoargenteus	1	0.05	1	1.56
Felidae	1	0.05		0.00
Panthera onca	1	0.05	1	1.56
Artiodactyla	1	0.05		0.00
Mazama sp.	1	0.05		0.00
Odocoileus virginianus	942	46.24	48	75.00
Pecari tajacu	2	0.10	1	1.56
Dasyprocta punctata	1	0.05	1	1.56
Sylvilagus sp.	4	0.20		0.00
Sylvilagus brasiliensis	1	0.05	1	1.56
Sylvilagus floridanus	1	0.05	1	1.56
Homo sapiens	58	2.85	7	10.94
Total	**2037**	**53.71**	**64**	**100.00**

Table 23. NISP and MNI calculations for *Operación* 114.

Taxon	NISP	%NISP	MNI	%MNI
medium/large mammal	97	54.80		
small/med mammal	10	5.65		
Carnivora	2	1.13		
Canis lupus familiaris	15	8.47	4	66.67
Odocoileus virginianus	53	29.94	2	33.33
Total	**177**	**100.00**	**6**	**100.00**

Table 24. NISP and MNI calculations for *Operación* 201.

Taxon	NISP	%NISP	MNI	%MNI
medium/large mammal	4	44.44		
Odocoileus virginianus	5	55.56	1	100.00
Total	**9**	**100.00**	**1**	**100.00**

Table 25. NISP and MNI calculations for *Operación* 202.

dog (*Canis lupus familiaris*) remains made up 1.08% of NISP and a MNI of two. All other species are present in very low percentages, and include two types of rabbit (*Sylvilagus brasiliensis* and *Sylvilagus floridanus*), gray fox (*Urocyon cinereoargenteus*), jaguar (*Panthera onca*), armadillo (*Dasypus novemcinctus*), agouti (*Dasyprocta punctata*), brocket deer (*Mazama* sp.), and peccary (*Pecari tajacu*), among other material that was identified to Family level (Table 23).

Some of the material displays carnivore, rodent and insect modifications, as well as different stages of weathering, and other natural modifications. Anthropogenic modifications are also present and include cut marks and burning. *Operación* 114 has been regarded as a context that is unique for many reasons; therefore, the detailed analysis of its material will be presented separately in Chapter eight.

Operación 201 (Chancalá)

It is important to note that this location was looted during the 2008 fieldwork (Liendo 2009b) and it was not possible to continue with the excavation; therefore, the results that are presented here may not represent the total material that was originally deposited. Nevertheless, this context is still the second largest after *Operación* 114, in terms of NISP and MNI, and we

can only guess how large this sample may have been, had it been possible to collect all the material. *Operación* 201 has been identified as a possible trash midden, because the context contains abundant ceramic, lithic and faunal fragments (Liendo 2009b:307). This interpretation is supported by the presence of faunal (carnivore chewing) and anthropogenic modifications (cut marks and burning), and the fact that the bone material displays different stages of weathering. Furthermore, it is possible that this midden reflects the activities that were carried out in the surrounding buildings, and, may therefore be a primary deposit (Liendo 2009b:311).

The majority of the material from *Operación* 201 was only identified as medium/large mammal (54.80%, n = 97). From those identified to species, deer is the most abundant (29.94%NISP, n = 53), with an MNI of two individuals. Dog remains are less numerous (8.47%NISP, n = 15), but represent four individuals. The remaining material includes carnivore (1.13%NISP, n = 2), and small/medium mammal remains (5.65%NISP, n = 10) (Table 24).

Operación 202 (San Juan Chancalaíto)

This locus was similar to *Operación* 201. It had very little material, most of which was identified as deer (55.56%NISP, n = 5) and represented one individual, the remaining material was identified as medium/large mammal (44.44%NISP, n = 4) (Table 25). Therefore, it is possible then that all the material from *Operación* 202 could potentially be deer (*sensus* Gautier 1987). All the remains were highly fragmented and eroded, and were chalky in texture, presenting damage caused by

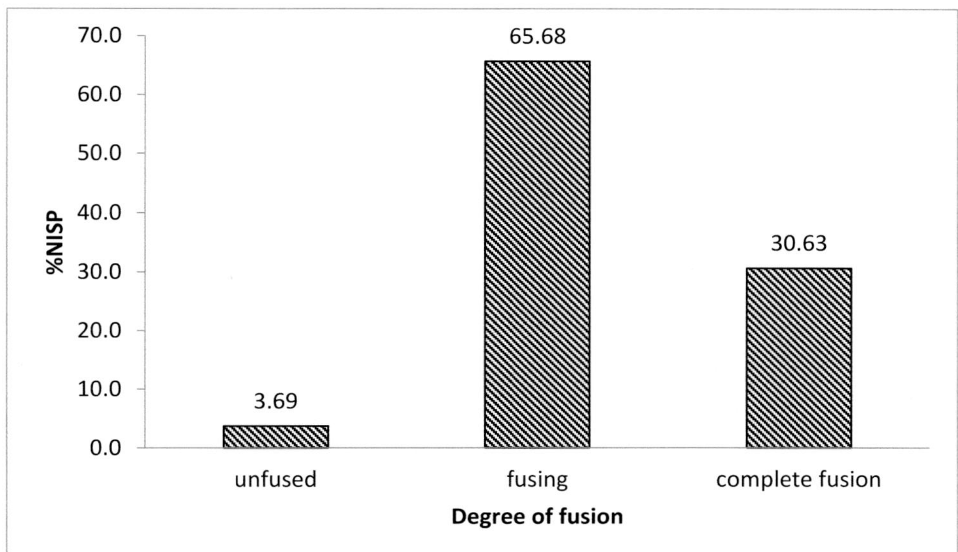

Figure 30. Degree of fusion present for all fauna (based on NISP).

moisture exposure, and indicating advanced stages of weathering; as such, it is suggested that this material could have been exposed for some time prior to its final deposit in this context. Because of this, it is considered likely that this material was exposed to the environment and redeposited in this context as a secondary deposit or fill.

Identification of age and sex

Age

Age profiles were generated based on methods discussed in Chapter four. An age interval was obtained only for identified species and resulted in 537 specimens that included dental and skeletal specimens, including white-tailed deer (*Odocoileus virginianus*), temazate (*Mazama* sp.), collared peccary (*Pecari tajacu*), domestic dog (*Canis lupus familiaris*), carnivore, and rabbit (*Sylvilagus* sp.). Age was identified in general by tooth eruption, wear patterns and by epiphyseal fusion. In some instances, it was only possible to identify a rough group category, but in other instances, due to the presence of a diagnostic trait, it was possible to assign a narrower specific age range (in months).

Identifying a specific age range was easier for some species than for others, depending on several factors, including the degree of fragmentation of the material and the availability of published studies to compare the sample with. As a result, the age range that could be most commonly identified for fragments from three categories, include the artiodactyls, the carnivores and the rabbits. Age groups were not identified for those specimens that were heavily fragmented or lacked a diagnostic element that would ensure a correct age group identification. Some species were only classifiable as young or adult, depending on the degree of postcranial fusion, including: armadillo (*Dasypus novemcinctus*), agouti (*Dasyprocta punctata*), jaguar (*Panthera onca*), and two particular types of rabbit (*Sylvilagus brasiliensis* and *Sylvilagus floridanus*). Finally, the ages for one specimen identified as Felidae and one identified as gray fox (*Urocyon cinereoargenteus*) were not calculated, as they were too fragmentary.

There were no complete animals present in any of the contexts analysed with most of the material representing disarticulated or semi-disarticulated remains. One of the problems with identifying age from disarticulated remains is that age based on early fusion and tooth eruption is the earliest age represented by an individual element, although the actual age of the animal could be greater. The dog remains exemplified this. At least four elements were identified as belonging to juveniles, mostly based on the eruption of a permanent tooth in the mandible, and all falling within the age bracket of 4-6 months. There was one mandible with a missing permanent premolar that suggests an age of at least 4 months, but it is possible that this individual may also present early fusing elements in the postcranial skeleton, making its true age around one year old.

Three major categories were created: complete unfused, fusing (which includes those with a degree of fusing in both early and late epiphyses), and complete fusion (Figure 30). The results indicate that the majority of the material presents some degree of fusion, in the early, late or both epiphyses (65.68%), followed by those with a complete fusion (30.63%), stressing the preference for young adults and adults in their prime age. Very small percentages (3.69%) of the faunal remains analysed were completely unfused or had deciduous teeth (suggesting juvenile animals).

These results broadly indicate the dominance of animals with some degree of epiphyseal fusion and/or presence of permanent dentition. In medium/large animals such as deer, these characteristics would be identified at around one year of age or older. In some of the smaller species, this degree of development can be reached at around four months of age, as is the case with dogs. Also, the period of rapid growth is reached at this age, and the maximum weight and size is reached (Davis 1987:39).

With species where a more specific age could be identified, specimens were classified in five general categories: juvenile, immature, immature+, sub-adult, and adult (Reitz and Wing 1999). A large proportion (41.94%; n = 229) of all the fauna was identified as immature, followed by the adults with 31.14% (n = 170), sub-adults (12.82%, n = 70) and juveniles (3.66%, n = 20). Another 10.44% (n = 57) of specimens were identified as immature+ and kept as an independent category, and includes those specimens that could be placed either in the sub-adult or adult age groups. Table 26 summarises these results.

Of the species for which age could be determined, deer was the only category containing specimens from all age groups, though most were immature (n = 229), or adult (n = 151). Sub-adults and juveniles were also present, but in lower proportions. The youngest fawn was two months old while the oldest deer was 7.5 years of age, with the majority of deer older than 12 months.

Figure 31 shows the percentages of each age range per species in months. It is possible to observe that for the deer, the majority were between 12 and 29 months (61.46%, n = 295), and 29-35 months of age (24.79%, n = 119), while 7.29% (n = 35) of deer were under 12 months and 6.46% (n = 31) were older than 35 months of age.

The other two artiodactyls, the brocket deer (*Mazama* sp.) and the collared peccary (*Pecari tajacu*), were both identified as adults, while the rabbit (*Sylvilagus* sp.) and canid (*Canis* sp.) were both younger than 12 months. For the dog, age was only identified in two broad categories, juveniles, of between 4 and 5 months (44.44%, n = 4) and adults, older than 12 months (55.56%, n = 5). 'Adult' in this case is a very broad category and could include individuals from one year up to 10-15 years of age. Nevertheless, no dog remains showed pathologies or any other modifications related to older ages, thus, there are no dogs in the old adult category, suggesting that dogs were killed primarily during the first year. This fact coincides with the analysis of dog remains from Preclassic Cuello deposits where Clutton-Brock and Hammond (1994) noticed that dogs were raised and killed at the end of their first year of life. Other small mammals, including rabbits, may have been also killed upon reaching maturity.

Taxon	Juvenile	%	Immature	%	Immature+	%	Sub-adult	%	Adult	%	n/a	%	Total	%
Odocoileus virginianus	14	70.00	229	100.00	57	100.00	70	100.00	151	88.82	483	93.60	1004	94.54
Mazama sp.									1	0.59			1	0.09
Pecari tajacu									2	1.18			2	0.19
Carnivora									2	1.18	2	0.39	4	0.38
Canis sp.	1	5.00									2	0.39	3	0.28
Canis lupus familiaris	4	20.00							5	2.94	29	5.62	38	3.58
Sylvilagus sp.	1	5.00							6	3.53			7	0.66
Dasypus novemcinctus									1	0.59			1	0.09
Dasyprocta punctate									1	0.59			1	0.09
Panthera onca									1	0.59			1	0.09
Total	20	100.00	229	100.00	57	100.00	70	100.00	170	100.00	516	100.00	1062	100.00

Table 26. Age categories for identified fauna from all *Operaciones*.

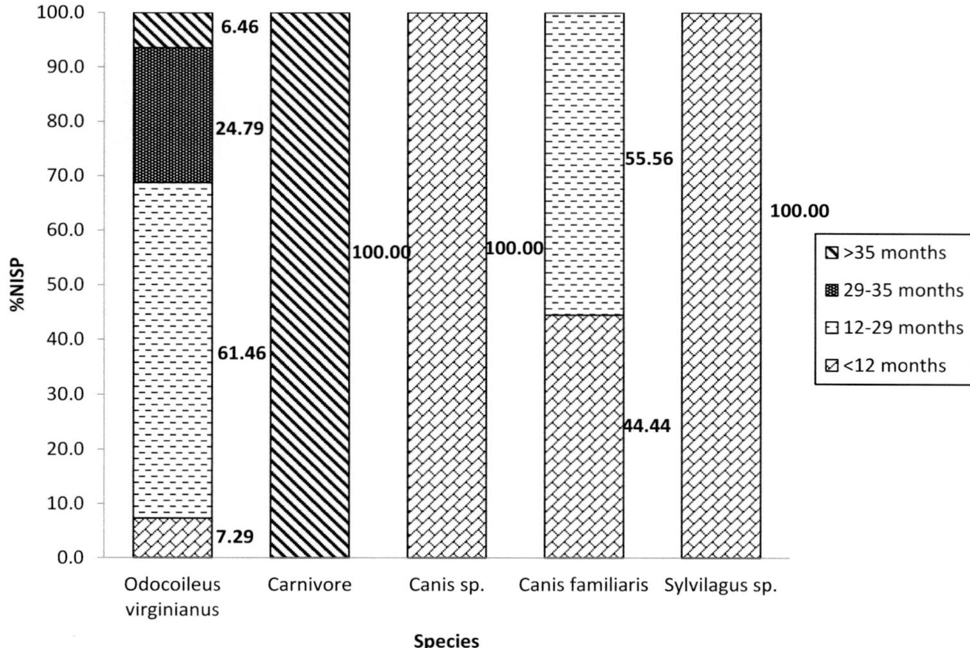

Figure 31. Distribution of species with an age identification in months (%NISP represent the total of each identified species).

When all the age data for Chinikihá are combined, the general age distribution for the fauna indicates that there were very few juveniles or old adults. There appears to have been a marked preference for young adults, or animals in their prime age. Since the natural pattern of mortality in most animals includes a high frequency of young and old adults known as an attritional profile, the overabundance of young adults in this sample suggest the targeting of individuals by age, and perhaps by sex (see below) (Steele 2003; Stiner 1990:317).

Loss of bones from very young animals may be due to carnivore activity or post-depositional destructive attrition, thus creating a bias towards adult animals (Klein and Cruz-Uribe 1984; Steele 1990:421). However, porous and small bones such as tarsals and carpals, were observed in the assemblage, indicating that all material had the same chances of survival and therefore, the selection of young adults represents the intentional targeting of this specific age group.

Sex

It has been suggested that the stag was a symbolic animal to the Maya associated with the *Cuch* ceremony (Pohl 1981). As a key ritual component, deer is linked to agriculture, sun, rain, prosperity, and the cyclical nature of time (Brown and Gerstle 2002). Hence, there is some significance attached to the identification of sex for deer remains. In Chinikihá, the sex was identified for 13 specimens, including two antlers, and 11 post-cranial fragments. In white-tailed deer, only male animals grow antlers, and as such, the two antler fragments represent two adult males, and the five post-cranial fragments can also be attributed to males. Stags therefore account for 54% (NISP = 7) of the deer remains, and were all found in *Operación* 114. Six females deer (46%NISP) were identified, one from *Operación* 201 and five from *Operación* 114. However, the number of specimens identified by sex is too small to determine if there was a deliberate selection of stags. It is expected that in the future, measurements of specific bones, such as the tibia, will clarify prey selection by sex.

Taphonomic modifications

Degree of fragmentation and type of fracture

All the *Operaciones* yielded material that was fragmented to different degrees. In total, 93.24% of the material was fragmented, while the other 6.76% comprised complete skeletal elements, though skeletal elements were not present in every *Operación*, or in the same proportions. It can be seen in Table 27 that all the material present in *Operaciones* 110, 111, 112, and 115 was fragmented. *Operaciones* 114, 201, and 202 possessed both complete bones and fragmented material. Overall, *Operación* 114 yielded the most complete bones, however, these represented only a small percentage of the material from this deposit. The fact that in all *Operaciones* most, if not all, of the material is fragmented, indicates that these contexts reflect a behaviour where the processing of carcasses is the main goal, as opposed to depositing complete carcasses, such as in the case of burials. In the latter, dismemberment or disarticulation is rarely seen.

	Op. 110	Op. 111	Op. 112	Op. 114	Op. 115	Op. 201	Op. 202	Total
Fragments	129	57	3	1882	2	170	8	2251
% by row	5.73	2.53	0.13	83.61	0.09	7.55	0.36	100.00
% by column	100.00	100.00	100.00	92.39	100.00	96.05	88.89	93.25
% by total	5.34	2.36	0.12	77.96	0.08	7.04	0.33	93.25
Complete				155		7	1	163
% by row				95.09		4.29	0.61	100.00
% by column				7.61		3.95	11.11	6.75
% by total				**6.42**		**0.29**	**0.04**	**6.75**
Total	**129**	**57**	**3**	**2037**	**2**	**177**	**9**	**2414**

Table 27. Distribution of fragmented and complete bones for all *Operaciones*.

The state of preservation was registered for 1053 bones (Figure 32). Fragmented bones represented 17.47% (n = 184), and fragmentary remains made up 82.52% (n = 869). Overall and regardless of the species, the bones that were most commonly complete included vertebrae (20% cervical, n = 38; 13.04% thoracic, n = 24; 10.33%, n = 19), followed by the tarsal bones (10.87%, n = 20). All other complete bones present were represented in low percentages. On the other hand, bones that were most commonly encountered in a fragmented state included pelvis (14.96%, n = 130), lumbar vertebrae (13.92, n = 121) and scapulae (13.35%, n = 116).

It is worth noting the low frequencies of long bones, both in complete (17.93%) and incomplete (16.91%) states of preservation. Vertebrae were in general the most abundant element, complete (44.02%) and fragmented (38.43%). The general absence of long bones in Chinikihá has been already noted (Montero 2008), and these new results stress again the fact that long bones are not present in the context and may have been removed or deposited elsewhere. On the other hand, the high percentage of vertebrae indicates that whole torsos were being processed *in situ*. While some of the vertebrae are being discarded complete, others show the transverse processes broken, probably from sectioning the column into smaller portions or to remove the loins.

Few skull fragments are present as either complete or fragmented, including the mandible. However, when mandible were present, more were fragmented than complete; many were broken at the ramus or displayed a fracture at the inferior margin, probably created during the extraction of bone marrow (Klein and Cruz-Uribe 1984:71).

Finally, complete scapulae and pelvis bones were seldom present, partially because of the morphology of these two bones, but also as a direct result of the processing methods which were being used.

Taxon	NISP	MNI	NISP:MNI ratio
small/medium mammal	67	0	
medium/large mammal	1222	0	
Dasypus novemcinctus	1	1	1.00
Carnivore	4	0	
Canis sp.	3	0	
Canis lupus familiaris	38	7	5.42
Urocyon cinereoargenteus	1	1	1.00
Felidae	1	0	
Panthera onca	1	1	1.00
Artiodactyla	1	0	
Mazama sp.	1	0	
Odocoileus virginianus	1004	54	18.59
Pecari tajacu	2	1	2.00
Dasyprocta punctata	1	1	1.00
Sylvilagus sp.	5	0	
Sylvilagus brasiliensis	1	1	1.00
Sylvilagus floridanus	1	1	1.00
Homo sapiens	60	9	6.67
Total	**2414**	**77**	**31.35**

Table 28. NISP:MNI ratio for all species.

When analysed by taxa (Table 28), the NISP:MNI ratios allows for some interesting comparisons. Although a NISP:MNI ratio could be potentially ambiguous due to the problems associated with obtaining MNI, it seems to be of some relevance when the skeletal elements present are the same. What this ratio does tell us is that the higher the ratio, the higher the degree of fragmentation (Marshall and Pilgram 1991), and these results could potentially be used to explore other taphonomic processes that may have affected the assemblage, such as human processing and post-depositional trampling. In this collection, deer, human and dog are the species with the highest ratios, deer being the highest (18.59%),

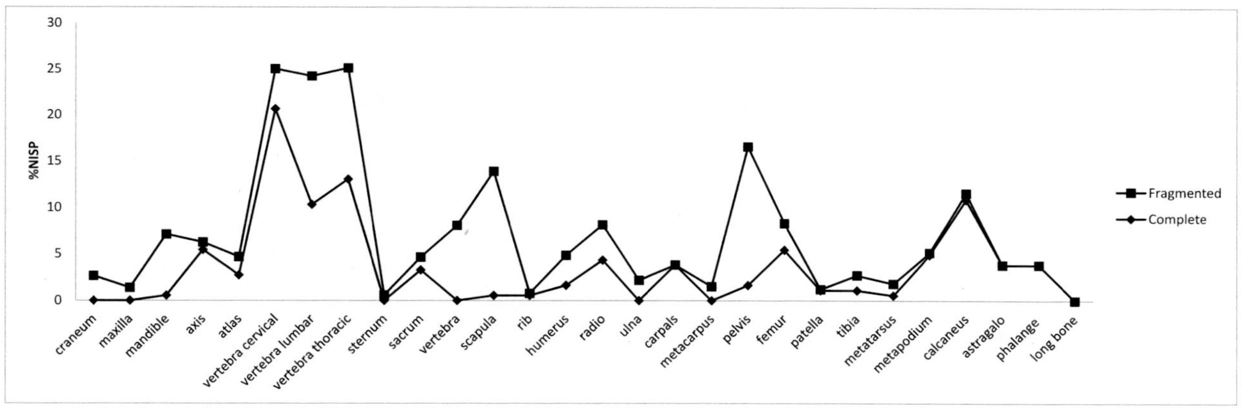

Figure 32. Distribution of complete and fragmented bones for all the assemblage (%NISP).

followed by human (6.67%), and domestic dog (5.42%). The NISP:MNI ratio suggests that these three species were more highly fragmented than the rest, although these results should be interpreted with caution as the other species were present only in low frequencies.

Presence of articulated remains

In several cases of foot bones and vertebrae (n = 62) there were two or more bones articulated (Table 29). During preliminary sorting, it was observed that some bags contained bones that belonged to the same individual, suggesting the remains were disposed of at the same time, probably still articulated, and were later subject to post-depositional movement. Material analysed from the same context (Montero 2008:112) contained two carpal and two tarsal bones still articulated, further supported this possibility. In the present analysis, all remains that were recovered still articulated come from *Operación* 114, and represent different body portions, mostly lower leg, and torso. There are elements present from both sides, left and right, and most fall in the immature and sub-adult categories. These elements do not belong to single individuals, but represent segments different individuals, suggesting that discarding these segments still articulated may have been a common practice. Furthermore, their presence in relative proximity to each other, in the same Square and Layer, and the fact that all articulated specimens show minimal or no weathering, suggests a rapid deposition, with materials being exposed *in situ*.

From all 62 bones that were recovered articulated, 16 exhibit cut marks that are consistent with filleting and skinning (Blasco 1992:113-116). These include multiple shallow perpendicular cuts on the apophysis of vertebrae (n = 8), and deep cut marks on lower limb elements, including metacarpus, astragalus, and calcaneus (n = 6). One axis with cut marks suggests the removal of the head. One case in particular is very interesting, as 17 vertebrae were found articulated, and

Bag Number	Square	Layer	Bones that articulate	Age
720	I1	II	1 astragalus and 1 calcaneus (left)	Immature
731	K1	II	1 cuboid-scaphoid, astragalus, and 1 calcaneus (left)	Immature
731	K1	II	2 cervical vertebrae	Immature+
709	L1	II	1 lumbar vertebra and 1 sacrum	Adult
709	L1	II	1 axis and 1 cervical vertebra	Immature
736	E2	III	2 metacarpals (left)	Immature
711	L1	III	1 cuboid-scaphoid, 1 astragalus, and 1 calcaneus (right)	Immature
711	L1	III	2 lumbar vertebrae	Sub-adult
738	I1	III	1 thoracic and 1 lumbar vertebra	Immature
799	J1	IV	2 innominates (1 left, 1 right)	Juvenile
759	K2	IV	2 cervical vertebrae	Immature
759	K2	IV	4 lumbar vertebrae	Immature
788	J2	IV	3 lumbar vertebrae	Immature
985	F1	V	1 cuboid-scaphoid, and 1 calcaneus (left)	Sub-adult
1009	F2	V	1 axis and 1 atlas	Immature
1009	F2	V	5 lumbar vertebrae	Immature
954	G1	V	1 cuboid-scaphoid, and 1 calcaneus (left)	Sub-adult
842	H2	V	2 lumbar vertebrae	Immature
816	I2	V	At least 17 vertebrae	Sub-adult
816	I2	V	2 lumbar vertebrae	Immature

Table 29. List of white-tailed deer bones that articulate, by square and layer, *Operación* 114.

Figure 33. Semi-articulated spinal column from a white-tailed deer in *Operación* 114, Square I2,
Layer V (Photograph by Coral Montero López).

none of them presented any cut marks, suggesting that in some cases, whole spines were discarded while still articulated and covered with flesh (Figure 33).

The predominance of semi-articulated axial (vertebrae), lower limb and distal elements (foot bones) contrasts dramatically with the absence of articulated long bones. This suggests that meat from higher value segments (such as the upper front and back limbs) were the prized body part, and were probably fully disarticulated or processed, while other body segments with less value were discarded semi-articulated, as their disarticulation may have been considered unnecessary. Alternatively, the presence of semi-articulated distal elements may suggest the removal of skins with foot bones still attached to them, and their posterior deposit in context *Operación* 114. The practice of leaving the foot bones with deer hides has been observed in many societies around the world. One example is the Iroquois in North America, who leave the distal elements still attached to deerskins (Engelbrecht 2003:11).

Presence of burned material

A low percentage of remains from the assemblage presented changes in colour and texture that indicated they were exposed directly or indirectly to fire. Very few bones were completely burned. These changes range from slight discolouration, localised brown areas, the presence of brown lines and small discrete patches, to completely charred with a distinctively black/white colouring all over the bone. Only three *Operaciones* displayed bones affected by exposure to fire (Table 30). *Operación* 114 had a total of 599 specimens that possibly indicated exposure to fire (15.49% of its total), while *Operación* 201 had only seven specimens (3.76%), and *Operación* 110 had only two (0.28%). In general, there were more fragments of small/medium and medium/large mammals with evidence of fire exposure, probably due to their overall larger presence in all three *Operaciones*. In terms of the identified taxa, the presence of burned material is not restricted

Taxon	Op. 110	Op. 114	Op. 201
small/medium mammal	1	4	1
medium/large mammal		353	2
Canis lupus familiaris		1	1
Odocoileus virginianus	1	239	3
Pecary tajacu		1	
Sylvilagus sp.		1	
Total	**2**	**599**	**7**

Table 30. Distribution of burned bones by *Operación*.

to a particular taxon, with examples of individual bones from the deer, dog, peccary, and rabbit remains exhibiting changes in colour and texture resulting from burning. White-tailed deer had the most of the burned materials, probably due to its dominance in the whole assemblage. Two human bones from *Operación* 114 were possibly boiled. None of the worked bones displayed changes in colour resulting from exposure to fire.

Faunal modifications

Faunal modifications—including carnivore chewing, rodent gnawing, and insect 'channelling'—were registered by the presence of these modifications on each specimen. This system assigned a '1' for the presence of a mark or a number of marks, without counting the number of marks if more than one mark was present. More than half of all the material collected from PRACH 2008 displayed evidence of faunal modifications (63.79%NISP). The counts did not include human remains recovered from the different *Operaciones*, as none of these remains presented any kind of faunal modification. Overall, carnivore chewing is significantly more frequent than rodent gnawing, and insect channelling. Carnivore chewing is only present in *Operaciones* 110, 111, 114, and 201, while *Operación* 114 is the only one that has bone elements with rodent gnawing and insect channelling (Table 31). When each assemblage is considered, *Operación* 114 has the

Location	Carnivore chewing	Column %	Rodent gnawing	Column %	Insect channeling	%Column	Row total	%Column (modified)	% Total
Operación 110	46	3.30					46	3.06	35.94
Operación 111	3	0.22					3	0.20	5.26
Operación 112								0.00	0.00
Operación 114	1197	85.87	103	100.00	4	100.00	1304	86.88	65.93
Operación 115								0.00	0.00
Operación 201	148	10.62					148	9.86	83.62
Operación 202								0.00	0.00
Total	**1394**	**100.00**	**103**	**100.00**	**4**	**100.00**	**1501**	**100.00**	**63.79**

Table 31. Frequency of modified specimens by fauna for all *Operaciones*.

	Op. 110	Op. 111	Op. 112	Op. 114	Op. 115	Op. 201	Op. 202
Total carnivorous/rodent/ insect modifications	46	3	0	1304	0	148	0
Total material	129	57	3	2037	2	177	9
%Total of modified	**35.66**	**5.26**	**0.00**	**64.02**	**0.00**	**83.62**	**0.00**

Table 32. Distribution of bones showing animal modifications (combined).

highest percentage of carnivore chewing (85.87%NISP), followed by *Operación* 201 (10.62%); *Operaciones* 110 and 111 have less than 5% each.

The high frequency of carnivore chewing in *Operaciones* 114 and 201 suggests that both contexts may have been associated with domestic activities or at least that these deposits partially contained materials that had been exposed where dogs and other carnivores could have had access to this food waste (e.g. Kent 1993). Furthermore, in *Operación* 114 the presence of carnivore, rodent and insect modifications may indicate that at least some of the bone fragments had been exposed for some time finally being deposited behind the Palace. There is however experimental data that indicates that carnivore chewing can occur within hours of discard, suggesting that the presence of carnivore chewing does not preclude a quick covering of the deposit (Munson and Garniewicz 2003).

When the three types of faunal modifications are combined (Table 32), *Operaciones* 114 and 201 present the highest percentages. In *Operación* 201, 83.62% of all materials were affected by faunal agents, while in *Operación* 114 64.02% of all materials present some modifications. *Operación* 110 had a third of its materials modified (35.66%) and *Operaciones* 112, 115, and 202 contained no materials exhibiting any kind of faunal modification, though this should be interpreted with caution, as these three *Operaciones* contained the fewest specimens. As such, no generalizations can be made at this point.

Upon consideration of the amount of material presenting faunal modifications, particularly dog chewing, it has been noted that there are low quantities of such modification within certain taxa. On the other hand, the absence of materials modified by faunal agents, including some faunal species and human remains, also indicates that these materials were not exposed to the same depositional conditions.

Human modifications

In this section, I first discuss the presence of cut marks that may have been the result of processing a carcass for human consumption, following which modifications of bone resulting from the manufacture of bone tools and ornaments will be discussed.

Processing of dietary taxa

The human modifications that were identified primarily include cut marks made with a fine tool implement, with hack marks and blows also noted. A total of 367 fragments of the entire mammal sample exhibit modifications made by a human agent (14.75%NISP), and it must be noted that examples with such modifications were not recovered from all *Operaciones* or all species. Cut marks are not present on any materials from *Operaciones* 111, 112, 115, and 202. Within the *Operaciones* that contained faunal remains modified by cut marks, *Operación* 114 had the greatest percentage, with 16.94% of the remains containing human modification, followed by *Operación* 201 (12.43%), and *Operación* 110 (3.88%). The presence of cut

Taxon	Op. 110	Op. 111	Op. 112	Op. 114	Op. 115	Op. 201	Op. 202	Total	% Total
Odocoileus virginianus				267 out of 942 = 28.34%		12 out of 53 = 22.64%		279 out of 1004	27.79
medium/large mammal	4 out of 119 = 3.36%			69 out of 943 = 7.31%		10 out of 97 = 10.30%		83 out of 1222	6.79
Homo sapiens				5 out of 58 = 8.62%				5 out of 60	8.33
small/medium mammal				2 out of 53 = 3.77%				2 out of 67	2.99
Canis lupus familiaris	1 out of 1 = 100%							1 out of 38	2.63
Pecari tajacu				1 out of 2 = 50%				1 out of 2	50.00
Artiodactyla				1 out of 1 = 100%				1 out of 1	100.00
Total cut marks	5 out of 129	0 out of 57	0 out of 3	340 out of 2037	0 out of 2	22 out of 177	0 out of 9	367 out of 2414	
% Total	3.88			16.69		12.43		15.20	

Table 33. Distribution of cut marks by species for all the identified material from PRACH 2008.

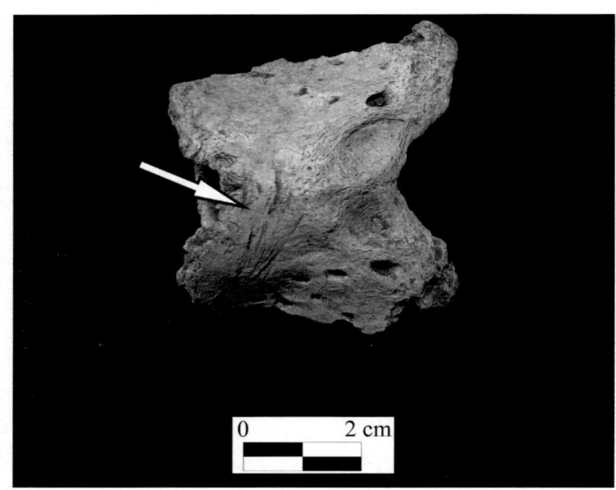

Figure 34. White-tailed deer (Odocoileus virginianus) atlas with perpendicular cut marks on the dorsal side, from *Operación* 114, Square E2, Layer V (Photograph by Coral Montero López).

marks on fragments from these three *Operaciones* was not unexpected, as they probably reflect the processing of carcasses for their consumption as food.

By species and regardless of context, 27.79% of all deer remains, (8.33%) of all human remains, and 6.79% of fragments from medium/large mammals displayed cut marks resulting from human activity (Table 33). When comparing among the different species, it is interesting to note that only two other species presented cut marks, collared peccary, and domestic dog. One hemi-mandible of a collared peccary and one innominate of an Artiodactila (possibly a peccary) present cut marks with the former displaying cutmarks on the ramus, and the latter on the pubic area. One dog innominate also displays cut marks above and under the acetabulum. Some anthropogenic modifications were also found on five human remains, including four clavicles and one fibula. Cut marks on deer may be present on all bones, and if present, they primarily appear on articulation surfaces (near epiphyses), on long bone shafts, and on vertebrae bodies. Other bones with cut marks include the innominate and scapula and in lesser proportions, phalanges. The regions where cut marks appear are consistent with butchering, skinning, and the disarticulation of carcasses, for the purposes of separating the meaty sections, filleting, or dividing the carcass in smaller sections in the case of ribs and vertebrae (Figure 34).

In terms of comparison with other sites, it can be noted that, in general, butchering has been scarce in the Maya area. In the Petén area, less than 13% of all the material combined from all sites and periods presented cut marks from butchery and skinning (Pohl 1990). In an analysis of ritual contexts, primarily caves, it was found that less than 1.5% of material had cut marks (Anderson 2009:63). Brown and Emery (2008:322) found that butchering marks on faunal remains recovered from two hunting caches comprised less than 10% of the total faunal assemblage. When present, cut marks are usually on the bones of edible species and are predominantly identified on deer remains.

It is important to mention that the potential identification of cut marks on osteological remains is intimately related to the preservation state of the remains. Emery (2010:126) mentions that for the Petexbatún assemblages only 0.1% display cut marks related to butchering and skinning, probably as a consequence of the poor preservation conditions in the area. Furthermore, Emery (2010:126) affirms that the lack in general of cut marks from other lowland samples is because the implements utilised do not leave a mark (in these cases, fine obsidian tools), and/or may be dependent upon the skill of the butchers. Finally, it is also considered possible that the process by which a carcass is butchered may be such that no marks are left on the bone, which would explain the lack of cut marks on osteological remains in the region.

Worked bone and shell

Basic information for registering worked bone included species, specimen, condition, and natural and cultural modifications. All worked material was photographed and weighed; however, no measurements were taken. In this analysis, I classified all the tools and ornaments following the typologies proposed by Moholy-Nagy (1994) and Emery (2010). It is important to consider that the choice of animals for the creation of tools and ornaments is not only based on the morphology of the bone intended for use as raw material.

In Chinikihá, there was a total of 91 modified bone and shell objects (400.8g) that could be identified as being the result of tool and ornament production (Table 34) (see Appendix C for full distribution). These objects were primarily made from faunal resources but at least two broken tools were manufactured using human bone. They show different degrees of modification, ranging from fragments at a variety of different stages in the manufacturing process, to finished tools and ornaments.

Modified shell fragments were the most numerous (38.46%), followed by remains only identified as Mammalia (28.57%); these were so highly modified that no further taxonomic identification was possible. Worked bone from medium/large mammal remains comprised 15.38%, with the remaining 17.58% composed of several identified species including dog, tapir, and turtle, which had been modified or showed alterations indicating an intention to create 'blank forms' to be used for tool or ornament manufacture.

Shell fragments were mostly identified as *Nephronaias* sp. and *Pachychilus* sp., although almost half of the shell fragments remained unidentified. *Nephronaias* sp. is a mollusc that has a pearly shell usually modified to create ornaments, including round beads, such as those found at *Operación* 114. *Pachychilus* sp. remains have been modified with a perforation, possibly to create a pendant or bead. It is possible that the animals were first consumed, and their shells subsequently used for the manufacture of ornamental beads (Emery 2007b:58).

It is important to note that in the collection of faunal remains, there were a large proportion of long bone splinters that could potentially be the result of a worked bone industry. However, due to the small amount of

Operación	Taxon	NISP	Artefact	Weight (g)
Operación 110				
	Mammalia	2	1 disc, 1 tube	5.4
	medium/large mammal	2	1 tube, 1 modified fragment	3.6
	unidentified shell	3	3 modified shell (1 perforated)	10.1
	Sub-total	7		19.1
Operación 111				
	Mammalia	1	1 *malacate*	6.1
	Sub-total	1		6.1
Operación 112				
	Pachychilus sp.	1	1 modified shell	2.7
	Sub-total	1		2.7
Operación 114				
	Mammalia	22	1 *manita*, 3 perforators, 8 needles, 1 disc, 1 tube, 1 ring, 1 spatula, 2 ornament, 4 blank forms	31.3
	medium/large mammal	10	1 perforator, 1 *raspador*, 1 *pulidor*, 7 blank forms	54.2
	Canis sp.	2	1 pendant, 1 blank form	2.3
	Odocoileus virginianus	5	1 *raspador*, 2 ornamental, 2 blank forms	50.1
	Tapirus bairdii	1	1 *pulidor*	3.1
	Homo sapiens	3	1 *güiro*, 2 blank form	72.0
	Testudines	5	5 ornaments	23.1
	Pachychilus sp.	1	1 pendant	4.1
	Nephronaias sp.	15	5 beads, 10 blank forms	35.4
	unidentified shell	13	1 tube, 1 pendant, 11 blank forms	54.9
	Sub-total	77		330.5
Operación 115				
	medium/large mammal	1	1 blank form	1.4
	Sub-total	1		1.4
Operación 201				
	Mammalia	1	1 perforator	2.4
	medium/large mammal	1	1 blank form	1.5
	Canis sp.	1	1 butt discarded	2.8
	Sub-total	3		6.7
No identified location				
	Pomacea flagellata	1	1 pendant	34.3
	Sub-total	1		34.3
Grand total		**91**		**400.8**

Table 34. Distribution of worked bone from Chinikihá.

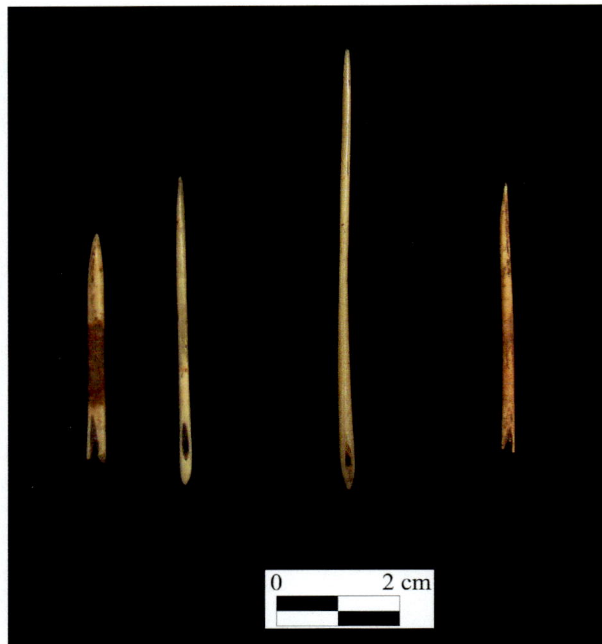

Figure 35. Bone needles from *Operación* 114 (from left to right: one fragmented and one complete needle from Square K1/Layer IV; one complete needle from Square F2/Layer V, and one fragmented needle from Square J2/Layer IV (Photograph by Coral Montero López).

modified bone for utilitarian or ornamental purposes and the extensive presence of carnivore and food processing marks, bone splinters are more probably the result of food processing or carnivore modification, rather than a result of the production of bone tools.

In order to understand the presence of certain faunal species, it is necessary to explore the possible role they played. Fauna can be classified into two main groups depending on their function, whether ceremonial, or as a subsistence resource. The distinction is made according to the location from which faunal remains are recovered, whether from a ceremonial or residential context (Emery 2010), the latter indicating an association with subsistence use (Teeter 2001:38). According to the classification system developed by Moholy-Nagy (1994), the objects present at Chinikihá can be placed under one of three classifications: technomic, sociotechnic, and idiotechnic. Most of the materials have been identified as ideotechnic. These items represent finished and incomplete objects, some of which display use-wear. Fourteen finished tools or ornaments, corresponding to Emery's (2010) Stage 5, were identified, with 13 from *Operación* 114 and one from *Operación* 111. These were eight needles, two flat discs with a central perforation, one perforator, one worked bone in the shape of a hand or *manita*, and one *malacate* (spinning whorl), this last being

the only artefact from *Operación* 111. Broken objects were present in all *Operaciones*, including discs, tubes, perforators, and ornamental pieces, some with carved glyphs or geometrical patterns. At this stage, it has not been possible to determine whether they were broken intentionally for deposit in this context, or if they had been broken before prior to their burial (Figure 35).

A large proportion of the modified bone and shell items displayed minimal modification, which is consistent with these pieces being transformed into blanks, awaiting further modification for the creation of tools. These included 18 bones and 21 shell fragments (42.85% of all modified bone and shell). Modifications include cuts, grooves, and polished edges intended to establish a smooth surface, creating a preform that would be further modified. Preforms were categorized as 'raw material blanks' or 'blank forms'. Also, a small number of bone fragments in the early stages of production, as defined by Emery (2010), were also observed, including one human ilium fragment in Stage 1, one deer metacarpus in Stage 2 (displaying deep longitudinal cut marks to divide the bone in two halves), and one dog radius distal epiphysis removal that correspond to the process of 'butt discarding'.

The presence of artefacts in different stages of production may suggest that some manufacture of tools and ornaments was being conducted at Chinikihá; however, it is also possible that some of the finished pieces arrived in Chinikihá as ready-made objects, via trade or exchange with other settlements. One such example is the presence of the Baird's tapir (*Tapirus bairdii*) rib, but even artefacts manufactured from bones of other, more locally available species, such as deer and dog, could have been imported, as they were valuable animals in the whole Maya area.

Among all the artefacts, there were two interesting objects that deserve further mention. One is a white-tailed deer mandible that was carved on both sides of the dentary. The depiction of a 'death eye' glyph is present on both sides of the mandible, so that the whole face is formed by the semi-circle figure next to it and the glyph would represent the eye of an animal; the teeth of this face would correspond to the upper dentary of a creature (Peter Mathews, personal communication 2011) (Figures 36 and 37). The function of this object was most probably ornamental or non-utilitarian, and it is possible that it was a musical instrument, as there are deep incisions or grooves along the margin of the mandible. In this way, the ramus of the mandible would have functioned as a handle to hold the instrument. The possibility that the mandible was a musical instrument is further supported by the inclusion of a human femur that also presents deep horizontal grooves along the diaphysis. Grooved long bones considered likely to have been used as musical instruments were common in the

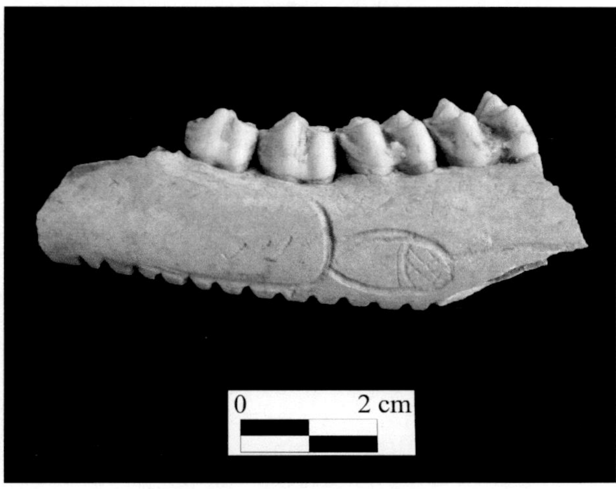

Figure 36. Carved white-tailed deer mandible with incised glyphs and incisions, *Operación* 114 (Photograph by Coral Montero López).

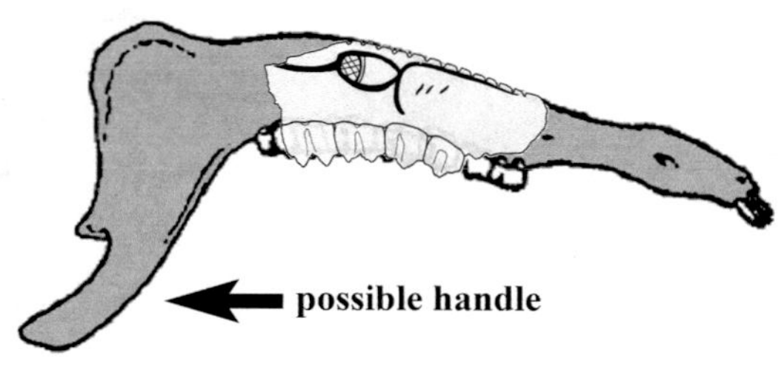

Figure 37. Hypothetical reconstruction of the carved mandible (modified from a drawing by Peter Mathews, reproduced with permission).

Mexican central highlands (see Pereira 2005 for further discussion).

The other artefact of particular interest is worked long bone with carved decoration depicting clothing, with a hand carved on one end, known as a *manita* (little hand) (Figure 38). Although the end opposite the hand appears to have been broken, it is considered to be a complete piece, as similar *manitas* from other archaeological deposits look the same. The bone is so modified that it was not possible to identify the species and was classified as belonging to a medium to large mammal. These *manitas* have been interpreted as instruments associated with scribers (Schmidt 2004), due to their similitude to the scribe glyph **a-TZ'B'-b'a** (Aj Tz'ihb'), and common appearance as burial offerings, as in the case of a burial Palenque from the Murciélagos phase which contained several objects, including bone needles and two *manitas* (Venegas 2005:63-64).

The 91 modified bone and shell specimens from Chinikihá represent only 1.87% of the whole assemblage. Although this is a very low proportion, it is comparable to other assemblages where modified bone items were intermingled with dietary remains, such as in Cozumel, where only 0.6% of the assemblage was composed of modified bone, all of which were deer metapodials (Hamblin 1984). This is particularly interesting considering that deer are not native to the island and therefore, had to be either imported or traded. Erin Kennedy Thornton (2008) reported that at the trade port of Trinidad de Nosotros in Guatemala, 4% of all faunal materials display artefactual modifications, and most of them are made of shell. When compared to other contexts at inland sites, the presence of modified materials in Chinikihá is very low. At Motul de San

José, 10% of all materials are artefacts, most of them finished objects made of bone (Thornton 2008), while in contexts representing construction fills at Structure A-1 from Xunantunich, Belize, 9% of all materials are artefacts, including needles, awls and manufacture debitage (Freiwald 2010:410).

The proportion of modified bone at Chinikihá seems even smaller when compared to a deposit associated with bone artefact production, such as L4-3 from Dos Pilas, where 40.63% of all materials reflect a production stage in the manufacturing of tools and ornaments (Emery 2010). What is interesting to note is that while some sites may have been importing or trading finished artefacts, most sites contain at least some evidence, in the form of items at different stages of the production sequence, that suggest exploitation of local resources and local tool manufacturing. At Chinikihá, the absence of tools and ornaments made from exotic species and the dominance of modified bone and shell from species used for dietary purposes, confirm a localised exploitation pattern. Most of the artefacts at Chinikihá come from *Operación* 114, a context associated with the Palace, suggesting that the elite may have controlled the production of tools and ornaments, especially those of ritual or idiotechnic importance. This however, does not preclude other segments of the society from having had access to other type of artefacts, particularly those of a utilitarian nature. In this sense, the presence of tools and ornaments is especially important, as they can be used to identify the function of a context.

In Piedras Negras, utilitarian artefacts made of modified bone and shell were common, but were not usually associated with ritual activities (Emery 2007b:59).

Figure 38. Worked bone in the shape of a hand or manita from *Operación* 114 (Photograph by Coral Montero López).

Examples of utilitarian artefacts retrieved from the site include needles, pins, perforators, and spatulas, as well as turtle shell and armadillo dermal bones (Emery 2007b:59). However, in deposits considered to be true ritual contexts such as caches, offerings and burials, the remains most commonly identified include marine shell, feline and artiodactyl species, noting that the first two of which are not local resources (Emery 2007a:59). In this sense, non-local species and probably human bones were considered exotic, and were therefore used for the manufacture of ornaments deposited in ritual contexts.

There are however, species that are multi-purpose and were used both as food and for ritual purposes, such as the deer. Often, species like the deer were first processed and consumed as a food resource, following which their bones would be used as a raw material for the production of tools and ornaments (Emery 2007b:58). Masson (1999:106) suggests that fauna favoured for ritual or upper class activities included large game animals (deer, tapir, peccary, crocodile, birds, and iguana), and that the supply of these may have been controlled by the elite, through butchering and redistribution.

Many studies in the Maya area have stressed that there was a differential access to faunal resources based on social classes (Emery 2003, 2004b; Pohl 1990). The upper classes had access to a greater range of animals, including non-local species, as well as ritually important and high-quality animals (Emery 2003:498). There are certain taxa that appear almost exclusively in elite contexts, and have symbolic connotations that associate them with the highest social strata (Pohl 1985b:111; Shaw 1991). This is exemplified by the jaguar (*Panthera onca*), which, because of its exoticism, it is related exclusively to the ruling classes (Saunders 1994). However, as has been mentioned previously, some species, such as deer, have been identified in varying contexts, including ritual and non-ceremonial deposits (Pohl 1985a).

A similar scenario is observable when studying the distribution of guinea pig (*Cavia porcellus*) remains in Perú (Sandefur 2002). In short, such animals are multi-purpose and interpreting their presence in a defined context requires consideration of other factors (Emery 2010; Montero 2013). More recent zooarchaeological studies have found that fitting results into a simple dichotomous elite/non-elite framework is very difficult, and trying to do so significantly limits our ability to understand the variability in the use of faunal resources by the Maya (Emery 2003:510) and furthermore, restricts the possibility of understanding the dynamic taphonomic history of the deposit.

Weathering stages

The degree of weathering was recorded for every specimen following Behrensmeyer's (1978) classification (Table 35). Specimens displayed various degrees of weathering, ranging from Stage 0 or no weathering, to Stage 4, which is characterised by a distinguishable bone surface that is coarsely fibrous and rough in texture; cracks are usually splintered and have rounded edges (Behrensmeyer 1978:151). No material from the Chinikihá assemblage was identified as having reached Stage 5, the most advanced degree of weathering in Behrensmeyer's system. The absence of bones in Stage 5 is not surprising, as bones in this category do not tend to survive in many archaeological settings (Reitz and Wing 1999:138).

In general terms, most of the material was found to have reached Stage 1 only (88.61%), displaying minimal weathering. In this stage some longitudinal cracking

Location	Stage 0	Stage 1	Stage 2	Stage 3	Stage 4	Total
Operación 110		61	21	41	6	129
Operación 111		57				57
Operación 112		1			2	3
Operación 114	16	1859	71	78	13	2037
Operación 115		1			1	2
Operación 201		158	7	11	1	177
Operación 202		2		7		9
Total	16	2139	99	137	23	2414
%Total	0.66	88.61	4.10	5.68	0.95	100.00

Table 35. Weathering stage for all the *Operaciones* (following Behrensmeyer 1978).

on long bones, and/or mosaic cracking on articular surfaces may be observed, sometimes appearing just a few days after deposition (Behrensmeyer 1978:151). Items exhibiting Stage 2 (4.10%) and Stage 3 (5.68%) weathering were present in comparatively smaller quantities than those in Stage 1, while bones at Stage 0 (0.66%) or Stage 4 (0.95%) were almost entirely absent. The distribution of specimens displaying different stages of weathering is not homogeneous in any of the *Operaciones*. The presence of bones with differing degrees of erosion in the same stratum stresses the fact that while some of the material was exposed to the environment for some time, other materials were probably deposited when fresh or right after being defleshed. Nevertheless, it is important to remember that weathering reflects climatic microvariation, and is also dependent on body size, age of the individual, and the type of bone that is affected (Behrensmeyer 1978; Reitz and Wing 1999).

By context, *Operación* 114 presented material in all stages, while *Operaciones* 110 and 201, presented materials in all stages except Stage 0. *Operación* 202 presented material in Stages 1 and 3, while *Operaciones* 112 and 115 presented materials in Stages 1 and 4. All the material in *Operación* 111 was recorded as Stage 1. An ANOVA test demonstrated that there is a significant difference between the degrees of weathering exhibited in different *Operaciones* (F = 0.5974; P = 0.6705; 0.5). Stage 0 was not included in this calculation due to its low numbers (n<20). This result strongly suggests that different formation processes have likely affected the different contexts. Where materials all exhibited weathering to the same stage within one *Operación* , as in *Operación* 111, it is likely that all material was affected by the same processes. The *Operaciones* with specimens in different stages of weathering were probably the result of a secondary and/or tertiary depositional history, or of their inclusion as construction fills.

Although it is difficult to determine the exposure time based on weathering stages (Lyman 1994:358), Behrensmeyer (1978:157) suggests that Stages 0 to 3 may represent materials that have lain exposed for three years or less. Therefore, the materials were then grouped in two broad categories, Stages 0-2 and 3-4 (Table 36). These groupings were used to explore which *Operaciones* were the result of a rapid accumulation and burial.

Operaciones 112 and 202 had a higher percentage of materials in Stages 3-4, while *Operaciones* 110, 114, and 201 had a predominance of materials in Stages 0-2, and a smaller percentage of materials in Stages 3-4. *Operación* 115 had one specimen in Stages 0-2 and one in stages 3-4. Finally, *Operación* 111 contained only material in Stages 0-2. Those *Operaciones* with a higher percentage of materials in Stages 0-2 are likely to have

Location	Stages 0-2	%NISP	Stages 3-4	%NISP	Total	%Total
Operación 110	82	63.57	47	36.43	129	100.00
Operación 111	57	100.00	0	0.00	57	100.00
Operación 112	1	33.33	2	66.67	3	100.00
Operación 114	1946	95.53	91	4.47	2037	100.00
Operación 115	1	50.00	1	50.00	2	100.00
Operación 201	165	93.22	12	6.78	177	100.00
Operación 202	2	22.22	7	77.78	9	100.00
Total	**2254**	**93.37**	**160**	**6.63**	**2414**	**100.00**

Table 36. Grouping of materials by weathering Stages 0-2 and 3-4.

undergone a more rapid deposition than the other *Operaciones*, and although some of the bones present in each of those *Operaciones* may have been exposed for a period of time, they were covered fairly quickly.

Correlating the faunal assemblage by context

The faunal assemblage has been analysed by taxonomic identification, age, degree of fragmentation, presence of human and faunal modifications, and presence of worked bone and shell for all *Operaciones*. When all of this information is combined, it is possible to discuss the differences between the different contexts. The materials from all *Operaciones* are consistent with an active occupation during the Late Classic period, and do not represent post-abandonment occupations, as they were integrated in the construction sequences of the structures with which they were associated.

The faunal assemblage in each *Operación* consists of highly fragmented material to a varying degree. Interestingly, faunal and human modifications were registered only for materials from some of the locations, including *Operaciones* 110, 111, 114, and 201. *Operaciones* 115 and 202 did not present any materials with taphonomic modifications. The presence of modifications such as cut marks, and breakage of bones for dismembering, filleting and general defleshing, indicates that the faunal resources were being processed for consumption as food. The high proportion of young mammal remains present suggests that animals in their prime age were purposely targeted, as they would yield the greatest amount of meat. The high numbers of modified *jute* shells present in almost all *Operaciones* confirm that these resources were being processed to be served as food.

Nevertheless, once they were processed for consumption, the way they entered the deposit may have differed between excavation units. *Operaciones* 110, 111, and 112 were initially considered to form part of construction fills, where *Operación* 110 was associated with a ballcourt, and *Operaciones* 111 and 112 as materials associated with a domestic residence with burials associated to it. *Operaciones* 114 and 201 were identified as middens associated with structures that formed small plazas, where *Operación* 114 is located at the ceremonial centre of Chinikihá, and *Operación* 201 at the smaller site of Chancalá. *Operación* 202 was identified as a deposit of materials above an occupational floor associated with a platform at San Juan Chancalaíto.

From these contexts, *Operación* 114 contained the highest faunal diversity, most of which was evidence of faunal exploitation as food consumption. The species present in *Operación* 114 included white-tailed deer, domestic dog, rabbit, agouti, armadillo, peccary, tapir, and jaguar, fauna that is commonly reported at other sites in the Maya region. Many of these were definitely consumed as food, but others were used for their pelts, teeth and claws, especially the carnivores (Sharer 1996:96). *Operación* 114 represents a large context associated directly with the Palace, and as such, allows us to explore the acquisition of certain taxa by the occupants of the Palace, and the use they made of each species. In the archaeological record of this *Operación*, several deposit events can be detected, as they have been defined by the laying of a stuccoed floor.

Summary

A total of 4849 bone and shell fragments were recovered from PRACH 2008. The most common species was a freshwater mollusc (*jute*), followed by white-tailed deer (*Odocoileus virginianus*), and human remains. White-tailed deer was the most abundant mammal identified for all *Operaciones*. Other fauna were present in lower proportions, but all taxa were obtained from the immediate vicinity of the settlement, and represent different microenvironmental zones, reflecting a local pattern of exploitation. Fauna remains were not distributed homogeneously within the different excavation contexts. *Operación* 114 made

up more than 84% of all the material analysed. The deposit with the highest density was *Operación* 114, which was also the richest and most diverse. The mammal assemblage reflects a selection by age with a preference for young adults (>12 months) or animals that are in their prime-age.

The osteofaunal material, despite being highly fragmented, was well-preserved, indicating that the degree of fragmentation may have been a result of other processes, primarily human processing for meat extraction and manufacturing of tools and ornaments, although the material had been affected to some degree by post-depositional faunal activity. A small but significant proportion of all the material displayed cut marks and other modifications consistent with primary and secondary butchering, supporting the observation of human processing for dietary purposes. The apex removal of numerous shell remains (mainly *Pachychilus* sp.) suggests their role as food, further contributing to the overall interpretation of the assemblage as food remains. Finally, a small proportion of bone and shell in the form either of finished tools and ornaments, or as items part way through being transformed when they were discarded, were recovered. Such objects were primarily found in *Operación* 114, contributing to the complexity of this deposit. The importance of the fauna present at Chinikihá is not only due to their dietary role but also may be related to their symbolism in the Maya cosmology. In the next chapter, *Operación* 114 is analysed in detail, using a set of three tests to explore if this deposit is indeed the result of ritual activity, more specifically, feasting.

Chapter eight

Detailed analysis of *Operación* 114

In this chapter, a detailed analysis of contextual data and faunal material from *Operación* 114 is presented, with the intention of addressing specific topics, including the investigation of the depositional history using zooarchaeological and taphonomic analysis. An assessment of whether the deposit or deposits were the result of ceremonial use or subsistence refuse is provided. The approach taken in this chapter is to combine the variables presented in Chapter five, but to focus exclusively on *Operación* 114, to test several hypotheses and models about faunal exploitation during the Late Classic period, and more specifically, to discern if there is a spatial patterning that can provide some information about the nature of the context.

As discussed in Chapter seven, the inhabitants of Chinikihá preferred white-tailed deer, so the analysis will focus primarily on this species so as to explore the formation process of the various deposits and ultimately, to explain the behaviour which may have led to their creation. In the previous chapter, it was possible to conclude that most faunal remains present in *Operación* 114 were the result of human consumption. This topic is further explored in this chapter in an attempt to identify spatial differences and clarify if this context could reflect single or multiple consumption events, since deer are found in overwhelming numbers and the remains include examples of all body portions. Thus, the focus on deer permits the exploitation of both the distribution patterns of the skeletal elements, and the degree to which carcass processing had occurred. Where appropriate, other species have been considered for the purpose of understanding how the elite accessed meat resources during the Late/Terminal Classic period, paying particular attention to the mammals with the second and third most abundant remains identified, the domestic dog and the human. A discussion on possible deer management as suggested by Carr (1996) and Pohl (1985a) is also included.

Deer remains are present in every layer and square in *Operación* 114, and their distribution seems to be continuous throughout the whole deposit except for the floor layer. Nevertheless, the archaeological materials found under the floor might represent earlier depositional episodes, suggesting a difference in contexts between the materials above and under the floor. Contextual analysis focused on the distribution of faunal remains by square/layer, age, seasonality, and taphonomical modifications (e.g. butchering and weathering marks).

To better manage the data, this chapter is divided into three parts. Part One tests for a spatial patterning that will ultimately work as a proxy to identify formation processes through the analysis of several variables including age, seasonality, and presence of anthropogenic and natural modifications. Some of the questions that derive from the spatial analysis include:

1. Is the material distributed homogeneously throughout the context?
2. Is the distribution of deer remains different from the other taxa? Was there a preference for a particular age group or body portion?
3. Have all the materials been subject to the same post-depositional processes?

Part Two explores the processing patterns by analysing the preferential exploitation of white-tailed deer, using the variables of body portion, skeletal completeness, sidedness, and utility indices. The analyses presented in Part Two seek to answer questions such as:

1. Was there a preference for a specific body part or side?
2. Were the carcasses arriving complete to the site and how were they being processed?
3. Can an age preference be discerned from this distribution?

Part Two also explores the butchering practices for the three main taxa identified in *Operación* 114, white-tailed deer, dog, and human remains, for the purpose of identifying the dietary contribution from these species. This is done by analysing the presence of cut marks and their distribution by body portion. A comparison between deer, dog, and human was also conducted to investigate whether all three taxa were exploited in a similar manner.

Finally, Part Three explores the possibility of a ritual use for certain faunal resources, including the deer, dog and human remains, and how these remains vary throughout the context. Questions addressed include:

1. Was there a different use of deer compared with other species?

Taxon	E1	E2	F1	F2	G1	G2	G3	H1	H2	I1	I2	J1	J2	K1	K2	L1	L2	n/a	Total	%Total
Medium/large mammal		32	78	73	4	22	6	15	36	8	42	60	178	268	54	58	6	3	943	46.29
Small/medium mammal			1	1		1			8	1		1	1	34	4	1			53	2.60
Dasypus novemcinctus																1			1	0.05
Carnivore														2					2	0.10
Canis sp.				1											1				2	0.10
Canis lupus familiaris		1	1	3	0	1				1	1	1	4	6	2			1	22	1.08
Urcyon cinereargentus				1															1	0.05
Felidae								1											1	0.05
Panthera onca					1														1	0.05
Artiodactyla									1										1	0.05
Mazama sp.														1					1	0.05
Odocoileus virginianus	9	42	34	59	22	58	1	34	38	22	57	51	158	187	85	66	5	14	942	46.24
Pecari tajacu									0					2					2	0.10
Dasyprocta punctata												1							1	0.05
Sylvilagus sp.			1					1						2					4	0.20
Sylvilagus brasiliensis														1					1	0.05
Sylvilagus floridanus															1				1	0.05
Homo sapiens		1	5	30		6		3	1			3		8	1				58	2.85
Total	9	76	120	168	27	88	7	54	84	32	100	117	341	511	148	126	11	18	2037	100.00
%Total	0.44	3.73	5.89	8.25	1.33	4.32	0.34	2.65	4.12	1.57	4.91	5.74	16.74	25.09	7.27	6.19	0.54	0.88	100.00	

Table 37. NISP distribution of species by square, *Operación* 114.

2. Does the material from under the floor represent a different type of context than that from above it?

The results from these three sections provide a basis for the discussion of feasting, and how it might be identified in the archaeological record. This discussion will be presented in Chapter ten.

Part one: Testing for a spatial patterning

The distribution of all materials by Square and Layer from *Operación* 114 will be assessed, in addition to a more specific focus on the distribution of white-tailed deer remains from *Operación* 114 by age, sex, and seasonality. This section aims to test if there is patterning based on the spatial distribution of the faunal sample. Then, spatial patterning is further explored by assessing a series of variables, including the presence of cut marks and bones modified by faunal and environmental agents. In this section, the distribution of the material relative to the floor area between Layers III and IV is evaluated to test for a change in context type within *Operación* 114.

Distribution of the material by square and layer

Spatially, it was observed that the materials in *Operación* 114 were concentrated primarily in two squares and were probably the result of at least two main dumping episodes (Table 37). Based on the NISP, concentrations have been identified in Squares K1 (25.09%) and J2 (16.74%), while the rest of the squares contained between 0.34% (square G3) and 8.25% (Square F2) of the total assemblage. In terms of taxa, medium/large mammals (46.29%), white-tailed deer (46.24%), and human remains (2.85%) were the most well-represented taxa, particularly the former two, remains of which were recovered from every Square. The rest of the species were present in small proportions, and only in some Squares. Squares J and K were situated near the back wall of the Palace and the high proportion of specimens found in these two squares suggests that this is the core, or at least the largest part of the deposit.

In the deepest layers of these squares, the faunal material was mixed with large quantities of ceramic fragments and large stones that were probably used as a base to lay the floor (Liendo 2009b). The ongoing ceramic analysis has revealed so far that squares K1 and J2 also yielded the highest concentration of sherds by weight, including service wares (plates, cooking vessels, and bowls), but also ritual ceramics, including incense burners, and other ritual paraphernalia such as ceramic drums and figurines (Mirón 2012). When faunal remains and service ceramics are considered together, the highest concentration of materials appears to have

been against the back wall behind the Palace, located to the left of the excavation grid in Figure 39.

Within the faunal assemblage, distribution by Layer showed that and regardless of the species, Layer IV produced the most material with 24.89%, followed by Layer II (23.56%), and Layer V (22.93%). Layer I had the least with only 7.36%, and no Layer information was obtained for 0.88% of the sample (Table 38).

It is important to remember the presence of a stuccoed floor between Layers III and IV, and to consider how its presence influences the distribution of materials within the context. A small section of this floor was discovered near the back wall of the Palace, and it is considered that this floor would have been extensive and formed an active surface. Thus, the material under it would be sealed and protected from post-depositional modifications. This suggests that two separate types of contexts exist within *Operación* 114, forming two units of analysis—above the floor (Layers I to III), and below it (Layers IV-V). Another factor that requires

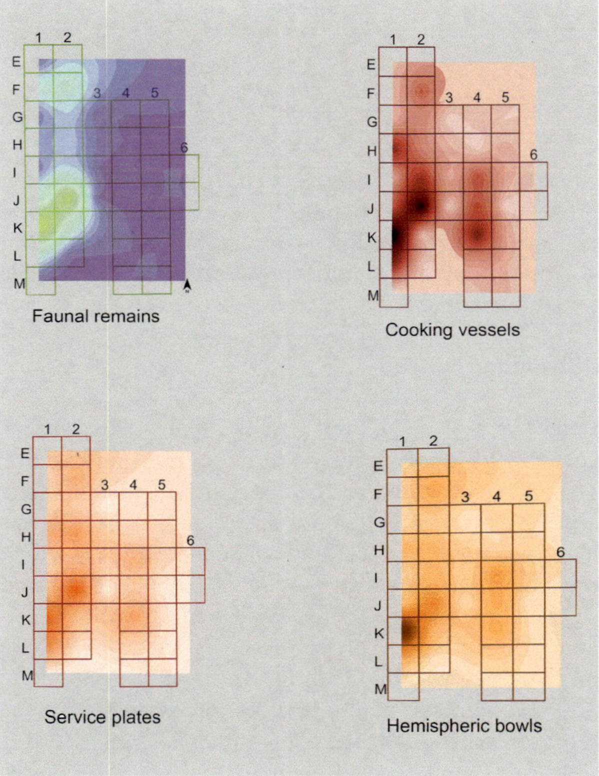

Figure 39. Distribution of faunal remains and serving vessels by Square in *Operación* 114 (modified from Mirón 2012, reproduced with permission).

Taxon	Layer I	Layer II	Layer III	Layer IV	Layer V	N.I.	Total	%Total
Medium/large mammal	85	260	139	225	231	3	943	46.29
Small/medium mammal	1	41	4	3	4		53	2.60
Dasypus novemcinctus		1					1	0.05
Carnivore		1		1			2	0.10
Canis sp.				1	1		2	0.10
Canis lupus familiaris	2	4	4	6	5	1	22	1.08
Urcyon cinereargentus					1		1	0.05
Felidae					1		1	0.05
Panthera onca				1			1	0.05
Artiodactyla					1		1	0.05
Mazama sp.				1			1	0.05
Odocoileus virginianus	62	172	206	266	222	14	942	46.24
Pecari tajacu			2				2	0.10
Dasyprocta punctata			1				1	0.05
Sylvilagus sp.		1		2	1		4	0.20
Sylvilagus brasiliensis				1			1	0.05
Sylvilagus floridanus			1				1	0.05
Homo sapiens		3	7	5	43		58	2.85
Total	**150**	**480**	**357**	**507**	**467**	**18**	**2037**	**100.00**
%Total	**7.36**	**23.56**	**17.53**	**24.89**	**22.93**	**0.88**	**100.00**	

Table 38. NISP distribution of species by layer in *Operación* 114.

consideration is the possibility that different formation processes, and/or changes in the function of the deposit, occurred during its accumulation. A statistical analysis showed no significant differences between the two sub-groups.

Distribution by age

From Tables 37 and 38, it is possible to observe that deer is the only species present in all squares and layers. The analysis focused on the distribution of deer by age and Layer (Table 39), and a specific age interval was identified for 495 white-tailed deer specimens of which the majority were in Layers IV (32.53%), V (23.64%), and III (21.82%). The age profile identified for white-tailed deer from epiphyseal fusion shows that there were more immature individuals (43.43%), with fewer adults (29.09%), and sub-adults (13.13%). Juvenile specimens represented a small percentage (3.23%), while 10.70% comprised immature+ specimens that could be either immature or adults.

When specific age groups (in months) were obtained for the white-tailed deer, the overall age distribution in *Operación* 114 mirrors the profile obtained for all the fauna from the total Chinikihá assemblage, discussed in Chapter six. The mortality profile for deer in *Operación* 114 indicates that animals in their prime age were targeted, with high proportions of animals between 12 and 29 months of age (60.04%), and between 29-35 months of age (24.90%). A small proportion of young animals (<12 months) (6.90%), and adults older than 35 months (8.16%) made up the total (Figure 40).

In the faunal assemblages identified as prey at other Maya sites, the deer were almost exclusively adults (Emery 2004a:108). Young and juvenile individuals are usually limited to ceremonial deposits related to fertility rituals or found primarily in elite deposits (Carr 1985; Pohl 1983; Wing 1975). Furthermore, immature animals may have been used for sacrifice and feasts, as a means of stressing the managerial role maintained over such resources by the elite, in a rather exclusionary way (Emery 2004a:108). Thus, a direct correlation between age and type of context (ritual or non-ritual) is expected to exist in the distribution of deer remains. With the aim of assessing differential patterning by layer, the specimens were grouped by age proportion above and below the floor (Figure 41). The grouping did not include those classified as immature+, as they could be either sub-adults or adults. The results show that although the remains of immature individuals dominated in both sub-groups, there was a slightly higher proportion of them under the floor (51.97%) than above it (46.93%). In contrast, there were proportionally more adults above the floor

Layer	Juvenile	Immature	Sub-adult	Immature+	Adult	Total	%Total
Layer I	0	13	2	6	9	30	6.06
Layer II	0	27	8	6	28	69	13.94
Layer III	3	44	14	16	31	108	21.82
Layer IV	8	86	15	9	43	161	32.53
Layer V	5	46	25	15	26	117	23.64
n/a	0	1	1	1	7	10	2.02
Total	16	217	65	53	144	495	100.00
%Total	3.23	43.83	13.13	10.70	29.09	100.00	

Table 39. NISP distribution of white-tailed deer and age groups by layer, *Operación* 114.

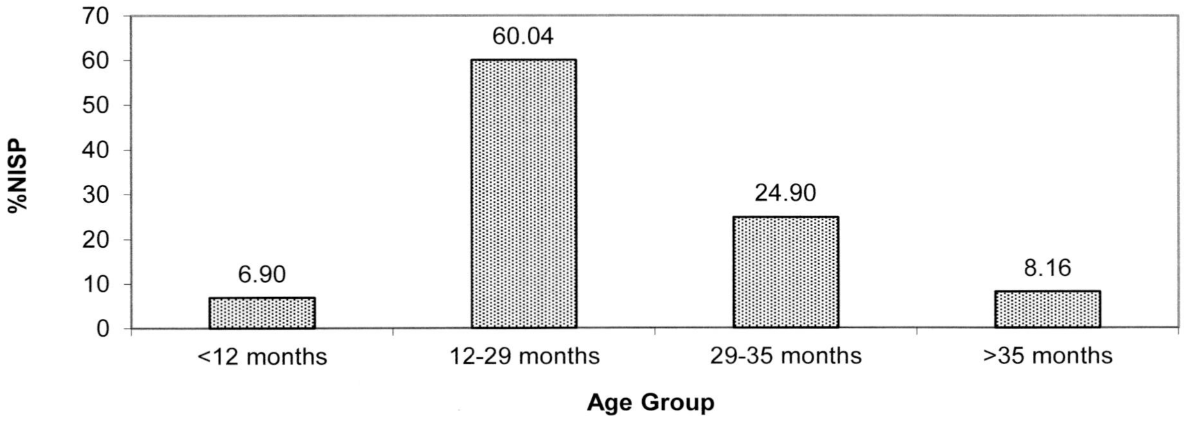

Figure 40. Distribution by age groups for white-tailed deer in
Operación 114.

(37.99%), than under it (27.17%). Remains in the sub-adult category were present in similar proportions in both sub-groups, making up 13.41% of the deer remains above the floor and 15.75% of those below the floor. Juvenile elements were more common under the floor (5.12%) than above it (1.68%), these low quantities being consistent with the whole assemblage. An observation of modern-day Guatemalan hunters suggests that juvenile animals are not generally favoured targets (Emery *et al.* 2009), but according to Pohl (1983:91), the Maya preferred young or juvenile deer for sacrifice in rituals associated with fertility. Therefore, the presence of remains in specific age groups may indicate specific roles for different animals within the contexts.

For statistical tests, the juvenile, immature, and sub-adult categories were merged into a single group (sub-adults). A non-parametric test indicated that when age categories were grouped in two large samples (sub-adult and adult), the differences were not significant. The non-apparent selection by age suggests that there is some continuity in the exploitation of white-tailed deer throughout the whole deposit, with a slight preference for individuals in their prime. These results contrast with earlier suggestions of young deer selection for ritual sacrifice (Pohl 1990:142), and their

deposition within sealed ritual contexts (Iglesias in Moholy-Nagy 1997). Although depositing young fragile bones in a sealed context would increase their chance of survival, by protecting them from factors such as carnivore chewing (Carr 1996:257), it was found that the distribution of animals in such contexts was not biased by age.

Distribution by sex

For Chinikihá's sample, the low proportions of skull fragments made sex differentiation difficult, with only two fragments of antler present. On the other hand, sexual dimorphism in white-tailed deer develops after 12 months of age, with does becoming sexually reproductive after 24 months of age, therefore, sex becomes more distinguishable through the study of the pelvis. In this assemblage, it was only possible to identify the sex of 10 pelvic specimens (Table 40), five of which were male and five were female. With the addition of the two antlers, male individuals add up to seven, or 58.33%, with the five females comprising 41.66% of the remains distinguishable by sex. The small sample of sexed specimens did not indicate any significant difference; thus, it is impossible to make any further comment on this aspect. However, the identification of

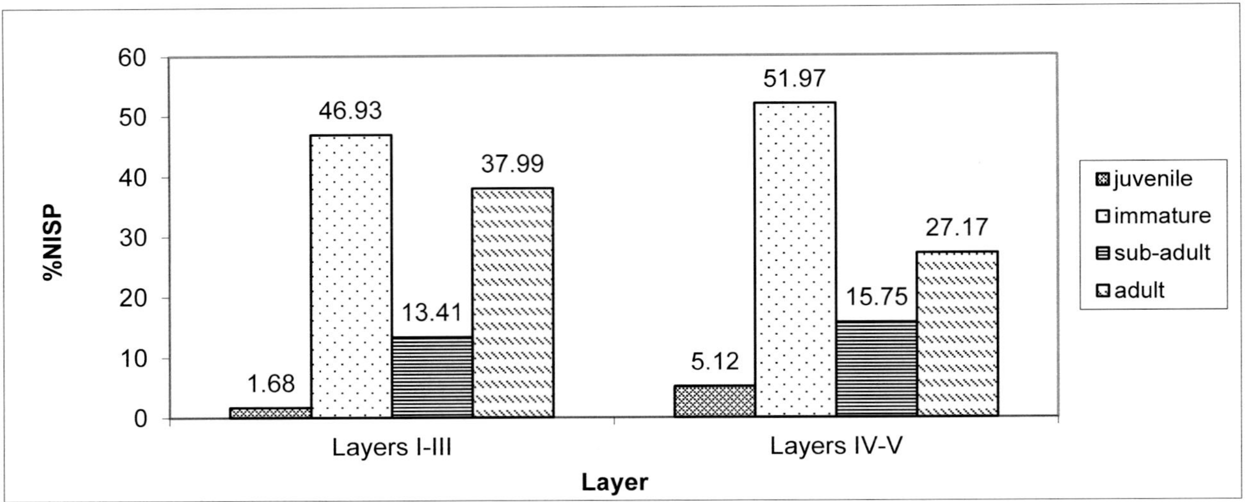

Figure 41. Distribution of white-tailed deer remains by age category and their
location regarding the floor in *Operación* 114.

Sex	Layer I	Layer II	Layer III	Layer IV	Layer V	Total
Female	1	3	0	1	0	5
Male	1	2	0	2	2	7
Total	2	5	0	3	2	12

Table 40. Distribution of white-tailed deer by sex in
Operación 114.

sex, especially in deer remains, should be considered in future studies as it has been suggested that male deer was preferred for use in ceremonies (Pohl 1981).

Mortality and seasonality profiles

Mortality profile

With the noticeable absence of fish and migratory birds in this assemblage, it was impossible to obtain any specific data on seasonality. Seasonality has been identified at other Maya archaeological sites based on the presence of pedicels in stag skulls and tooth eruption in young deer (Carr 1996:258), but in general, there is a lack of information on this topic. During the analysis of the 2008 material, no skulls with pedicels were observed, although a few pedicels have been reported for previous analysed material (Montero 2008). Due to the absence of skulls with pedicels in the current analysis, tooth eruption and wear patterns from the white-tailed deer were used to obtain a mortality profile and propose some interpretations regarding the seasonal exploitation of this animal.

White-tailed deer is a species in which females have a synchronised birth of one offspring per year, and each birth season can be expected at regular intervals. The

method used in this analysis is a modified version of Byers and Hill's (2009) study on pronghorn (*Antilocapra americana*), discussed in Chapter five. This method first requires that the teeth in the mandible be used to separate the remains into age groups, or cohorts. The overall presence of mandibles in this sample was extremely low (n = 44) and from those, it was only possible to assign a specific age (in months) to ten specimens, all from *Operación* 114. With these limitations in mind, the results were used to create a mortality profile, which would enable us to explore seasonality.

Age cohorts were grouped, with mortality profile, as follows: juvenile (1 week to 12 months), prime adult (12 months to 6.5 years), and old adult (over 6.5 years) (Figure 42). Prime adults clearly dominated the assemblage, making up 59.96% of the sample, followed by juveniles (30.03%). Older adults (10.01%) appear to have been the least favoured, reflecting a 'prime-age dominated' profile (Byers and Hill 2009; Stiner 1990). This profile is characterised by the selection of animals in the peak of their reproductive cycle, and usually with a full set of erupted permanent teeth. In a prime-aged dominated profile, there are a higher proportion of these animals compared to juvenile and older individuals (Byers and Hill 2009:303). It has been proposed that human predation is the sole cause of this pattern (Stiner 1990) (see Figure 42). The dominant presence of the prime-age group may imply selection (Stiner 1990:317), resulting in the capture of the healthiest and highest-return individuals (Byers and Hill 2009:303). Economically, prime-aged animals are considered by many as 'the optimum age to slaughter an animal [...] at the end of the juvenile period when the growth has stopped, and the meat gain does not increase relative to fodder input' (Davis 1987:39); this

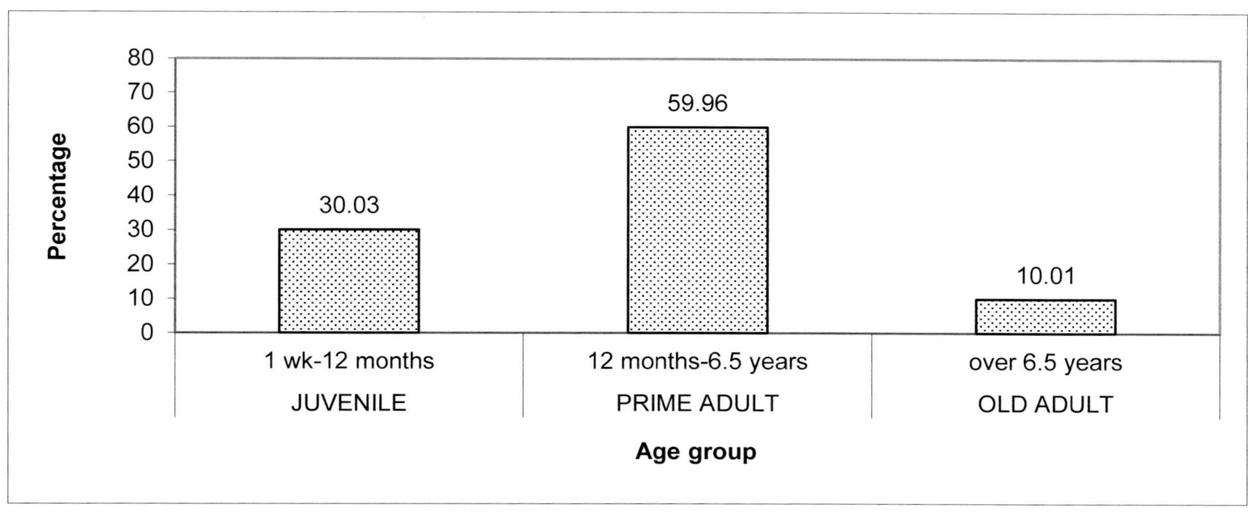

Figure 42. Mortality profile for white-tailed deer in *Operación* 114 by age cohorts.

is especially true for husbandry societies or those who manage domesticated animals.

This information, combined with the identification of some young adults with clear sexual dimorphism, suggests that hunters were probably targeting animals that were physically mature, and would yield the most weight or meat. The combined age distribution and mortality profile data can also be useful for exploring whether there was hunting pressure on deer through time. In general terms and for other areas around the world, hunting pressure has been identified as an increase in the presence of younger animals (Spiess *et al.* 2006), which, as mentioned earlier, clearly reflects a deliberate hunting strategy (Lyman 1994).

It is necessary to consider *Operación* 114 as a context which may reflect the hunting practices of the Maya during the Late Classic period at Chinikihá. The remains of prime-age adults dominate the entire assemblage from this location, indicating that there were no notable differences in their distribution throughout the whole deposit. It should be noted that there were more adults and fewer juveniles found in Layers I-III. If the deposit above the floor represented a later deposit than Layers IV-V beneath, the trend is the opposite to what would be expected if hunting pressure was a factor. Thus, it is possible that the preference for young adult deer at Chinikihá, especially in *Operación* 114, remained stable over 150 to 200 years.

Seasonality profile

A seasonality profile using ten mandibles was generated, again following Byers and Hill's model (2009), together with contemporary hunting data from Chiapas and the Yucatán Peninsula (Álvarez-Romero and Medellín 2005;

León and Montiel 2008; Mandujano and Rico-Gray 1991; Naranjo *et al.* 2010). The month of June was considered as the average month for birth, since it is the mid-point of the birth season in the area. Although the sample is very small, several conclusions can be drawn (Figure 43). It seems that the most kills occurred during winter, with 50% (n = 5) of deer killed during this season. Summer, and a combination of summer/autumn/ winter had 20% (n = 2) each, while one individual (10%) was identified as a possible winter/autumn kill.

This pattern perhaps shows that farmers, who usually carry out the hunting, are less occupied by their land during the winter, which corresponds to the dry season (Mandujano and Rico-Gray 1991:177). Although deer seems to have been procured all year round, there is a predominance of winter kills (December to March), an activity still favoured today in the Maya region (León and Montiel 2008; Naranjo *et al.* 2004:242). Hunting in the dry season may also be more practical since, as Pohl (1990:154) states, during this time '...swampy land dries out and game tends to congregate near sources of water' and hence, the animals would become easier to target. Deer hunting has been associated with ceremonies and rituals related to the rain god, *Chaak* (Mandujano and Rico-Gray 1991:179) and agricultural fertility (Pohl 1981), and as such it was necessary to perform a ritual during the winter to assure the return of the rains.

Furthermore, evidence for seasonal hunting can be observed in the distribution of seasonality by stratigraphic layers. The presence of teeth with different seasonality have been found in the same Layer, suggesting multiple depositional episodes. It may also indicate separate consumption episodes occurring in a cyclical pattern (Table 41). One of the limitations of this method is that only in very few cases can an absolute

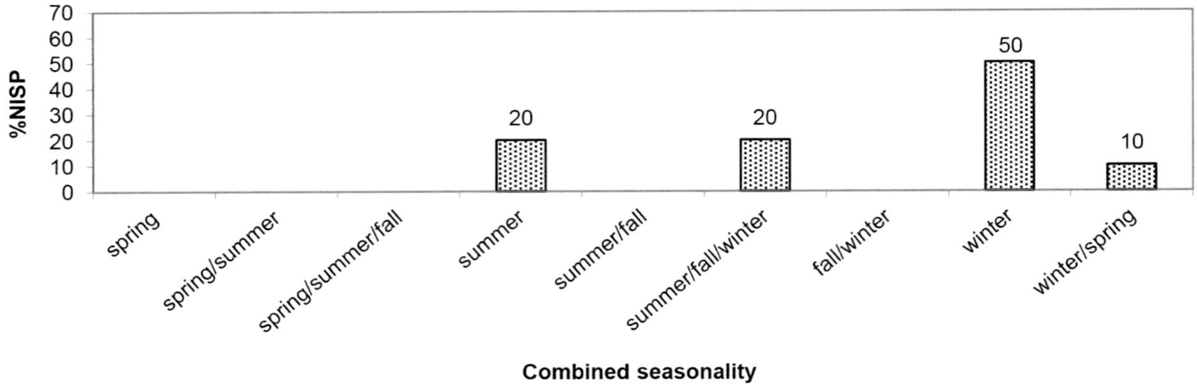

Figure 43. Frequency (in percentage) for white-tailed deer mandibles by combined seasonality.

season-of-death be identified, depending on the identification of a tight and definite age range. This can be influenced by many factors, such as micro-variation of birth seasons, animal population density and climate variation.

Unfortunately it was not possible to identify a specific age cohort for the rest of the species present in *Operación* 114, and no seasonality could be identified. Consequently, it was impossible to know if other animals were obtained during the dry season, or exploited in other seasons. The presence of remains from mature dogs and rabbits suggest that the procurement of these species followed a similar trend to that of the deer, with animals being targeted as prime-age adults. As to what time of the year they were being harvested, that information is unknown at present. In a contemporary analysis of hunting strategies in the Lacandón area, it was possible to observe hunters usually targeting larger animals, because of the meat yield per unit (Naranjo *et al.* 2004:235). In addition, ethnographic observations of modern Yucatec Maya suggests that peasant-hunters will only choose smaller species (iguana, agouti, and armadillo), when there is scarcity of larger species (>10kg of weight) (León and Montiel 2008:254). The reason for this seems to be based on the effort input and the return rates of meat (Pohl 1994:138). In other words, a lot of rabbits would be needed in order to obtain the same amount of meat procured from a deer. A similar logic may have been applied by hunters during the Late Classic.

Nevertheless, when the information regarding seasonality for white-tailed deer is combined with the data from the mortality profile, several interesting points can be drawn. First, there are few fawns, with the youngest specimen being two months old, and a few juveniles (<12 months of age). This suggests that this age group was not being targeted. Using the mortality data in combination with the seasonality study allows us to explore the ancient Mayan hunting strategies, which might have involved periodic kills of white-tailed deer throughout the year, but mostly during the dry season, targeting prime-aged animals (*sensus* Byers and Hill 2009). During the dry season, it has also been reported that deer stags tend to gather around the young fawns and females, forming larger groups (Pohl 1990:154). It is possible that young animals may have been killed unintentionally during the hunt for larger ones, as, if hunting pressure was a factor, a rise in the presence of young animals would have been observable in the assemblage. The results from this assemblage may reflect opportunistic hunting. There is no doubt that the main target group was the young prime aged adults for their large meat yield, but it is possible that some hunters may have decided to pursue fawns and females that were in the vicinity of adult males, if the opportunity arose.

In the Maya area, testing to determine whether pressure on faunal resources, especially during the Late Classic period, has been the aim of several studies (e.g. Emery 2010; Pohl 1990). It has been suggested that if there was some hunting pressure, the regular taking of younger animals would be expected, with fewer animals reaching maturity (Pohl 1990:152-153). However, data from several archaeological assemblages from the Maya region suggest that there was no hunting pressure during the Late Classic, or at least this pressure was not occurring across the whole area. Two sites that display minimal evidence of hunting pressure include Seibal and Altar de Sacrificios (Pohl 1990:153). In addition, it has been suggested that if hunting pressure was a factor, this would have affected the social classes differently. For the high classes, an increase of hunting pressure on some of their exclusively accessed resources may have forced them to use complete carcasses in a more efficient fashion (Emery 2010:122). In order to explore

Bag Number	Layer	Individual Number	Estimated season
689	II	12	summer
753	IV	2	Winter
753	IV	3	summer
1019	IV	9	Winter
1019	IV	10	Winter
788	IV	15	Winter
1012	V	1	Winter
842	V	4	summer/autumn/winter
842	V	5	spring/winter
842	V	6	summer/autumn/winter

Table 41. Distribution of individuals per layer and season for teeth in *Operación* 114.

this possibility, an analysis of the distribution of body portions and patterns of butchering was also conducted and will be presented in Part Two of this chapter.

Distribution of faunal modifications and environmental modifications

Carnivore chewing and rodent gnawing are the most common surface modifications present on the materials of *Operación* 114 (Figure 44). In Chapter seven, it was noted that a high percentage of the material had modifications, primarily carnivore chewing. In this chapter, the distribution of modified material by layer is explored, in order to see if it is possible to observe spatial associations between modifications. Carnivore chewing and rodent gnawing were considered independently from one another, resulting in the emergence of two different patterns, discussed below. The data from the faunal modifications is complemented with the information from environmental modifications in order to better understand the taphonomic history of this deposit.

Carnivore chewing

Carnivore chewing marks occurred frequently throughout all the material from *Operación* 114, regardless of taxon (60.56%), and their proportional frequency was relatively similar in all layers. When testing for a difference in context between those layers that were above the stuccoed floor (Layers I, II, and III), and those underneath it (Layers IV and V), there was no significant difference in the results that may have suggested that the material had been left exposed for a sufficient length of time to be affected by carnivores. The data on carnivore chewing needs to be considered in relation to

that regarding rodent gnawing and the distribution of weathered material, both discussed below.

Rodent gnawing

Bones modified by rodents were present in all layers, but were more frequent in Layers IV and V under the door. Statistical tests were also conducted and showed that there was a significant difference between the materials under the floor from those on top (X^2 = 31.2777; df = 1; p > 0.001) in terms of the presence of gnawing marks. This is interesting, as it was considered likely that this floor context was sealed. If this was true, then the presence of gnawing marks on the bones under the floor indicates that Layers IV and V may not have been deposited there deliberately, but were instead placed there unintentionally as part of the fill. However, at this point, it is not possible to make any further inferences.

The presence of both carnivore and rodent modifications suggests that the deposit remained open and uncovered for some time after the material was deposited. When carnivore chewing and rodent gnawing are combined, a Kolmogorov-Smirnov statistical test showed that their distribution by layer is not equal (Two Sample D = 0.2593), therefore, the presence of both types of marks supports the above interpretation, suggesting different formation processes.

Weathering stages

In *Operación* 114, weathering stages were identified for all species. Apart from the white-tailed deer, all other species present Stage 1 weathering, except for collared peccary, with two specimens in Stage 2. In the case of the deer, the overall material shows little to moderate weathering, with the majority of the material at Stage 1 (89.92%, n = 847), followed by Stage 2 (5.31%, n = 50), Stage 3 (3.29%, n = 31), Stage 0 (1.06%, n = 10), and Stage 4 (0.42%, n = 4). No material was registered at Stage 5 of weathering, as bones with this alteration 'tend to disintegrate to dust' (Lyman 1994:365). The material shows very little spatial patterning by layer, as Stage 1 was the dominant degree of weathering in all layers. There was no significant difference between the two deposits above and below the floor, probably due to the high proportion of bone displaying Stage 1 weathering, intermingled with bones with a higher degree of exposure (Figure 45). The dominance of materials displaying Stage 1 suggests that most of the materials were only minimally exposed to the environment.

When the data from the faunal modification analysis is compared with that of weathering, there appears to be a significant correlation between the presence of faunal modifications and the degree of erosion (Pearson's r = 0.684). This suggests that the time the

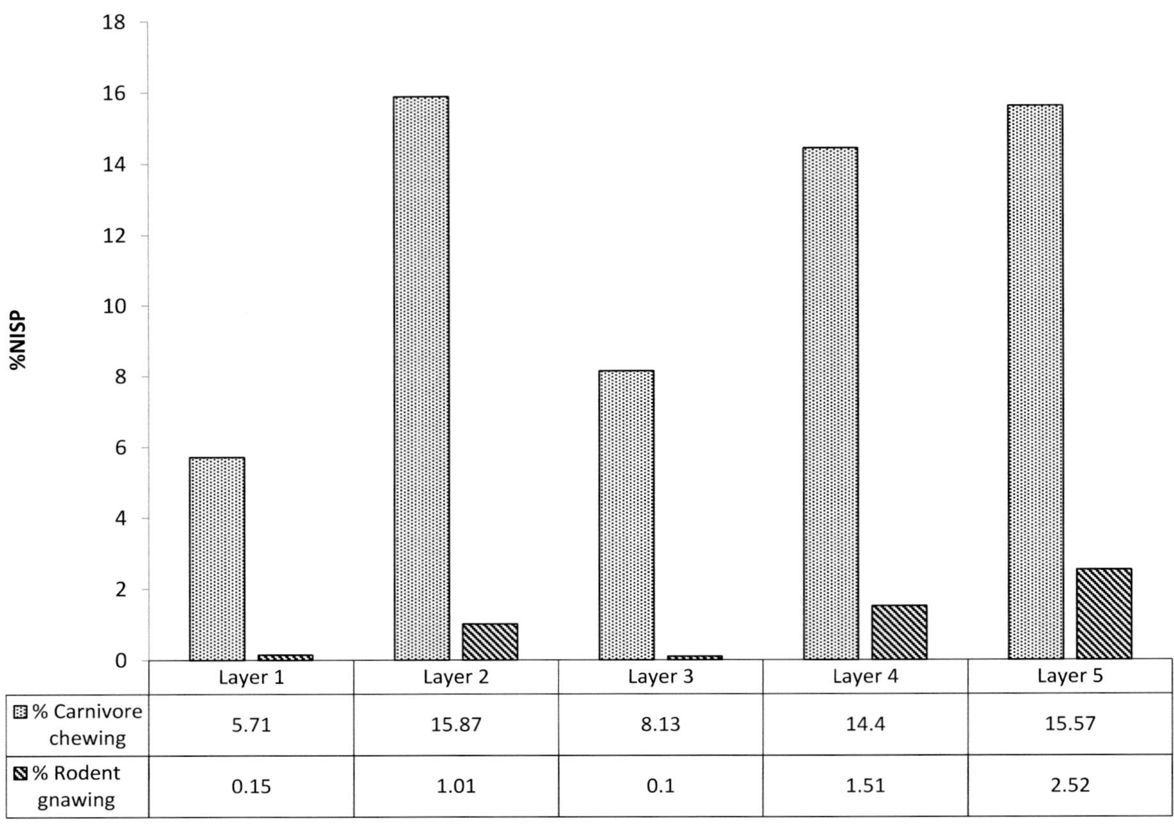

	Layer 1	Layer 2	Layer 3	Layer 4	Layer 5
% Carnivore chewing	5.71	15.87	8.13	14.4	15.57
% Rodent gnawing	0.15	1.01	0.1	1.51	2.52

Figure 44. Distribution of white-tailed deer bones with presence of carnivore chewing and rodent gnawing in *Operación* 114.

bone was exposed after deposition was too short to have had a severe effect. If a comparison is made with the weathering rates recorded from several carcasses of known death age (Gifford 1984), the proportions obtained for *Operación* 114 are consistent with those from a carcass that was exposed for between five months and a year. This is comparable to modern Maya practices of leaving domestic trash exposed for some time (see Stanton *et al.* 2008 for a discussion). Although it is impossible to know the exact amount of time the materials were exposed to the elements, this comparison suggests that the materials in *Operación* 114 were buried very quickly, and may represent a relatively short-term deposit or deposits (following Behrensmeyer 1978).

The deer assemblage showed that there is no spatial patterning in terms of age, sex, seasonality, and presence of taphonomic modifications. Furthermore, the data suggest that all deer were treated in a similar fashion. It is concluded that if there is a different formation process reflected by deer remains, it must be tested in terms of the presence of skeletal elements and body parts, the topic of Part Two.

Part two: testing for processing patterns

This section presents a more elaborate analysis of faunal processing, paying special attention to the white-tailed deer, as the remains of this species presented the most cultural modifications. The distribution of body parts by Layer is explored, followed by a discussion of the body part preference and skeletal completeness in *Operación* 114. This will explore the general efficiency with which deer carcasses were processed. This is then compared to the second most frequent species, the domestic dog, in order to explore differences by taxa. Further comparison between deer skeletal completeness is conducted using data from other sites, resulting from different activities, and include a bone workshop and a ritual deposit. The intensity of body part processing is analysed using the distribution of minimum number of elements (MNE), and minimum animal units (MAU). A comparison between fragmented and complete bones is also presented. These analyses are complementary, establishing a more complete picture of the exploitation of faunal resources and ultimately providing invaluable data on the resource processing patterns and the formation of the deposit. Such analysis will facilitate an examination into what behaviour or behaviours are

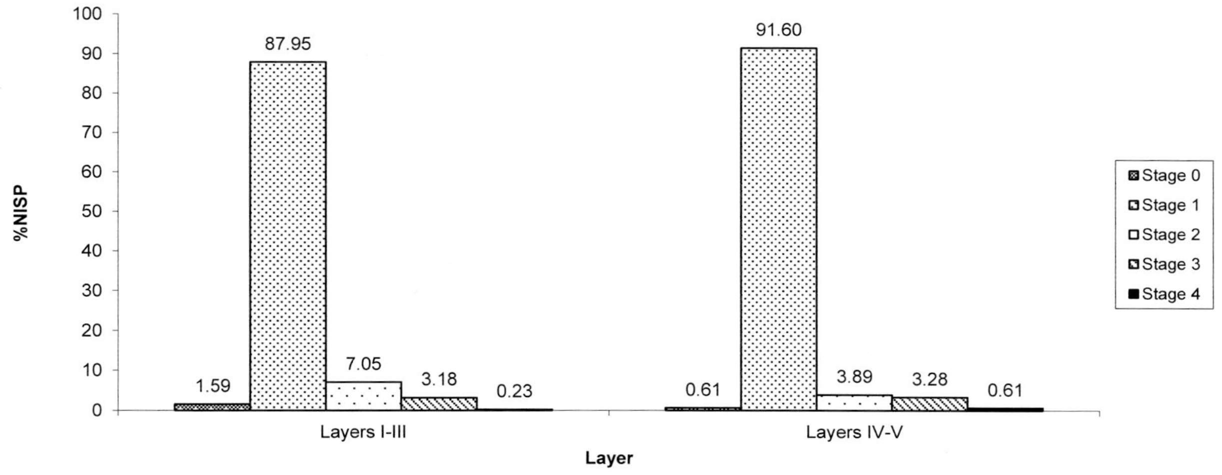

Figure 45. Weathering stage by layer (%NISP) for white-tailed deer, *Operación* 114.

behind these patterns. It has been seen that 'applying a wide range of procedures to the same datasets, we can see which patterns in the data area inherent to those data, and which are characteristic of a particular analytical technique' (O'Connor 2000:79).

Distribution of anatomical regions

To explore the possibility of a preference for specific anatomical regions, several analyses were carried out. First, raw counts (NISP) for body portions for all deer by Layer are presented in Table 42, with the overall proportions for each region present in Figure 46. Then, these proportions were grouped by their presence above (Layers I-III) and under the floor (Layers IV-V) to test if there was variation in distribution in relation to the floor. The distribution of body portions by age has been considered in order to explore if there was a different pattern in the exploitation of sub-adults and adults. Finally, the body portions are standardised considering their presence in a complete skeleton in order to assess what body parts are mostly represented,

and this result is then compared to other assemblages to see different patterns.

It is important to note that some bone elements, such as the carpals, were completely missing from this assemblage, or were in very low frequencies that do not reflect their real distribution. For example, ribs (NISP = 1), were rare, but were expected in much higher numbers. Unidentified rib fragments were grouped in the medium/large mammal category. Some of these may be deer, but because they did not present clear diagnostic characteristics, they were not included in the Artiodactyl or deer categories.

The most frequently occurring body part of the white-tailed deer was the torso (37.37%), followed by the upper back (15.39%), and upper front (14.86%) limbs. Lower front and lower back limbs occurred in very similar in proportions (5.84% and 5.73% respectively), and the distal element represents just 0.74%. A noted disparity is the difference between the neck (12%) and head parts (7.86%), as these elements are expected in similar

Layer	Head	Neck	Torso	Upper front	Lower front	Upper back	Lower back	Distal	Long bone	Total
Layer I	1	5	15	14	5	14	7	1		62
Layer II	14	24	58	31	7	22	13	1	2	172
Layer III	11	19	84	22	18	38	12	2		206
Layer IV	24	35	103	31	12	49	9	3		266
Layer V	24	27	86	40	11	22	12			222
n/a		3	6	2	2		1			14
Total	74	113	352	140	55	145	54	7	2	942
% total	7.86	12.00	37.37	14.86	5.84	15.39	5.73	0.74	0.21	100.00

Table 42. Distribution of skeletal regions by layer based on NISP for white-tailed deer in *Operación* 114.

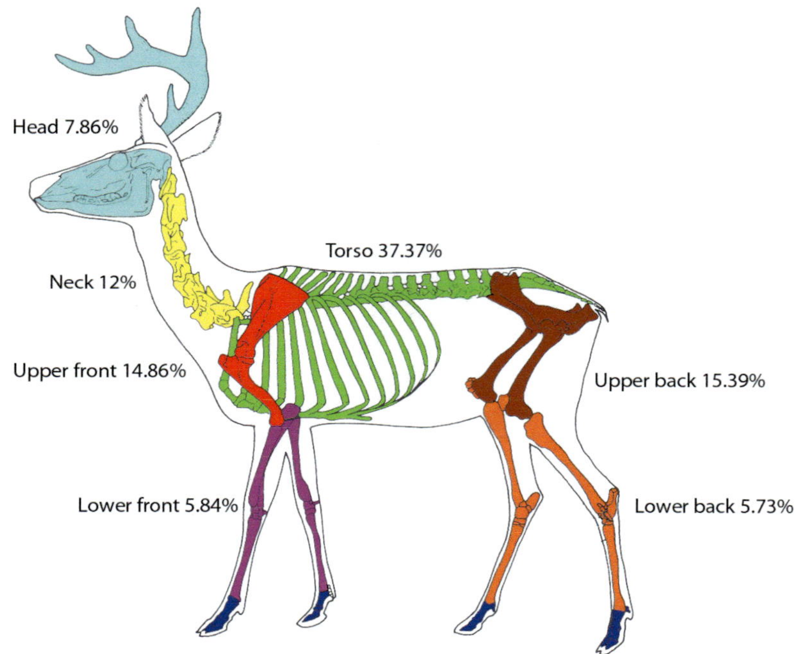

Figure 46. NISP distribution by body portion for white-tailed deer, *Operación* 114 (modified from Reitz and Wing 1999:171).

proportions. Skull fragments are very scarce, especially the occipital region (n = 4). No complete skulls were present, while there are at least 22 atlas and 17 axis elements, suggesting again that similar proportions of crania should be present. The presence of skull fragments suggests that complete animals may have been arriving to site, or were transported over short distances (Reitz and Wing 1999:203). The removal of skulls may have occurred during the initial butchering of carcasses, however, this would have resulted in the complete absence of skulls from this context. It is possible that skulls were being deposited elsewhere, as seen among contemporary Guatemalan Maya hunters who deposit skulls in hunting shrines inside caves (Brown 2009; Brown and Emery 2008). Other deposits where skulls and antlers are common elements include ritual deposits in caves and sink holes (Pohl 1983). The skulls could also have been smashed, as in the 16th century, when after a deer hunt, the Maya cooked the liver, heart, lungs and stomach, as well as the brains, breaking the skull to get access (Pohl 1990:161).

It is also interesting to note the difference in proportions of lower limb elements (5.75%) and the low proportions of distal elements (0.74%), since these two body portions should be present in similar proportions. During the excavation process it was observed that in many cases, tarsal bones were still semi-articulated when they were discarded. These, however, were not connected to a metatarsal or a phalange, although their presence supports the previous observation that whole animals were arriving to site. Distal elements were underrepresented in the sample, suggesting selective butchery.

While it is difficult to determine why the head and foot elements were underrepresented, it may be that head elements tend to be missing from consumption deposits because whole deer heads were used for decorative paraphernalia, tool manufacturing, decoration, and antlers could have been removed for use as tools (Brown 1996, 2002). It also appears that the head was sometimes removed from sacrificial animals, as seen in the burial of a headless deer in association with the Motmot marker in Copán (Storey 2005:329), and it is therefore possible that the heads were deposited elsewhere. Ethnographical data from Lake Atitlán, Guatemala suggest that the skulls may be removed to be deposited in hunting shrines (Brown and Emery 2008:318-319). The unexpected low representation of foot elements could be explained in several ways, including that they were split open to access the bone marrow (Lupo 1998), or that they were left as 'riders' (Binford 1981), still attached to the skins of animals, with just a few making their way to this deposit.

Pohl (1990:158) mentions that one explanation for the low numbers of medial and distal phalanges in archaeological contexts is because these bones remain attached to the skins when these are removed, therefore, these bones are expected to be present where skins are deposited, and not in meat-processing deposits. Another explanation could be that they are completely removed from the context by scavenging dogs and other fauna (Pohl 1990:158). In *Operación* 114 it was observed that there was a high frequency of bones with carnivore chewing, therefore, it is possible that at least some of the distal bones may be missing due to animal activity.

White-tailed deer body parts in Operación 114

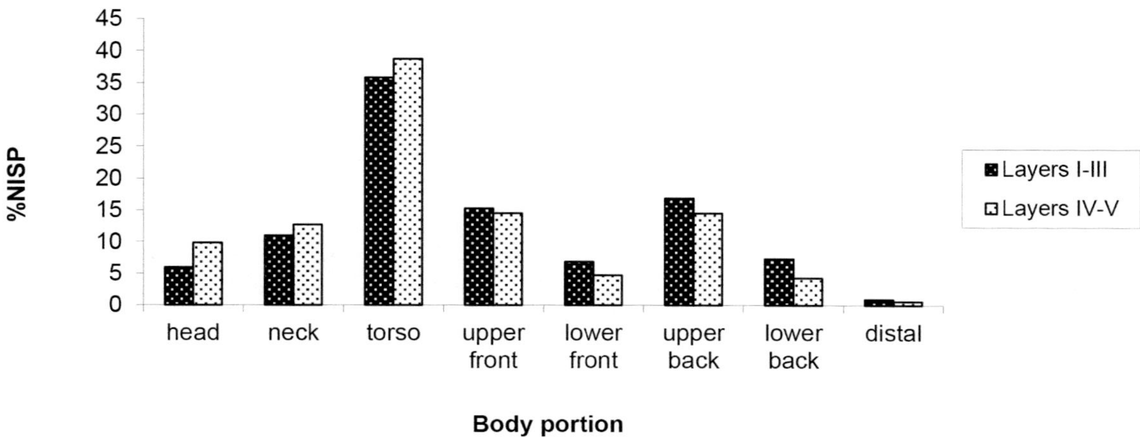

Figure 47. Distribution of body portions (%NISP) above and below the floor in *Operación* 114.

Neck and torso proportions are relatively high, and maybe accounted for by their high frequencies in a complete skeleton. The axial region has up to 54 individual bones, including ribs, cervical, thoracic, lumbar and sacral vertebrae (Emery 2010:199, Table 7.4). Their high proportions are expected in deposits where complete carcasses have arrived at a site and are being processed *in situ*.

The high percentage of torso elements may also be a consequence of their high frequencies in a complete skeleton. On the other hand, the high percentage of bones belonging to the upper sections of both, back limb and front limb, which include the scapula and humerus, and the upper back limb (innominate bones and femur), may represent a deliberate selection. These parts are prized, since they produce the largest meat packages. It is interesting to note however, that scapulae and innominate bones outnumber long bones in general. A further exploration of the observed presence of each bone in comparison to what is expected is presented in the Food Utility Index (FUI) section.

Torso and upper portions of the front and back limbs represented 67.62% of the whole sample. Since these carry the most meat, and/or are the most palatable, including meat cuts such as the ribs, loins and the haunch, their presence suggests selective butchery of high value parts. In contexts associated with the elite, especially in subsistence-type deposits (e.g. palaces), a high proportion of scapulae, humerus, vertebrae, innominate bones, and femur are expected, although this is not necessarily true in all cases (Emery 200b).

Figure 47 shows body portions grouped by stratigraphic level. Under the floor, there was a slightly larger percentage of head, neck and torso elements, while above the floor, there was a greater presence of the appendicular skeleton, including the upper front and back limbs, lower limb bones, and distal elements. The distribution seems very similar for both sub-groups, and is not statistically significant, suggesting a random distribution of body parts with no specific patterning throughout the whole deposit. This indicates that the disposal of white-tailed deer remains occurred in a similar way throughout the deposit.

As shown in Table 29, there were cases where discarded bones were still articulated, or semi-articulated, with the most common being axial, lower or distal elements of limbs, including vertebrae, ribs, and feet. In Layers I-III, there were 20 individual bones that formed 10 groupings of two and three bones, while in Layers IV-V there were 43 individual bones that formed 11 groupings of two or more bones, including a segment of 17 vertebrae. In Table 43, groups of articulated bones (axial, foot, and so on) were divided into two sub-samples (above and under the floor), in order to see the distribution of articulated segments.

In Layers I-III, there was approximately the same number of both axial and distal units, while in Layers IV-V there seems to be more axial units than distal ones. This distribution was not significant statistically when the two levels were compared. The distribution of articulated units mimics the distribution of body parts, with more appendicular body portions found in Layers I-III, and more head, neck and torso portions in Layers IV-V.

When grouped by age, the distribution of body portions also showed no significant difference between groups. Juvenile, immature, and sub-adult categories were grouped under 'sub-adult' and then compared to the

Layer	Axial unit	Distal unit	Total
Layers I-III	5	4	9
Layers IV-V	9	2	11
Total	**14**	**6**	**20**

Table 43. Distribution of articulated units considering the presence of floor (note that several bones may be included in each unit).

'adult' category (Figure 48). All body portions are present in the two age categories, and again, torso elements were the most frequent for both age groups. However, there were more adult specimens in the categories of head, upper and lower back, while there are more sub-adult specimens in the other categories.

To allow for comparisons between different body portions, a skeletal completeness calculation was conducted by standardising the observed values for body portions and comparing them with those of an expected frequency (Emery 2010:199). The skeletal completeness ratio (Reitz and Wing 1999:212) is based on the comparison between the observed percentage of elements and the expected percentage of elements in a complete skeleton. The logged ratio obtained for each body portion can be positive or negative, where zero indicates equal numbers of observed and expected elements in a complete skeleton. Positive values indicate an overrepresentation, and a negative value indicates underrepresentation. Since different studies classify bones in different anatomical portions (see Table 6), bone elements from *Operación* 114 were then

re-classified into these categories in other to compare at the intrasite levels. In Table 44 this classification is presented for white-tailed deer and dog. While the skeletal regions of deer that occurred more commonly were the torso or axial (45.84%), upper front limb (16.39%), and upper back limb (16.74%), dog remains occurred more frequently in the forms of cranial (22.72%) and distal segments (31.81%).

The ratio values of expected to observed for deer body portions are shown in Figure 49. The standardised values reflect the overall importance of the upper front and hind limbs (36.25% and 35% respectively). In this distribution, cranial fragments are highlighted, with cranial elements, mostly represented by hemimandibles, total 15.75%, while axial elements represent 7.35% of the skeleton. There is a lower representation of lower limb elements in general (11% for lower front and 2.25% for lower back limb) with a low presence of tibia, ulna, radio and metapodials. This could be due to their removal from the carcasses, as they are stronger bones that are often used for tool manufacture. Finally, distal elements (phalanges, carpals, and tarsals) represent 0.81%. These results contrast to those obtained by Teeter (2001:225) at Caracol, where a high proportion of skull and limb elements were associated with the elite.

The result from the observed to expected ratio analysis confirms that the upper limbs were probably the most important element in regards to the best meat cuts, reflecting a cultural predilection for them. An overall ratio for meat-bearing to non-meat bearing portions [(limb/(cranial+axial+distal elements)] was obtained following Emery (2010:42), that compared meat-

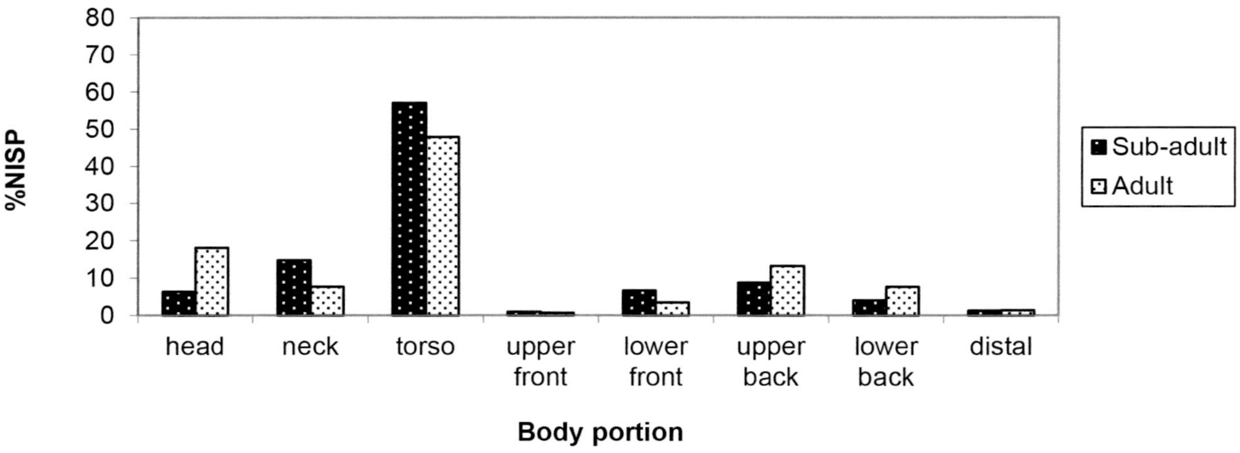

Figure 48. Distribution of body portions by age group (%NISP) for white-tailed deer in *Operación* 114.

Skeletal region	White-tailed deer	Domestic dog
Cranial	**8.42%**	**22.72%**
antler	2	0
hemi-mandible	44	4
skull	27	1
Axial	**45.84%**	**9.09%**
cervical vertebra	114	0
thoracic vertebra	126	0
lumbar vertebra	138	1
sacral vertebra	18	0
rib	1	1
Upper front limb	**16.39%**	**4.54%**
scapula	114	0
humerus	26	1
Lower front limb	**5.08%**	**13.63%**
radius	28	3
ulna	16	0
Upper hind limb	**16.74%**	**9.09%**
innominate	119	1
femur	26	1
Lower hind limb	**1.03%**	**9.09%**
tibia	9	2
fibula	0	0
Distal	**6.69%**	**31.81%**
phalanges	5	2
carpal/tarsal	32	1
metacarpal/metatarsal	21	4
Total	**866 (100%)**	**22 (100%)**

Table 44. NISP Distribution of white-tailed deer and domestic dog body parts (modified from Emery 2010:199).

bearing to non-meat bearing elements. This resulted in a value of 0.7252, suggesting that the proportion of meat to non-meat bearing elements is very similar, with both elements being used as a dietary staple. The ratio from Chinikihá contrasts with data from Petexbatún (1.31), where the proportion of front and hind limb bones was higher. The hind limb in particular was well represented, probably due to its high meat yield and the fact that the long bones of the leg could be used as raw materials for tool manufacture (Emery 2010:125).

When compared with all the other taxa present in *Operación* 114, it is clear that there is a regular distribution of white-tailed deer that reflects a deliberate choice of body portions (X^2 = 59.248; df = 8; p < 0.001), especially those with a higher meat value and/or utility index. Furthermore, when front and hind limb bones were compared, the hind limb bones were found to be more frequent than the front limb elements

(55.6%), a preference that is statistically significant (t = 3.611; df = 40; P < 0.001).

Using the skeletal completeness analysis by age sub-groups (Figure 50), the results again showed that there is no significant difference between the different deer age groups suggesting that the same body portions selected in adult individuals, were also selected in sub-adults. This may reflect a systematic use of deer carcasses regardless of age group. In both adults and sub-adults, the most popular body portion was the back haunch, which is not surprising as the Maya zooarchaeological literature mentions the back haunch is the meatiest and most economically attractive part of the deer, as 'the larger bones of the back leg would also have served as raw material for implements of various kinds' (Pohl 1985a:141).

As a comparison, domestic dog body portions were also re-grouped and graphed, following the skeletal completeness analysis used for deer. While there was a clear dominance of the haunch in deer, the most frequent body region which occurred among the domestic dog remains was the distal (31.82%NISP), followed by the cranial (18.18%NISP), lower front limb, and upper hind limb (13.64%NISP each). Axial and lower hind limb elements represent 9.09%NISP each, while upper front 4.55%NISP. When the observed distribution of elements was compared to the number of expected ones (Figure 51), the results suggest that most skeletal regions were present, in a more homogeneous distribution, with axial and distal elements being underrepresented. An ANOVA test showed that when dog body elements were compared to those from other species, excluding deer, there was no significant difference, in contrast with the result for white-tailed deer, which showed a clear selection of body parts.

The data obtained for white-tailed deer was then used to conduct direct comparisons between *Operación* 114 and other assemblages in the Maya area (Anderson 2009; Emery 2010). In Figure 52, a comparison between two other contexts with a high frequency of deer remains is presented. These include Cueva de los Quetzales (ritual deposit), and context L4-3 of Dos Pilas (tool manufacturing deposit). Cueva de los Quetzales is located inside the ceremonial centre of Las Pacayas site (300 BC - AD 500). The cave is located to the side of a large pyramid and it has been suggested that artefacts and other ritual objects were thrown into the cave once they were used (Anderson 2009). Group L4-3 is a small residential complex located in the centre of Dos Pilas and was largely occupied during the Late/Terminal Classic period; it mostly consists of debitage from bone working (Emery 2010:191).

While Anderson (2009) has stressed that bone distribution from Cueva de los Quetzales resembles hunting shrines,

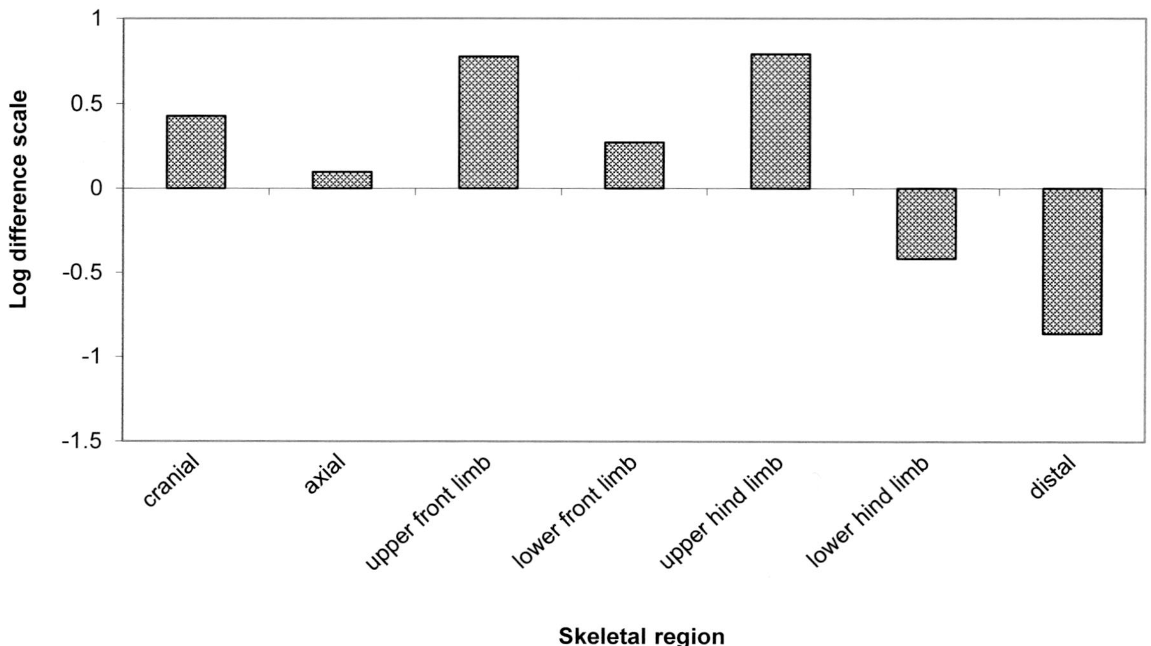

Figure 49. Ratio of expected to observed skeletal regions for white-tailed deer, *Operación* 114.

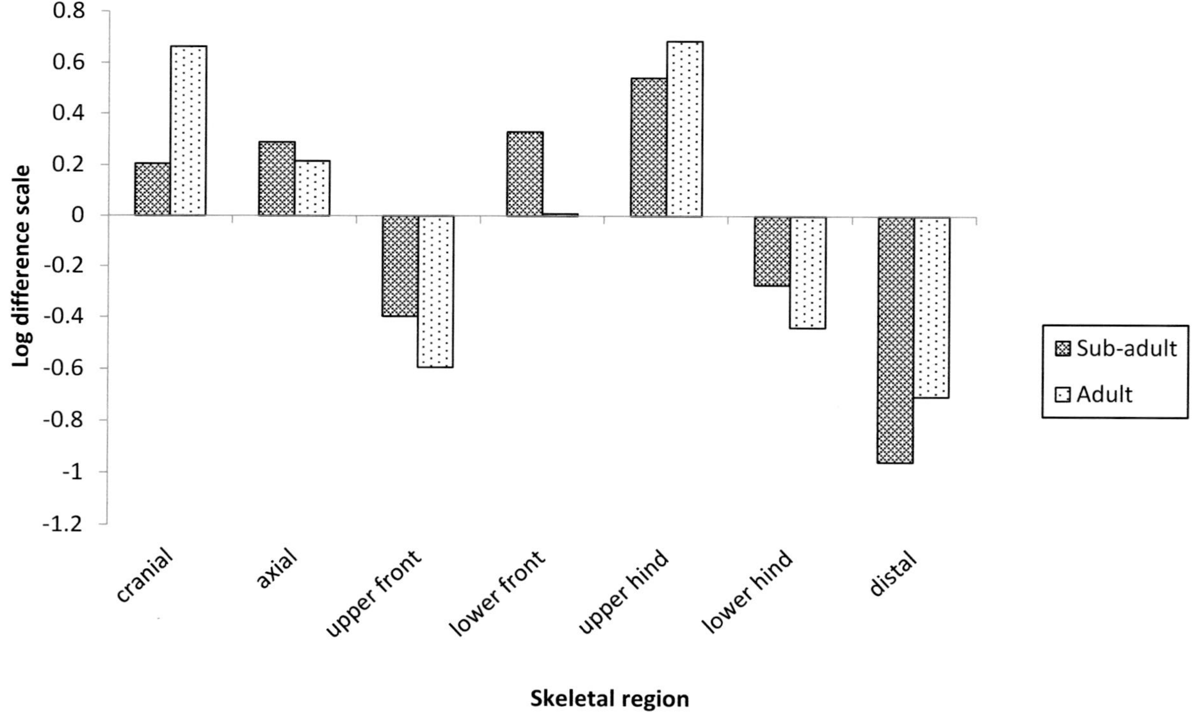

Figure 50. Skeletal completeness distribution for white-tailed deer by age group in *Operación* 114.

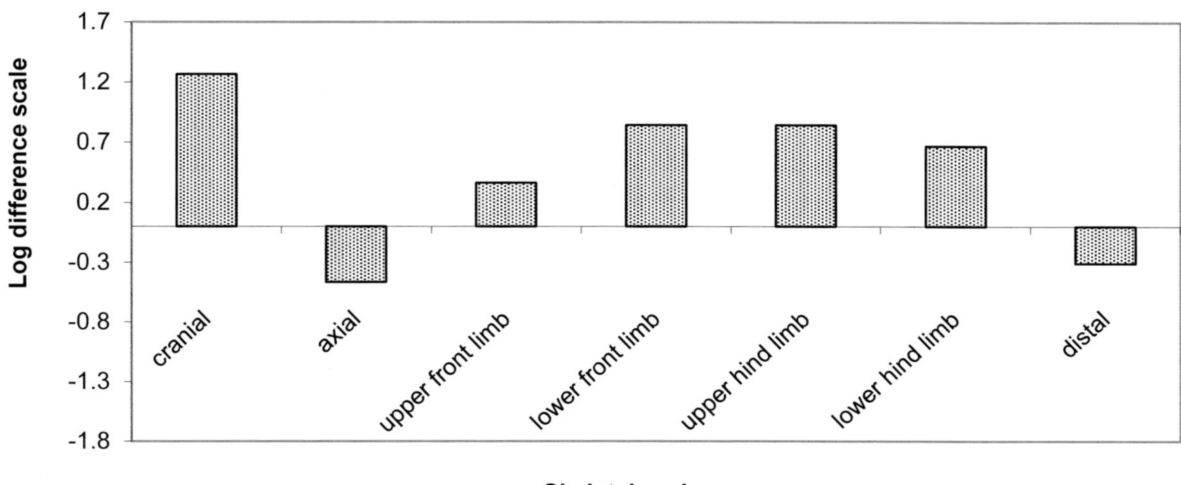

Figure 51. Ratio of expected to observed skeletal regions for domestic dog in *Operación* 114.

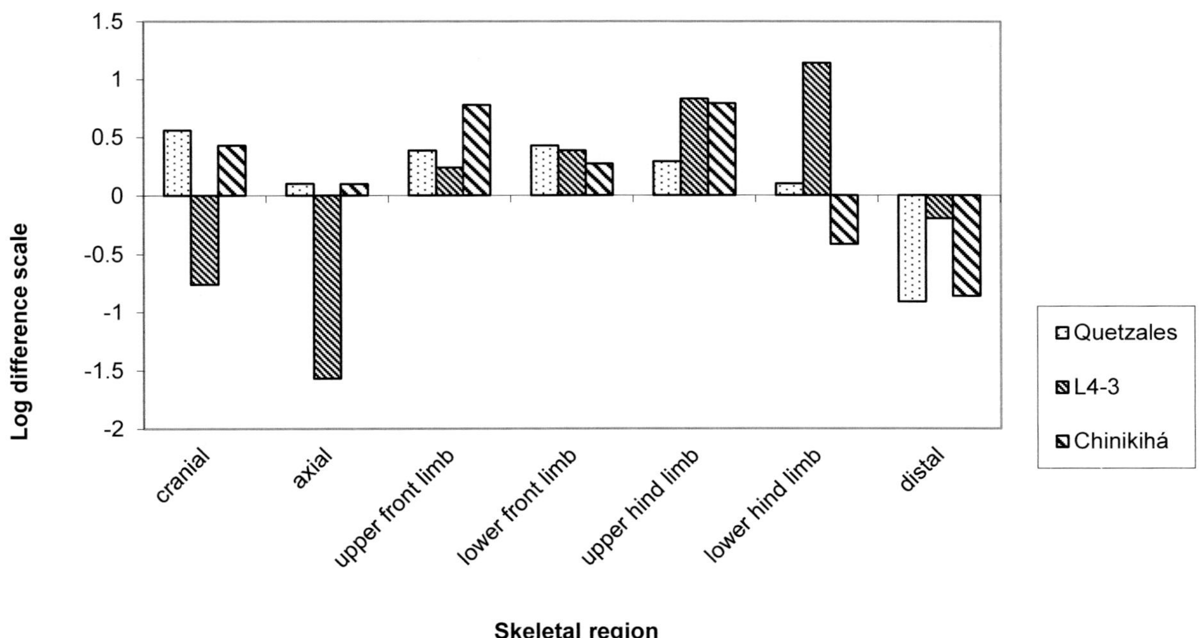

Figure 52. Skeletal completeness comparison between Chinikihá, Cueva de los Quetzales and Group L4-3.

while the Group L4-3 remains show a preference for those skeletal elements that can be transformed into bone tools. When Chinikihá is compared to those assemblages, it has a body portion distribution similar to Cueva de Quetzales, and both Chinikihá and Cueva de Quetzales are different from Group L4-3. In Group L4-3 there is a high representation of long bones from the upper and lower limbs, while head, torso, and distal elements are less frequent than expected. The majority of body portions from Cueva de Quetzales and Chinikihá are upper limbs and cranial parts.

Minimum number of elements (MNE) and minimum animal units (MAU)

To explore the processing patterns observed in deer, minimum number of elements (MNE) and minimum animal units (MAU) will be examined. MNE and MAU were calculated for each skeletal element (Table 45). MNE was calculated based on the most common portion of the skeletal element present. MNE values show a recurrent pattern of element selection for breakage is present, such as in the vertebrae as well as in different portions of the skull. MAU values are obtained by dividing the NISP by the expected number of each element present in a complete carcass—often referred to as the *modified count* (O'Connor 2000:71, original italics). For example, in the case of the scapula (70 MNE) it is divided by two (35 MAU), giving a better idea of the proportion of elements present.

When MNE is plotted against MAU (Figure 53), animal processing patterns can be seen. The torso elements have the highest value for MNE, while their MAU value is relatively low, as several vertebrae are grouped into a single unit. Upper front and back limbs, as well as the neck, have higher MAU values than the rest, and thus represent very compact units. There is a repetition of the same bone portions, indicating that each group is consistently treated in the same fashion. Head, lower limb, and both lower front and back limbs have relatively low MNE and MAU values, confirming once more the underrepresentation of these elements in the sample. These data also show the importance of the upper segments of both front and hind legs in the collection. Interestingly, there is a high value for neck MAU, suggesting that this was also a portion that was highly valued.

MAU values were then used to obtain %MAU, by taking the maximum value for MAU and using it as the relative maximum of the sample or standard by which all other elements are then multiplied by 100 to establish a normalised scale (Binford 1984:80-81). The information derived from %MAU then, is similar to that of the observed/expected ratio, and informs us about the

Skeletal element	NISP	MNE	MAU	%MAU
antler	2	2	1.00	2.86
skull	27	5	2.50	7.14
hemi-mandible	44	10	5.00	14.29
atlas	22	13	13.00	37.14
axis	17	16	16.00	45.71
cervical vertebrae	75	64	12.80	36.57
thoracic vertebrae	126	73	5.62	16.04
lumbar vertebrae	138	121	17.29	49.39
sacrum	18	16	16.00	45.71
sternum	5	1	1.00	2.86
rib	1	1	0.04	0.11
scapula	114	70	35.00	100.00
humerus	26	12	6.00	17.14
radius	28	12	6.00	17.14
ulna	16	10	5.00	14.29
carpal	0	0	0.00	0.00
metacarpal	11	4	2.00	5.71
innominate	119	62	31.00	88.57
femur	26	9	4.50	12.86
patella	3	3	1.50	4.29
tibia	9	4	2.00	5.71
tarsal	32	30	3.33	9.52
metatarsal	10	4	2.00	5.71
phalanges	5	5	0.21	0.60

Table 45. Distribution of NISP, MNE, MAU, and %MAU values for white-tailed deer.

over or underrepresentation of animal units. Since the values of %MAU are a derivative from NISP (Reitz and Wing 1999:217), %MAU values stress those body parts that are the most common. Body parts that are highly represented include cervical vertebrae (especially the atlas and the axis), while limb bones in general have a lower %MAU value. In the sample from Chinikihá, bones that have a high %MAU value include the scapula (100%) and the innominate bones (88.57%). However, their high %MAU value could also be a result of their survivorship in the assemblage as scapula and innominate are highly dense bones (Lyman 1994:258). Their economical utility, or the probability of a skeletal part to be transported back to a camp to be further used, also needs to be considered as an alternative explanation to %MAU (Lyman 1994:258). While the %MAU values point to a similar result from the observed/expected ratio, this does not assist in the determination of an appropriate explanation. In order to explain the high values of the scapulae and innominate, the Food Utility Index analysis was conducted.

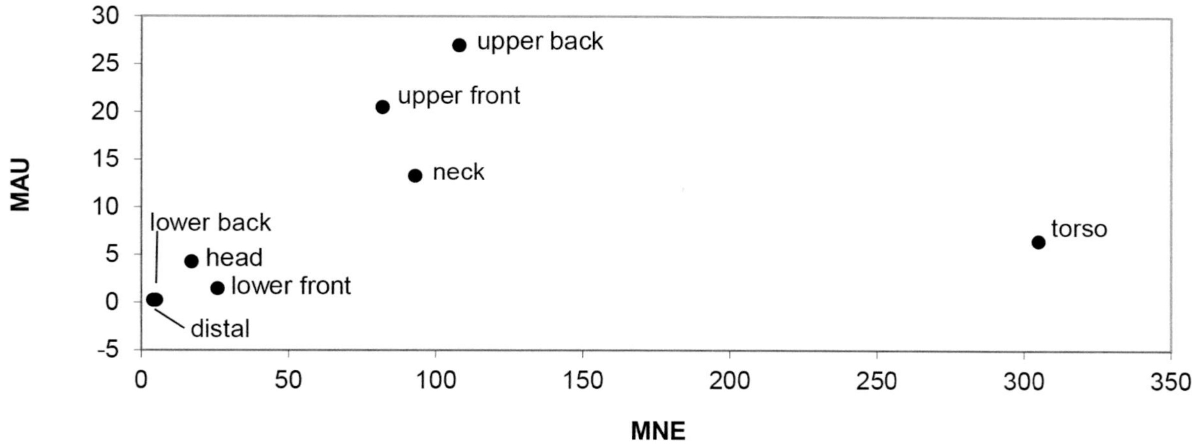

Figure 53. Distribution of MNE and MAU for white-tailed deer,
Operación 114.

Food utility index (FUI)

Element analysis by Food Utility Index (FUI) (Binford 1978; Jones and Metcalfe 1988; Metcalfe and Jones 1988; Reitz and Wing 1999) shows that there was not only an interest in the meatier parts, but also those that are the fattiest. Table 46 indicates which skeletal elements were more highly valued than others (following Kelly 2001; Metcalfe and Jones 1988). Among high-ranked elements, the scapula (12.79) and the innominate bones (11.33) are on top, along with some of the meat bearing long bones, which include the humerus, radius, ulna, femur, and tibia. The importance of the long bones is not only derived from their meat yield, but also from their potential for bone marrow extraction, and use as raw materials. It is necessary to consider the utility level of these bones for purposes other than diet. Long bones were traditionally modified to create tools and ornaments.

In the medium utility category, which includes all the vertebrae and ribs, the two top ranking elements are the lumbar (22.12) and thoracic (13.34) vertebrae. The relative importance of these skeletal elements relates to their meat yield, as two of the best meat cuts are obtained from these regions. Finally, the low utility elements include the head and distal body portions together. The two top ranked elements in the low utility group are the cervical vertebrae (11.70) and the tarsal bones (5.48). Evidence of cut marks on these two elements was primarily the result of removal of these sections.

What can be drawn from these series of analyses is that all the skeletal elements should be present in the same proportions as the most numerous or highest ranking elements, in this case, the scapula and innominate bones. In Figure 54, the observed distribution for each skeletal element is plotted against the expected range. Again, the scapula and the innominate bones have the highest index. In comparison, the two long bones that also form part of the upper limbs (humerus and femur) are significantly lower than expected. While this graph confirms again the low presence of long bones in general, it also suggests that other bones, such as the scapula, may be more often discarded in a context like this than expected. If this context reflects the consumption of meat, and a selection of the meatiest sections of the deer, then the relative high proportion of scapulae and innominate bones suggests they may be good indicators for identifying deposits that result from meat consumption.

Alternatively, the high percentage of scapulae and innominate bones may suggest that these two elements are being discarded more often in the same context where materials associated with dietary consumption are also present. This contrasts with Emery's (2007b:61) suggestion for the Piedras Negras assemblage, where scapulae and pelvis were often removed during butchering. Emery (2007b:61) also suggests that the femur and humerus are better suited to measure the use of preferred cuts (such as the haunch). The differences between Chinikihá and Piedras Negras are not well-understood at the moment, but a through taphonomic analysis may help to understand each site's unique formation process.

The combined data from the FUI distribution with the observed/expected ratio also stresses the fact that the high utility skeletal elements were not all important for the same reasons. The high FUI index of scapulae and innominate bones, combined with their significant presence in the deposit, suggests that they

Skeletal element	Low utility	Medium utility	High utility
antler	0.365631		
skull	0.914077		
hemi-mandible	1.828154		
atlas	2.376600		
axis	2.925046		
cervical vertebrae	11.70018		
sternum		0.182815	
thoracic vertebrae		13.34552	
lumbar vertebrae		22.12066	
sacral		2.925046	
rib		0.182815	
scapula			12.79707
humerus			2.193784
radius			2.193784
ulna			1.828154
innominate			11.33455
femur			1.645338
patella			0.548446
tibia			0.731261
carpal	n/a		
metacarpal	0.731261		
tarsal	5.484461		
metatarsal	0.731261		
phalanges	0.914077		

Table 46. Food Utility Index (FUI) distribution by skeletal element.

were important because of their meat yield, but once the meat had been removed, these bones had no other use. On the other hand, the humerus and femur were of high utility, not only associated with the amount of meat they have attached to them. Their infrequency in the same deposit as scapulae and innominate bones suggests that once the meat was stripped off the long bones, they were then converted into tools, or deposited elsewhere. This further suggests that once a complete deer carcass arrived at the site, it was first skinned, with the removal of head and distal elements, and then butchered in compact meat packages of which the upper haunches were favoured, and finally all carcass remnants were tossed in the same deposit.

Bone fragmentation

A question that arises from the above discussion is whether specific body portions or skeletal elements were further processed to obtain bone marrow. It is clear that the meatiest body portions were being targeted, not for just for subsistence, but probably for ceremonial use or consumption as an luxury item. This is supported by a comparison to the remains of feasting events in other parts of the world (e.g. Lau 2002; Munro and Grosman 2010; Pauketat *et al.* 2002). Among the material identified in *Operación* 114, there were several complete bones found, which were from various taxa. In Chapter seven, a summary of fragmented and complete bones was presented by context. This revealed that in *Operación* 114 more than 92% of the material was in a fragmentary state, contrasting with ritual sites, such as cave caches and offerings, where more complete bones are expected (see Anderson 2009).

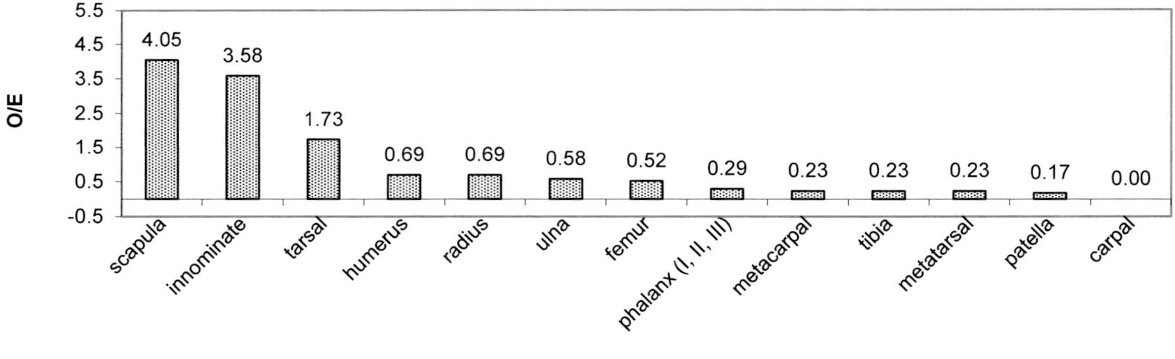

Figure 54. Distribution of skeletal elements ranked by observed/ expected index.

Of the identified deer bones (n = 938), there were at least 16.52% that were complete (n = 155), while 38.09% (n = 8) of all the dog remains were complete. Three rabbit bones—including *Sylvilagus* sp. (n = 2), and *Sylvilagus brasiliensis* (n = 1)—and a single bone of an armadillo were also complete. There was no spatial patterning in their distribution, and complete bones were retrieved from all stratigraphic layers. Cut marks were present exclusively on some of the complete bones from deer, while they were absent from complete bones of other species. At least a third (31.61%) of all complete deer bones exhibited cut marks and other modifications related to processing.

The presence of complete bones is interesting as some are skeletal elements that are rarely found in the archaeological record—such as vertebrae, innominate bones, and scapulae—due to their 'relative low structural density' (Kelly 2001:347), and are more prone to decay than more compact bone. Table 47 shows the complete and fragmented bones for white-tailed deer in *Operación* 114. A total of 81.91%NISP of the skeletal elements were fragments, and 18.09%NISP were complete bones. Solid compact bones like phalanges, axis, patella, and tarsals were more regularly retrieved than vertebrae, innominate bones, and scapulae, those these were more often retrieved still articulated. Other bones that were more commonly broken include the skull, mandible, some regions of the spine, and long bones such as the humerus, radius, and femur. The high frequency of broken scapulae and pelvic bones is probably a consequence of dismembering a carcass and preparing the front and back upper limbs. Hence, these bones were more frequently broken during the butchering. None of the skulls were complete, suggesting that either they were broken to access the brain, or they were broken to obtain the antlers. Long bones on the other hand, were represented by a mix of complete and fragmented bones.

Due to the high degree of fragmentation among the materials from the assemblage, identification to species level was difficult. In many cases, it was also impossible to identify a specific skeletal element, so they were classified according to the fragment they represent, including long bone fragment (splinter), rib, or other. When their frequency (%NISP) is plotted, the most common elements are rib fragments and long bone splinters (Figure 55). The fragmentary state of these two elements suggests that the torso and the legs were being heavily processed. In this sense, Pohl's observations among modern Maya are relevant, as she noticed that long bones would be purposely fractured to reduce them into a manageable size to be used as food or as tools (Pohl 1976:123). Another possible explanation is that these bones were broken as part of the butchering process itself, as seen in similar contexts in other parts

Skeletal element	NISP total	NISP complete	%NISP complete	NISP fragments	% NISP fragments
skull	17	0	0.00	17	100.00
hemi-mandible	44	1	2.27	43	97.73
atlas	22	5	22.73	17	77.27
axis	17	10	58.82	7	41.18
vertebra cervical	75	38	50.67	37	49.33
vertebra thoracic	126	22	17.46	104	82.54
vertebra lumbar	138	15	10.87	123	89.13
Sacrum	18	6	33.33	12	66.67
rib	1	1	100.00	0	0.00
scapula	114	1	0.88	113	99.12
humerus	26	3	11.54	23	88.46
radio	28	5	17.86	23	82.14
ulna	16	0	0.00	16	100.00
carpal	0	0	0.00	0	0.00
metacarpus	11	5	45.45	6	54.55
innominate	119	2	1.68	117	98.32
femur	26	5	19.23	21	80.77
patella	3	2	66.67	1	33.33
tibia	9	1	11.11	8	88.89
tarsal	32	28	87.50	4	12.50
metatarsus	10	0	0.00	10	100.00
phalanges	5	5	100.00	0	0.00
Total	**857**	**155**	**18.09**	**702**	**81.91**

Table 47. NISP values for complete and fragmented bones, by skeletal element (unidentified fragments are not included).

of the world (Kelly 2001:347). Bone splinters would also be expected if long bones were being processed for bone marrow extraction (Lyman 1994). Finally, in a bone collection that has been exposed for a period of time such as *Operación* 114, bones can be fragmented by carnivore activity and trampling.

The presence of cut marks on many of those rib fragments and long bone splinters supports the hypothesis that cutmark and fracture patterns resulted from butchering and other processing practices that included the preparation of carcasses to obtain meat and/or preparing them for their use as raw materials. However, we cannot discount that in some cases, bones were fractured with the aim of extracting the bone marrow, such as in the case of some long bones and the mandibles. While there is no study on bone marrow extraction for white-tailed deer in the Maya area, recent research has been conducted in order to understand the relationship between meat and bone

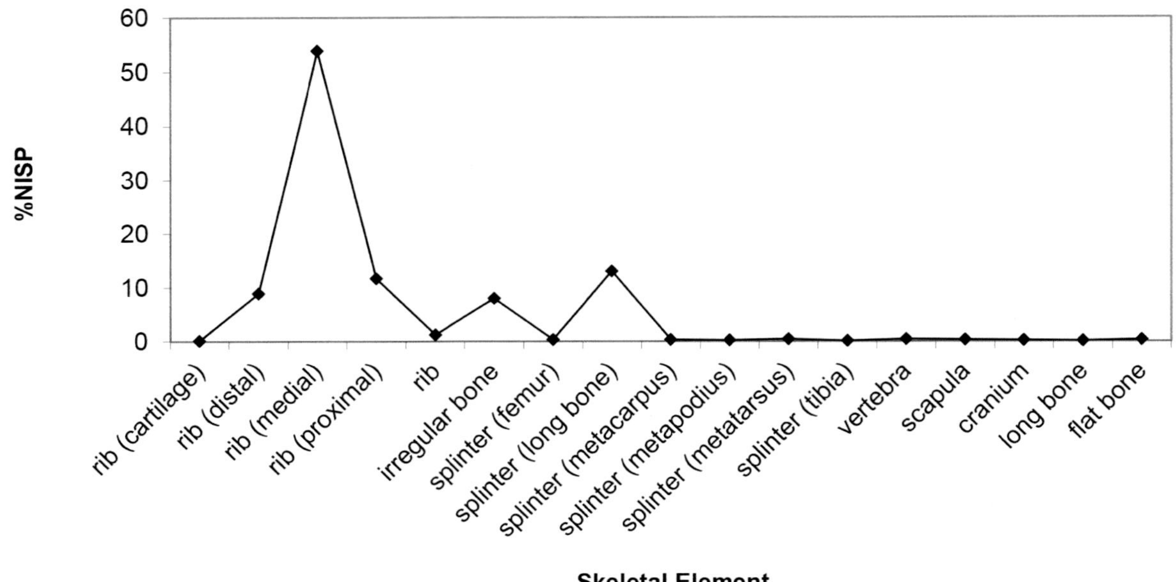

Figure 55. Distribution of small/medium and medium/large mammal bone
fragments by skeletal element.

marrow return in mammals, especially, white-tailed deer in North America (Madrigal and Zimmermann Holt 2002). This may indicate that people are systematically processing bones to obtain bone marrow, reflected in a preference for certain bones. These include those that carry unsaturated fatty acids in placental and non-placental mammals (Dietz 1946; Garvey 2011; West and Shaw 1975).

Research has indicated that those portions of bones that are located more distally from the torso carry bone marrow that is softer, oilier and apparently more palatable (Garvey 2011:769). The breakage pattern of these bones (humerus and proximal ulna in forelimb, and proximal and medial tibia in the hind limb) would suggest that bone marrow is being pursued. In summary, those bones with a high marrow yield are processed further after meat has been consumed (Madrigal and Zimmermann Holt 2002). The humerus, ulna, and tibia remains were highly fragmented in *Operación* 114 (see Table 47), suggesting that bone marrow may have been targeted, however, no definite explanation can be deduced at this point. The high percentage of long bone fractures could also be the result of other taphonomic processing including carnivore activity or post-depositional trampling. The presence of a few splintered mandibles at Seibal (Pohl 1985b:136), and fragments of long bones possibly broken intentionally at the Preclassic site of Urias (Emery 2002:4) suggests that these bones were cracked to obtain marrow. However, Emery (2002:4) has argued for the possibility that these bones were modified for the manufacture of tools.

The relatively scarce data for bone marrow extraction from deer bones contrasts with that for the domestic dog. A high frequency of crushed dog bones in Cuello may indicate bone marrow extraction, a process which may have included boiling the fragments into a stew rather than roasting them (Clutton-Brock and Hammond 1994:821). In this sense, it is imperative that more discussion and studies in this topic are conducted in the future in order to gain a better perspective of how the deer carcasses were processed for meat and any further processing that they may have been subject to.

Patterns of cut marks

Anthropogenic modifications were mostly identified as fine cut marks, possibly done with an obsidian flake (Montero 2008). Most of the cut marks registered in *Operación* 114 appear on white-tailed deer remains, with only two other species presenting cut marks: one possible cut mark identified on a collared peccary's (*Pecari tajacu*) hemi-mandible, and a cut on the pubis of an Artiodactyla (possibly identified as a peccary). The presence of processing marks on peccaries is not surprising, as these animals were also commonly hunted for their meat. No cut marks were identified on any of the dog remains present in *Operación* 114, although it is well documented that domestic dog was a major component of the Maya diet (Clutton-Brock and Hammond 1994; Wing 1978, 1981; Wing and Scudder 1991). The absence of cut marks on dog bones is also a characteristic at other sites and at different periods of time (Clutton-Brock and Hammond 1994:820; Hamblin 1984).

Regardless of the age categories, and excluding the unidentified fragments, a total of 264 white-tailed deer bones displaying cut marks were present in *Operación* 114, distributed through every layer. Three specimens were not attributed to a specific layer, and therefore, were not included in this analysis. The Layer with the most skeletal elements with cut marks is Layer IV (74 NISP), followed by Layer V (66 NISP), and Layer III (62 NISP). Layers I and II have less than 50 specimens with modifications. Considering each layer independently, the layer with the greatest percentage of modified materials is Layer III (30.10%NISP) and Layer I contained the least (25.81%NISP).

The materials were then grouped into two sub-samples, according to their location in relating to the stuccoed floor. Comparing the elements of cut marked to unmarked bones, each sub-sample had a similar percentage of bones with cut marks—28.69% below the floor and 28.18% above the floor. There is no significant difference between Layers I-III and IV-V, representing the deposits over and under the floor respectively. Therefore all the material—above and under the floor—was processed in a similar fashion (Table 48).

For the white-tailed deer sub-sample, cut marks were counted as one for each occurrence on every skeletal element, regardless of the amount of individual strikes. By age, Table 49 shows that the adult category had the highest number of cut marked bones (58 NISP), this count representing 40.28% of all adults, with the sub-adult category having the highest percentage (49.23%), followed by the immature category (23.96%), and the juveniles (18.75%). Immature+ individuals also present a high percentage of bones with cut marks (37.34%), but they could either represent immature or adult individuals. Specimens with no defined age were omitted from this analysis. Grouping the elements into two major categories (sub-adults and adults) resulted in a significant difference, due to the larger amount of sub-adults with processing marks (X^2 = 5.4100, df = 1, 0.05 > p > 0.01). This means that it is the younger animals that are being intensively processed over the adults, and probably reflects a cultural preference for meat from younger animals. This is interesting because some authors assume that younger or smaller animals would lack the presence of cut marks and other processing modifications because of their size (see Montero 2013 for discussion). Their presence necessarily stresses the fact that they are being processed for consumption and in a similar fashion to the adults. Overall, the intensive processing of sub-adult and younger animals may suggest that there is a marked preference for young

Layer	Presence of cut marks	%NISP	Absence of cut marks	%NISP	Total
Above floor	**124**	**28.18**	**316**	**71.82**	**440**
Layer I	16	25.81	46	74.19	62
Layer II	46	26.74	126	73.26	172
Layer III	62	30.10	144	69.90	206
Below floor	**140**	**28.69**	**348**	**71.31**	**488**
Layer IV	74	27.82	192	72.18	266
Layer V	66	29.73	156	70.27	222
Total	**264**	**28.45**	**664**	**71.55**	**928**

Table 48. Presence of cut marks on white-tailed deer bones (NISP) by layer in *Operación* 114.

animals, as they may taste better than older ones, or have a higher nutritional value.

Bones with cut marks in *Operación* 114 represent 33.33%, which is a much higher percentage in comparison with other, including *Operación* 201 (12.43%), and *Operación* 110 (3.88%) (see Table 33).

Several authors have mentioned the presence of anthropogenic modifications on deer and, in lesser proportions, dog remains in the Maya area. Modifications in the form of cut marks for butchery have been recorded at a variety of sites, including Cozumel (Hamblin 1984), Seibal (Pohl 1990), and Yaxchilán (Soto 1998). However, in general, the presence of cut marks occurs very rarely in most zooarchaeological collections, or alternatively, such marks have not been recorded when detected (Pohl 1990:157). This could be due to the fact that cut marks are unintentional during butchery, as opposed to bone marrow processing (Lyman 1995, although see Seetah 2006:114). In an ethnographic study among the Guatemalan Maya, it was noted though that there were few butchering marks on bone assemblages that appeared to be carefully curated before placing them in shrines (Emery *et al.* 2009). In Petexbatún, only 0.21% of the total assemblage had cut marks (n = 21) had evidence of butchering (Emery 2010:126). Emery (2010:126) mentions that the limited presence of altered remains may be the result of poor preservation conditions, where bone surfaces have been entirely removed, erasing the evidence of modifications. It is also proposed that the low number may be a consequence of the fine obsidian tools used (Brown and Emery 2008; Emery 2010:126). The large number of obsidian blades found in *Operación* 114 suggests that this type of implement may have been used for butchering and skinning (see Montero 2008).

Age group	Presence of cut marks	%NISP	Absence of cut marks	%NISP	Total
Immature	52	23.96	165	76.04	217
Immature+	20	37.74	33	62.26	53
Juvenile	3	18.75	13	81.25	16
Sub-adult	32	49.23	33	50.77	65
Adult	58	40.28	86	59.72	144
Total	165	33.33	330	66.67	495

Table 49. Presence of cut marks on white-tailed deer bone distributed by age groups in *Operación* 114.

Overall, the presence of cut marks in all age groups suggests that all individuals were processed in a similar fashion, and regardless of the age or type of deposit in which deer remains occur. Butchering marks have been identified in the same bone regions, suggesting that the dismemberment of a deer carcass primarily followed the animal's anatomy. This topic is discussed further in the next section. In summary, cut marks are expected if the carcass was being processed for meat and marrow extraction, unless they are obscured by post-depositional processes, such as erosion and carnivore chewing.

Patterns of skinning, dismemberment, and butchering

Cut marks on the bones were classified following Binford (1981), Blasco (1992), and Padró (2000). Overall, the highest frequencies of cut marks were identified on the torso (33.47%), and the upper back (22.71%). The upper front limb also had a high percentage (15.74%), and the rest of the body portions had less than 10%. Table 50 shows the distribution of cut marks by type, and these can be classified in three broad groups representing skinning, dismembering and butchering, or a combination of these. This classification is based on the stage of processing of a carcass and the location of cut marks on certain skeletal elements. The combination of cut marks is usually the result of a series of processes, where a single bone may be subject to a first treatment (e.g. dismembering) and processed further (e.g. butchering) until the desired product is obtained. Dismembering and butchering cut marks at the highest frequencies in the assemblage (44.22% and 39.84% respectively). A mix of dismembering and butchering was observed on 9.56% of elements. Skinning marks were less numerous (5.18%), but it is possible that these have been obscured by further processing, with subsequent marks obscuring those created by skinning. It was possible to identify at least some marks that correspond to periosteum removal (0.80%). In only one instance it was possible to observe a combination of skinning and dismembering marks (0.40%).

Skinning is defined as a series of deep, short, parallel cuts usually located on the skull, the distal section of the tarsals, phalanges, and metacarpals (Padró 2000). These cut marks are usually located on the extremes of the body, because the aim is to obtain a skin in one single piece. Bones with skinning marks were represented much less frequently in the assemblage, and were present only on lower limb and distal elements.

The aim of dismembering is to sub-divide a whole carcass into smaller sections for easy transportation (from the kill site), consumption, and/or storage. The head is removed by transversal cuts on the occipital condyles, and marks may also be present on the antero-ventral portion of the atlas. Binford (1981) identified that a tongue removal would leave marks on the condyles of the mandible or between PM3 and PM4. The torso would be dismembered by cutting big sections of vertebrae, sometimes with the proximal end of ribs still attached, though most proximal articulations of ribs appear broken from this first dismembering stage. Also, during this 'primary stage', the haunches are prepared in large blocks. Removing the femoral head from the acetabulum of the innominate disarticulates the back haunch. Cuts appear all around this area, and on the femoral head and trochanter. The front leg is removed by disarticulating the humerus from the scapula, by twisting the humerus and using the scapula as a lever. This process does not usually leave marks on the proximal humerus although some marks may be present on the neck of the scapulae.

Butchering can occur before or after cooking, and butchery marks usually appear on the lumbar vertebra, innominate bones, and distal limb elements. On long bones, the aim is to free the meat, so long shallow cuts along the diaphyses are expected, and may also be accompanied by short cuts on muscular insertions. Butchering marks also appear on irregular bones and on areas of protuberances, such as at the back of the humerus. Finally, the bone may be cleaned up in order to access the bone marrow, and in order to do so, the periosteum is stripped off the bone by scrapping it. The metatarsals usually have a high incidence of these marks.

The data from *Operación* 114 strongly suggests that the primary objective was the dismembering and butchering of large animal carcasses aiming to obtain the meat parcels, particularly those located on the torso, upper back and upper front body sections, with a minimal evidence of skinning or periosteal removal. Skinning may also have been important, as skins had a variety of uses. Deer skins were used to wrap sacred bundles and other ceremonial items (Miller and Taube 1993:75), and jaguar skins were used to make palanquins with which the kings displayed their power during the Classic period (Taube 2003:480).

According to Emery and Aoyama (2007:85), skinning and butchering marks seen at Aguateca in different contexts suggest that this activity should be considered a specialised craft, rather than simply a domestic activity. This is particularly true in those cases where animals were being butchered for ceremonies, as butchering would follow ritual prescriptions (Brown and Emery 2008:313).

The remains of torso section had the highest percentage of butchering and dismembering marks, probably as a result of producing smaller packages of ribs with meat still attached. When body parts are ranked by their utility index, the torso is considered to have less value than other body parts, including the upper front and back limbs.

To explore which of these two body portions was more heavily processed, all cut marks were regrouped according to the region in which they appear, focusing on the several articulations in the body in order to explore the differences in the intensification of the butchering process (following Lyman 2005:1726, Table 1). This analysis was based on the quantification of elements with cut mark occurrences, not the number of individual cut marks. The results are presented in Table 51. It can be observed that some articulations were more heavily processed, such as the knee (58.33%), the elbow (52.77%), and the ankle (48.64%), while other areas were less processed, for instance, the wrist joint (8.33%). This distribution suggests that the efforts were focused on disarticulating the meaty parts of the legs (upper front and back limbs). While the hip area displayed heavier processing (43.52%), the shoulder region showed less evidence of processing. However, it is important to remember that the quantity of strikes present on each bone was probably a result of not only the butcher's skill in dismembering a carcass, but also the amount of meat present on each element, the strength of the articulation itself, post-depositional modifications, and even the mode of preparation (stew or roast). All such factors need to be considered when interpreting the presence or absence of cut marks.

Finally, Figure 56 summarises the distribution of cut marks by body region and the relative proportion of each of those elements present in the *Operación* 114 assemblage. The distribution of butchering modifications is consistent with that of animals being processed for dietary consumption. It cannot be determined solely by the distribution of cut marks whether these animals were processed for ritual consumption or as part of a daily meal. While the distribution of cut marks on articulated bones seems to

Body portion	Skinning	%	Skinning and Dismembering	%	Dismembering	%	Dismembering and Butchering	%	Butchering	%	Periostial removal	%	Total	%
head	4	30.77			1	0.90							5	1.99
neck					21	18.92			5	5.00			26	10.36
torso					33	29.73			51	51.00			84	33.47
upper front					12	10.81	7	29.17	16	16.00	2	100.00	37	14.74
lower front	3	23.08			5	4.50	1	4.17	8	8.00			17	6.77
upper back					24	21.62	14	58.33	19	19.00			57	22.71
lower back	5	38.46	1	100.00	15	13.51	2	8.33	1	1.00			24	9.56
distal	1	7.69											1	0.40
Total	13	100.00	1	100.00	111	100.00	24	100.00	100	100.00	2	100.00	251	100.00

Table 50. Distribution of cut marks by type and body portions for white-tailed deer in *Operación* 114.

be a consequence of the logical way of dismembering a mammal's carcass, the high incidence of cut marks on the haunch suggest that butchering and preparing the best cut was the objective, as previously suggested by Pohl (1981) for feasting events.

The way in which large mammals would have been slaughtered has not been widely discussed in Maya zooarchaeology. We do not know whether they were dismembered immediately after being killed, or if carcasses were stored in a structure still fully dressed, awaiting other treatment. One of the best known butchery techniques is from the Romano-British period, where the difference between two practices has been explored (Seetah 2006). An animal that has been slaughtered, gutted and skinned on the ground, needs to be dismembered at the same time in order to avoid the accumulation of blood in the lower parts, which would make the meat unfit for consumption (Seetah 2006:111). If dismembering a fresh carcass is the norm, with large animals, such as with cattle in the Roman case, it is necessary to hang the animal from the posterior limbs, and cut marks will be shown especially on the ribs (the dorsal and inferior surfaces) and the vertebrae (Seetah 2006:111).

If we consider the location of cut marks on ribs and vertebrae for the white-tailed deer and add those from the medium/large mammal remains in *Operación* 114, it is possible to observe that more than 47.9% (n = 346) of rib fragments show one or several parallel cut marks. The remains of the middle rib section were the most modified, followed by the proximal and distal portions. On the vertebrae, 23.75% (n = 110) displayed butchering modifications, with the most concentrated on the lumbar and thoracic regions.

Cut marks on vertebrae from the thoracic and lumbar regions also suggest that these regions were being cut into smaller portions, as these body portions contain one of the most palatable cuts on large mammals, the tenderloin. However, it is not possible to ascertain whether the initial butchering and reduction to smaller and more manageable portions was conducted at the site or elsewhere, perhaps at the killing site. According to some authors, low proportions of head and feet elements are a result of their removal at the killing site (e.g. Kelly 2001), especially among hunter-gatherer societies that remove body parts of low value for ease of transportation (Masson 1999:103). In the Chinikihá assemblage, there was an almost total absence of head and distal elements. However, there was a high proportion of atlas and axis elements (first and second cervical vertebrae) that presented cut marks, with 40% (9 out of 22) of all atlases displaying one or more cut marks. Their presence in the assemblage suggests that complete carcasses were arriving to Chinikihá, and

	NISP	%	NISP with cut marks	%	Total by articulation
Shoulder					27.14
glenoid	69	98.57	19	100.00	
proximal humerus	1	1.43	0	0.00	
Total	**70**	**100.00**	**19**	**100.00**	
Wrist					8.33
distal ulna	1	8.33	0	0.00	
distal radio	7	58.33	1	100.00	
carpals	0	0.00	0	0.00	
proximal metacarpals	4	33.33	0	0.00	
Total	**12**	**100.00**	**1**	**100.00**	
Hip					43.52
acetabulum	79	92.94	35	94.59	
proximal femur	6	7.06	2	5.41	
Total	**85**	**7.06**	**37**	**100.00**	
Ankle					48.64
distal tibia	5	13.51	2	11.11	
tarsals	29	78.38	16	88.89	
proximal metatarsals	3	8.11	0	0.00	
Total	**37**	**100.00**	**18**	**100.00**	
Elbow					52.77
distal humerus	13	36.11	9	47.37	
proximal radius	12	33.33	4	21.05	
proximal ulna	11	30.56	6	31.58	
Total	**36**	**100.00**	**19**	**100.00**	
Knee					58.33
distal femur	8	66.67	5	71.43	
patella	3	25.00	1	14.29	
proximal tibia	1	8.33	1	14.29	
Total	**12**	**100.00**	**7**	**100.00**	

Table 51. Distribution of cut marks on white-tailed deer bones, grouped by articulation in *Operación* 114.

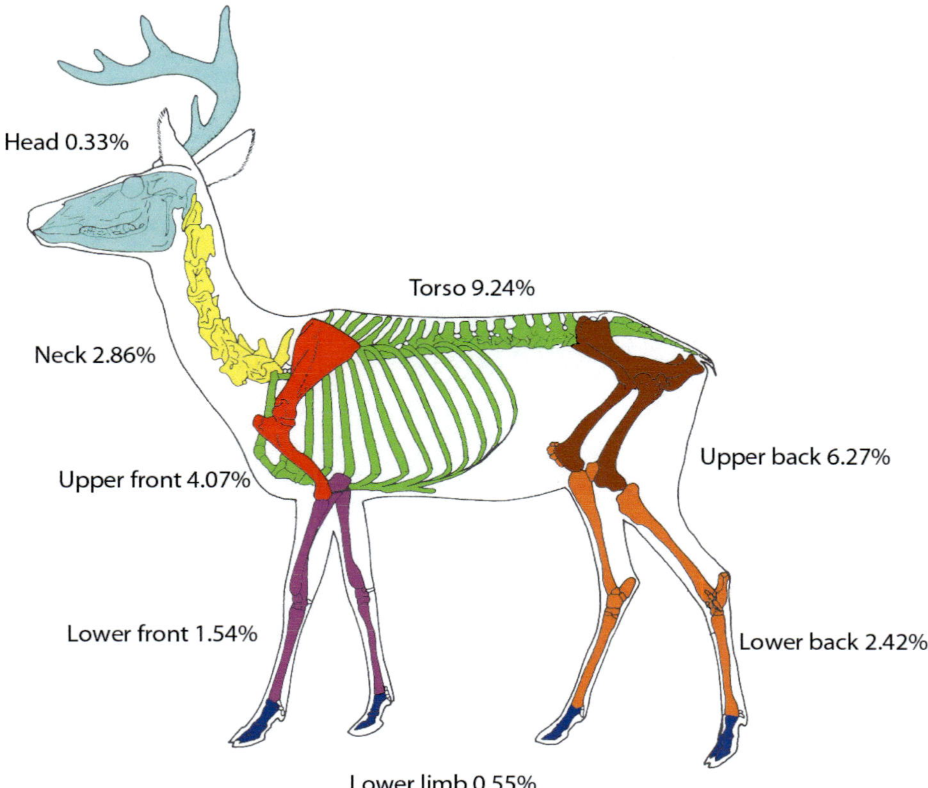

Figure 56. Presence of cut marks by body portion (%NISP) for white-tailed deer, *Operación* 114 (modified from Reitz and Wing 1999:171).

heads were being removed at the site, rather than at the primary location or killing site. Images of a hunted deer being carried on the back of a male character suggests that deer were complete when transported (Figure 57). Similarly, ankle elements also displayed a high proportion of cut marks, as did the astragalus and calcaneus. Twelve out of 19, or 63% of the calcaneus specimens displayed cut marks.

Burned bone

A total of 601 faunal and human bones with evidence of exposure to fire were detected in *Operación* 114. These were first separated into three main groups, white-tailed deer, other fauna (including dog, peccary, rabbit, small/medium, and medium/large mammals) and human. Burning or charring was detected on all bones from the deer, regardless of body portion. Burned bones from other fauna show a similar pattern, but the only human bones with changes in colour and texture were two clavicles that also had cut marks and fresh fractures on the proximal epiphyses. This possibly suggests they were boiled or exposed to a heat source for flesh removal.

When grouped relative to the floor (Table 52), most burned bone was retrieved from under the floor, although statistical tests showed that there was no significant difference between the two sub-groups, and that the distribution of burned elements might be considered as random, or as a result of the excavation and recovery strategies.

In summary, the presence of cut marks and burned bone might be helpful in identifying carcass processing for dietary consumption during ritual activities, a topic that is discussed more thoroughly in Part Three.

Part three: testing for rituality

Ritual activities may result in the different treatment of animal carcasses, such as the selection of specific segments from a specific side, associated with the role they play in offerings. In addition, the presence of exotic species and human remains can act as potential indicators of rituality in these contexts. Both of these issues will be explored in this section.

Figure 57. 'Deer Hunting Processing': stuccoed polychrome ceramic vessel from the Highlands in Guatemala, c. 700-900 DC (from http://www. famsi.org, vessel K808 from the Kerr Archives; Montero 2008:142, fig. 60).

Deer haunch sidedness

From the discussion in Part Two, it is clear that the meatiest body portions were being targeted, both for subsistence and probably for ceremonial use or consumption as a luxury item. This pattern is seen in the remains of feasting events in other parts of the world (e.g. Munro and Grosman 2010). This ritual use may be reflected in the selection of body elements from either the left or right side, as both were considered to be symbolically significant, not only among the Maya, but in Mesoamerica generally (Palka 2002). Among the Maya, deer were considered preferred animals for use as sacrificial victims, and the back haunch being particularly favoured with depictions of deer haunches being served as offerings common in the iconography (Pohl 1985a). Moreover, Pohl (1976, 1985a) has stated that left-sided back haunches were more common for ceremonial or ritual uses. It would then be expected that there would be a large majority of back limb bones, especially the left side, in deposits that were the result of ritual activities. To test this possibility, only sided bones from the front and back limbs were counted (Davis 1987:35).

Based on Pohl's statement, the assumption would be that for a ritual deposit, left-sided elements would occur in a greater quantity than right-sided elements, where in a non-ritual deposit, the left and right side should occur in corresponding proportions of approximately 50%. It was observed that there were less left elements than right ones (48.47%). In general, there was no marked preference for any side in *Operación* 114, and the difference between left and right was not statistically significant. In true ritual contexts, the dominant side is the left, as observed in the deer remains deposited in caves (Anderson 2009:109; Pohl 1983:89). Anderson (2009:103-104) found that there were a disproportionate number of left-sided front limb elements from white-tailed deer and dog, which may represent a ritual marker. However, it must be stressed that this trait may not necessarily be present in all species and bone elements at these types of sites (Anderson 2009).

Table 53 shows the distribution of bone elements grouped by limb and by divided by sidedness. Each skeletal element was considered individually. The analysis shows that elements were not equally distributed, with some, including the metacarpals (63.64%), the radius (55.56%), and the femur (52%), having higher percentages of left-sided specimens. The rest of the elements had an even distribution of left and right sides, or were altogether present in lower percentages.

Layer	White-tailed deer	Other fauna	Human	Total
Layers I-III	94	164	0	258
Layers IV-V	145	196	2	343
Total	**239**	**360**	**2**	**601**

Table 52. Distribution of burned bones by their presence above (Layers I-III) and under (Layers IV-V) the floor.

Left sided front and back limbs occurred in very similar percentages (44.40% front, and 44.63% back), as did the comparison of upper sections of both legs only (49.51% upper front, and 46.88% upper back limb). However, differences were noted upon comparing the left lower segments of both legs, with 57.14% front lower limb and only 38.77% for the back lower limb. It is clear from this analysis that there is no dominance of left elements in the back haunch as was expected, although Anderson (2009) observed this left-sided favouritism for the front lower limb in her data. In her analysis of rituality in caves, Anderson (2009:104) concluded that the preference for left-sided elements was more distinct for the front limb, rather than the back haunch as specified by Pohl (1985a). Due to the limited data regarding sidedness from other sites, it was not possible to conduct an inter-site comparison, and this may suggest that the consideration of specific bone sidedness should be included in future analyses to test the possibility of selection by bone for particular activities.

In terms of the spatial distribution, left elements were more numerous in the layers under the floor (56.41%), than above it (41.18%). The percentage of left-side elements, including front and back limbs, in Layers IV-V is not high. Statistical analysis indicates that there was no significant difference in the distribution of left specimens between Layers I-III and IV-V, and probably reflects a random distribution of left elements throughout the deposit (Table 54).

The overall results for sidedness in *Operación* 114 show no difference, and may suggest the primary role of deer at this location was related to food preferences. This result is similar to that observed at Caracol, with no marked preference for sidedness (Teeter 2001:275), and contrasts with Pohl's (1989:142) findings. The preference for specific sidedness may then be related to the age of the animals, but this hypothesis needs further testing in the Maya region.

Distribution of human remains

References to ritual deposits with a mixture of human and faunal bones are common among the zooarchaeological literature. More specifically, the presence of human remains with traces of burning and chewing marks in several midden and kitchen refuse contexts suggests that these remains may be the result of cannibalism.

Body portion			Left	Right	Total	%Left
Front limb:			**75**	**68**	**143**	**44.40**
	Upper limb		51	52	103	49.51
		scapula	39	40	79	49.37
		humerus	12	12	24	50.00
	Lower limb		24	18	42	57.14
		radius	15	12	27	55.56
		ulna	2	2	4	50.00
		carpal	0	0	0	0.00
		metacarpal	7	4	11	63.64
Back limb:			**79**	**98**	**177**	**44.63**
	Upper limb		60	68	128	46.88
		innominate	47	56	103	45.63
		femur	13	12	25	52.00
	Lower limb		19	30	49	38.77
		patella	0	3	3	0.00
		tibia	2	5	7	28.57
		tarsal	16	16	32	50.00
		metatarsal	1	6	7	14.29
		Total	**154**	**168**	**322**	**47.83**

Table 53. Distribution of sidedness for identifiable bones (NISP), for *Operación* 114.

Body portion	Layers I-III	% Layers I-III	Layers IV-V	% Layers IV-V	Total
Front limb:					
scapula	13	34.21	25	65.79	38
humerus	5	41.67	7	58.33	12
radius	4	26.67	11	73.33	15
ulna	5	71.43	2	28.57	7
metacarpal	5	71.43	2	28.57	7
Back limb:					
innominate	24	51.06	23	48.94	47
femur	4	30.77	9	69.23	13
patella	0		0		0
tibia	2	100.00	0	0.00	2
tarsal	8	50.00	8	50.00	16
metatarsal	0	0.00	1	100.00	1
Total	**70**	**44.30**	**88**	**55.70**	**158**

Table 54. Distribution of left-side elements in Layers I-III and Layers IV-V.

Skeletal element	NISP	%NISP
scapula	10	17.24
fibula	3	5.17
clavicle	10	17.24
pelvis	7	12.07
skull	6	10.34
humerus	1	1.72
vertebrae	8	13.79
metatarsus	5	8.62
ulna	1	1.72
radius	1	1.72
rib	4	6.90
hemi-mandible	1	1.72
femur	1	1.72
Total	**58**	**100.00**

Table 55. Summary of human remains present in *Operación* 114.

The consumption of human flesh in the Maya region was observed and recorded during the time of the Conquest and in recent times, more evidence has emerged from the archaeological record, including a midden context in the central acropolis of Tikal, and a kitchen midden associated to Structure D-2 in Seibal, reviewed by Pohl (1990:160).

Other authors have suggested that the presence of human remains in middens may be the result of the removal of bones from formal burials and their relocation to other deposits. These events have been seen as a way to inaugurate a ritual deposit (Harrison-Buck *et al.* 2007; Medina and Sánchez 2007) or to emphasise the 'social drama' associated with public feasting, related to fertility and female activities(Koželsky 2005:59).

In Chinikihá, 60 human bones were recovered from the PRACH 2008 excavations (see Appendix D). These remains were found in three different contexts: *Operación* 110 (n = 1), *Operación* 112 (n = 1), and *Operación* 114 (n = 58). Some of them presented similar taphonomic and anthropogenic modifications to the animal remains, especially those from *Operación* 114, and are considered separately from the non-human fauna in order to explore differences and then make a comparison between these and the animal sub-sample. In this study, it is suggested that they may be the result of human consumption by the elite at Chinikihá. Fifty-eight human remains were found in *Operación* 114 comprising 95% of all human remains recovered from PRACH 2008 excavations (Table 55). The other two human fragments were recovered in other contexts (*Operaciones* 110 and 112), but it is possible that those remains belong to burials located nearby. In contrast to *Operación* 114, human remains from other *Operaciones* do not display cut marks or heat exposure. None of the human remains were recovered still articulated, in sharp contrast to the materials in the faunal assemblage. This suggests that they may represent a non-funerary context.

Exact age was not identified from the clavicles, as the epiphyses of the sternum were missing from most of them. This epiphysis fuses between 20-25 years of age (Bass 1995:133), so these specimens were placed in the sub-adult age range. At least four scapulae were from individuals aged to 15 years of age, based on the coracoid fusion, while it was not possible to age the others due to their fragmentary state. None of the human bones were identified as children. One vertebra with pronounced osteophytosis was categorized as an old adult, and one hemi-mandible, was aged between 18-22 based on the absence of 3M and wear patterns present on M1 (White 2005:369). Sex was not identified for the post-cranial elements, but the hemi-mandible was from a male. Hence,

Skeletal element	Layers I-III	Layers IV-V
skull	5	1
hemi-mandible		1
scapula	3	6
clavicle	1	9 (5)
humerus		1
radius		1
ulna		1
vertebra		8
rib		4
pelvis		7
femur		1
fibula	1 (1)	2
metatarsus		5
Total	**10 (1)**	**48 (5)**

Table 56. Distribution of human bones by their location under (Layers IV-V) or above the floor (Layers I-III) in *Operación* 114 (numbers in parenthesis indicate number of bones with cut marks).

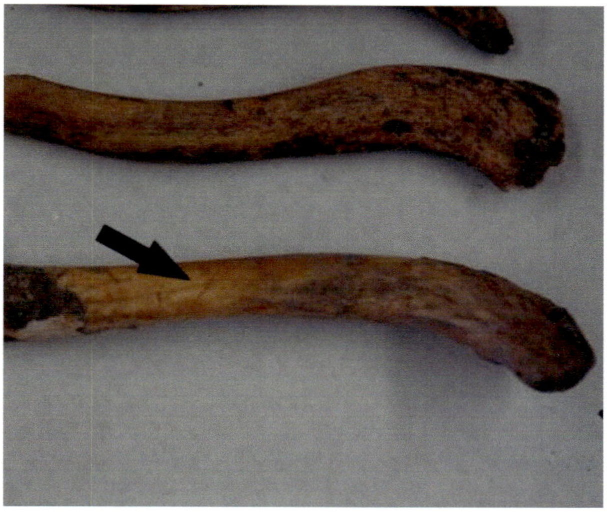

Figure 58. Human clavicles with evidence of fresh fractures on proximal epiphyses, and cut marks on diaphyses (showed by black arrow) Operación 114 (Photograph by Coral Montero Lopez).

the human sub-sample was made up mostly of young adults and adults. The MNI was calculated to be seven.

The modifications found on human remains were not marks associated with ante-mortem violence, but represented post-mortem or peri-mortem treatment (see Tiesler 2007). In general terms, the modifications found on the human sub-sample were similar to those present on the faunal remains in *Operación* 114. That both humans and animals may have been treated in a similar fashion has been interpreted as evidence of cannibalism in other parts of the world (Turner and Turner 1999; White 1991:394). In *Operación* 114, 17.24% (n = 10) bone fractures presented 'greenstick' patterns, occurring most commonly on the clavicles and scapulae. This is a modification commonly associated with disarticulation (Tiesler 2007:27). Cut marks were present on only a few bones, mostly on clavicles (n = 5) and a fibula (Table 56). A few marks were present on a skull fragment, but these were never confirmed securely as cut marks.

The cut marks and fractures present on the majority of the human remains from *Operación* 114 appeared mostly at the joint areas, especially around the shoulder on the clavicles and scapulae. It is particularly interesting that 10.41% of the human bones presented one or various paralleled cut marks, primarily on the clavicles, which have been identified as the result of flaying or skinning (Medina and Sanchez 2007:107; Tiesler 2007:27). Like faunal bones, changes in colour from heat exposition were also present on human bones (3.44%), and may be the result of bones being boiled.

The removal of human skeletal elements from the rest of the body is not uncommon in the Maya area and there are several examples of it in the Maya iconography, and this could explain the missing elements in the archaeological record, for example, in the case of the removal of the jaw from a sacrificial victim (Schele and Miller 1986:54). The removal of human bones from formal burials and their later deposition as construction fill materials, is a common practice by the Maya. The presence of deposited human remains in termination contexts is known from the Hershey site, Belize (Harrison-Buck *et al.* 2007), and Calakmul and Becán in México during the Late Classic period (Medina and Sánchez 2007). Thus, the cut marks recorded on the human bones may indicate their preparation for human consumption.

Statistical tests showed a significant correlation between the presence of cut marks on human and faunal bones ($X^2 = 3.6866$; df = 1; $0.05 > p > 0.02$). This may indicate that at least some human remains were being treated in a similar way to the animals which were being processed for dietary consumption, therefore exhibiting similar modifications (Figure 58). Other assemblages of human bone with similar modifications have been interpreted as the remains of sacrificial victims, whose bodies were reduced and their remains were scattered in a deposit (Harrison-Buck *et al.* 2007:81; White 1992). Nevertheless the occurrence of human remains with anthropogenic modifications in the Maya area is relatively infrequent. Caution is thus needed when interpreting these remains in such contexts with animals as a sign of ritual. It is a hypothesis in need of further testing.

The information on the potential dietary role of modified human remains scarce in the literature. There are only a few cases where human remains have been analysed in conjunction with faunal bones. When human bones were included in the reports, the information is incomplete, making it impossible to compare assemblages. One midden context has been identified where the presence of human remains from Late Classic Tikal shows burning and chewing, suggestive of cannibalism (Harrison in Pohl 1985b:110). Midden contexts containing isolated human remains mixed with animal remains during the Late/Terminal Classic are common, and include Dos Pilas (Emery 2009), Caracol (Teeter 2001), El Perú-Waka (Eppich 2009), Trinidad de Nosotros (Moriarty and Foias 2006), and Chichen Itzá (Götz 2008).

The workshop from Dos Pilas (L4-3), contained unmodified bones from 15 to 20 individuals intermingled with the faunal remains used in tool/ornament production (Emery 2009:462). Teeter (2001:168) reported the presence of modified human bones at Caracol in a mixed deposit. However, she did not mention how many bones were altered. Finally, in the Initial Series midden from Late Classic/Early Postclassic Chichen Itzá, some human bones were mixed with lithic flakes, thousands of ceramic sherds and faunal bones. No information was provided regarding the number of human bones, or whether any exhibited evidence of modification (Götz 2008). It is suggested here that the analysis of modified human remains needs to be included when they are present intermingled with faunal bones in the future.

Pohl (1981) analysed the modern *cuch* ritual or cargo celebration, a ceremony associated with fertility and agricultural prosperity. In the present day, a bull sacrifice is the main focus of this ceremony. Although there are some differences, such as the sacrificing of the bull instead of the deer stag, the *cuch* ritual has been performed since the early Maya and continues in the present day (Pohl 1981). Pohl (1981:517) also found that in some depictions, a man impersonating a deer is the sacrificial victim. According to Pohl and Feldman (1982) deer may have been substituted for human sacrifice victims in some ceremonies. Although there may have been some alterations to the ceremony, Pohl demonstrates that the symbolism may have remained the same, with the requirement for a human/deer/bull to be sacrificed in agricultural ceremonies, and that this may have also been linked to nobility and accession ceremonies (Pohl 1981:524). It is possible that men were sacrificed in the past, and then later substituted by deer, as images of deer sacrifices were more common in later periods (Pohl 1994:140).

The almost complete lack of carnivore chewing and/ or rodent gnawing on these human remains from

Operación 114 contrasts strongly with the presence of faunal modifications on the other bones. Faunal remains with rodent/dog modification are present on more than 60% of bones in *Operación* 114. It can be assumed that while the faunal specimens were the product of a series of primary and secondary depositions, the general condition of human bones suggests that great care was taken to bury them quickly, and they may represent an intentional deposit in this context.

Distribution of dog remains

From the Preclassic period, the Maya used dogs and deer as resources for domestic consumption, as raw materials for tools and ornaments and as components of rituals. Dog remains have been identified in variable proportions from sites dating to the Classic period, generally tending to occur in low frequencies. However by the Terminal Classic, it appears that, based on an overall increase in the presence of dog remains, it is possible that dogs were becoming more popular as a dietary staple, and this trend has been found to continue into the Postclassic period (Hamblin 1984; Pohl 1990). At the site of Cerros, dog remains appear in both elite and nonelite contexts (Carr 1986:7; Emery 1990:57; Hamblin 1984:109; Pohl 1985a:137). These authors point out however that it is the context within which dog remains are found that determines their role as either ritual or subsistence.

Ritual use of dog remains is usually inferred from the presence of dog elements in ceremonial assemblages, including deposits in caves (Emery 2003:505; Pohl 1990), and dog burials, a feature which became common during the Postclassic (Hamblin 1984; Wing 1978). Dog remains in middens were also found to be common at several sites from the Preclassic, suggesting dogs were raised for sacrifice and consumption (Clutton-Brock and Hammond 1994:821; Pohl 1983). In general, the most common body portions of dogs retrieved from archaeological sites include cranial and foot, at sites such as Dzibilchaltún, Lamanai, and Colha (Shaw 1991; Wing and Steadman 1980:326). Isotopic analyses of dogs remains from a midden from Lagartero indicated a corn-based diet (White *et al.* 2004), supporting the hypothesis that they were deliberately fed and then sacrificed for consumption as part of a ritual.

The distribution of elements were compared between dog and deer present in *Operación* 114 in order to explore patterns in their distribution (Figure 59), and their percentages of body portions (%NISP). As mentioned before, for deer, the pattern tends to indicate a preference for the torso and upper sections of both the front and back legs, while for the dog it seems that the lower front limb elements (the radius and especially the ulna) were favoured over the rest of the body

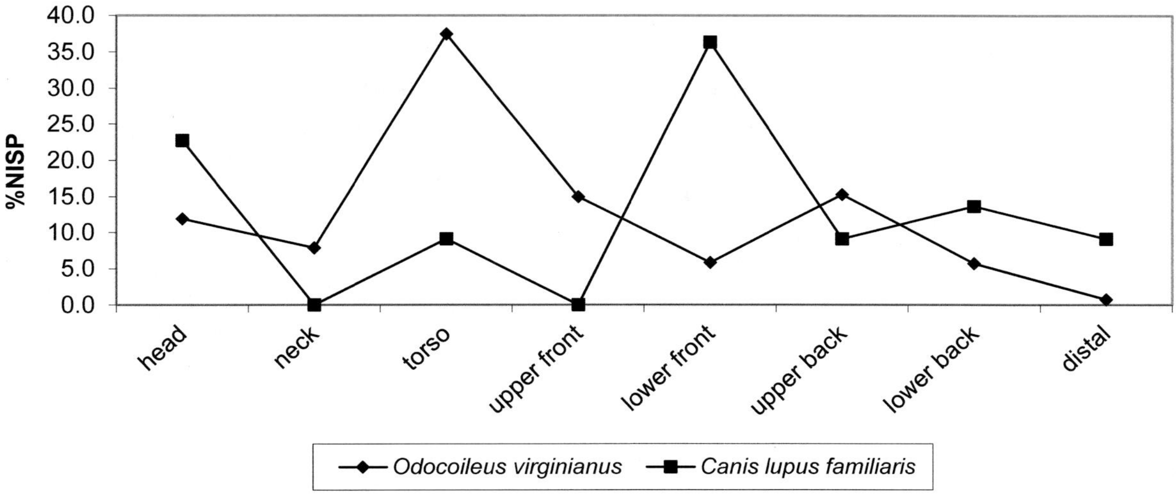

Figure 59. Comparison between the distribution of body portions for white-tailed deer and domestic dog in *Operación* 114 (%NISP).

portions. Slightly higher quantities of head elements from dogs were identified compared with those from deer, probably due to a greater presence of mandible elements and/or loose canid teeth in the assemblage.

None of the dog remains presented cut marks, in comparison to the 28.34% identified on deer. What does become clear is that, for dogs, lower front elements seem to be the dominant body part in the assemblage. The preference for the long bones of dogs, along with canine teeth, has also been identified at other sites, where long bones have been found in food refuse deposits indicating their dietary role (Teeter 2001:212). The canine teeth, however, may also have had a function as ornaments or for ceremonial use, as they can be perforated and transformed into pendants.

Comparison between white-tailed deer, dog, and human remains

In this section, the relationship between white-tailed deer and the other species is explored, in order to determine any correlations between them. I focused on the distribution of the three most common taxa, paying special attention to how dog and human remains were distributed in comparison with the white-tailed deer remains, considering that this chapter has determined that the deer had a dietary role in *Operación* 114 (Table 57). Deer, dog and human remains occurred in larger proportions under the floor than above it, and their distribution is very similar. However, statistical analysis suggest that the three categories are independent between each other. Also, there was no significant difference in the distribution of the three by Layer. It can be concluded that the distribution of these three categories is very similar under and above the floor, pointing to a possible continuity in their role throughout the whole deposit.

The other animal species were then added to the comparison, in order to explore differences between the three most common mammal remains and the rest of the faunal materials in *Operación* 114, and some interesting patterns emerged. While deer, dog and human remains occurred in slightly greater amounts under the floor (Layers IV-V) than above it (Layers I-III), quantities of *jute* shell remains increased dramatically from being scarcely represented in Layers IV-V to being notably abundant in Layers I-III. Modified bone, small/medium mammal, and medium/large mammal fragments occur in higher proportions in the layers above the floor than those below (Table 58).

From this analysis, two hypotheses can be drawn. First, there is a strong negative correlation between the categories and the Layer in which they appear (Kendal's tau-c = -0.01), suggesting that when one species increases, the others decrease. This is probably as a consequence of the high proportion of *jute* on the top layers, and the relatively homogeneous distribution of the other species all throughout the deposit. It is interesting to note that while the frequency of unidentified fragments increased, deer, dog, and human bone decreased. As suggested earlier, it is possible that some of the medium/large mammal fragments are indeed deer remains, but because of their degree of fragmentation and/or lack of landmarks, they could not be positively identified as such. Although not much more can be inferred from the distribution of unidentified fragments (small/medium and medium/

Layer	Deer	Dog	Human remains	Total
Layers I-III	440	10	10	460
Layers IV-V	488	12	48	548
Total	**928**	**22**	**58**	**1008**

Table 57. Distribution of the deer, dog, and human remains by Layer in *Operación* 114.

Layer	*Jute*	Dog	Other fauna	Deer	Modified bone	Human remains	Small/ medium	Medium/ large	Total
Layers I-III	1714	10	7	440	45	10	46	484	2756
Layers IV-V	4	12	12	488	32	48	7	456	1059
Total	**1718**	**22**	**19**	**928**	**77**	**58**	**53**	**940**	**3815**

Table 58. Distribution of all categories by Layer in *Operación* 114.

large mammals), the increase in their presence above the floor may suggest either a more intensive carcass processing occurring in Layers I-III, or more of the material is fragmented due to other taphonomic processes, including trampling, as the bone assemblage under the floor would have been protected.

Second, it is possible to observe that there were notably fewer freshwater shells present in Layers IV-V than in the upper Layers I-III, suggesting that there was a change in the pattern of exploitation of this resource. Their importance as foodstuff has been acknowledged elsewhere, but considering the limited amount of meat they can provide due to their small size, it is obvious that it would have required a large number of these shells to achieve a dietary value equivalent to that provided by a single deer (Emery 2010:117). However, during the Late Classic period, *jute* concentrations appear in different contexts, including deposits associated to the elite. Stanchly and Iannone (1997) suggest that the presence of *jute* in similar contexts, reflects more their inclusion as a ritual component, possibly as part of ritual feasting.

Certainly the large quantities of *jute* shells suggest that the Maya from Chinikihá were complementing their protein intake from large mammals by consuming other animal resources and during the Late/Terminal Classic. This is especially true towards the later moments in the history of the deposit. It also suggests that towards the end of the Late Classic period, it is possible that all social classes were consuming *jute* molluscs, rather than solely being the staple of the lower classes, as suggested in early literature (Nations 1979).

In conclusion, it appears that the distribution of the main dietary categories, the deer, dog and human remains could reflect the continual use of the same deposit through its life, but the appearance of more remains from molluscs and fragmentary mammal remains suggests that there is a difference in the formation of the deposit, or behaviour behind the two units under study (under and above the floor). In order to reach a more reliable interpretation of this deposit however, it would be necessary to include as much of other information related to this context as possible, including the distribution of ceramics, lithics, and macrobotanical remains, exploring their spatial distribution. Unfortunately, these analyses are not yet complete or ready to be integrated. Although the zooarchaeological analysis indicates some patterning of the materials, it is not sufficient to infer the role of the deposit.

Summary

The material in *Operación* 114 was not homogeneously distributed, either by square or by layer. There seems to have been a highly concentrated area of bone near the back wall of the Palace, and this could potentially indicate the core of the deposit. As indicated in the previous chapter, white-tailed deer was the most frequently occurring species, especially young adult animals. These would have been prime-aged animals that had reached their maximum meat yield; many of the animals were still young and their remains display unfused epiphyses (12-29 months of age). The mortality profile suggests that this context had multiple episodes of deer harvesting, primarily during the winter, but evidence for the killing of deer during all seasons appears to be present; hence, a recurrent use of this context is suggested, reflecting various episodes of meat consumption. These, however, should be taken with caution due to the low number of mandibles present and consequently used in the seasonality analysis.

A significant proportion of deer remains from all layers presented butchering marks (28.34%), reinforcing the idea that it was a favoured source of food. While deer was the preferred species, it was noted that not all body portions of this animal were present in the same quantities. There is a marked preference for torso, and upper front and back limb portions, and these three correspond to the meatiest sections of the carcass, regardless of the age of the animals. Also, the long bones that form the upper limb were highly regarded for their utility potential, as they could be processed to extract marrow and furthermore, were a potential raw material for tool and ornament manufacture. Head and distal elements were present in extremely low numbers, suggesting that they may have removed very early in the butchering process. The distribution of cut marks suggests the dismantling of the carcass into smaller portions. The preferred meat cuts appear to have been the tenderloin (torso) and the haunches. Although most of the material was fragmentary, the presence of complete bones also confirms that there was some waste, further indicated by the presence of articulated or semi-articulated skeletal elements. This distribution of faunal remains is consistent with that of feasting activities, where meat had an important role.

The presence of the stuccoed floor was incorporated into the analyses in order to test whether there were any observable differences between the material deposited above and underneath it. No patterning was discernible for the deer remains representing food debris. Furthermore, the whole assemblage exhibited low stages of weathering and carnivore chewing, which is consistent with the material laying exposed and uncovered only for a short period of time after being deposited. Dog and human remains also received similar treatment prior to be deposited, and their presence indicates their role as foodstuff. However, there was a significant difference in terms of where they were found (above and under the floor). While the use of deer and dog remains as food was consistent all through the deposit, human remains occurred more frequent under the floor, suggesting a different depositional history. It is suggested that the materials underneath the floor could have represented a construction fill, while the materials above it were the remains of feasting behaviour. Evidence of rodent gnawing is also more notable on remains from under the floor, therefore suggesting that some of the materials were exposed for a long time and along with the human remains, they could have been brought to serve as fill material.

Chapter nine

Results of the isotope analysis

In this chapter, the results of the bone diagenesis study are presented first, then the data from the isotope analysis of modern and archaeological bone are discussed, and finally, an interpretation of the palaeodiet of the fauna and human samples from Chinikihá is assessed.

The results for collagen (from bone and dentine) are presented in Tables 59 and 60 for δ^{13}C, and δ^{15}N for both human and fauna samples from Chinikihá. Results for apatite (from enamel) are presented in Table 61. The combined use of these analyses allows an interpretation of the human and animal ancient diets, as well an indication of the differences in plant and meat consumption by age, sex, status, and faunal domestication. The discussion is firstly centred on the fauna samples, followed by those from the human sample. All the results are reported as raw data, unless otherwise specified.

Diagenesis at Chinikihá

Proportion of carbon and nitrogen (%C and %N)

Overall, Chinikihá's values for %C range between 24.97 and 43.5, with a mean for animal and human samples of 37.46, and 36.05 respectively. The total sample %N values range between 7.65 to 15.58, with a mean of 12.82% for animals, and 12.9% for humans. Although some of the samples presented %N and %C outside the recommended range (see Chapter six), when the results were combined with C/N, it was apparent that the samples had only minor alterations resulting from diagenesis, and they were therefore included for further analysis.

Ratio of carbon to nitrogen (C/N)

Only one sample (CM16 bone collagen) was completely excluded from further analysis because its %C, %N, and C/N values were out of the accepted parameters probably caused by diagenesis. However, several other samples produced a high C/N ratio (slightly under or 3.8), but with δ^{13}C and δ^{15}N values similar to those from other sites in the Maya area. The correlation between C/N ratios and δ^{13}C$_{col}$ is non-existent for both fauna (r = -0.100) and human samples (r = -0.00); therefore, the samples were not systematically altered by diagenesis. Moreover, there is no correlation between C/N and δ^{15}N. This is also true for C/N and δ^{13}C$_{ap}$ for humans (r = -0.100).

Schoeninger and Moore (1992) report that for superficially well-preserved bone that has been cleaned chemically and mechanically and retains a percentage of organic residue equal to 50% or more of the original organics (organic residue > 10% of the original dry bone weight), the C:N ratio is unnecessary. For older samples (even older than 10,000 years, teeth samples are recommended, for collagen and enamel (Krueger 1991; Lee-Thorp and van der Merwe 1987). Thus, the combination of values from both dentine and cortical bone is used in this study as a means to control for diagenetic differences.

Crystallinity index (CI)

The three deer samples obtained have acceptable values for CI, with CM04 = 3.58, CM08 = 3.90 and CM09 = 3.25. These values are well within the proposed range of 2.8 to 4.0 (Wright and Schwarcz 1996), and show that there is no significant diagenesis, thus, the samples are suitable for further isotope analysis.

The results from testing Chinikihá's materials for diagenetic modification resulted in consistent values for apatite and collagen that reflect little or no diagenesis. However, some C/N ratios were out of the recommended range, and this could be a result of the bone chemical pre-treatment when preparing them for isotopic analysis (Ambrose 1990:446). Furthermore, it has been suggested (DeNiro *et al.* 1985) that the C:N ratios can be affected if bone has been exposed to heating, and in the case of Chinikihá's sample, more than 40% of the faunal remains show marks of direct and indirect heat exposure. Therefore, I consider that the samples are adequate for further isotopic analysis.

Limitations of the isotopic analysis

A total of 11 faunal samples were obtained from PRACH, including 10 samples from Chinikihá and one from Chancalá, in addition to eight human samples, all from Chinikihá. Original sampling included collagen from both cortical bone and dentine, and an apatite sample from dental enamel. Where possible, a set of three sub-samples was obtained per original sample.

From the fauna, three samples did not provide enough collagen from cortical bone (CM02, CM12, and CM66). These included two deer from Chinikihá, one deer

Lab code	Bag	Sq.	Level	Species	Tissue	Collagen $\delta^{15}N_{AIR}$ (‰)	Collagen $\delta^{13}C_{VPDB}$ (‰)	Collagen %N	Collagen %C	C/N
CM02	672	J2	III	White-tailed deer (*Odocoileus virginianus*)	3M	6.38	-20.50	13.8	41.1	3.0
					2M	5.19	-21.39	12.4	36.8	3.0
CM03	689	J1	II	White-tailed deer (*Odocoileus virginianus*)	Mandible	4.06	-19.84	13.8	38.8	2.8
					Mandible	5.28	-19.25	11.1	36.3	3.3
CM04	774	J2	III	White-tailed deer (*Odocoileus virginianus*)	3M	6.39	-18.68	14.1	38.9	2.8
					2M	5.60	-20.64	13.3	39.4	3.0
CM05	744	J1	III	White-tailed deer (*Odocoileus virginianus*)	Maxilla	5.20	-20.87	10.6	33.0	3.1
					2M	7.25	-21.57	12.9	39.5	3.0
CM06	753	I2	IV	White-tailed deer (*Odocoileus virginianus*)	Mandible	7.28	-21.97	9.5	28.6	3.0
CM07	1009	F2	V	White-tailed deer (*Odocoileus virginianus*)	Mandible	4.81	-20.23	15.1	41.4	2.7
CM08	1012	G2	V	White-tailed deer (*Odocoileus virginianus*)	2M	5.78	-18.89	14.0	37.6	2.7
CM09	1019	K1	IV	White-tailed deer (*Odocoileus virginianus*)	Mandible	7.13	-20.42	12.3	35.7	2.9
					3M	6.10	-19.15	14.1	41.3	2.9
CM10	826	K1	III	Collared peccary (*Pecari tajacu*)	Mandible	5.37	-19.53	11.1	33.6	3.0
CM12	1 (Chancalá)	n/a	III	White-tailed deer (*Odocoileus virginianus*)	2M	5.26	-19.37	14.3	42.0	2.9

Table 59. δ^{13}C and δ15N values from collagen for faunal samples under study.

Lab code	Bag/Burial No.	Level/ Individual	Description	Tissue	Collagen $\delta^{15}N_{AIR}$ (‰)	Collagen $\delta^{13}C_{VPDB}$ (‰)	Collagen %N	Collagen %C	C/N
				2M	8.43	-9.40	14.7	42.7	2.9
CM11	833	V	Adult male? (behind Palace)	Mandible	8.73	-9.09	7.9	25.0	3.2
				3M	8.71	-10.35	15.6	41.4	2.7
CM13	40	2	Adult fem. (Inner patio)	Femur	8.50	-9.53	14.9	39.8	2.7
CM14	42	4A	Adult male (Inner patio)	Femur	8.63	-9.17	14.1	37.8	2.7
				2M	11.73	-8.15	15.1	39.8	2.6
CM15	42	4B	Adult fem. (Inner patio)	Femur	10.45	-9.80	14.8	39.4	2.7
CM16	42	4C	Adult male (Inner patio)	1M	10.57	-8.52	15.4	40.6	2.6
CM17	43	1	Adult fem. (behind North Structure)	Femur	8.36	-10.44	7.7	25.0	3.3
				2M	9.90	-9.38	14.9	43.5	2.9
CM18	44	6B	Adult male (Inner patio)	Mandible	9.22	-10.34	9.2	27.8	3.0
				Femur	10.15	-10.37	13.0	36.8	2.8
CM19	45	7	Adult male (Inner patio)	1M	11.28	-11.89	10.5	29.1	2.8

Table 60. δ^{13}C and δ15N values from collagen for human samples under study.

Lab. Code	Bag	Level	Species	$\delta^{13}C_{VPDB}$ (‰)
CM 02	672	III	White-tailed deer (*Odocoileus virginianus*)	-13.07
CM 03	689	II	White-tailed deer (*Odocoileus virginianus*)	-14.05
CM 04	774	III	White-tailed deer (*Odocoileus virginianus*)	-11.00
CM 05	744	III	White-tailed deer (*Odocoileus virginianus*)	-11.62
CM 06	753	IV	White-tailed deer (*Odocoileus virginianus*)	-13.63
CM 07	1009	V	White-tailed deer (*Odocoileus virginianus*)	-13.93
CM 08	1012	V	White-tailed deer (*Odocoileus virginianus*)	-11.63
CM 09	1019	IV	White-tailed deer (*Odocoileus virginianus*)	-12.50
CM 66	774	III	Domestic dog (*Canis lupus familiaris*)	-7.40
CM 10	826	III	collared peccary (*Pecari tajacu*)	-11.71
CM 11	833	V	human (midden)	-2.00
CM 12	1 (Chancalá)	III	White-tailed deer (*Odocoileus virginianus*)	-10.90
CM 13	40	2	human (burial)	-2.31
CM 15	42	4B	human (burial)	-2.51
CM 16	42	4C	human (burial)	-3.00
CM 18	44	6B	human (burial)	-3.05
CM 19	45	7	human (burial)	-4.77

Table 61. $\delta^{13}C$ values from enamel apatite for animal and human samples under study.

from Chancalá and one dog from Chinikihá. No C/N was obtained for these. Collagen from dentine was not obtained for two deer samples (CM07 and CM09); the only dog sampled (CM66), though the dog sample did produce enough enamel apatite for analysis. Only one sample produced less %N than what is considered ideal (CM06, bone collagen = 9.5); however, the %C and C/N were in the accepted ranges, and therefore, this sample was considered to be in a suitable condition for further analysis.

In the case of the humans, collagen from cortical bone was obtained for all samples; however, because its %N, %C, and C/N values were out of the accepted parameters, two samples, CM16 (bone) and CM17 (bone), were not considered for further analysis. No teeth were sampled from CM14 and CM17, therefore, no dentine collagen or apatite from enamel was obtained.

It should also be mentioned that because of the limited number of human burials that have been sampled and considering that data is highly variable due to several factors already discussed by other researchers, the interpretations offered here are tentative.

Results

Reconstruction of the palaeodiet

The $\delta^{13}C$ and $\delta^{15}N$ for 31 modern plant samples and three faunal samples are presented in Figure 60 although modern plants with negative $\delta^{15}N$ values were not considered. These included achiote (*Bixa orellana*)

(sample CM26), green beans (*Phaseolus vulgaris*) (sample CM33S), mango (*Mangifera indica*) (sample CM42 S), and fig (*Ficus maxima*) (sample CM58).

The human and faunal samples from which collagen could be extracted from cortical bone are also included for comparative purposes, and as such, the dog sample is not included. The modern plant sample was limited, with one voucher specimen per species. To offset this, data was gathered from relevant literature and considered here in order to create hypothetical ranges of the values of C3 and C4 plants, as well as the expected values of freshwater fish and mollusc meat, as well as herbivorous animals (Coyston *et al.* 1999; Scherer *et al.* 2007; Tykot *et al.* 1996; White and Schwarcz 1989; White *et al.* 2001a; Williams *et al.* 2009; Wright 1997, 2006).

The range for modern C3 plants is $\delta^{13}C$ = -24.62‰ to -33.52‰, with a mean value of -28.47‰, while the only C4 plant had a value of $\delta^{13}C$ = -10.65‰. These values are consistent with those reported from other Maya archaeological sites, and modern samples (Gerry 1997; Wright 2006). The value for C3 plants is more negative than the expected range of -26.5 to -27.1‰ O'Leary 1988; Vogel and van der Merwe 1977) possibly due to the 'canopy effect' (van der Merwe and Medina 1991). The graph also shows the offset between human and animals with respect to the plants and is consistent with those values reported for a 5‰ offset between plants and consumers.

The fauna and human $\delta^{13}C$ and $\delta^{15}N$ values are distributed in a bimodal fashion, indicating that their diet was different (Figure 61). While most of the

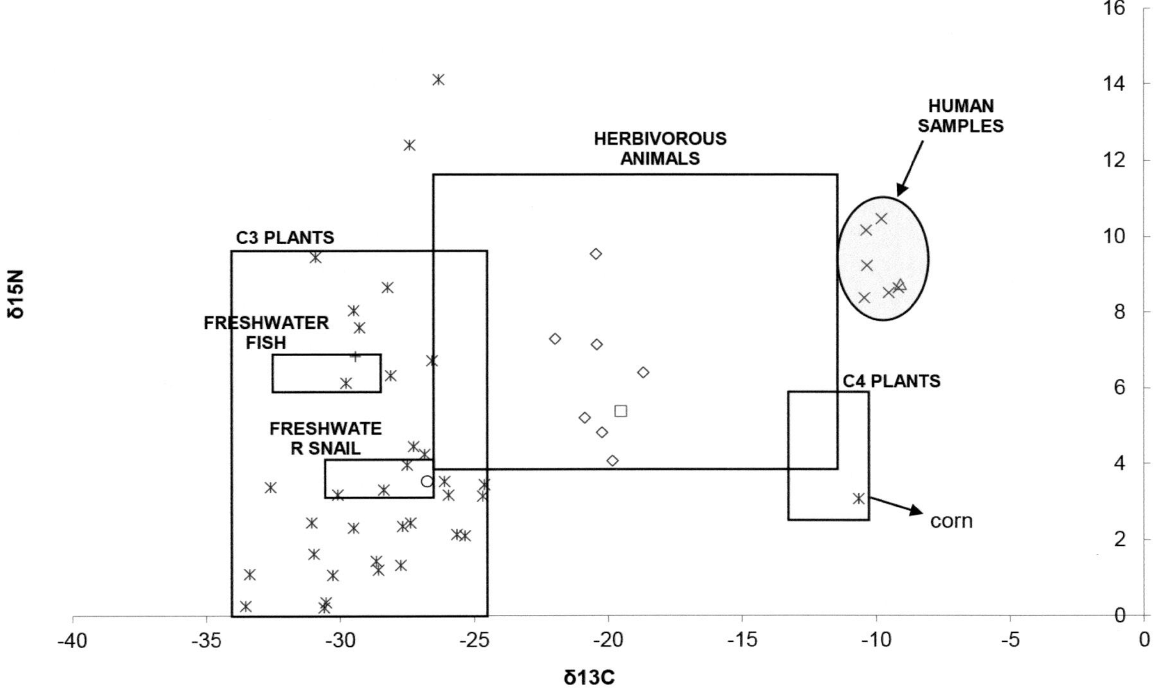

Figure 60. Stable carbon and nitrogen isotope ratios for modern and archaeological samples at Chinikihá. Boxes indicate the parameters for C3 and C4 plants, as well as for herbivorous animals, freshwater fish, and freshwater snail meat.

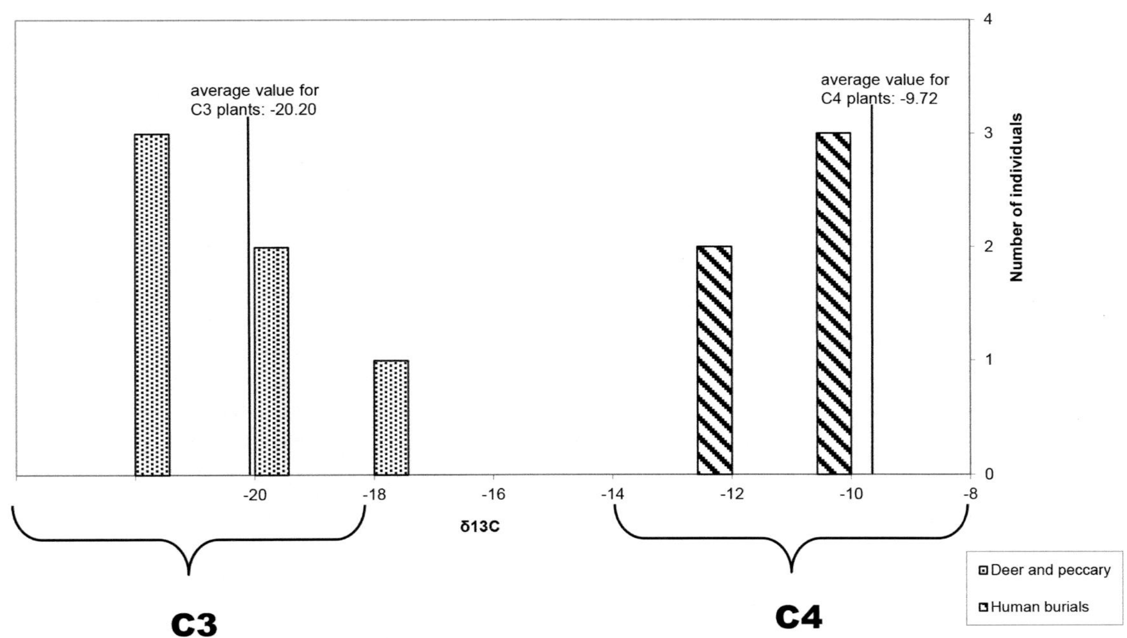

Figure 61. Bimodal distribution of δ13C values for humans and fauna from Chinikihá.

animals sampled reflect primarily a diet based on C3 plants, the human samples show a diet derived from C4 plants, principally corn. It is also important to mention that is possible that one deer had access to corn, as its values for $\delta^{13}C$ are closer to the C4 range.

Fauna

The range of $\delta^{13}C_{dent}$ for the faunal samples (-18.68‰ to -21.97‰, mean -20.20‰, s.d. 1.20) suggests primarily a C3 diet with an occasional intake of some C4 foods. The values for $\delta^{15}N$ range from 4.06‰ to 7.28‰, with a mean of 5.84‰ (s.d. 0.96), indicating an herbivorous diet. Some of the $\delta^{15}N$ values are surprisingly high which, according to some authors, may suggest animals from a different ecological origin (e.g. coastal and inland) reflecting different diets (Ambrose 1991; Katzenberg and Kelley 1991).

The mean $\Delta^{13}C_{sc-col}$ value for animal enamel and dentine is 7.73‰ (s.d. 0.56) and is consistent with the values for an herbivore diet (mean 6.8‰, s.d. 1.4). When reconstructing the diet from $\delta^{13}C_{sc}$ (mean -12.57‰) and $\delta^{13}C_{col}$ (mean -20.11‰), an enrichment of 10-12‰ for $\delta^{13}C_{sc-diet}$ (Ambrose and Norr 1993; DeNiro and Epstein 1978) is added and this results in a mean of the whole diet for apatite of -22.57‰ to -24.57‰. For collagen, the $\delta^{13}C_{sc-diet}$ is enriched by 3-7‰, returning values between -23.11‰ to -27.11‰ for the whole diet of the deer. These values are consistent with those obtained from modern plant samples collected in the region (as shown in Table 8), showing that the diet of the faunal sample was primarily based on C3 plants, with an occasional intake of corn. It is possible that deer were also ingesting *ramón* nuts and root crops, as both are C3. However, it is impossible to distinguish the individual plants isotopically (White and Schwarcz 1989:457).

The $\delta^{13}C_{col}$ values for the archaeological deer remains from Chinikihá contrast with those of modern North American deer that feed on corn, with a value of -17.8‰. Deer browsing in areas with no C4 plant products have a value of -23.3‰ (Cormie and Schwarcz 1994). However, there was variability among the individuals, especially in the plants they were eating, as suggested by the standard deviation values. Unfortunately, no $\delta^{13}C_{col}$ value was obtained for the dog sample, but its $\delta^{13}C_{sc}$ = -7.4‰ value is similar to those from the humans (ranging from -2‰ to -4.77‰) than to the other fauna (-10.90‰ to -14.05‰). The similarity between the values from the dog remains and the humans also has other implications, as it is possible that the dog was being fed with human food scraps or ate the garbage generated by humans at Chinikihá.

Humans

The values range for $\delta^{13}C_{dent}$ for the humans is -8.52‰ to -11.89‰, with a mean of -9.72‰ (s.d. 0.97). These values contrast with those obtained for the fauna and indicate that the human population relied more heavily on C4 plants and complemented them with some C3 plants. This is further confirmed by the values for $\delta^{13}C_{sc}$ and $\delta^{13}C_{col}$ with ranges between -12.94‰ to -14.94‰ and -12.61‰ to -16.61‰ respectively. This means that humans were eating more C4 plants, primarily corn, and complementing their diet with the ingestion of some C3 plants.

The source of protein is also different from the one expressed by the faunal sample, with values ranging from $\delta^{15}N$ = 8.43‰ to 11.73‰. These trophic level values are clearly in the omnivorous category (DeNiro and Epstein 1981; Schwarcz and Schoeninger 1991). While the $\delta^{13}C$ values show a diet predominantly focused on C4 plants for all the samples, the variability in the $\delta^{15}N$ values suggest a larger diversity in protein sources (Figure 62).

The 'spacing' between $\delta^{13}C_{sc}$ and $\delta^{13}C_{col}$ for enamel and dentine (collagen) suggest a similar trend, with a mean $\Delta^{13}C_{sc-col}$ value of 6.68‰ (s.d. 1.01), again, confirming an omnivorous diet (Lee-Thorp *et al.* 1989). These results, however, reflect the diet during childhood (Wright and Schwarcz 1999:1161), and vary according to the tooth sampled. Different diets reflected in the isotopes by different age groups will be discussed in the next section in more detail.

Corn consumption by fauna and humans

To determine how much corn was ingested, the $\delta^{13}C_{col}$ values from the long bone samples were used, as this value reflects the overall corn intake throughout the whole life of the animals or humans. It was not possible to establish a corn consumption value for the dog sample as only a $\delta^{13}C_{sc}$ was obtained and collagen amounts were too low for analysis.

The results indicate that the proportion of C4 plant intake by non-human animals at Chinikihá was extremely low, ranging from 3.71% to 13.24% with an average of 7.05% (s.d. 5.39). In some cases, no corn was consumed at all. In contrast, corn consumption by the humans was high, ranging from 65.05% to 73.00%, averaging 68.71% (s.d. 3.39) (Table 62). No corn consumption was calculated for the deer from Chancalá and the dog, as these samples did not produce enough collagen from cortical bone.

Overall, corn is not a particularly important foodstuff in the diet of the fauna, although the relatively higher values produced from one deer and the peccary sampled (13.24% and 11.59% of corn consumption) indicate that these two animals might have been browsing around cornfields. However, there is significant variation among the faunal samples, meaning that some of them could

Sample	Species/Description	Age	Sex	Collagen $\delta^{13}C_{VPDB}$ (‰)	% Corn consumption
CM03	white-tailed deer			-19.84	**9.76**
CM04	white-tailed deer			-19.25	**13.24**
CM05	white-tailed deer			-20.87	**3.71**
CM06	white-tailed deer			-21.97	**n/a**
CM07	white-tailed deer			-20.23	**7.47**
CM09	white-tailed deer			-20.42	**6.35**
CM10	collared peccary			-19.53	**11.59**
CM11	human from midden	adult	male	-9.09	**73.00**
CM13	Burial 40-2A	25-29	female	-9.53	**70.41**
CM14	Burial 42-4A	35-39	male	-9.17	**72.53**
CM15	Burial 42-4B	medium adult	female	-9.80	**68.82**
CM17	Burial 43-5A	medium adult	female	-10.44	**65.06**
CM18	Burial 44-6B	mature adult	male	-10.34	**65.65**
CM19	Burial 45-7A	adult	male	-10.37	**65.47**

* n/a represents values that are too small to be significant.

Table 62. Proportion of corn consumption by animals and humans at
Chinikihá (from cortical bone samples).

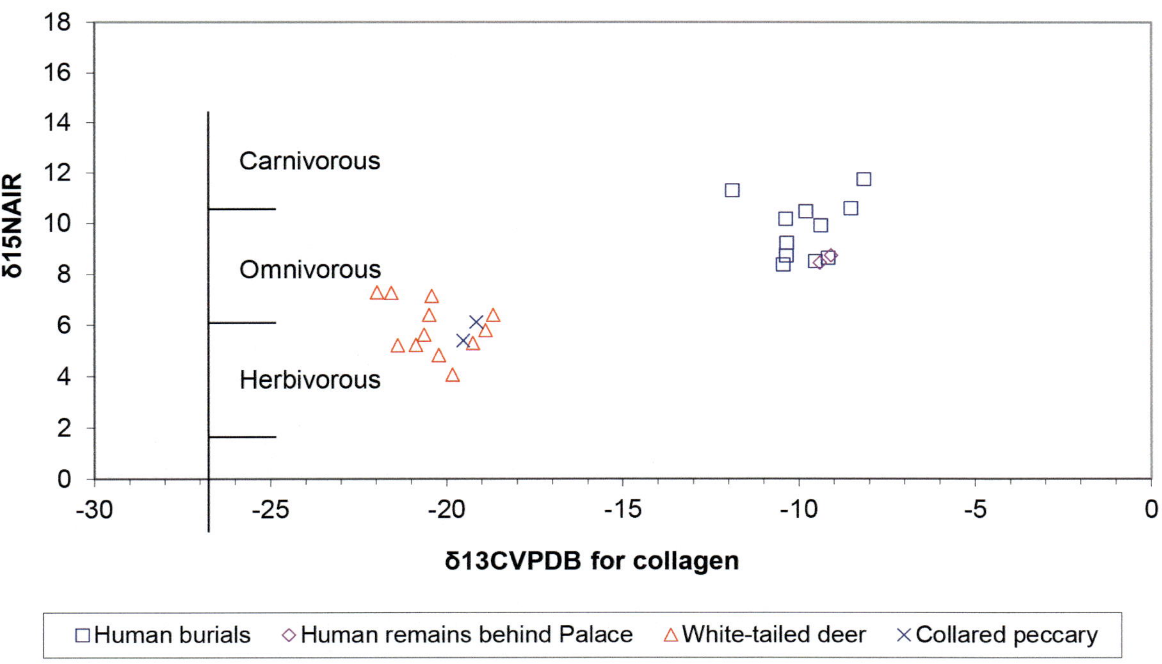

Figure 62. Distribution of $\delta^{13}C$ and $\delta^{15}N$ results for Chinikihá samples,
showing trophic levels.

have supplemented their diet with corn. This clearly contrasts with the deer and collared peccary results that apparently grazed in *milpas*, where corn made up a significant component of their diet (Wright 2006:96).

In contrast, corn was important in the human's diet where it constituted the base of their diet and contributed to more than 60% of their food. Although macrofossil preservation is not very good in the Maya region, corn macrobotanical remains have at least appeared in specific contexts in some archaeological sites, such as Copán, where it was deduced that corn accounted for at least 60% of the whole population's diet (Webster 2005:38). The values for corn consumption at Chinikihá are like those reported for Seibal, where corn consumption was 80% (Pohl 1990:159). Similar values were also found at other sites during the Classic period, including Caracol, Piedras Negras and several sites from the Petén area (Chase *et al.* 2001; Reed 1994; Wright 1994, 2006). Thus, the results obtained for Chinikihá fit well within what has been observed during the Classic period around the Maya area.

Deer domestication: Is it possible to identify?

By discussing the proportion of C3 and C4 plants that the animals were eating, we can also start discussing if there was a domestication process. As mentioned in Chapter three, the isotopic value calculated for animals that were being fed a diet that consisted entirely of corn for the purpose of ritual consumption, will resemble the values retrieved from human remains (White *et al.* 1993:359; White *et al.* 2001b:91; White *et al.* 2004:158). Deer on the other hand, was primarily hunted in the wild, although some authors have proposed that some animals may have been kept in captivity for a short period of time just before the celebration of a feast (Masson and Peraza 2008; White *et al.* 2004). In terms of the isotope analysis, where dogs were intentionally fed with corn, this will be reflected in the isotopic analysis of their remains (Hammond 1999:92; van der Merwe *et al.* 2000; White *et al.* 1993, 2001b, 2004). Evidence of corn consumption in deer is not so conclusive in terms of a scenario of domestication or captivity, due to their natural browsing behaviour.

The deer isotope values in Chinikihá for $\delta^{13}C$ are similar to those from other sites, including Preclassic sites such as Cuello, Belize (Hammond 1999; White *et al.* 2001b), and Classic Petexbatún in Guatemala (Emery *et al.* 2000), where the deer had a diet based on wild plants procured in forests, and only occasionally scavenged corn. The same pattern can be expected for the brocket deer and the peccary, which inhabit similar ecotones as the deer. The isotopic data on deer differ from those of the domestic dog, whose corn consumption during the Preclassic was significantly higher (Hammond 1999).

However, van der Merwe and colleagues (2000:24) suggest that a larger consumption of corn by deer may have happened during the Classic, and is truly observable during the Postclassic. Indeed, there are some limited examples of deer with high trace isotope values that point to the presence of corn in their diet—e.g. Lamanai (White and Schwarcz 1989), but cases like this are rare and the interpretations are biased because of limited samples.

Deer were apparently hunted in the wild, and there is no clear evidence of domestication yet (Emery *et al.* 2000; Montero and Núñez 2011; White *et al.* 2001b). However, the isotopic data is limited and other indicators for domestication—such as pathologies and genetic modification—would assist in clarifying this. An alternative explanation is that if deer were domesticated, they may still have been fed with wild plants (Montero *et al.* 2011; Tykot *et al.* 1996:358; Wright 1994). However, because humans were eating deer meat, if deer were being kept and fed on C3 plants, then humans should show similar $\delta^{13}C$ values as deer (Whittington and Reed 1997:160). The results from Chinikihá do not support this hypothesis.

Differences by age, sex, and status among the human samples

Differences by age: Dietary changes from childhood to adulthood

While the sample of burials from Chinikihá is small, there are some interesting trends. For example, the general values for Chinikihá are comparable to those reported from other sites for the Classic period, contributing significantly to the *corpus* of information about the diet of the Maya.

During childhood, the mean value of $\delta^{13}C_{sc}$ is -2.94‰ (n = 6, s.d. 0.98), $\delta^{13}C_{den}$ is -9.62‰ (n = 6, s.d. 1.35), and $\delta^{15}N$ averages 10.10‰ (n = 6, s.d. 1.94). The 'spacing' between $\Delta^{13}C_{sc\text{-}dent}$ for the whole childhood sample averages 6.68‰ (s.d. 1.01). When $\Delta^{13}C_{sc\text{-}dent}$ is correlated with the values for $\delta^{15}N$, the relationship between these two is negatively correlated (r = -0.69), meaning that for a bigger 'spacing' between carbonate and collagen, the $\delta^{15}N$ values would tend to be smaller—which in turn is related to lower trophic levels (e.g. from omnivores to herbivores)—as confirmed by controlled studies (Krueger and Sullivan 1984; Lee-Thorp *et al.* 1989). Having said this, the $\delta^{15}N$ values are markedly high—in the carnivore trophic level—probably due to the fact that 1M was selected for two individuals (CM16 and CM19). The results from 1M reflect the diet during early childhood (Wright and Schwarcz 1999). These individuals, therefore, probably were still being breastfed in early childhood. In these circumstances

Sample	$\delta^{13}C_{sc}$ (‰)	$\delta^{13}C_{den}$ (‰)	$\Delta^{13}C_{sc\text{-}den}$ (‰)	$\delta^{15}N$ (‰)	Tooth sampled	Age group by tooth
CM 11	-2.0	-9.4	7.4	8.43	2M	3-7 years of age; childhood diet (Coyston *et al.* 1999:226)
CM 13	-2.31	-10.35	8.04	8.71	3M	9.3-13 years of age; adulthood diet (Wright and Schwarcz 1999:1162; Coyston *et al.* 1999:226)
CM 15	-2.51	-8.15	5.64	11.73	2M	3-7 years of age; childhood diet (Coyston *et al.* 1999:226)
CM 16	-3.0	-8.52	5.52	10.57	1M	birth-3.7 years of age (Wright and Schwarcz 1999:1162)
CM 18	-3.05	-9.38	6.33	9.9	2M	3-7 years of age; childhood diet (Coyston *et al.* 1999:226)
CM 19	-4.77	-11.89	7.12	11.28	1M	birth-3.7 years of age (Wright and Schwarcz 1999:1162)

Table 63. Age group by tooth sampled for the $\delta^{13}C_{sc}$, $\delta^{13}C_{den}$, $\Delta^{13}C_{sc\text{-}den}$, and $\delta^{15}N$.

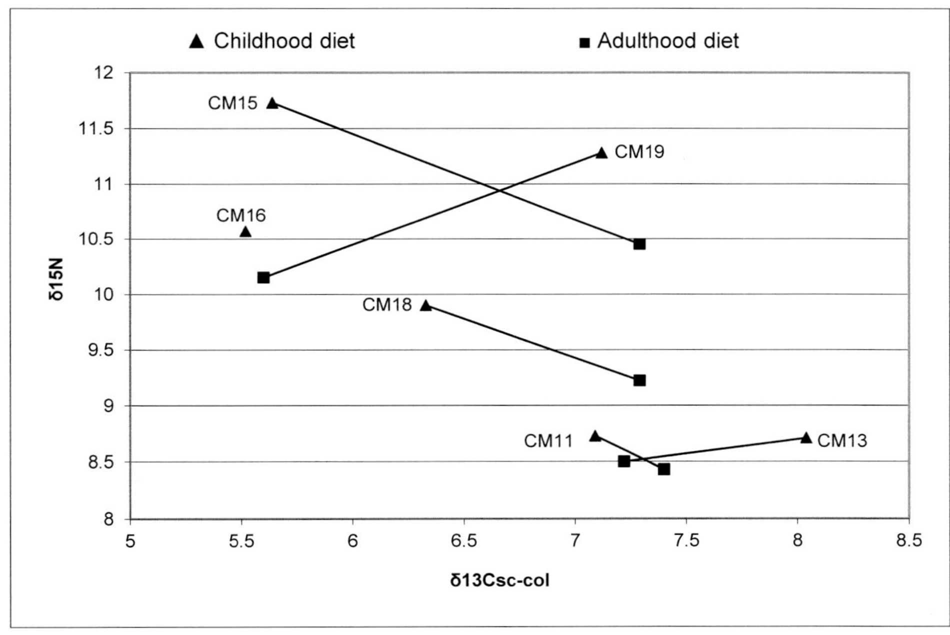

Figure 63. Differences between childhood and adulthood diet in the human samples (note that the length of the lines connecting both diets is equivalent to $\Delta^{13}C_{sc\text{-}lgbn}$).

breastfed infants usually display $\delta^{15}N$ values higher by 2‰ than the rest of the individuals, a value which reduces when solid foods are introduced (Fogel *et al.* 1989; Katzenberg 2008:428-429). The enrichment of $\delta^{15}N$ values between 0 and 3 years of age appears to be that of a carnivore because technically these individuals are 'eating their mothers (milk)' (Fogel *et al.* 1989; Wright and Schwarcz 1999).

In Table 63 we can see the results for each tooth that was used from the human samples. Information on which tooth was used is also provided, as each tooth will reflect different values according to the period in life of the individual.

The values for 2M are smaller (n = 3; $\Delta^{13}C_{sc\text{-}dent}$ = 6.45‰‰; $\delta^{15}N$ = 10.02‰) than those for 1M. Furthermore, the only value for 3M ($\Delta^{13}C_{sc\text{-}dent}$ = 8.04‰; $\delta^{15}N$ = 8.71‰) shows a larger 'spacing', and a lower value for trophic level, as marked by $\delta^{15}N$. Thus, it is possible to argue that after 3 years of age, some individuals would still be breastfed, but in general, the sub-adult population would be already eating a heavier C4 diet, complemented with some protein from C3-fed terrestrial animals (Figure 63).

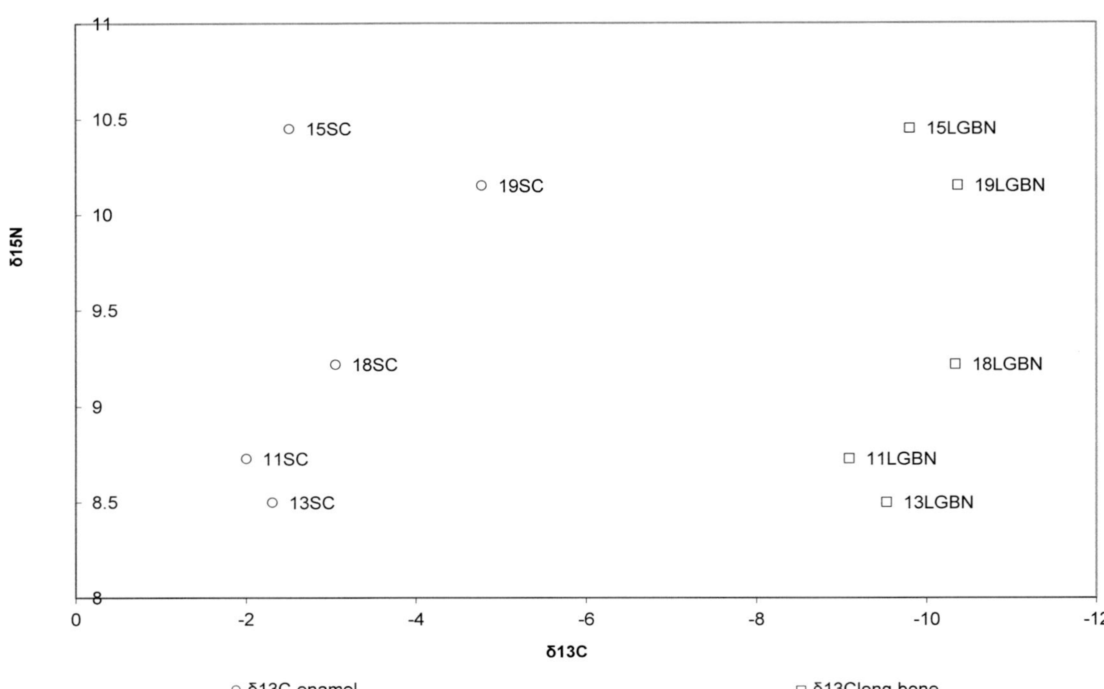

Figure 64. 'Spacing' between $\delta^{13}C$ collagen and apatite
data for human samples.

During adulthood—represented by values from long bones—values average $\delta^{13}C_{lgbn}$ = -9.22‰ (n = 8, s.d. 0.57), with a mean $\delta^{15}N$ of 9.14‰ (n = 8, s.d. 0.83). Where $\Delta^{13}C_{sc\text{-}lgbn}$ values average 6.89‰ (s.d. 0.73), and the correlation between this $\Delta^{13}C_{sc\text{-}lgbn}$ and $\delta^{15}N$ returned a value of r = -0.41‰, it indicates that there is a negative relationship between these two values. In Figure 64, the values for $\delta^{13}C_{sc}$ are more variable than those for $\delta^{13}C_{lgbn}$, pointing to a higher variability in diets during the earlier years of life. Smaller 'spacing' reflects higher meat consumption (Gerry 1997:56) and is consistent with a diet based on corn with little animal protein consumed, when combined with a high $\delta^{13}C$ and a low $\delta^{15}N$ value (Chase *et al.* 2001:111).

The changes in diet from childhood to adulthood are presented in Table 64. As values from enamel apatite represent childhood diet (Coyston *et al.* 1999), and values from long bone collagen represent the last 10-30 years of life (Krueger and Sullivan 1984), we can see an important change in the source of protein and carbohydrates with an increase in age. During childhood, the values for $\delta^{13}C$ are significantly high (mean $\delta^{13}C_{sc}$ = -2.94‰, s.d. 0.98), while in their adult life, values are comparable with those reported for other Maya sites (mean value of $\delta^{13}C_{lgbn}$ = -9.82‰, s.d. 0.57), and consistent with a reliance on corn horticulture (Wright

Sample	$\delta^{13}C_{sc}$ (‰)	$\delta^{13}C_{lgbn}$ (‰)	$\Delta^{13}C_{sc\text{-}lgbn}$ (‰)	$\delta^{15}N$ (‰)
CM 11	-2	-9.09	7.09	8.73
CM 13	-2.31	-9.53	7.22	8.5
CM14	--	-9.17		8.63
CM 15	-2.51	-9.8	7.29	10.45
CM 16	-3	--	--	--
CM17	--	-10.44	--	8.36
CM 18	-3.05	-10.34	7.29	9.22
CM 19	-4.77	-10.37	5.6	10.15

Table 64. Childhood diet reconstruction for the human sample values for $\delta^{13}C_{sc}$, $\delta^{13}C_{lgbn}$, $\Delta^{13}C_{sc\text{-}lgbn}$, and $\delta^{15}N$.

and White 1996). Access to protein during adulthood appears to have been similar among the individuals from the burials (mean $\delta^{15}N$ = 9.14‰, s.d. 0.8354), however there are some individuals that were eating more animal protein as they show a higher trophic level due different conditions. These are discussed below.

Differences by sex: differential access to resources

Other trends surface when sub-dividing the sample between females and males and using values from dentine and long bone collagen (Table 65). There is no significant difference between females and males for $\delta^{13}C$ and $\delta^{15}N$; however, some patterns can be observed.

According to the results in Figure 65 the distribution of female burials seems to be more compact and indicates less intra-group variation than the males. This means that women may have been accessing a larger diversity of meat resources than the men. Interestingly, the females had a bigger variation in $\delta^{15}N$, while the males had a difference in their $\delta^{13}C$ values.

During the Preclassic, at least in coastal sites, there was no significant difference between men and women (Tykot *et al.* 1996). It seems that all classes had access to a greater diversity of goods than were available in more varied ecotones (Tykot *et al.* 1996). Gender-based differences appear to have been significant during the Classic period in larger and more densely populated sites, such as Copán (Reed 1994:216; White *et al.* 2006a; Whittington 1999). These differences were not exclusive to the high class, but were also the case among low classes, distinction based on burial location within a site. The differences indicate that men had more access to exotic or sparse resources, such as meat (Whittington 1999), or corn in places where it was difficult to obtain (Hammond 1999:94). It has been suggested that men consumed corn as a beverage during the Preclassic, and later throughout the Classic period, regardless of a sites' location (Tykot *et al.* 1996; Whittington and Reed 1997:163). Christine White and colleagues (2006a:153), suggest that this is because men were engaging more often in ritual ceremonies that include consumption of meat and corn, although the participation of women in ritual activities may have varied temporally and/or regionally (White 2005:360). In short, women may not

Burial	Tissue	NISP	$\delta^{15}N_{AIR}$ (‰)	$\delta^{13}C_{VPDB}$ (‰)
Males	Bone	4	9.18	-9.74
	Dentine	3	9.63	-9.10
Females	Bone	3	9.10	-9.92
	Dentine	2	10.22	-9.25

Table 65. Distribution of $\delta^{15}N$ and $\delta^{13}C$ by sex (based on collagen values).

have been able to consume as many of the foods that had an ideological value (White *et al.* 2006a:152).

In coastal sites however, male burials with high values of $\delta^{13}C$ accompanied by high $\delta^{15}N$ values, could be reflecting a diet high in marine resources (White and Schwarcz 1989:464), and in fact, a low consumption of corn. Thus, understanding the archaeological context in which the remains were found is important. Equally important is the creation of an accurate framework from modern reference collections, to function as a baseline within which to interpret the results.

Differences by location: differences by social classes

Although the human sample is small, there are individuals from three different locations, including seven burials from the inner patio of a domestic compound, two burials from outside the same compound, and the human remains recovered from behind the Palace (Table 66).

The remains from the individual recovered from behind the Palace exhibit the lowest value for meat consumption, and the highest for corn consumption (Montero *et al.* 2011). There is a great variability among

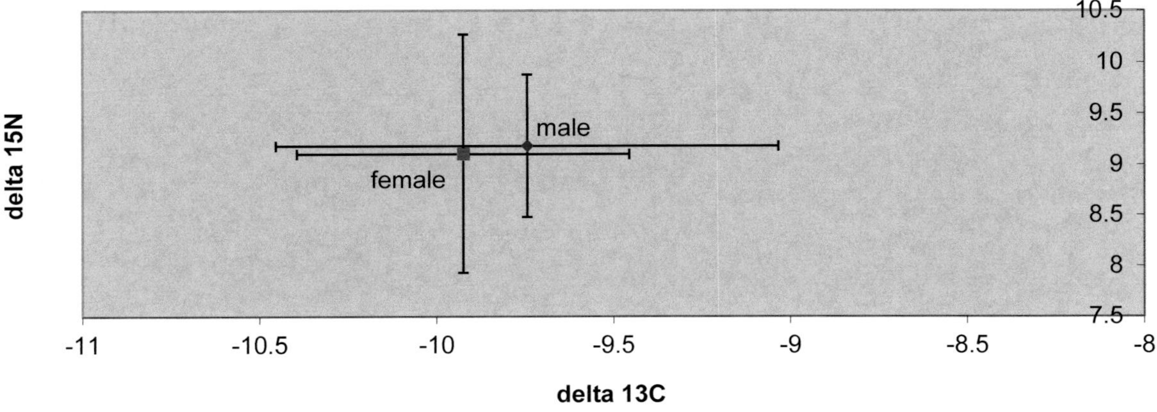

Figure 65. $\delta^{13}C$ and $\delta^{15}N$ isotope variation by sex at Chinikihá.

Location	Tissue	NISP	$\delta^{15}N_{AIR}$ (‰)	$\delta^{13}C_{VPDB}$ (‰)
Inner patio north structure	Bone	6	9.22	-9.94
	Teeth	4	10.23	-9.10
Behind north structure	Bone	1	8.36	-10.44
	Teeth	--	--	--
	Bone	1	8.73	-9.09
Behind palace	Teeth	1	8.43	-9.4

Table 66. Distribution of $\delta^{15}N$ and $\delta^{13}C$ by location (based on collagen values).

the burials from the inner patio (Figure 66), but this may be since very few burials from other areas have been sampled. Previously, individuals with high $\delta^{13}C$ values and a low $\delta^{15}N$ have been interpreted as members of the lower classes, including commoners and sacrificed victims (Hammond 1999a; Tykot *et al.* 1996; Whittington and Reed 1997). Chase and colleagues (2001, Chase and Chase 2010:6) identified that the diet of sacrificial victims, often treated as 'earth offerings', is different from the diet of proper burials found in the Acropolis of Caracol. Sacrificial victims could be from any age group, and children and adults have been included.

Low status members of the population have not been widely studied, since most isotope analyses in the Maya area have been focused almost exclusively on samples from elite graves, making comparisons hard to interpret. When the proportion of corn, as reflected in the isotopes from individuals, departs from the rest of the population, it has been interpreted to be an indicator of a person from a different geographical region, who was used as a sacrifice victim (Hammond

1999; Tykot *et al.* 1996:359). However, not all sacrificed people were foreigners—some were members of the local population, usually from the lower classes (White *et al.* 2006a:155).

Relationship between the isotope analysis and palaeopathology: a proxy approach to diet reconstruction

The values from $\delta^{13}C$ gradually increase from 1M and 2M (childhood diet) to 3M (adulthood diet). The only child (3-5 years) present in the burials was not sampled for isotope analysis, however, the presence of enamel hypoplasia on its deciduous canines suggest that this individual was also under nutritional stress. In long bones and tooth enamel, the most common marks of stress are Harris lines and dental hypoplasia respectively (Goodman *et al.* 1984:24). Judging by its age, this stress probably corresponds to the change of diet as consequence of weaning (Katzenberg 2008). Almost all the adults had enamel hypoplasia on their permanent teeth, except for burials 43-5A (CM17) and 45-7 (CM19). Interestingly, these two individuals also did not show carious lesions, usually associated with a high consumption of carbohydrates and starchy food items, such as corn. The $\delta^{13}C$ values for these individuals are also the lowest of all the collection, reflecting their low intake of corn.

On the other hand, the individual from behind the Palace presented high values of $\delta^{13}C$, indicative of a diet rich in carbohydrates. The dental diseases included an abscess and tooth loss of 1M, as well as carious lesions and an occlusal-wear pattern on all teeth (Figure 67).

Other pathologies that were present among the human remains include anaemic lesions, including

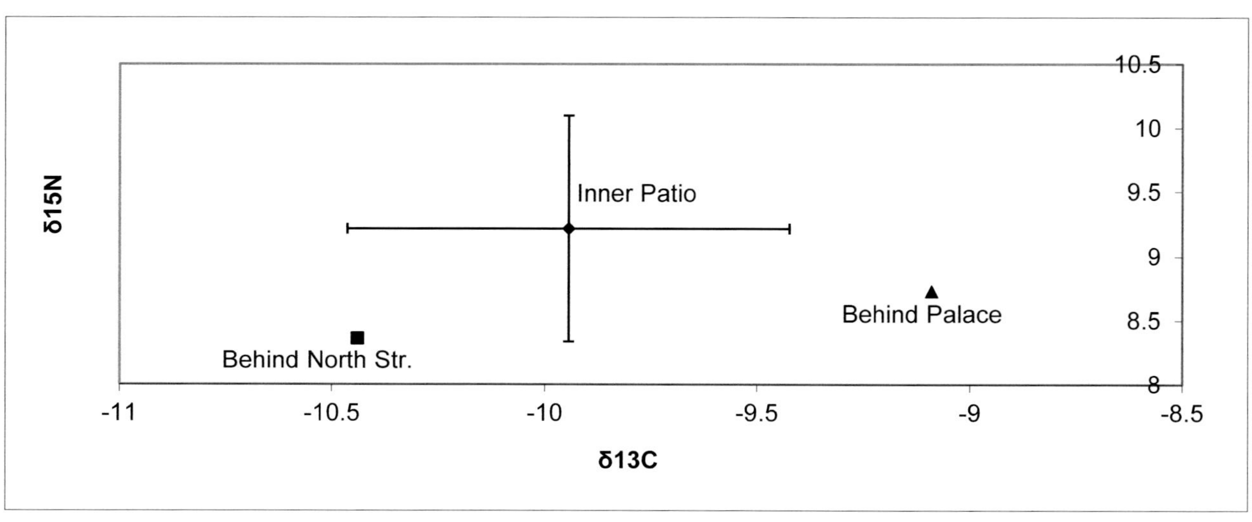

Figure 66. Distribution of $\delta^{13}C$ and $\delta^{15}N$ values by location at Chinikihá.

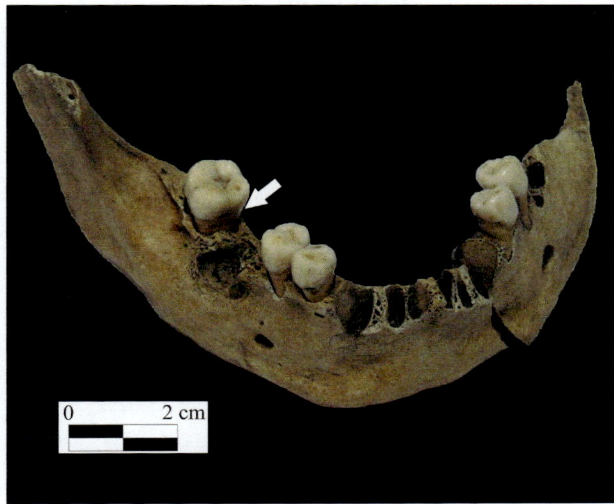

Figure 67. Mandible from sample CM11, showing an abscess at 1M on right side. Note the caries at the neck of 2M (red arrow), and the wear pattern on occlusal surfaces of all teeth present (Photograph by Coral Montero López).

cribra orbitalia and porotic hyperostosis (Luis Núñez, personal communication 2009), which usually forms after six months of breastfeeding, if not enough iron is taken in combination with a high intake of carbohydrates (Stuart-Macadam 1995). All the burials in the collection, except two (burial 41-3, not sampled and burial 45-7, sample CM19) presented at least one form of anaemia scarring, indicative of weaning stress. This trend is similar to that from other inland sites, where a high intake of corn and foods with little or no iron were being consumed (Wright and White 1996). These data clearly contrast with the low percentages of anaemia in coastal areas where iron-enriched marine food is available (White *et al.* 2006b).

Discussion

As pointed out, in the Maya region, social heterogeneity and small sample sizes are confounding factors when interpreting results of isotope analysis (White *et al.* 2006a:144). What can be seen from the above analysis is that it is difficult to single out specific diet components, as the values are highly variable. Although the data obtained from Chinikihá are limited, the results are important because they can be used to make inferences about the diet in smaller cities, and other topics such as the way these cities were obtaining faunal and plant resources, especially when exploring differences in the diet based on social class, and the possibility of ritual consumption of faunal resources.

As seen in Tables 67 and 68, there are sufficient data from different chronological and geographical areas to confirm that there was broad spectrum of corn consumption over temporal, spatial, and social variables (White 1999:XIV; White *et al.* 2006a:144; Wright 1993:173, 2006:114). Coastal sites show a more diverse diet, while inland sites appear to have had a much bigger reliance on corn as a basic food staple (Hammond 1999; White *et al.* 2001a). The results for Chinikihá are consistent and bring enough evidence to support the hypothesis that during the Balunté phase at Chinikihá (Classic period), the diet of the intermediate elite was based primarily on corn. However, the values from the human sample in general reflect a very heterogeneous diet, due to a great variability in the diet composition across the population (Wright 1993:173). Although some of the variability could be explained as a consequence of chronological differences, it is possible that these values are indeed pointing to a difference in status (Wright 1993).

The abundant data on corn dependence by humans is clear. On the other hand, access to meat and other exotic resources has ignited some debate in recent periods, especially those faunal remains in archaeological assemblages interpreted as the result of ritual activity. Identifying contexts that reflect a ritual behaviour is not an easy task, as argued in the previous chapters. Some authors (White *et al.* 2004:144) suggest that the isotope analysis of faunal remains can reveal whether they were domesticated and fed on corn for ritual purposes. Terrestrial animals fed on C3 plants have been part of the human diet in the Maya area since the Preclassic period (Metcalfe *et al.* 2009), but the quantity of such animals consumed for ritual meals is still under debate.

Deer remains from larger sites, such as Tikal and Copán, produced values that suggest most deer were wild or occasionally browsed in cornfields (White *et al.* 2004:152). Deer data contrast with those from the domestic dog, which more commonly produce higher values, pointing to a larger consumption of corn. However, in clearly ritual contexts—such as caches and offerings—both deer and dog remains seem to have higher $\delta^{13}C$ values.

The large faunal assemblage at Lagartero has been suggested as an example of ritual consumption of meat during the Classic period (White *et al.* 2004). However, mean values of deer bones from the ceremonial context reflect significant low corn consumption, ($\delta^{13}C$ = -18.2‰). One deer sample, however, resulted in a value of $\delta^{13}C$ = -7.3‰, reflecting a diet almost purely based on corn. Since samples from Lagartero are from cortical long bone, and reflect a long-term diet, we can assume that this animal was fed on corn since it was born. White and colleagues affirm 'it had a C4-restricted diet or was purposefully fed for *ritual consumption*' (White *et al.* 2004:151, italics mine). Moreover, these authors suggest that tamed deer were used to re-enact ceremonies with

Site	Preclassic		Classic		Posclassic		Context	References
Copán			$\delta^{13}C = -9.26$ $\delta^{15}N = 7.56$	(n = 48)				Reed 1994
Cuello	$\delta^{13}C = -12.9$ $\delta^{15}N = 8.9$	(n = 28)						Tykot *et al.* 1996; Van der Merwe *et al.* 2000:29, table 2.1
Lamanai	$\delta^{13}C = -12.4$ $\delta^{15}N = 10.2$	(n = 3)[a]	$\delta^{13}C = -13.37$ $\delta^{15}N = 10.27$	(n = 4)[b]			Burials at ceremonial core	[a]Wright and White 1996; [b]White and Schwarcz 1989
Kaminaljuyú			$\delta^{13}C = -9.8$ $\delta^{15}N = 7.2$	(n = 6)			Tombs at ceremonial core	Wright and Schwarcz 1999:1162
Chinikihá			$\delta^{13}C = -9.09$ $\delta^{15}N = 8.73$	(n = 1)			Scattered human remains behind Palace	This study
Chinikihá			$\delta^{13}C = -9.09$ $\delta^{15}N = 9.21$	(n = 6)			Burials assoc. to North Structure	This study
Yaxuná					$\delta^{13}C = -12.3$ $\delta^{15}N = 7.1$	(n = 3)		Mansell *et al.* 2006:175
Chunchucmil					$\delta^{13}C = -14.7$ $\delta^{15}N = 7.0$	(n = 3)		Mansell *et al.* 2006:175
Mayapán					$\delta^{13}C = -9$ to -12 $\delta^{15}N = 7.5$ to 11	(n = 34)		Wright 2009
Piedras Negras			$\delta^{13}C = -9.0$ to -8.1 $\delta^{15}N = 7.6$ to 9.8	(n = 7)			Royal and Elite burials	Scherer *et al.* 2007:92
Altun Ha			$\delta^{13}C = -11.76$ $\delta^{15}N = 10.69$	(n = 34)				White *et al.* 2001a:377, table 1

Table 67. $\delta^{13}C$ and $\delta^{15}N$ isotope values for human samples in the Maya region (from bone collagen).

mythological themes that commonly appear on Classic ceramics (White *et al.* 2004:151).

Summary

Ten faunal samples (eight deer, one dog, and one peccary), and six samples from a collection of human burials were prepared for isotope analysis. The preservation of the samples was good, with no diagenesis and thus, suitable for analysis. The results of the isotope analyses were inserted in a palaeodiet model that was generated with modern and archaeological data for this specific area in the Lowlands. In general, the deer and the peccary were eating more C3 plants than corn, although some animals may have been browsing in *milpas*, while human diet depended almost completely on corn with sporadic access to meat. The dogs were being fed deliberately or were scavenging among human leftovers, and thus, the isotope values from the dog remains appear similar to the human population. This is translated into a low percentage of corn consumption among wild fauna, while humans were heavily dependent on corn (over 60% of their diets).

The fact that deer values for corn consumption are not as high as the values from the human remains may suggest that the landscape was not significantly modified by corn agriculture. It is also suggested that

Site	Preclassic	Classic	Posclassic	Context	References
Lagartero		(n = 8) $\delta^{13}C$= -18.2 C/N = 3.3 $\delta^{15}N$= 5.4		Ceremonial dumping	White *et al.* 2004:149
Copán		(n = 20) $\delta^{13}C$= -20.35 C/N = 3.3 $\delta^{15}N$= 4.9		High class domestic refuse	White *et al.* 2004:149; Reed 1994; Gerry 1997
Tikal		(n = 4) $\delta^{13}C$= -20.5 C/N = 3.3 $\delta^{15}N$= 5.8		Midden	White *et al.* 2004:151
Colha	(n = 14) $\delta^{13}C$ = -21.0 C/N = 3.3 $\delta^{15}N$ = 5.0			Primary and secondary middens	White *et al.* 2001b:98
Cuello	(n = 5) $\delta^{13}C$ = -20.5 $\delta^{15}N$ = 5.8			n/a	Van der Merwe *et al.* 2000:29, table 2.1; Tykot *et al.* 1996
Pacbitun		(n = 5) $\delta^{13}C$ = -19.16 $\delta^{15}N$ = 9.61 $\delta^{15}N$ = 9.61			White *et al.* 1993:359, table 4
Petexbatún[a]		(n = 48) $\delta^{13}C$ = -20.55 C/N = 3.2 $\delta^{15}N$ = n/a		n/a	Emery *et al.* 2000:table 2
Chinikihá		(n = 8) $\delta^{13}C$ = -20.24 C/N = 2.9 $\delta^{15}N$ = 5.59			This study
Copán		(n = 3) $\delta^{13}C$ = -19.97‰ $\delta^{15}N$ = 4.07‰			Reed 1994
Mayapan			(n = 1) $\delta^{13}C$ = -21.1‰ $\delta^{15}N$ =5.3‰	n/a	Wright 2009
Marco González			(n = 2) $\delta^{13}C$ = -19.55 $\delta^{15}N$ = 5.4		Williams *et al.* 2009
Motul de San José		(n = 13) $\delta^{13}C$ = -20.17 $\delta^{15}N$ = n/a			Emery and Thornton (2008b)

[a]Arroyo de Piedra, Dos Pilas Tamarindito, Punta de Chimino, and Dos Pilas.
n/a: information not available or not published.

Table 68. $\delta^{13}C$ and $\delta^{15}N$ isotope values for deer samples in the Maya region (from bone collagen).

the values produced from the fauna and human remains represent exploitation largely of local resources, with perhaps a few animals having come from distant regions. In terms of the human diet, the information gained from the tooth samples was very important in assessing childhood health, and the beginning of social differentiation. In Chinikihá, there were differences in access to faunal resources based on age, sex, and social status. At least one individual was able to gain protein access since an early age, including meat and possibly an extended period of breastfeeding. Women on the other hand, may have had a more restricted access to meat, and reflect more variability in terms of the animals they might have eaten. Interestingly, the remains of an individual found in the midden display the highest $\delta^{13}C$ and the lowest $\delta^{14}N$ values, suggesting a diet almost exclusively of corn. This is interesting with regards to the discussion about the possible identity of sacrificial victims. The fact that his diet was different from the individuals from the other burial samples suggests that individuals that were chosen for sacrifice, or whose bones were removed and redeposited in ritual contexts, were not from the elite class.

Chapter ten

Discussion

The zooarchaeological and isotopic analyses presented here allow us to make several observations about the food procurement and exploitation techniques of the inhabitants of Chinikihá. Furthermore, these analyses provide enough data to allow us to explore the consumption patterns of the elite, through the distribution of faunal species used as food and the subsequent transformation of their remains into tools and ornaments, or ultimate discard and reuse as a construction fill. The analysis of the exploitation patterns of faunal resources as seen in this study suggests their dietary importance in smaller sites, such as Chinikihá, and allows a comparison with other similar sites during the Late/Terminal Classic period. Ultimately, the consumption of meat resources took place during feasting events and other activities in which the elite sought to promote and maintain their power. However, the identification of feasts in the archaeological record is not straightforward. In the Maya area, there are many examples of deposits containing large quantities of animal bones and ceramic fragments that have been identified as the remains of feasting events, creating a large *corpus* of data to which comparisons of the Chinikihá's assemblage can be drawn in order to define whether this deposit was formed by feasting activities.

This chapter will begin by discussing the results of the zooarchaeological analysis of Chinikihá's assemblage, in particular of *Operación* 114, a deposit that contains a set of attributes that could be interpreted to be the result of feasting activities. Particular attention will be paid to the taphonomic history of the deposit, as this is essential for the understanding of the behaviour or behaviours that contributed to its formation. To do so, a list of features that characterise feasts according to the anthropological literature will be used in comparison with the data from Chinikihá, in order to determine whether this deposit meets the criteria for a feasting event. This discussion is placed within the context of current interpretations regarding the Late/Terminal Classic, a period that has been defined by changes in the exploitation of faunal resources as a consequence of changes in the socio-political situation, and that had major consequences on the faunal exploitation by the elite (Emery 2010).

The isotopic analysis results conducted on human and animal samples in order to explore the faunal dietary contributions to human diet, and to characterise their

dietary consumption patterns during the Late/Terminal Classic period, will be used in support of this discussion. The isotopic evidence is very important as it allows us to explore how animals were treated. They may have been kept in captivity and fed specific diets by humans, as requited for many rituals during that period. Isotopic data also provides indirect information about faunal exploitation during periods of intense ritual activity and animal management during the Late/Terminal Classic period. Finally, the analysis of feasts and their importance in Chinikihá is part of a broader regional discussion comparing Chinikihá's data with other similar assemblages from other sites in the Maya area. Ultimately, this discussion aims to demonstrate the complexity of identifying feasting in the archaeological record, and to test its presence through zooarchaeological analysis.

Results of the zooarchaeological analysis

Using a traditional zooarchaeological approach, this dissertation has demonstrated that several hypotheses about the exploitation patterns of the elite in the Late/Terminal Classic Maya of Chinikihá can be evaluated. Three tests were applied with the aim to explore the distribution of faunal remains, and ultimately identify the distribution patterns of the remains. These tests were:

1. Testing for a spatial patterning
2. Testing for processing patterns
3. Testing for rituality

The presence of a stuccoed floor was used in order to explore possible differences in the distribution of the materials. The material was grouped into two units, under and above the floor (Layers IV-V and Layers I-III respectively). This involved the study of the spatial distribution of the materials in the context, the evidence of processing faunal remains, especially the white-tailed deer, and finally, the testing of the taphonomic history of deposition in order to identify the possibility that the assemblage was the result of ritual or feasting behaviour. The results from these tests are summarised in Table 69.

Testing for spatial patterning: results

Testing for spatial patterning considered the presence of a stuccoed floor between Layers III and IV of the deposit, analysing possible differences between the

	Hypothesis	Statistical test	Interpretation
Testing for spatial patterning	Discrete groupings of materials in the deposit	Not significant	No difference in the distribution of fauna by Layer; no difference under and above the floor
	Differential patterning by age	Not significant	No difference in the distribution of age by Layer; overall preference of animals in prime age
	Difference in the distribution of carnivore chewing	Not significant	No difference in the distribution of carnivore chewing by Layer; all materials were exposed for some time
	Differences in the distribution of rodent gnawing	Significant ($X^2 = 31.2777$, df $= 1$, p > 0.001)	There is more evidence of rodent gnawing under the floor (secondary fill)
	Differences in the distribution of weathering stages	Not significant	There is no difference: All materials were exposed briefly (six months to one year)
Testing for processing patterns	Selection of specific body portions	Not significant	No difference in the distribution of body portions by Layer: Torso, and upper limbs are preferred all throughout the deposit
	Selection of specific body portions by age	Not significant	No difference in the distribution of body parts by age: same parts selected for sub-adults and adults
	Selection of specific body portion by species	Very significant ($X^2 = 59.248$, df $= 8$, p >001) (t $= 3.611$, df $= 40$, p >0.001	The is a continual preference for deer haunches
	Cut marks by age	Significant ($X^2 = 5.4100$, df $= 1$, $0.05 > p > 0.01$	There are more sub-adults presenting more cut marks
	Cut marks by floor	Not significant	No difference in the distribution by Layer: Deer is processed in the same fashion
	Burning or heat exposure	Not significant	No difference in the distribution of burned materials by Layer:
Testing for ritual exploitation	Selection of left side for ritual	Not significant	No marked difference by sidedness by body portion nor by Layer
	More juvenile animals in ritual/ceremonial deposits	Not significant	No difference in the distribution by Layer
	Male animals were preferred for ritual activities	Not enough data	Not conclusive
	Similar treatment for fauna and humans	Significant ($X^2 = 3.6866$, df $= 1$, $0.05 > p > 0.02$	Similar processing of fauna and humans
	Distribution of separate groups (shell, modified fauna, humans, deer, dog, etc.)	Not significant	No difference in the distribution of all categories by Layer

Table 69. Results from the three tests conducted in *Operación* 114.

contexts under and above it. Firstly, the materials were grouped in two main categories, according to their distribution in the upper context (Layers I-III) and under the floor (Layers IV-V). It was thought that a different distribution pattern may have been identified through zooarchaeological analysis. This was done with the ultimate aim of identifying the behaviour behind the formation of *Operación* 114 and to identify the type of context this deposit represents. The results show that despite a floor being laid, there were no significant differences in the distribution of the materials, nor could a specific patterning be identified. Nonetheless, several generalisations can be made. The materials showed no specific distribution by Layer; however, the two largest concentrations of materials were identified against the back wall of the Palace. These concentrations may represent two separate 'dumps' located in Squares K1 (25.09%NISP) and J2 (16.74%NISP). These squares also contained the highest concentration of ceramic sherds, corresponding to preparation and serving wares. In the same location, the highest proportions of white-tailed deer, and domestic dog remains were identified, two species that played a critical dietary role in feasting and possessed symbolic importance. Coincidentally, the highest proportions of *jute* shells were also found in Square K1 (65.95%NISP), but in smaller concentrations in all other squares.

For most of the mammals present, there was no difference in distribution regarding age when the floor was considered, but it was noticed that there is a high proportion of prime-aged animals, including both immature (12-29 months) and sub-adult (29-35 months) animals. Other age categories such as juvenile and old were identified less frequently. This is particularly true in the case of the white-tailed deer. This distribution is often characterised as a 'prime-age mortality profile' (Stiner 1990), as the bulk of the sample is comprised of animals that are slaughtered when their maximum size and weight has been reached, returning the maximum amount of meat. A large percentage of the deer in their prime consisted of immature and sub-adult animals, although the animals may not have reached a complete fusion in all their skeletal elements. In the case of white-tailed deer, 59.96% of all deer remains fall into this category. The prime-age profile is also observable among the dog and rabbit remains through the analysis of epiphyseal closure, with dogs at the completion of their first year of life, and for rabbits, after four months of age. Therefore, there seems to be continuity in the selection of prime-aged animals throughout the whole context. The distribution of animals by age groups provides interesting information about the hunting strategies and faunal management systems of the inhabitants of Chinikihá. The presence of deer, dog, and rabbit in this context is consistent with that of other similar deposits. Further, the addition of *jute* shells in the later part of the deposit (above the floor), stresses their importance as a dietary resource for the elite during the Late Classic period (Pohl 1990).

Another factor that needed testing for spatial patterning was the distribution of non-human modifications and weathering stages observed on the faunal remains. When carnivore chewing was analysed independently, there was no observable difference in the distribution of marks on remains retrieved from under and above the floor. However, more than 60% of all faunal remains throughout the deposit presented some carnivore chewing all throughout the deposit. This suggests that the materials were left exposed for some time before being covered. Contrasting this with the high presence of carnivore chewing, rodent gnawing was relatively low (5.31%), and was concentrated in Layers IV-V. This suggests that the materials under the floor may have been part of a secondary deposit, used as a construction fill. The distribution of weathering stages throughout the context resulted in no significant difference, with most of the material being mildly exposed (Stage 1),

although some bones presented advanced stages of weathering. Combining the faunal modifications data with the distribution of weathering stages suggests that most faunal remains were left exposed for an average of six months up to a year, a practice that is common for domestic middens in ethnographic studies for the Maya region.

Testing for processing patterns: results

There is no doubt about the importance of deer as a dietary component, especially in *Operación* 114. As such, identifying the presence of specific age groups, body portions, and sidedness in the deposit was important for establishing butchery patterns. The results obtained showed that all body portions were present, suggesting complete carcasses were processed at the site, and elements from all body parts were present, including the discard of low utility parts, and the remains from dismembering and preparation of favoured parts for consumption. Although there is a high proportion of torso, upper front limb, and upper front back limb remains, there was no significant difference in the distribution of body parts by layer. The torso and upper segments of both limbs were the main body portions in the deposit, and their presence in all layers suggests that this pattern continued throughout the life of the deposit. There was also no significant difference by age, and the same three main body portions were selected from individuals of all ages. When body part values were normalised to contrast the great number of individual vertebrae present, there was a clear selection of the upper segments of front and back limbs, being the most prized section of deer, as it yields the largest quantities of meat. The argument that the haunch was deliberately selected was based on the high percentage of scapulae and innominate bones, as the femur and humerus were present in much smaller proportions.

There was a high proportion of bones from the meaty body portions presenting cut marks and other processing modifications in *Operación* 114 that suggest their processing for dietary consumption. There was no significant difference in the distribution of cut marks among the different layers, but there was a significant correlation between cut marks and age, with sub-adults presenting more cut marks than the adults. Other processing marks included heat exposure, as reflected by the presence of changes in colour and texture present on the bones, which added to a total of 16.11%, predominantly on white-tailed deer remains, but also other species, including dog, peccary, and rabbit. Specimens affected by burning included changes in the consistency and variations in colour, ranging from dark yellow to completely calcined bone, characterised by a white/black colour. Only two human bones presented changes consistent with boiling. However, the distribution of heat-exposed materials by Layer was not significant, and no grouping was observable.

Testing for ritual exploitation: results

The statistical analyses performed for this test aimed to identify a ritual use of faunal resources, considering their symbolic role in feasts. It was determined that there was no selection of body parts by sidedness, with left and right elements distributed randomly all throughout the deposit. A high percentage of juvenile animals, a common marker of ritual consumption, also resulted in no significance, and the scarce data by sex was too inconclusive to detect a preference for either sex. The similarity in treatment between isolated human remains and deer suggests their deliberate inclusion, and possible consumption in ritual ceremonies in *Operación* 114. However, when the distribution of all other analysed categories (worked bone, shell, and so on) was considered, no significant differences were detected.

Given the previous research on ritual, including studies of human and animal sacrifices, it is important to assess how this deposit reflects this pattern. According to Schele (1984) and Freidel (1986), sacrifice, especially of human victims, was seen as a vital component in the transmission of dynasties. The presence of human remains with clear anthropogenic modifications including cut marks, 'green stick' fractures, and changes in colour due to heat exposure are comparable to those present on the faunal remains. The inclusion of human remains in a context mainly derived from a consumption episode or episodes, suggests that at least some humans suffered a similar treatment to that of animals, and it may be interpreted as evidence of cannibalism (Turner and Turner 1999; White 1991:394). However, in this sense, the consumption of human flesh would have been highly restricted to certain segments of the society. The presence of human remains in *Operación* 114 supports the notion of ritual feasting, and along with dog remains, musical instruments, *incensarios* and other ritual paraphernalia, reinforces the notion that this was not the result of an ordinary meal, but one of a ritual nature (Emery 2004a:101). The topic of cannibalism and human and animal sacrifice, and how to recognise both in the archaeological record, needs further exploration in the future.

In summary, the results from the zooarchaeological analysis suggest that the composition of the deposit was very homogeneous, with truly little differentiating the context under the floor from those materials deposited above it. It was concluded that the materials under the floor may have entered the archaeological record as a secondary context, this is, as part of a construction fill. On the other hand, the context above the floor may

have been a primary deposit, where feasting activities was more discernible compared with the under-floor context. It is possible that the differences between the two units created by the presence of the floor could be the result of different formation processes or behaviours that were then combined as part of the taphonomic history of the deposit. This coincides with known practices of reutilisation of spaces by the Maya that result in mixed deposits and contexts; this is particularly common for ritual deposits (Lucero 2006). Ultimately, the context in which these remains appeared is directly associated with the construction sequence of the structures around the deposit, and the paths in which they are integrated in the archaeological record. Considering the temporal length of occupation of *Operación* 114, that is 100 to 150 years, the distribution of the materials suggests a periodical use of this context for the discard of feasting remains. Due to its large occupation however, deposits that reflect a long occupation become more complex, and their distinctive characteristics get obscured, often becoming more palimpsest-like (Hutson and Stanton 2007).

Results of the isotopic analysis

The results for the isotope analysis for the deer samples from *Operación* 114 confirmed that wild deer were mainly targeted, as most of these animals had a diet composed predominantly of wild plants, while only two samples (one deer and one peccary) indicated that they may have eaten some corn, probably from browsing in *milpas*. These results contrast sharply with deliberately fed deer from Lagartero, which produced results consistent with a diet either exclusively of corn since their infancy ($\delta^{13}C$ = -7.3‰) or for a short period of time, but long enough to be reflected in their long bones ($\delta^{13}C$ = -12.7‰) (White *et al.* 2004:150-151). These values could not be the result of opportunistic grazing in cornfields. In comparison, the results obtained for Chinikihá and Chancalá from ten deer and one peccary, showed $\delta^{13}C$ values averaging -20.30‰, indicating that their diet consisted mainly of C3 plants which may have included some wild grasses, legumes, and fruit trees, although some animals may have had access to maize fields. Furthermore, these results stress the fact that the deer were hunted in the wild, rather than kept in captivity.

Evidence of wild deer has been recovered from different sites and chronological periods, including the Preclassic sites of Colhá and Cuello, and the Classic period sites, including Lagartero, Copán, Tikal, the Petexbatún and the Pasión River regions (Emery *et al.* 2000; Masson 2004a; White *et al.* 2001b, 2004; Wright 2006). Overall, it seems that during the Classic period, the ancient Maya preferred to obtain their meat from wild resources (Wing 1978). However, it is important to acknowledge that there is still some debate regarding the animals in captivity, and whether they were being fed with corn (White *et al.* 2004:144). An alternative view suggests that if in captivity, these animals could have been fed with other plants including *ramón* leaves (*Brosimum alicastrum*) (Montero *et al.* 2011; Tykot *et al.* 1996:358; Wright 1994), resulting in a C3 signature indistinguishable from a varied wild diet.

In contrast to the exploitation of deer and other wild animals, the dog was one of the only true domesticates that the Maya had access to since the Preclassic period (Olsen 1985; Wing 1978). The use of dogs as food reflects a long-standing tradition in the Maya area and in all Mesoamerica in general, with use of the dog as a dietary resource was documented from the Preclassic (Clutton-Brock and Hammond 1994). It remained a constant staple through the Classic, and until Early Hispanic times (deFrance and Hanson 2008). The lack of processing marks on dogs has raised the question of how they were prepared for consumption. Hamblin (1984:116) suggested that the lack of cut marks in the Cozumel dog assemblage might be because dogs are stewed as opposed to roasting, while alternatives have been suggested (Clutton-Brock and Hammond 1994:820).

Domestic dogs were probably fed with household scraps, so little energy had to be put into their rearing. Only on special occasions, dogs would be fattened exclusively with corn, as a lead up to its ritual consumption (Shaw 1991:67). The preference for dog meat seen in various sites during the Preclassic seems to decline during the Classic period, when there are fewer examples of fattened dogs, only to be favoured again during the Postclassic period (Hamblin 1984).

For Chinikihá, only one enamel sample was obtained from a dog specimen. However, it was observed that the this dog's $\delta^{13}C$ value (-7.4‰) is more similar to the values of humans (-2.00 to -4.77‰) than to those of the deer sample (-10.90 to -13.63‰), suggesting that this dog may have been living in the same spaces as the humans, and being fed primarily with corn, or it was scavenging through food scraps left by humans (Clutton-Brock and Hammond 1994; White *et al.* 1993, 2001b, 2004).

Meat consumption has also been explored through $\delta^{13}C$ values of the animals consumed in such events. This technique is especially helpful when studying events where most or all the population would have participated, and allows us to examine minor differences in meat consumption by gender and social groups. It has been proposed that high class members consumed bigger quantities of corn as a beverage during rituals (LeCount 2001), or as food (Gerry and Krueger 1997), especially among those sites where maize was more socially valued (White *et al.* 1993). Finally, for some authors, the difference between social classes is in the diversity of their diet, especially plant diversity, being higher for the elite than for the lower classes (Lentz 1991; Reed 1994:216; White and Schwarcz 1989:465; Whittington and Reed 1997:160). The diet of the elite was greater in animal protein (Shaw 1999), but others suggest that meat consumption was minimal for all the social classes. These observations come from just a few sites that reflect distinctively higher meat consumption by the elite, including Caracol and the Petén area in Guatemala (Chase *et al.* 2001; Pohl 1985a, 1990). Ultimately, it is still not clear whether different social classes consumed differing amounts of meat.

rtheless, if elites were consuming more meat and/or a greater diversity of wild plants, it would be expected that the members of the higher class would have consumed proportionally less corn, and its $\delta^{13}C$ values would be less positive and a $\delta^{15}N$ more positive (Gerry 1997). Evidence for a differential corn and meat consumption by the elite has been obtained from different sites and chronological periods, including Altun Ha (White *et al.* 2001a), Lamanai (Coyston *et al.* 1999; White *et al.* 1994), and Pactibún (White *et al.* 1993) during the Preclassic period (White and Schwarcz 1989:458), and in the Petexbatún region, Caracol (Teeter 2004) and Copán during the Classic (Chase and Chase 2001; Reed 1999; White *et al.* 1993; Whittington and Reed 1997; Wright 1994, 2003). During the Late Classic period in particular, differential access to resources was based on gender and status (Scherer *et al.* 2007; Wright 1997). Contrasting data from the Postclassic show that there was no significant difference between people from different classes during the Postclassic (Williams *et al.* 2009; Wright 2009). In this analysis, the dietary patterns of the elite at Chinikihá were explored through an examination of their differential access to meat and plant resources. By studying their consumption patterns throughout their lives based on results from the long bone collagen and teeth apatite in the samples, an insight into their dietary habit was achieved.

While the $\delta^{13}C$ values indicate that the bulk of the human diet at Chinikihá was based on corn, it can be seen that women and members of different social strata (represented by the male remains in *Operación* 114) had a larger corn intake than male members of the elite. On the other hand, the $\delta^{15}N$ values highlight that there was a larger variability in the access to meat, with elite males consuming the most. The differential consumption of meat seems to be based not only on gender differences, but also by other socially-dictated practices, as at least one male individual had the highest meat consumption of the entire sample, and this access to meat may have started when he was a young boy. The two lowest $\delta^{15}N$

values came from a female buried outside the North Complex, and the remains of a male deposited in *Operación* 114. The differences observed in the isotopic analysis are corroborated by the burial treatment, grave location, and grave furniture from the burials. Because of the limited number of samples tested at Chinikihá, there were no significant differences recorded.

The isotopic information from the burial samples from Chinikihá is similar to that from other inland sites during the Late/Terminal Classic period (see Wright and White 1996), and suggests that meat consumption did not decline abruptly (Emery 2010:185). This tentatively suggests that in many sites during the Late/Terminal Classic, meat consumption remained constant. It may also be true for periods before and after this time, but more data is needed to examine this.

Situating the results within the dietary failure model

Emery (2010:121-122) enumerates a series of predicted occurrences that need to be identified in order to support the so-called model of dietary failure during the Late/Terminal Classic period. One of the predictions suggests that a change in the exploitation of faunal resources was observable, especially with relation of favoured species, resulting in an increase in hunting pressure. The consequences of this would translate into a rapid rise in the use of species of greater value, accompanied by an increase in the presence of meaty portions or primary cuts. This would be accompanied by a generalised inefficiency in carcass use that would result in waste (Emery 2010). Three predictions were then tested at *Operación* 114, including an increase in hunting pressure, an increase of meaty sections, and a generalised inefficiency in the processing of carcasses.

1. Hunting pressure, incremental use of favoured species and increased diversity

It has been proposed that the increase in demands for larger mammals during the Classic would have put pressure on the animal populations (Pohl 1985a), especially those species that were favoured. During the Preclassic, forest clearing for cultivation started and may actually have been a positive factor as deer would have been attracted to these new forest edge areas, bordering with savannah, making an increase in populations of deer possible in the initial stages of the Classic period (Pohl 1976:121). As human population increased to its maximum levels during the Late Classic, pressure was exerted on the wild resources (Pohl 1976:121).

During the Classic period then, demands for agricultural and meat resources rose, and it has been suggested that the profile of exploited species would show an increase

of juvenile or younger animals as a consequence of an earlier depletion of bigger animals (Emery 2010), with a marked increase in faunal diversity towards the Terminal period (Emery 2007a). Thus, juvenile animals are expected to be at their highest proportions during periods of highest political activity, accompanied by higher species diversity.

The increased exploitation of younger animals ultimately would have resulted in the exploitation of a higher diversity of species at the core of some ceremonial sites, but primarily in the periphery of larger sites (Pohl 1985a; Whittington and Reed 1997; Wright 1997). This trend is observed at sites from different regions. For example, during the Late and Terminal Classic, an increase in the amount of faunal remains was seen at Caracol (Teeter 2001:349-350). This is illustrated by an increase in the use of exotic fauna, such as birds, smaller fauna such as opossum, armadillo, margay, jaguar, racoon, tapir and coati, and their presence was restricted almost exclusively to elite contexts. Although some of these species were used as food, for ritual purposes, large mammals were still preferred rather than small and/or medium ones during the Late Classic (Masson 1999:106).

The evidence from Chinikihá suggests that there was not a noticeable increase in hunting pressure. From the age distribution of deer in all the layers of the assemblage, it can be seen that there was no important change in the age profile; the percentage of young fawns did not increase, but on the other hand, there were more remains of young adults in the top layers. Overall, the focus on animals in their prime throughout the context indicates a homogeneous exploitation pattern focused on young adults and the presence of a few juvenile individuals in the sample can be explained most readily as a result of opportunistic hunting or trampling, rather than a result of a shift in the exploitation patterns. This is similar to other sites in the Lowlands, such as Motul de San José, where deer numbers during the Late Classic remain fairly constant (Emery and Brown 2012:109).

Contrastingly, evidence of hunting pressure seems to vary depending on the location and temporality of a site. In the riverine site of Laguna de On, the scarcity of faunal bones during the Late Classic indicates that the hunting pressure on animal resources was high, possibly as a consequence of land clearing for the expansion of agricultural land (Masson 1999). Masson (1999:99) suggests that this conclusion can be extended to all of Belize. What we can observe is that there is a great variability at the regional and site level.

It has been suggested that new foods were introduces as an emergency measure in association with dietary scarcity, including less favoured 'famine' foodstuffs

(Emery 2010:122). One example of the introduction of such foods would be the appearance of freshwater shells or *jutes*, which generally carry a connotation of being lower class (Nations 1979), especially in the modern day. However, it has been observed that both deer and *jute* shells were symbolically linked to the concepts of fertility (Halperin *et al.* 2003; Pohl 1981); hence, it is not rare that after their consumption in ritual feasts, they were later discarded in the same contexts. According to some authors, there is substantial archaeological evidence of feasts involving mammals and *jute*, and this may have been an old tradition in the whole area (Halperin *et al.* 2003).

There was no evidence suggesting an increase in the diversity of species consumed, an occurrence directly linked to hunting pressure. On the contrary, data from Chinikihá is similar to that from other Late/Terminal Classic period sites, where intensification in the use of some resources has been reported. Intensification in the consumption of deer was accompanied by a change in the proportions of other species, with a decrease in proportions of dog and human remains from Layers IV-V to I-III. Emery and Brown (2012:105) state that there would be less taxonomic variability and fewer large game animals consumed in periods of political turmoil. Comparing with Motul de San José, there is a drop in the numbers of large game during the Late Classic, when there was more political activity.

In terms of diversity, *Operación* 114 has one of the lowest indices and the data therefore does not support the hypothesis of increasing diversity towards the Late Classic period. Futher, the data from Chinikihá provides new evidence that during the Late Classic period, deer populations must have remained stable, similarly to what occurred in the Petexbatún region (Emery 2010). The relatively low diversity that defines the different *Operaciones* under study, especially *Operación* 114, suggests that there was an ongoing selection of a few species, of which the white-tailed deer was the most important. Low diversity values are comparable to other elite deposits in the Lowlands characterised by a low diversity, accompanied by an emphasis on white-tailed deer, which, significantly, contains a high meat content (Emery 2003:498; Pohl 1976:192). Comparable sites include Seibal, Altar de Sacrificios, and Tikal, all analysed by Pohl (1990). Other sites include Caracol (Teeter 2001), Aguateca (Emery 1998), Dzibilchaltún (Wing and Steadman 1980), and Chichen Itzá (Götz 2005). The high frequency in which white-tailed deer was present, indicates that this species was probably an abundant resource through the whole Late Classic period, which represents at least 100-150 years of occupation (Murciélagos/Balunté phases). This species is present in different habitats, including the savannah and disturbed forests with secondary growth; hence, deer are naturally attracted to *milpas* and other human-modified landscapes.

The intensification in the exploitation of a few specific species is not only observable in evidence from the Late Classic period, but also from the Late Preclassic, another period of major social changes, characterised by the shift from small communities to hierarchical organised centres, as seen at Colhá, Belize, around 100 BC (Shaw 1991). During the Late Preclassic, a few species were the focus, these included terrestrial mammals—mainly the dog—but also marine resources that were obtained most likely through long-distance exchange (Shaw 1991). The main characteristic of the faunal exploitation seen during the Late Classic period is the overall predominance of the white-tailed deer in ritual and refuse contexts in sites including Seibal, Altar de Sacrificios, Toniná, Tikal, Piedras Negras, and Copán (Masson 1999; Olsen 1972; Pohl 1985a; Soto 1998; White *et al.* 2004). It is probable that the Maya of Chinikihá would have exercised some sort of resource management over the meat resources, primarily the deer, by avoiding killing young fawns, and sparing them for the future, in order to secure access to prime age animals for other consumption episodes. This would serve two objectives: to allow for some predictability of the meat resources, and also to maintain more stable deer populations.

This point is interesting, as some researchers have proposed that with the human population growth from the Preclassic to the Classic period, it would be expected that some sort of management of wild animals would be implemented to secure access to meat, especially for ritual ceremonies. This possibility has been considered at length by several authors because it is known that during the Postclassic period, populations of wild animals, including deer and peccaries, were home grown, especially for their use in rituals (Carr 1996; Pohl and Feldman 1982; White *et al.* 2001b). In recent times, several authors have explored the possibility of faunal management extending back to the Classic period (Clutton-Brock and Hammond 1994; White *et al.* 1993, 2001b).

Faunal management could take different forms, including the targeting of specific age groups such as young adults, in order to maintain the populations of adults in the wild for further reproduction. Another method of animal management imposed by the elite (Pohl 1985a:138) would have been included restricting access to, or taking control of, the forests the deer inhabited, along with other elite-favoured fauna, such as jaguar and monkey (Taube 2003). However, it is possible that the more permanent form of management, that of holding animals in captivity, may have occurred

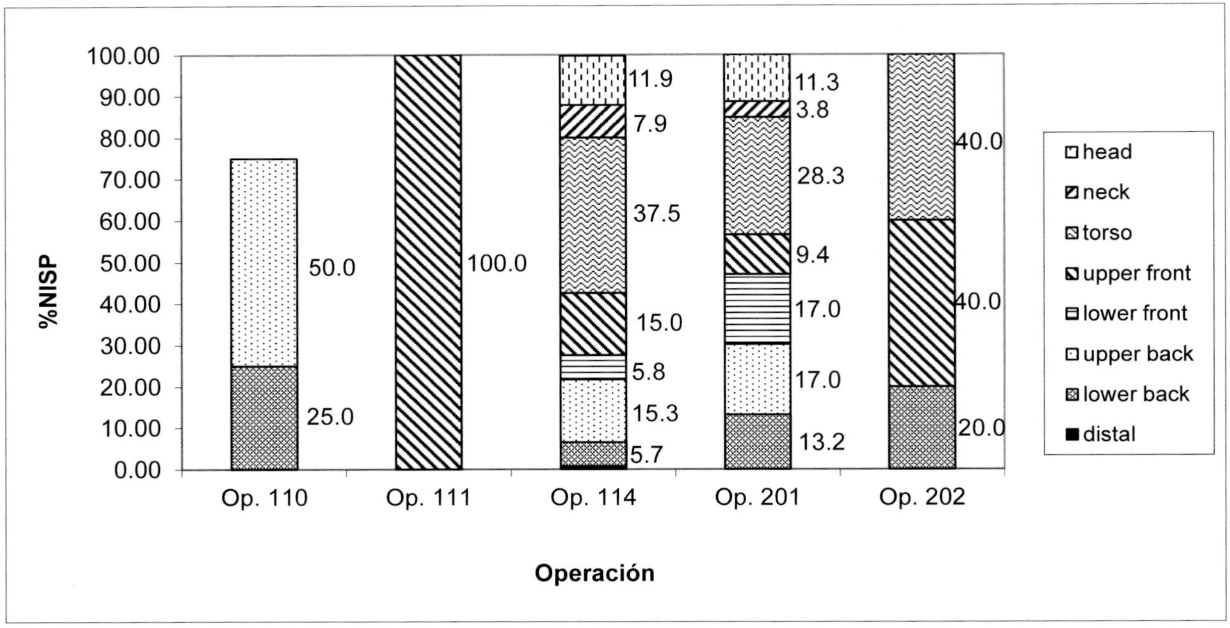

Figure 68. Distribution of white-tailed deer body portions by *Operación*.

(Carr 1996; Masson 1999; Masson and Peraza Lope 2008:173; Tykot *et al.* 1996). This would imply that some of these animals were tamed and hand-fed with corn. Management of wild animals in the Maya Lowlands during the Late Classic period was focused particularly on deer and peccary, two species that would produce large amounts of meat. Both species are known to adapt well to human contact, as seen in modern ethnographic accounts with young peccaries being breast-fed by Maya women (Kirchhoff 1963; Pohl 1976; Pohl and Feldman 1982; Tozzer 1941:127).

2. Associated increase in the use of meaty portions by elites

According to Emery (2010:122), in the period immediately before the collapse of the Late/Terminal Classic period, the increase of favoured species would also be accompanied by an increase in the use of the meatier portions favoured by the elite. Evidence of this may also include a change in preparation methods of butchering and cooking.

In the Maya literature, there are plenty of examples suggesting that specific elements were exclusive to the higher classes of the society, especially those body portions that correspond to the best meat cuts or carry the maximum meat yield. In the case of the white-tailed deer, the upper front and back limb sections have been related to the elite and priests by iconography and archaeological data (López 2006ñ Pohl 1985b, 1994).

In Chapter eight it was stated that the three most frequent body parts represented in *Operación* 114 were the torso, upper front and upper back limbs. Due to numerical differences between vertebrae and long bones from limbs in a complete skeleton, vertebrae values were normalised, stressing the real importance of the upper back limb, or haunch. With such a standardised distribution of animals by age and body part, the elite controlled the procurement of faunal resources for feasting events (Pohl 1976, 1985a; Shaw 1991). Moreover, the homogeneity in the distribution of body parts observed all throughout the deposit suggests that the resources were specifically targeted and brought back to the site for further processing.

To meet the prediction of an increase in meatier portions, not only would the haunch have to appear in exclusive association with elite contexts, but also, there should be an increase in their frequencies through time. In Figure 68 the distribution of deer body portions by *Operación* is presented. It is possible to observe that segments of high and low values are present in other contexts. Specifically, upper back limb remains were also found in other contexts, including *Operación* 110 (construction fill) and *Operación* 201 (midden). The haunch bones found in these two contexts include both femur and innominate, and this is interesting because the presence of both bones suggests that they might be related to dietary consumption, especially in the case of the innominate, discussed previously.

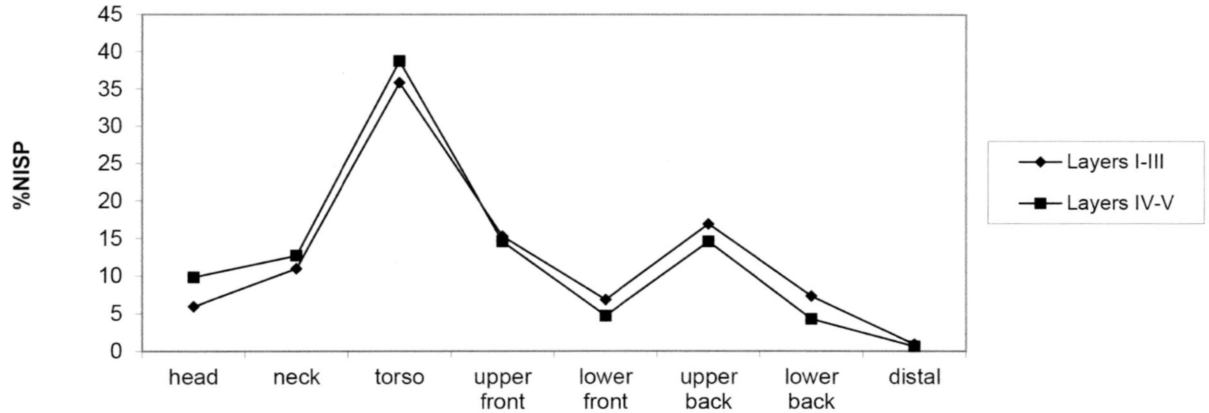

Figure 69. Distribution of meaty parts (axial and limb) and non-meaty (skull and distal) grouped by Layers I-III (above the floor), and Layers IV-V (under the floor) for *Operación* 114.

The presence of cut marks on deer bones in *Operación* 201, and the lack of tools or ornaments made of deer bones in both *Operaciones*, supports the role of deer as food in these two contexts. In comparison, during the Terminal Classic period, at least in Dos Pilas (specifically in L4-3 workshop), Emery (2010:184) did not observe a change through time in the distribution of meat-bearing elements Late Classic, but an intensification in carcass processing, especially in the use of limb and cranial bones, with particular reference to the upper hind and upper front limb bones for the manufacture of bone tools. This intensification however, reflected a shift in focus, from a purely subsistence usage of these resources, for tool production (Emery 2010:184).

The distribution of deer body portions in other *Operaciones* at Chinikihá, especially those parts considered more valuable and exclusive to the elite, can then be explained in different ways. First, that deer access was not as controlled as previously thought, and other segments of society were also able to access such important resources as deer for dietary consumption (Emery 2003:511). This is especially reflected in *Operación* 201, as the lower levels produced an assemblage considered to be a midden. It is possible then that satellite sites were allowed to keep and consume prime cuts, discarding them at their own locations (Emery 2007b:62). An alternative explanation would be that deer portions were redistributed during feasting events sponsored by the elite, who had the power to gather larger quantities of resources (Pohl and Pohl 1994). The amount of deer remains in all other *Operaciones* was too small to draw firm conclusions, but it is suggested that the presence of faunal remains in them could be a result of their inclusion as construction fill, a common practice among the Maya.

To test for an increase in high value meat portions through time, the distribution of meaty and non-meaty parts in *Operación* 114 is shown in Figure 69. The distribution of the deer remains in both units was very similar, with an over-representation of meaty parts and almost a complete lack of non-meaty sections. Age was not an influencing factor, and the favoured parts were the same for sub-adult animals and adults, both remaining fairly constant throughout the whole deposit. However, not all body parts were present in equal amounts, with head and distal elements being represented in very low proportions (7.86% and 0.74% respectively), while the upper front and back limbs were the most frequently occurring elements, adding up to a staggering 67.62%. The distribution of body parts also reflects a preference for those body portions that are meat bearing parts such as axial (neck and torso) and limb (upper front, lower front, upper back and lower back limbs). Non-meat bearing categories include the head and distal elements, and such remains were not present in significant quantities.

The prevailing representation of these body parts not only shows the preference of the elite for the highest meat yielding parts, but also could be interpreted as the removal of low utility body parts in the earlier parts of the butchering process. This is supported by the distribution of cut marks on distal elements that were still articulated, and other non-meaty articulations. Non-valuable body portions (with no meat yield or no potential use as raw material) are characteristically of distal elements from both front and back limb, and they seem to have been removed in areas where the upper section was being prepared for consumption, an occurrence also noted in Lagartero, another context that represents at least some feasting debris (Koželsky 2005:49). The high quantity of skulls and long bones in modern hunting shrines (Brown 2005; Brown and Emery 2008) suggests that it is possible that some head and distal elements might have been deposited elsewhere. Again, the variability in which body portions are distributed in assemblages identified as high elite, contributes to the difficulty in the identification of the behaviour that formed it.

There was a relatively high percentage of cut marks found on deer bones (28.45%) when compared to the rest of the fauna. These include primary and secondary butchery marks that indicate that most of the deer were arriving as whole carcasses to Chinikihá, where they were subsequently processed. This data combined with the fact that a sample of virtually every part of the deer skeleton was retrieved from Chinikihá, suggest that most of the animals were acquired locally in the surroundings of Chinikihá, where they were processed (see Montero 2008). However, it was not possible to observe a change in the butchering patterns over time.

Further evidence of changes in cooking methods is not very clear. For other feasting middens, it has been suggested that animals were prepared by roasting rather than boiling (Eppich 2009); this being especially true when preparing large animals. Pohl (1985a:140) suggests that deer forelimbs were given to the elite for their consumption, along with skulls, which were roasted or burned, in order to access the brain, tongue or marrow (Pohl 1976:19).

Boiling of smaller animals such as dogs was preferred over roasting (Clutton-Brock and Hammond 1994). For example, according to Pohl (1985a:139), deer were roasted in gridirons and then distributed to the community. Certainly, in *Operación* 114 there are very few cases of direct exposure to fire, with changes being more subtle, making it hard to identify the cooking process as roasting or boiling. Whether these two methods were complementary or if there was a preference for one or the other, is not possible to identify at the present. Nevertheless, the presence of plates with depictions of *tamales* being served at feasts, suggests that this may have been the preferred way of consuming meat. Evidence for this comes from the fact that plates and other ceramic vessels heaped with *tamales* are very common in the iconography, while deer legs being offered or consumed are rare (Bíró and Montero 2008). Alternatively, it is possible that both *tamales* and roasted legs were served together during the celebration of a feast, along with cacao-based and fermented drinks (LeCount 2001).

3. Generalised inefficiency in the use of carcasses

Emery (2010:137) suggested studying the distribution of meat-bearing elements through time to see changes in the access to meat resources. It is predicted here that during the 'collapse', the complete use of the carcasses, rather than just the favoured portions, would be observable. The presence at Chinikihá of torso and neck portions seems to support the exploitation of body parts considered to be of low and medium utility. More so, their presence indicates that the meat from the loins was being extracted, maximising the amount of meat available. One point of interest is that although we know that the meaty legs were being targeted, the ratio in which the upper long bones from both limbs appear against the scapula and pelvis indicates that the long bones may have been removed from the context, either for their use as raw materials in the manufacture of tools, or to be deposited elsewhere.

Although there were a few instances of semi-articulated bones present in *Operación* 114, these were not considered a sign of waste, since they include mainly low and medium utility segments, such as neck and torso, or distal segments. No haunch elements were found articulated, therefore, a generalised inefficiency of carcasses was not observed at Chinikihá.

In summary, there is no evidence for dietary failure at Chinikihá, with the results from *Operación* 114 suggesting that there was continuity in the exploitation patterns, at least during the Balunté/Murciélagos phases, during the Late/Terminal period. Data from Chinikihá coincides with the results from the Petexbatún region analysed by Emery (2010), concluding that there was no reduction of favoured species or a substantial increase in diversity during the Late Classic period. The introductions of less favoured dietary species, or an increase in the efficiency in the processing of carcasses, were also not observed at Chinikihá or Petexbatún.

The identification of function of *Operación* 114

The large spatial scale and enormous quantities of materials present in the *Operación* 114 deposit included thousands of ceramic fragments, lithics, bone and shell artefacts. The copious amounts of animal remains, allow us to pose questions about the nature of the deposit, such as its function as a reflection of ritual behaviours involving meat consumption. In order to do so, an examination of the depositional and taphonomic history of *Operación* 114 was undertaken in order to assess whether this deposit was intact and the result of feasting behaviour. *Operación* 114 was compared with *Operación* 201, another midden in the site of Chancalá, a smaller polity in the surroundings of Chinikihá. By comparing two similar deposits, the possibility of identifying differentiated access to resources could be evaluated. Furthermore, *Operación* 114 was then compared with deposits from other sites that were similar in composition, with large amounts of animal bones, mixed with other materials, including ceramics and artefacts. This intra-deposit comparison aimed to identify possible differences in the behaviour behind the formation of fauna-rich deposits that look alike. The relevance of conducting such comparisons comes from the significant difficulty in the Maya area in defining a context type, when the same suite of artefacts has been recovered from contexts known to have been created as a result of varied behaviours.

Three different contexts were selected: context L4-3 from Dos Pilas (bone workshop) (Emery 2008), Cueva de los Quetzales (ritual deposit) (Emery 2004a), and a feasting midden from Lagartero (Koželsky 2005). Having suggested previously in this chapter that the *Operación* 114 deposit was predominantly the result of dietary consumption, the results from the analysis of *Operación* 114 are contrasted with a set of zooarchaeological markers defined in Chapter one, in order to see if this deposit meets all the requirements to be classified as the result of feasting activities. The taphonomic history of the deposit was also considered, as this information can add vital data to the discussion. Finally, some general ideas about feasting during the Late/Terminal period are offered.

Operación 114 and its taphonomic history

Firstly, it is necessary to establish that this deposit is contemporary to the occupation of the Palace and not a post-abandonment deposit. From the history of deposition, it can be assumed that the whole deposit is contemporary to the Palace occupation for several reasons, including that there were no intrusive fauna such as dead rodents, birds, and other small species that would entered the deposit, if the deposit had been left open for longer periods. No disturbance by modern fauna has been identified either. This is important, as it has been suggested elsewhere that most middens only reflect the occupation around the time of abandonment (Pendergast 1992:70; Stanton *et al.* 2008). In this sense, it was observed that the materials were deposited and covered routinely, following a short period of exposure, but were not left completely exposed. Radiocarbon dates obtained from fauna samples and a glyph present on a plate support the notion that the midden corresponds to the period suggested by the ceramics typology, dating the bulk of the assemblage to the Balunté/Murciélagos phases (AD 700-850).

Furthermore, a large number of the decorated ceramics are very similar in style with those from Palenque, the controlling capital of the Hinterlands during the Late Classic period (Liendo 2005a). Chinikihá's own local lineage that may have started with *K'inich B'ah Tok'* (Stuart and Morales 2003), may have participated in the political network in which Palenque was involved, celebrating various rituals involving gatherings and feasts that would have produced large amounts of refuse.

Operación 114 may have been the result of such activities conducted during the Late/Terminal Classic period.

In terms of the distribution of the materials, *Operación* 114 was a closed deposit, with materials being placed in a pit that appears to have been purposely dug, though no walls have been observed. The materials were concentrated, with a homogenous distribution, rather than forming thin layers of materials, a characteristic of deposits associated with structures abruptly abandoned (Chase and Chase 2000). Nevertheless, drawing conclusions about how fast the materials were laid are not straightforward. It seems almost impossible to identify discrete episodes within the deposit, and most archaeologists would not even consider engaging in such an activity, because in most cases, feasting middens represent all types of feasts and include a mixture of ritual and mundane activities (Rosenwig 2007:5). This is particularly true for those deposits that reflect a long occupation sequence, such as *Operación* 114. Interestingly, the presence of a stuccoed floor sealed the materials under it, potentially indicating a difference in use or a transformation in the function of the whole deposit through time. It is through the zooarchaeological analysis that it was possible to detect some variation in how the materials were integrated to the archaeological record.

While a high presence of rodent-gnawed bones observed in the deepest section (Layers IV-V) indicates a secondary deposit, the rest of the deposit (Layers I-III) may represent one or various primary contexts throughout the life of the deposit. Although there were some minor differences detected in the distribution of the materials, statistical tests showed that these were not significant. On the contrary, the few significant tests suggest that the distribution of the remains all throughout the deposit reflect some continuity, with no major changes having occurred in a period of 100-150 years. Unfortunately, there are no results yet from the other materials retrieved from this deposit, including the complete analysis of all ritual ceramics, palynology and lithics, which need to be considered before a more definite interpretation of these patterns can be established.

Possible examples of different discard episodes include two major 'dumping' episodes behind the back wall of the Palace (Squares J1, K2), which produced the largest amounts of faunal and ceramic fragments present in the whole assemblage. The ceramics in these two squares included primarily processing and serving vessels, and both types were intermixed. Together, both preparation and serving wares in Square K1 represent 38.3kg and 31.4kg in Square J2. Cooking wares in these two squares were larger in size than the average for the rest of the context. The serving wares in these squares were also different from the rest, as fragments were more often characterised by better finishing or presented decoration in higher proportions. These two characteristics make the ceramic assemblage from *Operación* 114 different from other contexts within the site and even different from other sites in the Palenque Hinterlands region. A higher proportion of serving wares than storage vessels is considered to be a good marker for the identification of ritual feasting events (Fox 1996) and has been identified in other feasting deposits, such as Blue Creek's Special Deposit 1 (Clayton *et al.* 2005).

Other ceramic artefacts reflecting ritual activities were also found in Squares K1 and J2, and include ritual forms such as censers and figurines. In the ceramic analysis, Mirón (2012) suggests that the ceramic assemblage represents a mixed deposit of food preparation/consumption forms with other forms that represent ritual activities. Although the lithic analysis is not yet completed, a grinding stone or *mano* was registered in Square J2 (Layer IV), and is directly associated with processing plantstuffs for food. The presence of bone and shell artefacts in these squares was also high, with 41.5% of all artefacts/ornaments appearing in Squares K1 (24.6%NISP) and J2 (16.88%NISP).

A rapid deposition was also inferred by the presence of mortar-covered bones in the assemblage. A total of 333 faunal remains (8.93%) were covered with mortar to different degrees. Mortar or plaster seems to have been quickly splattered over the bones, with some bones completely covered and others containing mortar only on small areas on the surface. Of the 333 remains, most of them were located in Square K1 (49.25%) and Square K2 (30.34%), with fewer examples from all other squares. Mortar-covered bones were present in all layers, with slightly more under the floor (52.64%) than above it (45.17%); however, no patterning was observed by Layer. Mortar-covered specimens included many fauna species, but interestingly no human remains or tools were covered.

To summarise, the main function associated with *Operación* 114 seems to be consistent with that of a deposit of dietary remains that included primarily wild animals from the immediate surroundings, and domestic dogs. A few bone and shell artefacts, the majority of which were broken, were intermingled, as well as some isolated human remains. The materials were deposited by a series of different events throughout the Murciélagos/Balunté phases. The materials deposited during each of these events were quickly included in the deposit, as suggested by some materials being covered with fresh mortar, and the presence of various bones and ceramic fragments that refit. This characteristic has also been identified for other feasting deposits in the Maya area, for example at the site of Xunantunich, where 2% of all bones in

Group B refit (Freiwald 2010:411). Nevertheless, once the materials were deposited, it is possible that they were not covered immediately, as more than half of the remains were exposed long enough to be have been accessed by carnivores. Contrastingly, modified bone and human remains do not show any post-depositional modifications, suggesting that they may have been deposited in an expedient manner and through different pathways.

Given the size of this deposit, and considering the formation and post-depositional transformations, it is considered very unlikely to be an ordinary domestic midden. An MNI for deer in *Operación* 114 suggests at least 48 individuals were present, representing a large amount of meat. With feasts being held for multiple celebrations, including ball games (Fox 1996), end-of-cycle, dedication of structures (Ekholm 1990), and possibly feasts being held for marriages, deaths, and royal visits from important allies, it would be logical to expect that several feasts may have been held while *Operación* 114 was actively in use.

It is here suggested that although there are references in the anthropological literature that indicate that the consumption of large quantities of meat in a single event was the centre of ritual practices (see Albalá 2011), the taphonomic analysis of *Operación* 114 suggest otherwise. Periodical consumption episodes of symbolic resources, including meat, are commonly related to feasts around the world (Dietler and Hayden 2001). These events often coincide with seasonality and are a potential venue for studying the presence of several feasting episodes (Curet and Pestle 2010).

At Chinikihá, the possibility of several feasting events can be inferred through the study of seasonality. Evidence of seasonality is limited because of the minimal presence of mandibles (n = 10), but it was possible to observe that deer exploitation peaked during December and March. This is equivalent to the winter or dry season; however, deer was hunted in lower frequencies throughout the rest of the year. Specimens representing kills from different seasons were intermingled in the same layers, suggesting that there were several episodes of deer consumption. Furthermore, from the presence of these seasonally diverse specimens, it is possible to conclude that there was no shortage of deer. Hunters could have accessed them throughout the year as required by the elite, for the celebration of rituals involving meat consumption.

Deer may have been available all year long because of the implementation of different mechanisms, including wildlife management discussed above, but also, it is important to consider the possibilities of meat storage and preservation that the Maya may have practiced in the past (Shaw 1991). Examples of deer available through time include Caracol, Seibal, and Altar de Sacrificios, where deer was always available (Pohl 1990:153). Particularly for Caracol, it has been suggested that the regular availability of deer throughout the year was possibly a consequence of having managed deer by keeping them in environmental refuges (Teeter 2001:274). Meat could also have been preserved for future consumption. Unfortunately, there is very little information on meat storage and preservation, except for some data from Postclassic sites on the coast where salt production could have been used to preserve fish and other marine resources (Foster 2002:312).

More conclusively, the results from the isotopic analysis from a group of elite members suggest that meat consumption was not a regular activity, but may have been accessible at specific times, such as periodic feasting events. It is important to keep in mind that the consumption of meat perhaps had a larger symbolic importance than the action of eating large amounts of meat itself. The traditional way of preparing meat in *tamales,* does not require a large quantity of meat, therefore, it could be possible that all site occupants and visitors could have had access to meat during a feast. This is widely supported by the depictions of large plates heaped with *tamales* (Reents-Budet 2000:1026; Zender 2000:1044) presented to the royal class in what seems to be festive or public activities.

In light of the ongoing analysis of the assemblage and the evidence from other non-osteological markers, it is suggested that the assemblage in *Operación* 114 may have been the result of various feasting events. However, there is always the possibility that *Operación* 114 may represent a series of mixed deposits, a cumulative palimpsest of activities (Bailey 2007), including the remains of different types of feasting and other activities. The true extent of activities and behaviour present in this context may never be known. It is just not possible to discern between such activities at a finer scale.

Zooarchaeoological markers for feasting

There are many examples in the Maya literature that describe 'feasting deposits.' Other contexts containing similar assemblages have been identified as the result of feasting, including Altun Ha (Pendergast 1992), Lagartero (Koželsky 2005), Copán (Hendon 2003), El-Perú Waka (Eppich 2009), Trinidad de Nosotros (Moriarty and Foias 2006), Blue Creek (Guderjan *et al.* 2003), and an initial series midden at Late Classic in Chichen Itzá (Götz 2008). These deposits have been identified as feasting debris because of the presence of ceramics, food remains (faunal, botanical and isotopic data), and the presence of exotic goods.

In feasting deposits, an immense amount of debris left from the consumption activities would be expected, including the remains from food consumption in private or public events and the transformation of bone to tools, which is distinguishable in the archaeological record. Nevertheless, it is important to remember that other contexts from completely diverse activities may also resemble a feasting context, as many other ritual contexts present the same materials, including faunal remains and other ritual paraphernalia. All of these deposits have been previously grouped under the ambiguous term of 'problematic deposit', as defining the nature of such contexts has been very difficult. For example Pagliaro and colleagues (2003:77) determined that the high quantity of human bone, whole vessels, fragments, and large amounts of elite items and other material, including *manos, metate*s, projectile points, jade implements, shell, and animal bones, were indicative of a desecratory termination deposit. Similarly, Emery and colleagues (2009:787) defined the archaeological markers for feasts as 'typically identified based on the high frequencies of species preferred as food, with a high representation of all body parts or large quantities of those portions with the most meat.' Emery and colleagues however, caution that the same items could be a characteristic of ritual deposits such as a hunting shrine. Ultimately, it has been noted that the functions of objects do not reside in their forms, but in the variable pathways created by ritual and political agents (Walker and Lucero 2000:133).

Therefore the question is, are there any true markers for identifying feasts in the archaeological record? More relevant to this study, are there any zooarchaeological markers for feasting? In Chapter one, several markers were identified from the global literature in order to identify feasts through zooarchaeological analysis. In Chapters seven and eight, a thoroughly analysis was conducted for the whole Chinikihá assemblage, especially for *Operación* 114. As seen in Table 70, all attributes except two were identified, the presence of an associated kitchen and/or feasting area, and the presence of rare or costly animals used as food. Until now, no kitchen has been identified near the Palace, or in the excavations of Chinikihá as a whole. Similarly, no area has yet been defined as a feasting ground, and although the midden is directly associated with the construction sequence of the Palace and surrounding structures, it is impossible to determine where the feast took place.

There are many examples from the Late/Terminal Classic period where it was not possible to correlate a feasting midden directly with a kitchen or consumption area, including the N14-2 deposit at El Perú-Waka (Eppich 2009), and the A-8 midden at Altun Ha (Pendergast 1992).

Zooarchaeological marker	*Operación* 114
-High density of faunal and ceramics remains	More than 4000 faunal fragments (26.5kg.) mixed with more than 33,000 ceramic fragments (417.95kg)
-Special location or in a setting in association with ritual activities	Deposit associated with Palace in the core of the ceremonial centre of Chinikihá
-Associated cooking and preparation areas	Not identified
-Special foods, rarely eaten or costly to obtain	Not identified
-High proportions of butchered and processed remains	28.02% of deer remains display cut marks
-Special contexts that may be discrete deposits	High concentration of fauna and ceramic fragments in Squares K1, J2
-High proportions of symbolically important species	White-tailed deer comprises 24.37% of the deposit, but no difference by sidedness
-Focus on one species and low species diversity	Low diversity index (0.75), and focus on deer, and dog
-High frequency of young or immature animals	60.04% of all deer are immature
-Presence of articulated remains	6.68% of deer bones were still articulated
-Less taphonomic modifications of bones in feasting contexts (less burning, chewing and gnawing)	Most deer fragments display little weathering, and rodent gnawing, but heavy carnivore modifications (64.02%)

Table 70. Zooarchaeological markers and their correlates in *Operación* 114 (modified from Twiss 2008:420, Table 1).

Nonetheless, there are a few examples of kitchens or areas where large amounts of food were prepared for feasts (although not in the immediate vicinity), at sites such as Cerén and Kabah during the Classic period (Brown 2001; INAH Noticias 2011). The lack of an association with kitchen areas has prompted some researchers to suggest that maybe food was prepared in other locations and then transported to the consumption areas and served in the containers in which it was cooked, such as large unslipped jars (Eppich 2009:16). These vessels then would be discarded in the same deposits as the rest of the feast remains, including bones and other serving vessels, including highly valued polychrome wares. The combination of food remains, serving ceramics, and ritual vessels, along with other ritual paraphernalia used in feasts would then be considered a better marker for identifying feasts (Hendon 2003:225), especially when serving festival foods, such as *tamales* and chocolate (LeCount 1996:261).

In terms of the fauna used in rituals, most examples cited in literature refer to fauna that were locally available as the most common used in feasts. These mainly include, but are not limited to, deer, dog, rabbit, and freshwater molluscs, which are present in different proportions depending the environmental conditions of each site. Fish and other coastal resources would be considered costly in inland deposits, and these were not identified in *Operación* 114, stressing perhaps that the importance of fauna resources for feasts was more related to obtaining large quantities of meat from animals that are readily available.

The role that fauna played in the economic and political realms of Maya society is discussed below. Trying to identify a specific function of certain animals and molluscs is challenging. It has been stressed throughout this dissertation that some animals may have had several roles, including that of providing food and raw material for tools and ornaments (Emery 2007b:58). These include deer and *jute* shells. There is no doubt that certain animals considered as exotic (such as birds or wild cats) may have been more restricted in terms of who had access to them, and what their use was, all reflected in the type of deposits where their remains have been found. But deer, dog, and freshwater molluscs seem to appear in a variety of deposits, including both ritual or domestic, and in association with all segments of society. This suggests that their use was not as restricted or circumscribed as thought before.

That some species have been used in different ways has been identified as a characteristic of Maya faunal exploitation (Emery 2007b; Montero 2009). Deer in particular stands out as a 'multi-purpose' animal that was present in both non-elite and elite deposits. The deer's importance was not only related to its symbolic connotations with the concepts of fertility, and regeneration, but also to its dietary importance, as it is one of the largest animals in the region. These factors contribute to the confusion when trying to identify the nature of the deposit in which the materials are found.

Comparisons with other assemblages

Comparison with *Operación 201*

The distribution of body parts in *Operación* 114 (Chinikihá) and *Operación* 201 (Chancalá) are comparable in the proportions they exhibit (Figure 70), suggesting that the occupant of both of the sites may have had a similar access to meat sections of white-tailed deer, including the torso, upper front and upper back limbs. Furthermore, the presence of meat-bearing parts in *Operación* 201 suggests that even secondary

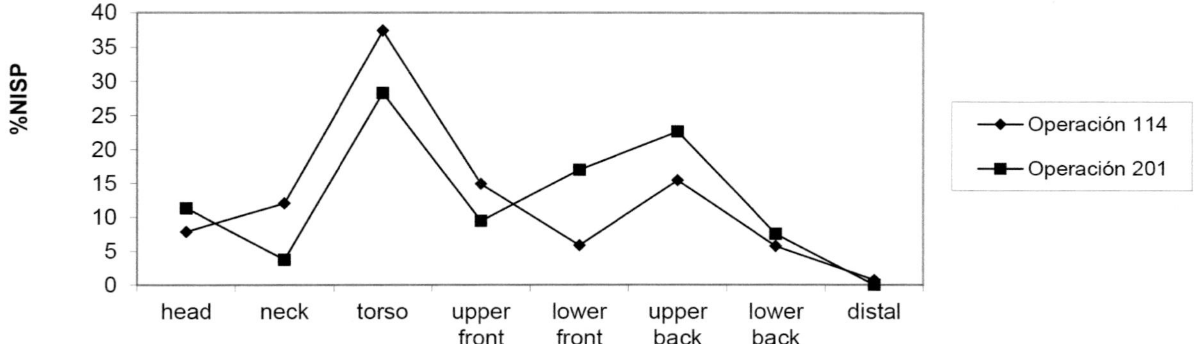

Figure 70. Comparison between *Operaciones* 114 (Chinikihá) and 201
(Chancalá) for white-tailed deer body portions (%NISP).

centres such as Chancalá, may have had access to faunal resources during the Late Classic period, and it is probable they were consumed at the site, since the bones were discarded locally, and most body portions are present in the deposit.

The low diversity of fauna at Chancalá is similar to that from Chinikihá, suggesting an exclusive use of a small number of animals in the diet, focused on white-tailed deer and dog in particular. No *jute* shells were recovered at all from *Operación* 201, and only three fragments of worked bone were recovered. However, when compared in terms of MNI, dog is more frequent at *Operación* 201 (4 MNI), than at Chinikihá (2 MNI). While smaller sites may have had access to meat for different reasons, the number of animals was not the same as that in larger sites, nor do the deposits from smaller sites contain remains of the same taxa. Both sites had their main period of occupation during the Murciélagos/Balunté phases (AD 700-850); however, Chinikihá is considered a Category I-1 site, along with Palenque, and therefore the emphasis on dogs at Chancalá may simply mean that in smaller polities these were the animals preferred or available, as larger game animals were restricted to the ruling elites.

The presence of faunal remains representing kills primarily from one season (winter), suggests that hunting may have been a specialized activity, with faunal remains uncommon in contexts outside of the elite (Pohl 1990:155). Nonetheless, control of faunal resources may have only just begun during the Classic period, as Leslie Shaw (1991:64) suggests that during the Late

Preclassic period at the site of Colhá, meat procurement from terrestrial and marine resources may have been conducted along with agriculture. This is especially true for those cases when faunal resources were captured with nets and traps, which were usually set up in or near agricultural land. Whether such activities were undertaken by farmers part time, by specialised hunters, or perhaps members of the elite classes themselves (Pohl 1990:155), is a topic requiring further study.

During the Classic period, deer, dog, and freshwater turtle were the three most popular animals chosen for feasting events around the Maya area, with the dog probably representing the only true domesticate (White *et al.* 2004:156). There were no turtle remains associated with dietary consumption found in *Operación* 114; however, the presence of deer and dog remains in feasting contexts is strongly related to the symbolic role each of them played in the Maya cosmology. Their presence in Classic sites reveals that there was some continuity from the Preclassic period in the practice of including domestic and wild fauna in feasting events.

Also, during the Late Classic period in the Maya area, each individual polity may have controlled their land surrounding, both for farming and hunting. However, larger polities began to exercise hegemony or temporal control over other polities (Santley *et al.* 1986:143). As a consequence, some of these sites were able to extend their access to land and faunal resources. Because of its geographical location, it is possible that Chinikihá may have been able to remain independent from other larger sites. It may also have been very attractive to

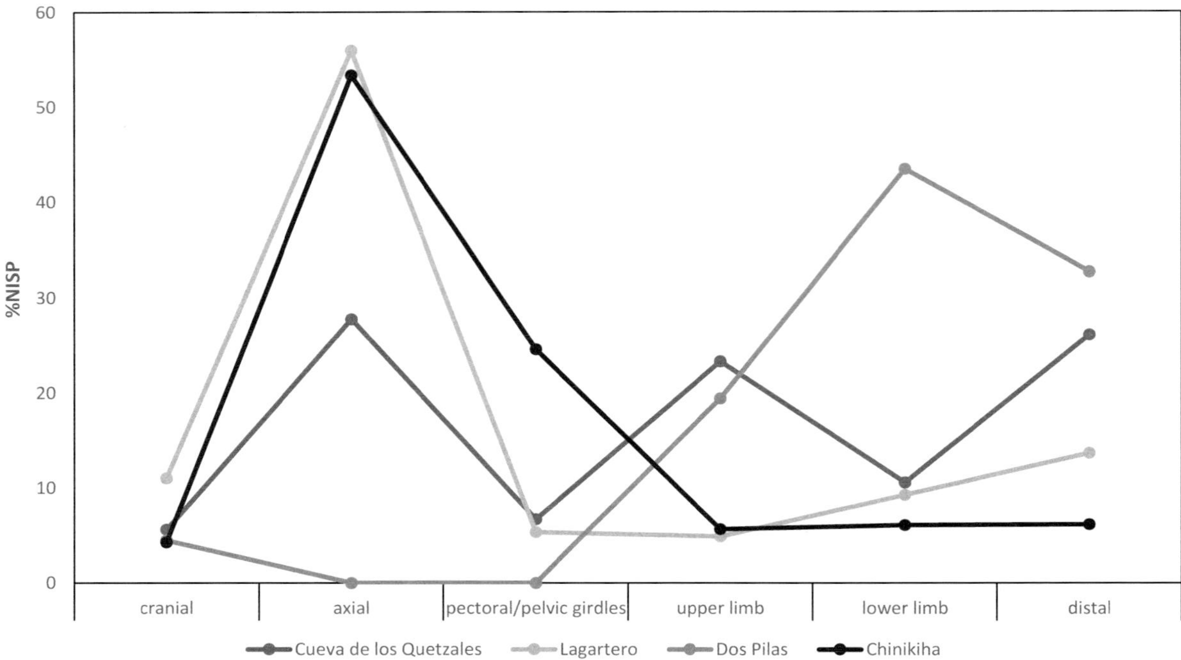

Figure 71. Comparison by body portion for similar contexts to Chinikihá
(modified from Emery 2004a, 2010; Koželsky 2005).

other settlements for a myriad of reasons. Chinikihá was not always able to remain independent, but was inserted in different spheres of influence and interacted with different sites, including Palenque, Piedras Negras and Pomoná.

In terms of the political networks, this result is interesting since it has been proposed that sites on the periphery had a larger diversity in their faunal resource access. Furthermore, if Chinikihá ever exercised control over Chancalá, there were still enough faunal resources for both sites to use for their own political/ritual agendas. However, if faunal resources were extracted from Chancalá and taken to a larger polity that was in power at that time, it is very hard to discern. The amount of faunal remains from Chancalá is very small, and therefore, 'it is difficult to distinguish faunal refuse resulting from daily subsistence from that resulting from butchering animals to be used as tribute', as seen in other parts of the world (Kelly 2001:341).

An alternative interpretation is that larger polities were losing control over highly-prized resources, as a consequence of their loss of power during the Late Classic period (Demarest 1992; Houston 1993; McAnany 1993), as suggested by the existence of deposits in smaller sites or peripheral locations around larger settlements where the presence of bone remains from elite-controlled species such as deer has also been observed, including Lamanai (Pendergast

1992:70), and Seibal (Pohl 1985a). At Seibal, there is evidence that lower status families gained access to better meat cuts including the tenderloin (located on the torso region), a cut that was usually reserved for the higher classes (Pohl 1985a:141). Nevertheless, the large quantities of deer remains at Chinikihá suggest that larger polities still had control and access to the favoured species.

Regional comparisons

Operación 114 is similar to other mixed contexts, including context L4-3 from Dos Pilas (Emery 2010), Cueva de los Quetzales (Emery 2004a), as well as a midden from Lagartero (Koželsky 2005). All of these contexts show similarities in artefacts, including large quantities of bones, lithics, ceramics, human remains and items associated with the elite. While Cueva de los Quetzales has been identified as a ritual dump, context L4-3 has been identified as a bone tool workshop and the contexts associated with Structure 1, Lagartero and *Operación* 114 have been identified as feasting deposits.

When animal body parts are plotted by site (Figure 71), Lagartero and Chinikihá are similar compared to the other two assemblages. There was a strong selection of prey, with the majority of the animals being young adults. A preference for specific body parts is also a characteristic, with strong bias towards 'more palatable meat', reflected as a high quantity of forelimb and hind limb bones; however, torso elements dominate both assemblages, reflecting their naturally greater abundances in a complete skeleton.

The Lagartero midden has been identified as the remains of a communal feast (Koželsky 2005). In this context, the predominant species was the domestic dog. Its presence, along with female paraphernalia, such as figurines and cotton production, 'functioned to assert the identity of Lagartero at a regional level' (Koželsky 2005:5). Ekholm (1990:456) originally identified this feast as a single episode of celebration for an end-of-year ceremony, which would be celebrated once every 52 years, and in direct association with the renewal of an architectural structure.

To analyse the assemblage from Lagartero, Koželsky (2005) considered Wiessner's ethnographic study of public feasting among the Enga groups in Papua New Guinea and used the six aspects that define feast according to Wiessner (2001:116-117), including: the aggregation of a large number of people, sharing or redistribution of goods, commemorating a specific occasion, public display, an abundance of available resources and an increase in demand to procure that abundance. Furthermore, Koželsky (2005:5) adds four archaeological expectations for feasting: 'the presence of a deposit in a public location, evidence of intentional deposition, the presence of artefacts or animals that were emphasised during the event, and the presence of a number of artefacts that are complete or can be reconstructed.'

Koželsky (2005:89) concluded that the deposit from Lagartero meets all the criteria as a feast where social drama was the driving force in forming an intentional deposit reflecting faunal consumption in a public location. However, due to the uniqueness and complexity of the *basurero*, Koželsky (2005:92) suggests that the origins of this deposit may never be known but suggests that it may be related to the Moon goddess, Ixchel, and more importantly, would have 'served to reflect and affirm the position of Lagartero in the Grijalva [River] region.' That the elite from Lagartero, just like the rulers from other sites may have tried to create a self-identity through the use of a specific animal by individual sites, may also explain the differences observed between sites, especially those located in a similar ecological setting, such as in the Palenque region.

While Chinikihá conforms to the regional model in which there was a preference for white-tailed deer, in Palenque there seems to be a marked preference for freshwater turtle (Zúñiga 2000). López (2006:7) suggests that the focus on freshwater resources in

Palenque, including turtles and fish, may be the result of a change in the environment that obliged people to substitute terrestrial mammals for aquatic resources. It is also possible that the focus on turtle may have been an attempt by the people of Palenque to distinguish themselves from other political entities, at least at a local level. As the isotope analysis from the deer sample from Chinikihá suggests, there is no sufficient evidence to support a change in the environment during the Late Classic, or the depletion of deer populations in the region. Therefore, the favouritism for a particular animal at the site level cannot be explained in terms of ecological restrictions, but it may reflect a political manipulation by the elites of each site. What can definitely be seen is that in periods of great political instability, the elite would try to increase their control of access to favoured resources, such as certain symbolic faunal species (Emery 2003:511).

When tools produced and associated refuse are compared, it is clear that the faunal assemblage from Chinikihá is not the result of an exclusive production of bone tools. A good comparison is the site of Dos Pilas, where axial and distal elements were almost completely missing, and there was a predominance of hind limb elements, especially the lower hind tibia, suggesting tool production (Emery 2010:201). Another site that produced a significant percentage of worked bone is Aguateca, where 46.81% of the faunal assemblage consisted of finished bone objects (Emery and Aoyama 2007:75). In contrast, the context behind the Palace at Chinikihá contained a small percentage of finished or incomplete artefacts and ornaments including bone needles, bone rings, pins, and other ritual paraphernalia. It suggests this was not simply a household rubbish dump. Furthermore, the specific absence of skull, vertebrae and ribs at the tool-manufacturing context of L4-3 in Dos Pilas (Emery 2010:126), contrasts with the presence of axial fragments at Lagartero (Koželsky 2005) and Chinikihá, as the latter may represent feasting contexts. During the Late Classic period, deposits identified as being the result of public feasting, contain low utility body parts that were not routinely exploited, and became more important due to their dietary contribution (Emery 2010).

Although Cueva de los Quetzales was believed to be a ceremonial site because of its location, Emery (2004a:109) concluded that it may reflect the final deposition of ritual activities carried out elsewhere. She also found that there was a majority of juvenile deer, dog, and other sacred animals, all with underworld connotations, present in her context. Although the deposit may have represented the remains of feasting, it must have been of a public exclusionary nature, where the focus was not on the meaty body portions, but on their symbolism, as represented by the selection of body parts based on sidedness. As Emery (2004a:111) puts it 'the fact that the body portions do not overemphasise the meaty haunches suggests that the ritual significance of side was more important in these offerings than the quality of the food it represented'. The significant presence of axial remains in Cueva de los Quetzales supports the hypothesis that the context was a result of a feast event, but the percentage of upper back limbs at the site, the highest of all four sites, further emphasises the importance of the haunch as an offering.

Feasting during the Late Classic period

Feasting in Mesoamerica has its roots in the Preclassic period, and is a long-standing tradition that is seen throughout Mesoamerica, and other cultural areas in the American continent. While the Preclassic period was accompanied by the institutionalisation of a ruler class (Hendon 1999) and an incipient population growth that would continue well into the Classic (Shaw 1991), the Late Classic period was marked by a generalised ecological and/or social tension, where the ever-growing ruling class would demand more and more resources, culminating in a major disruption towards the Terminal Classic. As the political competition also escalated during the Classic, elites all around the Maya area began to demand more natural resources for the celebration of feasts and the performance of other ritual-related activities, including animal and human sacrifice (Pohl 1985b). Hunting pressure varied individually according to the political involvement of each site. It would then be expected that sites that were more actively involved, would exhibit evidence of greater hunting pressure (Emery 2007a:191).

There is no homogeneity in the characteristics that define a feast but rather a great variability among the deposits identified as the result of feasting. Part of this is a consequence of the diversity of feasts, including the degree of involvement by the elite and the community and the particular event that the feast was being held for. Even though the term 'feast' is associated with a large variety of cultural practices (Dietler and Hayden 2001:3; Hayden 2001:28), a feasting event has been defined as the act of consuming food and drink in a communal manner, in a context other than the domestic. It is very difficult to positively identify feasting through a zooarchaeological analysis, as there are very few markers that could be used in an unequivocal way. Identification of feasts as a ritual act requires the identification of several associated acts (Brown 2001) that are distinguishable and function as an articulator between social relations (Dietler 2001). Therefore, if the aim is to understand social interaction, it is imperative to understand the role that feasting plays, as well as the differential consumption patterns that are associated with it and how feasting has been transformed through time (Dietler and Hayden 2001).

Exploring who was promoting feasting events, and who was participating in them, can be investigated through a range of archaeological attributes.

It has been suggested that feasts organised by the elite, could have been exclusionary, so that there was no sharing of food with the lower classes. This would have created an image of conspicuous consumption and waste, all as a mechanism employed by the elites to emphasise their power (Webster 2002:159). However, most feasts have a dual role (LeCount 1996) where emphasis is put on the celebration of feasts that were communal, and in order to create debt from the participants towards the emerging leaders (Hayden 1990; Joyce and Henderson 2007). For Joyce and Henderson (2007), feasts are seen as inclusive events where everybody probably shared food. The midden from Lagartero has been identified as 'the result of public, inclusionary, ritual actions' (Koželsky 2005:3). There are several examples of feasting deposits that have been identified as of an inclusionary nature, including Cerén and Kabah (Brown 2001; INAH Noticias 2011), and Lagartero (Koželsky 2005:3).

On the other hand, some authors see feasts as exclusive to a segment of the society, according to the distribution of archaeological remains (including type of food and location). One indicator could be the age of the animals consumed. According to Emery (2004a:108), the presence of very young animals that probably acted as sacrificial victims, could signal that they were then consumed as feast foods in a public exclusionary rituals performed by the elite members, who had the sole access to preferential animals, including the white-tailed deer.

There are two views as to how meat was consumed and distributed by the elite. The first one indicates that large amounts of food would have to be gathered by the elite and to be shared with the rest of the population. The food collected would be the result of tribute payment, by individuals or households (Pohl 1994:121). If we consider the second hypothesis, where only the elite would consume meat in a private ceremony, then the amount of meat per person would substantially increase, especially if meat consumption happened during a single event or over a few feasts. The consumption of very large amounts of meat during special occasions is not rare around the world, and is probably part of the ritual itself.

The forms of preparing food would also have had a major influence on the amount of food available during a celebration. It is important to remember that for the Classic Maya, as opposed to other Mesoamerican groups, there is very little evidence that they ate tortillas, but rather prepared dishes based on *tamales* (Taube 1989). *Tamales* are known to be very filling and

Figure 72. Representation of the deer
God with tamales placed in shallow bowls
(modified from Hellmuth 1978:182).

only a few would have been necessary per person. Although there are representations of deer haunches as offerings, complete images of deer as food are seldom represented (Bíró and Montero 2008). Inferences about deer being used as food can be drawn from glyphs on bowls that name the images of deer or deer-hunting and thus may indicate that the meal served on them during palace feasting ceremonies was deer (LeCount 2001; Reents-Budet 2000), especially in the form of *tamales* stuffed with deer meat. One interesting representation was found on a bowl where *tamales* are carried by a deer god, suggesting that such food items contained deer meat (Hellmuth 1978:182) (Figure 72).

The study of ritual feasts in the Maya area has been mainly approached through the analysis of ceramic vessels, especially vases for cacao drinking (LeCount 2001). This beverage was shared among the participants, along with food, such as maize-based foods, including *tamales*, stuffed with meat (LeCount 2001:943; Masson 1999; Tykot *et al.* 1996). Nowadays, festive foods include chicken and pigs (LeCount 2001), but during the 16th

century, peccary, deer, dog, and turkey were the norm. It is possible that the same animals were eaten during the Classic period (Pohl and Feldman 1982) in public ceremonies, although it is also possible that the elite may have consumed cacao drinks and meat-stuffed *tamales* more often than the rest of the population, as access to these foodstuffs was one of their prerogatives (Montero 2009; Pohl 1990:167; Yaeger and Robin 2004).

In the Maya area, it has been said that feasts were a means to bring elite and non-elite individuals together in order to establish alliances, and promote a social debt in benefit of the high class. In these events, a conspicuous consumption of large amounts of food and the display of symbols of power other valuable goods would be expected. Some have argued that it was the people from lower classes that would bring some of the goods to be consumed, including meat, which in turn would be re-distributed by the elite in order to create indebtedness on behalf of the commoners (Brown 2007:3; Jackson and Scott 2003). Such practices are known as 'palace economies' and occurred in other parts of the world, such as Crete; however, the Maya version would have been a much weaker one (Webster 2002:159) or may have been a mix of a palace economy with another ritual practice, including 'pot luck', such as the one seen among the Mississippian feasting ceremonies (Jackson and Scott 2003), where various members of the group provide items to be consumed collectively.

Without question, members of the higher social classes were consciously selecting certain species as a means of expressing their power. This would have resulted in a symbolic restriction of these resources being imposed on other social strata that, during periods of less political stress, would have been able to access such resources (Emery 2003:511). Thus, it is possible to expect that during periods of political stress, the number of species present should be lower or less diverse than during relatively conflict-free periods. Furthermore, the intensification in the use of faunal resources is also related to the increasing numbers of the elite members that demanded more and more resources for their feasts and ceremonies, especially those elites that were establishing themselves in new areas, or were emerging as a powerful centre during the Classic period (Eppich 2009:16). Feasts also were used to mitigate conflict between competitive neighbouring sites (Moriarty and Foias 2006:1135). It is possible this resulted in direct involvement in animal management, in order to ensure the access to meat required for their rituals (White *et al.* 2004:144).

There is no doubt that agricultural products, especially corn, were the foundation of the Maya diet. Nevertheless, there has been some debate about the practices of meat consumption by the Maya, and whether there were temporal or social differences. Some have even questioned whether the Maya consumed meat at all (Dillon 1988). During the Late Classic, there was an increase in the population that is intimately linked to an unprecedented increase in modified land for agriculture, which was in turn closely related to the agriculture expansion and the distribution of fauna, and its subsequent exploitation (Emery 2007a). Earlier evidence from different isotope analyses from human samples (Gerry and Krueger 1997; White 1997) showed that instead of intensification in the use of a few faunal resources, there was an increase in the dietary diversity as a means to combat the shortages brought by a diet relying almost exclusively on agricultural products (Masson 1999). However, new evidence introduced by more recent studies that combine both zooarchaeological and isotopic data, suggests that there was intensification in the use of a few large species, primarily the white-tailed deer (Emery 2010:271; Pohl 1994:138; Wright 2006), as the local elites would demand more and more large animals to be used in public events. The data from the zooarchaeological analysis at Chinikihá supports this later interpretation, with intensification in the exploitation of white-tailed deer, and the inclusion of other body parts rather than just the haunch.

The relationship between Chinikihá and other larger polities, such as Palenque and Pomoná, is also not well known, and we therefore do not know the extent of influence these polities might have had over Chinikihá when it was under their control, especially regarding access to faunal resources. We still need more data on this as well as full studies of the fauna exploitation at both Palenque and Pomoná in order to do inter-site comparisons. What we can see from the distribution of faunal remains is that Chinikihá remained independent and thus was able to maintain continual access to meat resources. This is similar to what might have happened at other sites, such as in Motul de San José and other sites in the Petexbatún region in Guatemala (Emery 2008:631; Thornton and Emery 2009:1184).

Furthermore, the evidence of ecological stability in the area proves that there was no hunting pressure on the deer populations. The political dominance that larger polities such as Palenque or Pomoná exercised did not jeopardise the access to resources by the local elite at Chinikihá. The high class had access to the choice of meat cuts, such as the haunch, for the performance of their own rituals throughout the Classic period, even at times of perceived political instability.

It is probable that the regional control Chinikihá exercised over restricted resources such as white-tailed deer, proved to be beneficial for political purposes. If public feasts were conducted at Chinikihá where the attendance of foreign guests would have been expected, and these guests witnessed the celebration of a feasting event or events where a relatively large number of animals were consumed and some of the meat was even wasted, then, Chinikihá would have looked like a powerful entity. This is still a very preliminary interpretation, and further comparisons with similar assemblages are required. Nevertheless, with more examples of feasting being discovered recently, including the deposit from *Operación* 114 at Chinikihá, it is now possible to start comparing these assemblages in a more specific manner and drawing conclusions based on similarities and differences between them.

Conclusion

The study of *Operación* 114, a context behind the Palace at Chinikihá, revealed the presence of thousands of animal bones and freshwater molluscs, intermingled with modified human remains, worked bone and complete ornaments and tools, ceramic figurines, exotic animals, and a large quantity of serving vessels. This assemblage is different from the rest of the *Operaciones* from Chinikihá but is comparable in size and characteristics to other deposits in other sites that have been identified as the result of feasting.

Large quantities of faunal bones and shell, human bones, worked bone (finished and unfinished), ceramic figurines, non-local or exotic animals, and extraordinarily large amounts of tableware have been identified as feasting markers. However, they all have been mentioned as key components in the identification of deposits that resulted from other ritual behaviours, such as termination and dedication offerings, construction fill, and even burials, creating further confusion as to how to identify feasting in the archaeological record. A series of ethnographic and archaeological comparisons using these markers as the base for identifying feasting in archaeology were established to test if *Operación* 114 was a feasting deposit. Zooarchaeological methods and isotope analyses were conducted to investigate this. The results indicated that this deposit is possibly the sum of various feasting episodes that occurred during the Late Classic period, a period when there was an increase in political competition in the Maya Lowlands. The results of these analyses also suggested that there is not a single criterion that is uniquely diagnostic of feasting (*sensus* Twiss 2008), but also stressed that the presence of all markers is not required in order to identify feasting behaviour.

It was concluded that *Operación* 114 represents the refuse from several feasting episodes, but in terms of identifying feasting events through the analysis of faunal remains, it was seen that there are very few zooarchaeological markers that can actually point to a positive identification of feasting events. Those factors that were considered of importance include age of the animal (preference for immature, prime-aged), presence of high density of materials with a low diversity (preference of specific species and body parts). If studies only focus on the zooarchaeological data without considering other associated materials that may be present, then defining a context as exclusively the result of feasting is difficult. Furthermore, this study stresses the importance of considering the taphonomic history of the deposit, and the way in which materials entered the archaeological record in order to understand how the function of a deposit may have changed through time. The ritual deposit of *Operación* 114 appears to be a periodical use of this context for the discard of feasting remains that was in use for 100 or 150 years.

The discussion presented here then stresses that there is no simple way to identify feasting (and other ritual activities for that matter) through the exclusive analysis of faunal remains, and emphasises the necessity of considering all the other materials present in the same context, as well as considering the taphonomical history of the deposit. There is no universal explanation for these deposits, and each must be viewed in conjunction with its own contexts and associations (Hill 1995). However, it should also be stressed that as the analysis of this type of deposits is approached by considering ritual and feasting as polythetic set of attributes with a multiplicity of overlapping phenomena, we should be acknowledging that there is no single fixed criterion to define it (Morris 2008:93).

When studying feasting in the Maya area, it is imperative to consider other practices, such as trash disposal and management of residues. However, this is not easy, as there are few studies on the disposal patterns of feasting remains and the variability represented by several similar contexts, making it difficult to identify middens from other deposits, such as termination and dedication rituals (Stanton *et al.* 2008). Feasting remains may be present in a myriad of deposits once the ritual part of the feast is over. Each context should be studied independently, considering the particularities and formation processes, as feasting remains are often treated the same as those from more mundane activities, creating a false sense of homogeneity in what should be expected from a feasting deposit. Furthermore, it seems that there is a general inability in identifying feasting activities in long occupation deposits, as they appear like palimpsests, reflecting a myriad of activities.

Operación 114 may have resulted from periodic feasting activities that were either conducted nearby or whose remains were transported from another location where feasts were conducted. Both cases involve large-scale preparation of foods for a communal ceremony. During the Classic period, rulers staged public events to promote and generate long-term benefits for themselves; as such these acts were conducted periodically to associate themselves with rituals that usually revolve around life cycles (birth, marriage, death, and so on) (Lucero 2003:523). They are also intrinsically associated with their discrete context, and the construction sequence of buildings where they were held, resulting in long sequences of deposits that are interconnected, usually by a ritual process (Lucero 2003; Walker and Lucero 2000). It is therefore suggested that the analysis consider the contexts as a whole, and take a life history approach, where different stratigraphic sequences can be used as units of analysis which are considered, but ultimately integrated, considering the relations between multiple variables in the sequence of deposits (Walker and Lucero 2000:135). Not only the contents but also the context should be analysed in an integrative fashion.

Despite all the shortcomings, this study does provide ample information on how large animals were considered of high value by the elite and how they were procured and processed, especially for dietary consumption. The consistent representation of preferred body portions, including the upper limbs and torso, and the remarkable dominance of a single mammal throughout the deposit, suggests that the elite controlled these animals and their highly valued body parts. Whether elite themselves, or a selected group of hunters oversaw bringing the animals back to the site is not presently understood. It is also suggested that the elite class may have exercised some type of management of wild deer to secure their availability in the future for a diversity of rituals that required the consumption of meat. The preferred animals were those in their prime age representing the largest yield of meat.

The representation of all body parts suggests that deer were brought back to the site where they would have been processed *in situ*. The preservation state of the archaeofaunal material was well suited to exploring the processing and selection of specific body parts, especially for the white-tailed deer. The favoured body part was the back haunch, followed by the front upper leg, and torso segments. This preference was observed in all age categories, suggesting that these body parts represent a conscious selection by the elite, and that the haunch may have had an integral role in ritual feasting.

The analysis of the distribution of species, body portion and age by layer suggested that there was little change in the patterns of consumption by the elite during the Late/Terminal Classic period, supporting Emery's conclusion that during this period there is no evidence for an ecological collapse, as previously thought (Emery 2010).

The application of isotope analysis provided evidence about the access to meat for members of minor elites,

as well as about the diet of deer. The results suggest that the inhabitants of Chinikihá had access to meat occasionally, but the bulk of their diet may have been plant-based, reliance on maize. Meat could have been prepared in different ways including being roasted, or stuffed *tamales*. Ample ceramic and iconographic evidence supports both interpretations. However, it is suggested here that *tamales* played an important role in rituals sponsored by the elite and may have been the favoured style of preparation.

It has been a while since Dietler and Hayden's seminal work *Feasts: Archaeological and Ethnographic Perspectives on Food, Politics, and Power* (2001), where several authors delineated what is nowadays known as the 'archaeological markers' of feasts that have been borrowed by many researchers around the world to identify feasts in archaeological contexts. While considering ethnographic cases, in the presence of literature, or in historical zooarchaeology, may be relatively easy, the study of feasts and other ritual activities that are liminal is a difficult task in archaeology, especially with the Maya, where certain animal taxa were, and are used for multiple purposes. As new evidence for feasting contexts from the Maya area is studied, we will be able to centre the discussion of feasting at a more regional level in order to understand the characteristics of such ritual behaviour.

Feasting in the Lowlands area has been a long-standing practice since the Preclassic period, being used by the elite as an important means to maintain control and promote themselves to the site's inhabitants, and also as a way of displaying their power in front of other elites that would participate in the ever-growing circuit of feasting and ritual activities that occurred during the Late Classic period. With this in mind, it is possible to confirm that the study of faunal exploitation can provide information about ritual activities such as feasting, but also the analysis of feasting remains offers an insight into other more mundane activities that are part of preparing a feast, such as butchery practices and food preparation. Ultimately, the study of faunal remains from Chinikihá may contribute to the study of broader topics, such as the economic, political, and social organisation within smaller polities during the Late/Terminal Classic period, and throughout the Maya Lowlands.

References

Adams, Richard E. W. 1977 *Prehistoric Mesoamerica*. Little Brown, New York.

Aimers, James J. 2007 What Maya Collapse? Terminal Classic Variation in the Maya Lowlands. *Journal of Archaeological Research* 15:329–377.

Albalá, Ken (editor) 2011 *Food Cultures of the World Encyclopedia*, Vol. 1. Greenwood, ABC-Clío, Santa Barbara.

Alcerreca A. Carlos, and Rafael Robles de B. 2005 *Mammals of the Yucatán Peninsula*. Dante, Biocenosis, Mérida.

Álvarez del Toro, Miguel 1977 Los Mamíferos de Chiapas. Serie Científica. Gobierno del Estado de Chiapas, Consejo Estatal de Fomento a la Investigación y Difusión de la Cultura, DIF-Chiapas/Instituto Chiapaneco de Cultura. UNACH, Tuxtla Gutiérrez.

Álvarez, Ticúl, and Aurelio Ocaña Informe Z-462: Análisis de la Fauna de Vertebrados Terrestres Procedentes de Palenque, Chiapas. Technical Report submitted to the Laboratorio de Zooarqueología. Instituto Nacional de Antropología e Historia (INAH), Mexico City.

Álvarez, Ticúl, Aurelio Ocaña, and Norma Valentín 1990 Identificación de los restos óseos procedentes de las excavaciones de Tonina, Chiapas. In *Toniná une Cite Maya du Chiapas*, tome IV, edited by P. Becquelin, and F. Taladoire, pp. 1832-1846. Collection Études Mésoaméricaines 6. Centre d'Etudes Mexicaines et Centraméricaines (CEMCA), Mexico City.

Álvarez-Romero, Jorge, and Rodrigo A. Medellín 2005 *Odocoileus virginianus*. Electronic document, http://www.conabio.gob.mx, accessed January 27, 2011. Comisión Nacional para el Conocimiento y Uso de la Biodiversidad (CONABIO).

Ambrose, Stanley H. 1993 Isotopic Analysis of Paleodiets: Methodological and Interpretive Considerations. In *Investigations of Ancient Human Tissues*, edited by M. K. Sandford, pp. 59-130. Gordon Breach, Switzerland.

1991 Effects of Diet, Climate, and Physiology on Nitrogen Isotope Abundances in Terrestrial Foodwebs. *Journal of Archaeological Science* 18:293-317.

1990 Preparation and Characterization of Bone and Tooth Collagen for Isotopic Analysis. *Journal of Archaeological Science* 17:431-451.

Ambrose, Stanley H., and Lynn Norr 1993 Experimental Evidence for the Relationship of the Carbon Isotope Ratios of Whole Diet and Dietary Protein to those of Bone Collagen and Carbonate. In *Prehistoric Human Bone: Archaeology at the Molecular Level*, edited by J. Lambert, and G. Grupe, pp. 1-37. Springer-Verlag, Berlin.

Anaya Hernández, Armando 2005 Strategic Location and Territorial Integrity: The Role of Subsidiary Sites in the Classic Maya Kingdoms of the Upper Usumacinta Region. Electronic document, http://intarch.ac.uk, accessed June 13, 2011. *Internet Archaeology* 19.

2001 *Site Interaction and Political Geography in the Upper Usumacinta Region during the Late Classic: A GIS Approach*. BAR International Series 994. John and Erica Hedges, Oxford.

Anaya Hernández, Armando, Stanley P. Guenter, and Marc U. Zender 2003 *Sak Tz'I*, a Classic Maya Centre: A Locational Model Based on GIS and Epigraphy. *Latin American Antiquity* 14(2):179-191.

Anderson, Elyse M. 2009 Exploring Maya Ritual Fauna: Caves and the Proposed Link with Contemporary Hunting Ceremonialism. Master's dissertation, University of Florida, Gainesville.

Anderson, E. N. 2010 Food and Feasting in the Zona Maya of Quintana Roo. In *Precolumbian Foodways: Interdisciplinary Approaches to Food, Culture, and Markets in Ancient Mesoamerica*, edited by J. E. Staller, and M. D. Carrasco, pp. 441-466. Springer, New York.

Andrews, E. Wyllys V 1986 Olmec Jades from Chacsinkin, Yucatán, and Maya Ceramics from La Venta, Tabasco. In *Research and Reflections in Archaeology and History, Essays in Honor of Doris Stone*, edited by E. Wyllys Andrews V, pp. 11-49. Middle American Research Institute, Publication 57. Tulane University, New Orleans.

Anselmetti, Flavio S. Anselmetti, David A. Hodell, Daniel Ariztegui, Mark Brenner, and Michael F. Rosenmeier 2007 Quantification of Soil Erosion Rates Related to Ancient Maya Deforestation. *Geology* 35(10):915–918.

Aoyama, Kazuo 2009 *Elite Craft Producers, Artists, and Warriors at Aguateca: Lithic Analysis: Monographs of the Aguateca Archaeological Project First Phase*, edited by T. Inomata and D. Triadan, Vol. 2. The University of Utah Press, Salt Lake City.

Arceo, Gloria, Salvador Mandujano, Sonia Gallina, and Luis Alfredo Perez-Jimenez 2005 Diet Diversity of White-Tailed Deer (*Odocoileus virginianus*) in a Tropical Dry Forest in Mexico. *Mammalia* 69(2):159-168.

Ashmore, Wendy 1989 Construction and Cosmology: Politics and Ideology in Lowland Maya Settlement Patterns. In *Word and Image in Maya Culture*, edited by W. F. Hanks, and D. S. Rice, pp. 272-286. University of Utah Press, Salt Lake City.

Ball, J. W. 1993 Pottery, Potters, Palaces and Polities: Some Socioeconomic and Political Implications of Late Classic Maya Ceramic Industries. In *Lowland Maya Civilization in the Eighth Century AD*, edited by J. A. Sabloff, and J. S. Henderson, pp. 243-272. Dumbarton Oaks, Washington, D. C.

Bailey, Geoff 2007 Time Perspectives, Palimpsests and the Archaeology of Time. *Journal of Anthropological Archaeology* 26:198-223.

Bass, William M. 1995 *Human Osteology: A Laboratory and Field Manual.* Special Publication 2, Missouri Archaeological Society, Columbia.

Becker, Marshall J. 1992 Burials as Caches; Caches as Burials: A New Interpretation of the Meaning of Ritual Deposits among the Classic Period Lowland Maya. In *New Theories on the Ancient Maya*, edited by E. C. Danien, and R. J. Sharer, pp. 185-196. University Museum Monograph 77. University of Pennsylvania, Philadelphia.

Beaudry-Corbet, Marilyn (with contributions by Ronald L. Bishop) 2002 Ceramics and Their Use at Cerén. In *Before the Volcano Erupted: the Ancient Cerén Village in Central America*, edited by P. Sheets, pp. 117-138. University of Texas Press, Austin.

Beaudry-Corbet, Marilyn, Scott E Simmons, and David B. Tucker 2002 Ancient Home and Garden: The View from Household 1 at Cerén. In *Before the Volcano Erupted: The Ancient Cerén Village in Central America*, edited by P. Sheets, pp. 45-57. University of Texas Press, Austin.

Behrensmeyer, Anna K. Taphonomic and Ecologic Information from Bone Weathering. *Paleobiology* 4:150-162.

Berlin, Heinrich 1955 News from the Maya World. *Ethnos* 20:201-209.

Binford, Lewis R. 1984 *Faunal Remains from Klasies River Mouth.* Academic Press, New York.

1981 *Bones: Ancient Man and Modern Myth.* Academic Press, New York.

1978 *Nunamiut Archaeology.* Academic Press, New York.

Bíró, Peter, and Coral Montero López 2008 Feast, Sacrifice and Deer Mountain in Iconography and Epigraphy: Can we identify them in Archaeology? Paper submitted to the Premio Palenque Contest 2008. Manuscript on file. INAH, Mexico City.

Bishop, Ronald 1994 Pre-Columbian Pottery: Research in the Maya Region. In *Archaeometry of Pre-Columbian Sites and Artifacts*, edited by D. A. Scott, and P. Meyers, pp. 15-65. Getty Conservation Institute, Los Angeles.

Blanco Padilla, Alicia, Bernardo Rodríguez Galicia, and Raúl Valadéz Azúa 2009 *Estudio de los Cánidos Arqueológicos del México Prehispánico.* Serie Textos Básicos y Manuales, Instituto Nacional de Antropología e Historia, Instituto de Investigaciones Antropológicas, Universidad Nacional Autónoma de México, Ciudad Universitaria.

Blanco, Alicia, Raúl Valadéz, and Bernardo Rodríguez 1999 Colección Arqueozoológica de Perros del Sitio Chac-Mool, Punta de Pájaros, Quintana Roo. *Arqueología* (segunda época) 22:89-106.

Blasco Sancho, María Fernanda *Tafonomía y Prehistoria: Métodos y Procedimientos de Investigación.* Departamento de Ciencias de la Antigüedad (Prehistoria), Universidad de Zaragoza, Departamento de Educación y Cultura, Aragón.

Bliege Bird, Rebecca, and Eric Alden Smith 2005 Signalling Theory, Strategic Interaction, and Symbolic Capital. *Current Anthropology* 46(2):221-248.

Bobrowsky, Peter T., and Bruce F. Ball 1989 The Theory and Mechanics of Ecological Diversity in Archaeology. In *Quantifying Diversity in Archaeology*, edited by R. D. Leonard, and G. T. Jones, pp. 4-12. Cambridge University Press, Cambridge.

Brock, Fiona, Bronk Ramsey, and Higham Thomas 2007 Quality Assurance of Ultrafiltered Bone Dating. *Radiocarbon* 49(2):187-192.

Brown, Kathryn M. 2007 *Ritual Ceramic Use in the Early and Middle Preclassic at the sites of Blackman Eddy and Cahal Pech, Belize.* Electronic document, http://www.famsi.org, accessed February 10, 2011. FAMSI.

2002 The Structure of Ritual Practice: An Ethnoarchaeological Exploration of Activity Areas at Rural Community Shrines in the Maya Highlands. PhD dissertation, University of Colorado, Boulder.

Brown, Linda A. 2009 Communal and Personal Hunting Shrines around LakeAtitlan, Guatemala. In *Maya Archaeology 1*, edited by C. Golden, S. Houston, and J. Skidmore, pp. 36-59. Precolumbia Mesoweb Press, San Francisco.

2005 Planting the Bones: Hunting Ceremonialism at Contemporary and Nineteenth-Century Shrines in the Guatemalan Highlands. *Latin American Antiquity* 16(2):131-146.

2001 Feasting on the Periphery: The Production of Ritual Feasting and Village Festivals at the Ceren Site, El Salvador. In *Feasts: Archaeological and Ethnographic Perspectives on Food, Politics, and Power*, edited by M. Dietler, and B. Hayden, pp. 368-390. Smithsonian Institution Press, Washington.

1996 Animals-as-Artifact/Animal-as-Representation: An Exploration of Household and Village Animal Use at the Ceren Site, El Salvador. Master's thesis, University of Colorado, Denver.

Brown, Linda A., and Kitty F. Emery 2008 Negotiations with the Animate Forest: Hunting Shrines in the Guatemalan Highlands. *Journal of Archaeological Method and Theory* 15:300-337.

Brown, Linda. A., and A. I. Gerstle 2002 Structure 10: Feasting and village festivals. In *Before the Volcano Erupted: The Ancient Ceren Village in Central America*, edited by P. Sheets, pp. 97-103. University of Texas Press, Austin.

Brumfiel, Elizabeth M. 1987 Elite and Utilitarian Crafts in the Aztec State. In *Specialization, Exchange, and Complex Societies*, edited by E. M. Brumfiel, and T. K. Earle, pp. 102-118. Cambridge University Press, New York.

Byers, David A., and Brenda L. Hill 2009 Pronghorn Dental Age Profiles and Holocene Hunting Strategies at Hogup Cave, Utah. *American Antiquity* 74(2):299-321.

Campiani, Arianna 2010 Los Conjuntos y Grupos Arquitectónicos de Chinikihá, Estudio Preliminar. In *Tercer Informe Parcial Proyecto Arqueologico Chinikihá, Temporada 2010*, coordinated by Rodrigo Liendo, pp. 21-52. Electronic document, http://www.famsi.com/resources/informes/Chinikihá2010, accessed December 3, 2011. FAMSI.

Carr, H. Sorayya 1996 Precolumbian Maya Exploitation and Management of Deer Populations. In *The Managed Mosaic: Ancient Maya Agriculture and Resource Use*, edited by S. L. Fedick, pp. 251-261. University of Utah Press, Salt Lake City.

1986 *Archaeology at Cerros, Belize, Central America: An interim report.* Vol. 1 of Archaeology at Cerros, Belize, Central America Series. Southern Methodist University Press, University Park.

1985 Subsistence and Ceremony: Faunal Utilization in a Late Preclassic Community at Cerros, Belize. In *Prehistoric Lowland Maya Environment and Subsistence Economy*, edited by M. D. Pohl, pp. 115-132. Papers of the Peabody Museum of Archaeology and Ethnology, Vol. 77. Harvard University Press, Cambridge.

Carr, H. S., and A. Fradkin 2008 Animal Resource Use in Ecological and Economic Context at Formative Period Cuello, Belize. *Quaternary International* 191:144-153.

Ceballos, Gerardo, and Giselle Oliva (cords.) 2005 *Los Mamiferos Silvestres de Mexico*. Fondo de Cultura Económica, Comisión Nacional para el Conocimiento y Uso de la Biodiversidad (CONABIO). Toppan Printing, Hong Kong.

Chaplin, Raymond E. 1971 *The Study of Animal Bones from Archaeological Sites*. Seminar Press, London.

Chase, Arlen F., and Diane Z. Chase 2010 The Context of Ritual: Examining the Archaeological Record at Caracol, Belize. *Research Reports in Belizean Archaeology* 7:3-15.

2001 The Royal Court of Caracol, Belize: Its Palaces and People. In *Royal Courts of the Ancient Maya*, Vol. II, edited by T. Inomata, and S. D. Houston, pp. 102-137. Westview, Boulder.

Chase, Arlen F., Diane Z. Chase, and Christine D. White 2001 El Paisaje Urbano Maya: La Integración de los Espacios Construidos y la Estructura Social en Caracol, Belice. In *Reconstruyendo la Ciudad Maya: el Urbanismo en las Sociedades Antiguas*, edited by A. Ciudad Ruiz, M. J. Iglesias Ponce de León, and M. del C. Martínez Martínez, pp. 95-122. Sociedad Española de Estudios Mayas, Madrid.

Chase, Diane Z. 1997 Southern Lowland Maya Archaeology and Human Skeletal Remains: Interpretations from Caracol (Belize), Santa Rita Corozal (Belize), and Tayasal (Guatemala). In *Bones of the Maya*, edited by S. L. Whittington, and D. M. Reed, pp. 15-27. Smithsonian Institution Press, Washington.

1985 Ganned but not Forgotten: Late Postclassical Archaeology and Ritual at Santa Rita Corozal, Belize. In *The Lowland Maya Postclassic*, edited by A. F. Chase, and P. M. Price, pp. 104-125. University of Texas Press, Austin.

Chase, Diane Z., and Arlen F. Chase 2000 Inferences about Abandonment: Maya Household Archaeology and Caracol, Belize. *Mayab* 13:67-77.

1998a The Architectural Context of Caches, Burials, and Other Ritual Activities for the Classic Period Maya (as Reflected at Caracol, Belize). In *Function and Meaning in Classic Maya Archaeology: A Symposium at Dumbarton Oaks 7th and 8th October, 1994*, edited by S. D. Houston, pp. 299-332. Dumbarton Oaks Research Library and Collection, Washington, D. C.

1998b Late Classic Maya Political Structure, Polity Size, and Warfare Arenas. In *Anatomía de una Civilización: Aproximaciones Interdisciplinarias a la Cultura Maya*, edited by A. Ciudad Ruiz, M. Y. Fernández Marquínez, J. M. García Campillo, M. J. Iglesias Ponce de León, A. Lacadena García-Gallo, and L. T. Sanz Castro, pp. 11-29. Sociedad Española de Estudios Mayas, Madrid.

1992 An Archaeological Assessment of Mesoamerican Elites. In *Mesoamerican Elites. An Archaeological Assessment*, edited by D. Z. Chase, and A. F. Chase, pp. 303-317. University of Oklahoma Press, Norman.

Chase, Arlen F., Diane Z. Chase, and Wendy Giddens Teeter 2004 Archaeology, Faunal Analysis and Interpretation: Lessons from Maya Studies. *Archaeofauna* 13:11-18.

Chisholm, M. S., D.E. Nelson, H.P. Schwarcz, and M. Knyf 1982 Carbon Isotope Measurement Techniques for Bone Collagen: Notes for the Archaeologist. *Journal of Archaeological Science* 10:335-360.

Christenson, Allen J. 2010 Maize was their Flesh: Ritual Feasting in the Maya Highlands. In *Precolumbian Foodways: Interdisciplinary Approaches to Food, Culture, and Markets in Ancient Mesoamerica*, edited by J. E. Staller, and M. Carrasco, pp. 577-600. Springer, New York.

Clark, John E. 2004 Mesoamerica Goes Public: Early Ceremonial Centres, Leaders, and Communities. In *Mesoamerican Archaeology*, edited by J. A. Hendon, and R. A. Joyce, pp. 43-72. Blackwell, Oxford.

Clark, J. E., and M. Blake 1994 The Power of Prestige: Competitive Generosity and the Emergence of Rank Society in Lowland Mesoamerica. In *Factional Competition and Political Development in the New World*, edited by E. M. Brumfiel, and J. W. Fox, pp. 17-30. Cambridge University Press, Cambridge.

Clarke, Michael J. 2001 Akha Feasting: An Ethnoarchaeological Perspective. In *Feasts: Archaeological and Ethnographic Perspectives on Food, Politics, and Power*, edited by M. Dietler, and B. Hayden, pp. 144-167. Smithsonian Institution Press, Washington.

Clayton, Sarah, David Driver, and Laura Kosakowsky 2005 Rubbish or Ritual? Contextualizing a Terminal Classic

Problematical Deposit at Blue Creek, Belize: A Response to 'Public Architecture, Ritual and Temporal Dynamics at the Maya Centre of Blue Creek' by Thomas Guderjan. *Ancient Mesoamerica* 16(1):119-131.

Clutton-Brock, Juliet and Norman Hammond 1994 Hot Dogs: Comestible Canids in Preclassic Maya Culture at Cuello, Belize. *Journal of Archaeological Science* 21:819-826.

Coe, Michael D. 1956 The Funerary Temple Among the Classic Maya. *Southwestern Journal of Anthropology* 12:387-394.

Coe, William R. 1990 *Excavations in the Great Plaza, North Terrace and North Acropolis of Tikal*. Tikal Reports, Vol. 14. University Museum, University of Pennsylvania, Philadelphia.

1959 *Piedras Negras Archaeology: Artifacts, Caches and Burials*. University Museum Monographs. University of Pennsylvania, Philadelphia.

Cohodas, Marvin 2002 Multiplicity and Discourse in Maya Gender Relations. In *Ancient Maya Gender Identity and Relations*, edited by L. Gustafson, and A. M. Trevelyan, pp. 11-53. Bergin and Garvey, Westport.

Collins, L. M. 2002 The Zooarchaeology of the Copan Valley: Social Status and the Search for a Maya Slave Class. PhD dissertation, Harvard University, Harvard.

Conlee, C. A. 2006 Regeneration as Transformation: Postcollapse Society in Nasca, Peru. In *After Collapse: The Regeneration of Complex Societies*, edited by G. M. Schwartz, and J. J. Nichols, pp. 99-13. The University of Arizona Press, Tucson.

Coplen, Tyler B. 1994 Reporting of Stable Hydrogen, Carbon and Oxygen Isotopic Abundances: *Pure and Applied Chemistry* 66:273-276.

1988 Normalization of Oxygen and Hydrogen Isotope Data. *Chemical Geology* (Isotope Geoscience Section) 72:293-297.

Coplen, Tyler B., Willi A. Brand, M. Gehre, M. Gröning, H. A. J. Meijer, B. Toman, and R. M. Verkouteren 2006 After two Decades a Second Anchor for the VPDB δ^{13}C Scale. *Rapid Communications in Mass Spectrometry* 20:3165-316.

Cormie, A. B., and H. P. Schwarcz 1994 Stable Isotopes of Nitrogen and Carbon of North American White-Tailed Deer and Implications for Paleodietary and Other Food Web Studies. *Palaeogeography, Palaeoclimatology, Palaeoecology* 107:227-241.

Corona-M, Eduardo 2008 The Origin of Zooarchaeology in Mexico: An Overview. *Quaternary International* 185:75-81.

Costin, Cathy L., and Timothy Earle 1989 Status Distinction and Legitimation of Power as Reflected in Changing Patterns of Consumption in Late Prehispanic Peru. *American Antiquity* 54:691-714.

Covich, Alan P. 1983 Mollusca: A Contrast in Species Diversity from Aquatic and Terrestrial Habitats. In *Pulltrouser Swamp: Ancient Maya Habitat, Agriculture, and Settlement in Northern Belize*, edited by B. L. Turner II, and P. D. Harrison, pp. 120-139. University of Texas Press, Austin.

Coyston, Shannon Louise 1995 An Application of Carbon Isotope Analysis of Bone Apatite to the Study of Maya Diets and Subsistence of Pachitún Lamanai, Belize. Master's thesis, Trent University, Peterborough.

Coyston, Shannon, Christine D. White, and Henry P. Schwarcz 1999 Dietary Carbonate Analysis of Bone and Enamel for Two Sites in Belize. In *Reconstructing Ancient Maya Diet*, edited by C. D. White, pp. 221-243. University of Utah Press, Salt Lake City.

Crabtree, Pam J. 2002 Ritual Feasting in the Irish Iron Age: Re-examining the Fauna from Dún Ailinne in Light of Contemporary Archaeological Theory. In *Behaviour Behind Bones: The Zooarchaeology of Ritual, Religion, Status and Identity*, edited by S. Jones O'Day, W. Van Neer, and A. Ervynck, pp. 62-65. Proceedings of the 9th ICAZ Conference, Durham. Oxbow Books, Oxford.

Craig, H. 1957 Isotope Standards for Carbon and Oxygen and Correction Factors for Mass-Spectrometric Analyses of Carbon Dioxide. *Geochimica et Cosmochimica Acta* 12:133-149. 1953 The Geochemistry of the Stable Carbon Isotopes. *Geochimica et Cosmochimica Acta* 3:53-92.

Crockford, Susan J. 2009 *A Practical Guide to In Situ Dog Remains for the Field Archaeologist*. Pacific Identifications, Victoria, British Columbia.

Cruz-Uribe, Kathryn 1988 The Use and Meaning of Species Diversity and Richness in Archaeological Faunas. *Journal of Archaeological Science* 15:179-196.

Culbert, T. Patrick 1988 The Collapse of Classic Maya Civilization. In *The Collapse of Ancient States and Civilizations*, edited by N. Yoffee, and G. L. Cowgill, pp. 69-101. University of Arizona, Tucson.

Curet, L. Antonio, and William J. Pestle 2010 Identifying High-Status Foods in the Archaeological Record. *Journal of Anthropological Archaeology* 29:413-431.

Dabney, Mary K., Paul Halstead and Patrick Thomas 2004 Mycenaean Feasting on Tsoungiza at Ancient Nemea. *Hesperia* 73(2):197-215 (Special issue: 'The Mycean Feast').

Dahlin, Bruce H., Daniel Bair, Tim Beach, Matthew Moriarty, and Richard Terry 2010 The Dirt on Food: Ancient Feasts and Markets among the Lowland Maya. In *Precolumbian Foodways: Interdisciplinary Approaches to Food, Culture, and Markets in Ancient Mesoamerica*, edited by J. E. Staller, and M. Carrasco, pp. 191-232. Springer, New York.

D'Altroy, Terence N. 1994 Factions and Political Development in the Central Andes. In *Factional Competition and Political Development in the New World*, edited by E. M. Brumfiel, and J. W. Fox, pp. 171-187. New Directions in Archaeology, Cambridge University Press, Cambridge.

Davis, Simon D. 1987 *The Archaeology of Animals*. Yale University Press, New Haven.

deFrance, Susanne D. 2009 Zooarchaeology in Complex Societies: Political Economy, Status, and Ideology. *Journal of Archaeological Research* 17:105–168.

deFrance, Susanne D., and Craig A. Hanson 2008 Labour, Population Movement, and Food in Sixteenth-Century Ek Balam, Yucatán. *Latin American Antiquity* 19(3):299-316.

Deines, Peter 1980 The Isotopic Composition of Reduced Organic Carbon. In *Handbook of Environmental Isotope Geochemistry*, edited by P. Fritz, and J. Ch. Fontes, pp. 329-406. Elsevier, Amsterdam.

Demarest, Arthur Andrew 2004 *Ancient Maya: The Rise and Fall of an Ancient Rainforest Civilization*. Cambridge University Press, Cambridge.

1992 Ideology in Ancient Maya Cultural Evolution: The Dynamics of Galactic Polities. In *Ideology and Pre-Columbian Civilizations*, edited by A. A. Demarest, and G. Conrad, pp. 135-157. School of American Research Seminar, School of American Research Press, Santa Fe.

Demarest, Arthur A., Prudence M. Rice, and Don S. Rice (editors) 2005 *The Terminal Classic in the Maya Lowlands: Collapse, Transition, and Transformation*. University Press of Colorado, Boulder.

De Montmollin, Olivier 1988 Settlement Scale and Theory in Maya Archaeology. In *Recent Studies in Precolumbian Archaeology*, edited by N. J. Saunders, and O. de Montmollin, pp. 63-101. BAR International Series 421, Oxford.

DeNiro, Michael J. 1987 Stable Isotopy and Archaeology. *American Scientist* 75:182-191.

1985 Post-Mortem Preservation and Alteration of 'in Vivo' Bone Collagen Ratios: Implications for Paleodietary Analysis. *Nature* 317:806-809.

DeNiro, Michael J., and Samuel Epstein Influence of Diet on the Distribution of Nitrogen Isotopes in Animals. *Geochimica et Cosmochimica Acta* 45:341-351.

1978 Influence of Diet on the Distribution of Carbon Isotopes in Animals. *Geochimica et Cosmochimica Acta* 42:495-506.

DeNiro, Michael J., and P. L.Walker 1986 Stable Nitrogen and Carbon Isotope Ratios in Bone Collagen as Indices of Prehistoric Dietary Dependence on Marine and Terrestrial Resources in Southern California. *American Journal of Physical Anthropology* 71:51-61.

DeNiro, Michael J., Margaret J. Schoeninger, and Christine A. Hastorf 1985 Effect of Heating on the Stable Carbon and Nitrogen Isotope Ratios of Bone Collagen. *Journal of Archaeological Science* 12:l-7.

Denys, Christiane 2002 Taphonomy and Experimentation. *Archaeometry* 44:469-484.

Devendhal, Kai 2005 Las Sedes del Poder: Arquitectura, Espacio, Función y Sociedad de los Conjuntos Palaciegos del Clásico Tardío en el Área Maya Evaluados desde la Arqueología y la Iconografía. PhD dissertation, IIA, UNAM, Mexico City.

Dietler, Michael 2001 Theorizing the feast: Rituals of Consumption, Commensal Politics, and Power in African Contexts. In *Feasts: Archaeological and Ethnographic Perspectives on Food, Politics, and Power*, edited by M. Dietler, and B. Hayden, pp. 65-114. Smithsonian Institution Press, Washington, D. C.

1996 Feasts and Commensal Politics in the Political Economy: Food, Power, and Status in Prehistoric Europe. In *Food and the Status Quest*, edited by P. Wiessner, and W. Schiefenhovel, pp. 87-125. Berghahn Books, Oxford.

Dietler, Michael, and Brian Hayden 2001 Digesting the Feast: Good to Eat, Good to Drink, Good to Think. In *Feasts: Archaeological and Ethnographic Perspectives on Food, Politics, and Power*, edited by M. Dietler, and B. Hayden, pp. 1-22. Smithsonian Institution Press, Washington, D. C.

Dietz, Albert A. 1946 Composition of Normal Bone Marrow in Rabbits. *Journal of Biological Chemistry* 165:505-511.

Dillon, Brian D. 1988 Meatless Maya? Ethnoarchaeological Implications for Ancient Subsistence. *Journal of New World Archaeology* 7(2-3):59-70.

Driesch, Angela von den 1976 *A Guide to the Measurement of Animal Bones from Archaeological Sites*. Peabody Museum Bulletins, Bulletin 1. Peabody Museum of Archaeology and Ethnology. Harvard University, Cambridge.

EA.FLMNH (volume II) 2003 Digital Photo Collection of Relevant Osteological Elements from 243 Neotropical and Neoartic Wild Species that Inhabit the Maya Area. Compiled by Christopher M. Götz based on the osteological collections at Florida Museum of Natural History, Gainesville, USA. Copyright by Kitty F. Emery, Environmental Archaeology, Florida Museum of Natural History.

Edwards, J. Kenneth, R. Larry Marchinton, and Gladys F. Smith Pelvic Girdle Criteria for Sex Determination of White-Tailed Deer. *Journal of Wildlife Management* 46:544-547.

Ekholm, Susanna 1990 Una Ceremonia de Fin-de-Ciclo: El Gran Basurero Ceremonial de Lagartero, Chiapas. In *La Época Clásica: Nuevos Hallazgos, Nuevas Ideas*, coordinated by A. Cardos de Méndez, pp. 455-463. Seminario de Arqueología Series. Museo Nacional de Antropología, INAH, Mexico City.

ElNesr, N. M., and J. K. Avery 1994 Tooth Eruption and Shedding. In *Oral Development and Histology*, edited by J. K. Avery, pp. 110-129. Thieme Medical Publishers, New York.

Emery, Kitty F. *Dietary, Environmental, and Societal Implications of Ancient Maya Animal Use in the Petexbatun: A Zooarchaeological Perspective on the Collapse*. Vanderbilt Institute of Mesoamerican Archaeology Series, Vol. 5. Vanderbilt University Press, Nashville.

2009 Perspectives on Ancient Maya Bone Crafting from a Classic Period Bone-Artifact Manufacturing Assemblage. *Journal of Anthropological Archaeology* 28:458-470.

2008 A Zooarchaeological Test for Dietary Resource Depression at the End of the Classic Period in the Petexbatun, Guatemala. *Human Ecology* 36:617-634.

2007a Assessing the impact of Ancient Animal Use. *Journal of Nature Conservation* 15:184-195.

2007b Aprovechamiento de la Fauna en Piedras Negras: Dieta, Ritual y Artesanía del Periodo Clásico Maya. *Mayab* 19:51-69.

2004a Animals from the Maya Underworld: Reconstructing Elite Maya Ritual at the Cueva de los Quetzales, Guatemala. In *Behaviour Behind Bones: The Zooarchaeology of Ritual, Religion, Status, and Identity*, edited by S. Jones O'Day, W. Van Neer, and A. Ervynck, pp. 101-113. Proceedings of the 9th Conference of the International Council of Archaeology, Durham, August 2002, Oxbow, Oxford.

2004b In Search of Assemblage Comparability: Methods in Maya Zooarchaeology. In *Maya Zooarchaeology: New Directions in Method and Theory*, edited by K. F. Emery, pp. 15-34. Cotsen Institute of Archaeology, UCLA Press, Los Angeles.

2004c Maya Zooarchaeology: In Pursuit of Social Variability and Environmental Heterogeneity. In *Continuity and Changes in Maya Archaeology: Perspectives at the Millenium*, edited by C. W. Golden, and G. Borgsted, pp. 193-217. Routledge, New York.

2004d In Search of the 'Maya Diet': Is Regional Comparison Possible in the Maya Tropics? *Archaeofauna* 13:37-56.

2004e (ed.) *Maya Zooarchaeology: New Directions in Method and Theory*. Cotsen Institute of Archaeology Monogram 51. University of California, Los Angeles.

2003 The Noble Beast: Status and Differential Access to Animals in the Maya World. *World Archaeology* 34: 498–515.

2002 Evidencia Temprana de Explotación Animal en el Altiplano de Guatemala. *Utz'ib* 3(2):1-16.

2001 Informe Zooarqueológico 2000: Utilización de Animales por la Élite de Piedras Negras. In *Proyecto Arqueológico Piedras Negras: Informe Preliminar No. 4, Cuarta Temporada, 2000*, edited by H. Escobedo, and S. D. Houston, pp. 559-566. Instituto de Antropología e Historia, Guatemala City.

2000 Isotopic Analysis of Ancient Deer Bone: Biotic Stability in Collapse Period Maya Land-Use. *Journal of Archaeological Science* 27:537-550.

1999 Zooarqueología y el Colapso Maya en Petexbatún. In *XII Simposio de Investigaciones Arqueológicas en Guatemala, 1998*, edited by J. P. Laporte, and H. L. Escobedo, pp. 834-849. Museo Nacional de Arqueología y Etnología, Guatemala.

1998 Uso de Fauna en Grupos Domésticos: Dieta y Ritual en Aguateca. In *Informe Preliminar del Proyecto Aguateca: La Temporada de 1998*, edited by T. Inomata, E. Ponciano, and D. Triadan, pp. 52-66. Instituto de Antropología e Historia de Guatemala, Guatemala City.

1997 The Maya Collapse: A Zooarchaeological Inquiry. PhD dissertation, Cornell University, Ithaca.

1990 Postclassic and Colonial Period Dietary Strategies in the Southern Maya Lowlands: Faunal Analyses from Lamanai and Tipu, Belize. MA thesis, University of Toronto, Toronto.

1986 Variation in a Tropical Gastropod Population: Implications for Ancient Maya Subsistence Patterns. BS dissertation, Trent University, Peterbourough, Ontario.

Emery, Kitty F., and K. Aoyama 2007 Bone, Shell, and Lithic Evidence for Crafting in Elite Maya Households at Aguateca, Guatemala. *Ancient Mesoamerica* 18:69-89.

Emery, Kitty F., and Linda A. Brown 2012 Maya Hunting Sustainability: Perspectives from Past and Present. In *The Ethics of Anthropology and Amerindian Research: Reporting on Environmental Degradation and Warfare*, edited by R. J. Chacon, and R. G. Mendoza, pp. 79-116. Springer, New York.

Emery, Kitty F., and Erin K. Thornton 2008a Zooarchaeological Habitat Analysis of Ancient Maya Landscape Changes. *Journal of Ethnobiology* 28(2):154-178.

2008b A Regional Perspective on Biotic Change during the Classic Maya Occupation using Zooarchaeological Isotopic Chemistry. *Quaternary International* 191(1):131-143.

Emery, Kitty F., Lori E. Wright, and Henry Schwarcz 2000 Isotopic Analysis of Ancient Deer Bone: Biotic Stability in Collapse Period Maya Land-Use. *Journal of Archaeological Science* 27:537-550.

Emery, Kitty F., Linda Brown, Elyse Anderson, Erin K. Thornton, and Michelle LeFebvre 2009 Etnozoología de Depósitos Rituales de los Mayas Modernos e Implicaciones para la Interpretación de la Dieta y del Ritual de los Antiguos Mayas. In *XXII Simposio de Investigaciones Arqueológicas en Guatemala*. Museo Nacional de Arqueología y Etnología, edited by J. P. Laporte, B. Arroyo, and H. E. Mejía, pp. 783-790. Ministerio de Cultura y Deportes; Instituto de Antropología e Historia, Asociación Tikal. Guatemala City.

Emmons, Louise H., and Francoise Feer 1997 *Neotropical Rainforest Mammals: A Field Guide*. University of Chicago Press, Chicago.

Engelbrecht, William 2003 *Iroquoia: The development of a Native World*. Syracuse University Press, Syracuse.

Eppich, Keith 2009 Feast and Sacrifice at El Perú-Waka': The N14-2 Deposit as Dedication. *The PARI Journal* 10(2):1-19.

Escobedo, Héctor, and Stephen Houston 2004 La Antigua Ciudad Maya de Piedras Negras, Guatemala. *Arqueología Mexicana* 66:52-55.

Fedick, Scott L. 2010 The Maya Forest: Destroyed or Cultivated by the Ancient Maya? *PNAS* 107(3):953-954.

Flannery, Kent V., and Marcus C. Winter 1976 Analysing Household Activities. In *The Early Mesoamerican Village*, edited by K. V. Flannery, pp. 34 47. Academic Press, Orlando.

Flores Esquivel, Atasta 2010 *Centros Cívico-Ceremoniales Menores o 'Sitios de Orden Secundario' en la Región de Palenque*. Electronic document, http://www.mesoweb.com/es/articulos/Flores/centros-secundarios-Palenque, accessed June 30, 2010. MESOWEB.

Fogel, M. L., N. Turros, and D. Owsley 1989 Nitrogen Isotope Tracers of Human Lactation in Modern and Archaeological Populations. *Annual Report of the Director, Geophysical Laboratory, Carnegie Institution of Washington, 1988-1989*, pp. 111-116. Carnegie Institution of Washington, Washington, D. C.

Fogelin, Lars 2007 The Archaeology of Religious Ritual. *The Annual Review of Anthropology* 36:55-71.

Foreman, Lyndsay 2004 The Truth about Deer, Turtles, and Dogs: An examination of Ancient Maya Human-Faunal Interactions. *Totem: The University of Western Ontario Journal of Anthropology*, 12(1):32-48.

Ford, Anabel 1991 Economic Variation of Ancient Maya Residential Settlement in the Upper Belize River Area. *Ancient Mesoamerica* 2:35-45.

Ford, Anabel, and Ronald Nigh 2009 Origins of the Maya Forest Garden: Maya Resource Management. *Journal of Ethnobiology* 29(2): 213–236.

Foster, Lynn V. 2002 *Handbook to Life in the Ancient Maya World*. Oxford University Press, Oxford.

Fox, John Gerard 1996 Playing with Power: Ballcourts and Political Ritual in Southern Mesoamerica. *Current Anthropology* 37(3):483-509.

Freidel, David 1992 Children of the First Father Skull: Terminal Classic Warfare in the Northern Maya Lowlands and the Transformation of Kingship and Elite Hierarchies. In *Mesoamerican Elites: An Archaeological Assessment*, edited by D. Z. Chase, and A. F. Chase, pp. 99-177. University of Oklahoma, Norman.

1986 Maya Warfare: An Example of Peer-Polity Interaction. In *Peer Polity Interaction and Socio-Political Change*, edited by C. Renfrew, and J. F. Cherry, pp. 93-108. Cambridge University Press, Cambridge.

Freidel, David A., and Linda Schele 1989 Dead Kings and Living Temples: Dedication and Termination Rituals among the Ancient Maya. In *Word and Image in Maya Culture*, edited by W. F. Hanks, and D. S. Rice, pp. 233-243. University of Utah Press, Salt Lake City.

Freidel, David A., Charles K. Suhler, and Rafael Cobos Palma 2010 *Termination Ritual Deposits at Yaxuna: Detecting the Historical in Archaeological Contexts*. Electronic document, http://maya.csuhayward.edu/yaxuna/termination.html, accessed June 11, 2010. Harvard University.

Freiwald, Carolyn R. 2010 Dietary Diversity in the Upper Belize River Valley: A Zooarchaeological and Isotopic Perspective. In *Pre-Columbian Foodways: Interdisciplinary Approaches to Food, Culture, and Markets in Ancient Mesoamerica*, edited by J. E. Staller, and M. D. Carrasco, pp. 399-420. Springer, New York.

Fridberg, Diana Peccaries in Ancient Maya Economy, Ideology, and Iconography. BA thesis, Harvard University, Cambridge.

Fried, Morton Herbert 1967 *The Evolution of Political Society: An Essay in Political Anthropology*. Studies in Anthropology 7. Random House, New York.

Garber, James F. 1989 *The Artifacts*. Series Archaeology at Cerros Belize, Central America, Vol. II, D. Freidel, series editor. Southern Methodist University Press, Dallas.

1983 Patterns of Jade Consumption and Disposal at Cerros, in Northern Belize. *American Antiquity* 48(4):800-807.

Garber, James F., W. David Driver, Lauren A. Sullivan, and David M. Glassman 1998 Bloody Bowls and Broken Pots: The Life, Death, and Rebirth of a Maya House. In *The Sowing and the Dawning: Termination, Dedication, and Transformation in the Archaeological and Ethnographic Record of Mesoamerica*, edited by S. Boteler Mock, pp. 124-133. University of New Mexico Press, Albuquerque.

García Moll, Roberto 2003 *La Arquitectura de Yaxchilán*. CONACULTA, INAH, Mexico City.

1996 Yaxchilán, Chiapas. *Arqueología Mexicana* 4(22):36-45.

Garvey, Jillian 2011 Bennett's Wallaby (*Macropus rufogriseus*) Marrow Quality vs. Quantity: Evaluating Human Decision-Making and Seasonal Occupation in Late Pleistocene Tasmania. *Journal of Archaeological Science* 38(4):763-783.

Gautier, Achiles 1987 Taphonomic Groups: How and Why. *Archaeozoologia* 12:47-52.

Gero, Joan M. 1990 Pottery, Power, and... Parties! *Archaeology* 1990:52-56.

Gerry, John Phillip 1997 Bone Isotope Ratios and Their Bearing on Elite Privilege Among the Classic Maya. *Geoarcharchaeology: An International Journal* 12(1):41-69.

1993 Diet and Status among the Classic Maya: An Isotopic Perspective. PhD dissertation, Harvard University, Cambridge.

Gerry, John P., and Harold W. Krueger 1997 Regional Diversity in Classic Maya diets. In *Bones of the Maya: Studies of Ancient Skeletons*, edited by S. Whittington, and D. M. Reed, pp. 196-207. Smithsonian Institution Press, Washington, D. C.

Gifford, Diane P. 1984 Taphonomic Specimens, Lake Turkana. *National Geographic Research Reports* 17:419-428.

Gilbert, F. 1966 Aging White-tailed Deer by Annuli in the Cementum of the First Incisor. *Journal of Wildlife Management* 30:200-202.Glassman, David M., James M. Conlon, and James F. Garber 1995 Survey and Initial Excavations at Floral Park. In *The Belize Valley Archaeology Project: Results of the 1994 Field Season*. Department of Archaeology, Belmopan, Belize.

Goodman, Alan H., Debra L. Martin, and George J. Armelagos 1984 Indications of Stress from Bone and Teeth. In *Paleopathology at the Origins of Agriculture*, edited by M. N. Cohen, and G. J. Armelagos, pp. 13-49. Academic Press, Orlando.

Golden, Charles, and Andrew Scherer 2006 Border problems: Recent archaeological research along the Usumacinta River. *The PARI Journal* 6(4):1-16.

Goldstein, David J., and Jon B. Hageman 2010 Power Plants: Paleobotanical evidence of rural feasting in Late Classic Belize. In *Precolumbian Foodways: Interdisciplinary Approaches to Food, Culture, and Markets in Ancient Mesoamerica*, edited by J. E. Staller, and M. Carrasco, pp. 421-440. Springer, New York.

Götz, Christopher 2008 Coastal and inland patterns of faunal exploitation in the Prehispanic northern Maya lowlands. *Quaternary International* 191 (2008) 154–169.

2005 La Fauna Arqueológica de Chichen Itzá: Nuevas Evidencias del Uso Prehispánico de Vertebrados con Base en las Recientes Excavaciones del INAH. Paper presented at the Segundo Congreso Internacional de Cultura Maya, March 13-19, 2005, Mérida, Mexico.

2004 Informe de los Resultados del Análisis Zooarqueológico de los Restos de Fauna Excavados en Dzibilchaltun, Yucatán. Technical Report submitted to Centro INAH-Yucatán, Mérida.

Grant, Annie 1991 Economic or Symbolic? Animals and Ritual Behaviour. In *Sacred and Profane: Proceedings of a Conference on Archaeology, Ritual and Religion, Oxford 1989*, edited by P. Garwood, D. Jennings, R. Skeates, and J. Toms, pp. 109-114. Oxford University Committee for Archaeology, Monograph 32. Institute of Archaeology, Oxford.

Grayson, Donald K. 1984 *Quantitative Zooarchaeology: Topics in the Analysis of Archaeological Faunas*. Academic Press, Orlando.

1978 Minimum Numbers and Sample Size in Vertebrate Faunal Analysis. *American Antiquity* 43(1):53-65.

Grave Tirado, Alfonso 1996 Patrón de Asentamiento en la Región de Palenque, Chiapas. BA thesis, ENAH, SEP, Mexico City.

Greene, Merle, R. L. Rands, and J. A. Graham 1972 *Maya Sculpture from the Southern Lowlands, the Highlands and Pacific Piedmont, Guatemala, Mexico, Honduras*. Lederer, Street, and Zeus, Berkeley.

Grube, Nikolai 1992 Classic Maya Dance: Evidence from Hieroglyphs and Iconography. *Ancient Mesoamerica* 3: 201–18.

Grupe, G., Ž. Mikic, J. Peters, and H. Manhart 2003 Vertebrate food webs and subsistence strategies of Meso- and Neolithic populations of Central Europe. In *Deciphering Ancient Bones*, edited by G. Grupe, and J. Peters, pp. 193-213. Documenta Archaeolbiologiae 1. Rohden/Westf, Leidorf.

Guderjan, Thomas H., Robert J. Lichtenstein, and C. Colleen Hanratty 2003 Elite Residences at Blue Creek, Belize. In *Maya Palaces: An Interdisciplinary Approach*, edited by J. J. Christie, pp. 13-45. University of Texas Press, Austin.

Gumerman, George IV 1997 Food and Complex Societies. *Journal of Archaeological Method and Theory* 4(2):105-139.

Hageman, Jon B. 2004 The Lineage Model and Archaeological Data in Late Classic Northwestern Belize. *Ancient Mesoamerica* 15:63-74.

Hale, James B. 1949 Aging Cottontail Rabbits by Bone Growth. *Journal of Wildlife Management* 13(2):216-225.

Hall, Raymond E. 1981 *The Mammals of North America*, Vols. I and II. Second Edition, John Wiley and Sons, New York.

Halperin, Christina T., and Antonia E. Foias 2010 Pottery Politics: Late Classic Maya Palace Production at Motul de San José, Petén, Guatemala. *Journal of Anthropological Archaeology* 29:392–411.

Halperin, Christina T., Sergio Garza, Keith M. Prufer, and James E. Brady 2003 Caves and Ancient Maya Ritual Use of *Jute*. *Latin American Antiquity* 14(2):207-219.

Hamblin, Nancy L. 1984 *Animal Use by the Cozumel Maya*. University of Arizona Press, Tucson.

1980 Animal utilization by the Cozumel Maya: Interpretation through faunal analysis. Unpublished PhD Dissertation, University of Arizona, Tucson.

Hamerow, Helena 2006 'Special Deposits' in Anglo-Saxon Settlements. *Medieval Archaeology* 50:1-30.

Hammond, Norman 1999 Ritual and Economy of the Preclassic Maya: Recent Evidences from Cuello, Belize. In *The Archaeology of Mesoamerica: Mexican and European Perspectives*, edited by W. Bray, and L. Manzanilla, pp. 83-96. British Museum Press, London.

Hammond, Norman, and Wendy Ashmore 1981 Lowland Maya Settlement: Geographical and Chronological Frameworks. In *Lowland Maya Settlement Patterns*, edited by W. Ashmore, pp. 19-35. School of American Research, Santa Fe.

Hansen, Richard D. 1998 Continuity and Disjunction: The Pre-Classic Antecedents of Classic Maya Architecture. In *Function and Meaning in Classic Maya Architecture*, edited by S. D. Houston, pp. 49-122. Dumbarton Oaks Research Library and Collection, Washington, D. C.

Harrison-Buck, Eleanor, Patricia A. McAnany, and Rebecca Storey 2007 Empowered and Disempowered During the Late to Terminal Classic Transition: Maya Burial and Termination Rituals in the Sibun Valley, Belize. In *New Perspectives on Human Sacrifice and Ritual Body Treatments in Ancient Maya Society*, edited by V. Tiesler, and A. Cucina, pp. 74-101. Springer, New York.

Hastorf, Christine A. 1993 *Agriculture and the Onset of Political Inequality before the Inka*. Cambridge University Press, Cambridge.

Haviland, William A. 1981 Dower Houses and Minor Centres at Tikal, Guatemala: An Investigation into the Valid Units in Settlement Hierarchies. In *Lowland Maya Settlement Patterns*, edited by W. Ashmore, pp. 89-117. University of New Mexico Press, Albuquerque.

Hayden, Brian 2009 Funerals as Feasts: Why are they so Important. *Cambridge Archaeological Journal* 19(1):29-52.

2001 Fabulous Feasts: A Prolegomenon to the Importance of Feasting. In *Feasts: Archaeological and Ethnographic Perspectives on Food, Politics, and Power*, edited by M. Dietler, and B. Hayden, pp. 23-64. Smithsonian Institution Press, Washington, D. C.

1996 Feasting in Prehistoric and Traditional Societies. In *Food and the Status Quest: An Interdisciplinary Perspective*, edited by P. Wiessner, and W. Schiefenhovel, pp. 127-147. Berghahn, Oxford.

1990 Nimrods, Piscators, Pluckers, and Planters: The Emergence of Food Production. *Journal of Anthropological Archaeology* 9:31-69.

Hayden, Brian, and Suzanne Villeneuve 2011 A Century of Feasting Studies. *Annual Review of Anthropology* 40:433-449.

Healy, Paul F., Kitty Emery, and Lori E. Wright 1990 Ancient and Modern Maya Exploitation of the *Jute* Snail (*Pachychilus*). *Latin American Antiquity* 1(2): 170-183.

Heaton, Timothy H. E., J. C. Vogel, Gertrude Chevallarie, and Gill Collet 1986 Climatic Influence on the Isotopic Composition of Bone Nitrogen. *Nature* 322:822-823.

Hedges, Robert E. M., Rhiannon E. Stevens, and Paul L. Koch 2006 Isotopes in Bone and Teeth. In *Isotopes in Paleoenvironmental Research*, edited by M. J. Leng, pp. 117-145. Developments in Paleoenvironmental Research 10. Springer, Dordrecht.

Hellmuth, N. 1978 *Tikal Copan Travel Guide: A General Introduction to Maya Art, Architecture, and Archaeology*. Foundation for Latin American Anthropological Research, St. Louis.

Hendon, Julia 2003 Feasting at Home: Community and House Solidarity among the Maya of Southeastern Mesoamerica. In *The Archaeology and Politics of Food and Feasting in Early States and Empires*, edited by T. L. Bray, pp. 203-233. Kluwer Academic/Plenum Publishers, New York.

2002 Household and State in Pre-Hispanic Maya Society: Gender, Identity and Practice. In *Ancient Maya Gender Identity and Relations*, edited by L. Gustafson, and A. M. Trevelyan, pp. 75-92. Bergin and Garvey, Westport.

1999 Multiple Sources of Prestige and the Social Evaluation of Women in Prehistoric Mesoamerica. In *Material Symbols: Culture and Economy in Prehistory*, edited by J. Robb, pp. 257-276. Occasional Paper 26. Centre for Archaeological Investigations, Southern Illinois University, Carbondale.

Women's Work, Women's Space, and Women's Status among the Classic-Period Maya Elite of the Copan Valley, Honduras. In *Women in Prehistory: North America and Mesoamerica*, edited by C. Claassen, and R. A. Joyce, pp. 33-46. University of Pennsylvania Press, Philadelphia.

Hesse, Brian, and Paula Wapnish 1985 *Animal Bone Archaeology: From Objectives to Analysis*. Manuals on Archaeology 5. Taraxacum, Washington, D. C.

Hill, Andrew 1980 Early Postmortem Damage to the Remains of Some Contemporary East African Mammals. In *Fossils in the Making*, edited by A. K. Behrensmeyer, pp. 131-152. University of Chicago Press, Chicago.

Hill, J. D. 1995 *Ritual and Rubbish in the Iron Age of Wessex: A Study on the Formation of a Specific Archaeological Record*. BAR British Series 242, Archaeopress, Oxford.

Hillson, Simon 2005 *Teeth*. Second Edition. Cambridge Manuals in Archaeology. Cambridge University Press, Cambridge.

Hodell, D. A., J. H. Curtis, and M. Brenner 1995 Possible Role of Climate in the Collapse of Classic Maya Civilization. *Nature* 375:391-394.

Hooton, E. A. 1940 Skeletons from the Cenote of Sacrifice at Chichen Itzá. In *The Maya and their Neighbours: Essays on Middle American Anthropology and Archaeology*, edited by C. L. Hay, R. L. Linton, S. K. Lothrop, H. Shapiro, and G. C. Vaillant, pp. 272-280. Appleton-Century, New York.

Hopkins, Mary Randolph 1992 Mammalian Remains. In *Artefacts from the Cenote of Sacrifice, Chichen Itzá, Yucatán*, pp.369-385. Memoirs of the Peabody of Archaeology and Ethnology, vol. 10, No. 3, edited by Clemency C. Coggins. Harvard University Press, Cambridge.

Houston, Stephen D. 1993 *Hieroglyphs and History at Dos Pilas: Dynastic Polities of the Classic Maya*. University of Texas Press, Austin.

Houston, S. D., and D. Stuart 2001 Peopling the Classic Maya Court. In *Royal Courts of the Ancient Maya: Theory, Comparison, and Synthesis*, Vol. 1, by T. Inomata, and S. D. Houston, pp. 54-83. Westview Press, Boulder.

Hülls, Matthias C., Pieter Grootes, and Marie-Josee Vadeau 2007 How Clean is Ultrafiltration Cleaning of Bone Collagen? *Radiocarbon* 49(2):193-200.

Hutson, Scott R., and Travis W. Stanton 2007 Cultural logic and practical reason: The Structure of Discard in Ancient Maya Houselots. *Cambridge Archaeological Journal* 17(2):123-144.

Hutson, Scott R., Travis W. Stanton, Aline Magnoni, Richard Terry, and Jason Craner Beyond the Buildings: Formation Processes of Ancient Maya Houselots and Methods for the Study of Non-architectural Space. *Journal of Anthropological Archaeology* 26:442-473.

INAH Noticias 2011 Descubren la Cocina Real de Kabah. Instituto Nacional de Antropología e Historia (INAH), Boletín 381. Electronic document, http://www. inahnoticias.mx, accessed 16 November 2011. INAH.

Inomata, Takeshi 2006 Plazas, Performers and Spectators: Political Theatres of the Classic Maya. *Current Anthropology* 47(5): 805-842.

2003 War, Destruction, and Abandonment: The Fall of the Classic Maya Centre of Aguateca, Guatemala. In *The Archaeology of Settlement Abandonment in Middle America*, edited by T. Inomata, and R. W. Webb, pp. 43-60. University of Utah Press, Salt Lake City.

Inomata, Takeshi, Daniela Triadan, Erick Ponciano, Estela Pinto, Richard E. Terry, and Markus Eberl 2002 Domestic and Political Lives of Classic Maya Elites: The Excavation of Rapidly Abandoned Structures at Aguateca, Guatemala. *Latin American Antiquity* 13(3):305-330.

Jackson, H. Edwin, and Susan L. Scott 2003 Patterns of Elite Faunal Utilization at Moundville, Alabama. *American Antiquity* 68(3):552-572.

James, S. R. 1997 Methodological Issues Concerning Screen Size Recovery Rates and Their Effects on Archaeofaunal Interpretations. *Journal of Archaeological Science* 24:385-397.

Jiménez, Socorro del P. 2009 Apuntes Preliminares y Catalogación de la Cerámica de Chinikihá, Chiapas: Temporada de Gabinete 2007-2009. In Segundo Informe Parcial Proyecto Arqueológico Chinikihá, Temporada 2008, edited by R. Liendo Stuardo. Electronic document, httm://*www.mesoweb.com/resources/informes/Chinikihá2008, accessed December 1*, 2009. MESOWEB.

Jing, Yuan, and Rowan Flad 2005 New Zooarchaeological Evidence for Changes in Shang Dynasty Animal Sacrifice. *Journal of Anthropological Archaeology* 24:252-270.

Johnson, Eileen Current Developments in Bone Technology. In *Advances in Archaeological Method and Theory*, edited by M. B. Schiffer, pp. 157-235. Academic Press, New York.

Jolón Morales, Mario Roberto 2005 Avances del Tema de Cacería en Guatemala: Diagnóstico. Centro de Estudios Conservacionistas (CECON), and Asociación de Profesionales en Biodiversidad y Medio Ambiente (PROBIOMA). Guatemala City.

Jones, Emily Lena Prey Choice, Mass Collecting, and the Wild European Rabbit (*Oryctolagus Cuniculus*). *Journal of Anthropological Archaeology* 25(3):275-289.

Jones, Kevin T., and Duncan Metcalfe Bare Bones Archaeology: Bones Marrow Indices and Efficiency. *Journal of Archaeological Science* 15:415-423.

Jones, G., T., and R. D. Leonard 1989 The Concept of Diversity: An Introduction. In *Quantifying Diversity in Archaeology*, edited by R. D. Leonard, and G. T. Jones, pp. 1-3. Cambridge University Press, Cambridge.

Joyce, Rosemary A. 2001 Archaeology of Ritual and Symbolism. In *International Encyclopedia of the Social and Behavioural Science*s, edited by N. J. Smelser, and P. B. Baltes, pp. 13371-13375. Elsevier, Oxford.

Joyce, Rosemary A., and John Henderson 2007 From Feasting to Cuisine: Implications of Archaeological Research in an Early Honduran Village. *American Anthropologist* 109(4):642–653.

Kan, Sergei 1989 *Symbolic Immortality: the Tlingit Potlatch of the 19th Century.* Smithsonian Institute Press, Washington, D. C.

Kansa, Sarah Whitcher, and Stuart Campbell 2004 Feasting with the dead? A ritual bone deposit at Domuztepe, South Eastern Turkey (*c.* 5550 BC). *Proceedings of the 9th ICAZ Conference, Durham 2002, vol 1: Behaviour Behind Bones*, edited by S. Jones O'Day, W. Van Neer, and A. Ervynck, pp. 2-13. International Council for Archaeozoology. Oxbow, Oxford.

Katzenberg, M. Ann 2008 Stable Isotope Analysis: A Tool for Studying Past Diet, Demography, and Life History. In *Biological Anthropology of the Human Skeleton*, edited by M. A. Katzenberg, and S. R. Saunders, pp.413-441. Wiley-Liss, New York.

Katzenberg, M. Anne, D. A. Herring, and Sally R. Saunders 1996 Weaning and Infant Mortality: Evaluating the Skeletal Evidence. *Yearbook of Physical Anthropology* 39:177-199.

Katzenberg, M. A., and J. H. Kelley 1991 Stable Isotope Analysis of Prehistoric Bone from the Sierra Blanca Region of New Mexico. In *Mogollon V: Proceedings of the 1988 Mogollon Conference*, edited by P. H. Beckett, pp. 207-209. COAS Publishing and Research, Las Cruces.

Katzenberg, M. Anne, and Nancy C. Lovell 1999 Stable Isotope Variation in Pathological Bone. *International Journal of Osteoarchaeology* 9:316-324.

Kay, M. 1974 Dental Annuli Age Determination on White-Tailed Deer from Archaeological Sites. *Plains Anthropologist* 19:224-227.

Keegan, William F., and Michael J. DeNiro 1988 Stable Carbon and Nitrogen-Isotope Ratios of Collagen used to Study Coral Reef and Terrestrial Components of Prehistoric Bahamian Diet. *American Antiquity* 53: 320-336.

Kelly, Lucretia S. 2001 A Case of Ritual Feasting at the Cahokia Site. In *Feasts: Archaeological and Ethnographic Perspectives on Food, Politics, and Power*, edited by M. Dietler, and B. Hayden, pp. 334-367. Smithsonian Institution Press, Washington, D. C.

Kent, Susan 1993. Variability in Faunal Assemblages: The Influence of Hunting Skill, Sharing, Dogs, and Mode of Cooking on Faunal Remains at a Sedentary Kalahari Community. *Journal of Anthropological Archaeology* 12:323-385.

Kidder, Alfred V. 1947 *The Artifacts of Uaxactun, Guatemala.* Carnegie Institution of Washington. Publication 576. Washington, D. C.

Kintigh, Keith W. 1989 Sample Size, Significance, and Measures of Diversity. In *Quantifying Diversity in Archaeology*, edited by R. D. Leonard, and G. T. Jones, pp. 25-36. Cambridge University Press, Cambridge.

Kirch, Patrick V. 2001 Polynesian Feasting in Ethnohistoric, Ethnographic, and Archaeological Contexts: A Comparison of Three Societies. In *Feasts: Archaeological and Ethnographic Perspectives on Food, Politics, and Power*, edited by M. Dietler, and B.

Hayden, pp. 168-184. Smithsonian Institution Press, Washington, D. C.

Kirchhoff, Paul 1963 The Tribes North of the Orinoco River. In *Handbook of South American Indians*, Vol. 4, edited by J. H. Steward, pp. 481-493. Cooper Square Publishers, New York.

Klein, Richard, and Kathryn Cruz-Uribe 1984 *The Analysis of Animal Bones from Archaeological Sites*. Prehistoric Archaeology and Ecology Series. University of Chicago Press, Chicago.

Koželsky, Kristin L. 2005 Identifying Social Drama in the Maya Region: Fauna from the Lagartero Basurero, Chiapas, Mexico. MA dissertation, Florida State University, Tallahasse.

Krueger, Harold W. 1991 Exchange of Carbon with Biological Apatite. *Journal of Archaeological Science* 18:355-361.

Krueger, Harold W., and Charles H. Sullivan 1984 Models for Carbon Isotope Fractionation between Diet and Bone. In *Stable Isotopes in Nutrition*, edited by J. F. Turnland, and P. E. Hohnson, pp. 205-220. ACS Symposium, American Chemical Society, Washington, D. C.

Kunen, Julie L., Mary Jo Galindo, and Erin Chase 2002 Pits and Bones: Identifying Maya Behaviour in the Archaeological Record. *Ancient Mesoamerica* 13:197-211.

LaMotta, Vincent M., and Michael B. Schiffer 2005 Archaeological Formation Processes. In *Archaeology: The Key Concepts*, edited by C. Renfrew, and P. Bahn, pp. 121-127. Routledge Key Guides, London.

Larsen, Clark Spencer 1997 *Bioarchaeology: Interpreting Behaviour from the Human Skeleton*. Cambridge Studies in Biological Anthropology 21. Cambridge University Press, Cambridge.

Lau, George F. 2002 Feasting and Ancestor Veneration at Chinchawas, North Highlands of Ancash, Peru. *Latin American Antiquity* 13(3):279-304.

LeCount, Lisa J. 2001 Like Water for Chocolate: Feasting and Political Ritual among the Late Classic Maya at Xunantunich, Belize. *American Anthropologist* 103(4):935-953.

1999 Polychrome Pottery and Political Strategies in Late and Terminal Classic Lowland Maya Society. *Latin American Antiquity* 10:239-258.

1996 Pottery and Power: Feasting, Gifting, and Displaying Wealth among the Late and Terminal Classic Lowland Maya. PhD dissertation, University of California, Los Angeles.

Lee-Thorp, Julia A., and Nikolaas J. van der Merwe 1987 Carbon Isotope Analysis of Fossil Bone Apatite. *South African Journal of Science* 83:71-74.

Lee-Thorp, Julia A., Nikolaas J. van der Merwe, and Judith C. Sealy 1989 Stable Carbon Isotope Ratio Differences between Bone Collagen and Bone Apatite, and their Relationship to Diet. *Journal of Archaeological Science* 16(6):585-599.

Lentz, David L. 1991 Maya Diets of the Rich and Poor: Paleoethnobotanical Evidence from Copan. *Latin American Antiquity* 2(3):269-287.

León, Perla, and Salvador Montiel 2008 Wild Meat Use and Traditional Hunting Practices in a Rural Mayan Community of the Yucatán Peninsula, Mexico. *Human Ecology* 36:249-257.

Lewall, E. F., and I. McT. Cowan Age Determination in Black-Tail Deer by Degree of Ossification of the Epiphyseal Plate in the Long Bones. *Canadian Journal of Zoology* 41:629-636.

Liendo Stuardo, Rodrigo 2012 *Cuarto Informe Parcial Proyecto Arqueológico Chinikihá, Temporada 2011*. Electronic document, http://www.famsi.com/resources/informes/Chinikihá2011, accessed April 12, 2012. FAMSI.

2010 *Tercer Informe Parcial Proyecto Arqueológico Chinikihá, Temporada 2010*. Electronic document, http://www.famsi.com/resources/informes/Chinikihá2010, accessed December 3, 2011. FAMSI.

2009a Inferencias sobre el Paisaje Político de Palenque en Época Prehispánica. In *La Estructura Política de las Capitales Mayas: Algunas Aportaciones*, edited by A. L. Izquierdo. Electronic document, http://www.mesoweb/es/articulos/liendo/Inferencias, accessed December 1, 2009, MESOWEB.

2009b *Segundo Informe Parcial Proyecto Arqueológico Chinikihá, Temporada 2008*. Electronic document, http://www.famsi.com/resources/informes/Chinikihá2008, accessed December 1, 2009. FAMSI.

2007a *Proyecto Arqueológico Chinikihá, Temporada 2006*. Electronic document, http://www.famsi.org, accessed February 12, 2011. FAMSI.

2007b The Problem of Political Integration in the Kingdom of Baak: A Regional Perspective for Settlement Patterns in the Palenque Region. In *Palenque: Recent Investigations at the Classic Maya Centre*, edited by D. B. Marken, pp. 85-106. Altamira, Lamham.

2005a An Archaeological Study of Settlement Distribution in the Palenque Area, Chiapas, Mexico. *Anthropological Notebooks* 11:31-44.

2005b Estrategias de Dominio Político Regional en el Reino de B'aak. *Mayab* 18:69-75.

2003 *La Organización de la Producción Agrícola en un Centro Maya del Clásico: Patrón de Asentamiento en la Región de Palenque, Chiapas, México*. Instituto Nacional de Antropología e Historia, University of Pittsburg, Mexico City.

1999 The Organization of Agricultural Production at a Classic Maya Centre: Settlement Patterns in the Palenque Region, Chiapas, Mexico. PhD dissertation, University of Pittsburgh, Pittsburgh.

López Bravo, Roberto 2006 Platillos Suculentos en Vajillas Elegantes: Un Acercamiento a la 'Alta Cocina' del Clásico Maya. *Lakamha'* (Segunda Época) 20: 3-8.

2005 El Preclásico Tardío en la Región de Palenque: Perspectivas de Investigación y Datos Recientes. *Mayab* 18:45-55.

Lucero, Lisa 2006 *Water and Ritual: The Rise and Fall of Classic Maya Rulers*. University of Texas Press, Austin.

2003 *The Politics of Ritual: The Emergence of Classic Maya Rulers. Current Anthropology 44(4): 523-558.*

Lupo, Karen 1998 Experimentally Derived Extraction Rates for Marrow: Implications for Body Part Exploitation Strategies of Plio-Pleistocene Hominid Scavengers. *Journal of Archaeological Science* 25(7): 657-675.

Lyman, R. Lee 2008 *Quantitative Paleozoology*. Cambridge Manuals in Archaeology. Cambridge University Press, New York.

2005 Analysing Cut Marks: Lessons from Artiodactyl Remains in the Northwestern United States. *Journal of Archaeological Science* 32:1722-1732.

1995 A Study of Variation in the Prehistoric Butchery of Large Artiodactyls. In *Ancient People and Landscapes*, edited by E. Johnson, pp. 233-253. Museum of Texas Tech University, Lubbock.

1994 *Vertebrate Taphonomy*. Cambridge Manuals in Archaeology. Cambridge University Press, Cambridge.

1979 Available Meat from Faunal Remains: A Consideration of Techniques. *American Antiquity* 44(3):536-546.

1976 A Cultural Analysis of Faunal Remains from the Alpowa Locality. MA thesis, Department of Anthropology, Washington State University, Vancouver.

Lyman, R. Lee, and G. L. Fox A Critical Evaluation of Bone Weathering as an Indication of Bone Assemblage Formation. *Journal of Archaeological Science* 16:293-317.

Madrigal, T. Cregg, and Julie Zimmermann Holt 2002 White-Tailed Deer Meat and Marrow Return Rates and Their Application to Eastern Woodlands Archaeology. *American Antiquity* 67(4): 745-759.

Maler, Teobert 1901 *Researches in the Central Portion of the Usumatsintla Valley: Report of Explorations for the Museum 1898-1900*. Memoirs of the Peabody Museum of Archaeology and Ethnology Vol. 2, Num. 1. Harvard University Press, Cambridge.

Mandujano, Salvador, and Víctor Rico-Gray 1991 Hunting, Use, and Knowledge of the Biology of the White-Tailed Deer (*Odocoileus virginianus*) by the Maya of Central Yucatán, Mexico. *Journal of Ethnobiology* 11(2):175-183.

Mansell, Eugenia Brown, Robert H. Tykot, David A. Freidel, Bruce H. Dahlin, and Traci Ardren 2006 Early to Terminal Classic Maya Diet in the Northern Lowlands of the Yucatán (Mexico). In *Histories of Maize: Multidisciplinary Approaches to the Prehistory, Linguistics, Biogeography, Domestication, and Evolution of Maize*, edited by J. E. Staller, R. H. Tykot, and B. F. Benz, pp. 173-185. Academic Press, Boston.

Marciniak, Arkadiusz 1999 Faunal Materials and Interpretive Archaeology—Epistemology Reconsidered. *Journal of Archaeological Method and Theory* 6(4):293-320.

Marcus, Joyce 1999 Men's and Women's Ritual in Formative Oaxaca. In *Social Patterns in Pre-Classic Mesoamerica*, edited by D. C. Grove, and R. A. Joyce, pp. 67-96. Dumbarton Oaks, Washington, D. C.

1993 Ancient Maya Political Organization. In *Lowland Maya Civilization in the Eighth Century AD*, edited by J. A. Sabloff, and J. S. Henderson, pp. 111-183. Dumbarton Oaks, Washington, D. C.

1976 *Emblem and State in the Classic Maya Lowlands: An Epigraphic Approach to Territorial Organization*. Dumbarton Oaks, Washington, D. C.

1973 Territorial Organization of the Lowland Classic Maya. *Science* 180: 911-916.

Marshall, Fiona, and Tom Pilgram 1991 Meat versus Within-Bone Nutrients: Another Look at the Meaning of Body Part Representation in Archaeological Sites. *Journal of Archaeological Science* 18:149-163.

Marken, Damien B., and Arnoldo González Cruz 2007 Elite Residential Compounds at Late Classic Palenque. In *Palenque: Recent Investigations at the Classic Maya Centre*, edited by D. B. Marken, pp. 135-160. Altamira Press, Lanham.

Marken, Damien B., and Kirk D. Straight 2007 Conclusion: Reconceptualizing the Palenque Polity. In *Palenque: Recent Investigations at the Classic Maya Centre*, edited by D. B. Marken, pp. 279-324. Altamira Press, Lanham.

Martin, Simon, and Nikolai Grube 2000 *Chronicle of the Maya Kings and Queens: Deciphering the Dynasties of the Ancient Maya*. Thames and Hudson, New York.

1995 Maya Superstates. *Archaeology* 48(6):41-46.

Marquina, Ignacio 1939 *Atlas Arqueológico de la República Mexicana*. Instituto Panamericano Geografía e Historia, Mexico City.

Masson, Marilyn A. 2004a Fauna Exploitation from the Preclassic to the Postclassic Periods at Four Maya Settlements in Northern Belize. In *Maya Zooarchaeology: New Directions in Method and Theory*, edited by K. Emery, pp. 97-124. Cotsen Institute of Archaeology, University of California, Los Angeles.

2004b Contribution of Fishing and Hunting to Subsistence and Symbolic Expression. In *K'axob: Ritual, Work, and Family in an Ancient Maya Village*, edited by P. A. McAnany, pp. 383-397. Monumenta Archaeologica 22. The Cotsen Institute of Archaeology, University of California, Los Angeles.

1999 Animal Resource Manipulation in Ritual and Domestic Contexts at Postclassic Maya Communities. *World Archaeology* 31:93-120.

1997 Cultural Transformation at the Maya Postclassic Community at Laguna de On, Belize. *Latin American Antiquity* 8(4):293-316.

Masson, Marilyn A., and Carlos Peraza Lope Animal Use at the Postclassic Maya Centre of Mayapan. *Quaternary International* 191:170-183.

2004 Commoners in Postclassic Maya Society. In *Ancient Maya Commoners*, edited by J. C. Lohse, and F. Valdez, Jr., pp. 197-223. University of Texas Press, Austin.

Mathews, Peter 2001 The Dates of Tonina and a Dark Horse in its History. *The PARI Journal* II(1):1-6.

1991 Classic Maya Emblem Glyphs. In *Classic Maya Political History: Hieroglyphic and Archaeological Evidence*, edited by T. P. Culbert, pp. 19-29. School of American Research Advanced Seminar Series. Cambridge University Press, Cambridge.

1985 Maya Early Classic Monuments and Inscriptions. In *A Consideration of the Early Classic Period in the Maya Lowlands,* edited by G. R. Willey, and P. Mathews, pp. 5-55. Institute for Mesoamerican Studies Publication 10. State University of New York, Albany.

n/d The Maya Dates Project. Manuscript on file, La Trobe University, Melbourne.

McAnany, Patricia 1995 *Living with the Ancestors: Kinship and Kingship in Ancient Maya Society.* University of Texas Press, Austin.

1993 The Economics of Social Power and Wealth among Eighth Century Maya Households. In *Lowland Maya Civilization in the Eighth Century AD*, edited by J. A. Sabloff, and J. S. Henderson, pp. 65-89. Dumbarton Oaks, Washington, D. C.

McAnany, Patricia A. (editor) 2004 *K'axob: Ritual, Work, and Family in an Ancient Maya Village.* Monumenta Archaeologica 22. The Cotsen Institute of Archaeology, University of California, Los Angeles.

McCrea, J. M. 1950 On the Isotopic Chemistry of Carbonates and Paleotemperature Scale. *The Journal of Chemical Physics* 18(6):849-857.

McEwan, Gordon F. 2006 Inca State Origins: Collapse and regeneration in the Southern Peruvian Andes. In After *Collapse: The Regeneration of Complex Societies*, edited by G. M. Schwartz, and J. J. Nichols, pp. 85-98. The University of Arizona Press, Tucson.

McKillop, Heather 2004 *The Ancient Maya: New Perspectives.* W.W. Norton & Co., New York.

1984 Prehistoric Maya Reliance on Marine Resources: Analysis of a Midden from Moho Cay, Belize. *Journal of Field Archaeology* 11(1):25-36.

McKillop, Heather, and Terance Winemiller 2004 Ancient Maya Environment, Settlement, and diet: Quantitative and GIS Spatial Analysis of Shell from Frenchman's Cay, Belize. In *Maya Zooarchaeology*, pp. 57-80, edited by K. F. Emery. Cotsen Institute of Archaeology, Monogram 51. University of California, Los Angeles.

Medina Martín, Cecilia, and Mirna Sánchez Vargas 2007 Posthumous Body Treatments and Ritual Meaning in the Classic Period Northern Petén: A Taphonomic Approach. In *New Perspectives on Human Sacrifice and Ritual Body Treatments in Ancient Maya Society*, edited by V. Tiesler, and A. Cucina, pp. 102-119. Springer, New York.

Metcalfe, Duncan, and K. T. Jones A Reconsideration of Animal Body-Part Utility Indices. *American Antiquity* 53:486-504.

Metcalfe, J. Z., C. D. White, F. J. Longstaffe, G. Wrobel, D. Collins Cook, and K. A. Pyburn 2009 Isotopic Evidence for Diet at Chau Hiix, Belize: Testing Regional Models of Hierarchy and Heterarchy. *Latin American Antiquity* 20(1): 15-36.

Miller, Mary E., and Karl Taube 1993 *The Gods and Symbols of Ancient Mexico and the Maya: An illustrated Dictionary of Mesoamerican Religion.* Thames and Hudson, London.

Milner, Nicky, and Preston Miracle 2002 Introduction: Patterning Data and Consuming Theory. In *Consuming Passions and Patterns of Consumption*, edited by P. Miracle, and N. Milner, pp. 1-5. McDonald Institute for Archaeological Research, McDonald Institute Monograph, University of Cambridge, Cambridge.

Miracle, Preston, and Nicky Milner (eds.) 2002 *Consuming Passions and Patterns of Consumption.* McDonald Institute for Archaeological Research, University of Cambridge, Cambridge.

Mirón Marván, Esteban 2014 Las prácticas culinarias y sus recipientes cerámicos en la región de Palenque y Chinikihá durante el Clásico Tardío. BA thesis, Escuela Nacional de Antropología e Historia (ENAH-SEP), Mexico City.

2012 Anexo 1: Análisis del Material Cerámico de la Operación 114. In *Cuarto Informe Parcial Proyecto Arqueológico Chinikihá, Temporada 2011*, coordinated by Rodrigo Liendo, pp. 340-363. Electronic document, http://www.famsi.com/resources/informes/Chinikihá2011, accessed April 12, 2012. FAMSI.

Mock, Shirley Boteler 1998 *The Sowing and the Dawning: Termination, Dedication, and Transformation in the Archaeological and Ethnographic Record of Mesoamerica.* University of New Mexico Press, Albuquerque.

Moholy-Nagy, Hattula 2003 *The Artifacts of Tikal: Utilitarian Artifacts and Unworked Material.* University Museum Monograph 118, Tikal Report 27B. University of Pennsylvania, Museum of Archaeology and Anthropology, Philadelphia.

1997 Middens, construction fill, and Offerings: Evidence for the Organization of Classic Period Craft Production at Tikal, Guatemala. *Journal of Field Archaeology* 24:293-313.

1994 Tikal Material Culture: Artifacts and Social Structure at a Classic Lowland Maya City. PhD dissertation, University of Michigan, Ann Arbor.

1978 The Utilization of *Pomacea* Snails at Tikal, Guatemala. *American Antiquity* 43(1):65-73.

Moholy-Nagy, Hattula, and William R. Coe 2008 *The Artifacts of Tikal: Ornamental and Ceremonial Artifacts and Unworked Material.* Tikal Report 27, Part A. University Museum Monograph 118, University of Pennsylvania Museum of Archaeology and Anthropology, Philadelphia.

Montero López, Coral 2013 Infiriendo el contexto arqueológico a través de la tafonomía: el uso del venado cola blanca (*Odocoileus virginianus*) en Chinikihá, Chiapas. In *The Archaeology of Mesoamerican Animals*, edited by C. Götz, and K. F. Emery. Lockwood Press, Atlanta.

2009 Sacrifice and Feasting among the Classic Maya Elite, and the Importance of White-Tailed Deer: Is There a Regional Pattern? *Journal of Historical and European Studies* 2:53-68.

2008 Infiriendo el Contexto de los Restos Faunísticos a través de la Tafonomía: El Análisis de un Basurero Asociado al Palacio de Chinikihá, Chiapas. MA thesis, UNAM, FFYL, IIA, Mexico City.

Montero López, Coral, and Luis Fernando Núñez Enríquez 2011 Salud y Dieta entre los Entierros de Chinikihá: Primeros Resultados. *Estudios de Antropología Biológica* XV:139-166.

Montero López, Coral, Luis Fernando Núñez, Pedro Morales, Edith Cienfuegos, and Francisco Otero 2011 Diet and Health at Chinikihá, Chiapas, Mexico: Some Preliminary Results. *Journal of Environmental Archaeology* 16(2):82-96.

Montoliú, María Algunos Aspectos del Venado en la Religión de los Mayas de Yucatán. *Estudios de Cultura Maya* 10:149-172.

Morales Puente, Pedro 2009 Reporte de Análisis. Technical Report from the Laboratorio de Espectrometría de Masas de Isotópos Estables. Manuscript on file, Instituto de Geología, UNAM.

Moriarty, Matthew D., and Antonia E. Foias 2006 El Juego de Pelota en el Centro de Petén: Evidencia Cerámica sobre Festejos Asociados al Juego de Pelota en La Trinidad de Nosotros, Petén. In *XX Simposio de Investigaciones Arqueológicas*, edited by J. P. Laporte, B. Arroyo, and H. E. Mejía, pp. 1127-1139. Ministerio de Cultura y Deportes, Instituto de Antropología e Historia, and Asociación Tikal: Fundación Arqueológica del Nuevo Mundo, Guatemala.

Morris, Craig 1982 The Infrastructure of Inka Control in the Peruvian Central Highlands. In *The Inca and Aztec States, 1400–1800: Anthropology and History*, edited by G. A. Collier, R. I. Rosaldo, and J. D. Wirth, pp. 153–171. Academic Press, New York.

Morris, James 2008 Associated Bone Groups: One Archaeologists Rubbish is Another's Ritual Deposition. In *Changing Perspectives on the First Millennium BC*, edited by O. Davis, N. Sharples, and K. Waddington, pp. 83-98. Oxbow Books, Oxford.

Munro, Natalie D., and Leore Grosman 2010 Early Evidence (ca. 12,000 B.P.) for Feasting at a Burial Cave in Israel. *PNAS* 107(35):15362-15366.

Munson, Patrick J., and Rexford C. Garniewicz 2003 Age-mediated Survivorship of Ungulate Mandibles and Teeth in Canid-ravaged Faunal Assemblages. *Journal of Archaeological Science* 30:405-416.

Murray, Priscilla 1980 Discard Location: The Ethnographic Data. *American Antiquity* 45(3):490-502.

Naranjo, Eduardo J., Juan Carlos López-Acosta, and Rodolfo Dirzo 2010 La Cacería en México. *Biodiversitas* 91:6-10.

Naranjo, Eduardo J., Michelle M. Guerra, Richard E. Bodmer, and Jorge E. Bolanos 2004 Subsistence Hunting by Three Ethnic Groups of the Lacandon Forest, Mexico. *Journal of Ethnobiology* 24(2):233-253.

Nations, James D. 1979 Snail Shells and Maize Preparation: A Lacandon Maya Analogy. *American Antiquity* 44 (3): 568-571.

Navarro Farr, Olivia Clementina 2009 Ritual, Process, and Continuity in the Late to Terminal Classic Transition: Investigations at Structure M13-1 in the Ancient Maya site of El Peru-Waka, Peten, Guatemala. PhD dissertation, Southern Methodist University, Dallas.

Nieto-Calleja, Rosalba 2005 Restos Animales Asociados a los Cambios Arquitectónicos en Palenque, Chiapas. Paper presented at the X Jornada Académica del Seminario Permanente de Arqueología, *Iconografía de la Fauna*, Mexico City.

O´Connor, Terry P. 2000 *The Archaeology of Animal Bones*. Texas A&M University Press, College Station.

1985 On Quantifying Vertebrates—Some Skeptical Observations. *Circaea* 3(1):27-30.

O'Day, Sharyn Jones, Wim Van Neer, and Anton Ervynck (eds) 2004 *Behaviour Behind Bones: The Zooarchaeology of Ritual, Religion, Status and Identity*. Proceedings of the 9th Conference of the International Council of Archaeozoology, Durham, August 2002. Oxbow Books, Oxford.

O'Leary, Marion H. 1988 Carbon Isotopes in Photosynthesis. *Bioscience* 38(5):328-336.

Odum, E.P. 1971 *Fundamentals of Ecology*. Third Edition, W.B. Saunders Company, Philadelphia.

Olivera Carrasco, Ma. Teresa 1997 La Arqueoictiofauna de Palenque, Chiapas, México. In *Homenaje al Profesor Ticúl Álvarez*, coordinated by J. Arroyo Cabrales, and O. J. Polaco, pp. 253-278. Colección Científica, INAH, Mexico City.

Olsen, Stanley J. 1985 *Origins of the Domestic Dog: The Fossil Record*. The University of Arizona Press, Tucson.

1982 *An Osteology of Some Mammals*. Papers of the Peabody Museum of Archaeology and Ethnology, Vol. 73. Harvard University Press, Cambridge.

1974 Early Domestic Dogs in North America and Their Origins. *Journal of Field Archaeology* 1(3/4):343-345.

1972 Animal Remains from Altar de Sacrificios. In *The Artifacts of Altar de Sacrificios*, pp. 243-246, edited by G. R. Willey. Papers of the Peabody Museum of Archaeology and Ethnology, Vol. 64, Num. 1. Harvard University Press, Cambridge.

1964 *Mammal Remains from Archaeological Sites Part I: Southeastern and Southwestern United States*. Papers of the Peabody Museum of Archaeology and Ethnology, Vol. 56, Num. 1. Harvard University Press, Cambridge.

Outram, Alan K. 2002 Bone Fracture and Within-bone Nutrients: An Experimentally Based Method for Investigating Levels of Marrow Extraction. In *Consuming Passions and Patterns of Consumption*, edited by P. Miracle, and N. Milner, pp. 51-63. McDonald

Institute Monographs, University of Cambridge, Cambridge.

Padró Irizarry, Virgen Johanna Artefactos en Asta y Hueso: Una Propuesta Metodológica para su Estudio a Partir de un Ejemplar Teotihuacano. MA thesis, Facultad de Filosofía y Letras (FFL), Instituto de Investigaciones Antropológicas (IIA). Universidad Nacional Autónoma de México (UNAM), Mexico City.

Pagliaro, Jonathan B., James F. Garber, and Travis W. Stanton 2003 Evaluating the Archaeological Signature of Maya Ritual and Conflict. In *Warfare and Conflict in Ancient Mesoamerica*, edited by M. K. Brown, and T. W. Stanton, pp. 75-108. Alta Mira, Walnut Creek.

Palka, Joel W. 2002 Left/Right Symbolism and the Body in Ancient Maya Iconography and Culture. *Latin American Antiquity* 13(4):419-443.

Pauketat, Timothy R., Lucretia S. Kelly, Gayle J. Fritz, Neal H. Lopinot, Scott Elias, and Eve Hargrave

2002 The Residues of Feasting and Public Ritual at Early Cahokia. *American Antiquity* 67(2):257-279.

Pendergast, David M. 2004 Where's the Meat? Maya Zooarchaeology from an Archaeological Perspective. In *Maya Zooarchaeology: New Directions in Method and Theory*, edited by K. F. Emery, pp. 239-248. Cotsen Institute of Archaeology Monograph 51. University of California, Los Angeles.

1992 Noblesse Oblige: The Elites of Altun Ha and Lamanai, Belize. In *Mesoamerican Elites: An Archaeological Assessment*, edited by D. E. Chase, and A. F. Chase, pp. 61-79. Oklahoma Press, Oklahoma.

Pereira, Gregory 2005 The Utilization of Grooved Human Bones: A Reanalysis of Artificially Modified Human Bones Excavated by Carl Lumholtz at Zacapu, Michoacan, Mexico. *Latin American Antiquity* 16(3):293-312.

Perkins, Dexter Jr., and Patricia Daly 1968 A Hunter's Village in Neolithic Turkey. *Scientific American* 219(5):96-106.

Plunket, Patricia 2002 Introduction. In *Domestic Ritual in Ancient Mesoamerica*, edited by Patricia Plunket, pp. 1-9. The Cotsen Institute of Archaeology Monograph 46. University of California, Los Angeles.

Pohl, Mary D. 1995 Appendix D: Late Classic Maya Fauna from Settlement in the Copan Valley, Honduras: Assertion of Social Status through Animal Consumption. In *Ceramics and Artifacts from Excavations at Copan Residential Zone*, edited by G. Willey, R. Leventhal, A. Demarest, and W. Fash, pp. 459-476. Papers of the Peabody Museum, Vol. 80. Peabody Museum Press, Cambridge.

1994 The Economics and Politics of Maya Meat Eating. In *The Economic Anthropology of the State*, edited by E. M. Brumfiel, pp. 119-148. Monographs in Economic Anthropology, Society for Economic Anthropology Monograph 11. University Press of America, Lanham.

The Ethnozoology of the Maya: Faunal Remains from Five Sites in the Petén, Guatemala. In *Excavations at Seibal, Guatemala*, edited by G. R. Willey, pp. 143-

174. Peabody Museum Monographs, Vol. 18, Num. 3. Harvard University Press, Cambridge.

1985a The Privileges of Maya Elites: Prehistoric Vertebrate Fauna from Seibal. In *Prehistoric Lowland Mayas Environment and Subsistence Economy*, edited by M. Pohl, pp. 133-143. Papers of the Peabody Museum of Archaeology and Ethnology, Vol. 77. Harvard University Press, Cambridge.

1985b Osteological Evidence for Subsistence and Status. In *Prehistoric Lowland Mayas Environment and Subsistence Economy*, edited by M. Pohl, pp. 109-113. Papers of the Peabody Museum of Archaeology and Ethnology, Vol. 77. Harvard University Press, Cambridge.

1983 Maya Ritual Faunas: Vertebrate Remains from Burials, Caches, Caves, and Cenotes in the Maya Lowlands. In *Civilization in the Ancient Americas: Essays in Honour of Gordon R. Willey*, edited by R. M. Leventhal, and A. L. Kolata, pp. 55-103. University of New Mexico and Peabody Museum of Archaeology and Ethnology, Cambridge.

1981 Ritual Continuity Transformation in Mesoamerica: Reconstructing the Ancient Maya *Cuch* Ritual. *American Antiquity* 46(3):513-529.

1976 Ethnozoology of the Maya: An Analysis of Fauna from Five Sites in Peten, Guatemala. PhD dissertation, Harvard University, Massachusetts.

Pohl, Mary E., and Lawrence H. Feldman 1982 The Traditional Role of Women and Animals in Lowland Maya Economy. In Maya *Subsistence: Studies in Memory of Dennis E. Puleston*, edited by K. V. Flannery, pp. 295-311. Academic Press, New York.

Pohl, Mary E., and John M. D. Pohl 1994 Cycles of Conflict: Political Factionalism in the Maya Lowlands. In *Factional Competition and Political Development in the New World*, edited by E. M. Brumfiel, and J. W. Fox, pp. 138-157. New Directions in Archaeology, Cambridge University Press, Cambridge.

Polaco, Oscar J., Adrián Méndez-B, and Hilda Heredia 1988 Hueso Modificado: Estudio Tafonómico Contemporáneo. *TRACE*:14: 73-81.

Potter, James M., and Scott G. Ortman 2004 Community and Cuisine in the Prehispanic American Southwest. In *Identity, Feasting, and the Archaeology of the Greater Southwest: Proceedings of the 2002 Southwest Symposium*, edited by B. J. Mills, pp. 173-191. University Press of Colorado, Boulder.

Powis, Terry G. 2004 Ancient Lowland Maya Utilization of Freshwater Pearly Mussels. In *Maya Zooarchaeology*, pp. 125-140, edited by K. F. Emery. Cotsen Institute of Archaeology 51. University of California, Los Angeles.

Powis, T. G., N. Stanchly, C. D. White, P. F. Healy, J. J. Awe, and F. J. Longstaffe 1999 A reconstruction of Middle Preclassic Maya Subsistence Economy at Cahal Pech, Belize. *Antiquity* 73:364-376.

Purdue, J. R. 1983a Epiphyseal Closure in White-Tailed Deer. *Journal of Wildlife Management* 47(4):1207-1213.

1983b Methods of Determining Sex and Body Size in Prehistoric Samples of White-Tailed Deer (*Odocoileus virginianus*). *Transactions of the Illinois State Academy of Science* 76(3-4):351-357.

Quitmyer, I. R. 2004 What Kind of Data are in the Backdirt? An Experiment on the Influence of Screen Size on Optimal Recovery. *Archaeofauna* 13:109-129.

Rands, Robert L 2007 Palenque and Selected Survey Sites in Chiapas and Tabasco: The Preclassic. In *Palenque: Recent Investigations at the Classic Maya Centre*, edited by D. B. Marken, pp. 25-56. Altamira Press, Lanham.

1977 The Classic Maya Collapse: Usumacinta Zone and the Northwestern Periphery. In *The Classic Maya Collapse*, edited by T. P. Culbert, pp. 165-205. University of New Mexico Press, Albuquerque.

1974 A Chronological Framework for Palenque. In *The Art, Iconography, and Dynastic History of Palenque, Part One. Primera Mesa Redonda de Palenque*, Vol. I, edited by M. Greene Robertson, pp. 35-40. Robert Louis Stevenson School, Pre-Columbian Art Research. Pebble Beach, California.

1967 Ceramica de la Región de Palenque, México. *Estudios de Cultura Maya* VII:111-147.

Rands, Robert L., and Ronald K. Bishop 1980 Resource Procurement Zones and Patterns of Ceramic Exchange in the Palenque Region, Mexico. In *Models and Methods in Regional Exchange*, edited by R. Fry, pp. 19-46. SAA Papers 1, Society for American Archaeology, Washington, D. C.

Rands, Robert L., Ronald K. Bishop, and Garman Harbottel 2002 Thematic and Compositional Variation in the Palenque-region Incensarios. Originally published in 1978, *Tercera Mesa Redonda*, edited by M. Greene Robertson. Electronic document, http://www.mesoweb.com/pari/publications/rt04/incensarios, accessed December 02, 2010. MESOWEB.

Randolph Hopkins, Mary 1992 Mammalian Remains. In *Artifacts from the Cenote of Sacrifice, Chichen Itzá, Yucatán*, edited by C. C. Coggins, pp. 369-385. Memoirs of the Peabody Museum of Archaeology and Ethnology, Harvard University Press, Cambridge.

Ransom, A. 1966 Determining age of White-Tailed Deer from Layers of Cementum of Molars. *Journal of Wildlife Management* 30:1977-1979.

Reed, D. M. 1999 Cuisine from Hun-Nal-Ye. In *Reconstructing Ancient Maya Diet*, edited by C. D. White, pp. 183-196. University of Utah Press, Salt Lake City.

1994 Ancient Diet at Copán, Honduras, as Determined through the Analysis of Stable Carbon and Nitrogen Isotopes. In *Paleonutrition: The Diet and Health of Prehistoric Americans*, edited by K. D. Sobolik, pp. 210-221. Centre for Archaeological Investigations, Southern Illinois University, Carbondale.

Reid, F. A. 1997 *A Field Guide to the Mammals of Central America and Southeast Mexico*. Oxford University Press, New York.

Reents-Budet, Dorie 2001 Classic Maya concepts of the royal court: an analysis of renderings on pictorial ceramics. In *Royal Courts of the Ancient Maya*, Vol. 1, edited by T. Inomata, and S. D. Houston, pp. 195–236. Westview, Boulder.

2000 Feasting among the Classic Maya: Evidence from the Pictorial Ceramics. In *The Maya Vase Book*, Vol. 6, edited by B. Kerr, and J. Kerr, pp. 1022-1038. Kerr Associates, New York.

1994 *Painting the Maya Universe: Royal Ceramics of the Classic Period*. Duke University Press, Durham.

Reitz, Elizabeth J., and Elizabeth S. Wing 1999 *Zooarchaeology*. Cambridge University Press, Cambridge.

Revez, Kinga M., Jurate M. Landwehr, and Jerry Keybl 2001 Measurement of δ^{13}C and δ^{18}O Isotopic Ratios of $CaCO_3$ using a Thermoquest Finnigan Gas Bench II Delta Plus XL Continuous Flow Isotope Ratio Mass Spectrometer with Application to Devil's Hole Core DH-11 Calcite, U.S. Geological Survey, Open-File Report 01-257.

Rice, Don S., and Prudence M. Rice 2004 History in the Future: Historical Data and Investigations in Lowland Maya Studies. In *Continuities and Changes in Maya Archaeology. Perspectives at the Millennium*, edited by C. S. Golden, and G. Borgstede, pp. 77-95. Routledge, New York.

Rice, Prudence M. 2009 On Classic Maya Political Economies. *Journal of Anthropological Archaeology* 28:70-84.

1981 Evolution of Specialized Pottery Production: A Trial Model. *Current Anthropology* 22:219-240.

Richardson, P. R. K. 1980 Carnivore Damage to Antelope Bones and its Archaeological Implications. *Paleontologia Africana* 23:109-125.

Ricketson, O. 1925 Burials in the Maya Area. *American Anthropologist* 27(3):381-401.

Ringrose, T. J. 1993 Bone Counts and Statistics: A Critique. *Journal of Archaeological Science* 20:121-157.

Roberts, S. J., C. I. Smith, A. Millard, and M. J. Collins 2002 The Taphonomy of Cooked Bone: Characterizing Boiling and its Physico-chemical Effects. *Archaeometry* 44(3):485-494.

Robin, Cynthia 2006 Gender, Farming and Long-Time Change: Maya Historical and Archaeological Perspectives. *Current Anthropology* 47(3): 409-433.

Rosenswig, Robert M. 2007 Beyond Identifying Elites: Feasting as a Means to Understand Early Middle Formative Society on the Pacific Coast of Mexico. *Journal of Anthropological Archaeology* 26: 1-27.

Sabloff, Jeremy A. 1986 Interaction Among Maya Polities: A Preliminary Examination. In *Peer Polity Interaction and Socio-Political Change*, edited by Colin Renfrew, and J. F. Cherry, pp. 109-116. Cambridge University Press, Cambridge.

Sandefur, Elsie C. 2002 Animal Husbandry and Meat Consumption. In *Empire and Domestic Economy*, edited by T. D'Altroy, and C. A. Hastorf, pp. 179-202. Interdisciplinary Contributions to Archaeology. Kluwer Academic Publishers, New York.

1988 Andean Zooarchaeology: Animal Use and the Inka Conquest of the Upper Mantaro Valley. PhD dissertation, University of California, Los Angeles.

Santley, Robert S., Thomas W. Killion, and M. T. Lycett 1986 On the Maya Collapse. *Journal of Anthropological Research* 42: 123-159.

Saul, F. P. 1972 *The Human Skeletal Remains of Altar de Sacrificios: An Osteobiographic Analysis.* Papers of the Peabody Museum of Archaeology and Ethnology 63(2). Harvard University, Cambridge.

Saunders, N. J. 1994 Tezcatlipoca: Jaguar Metaphors and the Aztec Mirror of Nature. In *Signifying Animals: Human Meaning in the Natural World*, edited by R. Willis, pp. 159-177. One World Archaeology 16. Routledge Press, London.

Scarborough, Vernon L. 1991 Courting the southern Maya Lowlands: A Study in Pre-Hispanic Ballgame Architecture. In *The Mesoamerican Ballgame*, edited by V. L. Scarborough, and D. R. Wilcox, pp. 129-144. The University of Arizona Press, Tucson.

Scarborough, Vernon L., and David Freidel 1991 *The Settlement System in a Late Preclassic Maya Community: Archaeology at Cerros, Belize, Central America*, edited by D. Freidel, Vol. III. Southern Methodist University Press, Dallas.

Schele, Linda 1984 Human sacrifice among the Classic Maya. In *Ritual Human Sacrifice in Mesoamerica,* edited by E. H. Boone, pp. 6-48. A Conference at Dumbarton Oaks, October 13th and 14th, 1979. Dumbarton Oaks, Washington, D. C.

Schele, Linda, and Mary Ellen Miller 1986 *The Blood of the Kings: Dynasty and Ritual in Maya Art.* Kimbell Art Museum, Fort Worth, Texas.

Schele, Linda, and Peter Mathews 1991 Royal Visits and Other Intersite Relationships among the Classic Maya. In *Classic Maya Political History: Hieroglyphic and Archaeological Evidence*, edited by T. P. Culbert, pp. 226-251. Cambridge University Press, Cambridge.

Scherer, Andrew K., Lori E. Wright, and Cassady J. Yoder 2007 Bioarchaeological Evidence for Social and Temporal Differences in Diet at Piedras Negras, Guatemala. *Latin American Antiquity* 18(1):85-104.

Schiffer, Michael B. *Formation Processes of the Archaeological Record.* University of New Mexico Press, Albuquerque.

Schlesinger, Victoria *Animals and Plants of the Ancient Maya: A Guide.* University of Texas Press, Austin.

Schmid, Elizabeth *Atlas of Animal Bones for Prehistorians, Archaeologists, and Quaternary Geologists.* Elsevier, Amsterdam.

Schmidt, Peter 2004 Las Máscaras de Oxkintok, Yucatán. *Arqueología Mexicana* (Edición Especial) 16:30-33.

Schoeninger, Margaret J. 1989 Reconstructing Prehistoric Human Diet. In *The Chemistry of Prehistoric Human Bone*, edited by D. T. Price, pp. 38-67. Cambridge University Press, Cambridge.

Schoeninger, Margaret J., and Michael J. DeNiro 1984 Nitrogen and Carbon Isotopic Composition of Bone Collagen from Marine and Terrestrial Animals. *Geochimica et Cosmochimica Acta* 48:625-639.

Schoeninger, Margaret J., and Katherine M. Moore 1992 Bone Stable Isotope Studies in Archaeology. *Journal of World Prehistory* 6: 247-296.

Schoeninger, Margaret J., Michael J. DeNiro, and Henrik Tauber 1983 Stable Nitrogen Isotope Ratios of Bone Collagen Reflect Marine and Terrestrial Components of Prehistoric Human Diet. *Science* 220:1381-1383.

Schoeninger, Margaret J., Katherine M. Moore, Mathew L. Murray, and John D. Kingston 1989 Detection of Bone Preservation in Archaeological and Fossil Samples. *Applied Geochemistry* 4:281-292.

Schwarcz, Henry P. 2006 Stable Carbon Isotope Analysis and Human Diet: A Synthesis. In *Histories of Maize: Multidisciplinary Approaches to the Prehistory, Linguistics, Biogeography, Domestication, and Evolution of Maize*, edited by J. P. Staller, R. H. Tykot, and B. F. Benz, pp. 315-321. Academic Press, New York.

2000 Some biochemical aspects of carbon isotopic paleodiet studies. In *Biogeochemical Approaches to Paleodietary Analysis*, edited by S. H. Ambrose, and M. A. Katzenberg, pp. 189-209. Advances in Archaeological and Museum Science 5. Plenum, New York.

1991 Some Theoretical Aspects of Isotope Paleodiet Studies. *Journal of Archaeological Science* 18:261-275.

Schwarcz, Henry P., and Margatet J. Schoeninger 1991 Stable Isotope Analyses in Human Nutritional Ecology. *Yearbook of Physical Anthropology* 34:283-321.

Schwarcz, Henry P., F. Jerome Melbye, M. Anne Katezenberg, and Martin Knyf 1985 Stable Isotopes in Human Skeletons of Southern Ontario: Reconstructing Paleodiet. *Journal of Archaeological Science* 12: 187-206.

Schwartz, M. 1997 *A History of Dogs in the Early Americas.* Yale University Press, New Haven.

Seetah, Krish 2006 Multidisciplinary Approach to Romano-British Cattle Butchery. In *Integrating Zooarchaeology*, edited by M. Maltby, pp. 108-116. Proceedings of the 9th ICAZ Conference, Durham 2002. Series Editors U. Albarella, K. Dobney, and P. Rowley-Conwy. Oxbow Books, Oxford.

Seinfeld, Daniel M., Christopher von Nagy, and Mary D. Pohl 2009 Determining Olmec Maize Use through Bulk Stable Carbon Isotope Analysis. *Journal of Archaeological Science* 36:2560–2565.

Severinghaus, C. W. Tooth Development and Wear as Criteria of Age in White-Tailed Deer. *Journal of Wildlife Management* 13(2):195-216.

Sharer, Robert J. 1996 *Daily Life in Maya Civilization.* Greenwood Press, Westport. 1994 *The Ancient Maya.* Fifth edition, Standford University Press, Standford.

Sharer, Robert J., and David W. Sedat 1987 *Archaeological Investigations in the Northern Maya Highlands Guatemala: Interpretation and the Development of Maya Civilization*. The University Museum Monograph 59. University of Pennsylvania, Philadelphia.

Sharer, Robert J. and Loa P. Traxler *The Ancient Maya*. Sixth Edition, Standford University Press, Standford.

Shaw, Leslie C. 1999 Social and Ecological Aspects of Preclassic Maya Meat Consumption at Colhá, Belize. In *Reconstructing Ancient Maya Diet*, edited by C. D. White, pp.83-100. University of Utah Press, Salt Lake City.

1991 The Articulation of Social Inequality and Faunal Resource Use in the Preclassic Community of Colha, Northern Belize. PhD dissertation, University of Massachusetts, Boston.

Sheets, Payson 2003 Uncommonly Good Food among Commoners: Growing and Consuming Food in Ancient Ceren. *Expedition* 45(2):17-21

Shemesh, Aldo 1990 Crystallinity and Diagenesis of Sedimentary Apatites. *Geochimica et Cosmochimica Acta* 54: 2433-2438.

Simpson, E. H. 1949 Measurement of Diversity. *Nature* 163(1949): 688.

Smith, Monica L. 2006 The Archaeology of Food Preference. *American Anthropologist* 108(3):480-493.

Solis, Wendy 2011 Ancient Maya Exploitation of *Jute* (*Pachychilus spp.*) at Minanha, West Central Belize. MA thesis, Trent University, Peterborough.

Soto Toral, Heriberto 1998 Estudio Arqueozoológico en la Ciudad Prehispánica Maya de Yaxchilán, Chiapas. BS thesis, Escuela Nacional de Ciencias Biológicas, IPN, Mexico City.

Soto Toral, Heriberto, and Oscar J. Polaco 1994 Informe Z-468: Hueso y Concha Procedentes de Yaxchilán, Chiapas. Technical Report submitted to the Laboratorio de Zooarqueología from Instituto Nacional de Antropología e Historia (INAH), Mexico City.

Spiess, Arthur, Kristin Sobolik, Diana Crader, John Mosher, and Deborah Wilson 2006 Cod, Clams and Deer: The Food Remains from Indiantown Island. *Archaeology of Eastern North America* 34:141-187.

Staller, John, Robert H. Tykot, and Bruce Benz *Histories of Maize: Multidisciplinary Approaches to the Prehistory, Linguistics, Biogeography, Domestication, and Evolution of Maize*. Academic Press, Boston.

Stanchly, Norbert 2004 Picks and Stones May Break My Bones: Taphonomy and Maya Zooarchaeology. In *Maya Zooarchaeology*, pp. 35-44, edited by K. F. Emery. Cotsen Institute of Archaeology 51. University of California, Los Angeles.

Stanchly, Norbert, and Gyles Iannone 1997 'A Royal Appetizer? The Use of Freshwater *Jute* Snail (*Pachychilus* spp.) in Ancient Maya Ritual Feasting.' Paper presented at the Annual Meeting of the Society for American Archaeology, Nashville.

Stanton, Travis W., M. Kathryn Brown, and Jonathan B. Pagliaro 2008 Garbage of the Gods? Refusal Disposal and Termination Rituals among the Ancient Maya. *Latin American Antiquity* 19(3):227-247.

Steele, Teresa E. 2003 Using Mortality Profiles to Infer Behaviour in the Fossil Record. *Journal of Mammalogy* 84(2):418–430.

Stiner, Mary C. 1994 *Honour among Thieves: A Zooarchaeological Study of Neandertal Ecology*. Princeton University Press, Princeton.

1990 The Use of Mortality Patterns in Archaeological Studies of Hominid Predatory Adaptations. *Journal of Anthropological Archaeology* 9:305-351.

Stocker, Sharon R., and Jack L. Davis 2004 Animal Sacrifice, Archives, and Feasting at the Palace of Nestor. *Hesperia* 73(2):179-195.

Stone, Andrea, and Marc Zender 2011 *Reading Maya Art: A Hieroglyphic Guide to Ancient Maya Painting and Sculpture*. Thames and Hudson, London.

Storey, Rebecca 2005 Health and Lifestyle (Before and After Death) among the Copan Elite. In *Copan: The History of an Ancient Maya Kingdom*, edited by E. Wyllys Andrews, and W. L. Fash, pp. 315-343. School of American Research Press, Santa Fe.

Stuart, David, and Alfonso C. Morales 2003 Chinikihá: Modern Threat to an Ancient Maya Kingdom. Electronic document, http://www.mesoweb.com/reports, accessed December 3, 2010. MESOWEB.

Stuart-Macadam, Patricia 1995 Breastfeeding in Prehistory. In *Breastfeeding: Biological Perspectives*, edited by P. Stuart-Macadam and K. A. Dettwyler, pp. 75-126. Aldine de Gruyter, Hawthorne.

Stuiver, M. 1978 Atmospheric Carbon Dioxide and Carbon Reservoir Changes. *Science* 199(4326):253–258.

Suhler, Charles 1996 Excavations in the North Acropolis, Yaxuna, Yucatán, Mexico. PhD dissertation, Southern Methodist University, Dallas.

Sullivan, Paul 1989 *Unfinished Conversations: Mayas and Foreigners between two Wars*. University of California Press, Berkeley.

Taube, Karl A. 2003 Ancient and Contemporary Maya Conceptions about Field and Forest. In *The Lowland Maya Area: Three Millenia at the Human-Wildlife Interface*, edited by A. Gomez Pompa, M. F. Allen, S. L. Fedick, and J. J. Jimenez-Osornio, pp. 461-492. Food Products Press, New York.

1989 The Maize Tamale in Classic Maya Diet, Epigraphy, and Art. *American Antiquity* 54(1):31-51.

Teeter, Wendy G. 2001 Maya Animal Utilization in a Growing City: Vertebrate Exploitation at Caracol, Belize. PhD dissertation, University of California, Los Angeles.

Thornton, Erin K. 2008 Resultados de Investigaciones Zooarqueológicas: Trinidad de Nosotros, Petén, Guatemala. Report submitted to the Guatemalan Instituto de Arqueología e Historia.

Thornton, Erin K., and Kitty F. Emery 2009 Uso e Intercambio Prehispánico de Recursos de Fauna en la Entidad Política de Motúl, Petén. In *XX Simposio de*

Investigaciones Arqueológicas, edited by J. P. Laporte, B. Arroyo, and H. Mejía, pp. 1181-1192. Instituto Nacional de Antropología, Asociación Tikal, Guatemala City.

Thornton, Erin K, Kitty F. Emery, David W. Steadman, Camilla Speller, Ray Matheny, and Dongya Yang 2012 Earliest Mexican Turkeys (*Meleagris gallopavo*) in the Maya Region: Implications for Pre-Hispanic Animal Trade and the Timing of Turkey Domestication. *PLoS ONE* 7(8): e42630. https://doi:10.1371/journal.pone.0042630.

Tiesler, Vera 2007 Funerary or Nonfunerary? New References in Identifying Ancient Maya Sacrificial and Postsacrificial Behaviors from Human Assemblages. In *New Perspectives on Human Sacrifice and Ritual Body Treatments in Ancient Maya Society*, edited by V. Tiesler, and A. Cucina, pp. 14-44. Springer, New York.

Tiesler, Vera, and Andrea Cucina (editors) 2001 *Janaab' Pakal de Palenque: Vida y Muerte de un Gobernante Maya*. UNAM, Universidad Autónoma de Yucatán (UADY), Mexico City.

Tieszen, Larry L. 1991 Natural Variations in the Carbon Isotope Values of Plants: Implications for Archaeology, Ecology, and Paleoecology. *Journal of Archaeological Science* 18:227-248.

Tieszen, Larry L., and Tim Fagre 1993a Effect of Diet Quality and Composition on the Isotopic Composition of Respiratory CO2, Bone Collagen, Bioapatite and Soft Tissues. In *Prehistoric Human Bone: Archaeology at the Molecular Level*, edited by J. B. Lambert, and G. Grupe, pp. 121-155. Springer-Verlag, Berlin.

1993b Carbon Isotopic Variability in Modern and Archaeological Maize. *Journal of Archaeological Science* 20:25-40.

Tieszen, Larry L., T. W. Boutton, K. G. Tesdahl, and N. A. Slade 1983 Fractionation and Turnover of Stable Carbon Isotopes in Animal Tissues: Implications for $\delta^{13}C$ Analysis of Diet. *Oecologia* (Berlin) 57:32-37.

Tito, Raul Y., Samuel L. Belknap III, Kristin D. Sobolik, Robert C. Ingraham, Lauren M. Cleeland, and Cecil M. Lewis, Jr. 2011 Brief Communication: DNA from Early Holocene American Dog. *American Journal of Physical Anthropology* 145(4):653-657.

Tozzer, Alfred M. 1967 *Animal Figures in the Maya Codices*. Peabody Papers Vol. 4, Num. 3. Harvard University Press, Cambridge.

1941 *Landa's Relaciones de las cosas de Yucatán* (translation). Papers of the Peabody Museum of Archaeology and Ethnology, Vol. 18. Harvard University Press, Cambridge.

Trabanino, Felipe 2012 Paleobotánica y Paleoambiente. In *Cuarto Informe Parcial Proyecto Arqueológico Chinikihá, Temporada 2011*, coordinated by Rodrigo Liendo, pp. 225-238. Electronic document, http://www.famsi.com/resources/informes/Chinikihá2011, accessed April 12, 2012. FAMSI.

2008 Análisis Arqueobotánico de los Macrorrestos Excavados en el Basurero del Palacio de Chinikihá, Señorío de Palenque, Chiapas, México. Third Report, September-November 2008 period. Manuscript in file, Secretaría de Relaciones Exteriores, Mexico City.

Turner, C. G., and J. A. Turner 1999 *Man, Corn. Cannibalism and Violence in the Prehistoric American Southwest*. The University of Utah Press, Salt Lake City.

Twiss, Katheryn C. 2008 Transformations in an Early Agricultural Society: Feasting in the Southern Levantine Pre-Pottery Neolithic. *Journal of Anthropological Archaeology* 27:418–442.

Tykot, Robert H. 2006 Isotope Analyses and the Histories of Maize. In *Histories of Maize: Multidisciplinary Approaches to the Prehistory, Linguistics, Biogeography, Domestication, and Evolution of Maize*, edited by J. E. Staller, R. H. Tykot, and B. F. Benz, pp. 131-142. Academic Press, Boston.

2002 Contribution of Stable Isotope Analysis to Understanding Dietary Variation among the Maya. In *Archaeological Chemistry: Materials, Methods, and Meaning*, edited by K. Jakes, pp. 214-230. American Chemical Society, Washington, D. C.

Tykot, R. H., F. Falabella, M. T. Planella, and E. Aspillaga 2009 Stable Isotopes and Archaeology in Central Chile: Methodological Insights and Interpretative Problems for Dietary Reconstruction. *International Journal of Osteoarchaeology* 19:156-170.

Tykot, R. H., N. J. van der Merwe, and N. Hammond 1996 Stable Isotope Analysis of Bone Collagen, Bone Apatite, and Tooth Enamel in the Reconstruction of Human Diet. In *Archaeological Chemistry: Organic, Inorganic and Biochemical Analysis*, edited by M. V. Orna, pp. 355-365. ACS Symposium Series 625, Washington.

Valentín Maldonado, Norma 2007 Registro Arqueológico del Caracol de Agua Dulce *Pachychilus* en el Estado de Chiapas, México. In *Los Moluscos Arqueológicos: Una Visión del Mundo Maya*, edited by A. Velázquez Castro, and L. S. Lowe, pp. 13-26. Cuaderno del Centro de Estudios Mayas, No. 34. UNAM, Mexico City.

van der Merwe, Nikolaas J., and Ernesto Medina 1991 The Canopy Effect, Carbon Isotope Ratios, and Foodwebs in Amazonia. *Journal of Archaeological Science* 18:249-259.

van der Merwe, N. J., and J. C. Vogel 1978 ^{13}C Content of Human Collagen as a Measure of Prehistoric Diet in Woodland North America. *Nature* 276(27/28):815-816.

van der Merwe, Nikolaas J., Robert H. Tykot, Norman Hammond, and Kim Oakberg 2000 Diet and Animal Husbandry of the Preclassic Maya at Cuello, Belize: Isotopic and Zooarchaeological Evidence. In *Biogeochemical Approaches to Paleodietary Analysis*, edited by S. Ambrose, and M. A. Katzenberg, pp. 23-38. Kluwer Academic, New York.

van Klinken, G. J. 1999 Bone Collagen Quality Indicators for Paleodietary and Radiocarbon Measurements. *Journal of Archaeological Science* 26(6): 687-695.

Valadéz, Raúl, Alicia Blanco, Bernardo Rodríguez, and Christopher Götz 2009 Perros Pelones del México Prehispánico. *Archaeobios* 3(1):5-19.

Varela Scherrer, Carlos Miguel 2019 Los peces en el registro arqueológico del grupo IV de Palenque. *Lakamha'* 58:4-5.

2012 La fauna arqueológica de Chinikihá, Chiapas: estatus y consumo animal, el caso del venado cola blanca (*Odocoileus virginianus*). BA thesis, Escuela Nacional de Antropología e Historia (ENAH-SEP), Mexico City.

Vega-Centeno, Rafael, and Sara Lafosse Construction, labour organization and feasting during the Late Archaic Period in the Central Andes. *Journal of Anthropological Archaeology* 26:150-171.

Venegas Durán, Benito J. 2005 En Busca de los Orígenes de Palenque: Investigaciones Recientes del Proyecto Crecimiento Urbano de la Antigua Ciudad de Palenque (PCU). *Mayab* 18:57-67.

Vogel, J. C., and Nikolaas J. van der Merwe 1977 Isotopic Evidence for Early Maize Cultivation in New York State. *American Antiquity* 42:238-242.

Vogt, Evon Z. 1993 *Tortillas for the Gods: A Symbolic Analysis of Zinacanteco Rituals*. University of Oklahoma Press, Norman.

Zinacantan: A Maya Community in the Highlands of Chiapas. Belknap Press, Harvard University, Cambridge.

Walker, William H. Ceremonial Trash? In *Expanding Archaeology*, edited by J. M. Skibo, W. H. Walker, and A. E. Nielsen, pp. 66-79. University of Utah Press, Salt Lake City.

Walker, William H., and Lisa J. Lucero 2000 The Depositional History of Ritual and Power. In *Agency in Archaeology*, edited by M.A. Dobres, and J. Robb, pp. 130-147. Routledge, London.

Wake, T. A. 2004 On the Paramount Importance of Adequate Comparative Collections and Recovery Techniques in the Identification and Interpretation of Vertebrate Archaeofaunas: A Reply to Vale and Gargett. *Archaeofauna* 13:173-182.

Webster, David 2005 Political Ecology, Political Economy, and the Culture History of Resource Management at Copan. In *Copan: The History of an Ancient Maya Kingdom*, edited by E. Wyllys Andrews, and W. L. Fash, pp. 33-72. School of American Research Press, Santa Fe.

The Fall of the Ancient Maya: Solving the Mystery of the Maya Collapse. Thames and Hudson, New York. 2001 Spatial Dimensions of Maya Courtly Life: Problems and Issues. In *Royal Courts of the Ancient Maya*, Vol. 1, edited by T. Inomata, and S. D. Houston, pp. 130-167. Westview Press, Boulder.

1997 Studying Maya Burials. In *Bones of the Maya*, edited by S. L. Whittington, and D. M. Reed, pp. 3-12. Smithsonian Institution Press, Washington.

Wells, E. Christian 2007 Faenas, Ferias, and Fiestas: Ritual Finance in Ancient and Modern Honduras. In *Mesoamerican Ritual Economy: Archaeological and Ethnological Perspectives*, edited by C. E. Wells, and K. L. Davis-Salazar, pp. 29-65. University Press of Colorado, Boulder.

West, G. C., and D. L. Shaw 1975 Fatty Acid Composition of Dall Sheep Bone Marrow. *Comp. Biochem. Physiol.* 50B:599-601.

White, Christine D. 2005 Gendered Food Behaviour among the Maya. *Journal of Social Archaeology* 5(3):356-382.

1999 Introduction: Ancient Maya Diet. In *Reconstructing Ancient Maya Diet*, edited by C. D. White, pp. IX-XXVII. University of Utah Press, Salt Lake City.

1997 Ancient Diet at Lamanai and Pacbitun: Implications for the Ecological Model of Collapse. In *Bones of the Maya: Studies of Ancient Skeletons*, edited by S. L. Whittington, and D. M. Reed, pp. 171-180. Smithsonian Institution Press, Washington, D. C.

White, Christine D., and Henry P. Schwarcz 1989 Ancient Maya Diet: As Inferred from Isotopic and Elemental Analysis of Human Bone. *Journal of Archaeological Science* 16:451-474.

White, Christine D., Paul F. Healy, and Henry P. Schwarcz 1993 Intensive Agriculture, Social Status, and Maya Diet at Pacbitun, Belize. *Journal of Anthropological Research* 49:347-375.

White, Christine D., Fred J. Longstaffe, and Henry P. Schwarcz 2006a Social Directions in the Isotopic Anthropology of Maize in the Maya Region. In *Histories of Maize: Multidisciplinary Approaches to the Prehistory, Linguistics, Biogeography, Domestication, and Evolution of Maize*, edited by J. Staller, R. H. Tykot, and B. Benz, pp. 143-159. Academic Press, Boston.

White, Christine D., David M. Pendergast, Fred J. Longstaffe, and Kimberley R. Law 2001a Social Complexity and Food Systems at Altun Ha, Belize: The Isotopic Evidence. *Latin American Antiquity* 12:371-393.

White, Christine D., Mary E. D. Pohl, Henry P. Schwarcz, and Fred. J. Longstaffe 2004 Feast, Field, and Forest: Deer and Dog Diets at Lagartero, Tikal, and Copan. In *Maya Zooarchaeology*, edited by K. F. Emery, pp. 141-158. Cotsen Institute of Archaeology, University of California, Los Angeles.

2001b Isotopic Evidence for Maya Patterns of Deer and Dog Use at Preclassic Colha. *Journal of Archaeological Science* 28: 89-107.

White, Christine D., Jay Maxwell, Alexis Dolphin, Jocelyn Williams, and Fred Longstaffe 2006b Pathoecology and Paleodiet in Postclassic/Historic Maya from Northern Coastal Belize. *Memorias do Instituto Oswaldo Cruz* 101, suppl. II, pp. 35-42.

White, Theodore E. 1953 A Method of Calculating the Dietary Percentage of Various Food Animals Utilized by Aboriginal People. *American Antiquity* 18(4):396-398.

White, Tim D. 1992 *Prehistoric Cannibalism at Mancos 5MTUMR-2346*. Princeton University, Princeton.

1991 *Human Osteology*. Academic Press, San Diego.

Whittington, Stephen L. 1999 Caries and Antemortem Tooth Loss at Copan: Implications for Commoner Diet. In *Reconstructing Ancient Maya Diet*, edited by C. D. White, pp. 151-167. University of Utah Press, Salt Lake City.

Whittington, Stephen L., and David M. Reed 1997 Commoner Diet at Copan: Insights from Stable Isotopes and Porotic Hyperostosis. In *Bones of the Maya*, edited by S. L. Whittington, and D. M. Reed, pp. 157-170. Smithsonian Institution Press, Washington, D. C.

Wiessner, Polly 2001 Of Feasting and Value: Enga Feasts in a Historical Perspective (Papua New Guinea). In *Feasts: Archaeological and Ethnographic Perspectives on Food, Politics, and Power*, edited by M. Dietler, and B. Hayden, pp. 115-143. Smithsonian Institution Press, Washington.

Williams, Jocelyn S., Christine D. White, and Fred J. Longstaffe 2009 Maya Marine Subsistence: Isotopic Evidence from Marco Gonzalez and San Pedro, Belize. *Latin American Antiquity* 20(1):37-56.

Williamson, Richard 1996 Excavations, Interpretations, and Implications of the Earliest Structures Beneath Structure 10L-26 at Copan, Honduras (originally published in Eighth Palenque Round Table, 1993, edited by M. J. Macri, and J. McHargue. Pre-Columbian Art Research Institute (PARI), Vol. X). Electronic document, http://www.mesoweb.com/pari/publications/RT10/17_Excavations, accessed February 25, 2011. FAMSI.

Wing, Elizabeth S. 1981 A Comparison of Olmec and Maya Foodways. In *The Olmec and Their Neighbors*, pp. 20-28, edited by E. Benson. Dumbarton Oaks, Washington, D. C.

1978 Use of Dogs for Food: An Adaptation to the Coastal Environment. In *Prehistoric Coastal Adaptation: The Economy and Ecology of Maritime Middle America*, edited by B. L. Stark, and B. Voorhies, pp. 29-41. Academic Press, New York.

1975 Animal Remains from Luubantun. In *Luubantun, a Classic Maya Realm*, edited by N. Hammond, pp. 379-383. Peabody Museum Monograph No. 2. Harvard University, Cambridge.

Wing, Elizabeth S., and Sylvia J. Scudder 1991 The Exploitation of Animals. In *Cuello: An Early Maya Community in Belize*, edited by N. Hammond, pp. 84-97. Cambridge University Press, Cambridge.

Wing, Elizabeth S., and David Steadman 1980 Vertebrate Faunal Remains from Dzibilchaltun. In *Excavations at, Dzibilchaltun Yucatán, Mexico*, edited by E. Andrews IV and E. Andrews V, pp. 326-331. MARI Publication 48, New Orleans.

Woodburne, Michael O. 1968 *The Cranial Myology and Osteology of Dicotyles tajacu, the Collared Peccary, and its Bearing on Classification*. Memoirs of the Southern California Academy of Sciences, Vol. 7. Anderson, Ritchie & Simon, Los Angeles.

Wright, Lori E. 2009 Etnicidad e Isotopos en Mayapan. Electronic document, http://www.famsi.org, accessed March 29 2010. FAMSI.

2006 *Diet, Health, and Status among the Pasion Maya: A Reappraisal of the Collapse*. Vanderbilt Institute of Mesoamerican Archaeology. Vanderbilt University Press, Nashville.

2004 Osteological Investigations of Ancient Maya Lives. In *Continuities and Change in Maya Archaeology*, edited by C. Golden, and G. Borgsted, pp. 201-215. Routledge Press, New York.

2003 La Muerte y Estatus Económico: Investigando el Simbolismo Mortuorio y el Acceso a los Recursos Alimenticios entre los Mayas. In *Antropología de la Eternidad: La Muerte en la Cultura Maya*, edited by A. Ciudad Ruiz, H. Ruz Soza, and M. J. Ponce de León, pp. 173-193. Sociedad Española de Estudios Mayas, Madrid.

1999a The Elements of Maya Diets: Alkaline Earth Baselines and Paleodietary Reconstruction in the Pasion Region. In *Reconstructing Ancient Maya Diet*, edited by C. D. White, pp. 197-219. The University of Utah Press, Salt Lake City.

1999b Los Niños de Kaminaljuyú: Isótopos, Dieta y Etnicidad en el Altiplano Guatemalteco. In *XII Simposio de Investigaciones Arqueológicas en Guatemala 1998*, edited by J. P. Laporte, and H. L. Escobedo, pp. 434-444. Museo Nacional de Arqueología y Etnología, Asociación Tikal, Guatemala City.

1997 Ecology or Society? Paleodiet and the Collapse of the Pasion Maya Lowlands. In *Bones of the Maya*, edited by S. L. Whittington, and D. M. Reed, pp. 181-195. Smithsonian Institution Press, Washington, D. C.

1994 Sacrifice of Earth? Diet, Health and Inequality in the Passion Maya Lowlands, Vols. 1 and 2. PhD dissertation, University of Chicago, Carbondale.

1993 La Dieta Antigua en la Región de La Pasión. In *VI Simposio de Investigaciones Arqueológicas en Guatemala, 1992*, edited by J. P. Laporte, H. Escobedo, and S. Villagrán de Brady, pp. 172-179. Museo Nacional de Arqueología y Etnología, Guatemala.

Wright, Lori E., and Henry P. Schwarcz 1999 Correspondence between Stable Carbon, Oxygen and Nitrogen Isotopes in Human Tooth Enamel and Dentine: Infant Diets at Kaminaljuyu. *Journal of Archaeological Science* 26:1159-1170.

1996 Infrared and Isotopic Evidence for Diagenesis of Bone Apatite at Dos Pilas, Guatemala: Paleodietary Implications. *Journal of Archaeological Science* 23(6):933-944.

Wright, Lori E., and Christine D. White 1996 Human Biology in the Classic Maya Collapse: Evidence from Paleopathology and Paleodiet. *Journal of World Prehistory* 10(2):147-198.

Wright, Lori E., Juan Antonio Valdes, James H. Burton, T. Douglas Price, and Henry P. Schwarcz 2010 The Children of Kaminaljuyu: Isotopic Insight into Diet and Long Distance Interaction in Mesoamerica. *Journal of Anthropological Archaeology* 29(2):155-178.

Yaeger, Jason 2000 Changing Patterns of Social Organization: The Late and Terminal Classic Communities at San Lorenzo, Cayo District, Belize. PhD dissertation, University of Pennsylvania, Pennsylvania.

Yaeger, Jason, and Cynthia Robin 2004 Heterogeneous Hinterlands: The Social and Political Organization of Commoner Settlements near Xunantunich, Belize. In *Ancient Maya Commoners*, edited by J. C. Lohse, and F. Valdez, Jr., pp. 147-174. University of Texas Press, Austin.

Zender, Marc U. 2000 A Study of Two Uaxactun-Style Tamale-Serving Vessels. In *The Maya Vase Book*, Vol. 6, edited by B. Kerr, and J. Kerr, pp. 1038-1055. Kerr Associates, New York.

Zúñiga Arellano, Belem 2000 Identificación y Análisis de Restos Animales Recuperados en las Excavaciones Efectuadas en Palenque, Chiapas 1991-1994. Proyecto Arqueológico Palenque. Manuscript on file, Instituto Nacional de Antropología e Historia (INAH), Mexico City.

Appendix A

List of isolated teeth by *Operación*

Operation	Square	Layer	NISP	Species	Element
110	B5	II	1	Odocoileus virginianus	3PM
114	K1	II	1	Carnivora	M1
114	K1	II	1	Odocoileus virginianus	PM?
114	K1	II	2	Odocoileus virginianus	1 premolar and 1 molar
114	K1	II	1	Carnivora	1M
114	K1	II	1	Rodentia	incisor
114	J1	III	1	Odocoileus virginianus	3M
114	G1	IV	3	Odocoileus virginianus	molar
114	I2	IV	2	Odocoileus virginianus	molar
114	G2	V	1	Odocoileus virginianus	1PM
114	F2	V	1	Odocoileus virginianus	3M
114	F2	V	1	Odocoileus virginianus	molar
114	E2	V	1	Odocoileus virginianus	3M
114	G1	V	1	Odocoileus virginianus	3M
114	G1	V	1	Odocoileus virginianus	molar
114	F2	V	1	Odocoileus virginianus	1M
201	external wall	3 metric level	1	Carnivora	molar
201	n/a	Layer II/level 2	1	*Canis* sp.	M1
201	n/a	Layer II/level 2	2	Odocoileus virginianus	(2PM, 2M)
201	n/a	Layer II/level 2	1	Odocoileus virginianus	molar
201	n/a	Layer II/level 2	1	Canis lupus familiaris	canine

Appendix B

List of material identified by *Operación*

Operacion 110

Bag number	Square	Layer	NISP	Species	Specimen	Side
185	n.i.	I	1	*Canis lupus familiaris*	innominate	right
192	n.i.	II	1	n.i.	long bone (diaphysis)	n/a
304	C6, C7	II	22	medium/large mammal	long bone splinter	n/a
309	A1, B1, C1	II	1	medium/large mammal	irregular	n/a
325	C7	II	2	medium/large mammal	irregular	n/a
325	C7	II	1	*Odocoileus virginianus*	ilium	right
346	C6-C7	II	2	medium/large mammal	rib (middle)	n/a
850	B5	II	16	medium/large mammal	long bone splinter	n/a
872	B5	II	12	medium/large mammal	long bone splinter	n/a
886	A, B, E	II	1	*Odocoileus virginianus*	ilium	right
886	A, B, E	II	1	medium/large mammal	irregular	n/a
900	C2	II	2	small/medium mammal	long bone (diaphysis)	n/a
904	C1	II	3	medium/large mammal	irregular	n/a
911	A3	II	2	medium/large mammal	long bone splinter	n/a
929	A2, B2	III	1	n.i.	irregular	n/a
929	A2, B2	III	1	*Odocoileus virginianus*	astragalus	right
941	B2	IV	1	n.i.	long bone (diaphysis)	n/a
947	n.i.	IV	1	small/medium mammal	irregular	n/a
947	n.i.	IV	1	medium/large mammal	long bone splinter	n/a
1066	A1, A2	IV, V	1	small/medium mammal	long bone splinter	n/a
1066	A1, A2	IV-V	8	medium/large mammal	rib (middle)	n/a
1066	A1, A2	IV-V	2	medium/large mammal	long bone (diaphysis)	n/a
1066	A1, A2	IV-V	4	medium/large mammal	flat bone	n/a
1066	A1, A2	IV-V	29	medium/large mammal	irregular	n/a
1066	A1, A2	IV-V	7	medium/large mammal	long bone splinter	n/a
1089	n.i.	II	1	*Sylvilagus sp.*	femur	right
1089	n.i.	II	3	medium/large mammal	rib (middle)	n/a
1089	n.i.	II	1	medium/large mammal	long bone splinter	n/a
n/a	A1-A2	IV-V	1	medium/large mammal	rib (middle)	n/a
n/a	A1-A2	IV-V	2	medium/large mammal	long bone splinter	n/a

Operacion 111

Bag number	Square	Layer	NISP	Species	Specimen	Side
230	CI-4	n.i.	1	*Canis sp.*	hemi-mandible	left
576	II-1	n.i.	9	medium/large mammal	irregular	n/a
576	II-1	n.i.	3	medium/large mammal	long bone	n/a
1107	ext. North	III	8	n.i.	irregular	n/a
1120	ext. North	III	1	*Odocoileus virginianus*	scapula	right
1120	ext. North	III	43	medium/large mammal	long bone	n/a

Operacion 112

Bag number	Square	Layer	NISP	Species	Specimen	Side
581	North Structure	Construction fill	2	medium/large mammal	long bone splinter	n/a

Operacion 115

Bag number	Square	Layer	NISP	Species	Specimen	Side
1072	N1	II	1	medium/large mammal	long bone splinter	n/a
1076	I	N1	1	medium/large mammal	long bone splinter	n/a

Operacion 114

Bag number	Square	Layer	NISP	Species	Specimen	Side
114	J1	III	1	*Canis lupus familiaris*	metatarsus	n/a
114	J1	III	1	*Dasyprocta puntata*	femur	left
114	J1	III	1	small/medium mammal	rib (middle)	n/a
135	J2	I	1	*Odocoileus virginianus*	humerus	right
135	J2	I	1	*Odocoileus virginianus*	femur	right
135	J2	I	2	*Odocoileus virginianus*	radius	right
135	J2	I	1	*Odocoileus virginianus*	metarcapus	right
135	J2	I	1	*Odocoileus virginianus*	ilium	left
135	J2	I	1	*Odocoileus virginianus*	innominate	left
135	J2	I	1	*Odocoileus virginianus*	pubis	left
135	J2	I	1	*Odocoileus virginianus*	phalange I	n/a
135	J2	I	2	*Odocoileus virginianus*	scapula	n/a
135	J2	I	2	*Odocoileus virginianus*	cervical vertebra	n/a
135	J2	I	2	*Odocoileus virginianus*	thoracic vertebra	n/a
135	J2	I	1	*Odocoileus virginianus*	vertebra	n/a
135	J2	I	3	*Odocoileus virginianus*	lumbar vertebra	n/a
135	J2	I	8	medium/large mammal	rib (middle)	n/a
135	J2	I	2	medium/large mammal	rib (proximal)	n/a
135	J2	I	7	medium/large mammal	irregular	n/a
135	J2	I	15	medium/large mammal	long bone splinter	n/a
143	K2	I	1	*Odocoileus virginianus*	ischium	right
143	K2	I	1	*Odocoileus virginianus*	metacarpus II	left (ext)
143	K2	I	1	*Odocoileus virginianus*	cervical vertebra	n/a
143	K2	I	1	*Odocoileus virginianus*	scapula	right
143	K2	I	1	*Odocoileus virginianus*	ilium	right
143	K2	I	1	*Odocoileus virginianus*	scapula	n/a
143	K2	II	3	*Odocoileus virginianus*	thoracic vertebra	n/a
143	K2	I	1	*Canis lupus familiaris*	tibia	right
143	K2	I	1	small/medium mammal	long bone (diaphysis)	n/a
143	K2	I	6	medium/large mammal	rib (middle)	n/a
143	K2	I	8	medium/large mammal	long bone splinter	n/a
650	K1	I	1	*Odocoileus virginianus*	metatarsus	right
650	K1	I	1	*Odocoileus virginianus*	scapula	right
650	K1	I	3	*Odocoileus virginianus*	scapula	left
650	K1	I	1	*Odocoileus virginianus*	humerus	right
650	K1	I	1	*Odocoileus virginianus*	calcaneus	right
650	K1	I	1	*Odocoileus virginianus*	astragalus	left
650	K1	I	1	*Odocoileus virginianus*	pubis	n/a
650	K1	I	2	*Odocoileus virginianus*	ischium	n/a

Bag number	Square	Layer	NISP	Species	Specimen	Side
650	K1	I	1	*Odocoileus virginianus*	cervical vertebra	n/a
650	K1	I	1	*Odocoileus virginianus*	lumbar vertebra	n/a
650	K1	I	1	*Odocoileus virginianus*	thoracic vertebra	n/a
650	K1	I	1	*Canis lupus familiaris*	femur	n/a
650	K1	I	4	medium/large mammal	rib (distal)	n/a
650	K1	I	4	medium/large mammal	rib (middle)	n/a
650	K1	I	4	medium/large mammal	long bone splinter	n/a
653	G3	I	1	*Odocoileus virginianus*	astragalus	left
653	G3	I	1	medium/large mammal	femur splinter	n/a
658	L1	I	1	*Odocoileus virginianus*	patella	right
658	L1	I	1	*Odocoileus virginianus*	ilium	left
658	L1	I	1	*Odocoileus virginianus*	radius	left
658	L1	I	1	*Odocoileus virginianus*	tibia	left
658	L1	I	1	*Odocoileus virginianus*	hemi-mandible	right
658	L1	I	1	*Odocoileus virginianus*	ilium	left
658	L1	I	1	*Odocoileus virginianus*	thoracic vertebra	n/a
658	L1	I	1	*Odocoileus virginianus*	ischium	right
658	L1	I	1	*Odocoileus virginianus*	sacrum	n/a
658	L1	I	2	*Odocoileus virginianus*	scapula	n/a
658	L1	I	2	*Odocoileus virginianus*	scapula	right
658	L1	I	1	*Odocoileus virginianus*	femur	n/a
658	L1	I	11	medium/large mammal	rib (middle)	n/a
658	L1	I	1	medium/large mammal	rib (proximal)	n/a
658	L1	I	1	medium/large mammal	long bone	n/a
658	L1	I	3	medium/large mammal	irregular	n/a
658	L1	I	1	medium/large mammal	femur splinter	n/a
658	L1	I	2	medium/large mammal	long bone splinter	n/a
658	L1	I	1	medium/large mammal	metapodium splinter	n/a
661	L2	I	1	*Odocoileus virginianus*	patella	right
661	L2	I	1	*Odocoileus virginianus*	cervical vertebra	n/a
661	L2	I	2	*Odocoileus virginianus*	lumbar vertebra	n/a
661	L2	I	1	*Odocoileus virginianus*	pubis	right
661	L2	I	3	medium/large mammal	rib (middle)	n/a
661	L2	I	3	medium/large mammal	long bone splinter	n/a
664	J2	II	2	*Odocoileus virginianus*	scapula	right
664	J2	II	1	*Odocoileus virginianus*	calcaneus	right
664	J2	II	1	*Odocoileus virginianus*	scapula	n/a
664	J2	II	2	*Odocoileus virginianus*	hemi-mandible	n/a
664	J2	II	2	*Odocoileus virginianus*	vertebra	n/a
664	J2	II	3	*Odocoileus virginianus*	thoracic vertebra	n/a
664	J2	II	3	medium/large mammal	rib (middle)	n/a
664	J2	II	1	medium/large mammal	irregular	n/a
664	J2	II	6	medium/large mammal	long bone splinter	n/a
667	G2	II	1	*Odocoileus virginianus*	calcaneus	right
667	G2	II	1	medium/large mammal	irregular	n/a
667	G2	II	1	medium/large mammal	long bone splinter	n/a
672	J2	III	1	*Odocoileus virginianus*	humerus	left
672	J2	III	1	*Odocoileus virginianus*	tibia	right
672	J2	III	1	*Odocoileus virginianus*	scapula	left
672	J2	III	1	*Odocoileus virginianus*	metacarpus	left
672	J2	III	1	*Odocoileus virginianus*	scapula	right
672	J2	III	1	*Odocoileus virginianus*	innominate	left
672	J2	III	1	*Odocoileus virginianus*	ischium	right

Bag number	Square	Layer	NISP	Species	Specimen	Side
672	J2	III	1	*Odocoileus virginianus*	ilium	left
672	J2	III	1	*Odocoileus virginianus*	ilium	right
672	J2	III	1	*Odocoileus virginianus*	innominate	left
672	J2	III	2	*Odocoileus virginianus*	axis	n/a
672	J2	III	1	*Odocoileus virginianus*	thoracic vertebra	n/a
672	J2	III	2	*Odocoileus virginianus*	cervical vertebra	n/a
672	J2	III	4	*Odocoileus virginianus*	lumbar vertebra	n/a
672	J2	III	1	*Odocoileus virginianus*	vertebra	n/a
672	J2	III	13	medium/large mammal	rib (middle)	n/a
672	J2	III	2	medium/large mammal	rib (proximal)	n/a
672	J2	III	7	medium/large mammal	long bone splinter	n/a
675	G3	II	2	medium/large mammal	irregular	n/a
675	G3	II	3	medium/large mammal	long bone splinter	n/a
683	H2	II	4	medium/large mammal	rib (middle)	n/a
683	H2	II	8	small/medium mammal	irregular	n/a
684	G2	III	2	*Odocoileus virginianus*	femur	left
684	G2	III	2	*Odocoileus virginianus*	femur	right
684	G2	III	1	*Odocoileus virginianus*	scapula	left
684	G2	III	2	*Odocoileus virginianus*	ilium	right
684	G2	III	1	*Odocoileus virginianus*	thoracic vertebra	n/a
684	G2	III	1	*Odocoileus virginianus*	ischium	left
684	G2	III	1	*Odocoileus virginianus*	ilium	left
684	G2	III	1	*Odocoileus virginianus*	tibia	right
684	G2	III	1	medium/large mammal	rib (middle)	n/a
684	G2	III	2	medium/large mammal	rib (proximal)	n/a
684	G2	III	1	medium/large mammal	femur splinter	n/a
689	J1	II	1	*Odocoileus virginianus*	radius	left
689	J1	II	2	*Odocoileus virginianus*	femur	right
689	J1	II	1	*Odocoileus virginianus*	humerus	left
689	J1	II	2	*Odocoileus virginianus*	scapula	right
689	J1	II	3	*Odocoileus virginianus*	hemi-mandible	left
689	J1	II	1	*Odocoileus virginianus*	hemi-mandible	right
689	J1	II	1	*Odocoileus virginianus*	metapodium	n/a
689	J1	II	1	*Odocoileus virginianus*	ilium	right
689	J1	II	3	*Odocoileus virginianus*	hemi-mandible	n/a
689	J1	II	1	*Odocoileus virginianus*	ulna	n/a
689	J1	II	1	*Odocoileus virginianus*	scapula	n/a
689	J1	II	1	*Odocoileus virginianus*	cervical vertebra	n/a
689	J1	II	2	*Odocoileus virginianus*	lumbar vertebra	n/a
689	J1	II	1	*Odocoileus virginianus*	sacrum	n/a
689	J1	II	1	*Odocoileus virginianus*	maxilla	n/a
689	J1	II	12	medium/large mammal	rib (distal)	n/a
689	J1	II	12	medium/large mammal	rib (middle)	n/a
689	J1	II	4	medium/large mammal	irregular	n/a
689	J1	II	1	medium/large mammal	metatarsus splinter	n/a
693	H2	III	2	medium/large mammal	rib (proximal)	n/a
693	H2	III	2	medium/large mammal	irregular	n/a
695	H1	III	1	*Odocoileus virginianus*	femur	left
695	H1	III	2	*Odocoileus virginianus*	humerus	right
695	H1	III	1	*Odocoileus virginianus*	thoracic vertebra	n/a
695	H1	III	1	*Odocoileus virginianus*	lumbar vertebra	n/a
695	H1	III	2	medium/large mammal	rib (middle)	n/a
695	H1	III	1	medium/large mammal	long bone splinter	n/a

Bag number	Square	Layer	NISP	Species	Specimen	Side
704	H1	III	1	*Odocoileus virginianus*	tibia	right
704	H1	III	1	*Odocoileus virginianus*	cervical vertebra	n/a
709	L1	II	1	*Odocoileus virginianus*	sacrum	n/a
709	L1	II	5	*Odocoileus virginianus*	lumbar vertebra	n/a
709	L1	II	1	*Odocoileus virginianus*	scapula	right
709	L1	II	1	*Odocoileus virginianus*	innominate	right
709	L1	II	1	*Odocoileus virginianus*	innominate	left
709	L1	II	1	*Odocoileus virginianus*	metatarsus	right
709	L1	II	1	*Odocoileus virginianus*	calcaneus	right
709	L1	II	1	*Odocoileus virginianus*	ilium	left
709	L1	II	2	*Odocoileus virginianus*	axis	n/a
709	L1	II	1	*Odocoileus virginianus*	cervical vertebra (C3)	n/a
709	L1	II	7	*Odocoileus virginianus*	cervical vertebra	n/a
709	L1	II	1	*Odocoileus virginianus*	thoracic vertebra (T1)	n/a
709	L1	II	4	*Odocoileus virginianus*	thoracic vertebra	n/a
709	L1	II	1	*Odocoileus virginianus*	sacrum I	n/a
709	L1	II	2	*Odocoileus virginianus*	skull	n/a
709	L1	II	4	*Odocoileus virginianus*	scapula	n/a
709	L1	II	1	*Dasypus novemcinctus*	tibia	right
709	L1	II	2	medium/large mammal	rib (distal)	n/a
709	L1	II	19	medium/large mammal	rib (middle)	n/a
709	L1	II	1	medium/large mammal	rib (proximal)	n/a
709	L1	II	3	medium/large mammal	irregular	n/a
709	L1	II	1	medium/large mammal	long bone splinter	n/a
711	L1	III	1	*Odocoileus virginianus*	atlas	n/a
711	L1	III	1	*Odocoileus virginianus*	thoracic vertebra (T1)	n/a
711	L1	III	1	*Odocoileus virginianus*	innominate	left
711	L1	III	1	*Odocoileus virginianus*	metacarpus	left
711	L1	III	1	*Odocoileus virginianus*	scapula	right
711	L1	III	1	*Odocoileus virginianus*	metatarsus	right
711	L1	III	1	*Odocoileus virginianus*	ulna	left
711	L1	III	3	*Odocoileus virginianus*	thoracic vertebra	n/a
711	L1	III	2	*Odocoileus virginianus*	sternum	n/a
711	L1	III	2	*Odocoileus virginianus*	lumbar vertebra	n/a
711	L1	III	1	*Odocoileus virginianus*	calcaneus	right
711	L1	III	1	*Odocoileus virginianus*	astragalus	right
711	L1	III	1	*Odocoileus virginianus*	cuboides-escafoides	right
711	L1	III	1	*Odocoileus virginianus*	tibia	left
711	L1	III	1	small/medium mammal	rib (middle)	n/a
711	L1	III	1	medium/large mammal	rib (cartilage)	n/a
711	L1	III	1	medium/large mammal	rib (distal)	n/a
711	L1	III	7	medium/large mammal	rib (middle)	n/a
711	L1	III	3	medium/large mammal	rib (proximal)	n/a
713	I2	II	2	*Odocoileus virginianus*	lumbar vertebra	n/a
713	I2	II	2	*Odocoileus virginianus*	long bone	n/a
713	I2	II	1	medium/large mammal	rib (proximal)	n/a
713	I2	II	1	medium/large mammal	long bone splinter	n/a
720	I1	II	1	*Odocoileus virginianus*	femur	right
720	I1	II	1	*Odocoileus virginianus*	scapula	left
720	I1	II	1	*Odocoileus virginianus*	calcaneus	left
720	I1	II	1	*Odocoileus virginianus*	astragalus	left
720	I1	II	1	*Odocoileus virginianus*	thoracic vertebra	n/a
720	I1	II	1	medium/large mammal	rib (middle)	n/a

Bag number	Square	Layer	NISP	Species	Specimen	Side
727	I2	III	1	*Odocoileus virginianus*	ilium	left
727	I2	III	1	*Odocoileus virginianus*	metatarsus	right
727	I2	III	3	*Odocoileus virginianus*	scapula	right
727	I2	III	2	*Odocoileus virginianus*	lumbar vertebra	n/a
727	I2	III	1	n.i.	long bone (proximal)	n/a
727	I2	III	5	medium/large mammal	rib (middle)	n/a
729	I2	III	1	*Odocoileus virginianus*	tibia	right
731	K1	II	4	*Odocoileus virginianus*	scapula	left
731	K1	II	6	*Odocoileus virginianus*	scapula	n/a
731	K1	II	2	*Odocoileus virginianus*	calcaneus	right
731	K1	II	2	*Odocoileus virginianus*	ulna	right
731	K1	II	1	*Odocoileus virginianus*	humerus	left
731	K1	II	1	*Odocoileus virginianus*	humerus	right
731	K1	II	1	*Odocoileus virginianus*	humerus	n/a
731	K1	II	1	*Odocoileus virginianus*	ischium	left
731	K1	II	1	*Odocoileus virginianus*	innominate	right
731	K1	II	1	*Odocoileus virginianus*	ilium	right
731	K1	II	1	*Odocoileus virginianus*	pubis	left
731	K1	II	1	*Odocoileus virginianus*	pubis	right
731	K1	II	1	*Odocoileus virginianus*	ilium	right
731	K1	II	1	*Odocoileus virginianus*	calcaneus	left
731	K1	II	1	*Odocoileus virginianus*	astragalus	left
731	K1	II	1	*Odocoileus virginianus*	cuboides-escafoides	left
731	K1	II	1	*Odocoileus virginianus*	axis	n/a
731	K1	II	8	*Odocoileus virginianus*	cervical vertebra	n/a
731	K1	II	2	*Odocoileus virginianus*	thoracic vertebra (T1)	n/a
731	K1	II	7	*Odocoileus virginianus*	thoracic vertebra	n/a
731	K1	II	4	*Odocoileus virginianus*	lumbar vertebra	n/a
731	K1	II	2	*Odocoileus virginianus*	sacrum I	n/a
731	K1	II	13	*Odocoileus virginianus*	vertebra	n/a
731	K1	II	1	*Odocoileus virginianus*	ulna	n/a
731	K1	II	1	*Odocoileus virginianus*	pubis	right
731	K1	II	1	*Sylvilagus* sp. (possibly *S. brasiliensis*)	femur	right
731	K1	II	3	medium/large mammal	rib (distal)	n/a
731	K1	II	39	medium/large mammal	rib (middle)	n/a
731	K1	II	3	small/medium mammal	rib (middle)	n/a
731	K1	II	7	medium/large mammal	rib (proximal)	n/a
731	K1	II	2	small/medium mammal	rib (proximal)	n/a
731	K1	II	8	medium/large mammal	irregular	n/a
731	K1	II	7	medium/large mammal	long bone splinter	n/a
733	K2	III	1	*Canis lupus familiaris*	hemi-mandible	right
733	K2	III	1	*Odocoileus virginianus*	radius	right
733	K2	III	1	*Odocoileus virginianus*	scapula	right
733	K2	III	1	*Odocoileus virginianus*	humerus	left
733	K2	III	2	*Odocoileus virginianus*	femur	right
733	K2	III	1	*Odocoileus virginianus*	ulna	right
733	K2	III	1	*Odocoileus virginianus*	scapula	left
733	K2	III	1	*Odocoileus virginianus*	sternum	n/a
733	K2	III	3	*Odocoileus virginianus*	ilium	right
733	K2	III	1	*Odocoileus virginianus*	pubis	right
733	K2	III	3	*Odocoileus virginianus*	ischium	right
733	K2	III	2	*Odocoileus virginianus*	ischium	left

Bag number	Square	Layer	NISP	Species	Specimen	Side
733	K2	III	4	*Odocoileus virginianus*	pelvis (central)	n/a
733	K2	III	1	*Odocoileus virginianus*	scapula	n/a
733	K2	III	1	*Odocoileus virginianus*	radius	right
733	K2	III	2	*Odocoileus virginianus*	thoracic vertebra	n/a
733	K2	III	1	*Odocoileus virginianus*	axis	n/a
733	K2	III	4	*Odocoileus virginianus*	cervical vertebra	n/a
733	K2	III	8	*Odocoileus virginianus*	vertebra	n/a
733	K2	III	3	*Odocoileus viriniaris*	lumbar vertebra	n/a
733	K2	III	2	*Odocoileus virginianus*	thoracic vertebra	n/a
733	K2	III	1	*Sylvilagus floridanus*	innominate	right
733	K2	III	1	*Odocoileus virginianus*	maxilla	right
733	K2	III	19	medium/large mammal	rib (middle)	n/a
733	K2	III	2	small/medium mammal	rib (middle)	n/a
733	K2	III	3	medium/large mammal	rib (proximal)	n/a
733	K2	III	3	medium/large mammal	long bone splinter	n/a
736	E2	III	1	*Odocoileus virginianus*	humerus	right
736	E2	III	1	*Odocoileus virginianus*	humerus	left
736	E2	III	1	*Odocoileus virginianus*	femur	left
736	E2	III	1	*Odocoileus virginianus*	femur	right
736	E2	III	1	*Odocoileus virginianus*	innominate	right
736	E2	III	1	*Odocoileus virginianus*	metacarpus I	left
736	E2	III	1	*Odocoileus virginianus*	metacarpus II	left
736	E2	III	3	*Odocoileus virginianus*	thoracic vertebra	n/a
736	E2	III	3	*Odocoileus virginianus*	lumbar vertebra	n/a
736	E2	III	1	n.i.	rib (proximal)	n/a
736	E2	III	5	medium/large mammal	rib (middle)	n/a
736	E2	III	1	medium/large mammal	rib (proximal)	n/a
736	E2	III	4	medium/large mammal	irregular	n/a
736	E2	III	3	medium/large mammal	long bone splinter	n/a
738	I1	III	1	*Odocoileus virginianus*	radius	left
738	I1	III	1	*Odocoileus virginianus*	radius	right
738	I1	III	1	*Odocoileus virginianus*	ulna	left
738	I1	III	1	*Odocoileus virginianus*	ulna	right
738	I1	III	1	*Odocoileus virginianus*	scapula	right
738	I1	III	1	*Odocoileus virginianus*	metacarpus	right
738	I1	III	1	*Odocoileus virginianus*	ischium	left
738	I1	III	6	*Odocoileus virginianus*	thoracic vertebra	n/a
738	I1	III	1	*Odocoileus virginianus*	thoracic vertebra (T13)	n/a
738	I1	III	1	*Odocoileus virginianus*	lumbar vertebra (L1)	n/a
738	I1	III	1	*Canis lupus familiaris*	innominate	right
738	I1	III	1	n.i.	humerus	n/a
738	I1	III	3	medium/large mammal	rib (middle)	n/a
738	I1	III	2	medium/large mammal	rib (proximal)	n/a
738	I1	III	1	medium/large mammal	metacarpus splinter	n/a
744	J1	III	1	*Odocoileus virginianus*	atlas	n/a
744	J1	III	1	*Odocoileus virginianus*	cervical vertebra	n/a
744	J1	III	5	*Odocoileus virginianus*	lumbar vertebra	n/a
744	J1	III	1	*Odocoileus virginianus*	radius	right
744	J1	III	1	*Odocoileus virginianus*	hemi-mandible	right
744	J1	III	1	*Odocoileus virginianus*	hemi-mandible	left
744	J1	III	1	*Odocoileus virginianus*	radius	right
744	J1	III	1	*Odocoileus virginianus*	skull	n/a
744	J1	III	1	*Odocoileus virginianus*	calcaneus	left

Bag number	Square	Layer	NISP	Species	Specimen	Side
744	J1	III	5	*Odocoileus virginianus*	thoracic vertebra	n/a
744	J1	III	1	*Odocoileus virginianus*	maxilla	left
744	J1	III	2	medium/large mammal	rib (distal)	n/a
744	J1	III	11	medium/large mammal	rib (middle)	n/a
744	J1	III	6	medium/large mammal	rib (proximal)	n/a
744	J1	III	3	medium/large mammal	scapula	n/a
744	J1	III	1	medium/large mammal	long bone splinter	n/a
744	J1	III	1	medium/large mammal	vertebra	n/a
746	K1	II	1	medium/large mammal	metatarsus splinter	n/a
747	K1	II	1	*Odocoileus virginianus*	maxilla	left
747	K1	II	1	*Odocoileus virginianus*	skull	left
747	K1	II	1	*Odocoileus virginianus*	innominate	left
747	K1	II	1	*Odocoileus virginianus*	radius	right
747	K1	II	2	*Odocoileus virginianus*	atlas	n/a
747	K1	II	1	*Odocoileus virginianus*	lumbar vertebra	n/a
747	K1	II	11	medium/large mammal	rib (middle)	n/a
747	K1	II	1	medium/large mammal	rib (proximal)	n/a
747	K1	II	4	medium/large mammal	irregular	n/a
749	K1	II	1	*Odocoileus virginianus*	scapula	right
749	K1	II	1	*Odocoileus virginianus*	calcaneus	right
749	K1	II	2	*Odocoileus virginianus*	axis	n/a
749	K1	II	1	*Odocoileus virginianus*	ischium	right
749	K1	II	1	*Odocoileus virginianus*	innominate	right
749	K1	II	4	*Odocoileus virginianus*	pelvis (central)	n/a
749	K1	II	1	*Odocoileus virginianus*	scapula	left
749	K1	II	2	*Odocoileus virginianus*	scapula	n/a
749	K1	II	1	*Odocoileus virginianus*	metatarsus	n/a
749	K1	II	2	*Odocoileus virginianus*	lumbar vertebra	n/a
749	K1	II	5	medium/large mammal	rib (middle)	n/a
749	K1	II	2	medium/large mammal	irregular	n/a
749	K1	II	1	*Odocoileus virginianus*	pubis	right
753	I2	IV	1	*Odocoileus virginianus*	hemi-mandible	right
753	I2	IV	1	*Odocoileus virginianus*	scapula	left
753	I2	IV	1	*Odocoileus virginianus*	innominate	right
753	I2	IV	1	*Odocoileus virginianus*	ischium	right
753	I2	IV	1	*Odocoileus virginianus*	ilium	left
753	I2	IV	1	*Odocoileus virginianus*	ilium	right
753	I2	IV	1	*Odocoileus virginianus*	ischium	left
753	I2	IV	1	*Odocoileus virginianus*	patella	right
753	I2	IV	1	*Odocoileus virginianus*	femur	left
753	I2	IV	1	*Odocoileus virginianus*	metatarsus	right
753	I2	IV	1	*Odocoileus virginianus*	thoracic vertebra	n/a
753	I2	IV	1	*Canis lupus familiaris*	radius	left
753	I2	IV	3	*Odocoileus virginianus*	hemi-mandible	right
753	I2	IV	2	*Odocoileus virginianus*	hemi-mandible	left
753	I2	IV	1	*Odocoileus virginianus*	ilium	right
753	I2	IV	4	medium/large mammal	rib (distal)	n/a
753	I2	IV	14	medium/large mammal	rib (middle)	n/a
753	I2	IV	1	medium/large mammal	rib (proximal)	n/a
753	I2	IV	1	medium/large mammal	long bone splinter	n/a
759	K2	IV	1	*Odocoileus virginianus*	pubis	right
759	K2	IV	1	*Odocoileus virginianus*	innominate	right
759	K2	IV	1	*Odocoileus virginianus*	innominate	left

Bag number	Square	Layer	NISP	Species	Specimen	Side
759	K2	IV	1	*Odocoileus virginianus*	scapula	left
759	K2	IV	1	*Odocoileus virginianus*	pubis	n/a
759	K2	IV	1	*Odocoileus virginianus*	ischium	n/a
759	K2	IV	1	*Odocoileus virginianus*	hemi-mandible	left
759	K2	IV	1	*Odocoileus virginianus*	lumbar vertebra (L2)	n/a
759	K2	IV	1	*Odocoileus virginianus*	lumbar vertebra (L3)	n/a
759	K2	IV	1	*Odocoileus virginianus*	lumbar vertebra (L4)	n/a
759	K2	IV	1	*Odocoileus virginianus*	lumbar vertebra (L5)	n/a
759	K2	IV	1	*Odocoileus virginianus*	axis	n/a
759	K2	IV	2	*Odocoileus virginianus*	cervical vertebra	n/a
759	K2	IV	4	*Odocoileus virginianus*	thoracic vertebra	n/a
759	K2	IV	1	*Odocoileus virginianus*	sacrum	n/a
759	K2	IV	10	*Odocoileus virginianus*	lumbar vertebra	n/a
759	K2	IV	1	*Odocoileus virginianus*	skull	n/a
759	K2	IV	1	*Canis* sp.	tibia	left
759	K2	IV	1	*Odocoileus virginianus*	maxilla	left
759	K2	IV	1	*Odocoileus virginianus*	maxilla	right
759	K2	IV	13	medium/large mammal	rib (middle)	n/a
759	K2	IV	2	medium/large mammal	rib (proximal)	n/a
759	K2	IV	1	small/medium mammal	rib (proximal)	n/a
767	I2	II	1	*Odocoileus virginianus*	ulna	left
767	I2	II	1	medium/large mammal	rib (middle)	n/a
770	I1	III	1	*Odocoileus virginianus*	ulna	left
770	I1	III	1	*Odocoileus virginianus*	scapula	left
770	I1	III	1	medium/large mammal	long bone splinter	n/a
774	J2	III	1	*Odocoileus virginianus*	humerus	right
774	J2	III	1	*Odocoileus virginianus*	radius	left
774	J2	III	1	*Odocoileus virginianus*	humerus	right
774	J2	III	1	*Odocoileus virginianus*	ulna	left
774	J2	III	1	*Odocoileus virginianus*	calcaneus	right
774	J2	III	1	*Odocoileus virginianus*	phalange	n/a
774	J2	III	5	*Odocoileus virginianus*	cervical vertebra	n/a
774	J2	III	2	*Odocoileus virginianus*	thoracic vertebra	n/a
774	J2	III	3	*Odocoileus virginianus*	lumbar vertebra	n/a
774	J2	III	11	*Odocoileus virginianus*	vertebra	n/a
774	J2	III	1	*Canis lupus familiaris*	hemi-mandible	left
774	J2	III	1	*Odocoileus virginianus*	hemi-mandible	right
774	J2	III	1	*Odocoileus virginianus*	maxilla	left
774	J2	III	1	*Odocoileus virginianus*	maxilla	right
774	J2	III	1	*Odocoileus virginianus*	hemi-mandible	left
774	J2	III	8	medium/large mammal	rib (middle)	n/a
774	J2	III	5	medium/large mammal	rib (proximal)	n/a
774	J2	III	2	medium/large mammal	long bone splinter	n/a
788	J2	IV	1	*Odocoileus virginianus*	metacarpus	left
788	J2	IV	1	*Odocoileus virginianus*	metatarsus	n/a
788	J2	IV	12	*Odocoileus virginianus*	thoracic vertebra	n/a
788	J2	IV	15	*Odocoileus virginianus*	lumbar vertebra	n/a
788	J2	IV	1	*Odocoileus virginianus*	sacrum	n/a
788	J2	IV	1	*Odocoileus virginianus*	ischium	right
788	J2	IV	2	*Odocoileus virginianus*	ilium	right
788	J2	IV	1	*Odocoileus virginianus*	ischium	right
788	J2	IV	1	*Odocoileus virginianus*	ilium	left
788	J2	IV	10	*Odocoileus virginianus*	cervical vertebra	n/a

Bag number	Square	Layer	NISP	Species	Specimen	Side
788	J2	IV	1	*Odocoileus virginianus*	cervical vertebra (C7)	n/a
788	J2	IV	1	*Odocoileus virginianus*	lumbar vertebra (L5)	n/a
788	J2	IV	2	*Odocoileus virginianus*	axis	n/a
788	J2	IV	1	*Odocoileus virginianus*	atlas	n/a
788	J2	IV	3	*Odocoileus virginianus*	sacrum I	n/a
788	J2	IV	1	*Odocoileus virginianus*	humerus	right
788	J2	IV	1	*Odocoileus virginianus*	humerus	n/a
788	J2	IV	1	*Odocoileus virginianus*	metacarpus	left
788	J2	IV	1	*Odocoileus virginianus*	calcaneus	right
788	J2	IV	1	*Odocoileus virginianus*	phalange II	n/a
788	J2	IV	3	*Odocoileus virginianus*	scapula	left
788	J2	IV	2	*Odocoileus virginianus*	scapula	n/a
788	J2	IV	1	*Odocoileus virginianus*	innominate	left
788	J2	IV	1	*Odocoileus virginianus*	innominate	right
788	J2	IV	5	*Odocoileus virginianus*	skull	n/a
788	J2	IV	1	*Canis lupus familiaris*	tibia	right
788	J2	IV	1	*Canis lupus familiaris*	humerus	right
788	J2	IV	1	*Canis lupus familiaris*	lumbar vertebra	n/a
788	J2	IV	1	*Odocoileus virginianus*	hemi-mandible	right
788	J2	IV	1	n.i.	rib (middle)	n/a
788	J2	IV	6	medium/large mammal	rib (distal)	n/a
788	J2	IV	53	medium/large mammal	rib (middle)	n/a
788	J2	IV	1	medium/large mammal	rib (proximal)	n/a
788	J2	IV	9	medium/large mammal	rib (proximal)	n/a
788	J2	IV	2	medium/large mammal	skull	n/a
788	J2	IV	3	medium/large mammal	vertebra	n/a
788	J2	IV	8	medium/large mammal	irregular	n/a
788	J2	IV	1	medium/large mammal	metatarsus splinter	n/a
796	H1	IV	1	*Odocoileus virginianus*	radius	right
796	H1	IV	1	*Odocoileus virginianus*	humerus	right
796	H1	IV	1	*Odocoileus virginianus*	femur	right
796	H1	IV	1	*Odocoileus virginianus*	radius	left
796	H1	IV	2	*Odocoileus virginianus*	scapula	right
796	H1	IV	1	*Odocoileus virginianus*	ilium	left
796	H1	IV	1	*Odocoileus virginianus*	ischium	right
796	H1	IV	1	*Odocoileus virginianus*	thoracic vertebra (T1)	n/a
796	H1	IV	2	*Odocoileus virginianus*	thoracic vertebra	n/a
796	H1	IV	1	*Odocoileus virginianus*	lumbar vertebra	n/a
796	H1	IV	1	*Odocoileus virginianus*	ischium	n/a
796	H1	IV	1	*Odocoileus virginianus*	pubis	n/a
796	H1	IV	1	*Odocoileus virginianus*	sacrum I	right
796	H1	IV	1	*Odocoileus virginianus*	cuboides-escafoides	left
796	H1	IV	1	*Sylvilagus* sp. (possibly *S. brasiliensis*)	innominate	right
796	H1	IV	1	*Odocoileus virginianus*	1st rib	n/a
796	H1	IV	4	medium/large mammal	rib (middle)	n/a
796	H1	IV	1	medium/large mammal	tibia splinter	n/a
799	J1	IV	1	*Odocoileus virginianus*	thoracic vertebra (T1)	n/a
799	J1	IV	1	*Odocoileus virginianus*	radius	left
799	J1	IV	2	*Odocoileus virginianus*	innominate	left
799	J1	IV	2	*Odocoileus virginianus*	innominate	right
799	J1	IV	1	*Odocoileus virginianus*	scapula	left
799	J1	IV	1	*Odocoileus virginianus*	scapula	right

Bag number	Square	Layer	NISP	Species	Specimen	Side
799	J1	IV	2	*Odocoileus virginianus*	thoracic vertebra	n/a
799	J1	IV	1	n.i.	long bone (diaphysis)	n/a
799	J1	IV	5	medium/large mammal	rib (middle)	n/a
799	J1	IV	1	medium/large mammal	rib (proximal)	n/a
799	J1	IV	1	medium/large mammal	long bone splinter	n/a
800	H2	III	1	medium/large mammal	rib (middle)	n/a
801	J2	V	1	*Odocoileus virginianus*	thoracic vertebra	n/a
801	J2	V	3	*Odocoileus virginianus*	lumbar vertebra	n/a
801	J2	V	1	*Odocoileus virginianus*	scapula	n/a
801	J2	V	1	*Odocoileus virginianus*	hemi-mandible	right
801	J2	V	3	medium/large mammal	rib (middle)	n/a
801	J2	V	1	medium/large mammal	rib (proximal)	n/a
801	J2	V	3	medium/large mammal	flat bone	n/a
801	J2	V	9	medium/large mammal	irregular	n/a
801	J2	V	1	small/medium mammal	long bone (diaphysis)	n/a
805	E2	V	1	*Odocoileus virginianus*	scapula	left
805	E2	V	2	*Odocoileus virginianus*	atlas	n/a
805	E2	V	1	*Odocoileus virginianus*	ischium	right
805	E2	V	1	*Odocoileus virginianus*	ischium	left
805	E2	V	1	*Odocoileus virginianus*	cuboides-escafoides	left
805	E2	V	1	*Odocoileus virginianus*	hemi-mandible	left
805	E2	V	1	*Odocoileus virginianus*	radius	n/a
805	E2	V	2	*Odocoileus virginianus*	vertebra	n/a
805	E2	V	1	n.i.	rib (proximal)	n/a
805	E2	V	2	medium/large mammal	rib (middle)	n/a
805	E2	V	1	medium/large mammal	rib (proximal)	n/a
805	E2	V	2	medium/large mammal	long bone splinter	n/a
807	G2	IV	1	*Odocoileus virginianus*	femur	left
807	G2	IV	1	*Odocoileus virginianus*	scapula	right
807	G2	IV	2	*Odocoileus virginianus*	ilium	right
807	G2	IV	1	*Odocoileus virginianus*	astragalus	right
807	G2	IV	1	*Odocoileus virginianus*	ischium	left
807	G2	IV	1	*Odocoileus virginianus*	atlas	n/a
807	G2	IV	1	*Odocoileus virginianus*	ulna	left
807	G2	IV	1	*Odocoileus virginianus*	radius	left
807	G2	IV	1	*Odocoileus virginianus*	lumbar vertebra	n/a
807	G2	IV	1	*Odocoileus virginianus*	scapula	right
807	G2	IV	1	*Odocoileus virginianus*	ilium	left
807	G2	IV	1	*Odocoileus virginianus*	ischium	right
807	G2	IV	1	*Odocoileus virginianus*	metapodium	n/a
807	G2	IV	1	*Odocoileus virginianus*	thoracic vertebra	n/a
807	G2	IV	3	medium/large mammal	rib (distal)	n/a
807	G2	IV	2	medium/large mammal	rib (proximal)	n/a
807	G2	IV	1	medium/large mammal	irregular	n/a
807	G2	IV	1	medium/large mammal	long bone splinter	n/a
807	G2	IV	1	small/medium mammal	long bone (proximal)	n/a
811	G1	IV	1	*Odocoileus virginianus*	radius	right
811	G1	IV	1	*Odocoileus virginianus*	femur	left
811	G1	IV	3	*Odocoileus virginianus*	scapula	left
811	G1	IV	1	*Odocoileus virginianus*	scapula	right
811	G1	IV	1	*Odocoileus virginianus*	innominate	right
811	G1	IV	1	*Odocoileus virginianus*	ischium	right
811	G1	IV	1	*Odocoileus virginianus*	atlas	n/a

Bag number	Square	Layer	NISP	Species	Specimen	Side
811	G1	IV	2	*Odocoileus virginianus*	cervical vertebra	n/a
811	G1	IV	2	*Odocoileus virginianus*	thoracic vertebra	n/a
811	G1	IV	2	*Odocoileus virginianus*	lumbar vertebra	n/a
811	G1	IV	1	*Panthera onca*	ulna	left
811	G1	IV	1	medium/large mammal	rib (middle)	n/a
816	I2	V	1	*Odocoileus virginianus*	ischium	right
816	I2	V	2	*Odocoileus virginianus*	thoracic vertebra	n/a
816	I2	V	7	*Odocoileus virginianus*	lumbar vertebra	n/a
816	I2	V	17	*Odocoileus virginianus*	vertebra	n/a
816	I2	V	1	small/medium mammal	tibia	n/a
816	I2	V	2	medium/large mammal	rib (distal)	n/a
816	I2	V	9	medium/large mammal	rib (middle)	n/a
816	I2	V	2	medium/large mammal	rib (proximal)	n/a
816	I2	V	1	medium/large mammal	long bone splinter	n/a
818	H1	V	1	*Odocoileus virginianus*	tibia	n/a
818	H1	V	1	medium/large mammal	rib (middle)	n/a
818	H1	V	1	medium/large mammal	long bone splinter	n/a
820	H2	IV	1	*Odocoileus virginianus*	cervical vertebra	n/a
820	H2	IV	1	*Odocoileus virginianus*	thoracic vertebra	n/a
820	H2	IV	2	medium/large mammal	rib (middle)	n/a
823	K1	III	1	*Odocoileus virginianus*	skull	n/a
823	K1	III	2	*Odocoileus virginianus*	scapula	right
823	K1	III	1	*Odocoileus virginianus*	ilium	right
823	K1	III	1	*Odocoileus virginianus*	innominate	left
823	K1	III	1	*Odocoileus virginianus*	ischium	left
823	K1	III	1	*Odocoileus virginianus*	hemi-mandible	left
823	K1	III	1	*Odocoileus virginianus*	phalange I	n/a
823	K1	III	1	*Odocoileus virginianus*	sternum	n/a
823	K1	III	5	*Odocoileus virginianus*	thoracic vertebra	n/a
823	K1	III	1	*Odocoileus virginianus*	cervical vertebra	n/a
823	K1	III	2	*Odocoileus virginianus*	lumbar vertebra	n/a
823	K1	III	1	*Odocoileus virginianus*	sacrum I	n/a
823	K1	III	2	medium/large mammal	rib (middle)	n/a
823	K1	III	1	medium/large mammal	rib (proximal)	n/a
823	K1	III	1	medium/large mammal	long bone splinter	n/a
826	K1	III	1	*Pecari tajacu*	hemi-mandible	left
826	K1	III	1	*Pecari tajacu*	hemi-mandible	right
833	G2	V	1	*Odocoileus virginianus*	radius	left
833	G2	V	1	*Odocoileus virginianus*	metatarsus	right
833	G2	V	1	*Odocoileus virginianus*	femur	left
833	G2	V	1	*Odocoileus virginianus*	calcaneus	right
833	G2	V	1	*Odocoileus virginianus*	humerus	left
833	G2	V	1	*Odocoileus virginianus*	radius	left
833	G2	V	1	*Odocoileus virginianus*	innominate	right
833	G2	V	3	*Odocoileus virginianus*	scapula	right
833	G2	V	3	*Odocoileus virginianus*	ilium	right
833	G2	V	1	*Odocoileus virginianus*	innominate	left
833	G2	V	3	*Odocoileus virginianus*	scapula	left
833	G2	V	2	*Odocoileus virginianus*	thoracic vertebra	n/a
833	G2	V	4	*Odocoileus virginianus*	lumbar vertebra	n/a
833	G2	V	1	*Odocoileus virginianus*	cervical vertebra	n/a
833	G2	V	3	medium/large mammal	rib (middle)	n/a
833	G2	V	1	medium/large mammal	long bone splinter	n/a

Bag number	Square	Layer	NISP	Species	Specimen	Side
842	H2	V	1	*Odocoileus virginianus*	skull	n/a
842	H2	V	1	*Odocoileus virginianus*	skull	right
842	H2	V	1	*Odocoileus virginianus*	skull	left
842	H2	V	1	*Odocoileus virginianus*	hemi-mandible	n/a
842	H2	V	1	*Odocoileus virginianus*	scapula	right
842	H2	V	1	*Odocoileus virginianus*	calcaneus	left
842	H2	V	1	*Odocoileus virginianus*	radius	left
842	H2	V	1	*Odocoileus virginianus*	humerus	left
842	H2	V	2	*Odocoileus virginianus*	radius	left
842	H2	V	1	*Odocoileus virginianus*	scapula	right
842	H2	V	1	*Odocoileus virginianus*	ischium	right
842	H2	V	1	*Odocoileus virginianus*	metacarpus	left
842	H2	V	4	*Odocoileus virginianus*	hemi-mandible	left
842	H2	V	3	*Odocoileus virginianus*	hemi-mandible	right
842	H2	V	1	*Odocoileus virginianus*	atlas	n/a
842	H2	V	3	*Odocoileus virginianus*	femur	left
842	H2	V	6	*Odocoileus virginianus*	lumbar vertebra	n/a
842	H2	V	4	*Odocoileus virginianus*	cervical vertebra	n/a
842	H2	V	2	*Odocoileus virginianus*	thoracic vertebra	n/a
842	H2	V	1	*Artiodactyla* (posibly *Pecari tajacu*)	innominate	right
842	H2	V	1	n.i.	scapula	n/a
842	H2	V	2	medium/large mammal	skull (zygomatic)	n/a
842	H2	V	2	medium/large mammal	rib (distal)	n/a
842	H2	V	14	medium/large mammal	rib (middle)	n/a
842	H2	V	6	medium/large mammal	rib (proximal)	n/a
842	H2	V	1	medium/large mammal	metacarpus splinter	n/a
950	H1	V	4	*Odocoileus virginianus*	thoracic vertebra (T1)	n/a
950	H1	V	2	*Odocoileus virginianus*	cervical vertebra	n/a
950	H1	V	2	*Odocoileus virginianus*	hemi-mandible	n/a
950	H1	V	1	Felidae	cervical vertebra	n/a
950	H1	V	1	*Odocoileus virginianus*	hemi-mandible	right
950	H1	V	1	medium/large mammal	rib (distal)	n/a
950	H1	V	1	medium/large mammal	rib (middle)	n/a
950	H1	V	3	medium/large mammal	rib (proximal)	n/a
954	G1	V	1	*Odocoileus virginianus*	calcaneus	left
954	G1	V	1	*Odocoileus virginianus*	cuboides-escafoides	left
954	G1	V	1	*Odocoileus virginianus*	metatarsus	left
954	G1	V	1	*Odocoileus virginianus*	hemi-mandible	right
954	G1	V	1	*Odocoileus virginianus*	sacrum I	n/a
954	G1	V	2	*Odocoileus virginianus*	thoracic vertebra	n/a
954	G1	V	1	medium/large mammal	rib (distal)	n/a
954	G1	V	1	medium/large mammal	rib (proximal)	n/a
954	G1	V	1	medium/large mammal	long bone splinter	n/a
961	F1	IV	1	*Odocoileus virginianus*	ilium	left
961	F1	IV	1	*Odocoileus virginianus*	scapula	right
961	F1	IV	2	*Odocoileus virginianus*	thoracic vertebra	n/a
961	F1	IV	3	*Odocoileus virginianus*	lumbar vertebra	n/a
961	F1	IV	1	*Odocoileus virginianus*	sacrum I	n/a
961	F1	IV	1	medium/large mammal	rib (distal)	n/a
961	F1	IV	4	medium/large mammal	rib (middle)	n/a
965	E2	IV	1	*Odocoileus virginianus*	metatarsus	n/a
965	E2	IV	1	*Odocoileus virginianus*	ilium	left
965	E2	IV	1	*Odocoileus virginianus*	ischium	right

Bag number	Square	Layer	NISP	Species	Specimen	Side
965	E2	IV	1	*Odocoileus virginianus*	phalange I	n/a
965	E2	IV	1	*Odocoileus virginianus*	lumbar vertebra	n/a
965	E2	IV	1	*Odocoileus virginianus*	sacrum I	n/a
965	E2	IV	1	*Canis lupus familiaris*	hemi-mandible	right
965	E2	IV	6	medium/large mammal	rib (middle)	n/a
965	E2	IV	1	medium/large mammal	metacarpus splinter	n/a
967	E1	IV	4	*Odocoileus virginianus*	lumbar vertebra	n/a
967	E1	IV	1	*Odocoileus virginianus*	vertebra	n/a
967	E1	IV	4	*Odocoileus virginianus*	atlas	n/a
969	F2	IV	2	*Odocoileus virginianus*	ilium	left
969	F2	IV	1	*Odocoileus virginianus*	humerus	right
969	F2	IV	1	medium/large mammal	long bone splinter	n/a
975	F2	V	1	*Odocoileus virginianus*	humerus	left
975	F2	V	2	*Odocoileus virginianus*	ilium	left
975	F2	V	1	*Odocoileus virginianus*	scapula	left
975	F2	V	1	*Odocoileus virginianus*	humerus	left
975	F2	V	2	*Odocoileus virginianus*	axis	n/a
975	F2	V	1	*Odocoileus virginianus*	atlas	n/a
975	F2	V	1	*Odocoileus virginianus*	thoracic vertebra	n/a
975	F2	V	2	*Odocoileus virginianus*	lumbar vertebra	n/a
975	F2	V	3	*Odocoileus virginianus*	vertebra	n/a
975	F2	V	1	*Odocoileus virginianus*	scapula	n/a
975	F2	V	1	small/medium mammal	rib (middle)	n/a
975	F2	V	1	n.i.	rib (proximal)	n/a
975	F2	V	12	medium/large mammal	rib (middle)	n/a
975	F2	V	7	medium/large mammal	rib (proximal)	n/a
975	F2	V	2	medium/large mammal	long bone splinter	n/a
980	F1	V	1	*Odocoileus virginianus*	humerus	left
980	F1	V	2	*Odocoileus virginianus*	scapula	right
980	F1	V	1	*Odocoileus virginianus*	cervical vertebra	n/a
980	F1	V	1	*Odocoileus virginianus*	thoracic vertebra	n/a
980	F1	V	2	*Odocoileus virginianus*	lumbar vertebra	n/a
980	F1	V	1	*Odocoileus virginianus*	sternum	n/a
980	F1	V	1	*Odocoileus virginianus*	maxilla	left
980	F1	V	3	medium/large mammal	long bone splinter	n/a
980	F1	V	2	medium/large mammal	rib (distal)	n/a
980	F1	V	19	medium/large mammal	rib (middle)	n/a
980	F1	V	2	medium/large mammal	rib (proximal)	n/a
985	F1	V	1	*Odocoileus virginianus*	scapula	right
985	F1	V	1	*Odocoileus virginianus*	scapula	left
985	F1	V	2	*Odocoileus virginianus*	innominate	left
985	F1	V	1	*Odocoileus virginianus*	calcaneus	left
985	F1	V	1	*Odocoileus virginianus*	cuboides-escafoides	left
985	F1	V	1	*Odocoileus virginianus*	scapula	n/a
985	F1	V	1	*Odocoileus virginianus*	atlas	n/a
985	F1	V	3	*Odocoileus virginianus*	cervical vertebra	n/a
985	F1	V	4	*Odocoileus virginianus*	thoracic vertebra	n/a
985	F1	V	2	*Odocoileus virginianus*	lumbar vertebra	n/a
985	F1	V	1	*Sylvilagus* sp. (posibly *S. brasiliensis*)	femur	right
985	F1	V	1	n.i.	long bone (diaphysis)	n/a
985	F1	V	1	small/medium mammal	rib (middle)	n/a
985	F1	V	32	medium/large mammal	rib (distal)	n/a

Bag number	Square	Layer	NISP	Species	Specimen	Side
985	F1	V	7	medium/large mammal	rib (proximal)	n/a
985	F1	V	8	medium/large mammal	long bone splinter	n/a
989	E2	V	1	*Odocoileus virginianus*	femur	left
989	E2	V	1	*Odocoileus virginianus*	femur	right
989	E2	V	1	*Odocoileus virginianus*	atlas	n/a
989	E2	V	2	*Odocoileus virginianus*	cervical vertebra	n/a
989	E2	V	2	*Odocoileus virginianus*	scapula	left
989	E2	V	1	*Odocoileus virginianus*	scapula	right
989	E2	V	1	*Odocoileus virginianus*	hemi-mandible	n/a
989	E2	V	3	*Odocoileus virginianus*	lumbar vertebra	n/a
989	E2	V	1	*Odocoileus virginianus*	antler	right
989	E2	V	4	medium/large mammal	rib (middle)	n/a
989	E2	V	1	medium/large mammal	rib (proximal)	n/a
989	E2	V	1	medium/large mammal	long bone splinter	n/a
989	E2	V	1	medium/large mammal	metatarsus splinter	n/a
993	F2	V	1	*Odocoileus virginianus*	tibia	right
993	F2	V	6	*Odocoileus virginianus*	scapula	n/a
993	F2	V	1	*Odocoileus virginianus*	innominate	right
993	F2	V	1	*Odocoileus virginianus*	radius	left
993	F2	V	1	*Odocoileus virginianus*	calcaneus	left
993	F2	V	1	*Odocoileus virginianus*	radius	left
993	F2	V	1	*Odocoileus virginianus*	humerus	left
993	F2	V	4	*Odocoileus virginianus*	scapula	left
993	F2	V	1	*Odocoileus virginianus*	scapula	right
993	F2	V	2	*Odocoileus virginianus*	ulna	right
993	F2	V	1	*Odocoileus virginianus*	hemi-mandible	left
993	F2	V	1	*Odocoileus virginianus*	hemi-mandible	n/a
993	F2	V	1	*Odocoileus virginianus*	ischium	left
993	F2	V	4	*Odocoileus virginianus*	thoracic vertebra	n/a
993	F2	V	6	*Odocoileus virginianus*	lumbar vertebra	n/a
993	F2	V	2	*Odocoileus virginianus*	cervical vertebra	n/a
993	F2	V	1	*Odocoileus virginianus*	atlas	n/a
993	F2	V	4	*Odocoileus virginianus*	vertebra	n/a
993	F2	V	1	*Odocoileus virginianus*	ilium	n/a
993	F2	V	1	*Canis lupus familiaris*	metacarpus	n/a
993	F2	V	1	*Canis lupus familiaris*	rib	n/a
993	F2	V	1	*Urocyon cinereoargenteus*	skull	left
993	F2	V	30	medium/large mammal	rib (middle)	n/a
993	F2	V	5	medium/large mammal	rib (proximal)	n/a
993	F2	V	15	medium/large mammal	long bone splinter	n/a
993	F2	V	1	medium/large mammal	metapodium splinter	n/a
1009	F2	V	1	*Odocoileus virginianus*	hemi-mandible	left
1009	F2	V	1	*Canis* sp.	hemi-mandible	left
1009	F2	V	1	*Canis lupus familiaris*	hemi-mandible	left
1012	G2	V	3	*Odocoileus virginianus*	scapula	right
1012	G2	V	2	*Odocoileus virginianus*	cervical vertebra	n/a
1012	G2	V	1	*Odocoileus virginianus*	axis	n/a
1012	G2	V	1	*Odocoileus virginianus*	maxilla	n/a
1012	G2	V	3	medium/large mammal	rib (middle)	n/a
1012	G2	V	2	medium/large mammal	irregular	n/a
1019	K1	IV	1	*Odocoileus virginianus*	skull	right
1019	K1	IV	1	*Odocoileus virginianus*	scapula	n/a
1019	K1	IV	1	*Odocoileus virginianus*	thoracic vertebra (T1)	n/a

Bag number	Square	Layer	NISP	Species	Specimen	Side
1019	K1	IV	1	*Odocoileus virginianus*	skull	left
1019	K1	IV	1	*Odocoileus virginianus*	tibia	n/a
1019	K1	IV	1	*Odocoileus virginianus*	skull	n/a
1019	K1	IV	1	*Odocoileus virginianus*	radius	left
1019	K1	IV	3	*Odocoileus virginianus*	scapula	left
1019	K1	IV	1	*Odocoileus virginianus*	humerus	right
1019	K1	IV	1	*Odocoileus virginianus*	radius	right
1019	K1	IV	1	*Odocoileus virginianus*	ulna	left
1019	K1	IV	1	*Odocoileus virginianus*	humerus	left
1019	K1	IV	1	*Odocoileus virginianus*	astragalus	right
1019	K1	IV	1	*Odocoileus virginianus*	femur	right
1019	K1	IV	1	*Odocoileus virginianus*	femur	left
1019	K1	IV	3	*Odocoileus virginianus*	atlas	n/a
1019	K1	IV	1	*Odocoileus virginianus*	axis	n/a
1019	K1	IV	5	*Odocoileus virginianus*	cervical vertebra	n/a
1019	K1	IV	5	*Odocoileus virginianus*	lumbar vertebra	n/a
1019	K1	IV	1	*Odocoileus virginianus*	sacrum	n/a
1019	K1	IV	13	*Odocoileus virginianus*	thoracic vertebra	n/a
1019	K1	IV	1	*Odocoileus virginianus*	ulna	right
1019	K1	IV	1	*Odocoileus virginianus*	hemi-mandible	n/a
1019	K1	IV	1	*Sylvilagus brasiliensis*	femur	right
1019	K1	IV	1	*Sylvilagus sp.*	hemi-mandible	left
1019	K1	IV	1	carnivore	hemi-mandible	left
1019	K1	IV	2	*Odocoileus virginianus*	hemi-mandible	right
1019	K1	IV	1	*Odocoileus virginianus*	antler	n/a
1019	K1	IV	45	medium/large mammal	rib (middle)	n/a
1019	K1	IV	3	medium/large mammal	rib (proximal)	n/a
1019	K1	IV	11	medium/large mammal	rib	n/a
1019	K1	IV	1	medium/large mammal	irregular	n/a
1019	K1	IV	5	medium/large mammal	long bone splinter	n/a
1035	K1	IV	1	*Odocoileus virginianus*	scapula	right
1035	K1	IV	1	*Odocoileus virginianus*	scapula	left
1035	K1	IV	4	*Odocoileus virginianus*	innominate	left
1035	K1	IV	1	*Odocoileus virginianus*	ischium	right
1035	K1	IV	1	*Odocoileus virginianus*	scapula	n/a
1035	K1	IV	1	*Odocoileus virginianus*	axis	n/a
1035	K1	IV	2	*Odocoileus virginianus*	lumbar vertebra	n/a
1035	K1	IV	1	*Mazama sp.*	hemi-mandible	left
1035	K1	IV	1	small/medium mammal	rib (middle)	n/a
1035	K1	IV	6	medium/large mammal	rib (middle)	n/a
1035	K1	IV	1	medium/large mammal	rib (proximal)	n/a
1035	K1	IV	1	*Canis lupus familiaris*	radius	right
1009/678	F1	V	1	*Canis lupus familiaris*	skull	left
1009/678	F2	V	1	n.i.	irregular	n/a
1009/678	F2/H1	V/II	1	*Odocoileus virginianus*	scapula	left
1009/678	F2/H1	V/II	1	*Odocoileus virginianus*	radius	right
1009/678	F2/H1	V/II	1	*Odocoileus virginianus*	scapula	n/a
1009/678	F2/H1	V/II	1	*Odocoileus virginianus*	calcaneus	right
1009/678	F2/H1	V/II	1	*Odocoileus virginianus*	metacarpus I	right (int)
1009/678	F2/H1	V/II	1	*Odocoileus virginianus*	atlas	n/a
1009/678	F2/H1	V/II	1	*Odocoileus virginianus*	axis	n/a
1009/678	F2/H1	V/II	6	*Odocoileus virginianus*	lumbar vertebra	n/a
1009/678	F2/H1	V/II	1	*Odocoileus virginianus*	cervical vertebra	n/a

Bag number	Square	Layer	NISP	Species	Specimen	Side
1009/678	F2/H1	V/II	3	medium/large mammal	rib (middle)	n/a
731/801	J2/K1	V/II	1	*Canis lupus familiaris*	radius	left
n/a	G2	V	1	*Canis lupus familiaris*	phalange II	n/a
n/a	K1	II	2	*Odocoileus virginianus*	thoracic vertebra	n/a
n/a	K1	II	1	*Odocoileus virginianus*	vertebra	n/a
n/a	K1	II	1	*Odocoileus virginianus*	scapula	n/a
n/a	K1	II	1	*Odocoileus virginianus*	sacrum I	n/a
n/a	K1	II	1	*Canis lupus familiaris*	carpus	left
n/a	K1	II	1	*Canis lupus familiaris*	phalange I	left
n/a	K1	II	1	*Canis lupus familiaris*	metacarpus II	left
n/a	K1	II	1	*Canis lupus familiaris*	metacarpus III	left
n/a	K1	II	1	carnivore	radius	left
n/a	K1	II	7	medium/large mammal	rib (middle)	n/a
n/a	K1	II	1	medium/large mammal	rib (proximal)	n/a
n/a	K1	II	2	small/medium mammal	rib (proximal)	n/a
n/a	K1	II	43	medium/large mammal	rib (middle)	n/a
n/a	K1	II	11	medium/large mammal	long bone splinter	n/a
n/a	K1	II	27	medium/large mammal	irregular	n/a
n/a	K1	II	1	medium/large mammal	vertebra	n/a
n/a	K1	II	1	n.i.	rib (proximal)	n/a
n/a	K1	II	1	n.i.	long bone (diaphysis)	n/a
n/a	K1	II	1	n.i.	long bone (distal)	n/a
n/a	K1	II	1	small/medium mammal	long bone	n/a
n/a	K1	II	5	small/medium mammal	irregular	n/a
n/a	K1	II	12	small/medium mammal	long bone (diaphysis)	n/a
n/a	K1	II	2	medium/large mammal	rib (middle)	n/a
n/a	K1	II	8	small/medium mammal	rib (middle)	n/a
n/a	K1	II	1	n.i.	hemi-mandible	n/a

Operacion 201

Bag number	Square	Layer	NISP	Species	Specimen	Side
n/a	2 level	II	1	medium/large mammal	long bone (proximal)	n/a
n/a	2 level	II	2	small/medium mammal	long bone (diaphysis)	n/a
n/a	2 level	II	1	small/medium mammal	skull	n/a
n/a	2 level	II	1	small/medium mammal	pelvis	n/a
n/a	2 level	II	1	small/medium mammal	long bone spinter	n/a
n/a	ext wall	III	2	*Canis lupus familiaris*	radius	left
n/a	ext wall	III	1	*Canis lupus familiaris*	ulna	right
n/a	ext wall	III	1	*Canis lupus familiaris*	metacarpus	n/a
n/a	ext wall	III	1	carnivore	lumbar vertebra	n/a
n/a	ext wall	III	1	carnivore	maxilla	n/a
n/a	ext wall	III	18	medium/large mammal	long bone spinter	n/a
n/a	ext wall	III	1	medium/large mammal	rib (distal)	n/a
n/a	ext wall	III	27	medium/large mammal	rib (middle)	n/a
n/a	ext wall	III	5	medium/large mammal	rib (proximal)	n/a
n/a	ext wall	III	8	medium/large mammal	irregular	n/a
n/a	ext wall	III	1	*Odocoileus virginianus*	skull	n/a
n/a	ext wall	III	1	*Odocoileus virginianus*	femur	left
n/a	ext wall	III	1	*Odocoileus virginianus*	innominate	left
n/a	ext wall	III	1	*Odocoileus virginianus*	innominate	right
n/a	ext wall	III	1	*Odocoileus virginianus*	pubis	left
n/a	ext wall	III	2	*Odocoileus virginianus*	calcaneus	right

Bag number	Square	Layer	NISP	Species	Specimen	Side
n/a	ext wall	III	1	*Odocoileus virginianus*	scapula	right
n/a	ext wall	III	1	*Odocoileus virginianus*	scapula	n/a
n/a	ext wall	III	1	*Odocoileus virginianus*	radius	left
n/a	ext wall	III	1	*Odocoileus virginianus*	metacarpus	left
n/a	ext wall	III	1	*Odocoileus virginianus*	metatarsus	right
n/a	ext wall	III	1	*Odocoileus virginianus*	radius	right
n/a	ext wall	III	1	*Odocoileus virginianus*	calcaneus	left
n/a	ext wall	III	1	*Odocoileus virginianus*	femur	left
n/a	ext wall	III	2	*Odocoileus virginianus*	cervical vertebra	n/a
n/a	ext wall	III	2	*Odocoileus virginianus*	thoracic vertebra	n/a
n/a	ext wall	III	8	*Odocoileus virginianus*	vertebra	n/a
n/a	ext wall	III	1	*Odocoileus virginianus*	humerus	left
n/a	ext wall	III	1	*Odocoileus virginianus*	metacarpus	n/a
n/a	ext wall	III	1	*Odocoileus virginianus*	humerus	n/a
n/a	ext wall	III	1	*Odocoileus virginianus*	ischium	n/a
n/a	ext wall	III	1	*Odocoileus virginianus*	ischium	n/a
n/a	ext wall	III	1	*Odocoileus virginianus*	maxilla	right
n/a	ext wall	III	5	small/medium mammal	long bone (diaphysis)	n/a
n/a	2 level	II	26	medium/large mammal	long bone spinter	n/a
n/a	2 level	II	8	medium/large mammal	rib (middle)	n/a
n/a	2 level	II	3	medium/large mammal	femur splinter	n/a
n/a	2 level	II	1	*Canis lupus familiaris*	metacarpus	n/a
n/a	2 level	II	2	*Canis lupus familiaris*	calcaneus	right
n/a	2 level	II	1	*Canis lupus familiaris*	metacarpus V	left
n/a	2 level	II	3	*Canis lupus familiaris*	radius	left
n/a	2 level	II	1	*Canis lupus familiaris*	radius	right
n/a	2 level	II	1	*Canis lupus familiaris*	radius	n/a
n/a	2 level	II	1	*Canis lupus familiaris*	femur	right
n/a	2 level	II	1	*Canis lupus familiaris*	rib (proximal)	n/a
n/a	2 level	II	1	*Odocoileus virginianus*	skull	n/a
n/a	2 level	II	1	*Odocoileus virginianus*	thoracic vertebra	n/a
n/a	2 level	II	1	*Odocoileus virginianus*	metacarpus I	right (ext)
n/a	2 level	II	1	*Odocoileus virginianus*	metacarpus II	right(int)
n/a	2 level	II	1	*Odocoileus virginianus*	ulna	left
n/a	2 level	II	1	*Odocoileus virginianus*	humerus	left
n/a	2 level	II	1	*Odocoileus virginianus*	metacarpus	right
n/a	2 level	II	1	*Odocoileus virginianus*	radius	left
n/a	2 level	II	1	*Odocoileus virginianus*	tibia	right
n/a	2 level	II	2	*Odocoileus virginianus*	hemi-mandible	right
n/a	2 level	II	1	*Odocoileus virginianus*	hemi-mandible	left
n/a	2 level	II	2	*Odocoileus virginianus*	ilium	right
n/a	2 level	II	4	*Odocoileus virginianus*	vertebra	n/a
n/a	2 level	II	2	*Odocoileus virginianus*	tibia	left

Operacion 202

Bag number	Square	Layer	NISP	Species	Specimen	Side
n/a	n/a	3 metric level	1	*Odocoileus virginianus*	humerus	right
n/a	n/a	3 metric level	1	*Odocoileus virginianus*	scapula	n/a
n/a	n/a	3 metric level	1	*Odocoileus virginianus*	calcaneus	right
n/a	n/a	3 metric level	2	*Odocoileus virginianus*	vertebra	n/a
n/a	n/a	3 metric level	3	medium/large mammal	long bone splinter	n/a
n/a	n/a	3 metric level	1	medium/large mammal	irregular	n/a

Appendix C

List of modified bone and shell studied

Operación	Bag Number	Square	Layer	NISP	Species	Specimen	Tool	Weight (g)
110	276	A1, B1	IV	1	unidentified shell	n/a	modified frag.	5.7
110	309	A1, B1, C1	II	1	medium/large mammal	rib (middle)	modified frag.	1.1
110	892	A1, B1	III, IV	1	Mammalia	n/a	disc (centred perforation)	4.5
110	892	A1B1	II, III	1	unidentified shell	n/a	modified frag.	3.5
110	920	A2B2	II	1	unidentified shell	n/a	modified frag.	0.9
110	929	A2, B2	III	1	Mammalia	long bone	tube	0.9
110	1066	A1, A2	IV, V	1	medium/large mammal	n/a	tube	2.5
111	230	C1	IV	1	Mammalia	n/a	*malacate*	6.1
112	580	112-EW	N/A	1	*Pachychilus* sp.	n/a	modified shell	2.7
114	796	H1	IV	1	medium/large mammal	rib (middle)	*pulidor*	1.4
114	842	H2	V	1	Testudines	plaque plastron	ornament	7.4
114	842	H2	V	1	*Odocoileus virginianus*	metapodium	ornament	7.4
114	664	J2	II	1	*Odocoileus virginianus*	femur (distal)	*raspador*	3.0
114	744	J1	III	1	Mammalia	n/a	*manita*	3.1
114	709	L1	II	1	*Tapirus bairdii*	rib (middle)	*pulidor*	3.1
114	672	J2	III	1	Mammalia	n/a	ornament	1.3
114	672	J2	III	1	*Homo sapiens*	ilium	blank form	13.0
114	672	J2	III	1	Mammalia	tibia	spatula	4.0
114	731	K1	II	1	Mammalia	rib	ornament	0.4
114	801	J2	V	2	Mammalia	long bone	blank form	3.8
114	950	H1	V	2	Testudines	plaque plastron	ornament	6.3
114	744	J1	III	1	*Canis* sp.	metapodium	blank form	1.3
114	1019	K1	IV	1	medium/large mammal	metapodium	blank form	4.1
114	689	J1	II	1	medium/large mammal	long bone	blank form	3.3
114	997	F2	V	1	Mammalia	n/a	needle	0.7
114	n/a	I1	III	1	Testudines	plaque plastron	ornament	5.8
114	680	G2	III	1	Mammalia	n/a	disc	4.4
114	n/a	K1	II	2	Mammalia	n/a	needle	1.0
114	825	K1	III	1	medium/large mammal	long bone	perforator	3.5
114	711	L1	III	1	medium/large mammal	scapula	blank form	2.7
114	842	H2	V	1	medium/large mammal	antler	blank form	8.3
114	999	F2	V	1	Testudines	plaque plastron	ornament	3.6
114	747	K1	II	1	medium/large mammal	rib (middle)	blank form	1.6
114	731	K1	II	1	medium/large mammal	rib (middle)	blank form	0.8

Operación	Bag Number	Square	Layer	NISP	Species	Specimen	Tool	Weight (g)
114	n/a	K2	III	1	Mammalia	n/a	perforator	1.6
114	766	J1	III	1	*Canis* sp.	carnassial	pendant	1.0
114	985	F1	V	1	Mammalia	n/a	blank form	1.5
114	823	K1	III	1	*Homo sapiens*	skull	blank form	9.3
114	746	K1	II	1	Mammalia	n/a	ring	0.5
114	n/a	K1	II	1	unidentified shell	n/a	pendant	0.2
114	816	I2	V	1	*Odocoileus virginianus*	metacarpus	blank form	20.2
114	777	J2	IV	1	Mammalia	n/a	needle	0.3
114	970	F2	V	1	Mammalia	n/a	needle	0.4
114	n/a	K2	III	2	Mammalia	n/a	needle	0.8
114	753	I2	IV	1	medium/large mammal	irregular	blank form	7.9
114	675	G3	II	1	Mammalia	n/a	blank form	3.3
114	n/a	K1	II	1	n/a	long bone	tube	1.9
114	961	F1	IV	1	*Odocoileus virginianus*	metapodium	blank form	8.6
114	961	F1	IV	1	Mammalia	long bone	perforator	1.8
114	801	J2	V	1	medium/large mammal	tibia	*raspador*	20.6
114	n/a	K2	III	2	*Nephronaias* sp.	n/a	bead	0.3
114	823	K1	III	1	*Homo sapiens*	long bone	guiro	49.7
114	n/a	K1	II	1	Mammalia	n/a	needle	0.5
114	1012	G2	V	1	*Odocoileus virginianus*	hemi-mandible	ornament	10.9
114	845	H1	V	1	unidentified shell	n/a	pendant	8.2
114	993	F2	V	1	*Pachychilus* sp.	n/a	pendant	4.1
114	762	K1	III	1	*Nephronaias* sp.	n/a	bead	0.1
114	n/a	K1	II	1	*Nephronaias* sp.	n/a	bead	0.1
114	747	K2	II	5	*Nephronaias* sp.	n/a	n/a	6.9
114	746	K2	II	2	*Nephronaias* sp.	n/a	n/a	4.7
114	675	G3	II	1	unidentified shell	n/a	blank form	1
114	818	I1	V	1	unidentified shell	n/a	blank form	6.8
114	744	J1	III	1	unidentified shell	n/a	blank form	7.7
114	746	K2	II	1	*Nephronaias* sp.	n/a	bead	2.8
114	731	K1	II	3	unidentified shell	n/a	blank form	7.9
114	844	H2	V	1	*Nephronaias* sp.	n/a	n/a	8.2
114	820	H2	IV	1	*Nephronaias* sp.	n/a	n/a	9.9
114	788	J2	IV	5	unidenfied shell	n/a	blank form	23.1
114	689	J1	II	1	*Nephronaias* sp.	n/a	n/a	2.4
115	1091	N2	III	1	medium/large mammal	rib (middle)	1 blank form	1.4
201	n/a	Layer 2	II	1	*Canis lupus familiaris*	radius	1 refuse distal epifisis removal 'butt discarded'	2.8
201	n/a	Layer 2	II	1	Mammalia	n/a	perforator	2.4
201	n/a	Layer 2	II	1	medium/large mammal	long bone	1 blank form	1.5
n/a	1020	n/a	n/a	1	*Pomacea flagellata*	n/a	1 pendant	34.3

List of human remains studied

Operación	Bag number	Square	Layer	NISP	Specimen	Side
110	879	B3	II	1	phalange	n/a
112	617	n/a	n/a	1	clavicle	right
114	667	G2	II	1	fibula	n/a
114	684	G2	III	1	scapula	right
114	744	J1	III	1	scapula	left
114	749	K1	II	1	scapula	right
114	759	K2	IV	1	pelvis	n/a
114	796	H1	IV	1	scapula	left
114	799	J1	IV	1	clavicle	left
114	799	J1	IV	1	clavicle	right
114	805	E2	V	1	clavicle	left
114	823	K1	III	5	skull	n/a
114	833	G2	V	1	scapula	left
114	833	G2	V	1	scapula	right
114	833	G2	V	1	scapula	right
114	833	G2	V	1	hemi-mandible	right
114	842	H2	V	1	scapula	left
114	950	H1	V	2	clavicle	left
114	975	F2	V	2	metatarsus	n/a
114	975	F2	V	1	ulna	right
114	980	F1	V	1	fibula	n/a
114	985	F1	V	2	clavicle	left
114	985	F1	V	1	pelvis	right
114	985	F1	V	1	skull (temporal)	right
114	993	F2	V	3	lumbar vertebra	n/a
114	993	F2	V	1	metatarsus	n/a
114	993	F2	V	1	fibula	n/a
114	993	F2	V	1	radius	left
114	993	F2	V	2	fibula	n/a
114	993	F2	V	3	rib	n/a
114	993	F2	V	1	femur	n/a
114	993	F2	V	2	pelvis	n/a
114	993	F2	V	1	rib	n/a
114	993	F2	V	1	scapula	right
114	993	F2	V	3	pelvis	n/a
114	1019	K1	IV	1	clavicle	right
114	1009/678	F2	V	1	scapula	right